# Teacher's Edition

# SRA OPEN COURT READING

## Level 3 • Unit 1

## Friendship

— PROGRAM AUTHORS —

| | | |
|---|---|---|
| Carl Bereiter | Robbie Case | Marsha Roit |
| Ann Brown | Jan Hirshberg | Marlene Scardamalia |
| Joe Campione | Marilyn Jager Adams | Marcy Stein |
| Iva Carruthers | Anne McKeough | Gerald H. Treadway, Jr. |
| | Michael Pressley | |

A Division of The McGraw-Hill Companies

Columbus, Ohio

## Acknowledgments

Grateful acknowledgment is given to the following publishers and copyright owners for permissions granted to reprint selections from their publications. All possible care has been taken to trace ownership and secure permission for each selection included. In case of any errors or omissions, the Publisher will be pleased to make suitable acknowledgments in future editions.

AMOS & BORIS by William Steig. Copyright © 1971 by William Steig. Reprinted by permission of Farrar, Straus & Giroux, LLC.

From STORIES JULIAN TELLS by Ann Cameron, illustrated by Ann Strugnell. Text copyright © 1981 by Ann Cameron. Illustrations copyright © 1981 by Ann Strugnell. Reprinted by permission of Pantheon Books, a division of Random House, Inc.

From Angel Child, Dragon Child, by Michele Maria Surat. © 1983 by Raintree/Steck-Vaughn. All rights reserved. Reproduced by arrangement with Steck-Vaughn Company.

JANEY by Charlotte Zolotow. COPYRIGHT © 1973 BY CHARLOTTE ZOLOTOW. Used by permission of HarperCollins Publishers.

"The Tree House" from THE BIG BOOK OF PEACE. Reprinted by permission of Harold Ober Associates Incorporated. Copyright © 1990 by Lois Lowry. Illustration © Trina Schart Hyman.

From RUGBY & ROSIE, copyright © 1997 by Nan Parson Rossiter. Reprinted with permission of Dutton Children's Books, a division of Penguin Putnam. All rights reserved.

TEAMMATES by Peter Golenbock, text copyright © 1990 by Golenbock Communications, illustrations copyright © 1990 by Paul Bacon, reprinted by permission of Harcourt, Inc.

"The Legend of Damon and Pythias" from THE BAG OF FIRE AND OTHER PLAYS by Fan Kissen. Copyright © 1964 by Houghton Mifflin Company, renewed © 1993 by John Kissen Heaslip. Reprinted by permission of Houghton Mifflin Company. All rights reserved.

**www.sra4kids.com**

*SRA/McGraw-Hill*

*A Division of The McGraw·Hill Companies*

Send all inquiries to:
SRA/McGraw-Hill
8787 Orion Place
Columbus, OH 43240-4027

Printed in the United States of America.

ISBN 0-07-569663-0

2 3 4 5 6 7 8 9 WEB 07 06 05 04 03 02

# Welcome to

## SRA OpenCourt Reading

# Open Court Reading: The Most Complete, Effective Reading Program Available

*Open Court Reading* is the only reading program that provides:

- An **educational philosophy** based on scientific research and **nearly 40 years** of practical classroom experience
- A program that has been **proven successful in schools** nationwide
- A **well-defined plan of systematic, explicit instruction** for teaching the strategies and skills of reading
- A **partnership through training** that will help teachers and administrators successfully implement *Open Court Reading*

*Open Court Reading* is a **research-based** curriculum grounded in **systematic, explicit instruction** of:

- Phonemic awareness, phonics, and word knowledge
- Comprehension skills and strategies
- Inquiry skills and strategies
- Writing and language arts skills and strategies

The program creates a **literature-rich environment** that instills a passion for lifelong reading and a love of literature and the written word.

Our basic **philosophy** has remained consistent for nearly **40 years**. *Open Court Reading* has always contained the keys to teaching children how to read and read to learn.

# Open Court Reading
# Creates Confident Learners

*Open Court Reading* provides:

- Research-based instruction
- Strong authorship
- A systematic, explicit instructional plan
- Literature with a purpose
- Differentiating instruction for meeting students' individual needs

## Research-Based Instruction

*Open Court Reading* is built on a solid foundation of nearly **40 years of research**. Test results repeatedly prove its effectiveness. Reading instruction trends may have changed; *Open Court Reading* has remained true to the fact that children learn best when taught using what has been researched and proven to work.

*Open Court Reading* is based on four types of research:

1. Academic
2. Most effective practices in education
3. Field testing
4. Learner verification results

*Open Court Reading* is the **only** program that guarantees all four.

## Strong Authorship

The authors of *Open Court Reading* bring expertise in specific areas of educational research to our program. Their widely published books, journal articles, and research studies lead the field in areas such as phonemic awareness and phonics instruction and comprehension skills and strategies instruction.

*Research in Action* articles found throughout the program provide information showing how the work of our authors and others respected in the field of educational research have been incorporated into our program. These articles provide more information on how *Open Court Reading* works and why it is so successful.

## Systematic, Explicit Instructional Plan

Students are most successful when they learn through a balance of systematic direct instruction in sound and word recognition, guided practice, and application of skills with extensive reading of decodable text and authentic literature.

Through systematic, explicit instruction, *Open Court Reading* has organized lessons in the most logical and efficient way possible for teaching children to read and write with skill and confidence. All strategies and skills are arranged from the simplest to the most complex. Because the skills build upon one another, children are able to grasp complex concepts more easily.

*Open Court Reading* provides more comprehensive Teacher Editions than any other program. The presentation of concepts, skills, and practice is detailed – all you need to do is follow the directions. Reading and writing strategies are delivered in a manner that has been proven through research to be the most effective.

### Research in Action
#### Phonemic Awareness

The goal of phonemic awareness activities is to lead students to understand that spoken words are made up of chains of smaller sounds—the syllables and phonemes. Because students are accustomed to producing and hearing words as unbreakable wholes, this is not a natural insight. Nevertheless, for understanding an alphabetic language in which the letters and letter patterns represent the sub-sounds of words, it is a critical insight. After students have learned to think about words in terms of their component sounds, decoding will make sense and inventive spelling will come easily. Conversely, poorly developed phonemic awareness is believed to be the single greatest cause of reading disability. *(Marilyn J. Adams)*

## Literature With a Purpose

*Open Court Reading* provides a **survey course of literature**, exposing students to a variety of different **writing styles** and **genres**. We guide students in understanding the strategies and skills necessary for reading text in the **real world**. Literature in *Open Court Reading* is found in:

- Big Books
- Anthologies
- Teacher Read Alouds
- Story Time Selections (Kindergarten)
- Online bibliography

**In *Open Court Reading*, students read literature written by trade book authors by the middle of Grade 1.** Our compilation of literature selections is so tightly woven that our students are involved in independent **Inquiry and Investigation** on complicated subjects much sooner and with more ease.

## Differentiating Instruction for Meeting Individual Needs

*Open Court Reading* provides a variety of proven experiences for accommodating individual students' needs.

- Reteach
- Intervention
- Challenge
- English-Language Learners

# Research and Results

**Open Court Reading Is the Most Thoroughly Researched Program Available**

## Research Shows:

Students who are early independent readers:

- Learn better throughout their school years
- Become motivated readers who typically read more than children who learn to read later
- Develop increased:
  - Vocabulary
  - Understanding of abstract concepts
  - Appreciation of a diverse array of literature and writing styles
  - General knowledge

While current educational standards call for students to be reading by the end of Grade 3, *Open Court Reading* is structured to ensure that students are reading fluently and comprehending what they read **by the end of Grade 1.**

## The Open Court Response:

Open Court has always included those essential concepts that research has repeatedly shown are necessary for learning to read. By using established routines throughout the program, *Open Court Reading* systematically and explicitly teaches each of these essential concepts:

- The alphabetic principle
- Print awareness
- Phonemic awareness
- Systematic, explicit phonics
- Comprehension strategies and skills
- Inquiry techniques and strategies
- The writing process and writing skills
- Spelling and vocabulary
- Grammar, usage, and mechanics

## A Success Story 40 Years in the Making

Since the early 1960s, Open Court has included the fundamental elements that research has shown are necessary for teaching children how to read.

For nearly 40 years, Open Court has monitored and learned from the research that experts in the field of reading have conducted, incorporating these important findings into the programs.

SRA is proud to note that many of those same researchers hold *Open Court Reading* in high esteem as a well-balanced program that teaches students not only how to read, but also how to comprehend and make the most of reading content.

# A Reading Program Rooted In Research

## Academic Research

Leaders in educational research, the authors of *Open Court Reading* are experts on how children learn to read and read to learn. Together, they have created *Open Court Reading* to most effectively help expand students' reading and learning capabilities.

- **Phonemic awareness and systematic, explicit phonics** instruction is based on the work of **Dr. Marilyn Jager Adams**, author of the most frequently cited book on beginning reading, *Beginning to Read: Thinking and Learning about Print* (1990).

- **Comprehension skills and strategies** instruction is based on the work of **Dr. Ann Brown's** reciprocal teaching model and **Dr. Michael Pressley's** transactional strategy instruction model.

- **Dr. Marlene Scardamalia** lends the benefit of extensive research in the psychology of writing.

- Research conducted by **Dr. Carl Bereiter** is incorporated into the **Inquiry and Investigation** part of each lesson.

- A **Professional Development** plan has been developed and is expertly guided by **Dr. Marsha Roit**.

- The **Intervention** materials were created under the direction of **Dr. Marcy Stein**, who is widely published on the subject of special education, and **Dr. Marsha Roit** who, through her work in classrooms, brings a unique perspective to these materials.

## Most Effective Practices in Education

- A comprehensive report by the **National Reading Panel** (2000) endorses the instructional model that *Open Court Reading* has used for nearly 40 years.

- Findings from studies being conducted by the **National Institute of Child Health and Human Development (NICHD)**, as well as conclusions from comprehensive reviews of beginning reading research, all indicate that effective reading instruction should include the strategies found in *Open Court Reading* for teaching children how to read.

- The **American Federation of Teachers (AFT)** reviewed current reading programs and issued a statement called *What Works*. In this statement, Open Court was identified as a program that incorporates research-based instruction and has classroom data to support its effectiveness.

- The **U.S. Department of Education's** Reading Excellence Act has awarded state grants to improve reading achievement mandating that schools choose programs that show "scientifically based research and effective practices that have been replicated effectively." Open Court has been the program of choice for schools throughout the nation who are being awarded this grant.

- An independent study (**Educational Research Analysis**, 2000) states that "*Open Court Reading* has the highest decodability, comprehensiveness, intensiveness, and consistency of any reading program." It was ranked best of all programs reviewed.

## Field Testing

A study conducted by Foorman, et al. (1996) compared the effectiveness of the explicit, systematic program, Open Court, to other approaches. Results of this study found that Open Court's direct instruction approach was more effective with students at risk of reading failure than the other approaches as measured by a variety of tests, including standardized measures.

## Learner Verification Results

In a study conducted by Douglas J. McRae, educational measurement specialist, Stanford/9 test scores from the STAR program were analyzed. The results of that study indicate:

- Open Court schools had higher gain scores statewide.

- Open Court provided the largest gain scores for schools with high concentration of both LEP (Limited English Proficient) and Low-SES (Socio-Economic Status) students.

- Scores show cumulative advantage over the span of two years with Open Court.

The conclusion of this study was that using Open Court made a difference. These schools (a sampling of over 150,000 students) showed greater gains than either statewide gains or gains from a demographically matched set of schools.

### Grade 2 Scores

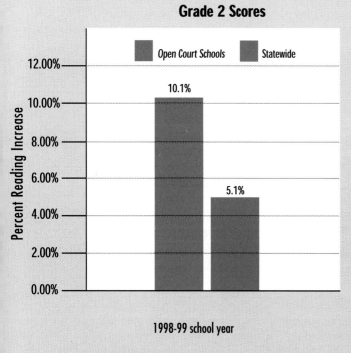

1998-99 school year

### Grade 2 Results

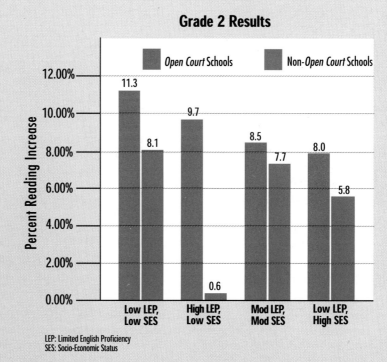

LEP: Limited English Proficiency
SES: Socio-Economic Status

For a complete look at this study, please call 1-800-772-4543 and ask for Research Findings: The Research-Based Reading Materials You Choose May Have a Direct Impact on Your Students' Reading Performance, ISBN# R80000456.

# Open Court Reading Authors
## Bring Research Into Your Classroom

### MARILYN JAGER ADAMS, PH.D.

Cited in the *2000 Politics of Education Yearbook* as one of the most influential people in the national reading policy arena, Dr. Adams has worked closely with a number of agencies to develop reading standards, policies, and staff development strategies.

- Author/co-author of:
  - *Beginning to Read: Thinking and Learning about Print*
  - *Preventing Reading Difficulties in Young Children*
  - *Fox in a Box* Assessment Program
  - *Phonemic Awareness in Young Children*
  - *Odyssey: A Curriculum for Thinking*
- Advisor to *Sesame Street* and *Between the Lions*

### CARL BEREITER, PH.D.

An accomplished author, researcher, and professor, Dr. Bereiter has published extensively on teaching and learning.

- Invented CSILE (Computer Supported Intentional Learning Environments), the first networked collaborative learning environment in schools, with Dr. Marlene Scardamalia; the current version, *Knowledge Forum®*, is in use in 12 countries
- Co-author of:
  - *The Psychology of Written Composition*
  - *Surpassing Ourselves: The Nature and Implications of Expertise*
- Author of *Education and the Mind of the Knowledge Age*
- Professor at Centre for Applied Cognitive Science, Ontario Institute for Studies in Education
- One of 100 people honored in the Routledge Great Thinkers in Education
- Member of the National Academy of Education

### JOE CAMPIONE, PH.D.

A leading researcher on cognitive development, individual differences, assessment, and the design of innovative learning environments, Dr. Campione is currently a Professor in the School of Education at University of California at Berkeley.

- Most recent work has focused on methods to restructure elementary schools
- Has created curriculums that introduce students as early as Grade 1 to the research process

### IVA CARRUTHERS, PH.D.

Equipped with both hands-on and academic experience, Dr. Carruthers serves as a consultant and lecturer in both educational technology and matters of multicultural inclusion.

- President of Nexus Unlimited, Inc., a human resources development and computer services consulting firm
- Consultant, U.S. Advisory Council on the National Information Infrastructure
- Former Chairperson and Professor of the Sociology Department at Northeastern Illinois University
- Has developed software for teaching African-American history and inter-disciplinary subjects
- Co-producer of *Know Your Heritage*, a televised academic quiz show
- Has also been an elementary school teacher, high school counselor, and research historian

### JAN HIRSHBERG, ED.D.

Focusing on how children learn to read and write and the logistics of teaching reading and writing in the early grades, Dr. Hirshberg is currently working as a language arts resource teacher and consultant in Alexandria, Virginia.

- Author/co-author of:
  - *Open Court 1989, Kindergarten and Grade 1 Reading and Writing Program*
  - *Collections for Young Scholars*
  - *Open Court 1995* and *2000*, reading, writing, and learning program

- Former teaching fellow, research assistant, instructor, and lecturer at the Graduate School of Education at Harvard University
- Former elementary school teacher and school district reading consultant

### ANNE MCKEOUGH, PH.D.

A Professor in the Division of Applied Psychology and Chair of the Human Learning and Development program at the University of Calgary, Dr. McKeough has received a number of research awards and grants.

- Co-editor of several volumes, including:
  - *Toward the Practice of Theory Based Instruction: Current Cognitive Theories and Their Educational Promise*
  - *Teaching for Transfer: Fostering Generalization in Learning*
  - *Schools in Transition*
- Has authored numerous articles advocating the benefits of a continued and reflective partnership between teaching practices and child development research
- Current research focuses on cognitive development and developmentally based instruction

### MICHAEL PRESSLEY, PH.D.

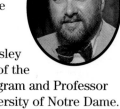

Most recently honored by the National Reading Conference as the 2000 recipient of the Oscar Causey Award for career contributions to reading research, Dr. Pressley is the Academic Director of the Masters of Education Program and Professor of Psychology at the University of Notre Dame.

- Editor of *Journal of Educational Psychology*
- Author of *Reading Instruction That Works: The Case for Balanced Teaching* and co-author of *Learning to Read: Lessons from Exemplary First-Grade Classrooms*
- An expert in comprehension instruction and in the ethnographic study of the elementary classroom experience
- Author of more than 200 scientific articles

## MARSHA ROIT, ED.D.

The Director of Professional Development for SRA/McGraw-Hill, Dr. Roit spends considerable time in classrooms developing reading and writing curricula and training teachers and administrators in effective instructional practices.

- Works directly with school districts creating staff development models that support research-based instruction and its effectiveness
- Has focused research on strategy instruction with both mainstream and English-Language Learners
- Has published in a variety of professional journals, including:
  - *Exceptional Children*
  - *Journal of Learning Disabilities*
  - *The Elementary School Journal*

## MARLENE SCARDAMALIA, PH.D.

A Professor at the Centre for Applied Cognitive Science and Department of Curriculum Teaching and Learning, Ontario Institute for Studies in Education, Dr. Scardamalia has conducted research and been published in the areas of cognitive development, psychology of writing, intentional learning, the nature of expertise, and educational uses of computers.

- Invented CSILE (Computer Supported Intentional Learning Environments), the first networked collaborative learning environment in schools, with Dr. Carl Bereiter; the current version, *Knowledge Forum®*, is in use in 12 countries
- Member of the U.S. National Academy of Education
- While a fellow at the Center for Advanced Study in Behavioral Sciences, headed "Cognitive Bases of Educational Reform," from which grew "Schools of Thought," a school reform program noted for its synthesis of major cognitive-based learning initiatives

## MARCY STEIN, PH.D.

An Associate Professor and founding faculty member of the education program at the University of Washington, Tacoma, Dr. Stein currently coordinates At-Risk and Special Education graduate programs, and teaches in the teacher certification program. She has served as consultant to departments of education on the translation of reading research to instructional practice.

- She has published extensively on topics including:
  - Beginning and remedial reading instruction
  - Vocabulary acquisition
  - Curriculum and textbook analysis
- She has served on many national and local committees and in consultant positions, including:
  - Los Angeles Unified School District, Consultant
  - Washington State Special Education Improvement Grant Steering Committee, Invited Member
  - *Remedial and Special Education* journal, consulting editor

## GERALD H. TREADWAY, JR., PH.D.

Professor at San Diego State University, Dr. Treadway teaches reading methods, balanced reading programs, and reading comprehension.

- Member of California's Reading Task Force and the Reading Credentials Task Force
- Member of California Academic Standards Commission
- Associate Director of the California Reading and Literature Project
- Contributing author to *Fox in a Box*, a diagnostic reading assessment for students in Grades K-2
- Former member and Chair of the California Curriculum Commission
- Former elementary school teacher

## ANN BROWN, PH.D.

The past President of the American Education Research Association, Dr. Brown conducted a great deal of research in the area of distributed expertise in the classroom.

- Worked as a professor of math, science, and technology in the Graduate School of Education at the University of California at Berkeley
- Served on the congressional panel to monitor National Assessment of Education Progress state-by-state assessments
- Received many honors and awards in both the United States and England for her contributions to educational research

## ROBBIE CASE, PH.D.

Beginning in the mid-1970s, Dr. Case conducted research on the relationship between children's learning and their cognitive development during elementary school.

- Former Professor of Education at Stanford University
- Former Director of the Laidlaw-Centre at the Institute of Child Study, University of Toronto
- Authored books and scholarly articles on cognitive development that are sold throughout the world

# Open Court Reading
# Instructional Plan

## Systematic and Explicit

**Explicit instruction** is teacher-directed identification of learning goals, specific presentation to students, teacher modeling, student practice, and assessment.

**Systematic instruction** outlines the logical sequence of skill presentation and research-based, effective learning routines.

## Teacher Modeling

Teacher modeling is key to systematic, explicit instruction. Starting in Kindergarten, teachers model a repertoire of skills and strategies students learn to apply independently. Every lesson includes multiple opportunities to model the process that good readers use. Students then practice and apply the modeled strategies to work up to independent use of the strategies.

*Open Court Reading* provides systematic and explicit instruction for every skill throughout the program.

### 1 Preparing to Read

- Sounds and letters
- Phonemic awareness
- Phonics and fluency
- Word knowledge

In Kindergarten and Grade 1, Part 1 of every lesson carefully teaches letter names, sounds, and spellings in a carefully crafted sequence that enables students to begin reading real words as soon as possible. Phonemic awareness, phonics, and fluency skills are all presented using research-based strategies that include blending and segmentation. Students quickly, efficiently, and effectively learn the sound patterns that make up English words. Practice and review of these key skills are systematically built into the curriculum to ensure mastery. In later grades, word knowledge is presented with the same careful attention. At the same time, students increase vocabulary skills through careful presentation and practice using vocabulary from the literature selection.

### 2 Reading and Responding

**Comprehension Skills and Strategies**

Part 2 of every lesson teaches specific comprehension skills and strategies in conjunction with the excellent literature that forms the core of each lesson. Comprehension strategies, such as clarifying, summarizing, and predicting, are modeled, practiced, and reviewed in the first reading of the literature.

Comprehension skills, including sequence and drawing conclusions, are modeled, practiced, and reviewed in the second reading of the literature. This comprehensive development of skills and strategies builds life-long confidence.

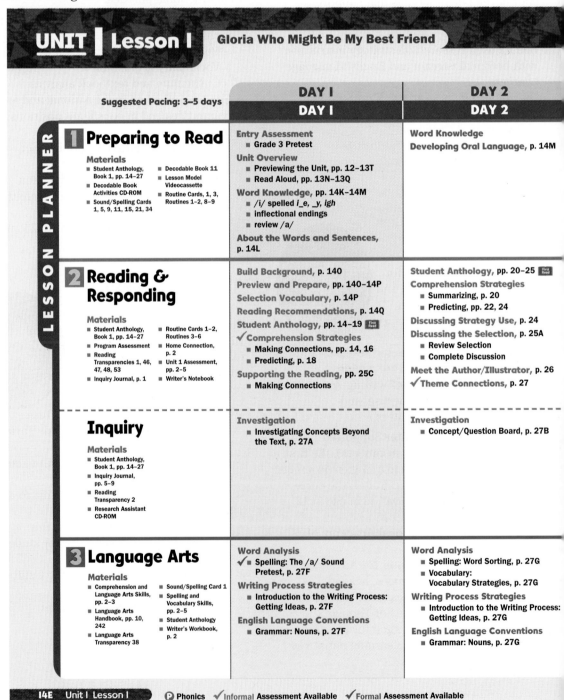

## Inquiry

Inquiry and investigation strategies are thoughtfully developed to teach students how to ask questions and find the answers to their questions. With Inquiry, students apply all of the reading, comprehension, and language arts skills they are learning in order to develop and present their investigations.

## 3 Language Arts

- Spelling
- Vocabulary
- Writing process strategies
- Writer's craft
- English language conventions
- Grammar, usage, and mechanics
- Listening, speaking, and viewing
- Penmanship
- Basic computer skills

Part 3 of every lesson includes systematic and explicit development of language arts skills, including the writing process, writing traits, writer's craft, and structures of writing in different genres. Each skill is explicitly taught using teacher models or models from the *Language Arts Handbook* and practiced in reading and/or writing activities. These activities show how the skill is connected to the other parts of the lesson. Like the phonics and comprehension skills, the language arts skills are added to each student's knowledge toolbox, so that students can employ appropriate skills when developing their investigations, or in other contexts.

## Assessment

Continuous assessment enables teachers to gauge the progress of their students so that no student misses needed instruction.

The assessment section of *Open Court Reading* contains:

- Program Assessment
  - Teacher's Observation Log
  - Pretest
  - Midyear test
  - Posttest
- Unit Assessments
  Includes assessments for all skills taught. Unit Assessments contain:
  - Oral Fluency Assessments
  - Writing assessments
  - Spelling assessments
  - Vocabulary assessments
  - Listening assessments
  - Grammar, usage, and mechanics assessments
  - Comprehension assessments
  - Literature assessments
  - Class assessment record
  - Student assessment record
- Diagnostic Assessment
  Provides more focused assessment opportunities to aid in individualizing instruction.

---

**Theme: Friendship**

| DAY 2 continued / DAY 3 | DAY 3 / DAY 4 | DAY 5 |
|---|---|---|
| **Phonics and Fluency, pp. 14M–14N**<br>■ Review short vowels<br>**About the Words and Sentences, 14M** | ℗ **Phonics and Fluency**<br>Developing Oral Language, p. 14N<br>Dictation, p. 14N | General Review |
| **Student Anthology, pp. 14–19** Second Read<br>**Comprehension Skills**<br>■ Classify and Categorize, pp. 15, 17, 19<br>**Social Studies Connection**<br>■ Maps, p. 25E | **Student Anthology, pp. 20–25** Second Read<br>**Comprehension Skills**<br>■ Classify and Categorize, pp. 21, 23, 25<br>**Checking Comprehension, p. 25**<br>**Review Selection Vocabulary, p. 25B**<br>**Literary Elements, p. 25D**<br>■ Point of View | ✓ **Selection Assessment**<br>■ "Gloria Who Might Be My Best Friend," pp. 2–5<br>**Home Connection, p. 25B**<br>**Science Connection**<br>■ Enegy and the Wind, p. 25F |
| **Investigation**<br>■ Generating Questions to Investigate, p. 27C | **Supporting the Investigation**<br>■ Interviewing, p. 27D | **Investigation**<br>■ Unit Investigation Continued<br>■ Update Concept/Question Board |
| **Word Analysis**<br>■ Spelling: The /a/ Sound, p. 27H<br>■ Vocabulary:<br>  Vocabulary Strategies, p. 27H<br>**Writing Process Strategies**<br>■ Introduction to the Writing Process: Getting Ideas, p. 27H<br>**English Language Conventions**<br>■ Grammar: Nouns, p. 27H | **Word Analysis**<br>■ Spelling: The /a/ Sound, p. 27I<br>■ Vocabulary:<br>  Vocabulary Strategies, p. 27I<br>**Writing Process Strategies**<br>■ Introduction to the Writing Process: Getting Ideas, p. 27I<br>**English Language Conventions**<br>✓ ■ Listening, Speaking, Viewing<br>  Listening: Being a Good Listener, p. 27I | **Word Analysis**<br>■ Spelling: The /a/ Sound<br>✓ Final Test<br>✓ Vocabulary:<br>  Vocabulary Strategies, p. 27J<br>**Writing Process Strategies**<br>■ Introduction to the Writing Process: Getting Ideas, p. 27J<br>**English Language Conventions**<br>✓ ■ Penmanship:<br>  Cursive Letters *i* and *t*, p. 27J |

# Open Court Reading
## Literature

## In-Depth Literary Theme Perspectives

The goal of *Open Court Reading* is to efficiently and effectively teach children to decode and comprehend so that they can read a variety of literature types. All of the skills development throughout the program serve this purpose. From the very beginning, the program has emphasized the quality of the literature students read and the organization of that literature around big ideas to promote understanding and discussion.

Each unit throughout the program explores a comprehensive theme. The literature in each unit of *Open Court Reading* is organized around one of two types of themes:

- **Universal themes**, such as Keep Trying, Friendship, and Survival, encourage in-depth and critical thinking.
- **Research themes**, such as Weather, Astronomy, and Ancient Civilizations, develop inquiry and research in science and social studies content areas.

## Inquiry and Investigation

Throughout lessons in *Open Court Reading*, students do more than just read literature. They also ask questions, discuss, research, write about, and think about the concepts and ideas centered around the themes they read.

## Quality Literature Organized into Unit Themes

| | UNIT 1 | UNIT 2 | UNIT 3 | UNIT 4 |
|---|---|---|---|---|
| **LEVEL K** BIG BOOKS | School | Shadows | Finding Friends | The Wind |
| **LEVEL 1** BIG BOOKS | Let's Read! | Animals | Things That Go | Our Neighborhood at Work |
| **LEVEL 2** STUDENT ANTHOLOGIES | Sharing Stories | Kindness | Look Again | Fossils |
| **LEVEL 3** STUDENT ANTHOLOGIES | Friendship | City Wildlife | Imagination | Money |
| **LEVEL 4** STUDENT ANTHOLOGY | Risks and Consequences | Dollars and Sense | From Mystery to Medicine | Survival |
| **LEVEL 5** STUDENT ANTHOLOGY | Cooperation and Competition | Astronomy | Heritage | Making a New Nation |
| **LEVEL 6** STUDENT ANTHOLOGY | Perseverance | Ancient Civilizations | Taking a Stand | Beyond the Notes |

| UNIT 5 | UNIT 6 | UNIT 7 | UNIT 8 | UNIT 9 | UNIT 10 |
|---|---|---|---|---|---|
| Stick to It | Red, White, and Blue | Teamwork | By the Sea | | |
| STUDENT ANTHOLOGIES | | | | | |
| Weather | Journeys | Keep Trying | Games | Being Afraid | Homes |
| Courage | Our Country and Its People | | | | |
| Storytelling | Country Life | | | | |
| Communication | A Changing America | | | | |
| Going West | Journeys and Quests | | | | |
| Ecology | A Question of Value | | | | |

Focus Questions  In what ways can we show kindness to nature? Have you ever had to "let go" of something you love because it was the kind thing to do?

Butterfly House
by Eve Bunting
illustrated by Greg Shed

When I was just a little girl
I saw a small black creature
like a tiny worm,
and saved it from a greedy jay
who wanted it
for lunch. ❶

I carried it inside,
safe on its wide green leaf.
My grandpa said
it was a larva
and soon would be
a butterfly. ❷

156

157

# Open Court Reading
# Literature

## Excellent Examples of a Variety of Literature

Interesting and high-quality literature is introduced in *Open Court Reading* as soon as students begin school. The literature provides the foundation of each lesson throughout the program. Comprehension skills and strategies, spelling and vocabulary, writing process strategies, and English language conventions all connect to the lesson selection.

Each literature selection in the Big Books and Anthologies was painstakingly selected with the following goals in mind:

- **Unique theme perspectives** encourage student inquiry. Each selection in a unit adds a new concept or idea about the theme.

- **A variety of literature** provides fiction and nonfiction genres, including novels, short stories, poems, essays, dramas, mysteries, and informational articles so students experience many different forms of literature.

- **Reading practice** includes grade-level appropriate literature.

- **Excellent examples of writing** in literature provide superior models for students' writing.

- **Classic and contemporary literature** works together to broaden students' perspectives.

- **Author Styles** offer award-winning works and different styles of writing so students develop a cultural literacy.

In addition to the literature in the Big Books and Anthologies, these components provide further exposure to literature in each unit:

- Teacher Read Alouds (K-6)
- Story Time Selections (K)
- Leveled Libraries (K-6)
- Online Bibliography (K-6)

## Literature Selections Provide Foundation for Independent Inquiry and Investigation

Chart from Unit Overview found on the following page provides information on how the literature furthers theme-based study.

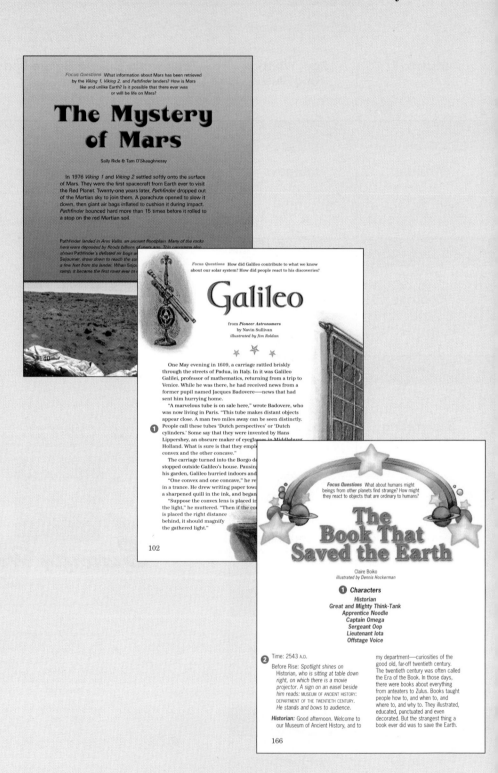

| | OVERVIEW OF SELECTION | LINK TO THE THEME | UNIT INVESTIGATIONS | SUPPORTING STUDENT INVESTIGATIONS |
|---|---|---|---|---|
| **Lesson 1**<br>*Galileo* | ■ In this biographical selection, Galileo's telescope reveals things about the heavens that eventually put him at odds with church authorities. | ■ Galileo introduced many people to the faraway planets, satellites, and stars studied in astronomy. | ■ Generate questions and ideas to investigate | ■ Investigation activities<br>■ Learn to use charts |
| **Lesson 2**<br>*Telescopes* | ■ This nonfiction selection explains how different kinds of telescopes work, including the Hubble space telescope. | ■ Telescopes, the basic tools of astronomy since the 1600s, have become more powerful and sophisticated. | ■ Formulate questions and problems | ■ Investigation activities<br>■ Learn to use diagrams |
| **Lesson 3**<br>*The Heavenly Zoo* | ■ The origins of three astrological patterns are explained by ancient myths from different cultures. | ■ Lacking scientific knowledge of the stars, ancient peoples created myths to give meaning to these phenomena.<br>■ Constellation myths helped ancient people remember, locate, and identify stars. | ■ Make conjectures | ■ Investigation activities<br>■ Learn to use card and computer catalogs |
| **Lesson 4**<br>*Circles, Squares, and Daggers* | ■ This nonfiction selection illustrates how Native Americans of long ago created structures to mark the cycles of seasons and the passing of time. | ■ Archaeoastronomy is a field of study that combines archaeology and astronomy. | ■ Establish investigation needs | ■ Investigation activities<br>■ Learn to use outlines |
| **Lesson 5**<br>*The Mystery of Mars* | ■ This nonfiction selection illustrates how astronomers learned a great deal about Mars from the journeys of the *Viking 1*, *Viking 2*, and *Pathfinder* spacecraft. | ■ Space missions to Mars have broadened our knowledge of the field of astronomy. | ■ Establish investigation plans | ■ Investigation activities<br>■ Learn to use indices |
| **Lesson 6**<br>*Stars* | ■ This nonfiction selection provides an introduction to the different kinds of distant objects and systems that modern astronomers investigate. | ■ Nebulas, supernovas, and quasars are some of the types of stars in the universe that have been discovered through astronomy. | ■ Continue investigation<br>■ Make informal presentations | ■ Investigation activities<br>■ Learn note-taking skills |
| **Lesson 7**<br>*The Book That Saved the Earth* | ■ This humorous science fiction play suggests that some aliens may not be as intelligent as we think. | ■ The study of astronomy leads some to wonder what alien life-forms would think of our culture if they should discover us first. | ■ Present investigation findings | ■ Investigation activities<br>■ Self-evaluate investigations |

# Open Court Reading

## Provides a Balanced and Integrated Reading Program for Florida

*Open Court Reading* is aligned with critical elements for teaching reading and language arts that have been adopted by the state of Florida. Every lesson shows how our program correlates to these standards.

Furthermore, the following books that Florida has adopted as the basis for state reading specifications relate to *Open Court Reading*:

- *Preventing Reading Difficulties in Young Children* – references works of several *Open Court Reading* authors.

- *Starting Out Right: A Guide to Promoting Children's Reading Success* – uses Open Court as *the* example of a balanced reading program.

### Every Child a Reader

The instructional models in *Open Court Reading* ensure that every child has the benefit of the best reading instruction available.

### Whole Group Instruction

Every lesson begins with whole-group teacher-directed lessons so that all children have access to the same models and information.

### Differentiating Instruction: Workshop

Workshop is a period of time devoted to collaborating on investigations of unit concepts, working independently, or meeting individual needs. Workshop items and procedures are introduced to the whole group through direct-teaching sessions. Then students are released gradually from directed-teaching to work independently or in collaborative groups. Teachers work with individuals or small groups as needed.

### Independent Learning

As part of the *Inquiry* strand, the Concept/Question Board is a place for students to ask questions and find answers that will give them a better understanding of the unit theme. It is also a place to publish the results of their investigations.

### Universal Access: Meeting Individual Needs

By making no assumptions about prior knowledge, *Open Court Reading* provides a variety of proven experiences that accommodate different student needs:

- **Reteach** lessons are available for all skills for those students who need extra support.

- **Intervention** lessons are for students who need more intensive support and instruction. Intervention includes controlled vocabulary selections based on unit themes and specific skill lessons to bring students up to grade level.

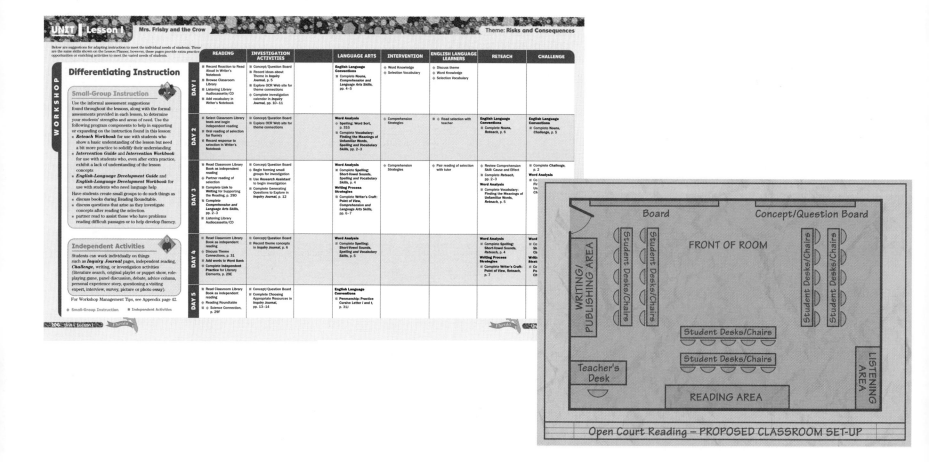

- **Challenge** activities are included to provide continued stimulation for those students working above level and beyond the capabilities of the average readers in the class.

- **English-Language Development** lessons address the needs of today's increasingly diverse classrooms. This instructional support complements the *Open Court Reading* lessons. Also, Home Connections Blackline Masters include parent letters in both Spanish and English to communicate classroom progress, including unit themes and activities.

## Activating prior knowledge and natural inquiries with the Concept/Question Board

The *Concept/Question Board* is used throughout lessons in *Open Court Reading* to encourage students to think independently and flexibly.

At the opening of each unit, students examine a concept-related picture and discuss what about it looks familiar. Students write what they know about the concept, and post it on the *Concept* side of the board. Some questions teachers can ask to spur discussion and activate prior knowledge are provided in the Unit Opener.

Next, the class discusses what more they would like to know about the concept. The questions that come from this discussion are posted on the *Question* side of the board. Throughout the lessons in the unit, the class investigates these questions by searching for answers in the literature and in outside sources.

This ongoing learning process encourages inquiry and investigation, helping students to form independent thinking strategies, and build effective thinking habits.

**A second grade Concept/Question Board from Karen Hansill in Georgia**

# Program Components

**Teacher Support** (K-6)
(Teacher Editions, Online Support, Training Video Collection, Professional Development Guides)

Teacher Editions provide the information necessary for teaching systematic, explicit skills instruction centered around quality literature selections. Professional Development Guides and Lesson Model Videos offer a deeper understanding of the program, how it works, and why.

**First Reader** (2)
This reader contains real literature for review and reinforcement of skills is used during the Getting Started lessons at the beginning of Grade 2.

**Big Books and Little Big Books** (K-1)
Contain multiple literature selections and fine art to promote reading and shared reading experiences.

**Story Time Selections**
Trade books used to support each unit in kindergarten.

**Blackline Masters and Workbooks**
Sounds and Letters Skills (K), Language Arts Skills (K), Phonics Skills (1), Comprehension and Language Arts Skills (1-6), Inquiry Journal (2-6), Spelling and Vocabulary Skills (1-6), and Writer's Workbook (K-6) are used to help reinforce and practice skills taught.

**Student Anthologies** (1-6)
Collections of literature based on themes. Each selection is chosen for the content it adds to the theme.

**Science/Social Studies Connection Centers** (K-6)
Reinforce reading across the curriculum by linking science and social studies content to the *Open Court Reading* lessons.

**Technology**
Alphabet Book Activities (K), Decodable Book Activities (1-3), Spelling (1-6), Writing (K-3, 4-6), Assessment (K-6), Research Assistant (2-6), and Management (K-6) CD-ROMs; Audiocassette or CD Listening Libraries (K-6), Alphabet Sound Card Stories Audiocassette or CD (K), Sound/Spelling Card Stories Audiocassette or CD (1-3), Lesson Models Video Collection (K-3), Online Bibliography (K-6), Online Teacher Support (K-6), and Leap into Phonics (K-3)

## Decodable Text (K-3)
(Pre-Decodable and Decodable Books and Takehomes)

These books give students the opportunity to practice the blending strategies and high-frequency words they are learning during Part 1 of the lesson. Individual (1 copy of each book) and Classroom Sets (6 copies of each book) are available. These also come in a tear-out Takehome format in which books are made by students to use during class or to take home to practice with parents. Takehomes are available in 4-color or black & white versions.

## First Reader, Second Reader (1)

These readers help transition students from reading decodable text and high-frequency sight words to reading authentic trade-book literature in the Anthologies and Leveled Classroom Libraries. Although still somewhat controlled, the text in these engaging readers about the unit theme provides students with more of the challenges found in completely uncontrolled trade-book text. They provide the perfect step between the completely controlled Decodable Text and the text found in the Anthologies.

## Assessment Blackline Masters or Workbooks (K-6)
Diagnostic, Program, Unit, and Standardized Test have specific assessments that help evaluate the progress of each student using various types of formal assessment.

## Phonics Packages (K-3)
Contain the manipulatives necessary for teaching the phonemic awareness and phonics instruction. The Story Crafting components can also be found in the Kindergarten Reading, Phonemic Awareness, and Phonics Package.

## Language Arts Handbook (K-1)
## Language Arts Big Book (2-6)

Contains models of the writing process, writing traits, writer's craft, and structures of writing.

## Additional Literature
Selections chosen to supplement the literature in the Big Books and Anthologies can be found in Teacher Read Aloud Selections, Leveled Classroom Libraries, Online Bibliography (K-6). Leveled Libraries contain trade book selections that are leveled easy, average, and advanced and provide more information for unit investigations.

## Practice Books (K-6)
(Challenge, Reteach, Intervention, English-Language Development)

For use during Differentiating Instruction in Workshop. These practice books remediate, reinforce, and extend lessons for meeting the needs of all learners in your classroom. They are available in both workbook and blackline master formats.

# Every Child a Reader,
## Every Teacher a Success

### Every Child Deserves to Read

According to educational researchers:

- Children who learn to read by the end of Grade 1 perform better in school and beyond.
- Children who enjoy reading learn more quickly and read more.

Literacy in today's society means more than simply being able to read the billboards stretched along the interstates, sign a name to a bank account, or read a newspaper article. In today's workplaces, literacy means being able to pursue multiple tasks at one time, being able to understand written and spoken language, and even knowing how to research and solve problems.

**All children, regardless of background, deserve an equal opportunity to excel**. Children should be invigorated and excited about having the opportunity to acquire knowledge. This will only happen if all children are given equal access to those practices that are proven to work in the classroom.

***Open Court Reading* is *the* proven curriculum for teaching children how to read, comprehend, and gain knowledge from what they read**. The instructional plan found in *Open Court Reading* prepares our children for the reality of a literate future. The research and results that support *Open Court Reading* have shown this to be true.

When children are given the structure they need from the beginning, they move beyond that which any program or teacher can provide. Equal access is the right of every child that we are asked to educate. Every child must be taught to read fluently and independently by the end of Grade 1. With *Open Court Reading*, this is a reality, not a chance.

## Every Teacher Deserves the Best Program and Support for Teaching It

### The Best Program

According to the latest research, the classrooms of the most effective teachers are characterized by:

- High academic engagement
- Excellent classroom management
- Positive reinforcement and cooperation
- Explicit teaching of skills
- An emphasis on literature
- Plenty of reading and writing practice
- Matching of task demands to student competence
- Encouragement of student self-regulation
- Strong cross-curricular connections

(CELA Report Number 11007)

Only a reading program such as *Open Court Reading* can help you accomplish such a daunting list of tasks.

*Open Court Reading* is the only reading program that provides:

- **An educational philosophy based on scientific research and nearly 40 years of practical classroom experience**
- **A program that has been successful in classrooms nationwide**
- **A partnership through training that will help you not only successfully implement *Open Court Reading*, but also understand solid reading instruction**

What does this mean to you? **Success**, and the added assurance that the children in your classroom are getting **the best program available**.

## What Open Court Means to Me

"Personally, I find your program very helpful for teaching my students. I teach at a high-risk school, and this series is not just for accelerated readers."

– Ryan Williams, Teacher

"Open Court is the most complete program that I have seen in my career."

– Linda LaMarre, Superintendent

"Open Court is not just phonics-oriented, but it includes phonics, comprehension, and writing…It is important to consider all aspects of reading instruction. If a school chooses a program that relies on phonics alone, teachers will abandon the program when they realize it does not offer the balanced instruction that Open Court does."

– Marge Thompson, Principal

"In 26 years of work in education, I have never experienced the high level of support we received from SRA. It's really amazing!"

– Lois Zercher, Assistant Superintendent

"People are always looking for quick fixes to education problems in this country and there aren't any. Open Court requires a lot of work on the part of the teacher and students, but we're happy to work hard if we're going to keep getting such great results."

– Diane Yules, Reading Specialist

For more Open Court Success Stories, call 1-800-SRA-4543 or visit SRA's web site at www.sra4kids.com.

## Support for Teaching

One component of the success of *Open Court Reading* is SRA's strong commitment to professional development. SRA is dedicated not only to the education of students, but of educators as well.

During one of our many training events, you learn not only how to successfully implement *Open Court Reading*, but also how to successfully implement the best educational practices in your classroom. Our professional team of consultants are former classroom and Open Court teachers who know our program intimately. They continuously participate in professional development training in order to make sure that the information they share with you is the best and the most current.

We provide support through:

- In-service training
- On-site follow-up
- Weekend seminars
- Online training
- Summer institutes
- Professional development guides
- Training video collection

Teachers and administrators may get information about training sessions by calling the Teacher Learning Exchange at 1-800-382-7670 or by visiting www.tlexchange.com

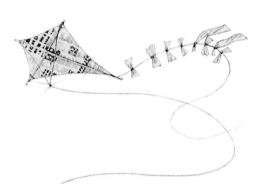

**Lesson I**

## Gloria Who Might Be My Best Friend     14A

*realistic fiction written by* Ann Cameron • *illustrated by* Ann Strugnell

**Lesson Skills**

| Phonics and Fluency | Word Knowledge | Comprehension | Language Arts |
| --- | --- | --- | --- |
| • Short Vowels | • /ī/ Spelled i_e, _y, igh<br>• Inflectional Endings<br>• /a/ | **Strategies**<br>• Making Connections<br>• Predicting<br>• Summarizing<br>**Skills**<br>• Classify and Categorize | • The /a/ Sound<br>• Writing: Autobiography<br>  Getting Ideas<br>• Nouns |

**Lesson 2**

## Angel Child, Dragon Child     28A

*realistic fiction written by* Michele Maria Surat • *illustrated by* Vo-Dinh Mai
🏅 *ALA Booklist Editor's Choice*

**Lesson Skills**

| Phonics and Fluency | Word Knowledge | Comprehension | Language Arts |
| --- | --- | --- | --- |
| • /m/ Spelled -mb<br>• /e/ Spelled ea<br>• Short Vowels<br>• Closed Syllables | • Plural -s<br>• Inflectional Endings<br>• Homographs<br>• Comparative and<br>  Superlative Adjectives<br>• /e/ Spelled e | **Strategies**<br>• Visualizing<br>• Summarizing<br>• Asking Questions<br>**Skills**<br>• Cause and Effect | • The /e/ Sound<br>• Writing: Autobiography<br>  Prewriting<br>• Pronouns |

**Lesson 3**

## The Tree House     48A

*realistic fiction written by* Lois Lowry • *illustrated by* Trina Schart Hyman

**Lesson Skills**

| Phonics and Fluency | Word Knowledge | Comprehension | Language Arts |
| --- | --- | --- | --- |
| • /ā/ Spelled a, ai_, a_e,<br>  _ay | • Antonyms<br>• Homophones<br>• Prefix re-<br>• Related Words<br>• Review /i/ | **Strategies**<br>• Asking Questions<br>• Making Connections<br>• Visualizing<br>**Skills**<br>• Compare and Contrast | • The /i/ Sound<br>• Writing: Autobiography<br>  Drafting<br>• Action Verbs |

# Getting Started

## Preparing to Use

**SRA Open Court Reading**

This section provides an overview of classroom management issues and introductory activities that explain the function of the *SRA/Open Court Reading* program elements and how to use them.

# Introductory Lessons

The major goals of the **Getting Started** introductory lessons are:

- to help students review and restart those skills learned in earlier grade levels.
- to help you obtain a clear picture of your students' strengths, needs, and prior learning.

## Why a Special Getting Started Section?

Reading programs are often set up as if the first day of a new school year happens the day after the last day of the previous school year. This approach ignores the fact that students have approximately two months between the end of the school year and the beginning of the next. *SRA/Open Court Reading* recognizes this fact, and the fact that many students do little during those two months to retain and strengthen the skills and knowledge they acquired during the previous school year. This special **Getting Started** section is a quick review of important reading skills that will remind students of previous learning and get them ready for learning in the new school year.

These lessons also introduce key elements of the program, such as the Word Bank, Discussion, Writing Seminar, Concept/Question Board, and Writing Center in context.

In addition, the **Getting Started** section offers you an effective way to evaluate what your students already know and what they need to know in order to be successful in your class. This knowledge will allow you to base your reading instruction on fact rather than on assumptions, giving you and the students an opportunity to build on previous learning and to learn new and vital skills.

Most important, the **Getting Started** activities allow students to begin Unit 1 of regular instruction knowing that they possess the necessary skills.

## Pacing

Whereas the *SRA/Open Court Reading Student Anthology* lessons are intended to fill three to five days, the five **Getting Started** lessons are presented in a daily lesson format and should be completed in about a week. You may spend more or less time on a specific lesson, depending on the needs of your students. If your students had the *SRA/Open Court Reading* program in the past, they should move quickly. These students should soon remember and start using the skills they learned in earlier grade levels.

The atmosphere should be relaxed, and both you and the students should view **Getting Started** as a period of rediscovery before taking on the new challenges of this grade level. Point out to students that the purposes of the lessons are, first, to review quickly what they learned the previous year, and, second, to give them a preview of the kind of wonderful stories they will read in this grade level.

# Organizing Your Classroom

## Phonics Instruction

In the *SRA/Open Court Reading* program, early reading instruction does not assume that students already know the alphabetic principle. Instruction involves the systematic, explicit teaching of sound/spellings, the blending of sounds into words, and the application of this knowledge to reading and writing.

## Sound/Spelling Cards

The *Sound/Spelling Cards,* are used to introduce or review sound/spellings. Each card contains the common spelling or spellings of a sound. With the exception of the long vowel *Sound/Spelling Cards,* each card depicts both an action-sound association and a picture of something whose name includes the sound. Alliterative stories for the cards are found in the Appendix of this guide.

The *Sound/Spelling Cards* are numbered and should be displayed in order. Place them in a prominent place in the classroom so that all students can see them and use them for reference. As you proceed through the *Getting Started* activities and through the first three units of regular instruction, you and your students may need to point out specific cards as a review. Therefore, the cards should be placed low enough to make this possible but high enough for all students to have an unobstructed view of them.

Although they are not specifically referenced in the final three units, the *Sound/Spelling Cards* should remain on display for the entire school year. They are an invaluable tool for the students in both their reading and their writing.

## Decodable Books

Students need to remain mindful of the ultimate goal of phonics and word knowledge instruction: real reading and writing. Since the best way to practice reading is to read, *SRA/Open Court Reading* provides a wealth of reading materials at each step along the way. Even after students have learned sounds, there are books for students to read for extra practice. Practice reading is most effective when the material is decodable with sounds and spellings students already know and sight words they have learned. The *Decodable Books* are carefully crafted so that students practice the skills they learned with connected text, thereby gaining confidence in their reading abilities.

The *Decodable Books* are simple, colorfully illustrated stories available to be read again and again. They are also available in consumable and blackline forms that children can decorate and take home to share with their families. Two *Decodable Books* are designated for each of the five **Getting Started** lessons. One *Decodable Book* is designed to go along with each lesson in Units 1–4.

## Reading

For students to become more than competent decoders, they must become strategic readers. That is, they must learn how to think about what they read and to use specific reading strategies and behaviors. Teachers help students become strategic readers by modeling the key reading strategies used by expert readers and by providing them with multiple opportunities to read fine literature. First-rate reading selections illustrate for students the best possible use of language and stimulate them to think about, write about, and discuss important ideas and concepts.

## Oral Reading

Reading aloud is one of the best ways for students to develop their reading skills. In the course of the daily lessons, students will read orally from the *Student Anthology* selections. To promote students' reading growth, however, you will want multiple opportunities for oral reading. For example, you may:

- ask students to reread in pairs the anthology selections.
- set aside a period of time each day for oral reading of trade books.
- set up a home reading log, asking parents to read with their children.
- have students partner-read content area texts from other subjects your class is studying.
- Read *Decodable Books* for extra practice with phonics and word knowledge lessons.

However you do it, you will find that every minute of oral reading by students pays off in terms of reading growth.

On a regular basis, take time to listen to students as they read favorite stories and books aloud. Listening to students read from an anthology selection provides you with information about their ability to manage the vocabulary and concepts of the text, as well as to gauge their reading fluency. Listening to students read orally allows you to evaluate their developing fluency and to identify particular areas with which they need more work. To complement these activities, you may also want to listen to students read books they have selected for themselves. This will give you insights into their taste in reading materials, their own opinion of their reading ability, as well as their reading progress.

## Reading Area

Provide as many books as possible for your classroom Reading Area. During the course of the year the students will be asked to do much reading on specific subjects. Prepare your classroom ahead of time by bringing in books on the concepts or themes the students will be studying. You may choose to order the *Leveled Classroom Library* that accompanies the program or you may decide to provide your own library. In either case, you should encourage students to bring in books that they have enjoyed and want to share with their classmates.

## Listening Area

Each selection in the *Student Anthology* is recorded on audiocassette and CD for use in your classroom. As you read each selection, encourage students to listen to the recording during Workshop. Provide one or two tape recorders or CD players that work both with and without earphones. In this way, individual students may listen to selections without disturbing the rest of the class. You will also be able to play the selections for the whole class if you choose.

You should also encourage students to record their own stories, then share these stories with their classmates.

# Writing

Reading and writing are interwoven processes, and each helps build and strengthen the other. Throughout the year, students do a tremendous amount of writing, both independently and collaboratively. They write for an array of purposes and audiences. Extended writing includes stories and various nonfiction pieces such as research reports, biographies, persuasive papers, and letters. In addition, they write daily in the form of note taking, making lists, and making journal entries.

To assure success in writing, the students will need:

- **A Writer's Notebook**
  Each student should provide his or her own Writer's Notebook. This journal can be a three-ring binder with tabbed sections; however, a spiral notebook with sections will work also.

- **A Writing Folder**
  Students should be encouraged continually to revise and edit their writing. Each student should have a folder in which to keep this writing-in-progress. Any pocket folder will work for this purpose; however, you may choose to order the *Writing Folders* that accompany the *SRA/Open Court Reading* program. In addition to pockets to hold student writing, these folders contain a list of proofreading marks and tips for revising that students will find useful.

- **A Writing Portfolio**
  An artist's portfolio contains pieces that the artist considers the best of his or her work. Help students to develop a similar portfolio of their writing. From time to time, hold conferences with individual students so that they can show you the work they have put in their portfolios and explain what they particularly like about the pieces they have chosen to keep.

  You should keep your own portfolio for each student in which you place samples of written work that show the student's progress throughout the year.

## Writing Area

The Writing Area should contain materials students can use to write and illustrate their work and to facilitate the students' efforts as they work together on unit investigations, including:

- pencil and crayons
- pens
- white paper
- colored paper
- old magazines they can cut up
- scissors
- staplers
- reference books such as dictionaries and encyclopedias.
- computers—preferably with Internet access. The SRA Home Page (see www.sra4kids.com) includes materials specifically related to the themes the students are studying.
- books on the themes the students are studying. You may choose to order the *Leveled Classroom Library* that accompanies the program. In addition, bibliographies of additional related books can be found in the unit overviews of the *Teacher's Editions*.

# Inquiry: Reflection and Investigation

In *SRA/Open Court Reading*, lessons are integrated through extensive reading, writing, and discussion. In turn, the lessons are organized into learning units, with each selection in a unit adding more information or a different perspective to the students' growing knowledge of a theme or concept.

Some units allow students to expand their perspectives on universal themes such as kindness, courage, perseverance, and friendship by relating what they read to their own experiences.

Other units involve students in the research process, giving them the tools they need to discover and learn on their own and as part of a collaborative group. Inquiry activities provide students with a systematic structure for investigation that is driven by their own interests and conjectures.

All units are designed to help students:

- deepen their comprehension by enabling them to apply the skills they are learning to texts and activities of their own choosing.

- synthesize and organize what they are learning in order to present their findings to their classmates.
- determine suitable avenues of inquiry and methods of presentation.
- become more independent and responsible about their time and efforts.
- work efficiently in collaborative groups.

## Concept/Question Board

One of the primary goals of *SRA/Open Court Reading* is to help you and your students form a community of learners. To do this, sharing information is essential. The Concept/Question Board is a bulletin board or chart. The students can share their growing knowledge about a unit theme or concept by posting on the Board newspaper clippings, magazine articles, information taken from the Internet, photographs, and other items that might be of interest to or help for their classmates. As the class progresses through a unit, the Board serves as the place where common interests become evident. As these interests emerge, the students can use them as the basis for forming collaborative groups to investigate ideas in greater depth.

In addition, the Board gives students an outlet for questions that arise as they read on their own. The questions can be written directly on a sheet of paper attached to the Board, or they can be written on separate slips of paper and pinned to it. Self-sticking notepads can also be used. The Concept/Question Board lets students know that questions are not problems but a way of learning. Questions thus become a springboard to further investigation. Collaborative groups can be formed around common questions.

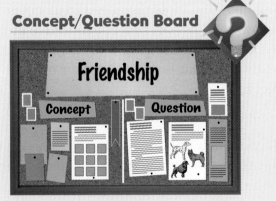

**Concept/Question Board**

Friendship

Concept    Question

The Board should change constantly, reflecting the developing and changing interests of the class. For the **Getting Started** section you can give the Board a title, such as "Reading and Writing."

## Differentiating Instruction: Workshop

Workshop is integral to *SRA/Open Court Reading*. It is during this time, which you designate as a part of each class day, that students gain the experience of managing their own learning process. During Workshop, students work on their own or collaboratively to practice and review material taught in the lessons or to complete projects of their own choosing. As the students gradually take more responsibility for their work, they learn to set learning goals, to make decisions about the use of time and materials, and to collaborate with classmates. Of equal importance, Workshop gives you a designated time each day to work with students one-on-one or in small groups.

During Workshop, your students can:

- read to each other for pleasure and to increase fluency.
- work independently and in small collaborative groups on their investigations.
- work on unfinished writing projects.
- work on any unfinished projects or assignments they have.
- assess what projects they have that need work, prioritize their time, and direct their own efforts.

During Workshop, you can:

- work with individuals and small groups who have shown a need for additional instruction.
- listen to individuals read in order to assess informally their progress and help them gain fluency.
- conduct writing conferences with individual students to discuss their progress as writers.

The Reading, Listening, and Writing Areas will be used extensively during Workshop. If possible, equip these areas with furniture that is easy to move and will allow for both independent work and small group work.

# Getting Started Checklist

This checklist will help you be prepared for the school year. Look back over the Getting Started section if you have any questions about these program elements.

- ○ **Organize Student Anthologies and Workbooks**
- ○ **Set Up Reading Area**
- ○ **Establish Listening Area**
- ○ **Plan for Discussions**
- ○ **Plan for Writing Notebook**
- ○ **Establish Writing Folder**
- ○ **Establish Writing Area**
- ○ **Develop Concept/Question Board**
- ○ **Plan for Workshop**

*Inquiry*
*hardcard/Rolodex with website addresses*

*★ make Chart ★*

*Comp. Strategies*
*ask questions*
*clarify*
*make connections*
*  "  predictions*
*summarize*
*visualize*

*Genre*
*historical Fiction*
*mystery*
*fiction believable*
*poem fable; folktale*
*Non-Fiction*
*autobiography*
*biography*
*journal*

*Comp. Skills*

# Day 1

## Getting Acquainted

Have students introduce themselves to each other. Have students tell which of the other students they have had in their class before. Encourage new students to the school to tell a little about themselves—where they came from, what school they went to, etc.

## Reading

### Background Knowledge

To activate the students' background knowledge, have them discuss what they know about reading. List their comments on the board or on paper.

Encourage students to bring to class their favorite books or stories. Each day, invite a volunteer to read a story. You might want to tell students to practice reading their stories out loud before they read them for the class.

Listeners should be encouraged to politely ask for clarification whenever unfamiliar words or ideas are presented in the reading. Learning to ask politely for assistance should always be fostered during reading.

Read *Decodable Book 1,* "Dave the Brave" and *Decodable Book 2,* "Sleepy Steve" for practice.

## Discussion

Discussion is an integral part of learning. Through discussion, students are exposed to different points of view and reactions to text. They also learn to express their thoughts and opinions coherently as well as to respect the ideas and opinions of others.

Listening and responding to each other's ideas and questions is fundamental to learning. Throughout the program students are expected to listen and respond to each other—during Writing Seminar, collaborative activities, exploration of the unit concepts—not just in a discussion about a story. Talk about what a discussion is and what is expected of participants during a discussion. Students must listen to what others are saying and respond to what is being said. Students should not interrupt, raise their hands when they want to say something, ask questions of each other, not talk while others are speaking, take turns, and respond to the question or idea rather than going off on a different or unrelated thought or tangent.

### Handing off

Through a process called *handing off,* students learn to take the primary responsibility for holding and controlling a discussion. *Handing off* simply means that each student who responds in a discussion is responsible for drawing another student into the discussion.

During this initial lesson, you may want to begin a discussion by asking a question or making a statement. Have a student respond to your question, ask a question, or make a comment of his or her own, calling on another student to respond or react.

## Concept/Question Board

Encourage students to add to the Concept/Question Board throughout the **Getting Started** lessons. They can write what they know about reading, writing, and learning, find articles and pictures, or add information about their favorite books.

Talk about reading and any problems the students had learning to read. Ask what they read, what they liked, and what they learned. Encourage students to ask questions as well. Write these on pieces of paper and put them on the Concept/Question Board.

## Writing

The writing process will be formally introduced in the first unit. Talking about the process here will help you evaluate your students' understanding of writing. Talk about the idea that one of the most important things that good writers do is take time to think before they write. They think about what they know, what they want to write about, and whether they need to get more information. Have the students talk about reading, problems they have had, favorite stories they have read, and the like. Make a list of possible writing ideas and keep it for tomorrow. Tell the students that they will start to think about these ideas and that tomorrow you will review them and add any more ideas if the students have them.

# Day 2

## Reading

Ask students to share some of the stories or books they have brought in. If any of the students are ready, have them read aloud a story to the rest of the class. Start a Word Bank with any words the students have difficulty with. Tell students that the Word Bank will grow as the year goes on and that in addition to problematic words, they will add words that have to do with particular ideas or concepts and words that they particularly like.

Read *Decodable Book 3,* "The Shy Bird's Trick" and *Decodable Book 4,* "Chinlow of Singboat" for practice.

## Discussion

Quickly review what good participants do during a discussion. Remind the students of the discussion they had yesterday and how they led the discussion using *handing off*. Once again, you may have to get the students started with questions or statements such as, "That was interesting, tell me what you like best about the story." When the first student is finished responding, he or she should select the next student to continue the discussion.

### Concept/Question Board

Have students place any new questions or comments they have about reading and writing on the Concept/Question Board. Be sure to note any articles, books, or pictures any of the students have brought in and put on the Board.

## Writing

### Writing Area

Discuss with the students the purposes of the Writing Area. Walk the students through the different materials you have in the center: pencils, crayons, markers, pens, white paper, colored paper, old magazines for ideas and illustrations, scissors, staplers, and dictionaries and a thesaurus as reference tools.

### Writing Folder

Distribute the *SRA/Open Court Reading Writing Folder* to the students. Have the students write their names on the folders. Give the students time to look over the folders and comment on them. Tell the students that they will use these folders all year to hold the writing pieces they are working on.

If you didn't order the *SRA/Open Court Reading Writing Folder,* have students each bring a pocket folder to use as a writing folder.

### Drafting

Review the ideas for writing that the students generated yesterday and ask if there are new ideas that they would like to add to the list. Explain to the students that after writers think about what they might want to write, they begin writing a first draft. Tell the students that they don't have to worry about this being neat or perfect. Encourage students to leave a line or two between each line they write. This will give them room to make changes later. They will have a chance to rewrite their story after they have read it and made any changes they want. The point of writing in **Getting Started** is for you to get a sense of the students' knowledge of the writing process and writing skills including spelling, grammar, and mechanics.

Have the students choose a topic from the list or a topic of their own and begin writing. As the students are writing, conference with individual students. Holding conferences with students helps them identify and solve problems. Conferences during this drafting phase help students identify and refine a topic. This is also a good time to observe students as they are writing. Remember, as you are conferencing:

- You don't have to meet with every student every day.
- Conferences should be brief.
- Don't take ownership of the student's work.
- Encourage students to identify what is good and what problems they are having.
- Leave students with a positive comment.

At the end of the writing time, have the students put their drafts in their writing folders and either put their folders in their desks or in a file box in the Writing Area.

# Day 3

## Reading

Give students the grade level pretest. Tell students that this test is a little different from others they have taken; they will not get a grade on this test. This test is to help you know what the students remember from last year. There will be another test like this at the end of the year that will show how much they have learned this year. If the students don't know some of the answers, tell them not to worry. There is a lot to learn about reading and writing and they will be able to meet the challenge and do it by the end of the year.

Read **Decodable Book 5,** "Mrs. Music" and **Decodable Book 6,** "Paul, Aunt Maud, and Claude" for review and practice.

## Writing

### Continue Writing

Remind students of the Writing Area. During writing today, they can go to the center if they need any materials. Have the students continue the story they began yesterday. Conference with students, noting those that might have something to share during Seminar which will be introduced today. Look for students with interesting ideas, creative topics, extended sentences, etc.

### Writing Seminar

Introduce the students to the idea of Seminar. Seminar is a time when the students will be able to share their work with each other. This is a time when two or three students will share their work with the class and then their classmates will have time to give feedback. Seminar participants must listen carefully and politely, just as they do during discussion and *handing off.* When the author is finished reading, the other students should say something positive about what the author wrote. They can tell what they liked and why; how the author's story made them feel good; and what the author's story reminded them of. You may need to

model this in the beginning by telling what you liked about the story and why. Be sure to let students know that over the next few days everyone will have a chance to share their stories.

## Differentiating Instruction: Workshop

Introduce the idea of Workshop. Workshop is a period of time each day in which the students will work collaboratively or independently to practice and review material taught in the lesson or to complete projects related to the unit theme. Tell the students that every day, there will be a time when they will be working without you on their own or in small groups. During that time, they may be working on materials that you assign or they may be partner reading, reading independently, working on writing or a unit investigation, or meeting with you.

Meet with the students and establish rules for Workshop. These might include:

- Be polite.
- Share with others.
- Use your inside voice (or whisper).
- Take only the material you need.
- When you are finished, clean up and put away the materials you used.

You may want to post these rules, review them periodically, and revise them if necessary.

## Reading Area

The students have already learned about the Writing Area. Introduce the Reading Area today. In this area, students will find books, magazines, newspapers, and other reading materials. Students should be encouraged to bring in favorite books and share them in the center. Let students know they can come and choose a book any time they have free time, not just during Workshop.

## Concept/Question Board

While you are not reading with the students today, give them a few minutes to add to the Concept/Question Board.

# Day 4

## Reading

In preparation for beginning the first unit, you might ask the students if they have read any stories about the unit theme. Encourage the students who have read such stories to retell them and tell what they thought of them. Gently encourage students to be specific in their comments. Instead of settling for "I liked the story," have the students elaborate on their thoughts by explaining what it was about the story that they liked.

Read *Decodable Book 7,* "Flower the Cow" and *Decodable Book 8,* "Toy Store Explorer" for review and practice.

## Writer's Notebook

Throughout the course of the year, your students will be asked to do a tremendous amount of writing. Reading and writing are closely interwoven and each will help build and strengthen the other. In order to assure the best results and success in writing, the students will need a Writer's Notebook. Each student should provide his or her own Writer's Notebook. This notebook can be a three-ring binder with tabbed sections; however, a spiral notebook with sections works also. Use time during **Getting Started** to let the students prepare their Writer's Notebooks. The following sections are suggested:

- **Response Journal** in which students will write a personal response to the literature they read
- **Vocabulary** in which students will record vocabulary or spelling words they need to learn
- **Writing Ideas** in which students record ideas for future writing they want to do as well as ideas gained during brainstorming sessions
- **Personal Dictionary** in which students record concept related words or any new word they learn and want to remember

Take time to have students put together their Writer's Notebooks. If some students don't finish, have them complete their notebooks during Workshop.

## Listening Area

Remind the students of the Writing Area and the materials that are there and the fact that students can use them at any time during writing, Workshop or free time. Today introduce the Listening Area. Tell students that there will be an audiocassette and CD of all the selections in their anthology.

## Workshop

Review the rules for Workshop. Tell the students that today they can continue work on their stories or they may want to begin a new story. They can also go to the Reading Area, Listening Area, or complete or decorate their Writer's Notebooks. Since this is the first time students are involved in Workshop, you may want to assign students to the different areas. Circulate as students are working.

## Concept/Question Board

Give students a few minutes to add to the Concept/Question Board information about what they learned today or any questions they have.

# Day 5

## Reading

If you have favorite stories about the unit theme, read them to the students. As you read these stories, encourage discussion about how they are alike and how they are different. Stories on the same topic generally approach the subjects differently, which adds new perspectives. The ability of the students to see these perspectives will be very important to them as they progress through their school careers.

Read **Decodable Book 9,** "A Book for Mr. Hook" and **Decodable Book 10,** "Root Stew" for review and practice.

## Writing

Today you will introduce the students to revision and proofreading. Have one or two students read their stories in Seminar. As students are reading their stories, listen for short sentences that could be extended. After students have read their stories, encourage them to extend some of the sentences. Explain that extending sentences makes stories more interesting for the reader. Have students work on revising their stories by extending sentences. Show students how they can do this by putting in a carat (^) and writing their extensions in the blank lines they have left. Conference with individual students or small groups of students as they are revising their stories. At the end, have several students share sentences they have extended.

### Proofreading

Today, students will also be informally introduced to proofreading. Tell students that when proofreading, if they find a mistake or problem, they should circle the word and write it correctly. Explain to students that they will proofread their stories to be sure the words are spelled correctly, that they have used capitals and punctuation correctly, and that they have used words correctly.

## Sentence Lifting

Sentence Lifting is an effective and engaging way to model proofreading using sentences taken from the students' writing. Students are expected to identify and correct their own errors. Since you should use both sentences with errors and sentences without errors, the students see examples of correct writing. The focus is a positive one and helps students understand that all writers make mistakes and need to improve on their writing.

In preparation for sentence lifting, look through the students' writing folders for common errors in capitalization, punctuation, or spelling. Select some sentences that contain errors and others that don't. Copy the sentences on the board or on an overhead transparency.

Read the first sentence with a mistake. Have students identify what needs to be changed. Circle the errors and have the students tell you how to write it correctly. Help the students with spellings they are unsure of. Point out any errors that the students miss.

Give students additional time to proofread their own papers and make changes. Conference with students who need help. You may wish to spend additional time with them during Workshop.

## Concept/Question Board

Give the students a few minutes to add to the Concept/Question Board information about what they learned today or any questions they have.

## Workshop

Remind students that as they begin their unit investigations, they will need resources to help them. Show students what has been supplied for inquiry purposes in the Writing Area and where the supplies are kept.

By this time, students should be comfortable with the set up of the room, acquainted with you and each other, and ready to move into the anthology.

# SRA

# OpenCourt READING

## Level 3 • Unit 1
# Friendship

## UNIT I  Friendship

**F**riendship can be confusing, nice, sad, and very, very important. What is a friend? How do you become a friend? What can you expect of a friend? Everyone has these questions, but what are the answers?

12

13

# Exploring the Theme

## Introduction

Friendship is one of the most consuming concerns of students in middle childhood. Students have many ideas about what makes, and what breaks, a friendship. Although relationships within the family are still primary in Grade 3, relationships outside the family start to play a more dominant role. As students investigate this world, they learn in a new way about the joys and pitfalls inherent in friendship.

Listening to students' ideas about what constitutes a good friendship and helping them clarify their own views are crucial activities at this point. Starting with their current understanding of friendship greatly increases the possibility of their gaining a deeper understanding of the concept by the unit's end.

*Teacher's Edition* page numbers correspond to page numbers in the *Student Anthology.*

# Investigation Goals

The investigation goals for this unit are as follows:

- To deepen knowledge of what friendship is.
- To create an awareness of who can be friends and how to make friends.
- To investigate how to mend damaged friendships.
- To develop an understanding of what makes a good friend.
- To use the research cycle to investigate questions related to the concept of friendship.

# Learning Goals

Within each of the general investigation goals, a number of more specific learning goals are pursued. Students will:

- **learn** to read.
- **listen, write, and speak** on the topic of friendship.
- **participate in small and large group discussions** about friendship.
- **ask and answer questions** relevant to friendship.
- **relate the ideas and experiences of the texts** to their own ideas and experiences.
- **develop** a vocabulary about friendship.
- **make cultural connections** by reading the selections.
- **identify different types of literature.**
- **identify the writer's craft** in the narrative genre.
- **conduct and report** on interviews of immigrants and other experts.
- **create and perform** fictional scenes related to the area of investigation.
- **lead panel discussions** about concepts.

**Teacher Tip** To facilitate your own understanding of and feelings about friendship, you might wish to consider the following questions:

- ✓ Is it better to have a large number of friends or a few close ones?
- ✓ Can you be better friends with someone you have known for a few days than with someone you have known for years?
- ✓ Is it okay to tell a lie to keep a friend from getting into trouble?
- ✓ What is the most important thing you look for in a friend?
- ✓ Being friends with some people is easy, but with others it is hard work. Should that fact be the determining factor in deciding who will be your friend?
- ✓ What are the benefits and hardships of having friends?
- ✓ Why are friends so essential in our lives?

# Exploring the Theme

## Supporting Student Investigations

Students are encouraged to deepen their knowledge of each of the themes presented throughout **Open Court Reading.** In learning more about friendship, students will need to talk to people about it, as well as read stories and articles that revolve around the theme of Friendship.

Encourage students to use their personal experiences to interpret the literature they read about friendship. Because it is also important for students to extend their thinking and for their views to be challenged and developed, encourage them to use this literature to reinterpret their personal experiences.

Explain to students that they will gain a better understanding of the concept of friendship as they progress through the unit's selections and as they work on the unit investigation.

Following are some formats students may want to use for the presentation of their investigations. Be sure to tell students that this is just a list of suggestions and they are encouraged to propose their own ideas.

- A miniplay or puppet show about friendship
- A role-playing game to work out a problem about friendship
- A panel discussion about friendship-related issues
- A debate on an issue related to friendship
- A newspaper column dealing with friendship-related problems
- A personal experience story about friendship

Explain to the students that they may work on their investigations alone, with partners, or in small groups. Throughout each lesson, monitor student progress and encourage students to report problems they encounter in preparing their investigations.

## Unit Investigations

Unit investigations are student-driven and should emerge from students' interests, encouraged or ignited by their reading and class discussions. Unit investigations should involve reading beyond the program material and should address the conceptual aims of the unit.

### Suggested Activities

The suggested activities below are intended to support the unit investigation.

- Students might want to discuss ideas about who can be friends. For example, can third grade girls and boys really be friends?
- Students might choose to investigate how people who have immigrated to this country have gone about making friends and being understood by conducting interviews or inviting a guest speaker to class.
- Students might discuss methods for repairing damaged friendships.
- Students can conduct a literature search to identify qualities, such as courage, that make up good friendships.
- Students invite a guest speaker to class to discuss ideas about team spirit and the qualities important to being a team member.
- Students interview each other or other teachers about the meaning of trust and loyalty and how they relate to friendship.

| | OVERVIEW OF SELECTION | LINK TO THE THEME | UNIT INVESTIGATIONS | SUPPORTING STUDENT INVESTIGATIONS |
|---|---|---|---|---|
| **Lesson 1** *Gloria Who Might Be My Best Friend* | ■ In this piece of realistic fiction, Julian tests his skills at making friends with the new kid on the block, who just happens to be a girl. | ■ Julian models for readers how they might try making friends with someone they wouldn't initially consider their type of friend. | ■ Facilitate discussion of questions about friendship. | ■ Introduce the research cycle.<br>■ Introduce the Concept/Question Board. |
| **Lesson 2** *Angel Child, Dragon Child* | ■ This moving story tells of a Vietnamese child's first experiences in an American school—her feelings of separation and alienation, and her subsequent joy as she is understood and accepted. | ■ The importance of talking and listening to others becomes obvious as readers discover that getting to know someone better can help to create a lasting friendship. | ■ Students can investigate the challenges of friendship related to immigration. They can host guest speakers to class or conduct their own interviews. | ■ Review options for investigations.<br>■ Introduce a schedule for investigations.<br>■ Model investigation questions and problems.<br>■ Students form groups based on areas of interest. |
| **Lesson 3** *The Tree House* | ■ Chrissy and Leah both refuse to let the other visit as they quarrel over whose tree house is best. Finally, though, the girls discover that sharing something increases its worth. | ■ Chrissy learns that sharing her tree house with a friend makes it, and their friendship, even more special. | ■ Students discuss mending damaged friendships. | ■ Investigation groups form conjectures and identify research needs.<br>■ Assist students in forming investigation questions, as necessary.<br>■ Guide students in identifying their investigation needs. |
| **Lesson 4** *Rugby & Rosie* | ■ This selection tells the story of friendship between pets and people. When a puppy comes to stay for just a year, existing relationships change. Will the puppy have to leave? If so, how will things change again? | ■ The characters in this story help readers understand what it's like to have a pet for a best friend. They teach us that sometimes friends have to say goodbye and that even in the midst of sadness over separation, new friendships can begin. | ■ Students discuss the qualities that make good friendships. | ■ Students identify investigation needs and plans.<br>■ Help students revise plans if necessary.<br>■ Help students focus on their investigation questions and needs.<br>■ List knowledge needs and possible sources of information. |
| **Lesson 5** *Teammates* | ■ This piece chronicles the challenges that Jackie Robinson faced as the first African-American baseball player in the major leagues, and the integrity of those who supported him. | ■ This story illustrates a special kind of friendship—one that develops between people who share common goals and beliefs. | ■ Students invite a guest speaker to class to discuss the qualities of a team. | ■ Investigation continues and students expand their source materials.<br>■ Verify information and sources.<br>■ Conduct class discussions to help identify knowledge needs and to consider changes based on investigation problems. |
| **Lesson 6** *The Legend of Damon and Pythias* | ■ Damon and Pythias are legendary figures passed down from the Greek tradition. Their trust and loyalty in each other have made them examples of true friendship. The sacrifice they were willing to make for each other is a lesson in the beautiful potential of friendship. | ■ True friends are loyal to each other because they trust each other.<br>■ Sometimes friendship requires a sacrifice. | ■ Students discuss the meaning of trust and loyalty. | ■ Groups present their investigations.<br>■ Raise new questions for further investigations. |

**PROGRAM RESOURCES**

## Student Materials

**Student Anthology**
**Pages 12–111**

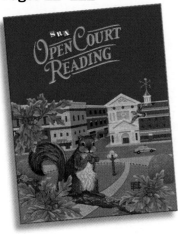

**Inquiry Journal**
**Pages 1–27**

**Writer's Workbook**
**Pages 2–5**

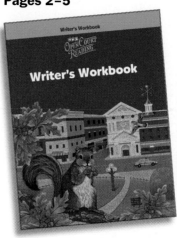

**Comprehension and Language Arts Skills**
**Pages 2–25**

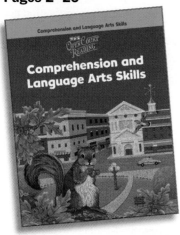

**Spelling and Vocabulary Skills**
**Pages 2–25**

**Language Arts Handbook**

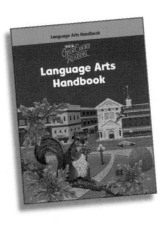

### Additional Materials
- Listening Library Audiocassettes/CDs
- Program Assessment
- Unit 1 Assessment
- Writing Folder
- Student Research Assistant

### Meeting Individual Needs
- ELD Workbook
- Intervention Workbook
- Reteach
- Challenge
- Decodable Books
- Decodable Takehome Books
- Decodable Book Activities CD-ROM
- Leveled Classroom Library

# Teacher Materials

### Teacher's Edition, Book 1
**Pages 12–111P**

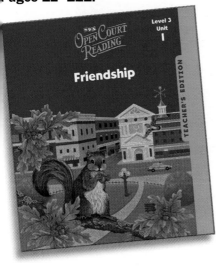

### Read Aloud
*Amos & Boris*

### Home Connection
**Pages 1–14**

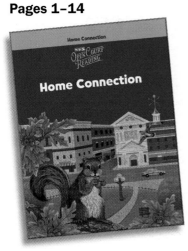

### Comprehension and Language Arts Skills Teacher's Edition
**Pages 2–25**

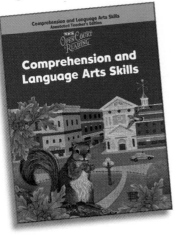

### Spelling and Vocabulary Skills Teacher's Edition
**Pages 2–25**

### Writer's Workbook Teacher's Edition
**Pages 2–5**

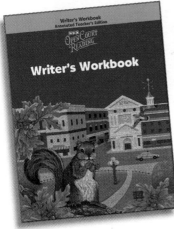

### Overhead Transparencies
Reading Numbers 1–9, 46–53
Language Arts Numbers 2, 7–10, 17–21, 24–25, 27–31, 33, 38

## Additional Materials

- Teacher's Professional Guides
- Phonics Lesson Cards
- Manipulative Package

## Meeting Individual Needs

- ELD Guide
- ELD Glossary
- Intervention Guide
- Intervention Annotated Bibliography
- Reteach Teacher's Edition
- Challenge Teacher's Edition

PROGRAM RESOURCES

## Leveled Classroom Library*

"Stevie" – trade book

| Easy | Average | Advanced |
|------|---------|----------|

## Bibliography**

*Captain Snap and the Children of Vinegar Lane* by Roni Schotter

*Officer Buckle and Gloria* by Peggy Rathmann

*On Call Back Mountain* by Eve Bunting

*Rosie and Michael* by Judith Viorst

*My First American Friend* by Sarunna Jin

*The Tin Heart* by Karen Ackerman

*The Stories Julian Tells* by Ann Cameron

Note: Teachers should preview any trade books and videos for appropriateness in their classrooms before recommending them to students.

\* These books, which all support the unit theme Friendship, are part of a 36-book *Leveled Classroom Library* available for purchase from SRA/McGraw-Hill.

\*\* Check libraries or bookstores for availability.

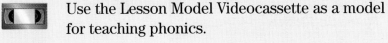

# TECHNOLOGY

## Web Connections

**www.sra4kids.com**

**Friendship Web Sites**

Information about Friendship and links to sites concerning Friendship can be found at www.sra4kids.com.

## CD-ROMs

**\* Decodable Book Activities**

**SRA/MCGRAW-HILL, 2002**

Use the **Decodable Book Activities CD-ROM** activities to support the phonics review in this unit.

**\* Research Assistant**

**SRA/MCGRAW-HILL, 2002**

As students continue their investigation of friendship, encourage them to use the **Research Assistant CD-ROM** program to help them organize and share their findings.

**\* OCR Spelling**

**SRA/MCGRAW-HILL, 2002**

Use this software for extra spelling review in this unit.

**\* The Ultimate Writing and Creativity Center**

**THE LEARNING COMPANY, 2002**

Students can use this word processing software to get ideas, draft, revise, edit, and publish their Writing Process Strategies activities in this unit.

## Computer Skills

**\* Basic Computer Skills**

The **SRA Basic Computer Skills** program can be used to help students develop computer skills within the context of the unit theme.

## Videocassettes

Use the Lesson Model Videocassette as a model for teaching phonics.

**\* All I See**

A boy begins to realize his own artistic vision through his friendship with an artist who sees and paints only whales. Videocassette; 8 min.

**\* The Fledgling**

The mysterious Goose Prince befriends Georgie Hall and helps her to realize her dream of flying. Videocassette; 38 min.

**\* Henry and Mudge Video**

Mudge is Henry's dog and best friend. Enjoy their adventures in *Henry and Mudge in Puddle Trouble*, *Henry and Mudge in the Green Time*, *Henry and Mudge Under the Yellow Moon*, and *Henry and Mudge in the Sparkle Days*. Videocassette; 4 vol. 43 min.

**\* Like Jake and Me**

Alex finally finds a common bond and friendship with his stepfather, Jake, when Alex saves him from a spider. Videocassette; 16 min.

## Audiocassettes/CDs

**\* Listening Library: Friendship**

**SRA/MCGRAW-HILL, 2002**

Students will enjoy listening to the selections they have read. Encourage them to listen during Workshop.

**\* Sound/Spelling Card Stories**

**SRA/MCGRAW-HILL, 2002**

Students can listen to and practice the **Sound/Spelling Stories** during Workshop.

Titles preceded by an asterisk (\*) are available through SRA/McGraw-Hill. Other titles can be obtained by contacting the publisher listed with the title.

# UNIT | OVERVIEW

| | WORD KNOWLEDGE/ PHONICS & FLUENCY | COMPREHENSION | LITERARY ELEMENTS |
|---|---|---|---|
| **Lesson 1** *Gloria Who Might Be My Best Friend* **Genre: Realistic Fiction** | ■ Set 1: /ī/ spelled *i_e*, *_y*, *igh*; inflectional endings; review /a/ ■ Set 2: review short vowels | **Strategies** ■ Making Connections ■ Summarizing ■ Predicting **Skills** ■ Classify and Categorize | ■ Point of View |
| **Lesson 2** *Angel Child, Dragon Child* **Genre: Realistic Fiction** | ■ Set 1: plural *-s*; inflectional endings; homographs; comparative and superlative adjectives; /e/ spelled *e* ■ Set 2: review short vowels; /m/ spelled *-mb*; short e spelled *ea*; closed syllables | **Strategies** ■ Asking Questions ■ Summarizing ■ Visualizing **Skills** ■ Cause and Effect | ■ Plot |
| **Lesson 3** *The Tree House* **Genre: Realistic Fiction** | ■ Set 1: antonyms; homophones; prefix *re-*; related words; review /i/ ■ Set 2: /ā/ spelled *a*, *ai_*, *a_e*, *_ay* | **Strategies** ■ Making Connections ■ Asking Questions ■ Visualizing **Skills** ■ Compare and Contrast | ■ Dialogue |
| **Lesson 4** *Rugby & Rosie* **Genre: Realistic Fiction** | ■ Set 1: suffixes *-ly*, *-ed*, *-ing*; irregular past tense verbs; contractions; /ō/ spellings ■ Set 2: review /ē/ spelled *e*, *ea*, *e_e*, *_y*, *ee*, *ie_* | **Strategies** ■ Predicting ■ Asking Questions ■ Making Connections **Skills** ■ Cause and Effect | ■ Characterization: Analyzing Character Traits |
| **Lesson 5** *Teammates* **Genre: Biography** | ■ Set 1: suffix *-tion*; prefixes and suffixes; frequently misspelled words; plural forms of nouns that end in *-y*; /u/ ■ Set 2: review /ī/ spelled *i*, *_y*, *i_e*, *_ie*, *igh* | **Strategies** ■ Monitoring and Clarifying ■ Summarizing ■ Predicting **Skills** ■ Main Idea and Details | ■ Characteristics of Nonfiction |
| **Lesson 6** *The Legend of Damon and Pythias* **Genre: Myth** | ■ Set 1: inflectional endings and suffixes added to root words; /k/; nouns; short vowels ■ Set 2: review /ō/ spelled *o*, *_ow*, *o_e*, *oa_*, *_oe* | **Strategies** ■ Asking Questions ■ Monitoring and Adjusting Reading Speed ■ Summarizing **Skills** ■ Sequence | ■ Features of a Play |

| INQUIRY | WORD ANALYSIS | WRITING PROCESS STRATEGIES | ENGLISH LANGUAGE CONVENTIONS |
|---|---|---|---|
| ■ Interviewing | **Spelling**<br>■ The /a/ Sound<br>**Vocabulary**<br>■ Vocabulary Strategies | **Introduction to the Writing Process**<br>■ Getting Ideas | **Grammar**<br>■ Nouns<br>**Listening, Speaking, Viewing**<br>■ Listening: Being a Good Listener<br>**Penmanship**<br>■ Cursive Letters $i$ and $t$ |
| ■ Choosing Appropriate Sources | **Spelling**<br>■ The /e/ Sound<br>**Vocabulary**<br>■ Context Clues | **Introduction to the Writing Process**<br>■ Prewriting | **Grammar**<br>■ Pronouns<br>**Listening, Speaking, Viewing**<br>■ Speaking: Speaking Clearly<br>**Penmanship**<br>■ Cursive Letters $u$ and $w$ |
| ■ ABC Order | **Spelling**<br>■ The /i/ Sound<br>**Vocabulary**<br>■ Word Structure | **Introduction to the Writing Process**<br>■ Drafting<br>**Writer's Craft**<br>■ Topic Sentences | **Grammar**<br>■ Verbs: Action, State of Being, Linking<br>**Listening, Speaking, Viewing**<br>■ Language: Changing Our Speech<br>**Penmanship**<br>■ Cursive Letters $r$ and $s$ |
| ■ Following Directions | **Spelling**<br>■ The /o/ Sound<br>**Vocabulary**<br>■ Dictionary Strategy | **Introduction to the Writing Process**<br>■ Revising<br>**Writer's Craft**<br>■ Sentence Variety | **Grammar**<br>■ Verbs: Verb Phrase, Main Verb, Helping Verb<br>**Listening, Speaking, Viewing**<br>■ Viewing: Learning from Pictures<br>**Penmanship**<br>■ Cursive Letters $p$ and $j$ |
| ■ Parts of a Book | **Spelling**<br>■ The /u/ Sound<br>**Vocabulary**<br>■ Thesaurus Strategy | **Introduction to the Writing Process**<br>■ Editing/Proofreading<br>**Writer's Craft**<br>■ Staying on Topic | **Grammar**<br>■ Sentences: The Four Types, End Punctuation, Capitalization of First Letter<br>**Listening, Speaking, Viewing**<br>■ Interacting: Using Gestures<br>**Penmanship**<br>■ Cursive Letters $a$, $c$, and $d$ |
| ■ ABC Order | **Spelling**<br>■ Review Short Vowels<br>**Vocabulary**<br>■ Word Mapping, Word Grouping, and Comparisons | **Introduction to the Writing Process**<br>■ Publishing | **Grammar**<br>■ Review<br>**Listening, Speaking, Viewing**<br>■ Presenting: Sharing Information<br>**Penmanship**<br>■ Cursive Letters $q$, $g$, and $o$ |

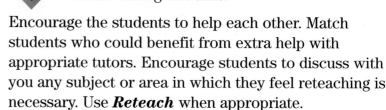

**WORKSHOP**

# Differentiating Instruction

Explain to students that there will be a time every day when they will be expected to work on activities. This time, called Workshop, will be devoted to collaborating on their investigations of unit concepts and working independently to meet each of their individual needs. Students will work on their own, in pairs, or in small groups independently.

Workshop is a means of leading students to make good use of free time. It assures that the needs of all students will be met, from those who require any extra help to the advanced learners. During this time, encourage them all to become independent, self-motivated learners. During Workshop, students will learn to make good use of their time; make decisions about activities, materials, and work; understand organization and care of materials; share and cooperate with others; and adapt skills learned from direct teaching in self-teaching situations.

Students can make the best use of Workshop when:

- A set of rules, such as "be polite, share, and whisper," is posted and observed.
- A set of classroom materials necessary for the various activities is available.
- The physical organization of the classroom facilitates both independent and group activities.
- The teacher closely supervises this time.

Because students will be working on a variety of activities, you will be afforded time and opportunity to differentiate instruction to address the special needs of all students. At this time, you may want to reteach and reinforce previous lessons or preteach upcoming lessons with students who need help, or you might provide individual or small-group lessons related to the students' investigations.

## Meeting Individual Needs

The following are examples of the types of activities that you might have going on during Workshop.

**Collaborating on Investigation**
Students will meet in small groups to formulate questions about the unit concept. They may make assignments that can be investigated individually in order to answer the questions. During this time students may also share and evaluate materials for their investigations. Groups will then meet with the teacher to discuss their goals and assignments.

**Preteaching/Reteaching** The time you set aside for Workshop will also allow you to help individuals or small groups of students who have exhibited a need in any area. If you have students who would benefit from preteaching or reteaching, you have several different options to use during this time.

Encourage the students to help each other. Match students who could benefit from extra help with appropriate tutors. Encourage students to discuss with you any subject or area in which they feel reteaching is necessary. Use **Reteach** when appropriate.

**Independent Reading** Suggest that students find and read other books by authors featured in the unit. Students may wish to read the books listed in the ***Leveled Classroom Library,*** as they will enhance their investigations of the unit theme. Students should also be reading books outside the classroom for 30 minutes daily.

**Partner Reading** Provide time every day for students to read with a partner. Encourage students to reread their anthology selections, taking alternate paragraphs, as well as reading other stories to each other for practice and enjoyment. This is also a time for students to practice reading Decodable books to increase fluency.

**Reading Roundtable** Students may share information about additional books they have read independently and discuss how those books support the unit theme or simply what they thought of their readings: Did they enjoy the books? Why or why not? Would they recommend the books? Reading Roundtable is much like a book club, in which all members read the same book and share their reactions to the story or book.

**Writing Seminar** This is a time students can share their writing and conference with peers.

# Setting Up the Classroom

Setting up your classroom to accommodate different activities will help ensure that Workshop progresses smoothly and effectively. While setting up your classroom, keep in mind the primary activities of Workshop. Since students will be doing both independent and collaborative reading and writing, it is suggested that you provide the following space and materials:

- A reading area supplied with books and magazines.

- A writing and publishing area supplied with paper, pencils, rulers, colored markers, crayons, tape, string, and scissors.

- A listening area that includes a tape recorder (or CD player) and audiocassettes (or CDs) of stories, poems, and songs for students to hear. You might want to provide blank cassettes and encourage the students to use them for writing projects or for other investigations.

- The ***Sound/Spelling Cards*** should line the front wall above the board so that students can easily see the cards.

Students work much better independently when there is adequate space and a sense of order. The room arrangement below is one possibility, but it is not the only way to arrange your classroom, especially if space is an issue. The proposed arrangement provides for easy movement of the students, leaves a large open space on the floor for whole-class and individual activities, facilitates easy access for the teacher, and organizes the class into manageable sections. It also allows the placement of those with visual, auditory, and other impairments in advantageous positions near the front of the room. Students should not be grouped at desks or tables according to ability. They should be heterogeneously grouped.

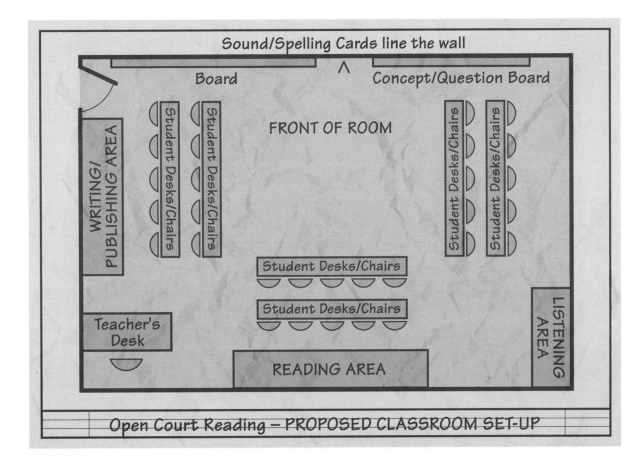

Sound/Spelling Cards line the wall

Board

Concept/Question Board

WRITING/ PUBLISHING AREA

Student Desks/Chairs

Student Desks/Chairs

FRONT OF ROOM

Student Desks/Chairs

Student Desks/Chairs

Student Desks/Chairs

Student Desks/Chairs

Teacher's Desk

LISTENING AREA

READING AREA

Open Court Reading – PROPOSED CLASSROOM SET-UP

## MEETING INDIVIDUAL NEEDS

| | Reteach | ELL | Challenge | Intervention |
|---|---|---|---|---|
| **Lesson 1**<br>*Gloria Who Might Be My Best Friend* | **Language Arts**<br>■ **Spelling:** The /a/ Sound<br>■ **Vocabulary:** Vocabulary Strategies<br>■ **Grammar:** Nouns | **Preparing to Read**<br>■ Word Knowledge<br>**Reading and Responding**<br>■ Selection Vocabulary<br>**Language Arts**<br>■ Vocabulary Strategies; Grammar, Usage, and Mechanics | **Language Arts**<br>■ **Spelling:** The /a/ Sound<br>■ **Vocabulary:** Vocabulary Strategies<br>■ **Grammar:** Nouns | **Preparing to Read**<br>■ Word Knowledge<br>**Reading and Responding**<br>■ Selection Vocabulary<br>**Language Arts**<br>■ Vocabulary Strategies; Grammar, Usage, and Mechanics |
| **Lesson 2**<br>*Angel Child, Dragon Child* | **Reading and Responding**<br>■ Cause and Effect<br>**Language Arts**<br>■ **Spelling:** The /e/ Sound<br>■ **Vocabulary:** Context Clues<br>■ **Grammar:** Pronouns | **Preparing to Read**<br>■ Word Knowledge<br>**Reading and Responding**<br>■ Selection Vocabulary<br>**Language Arts**<br>■ Vocabulary Strategies; Grammar, Usage, and Mechanics | **Reading and Responding**<br>■ Cause and Effect<br>**Language Arts**<br>■ **Spelling:** The /e/ Sound<br>■ **Vocabulary:** Context Clues<br>■ **Grammar:** Pronouns | **Preparing to Read**<br>■ Word Knowledge<br>**Reading and Responding**<br>■ Selection Vocabulary<br>**Language Arts**<br>■ Vocabulary Strategies; Grammar, Usage, and Mechanics |
| **Lesson 3**<br>*The Tree House* | **Reading and Responding**<br>■ Compare and Contrast<br>**Language Arts**<br>■ **Spelling:** The /i/ Sound<br>■ **Vocabulary:** Word Structure<br>■ **Grammar:** Verbs<br>■ **Writer's Craft:** Topic Sentences | **Preparing to Read**<br>■ Word Knowledge<br>**Reading and Responding**<br>■ Selection Vocabulary<br>**Language Arts**<br>■ Vocabulary Strategies; Grammar, Usage, and Mechanics | **Reading and Responding**<br>■ Compare and Contrast<br>**Language Arts**<br>■ **Spelling:** The /i/ Sound<br>■ **Vocabulary:** Word Structure<br>■ **Grammar:** Verbs<br>■ **Writer's Craft:** Topic Sentences | **Preparing to Read**<br>■ Word Knowledge<br>**Reading and Responding**<br>■ Selection Vocabulary<br>**Language Arts**<br>■ Vocabulary Strategies; Grammar, Usage, and Mechanics |
| **Lesson 4**<br>*Rugby & Rosie* | **Language Arts**<br>■ **Spelling:** The /o/ Sound<br>■ **Vocabulary:** Dictionary Strategy<br>■ **Grammar:** Verbs<br>■ **Writer's Craft:** Sentence Variety | **Preparing to Read**<br>■ Word Knowledge<br>**Reading and Responding**<br>■ Selection Vocabulary<br>**Language Arts**<br>■ Vocabulary Strategies; Grammar, Usage, and Mechanics | **Language Arts**<br>■ **Spelling:** The /o/ Sound<br>■ **Vocabulary:** Dictionary Strategy<br>■ **Grammar:** Verbs<br>■ **Writer's Craft:** Sentence Variety | **Preparing to Read**<br>■ Word Knowledge<br>**Reading and Responding**<br>■ Selection Vocabulary<br>**Language Arts**<br>■ Vocabulary Strategies; Grammar, Usage, and Mechanics |
| **Lesson 5**<br>*Teammates* | **Reading and Responding**<br>■ Main Ideas and Details<br>**Language Arts**<br>■ **Spelling:** The /u/ Sound<br>■ **Vocabulary:** Thesaurus Strategy<br>■ **Grammar:** Sentences<br>■ **Writer's Craft:** Staying on Topic | **Preparing to Read**<br>■ Word Knowledge<br>**Reading and Responding**<br>■ Selection Vocabulary<br>**Language Arts**<br>■ Vocabulary Strategies; Grammar, Usage, and Mechanics | **Reading and Responding**<br>■ Main Ideas and Details<br>**Language Arts**<br>■ **Spelling:** The /u/ Sound<br>■ **Vocabulary:** Thesaurus Strategy<br>■ **Grammar:** Sentences<br>■ **Writer's Craft:** Staying on Topic | **Preparing to Read**<br>■ Word Knowledge<br>**Reading and Responding**<br>■ Selection Vocabulary<br>**Language Arts**<br>■ Vocabulary Strategies; Grammar, Usage, and Mechanics |
| **Lesson 6**<br>*The Legend of Damon and Pythias* | **Language Arts**<br>■ **Spelling:** Review Short Vowels<br>■ **Vocabulary:** Vocabulary Strategies<br>■ **Grammar:** Review | **Preparing to Read**<br>■ Word Knowledge<br>**Reading and Responding**<br>■ Selection Vocabulary<br>**Language Arts**<br>■ Vocabulary Strategies; Grammar, Usage, and Mechanics | **Language Arts**<br>■ **Spelling:** Review Short Vowels<br>■ **Vocabulary:** Vocabulary Strategies<br>■ **Grammar:** Review | **Preparing to Read**<br>■ Word Knowledge<br>**Reading and Responding**<br>■ Selection Vocabulary<br>**Language Arts**<br>■ Vocabulary Strategies; Grammar, Usage, and Mechanics |

Above are suggestions for adapting instruction to meet the individual needs of students. These are the same skills shown on the Unit Skills Overview; however, these pages provide extra practice opportunities or enriching activities to meet the varied needs of students.

| ◆ **Informal Assessment** | **Progress Assessment** | ◆ **Formal Assessment** | |
|---|---|---|---|
| Comprehension Strategies, 14J, 14<br>Theme Connection, 27<br>Grammar, Usage, and Mechanics, 27H<br>Listening, Speaking, Viewing, 27I<br>Vocabulary, 27J<br>*Penmanship, 27J | Comprehension and Language<br>  Arts Skills, 2–3<br>Reteach, 2–4<br>Challenge, 2–4<br>Writer's Workbook, 2<br>Spelling and Vocabulary Skills, 2–5<br>Inquiry Journal, 1, 5–9 | Unit 1 Assessment<br>■ Selection Assessment, 2–5<br>■ Spelling Pretest, 26<br>■ Spelling Final Test, 27<br>■ Research Rubrics, 14J<br>*Writing Process Assessment Rubrics, 27J<br>■ Program Assessment<br>  ■ Pretest, 2–9 | Lesson 1 |
| Comprehension Strategies, 28J, 28<br>Theme Connection, 45<br>Grammar, Usage, and Mechanics, 45H<br>Listening, Speaking, Viewing, 45I<br>Vocabulary, 45J<br>*Penmanship, 45J | Comprehension and Language<br>  Arts Skills, 4–7<br>Reteach, 5–9<br>Challenge, 5–8<br>Writer's Workbook, 3<br>Spelling and Vocabulary Skills, 6–9<br>Inquiry Journal, 2, 10–15 | Unit 1 Assessment<br>■ Selection Assessment, 6–9<br>■ Spelling Pretest, 28<br>■ Spelling Final Test, 29<br>■ Research Rubrics, 28J<br>*Writing Process Assessment Rubrics, 45J | Lesson 2 |
| Comprehension Strategies, 48J, 48<br>Theme Connection, 61<br>Grammar, Usage, and Mechanics, 61H<br>Listening, Speaking, Viewing, 61I<br>Vocabulary, 61J<br>*Penmanship, 61J | Comprehension and Language<br>  Arts Skills, 8–13<br>Reteach, 10–15<br>Challenge, 9–13<br>Writer's Workbook, 3<br>Spelling and Vocabulary Skills, 10–13<br>Inquiry Journal, 3, 16–19 | Unit 1 Assessment<br>■ Selection Assessment, 10–13<br>■ Spelling Pretest, 30<br>■ Spelling Final Test, 31<br>■ Research Rubrics, 48J<br>*Writing Process Assessment Rubrics, 61J | Lesson 3 |
| Comprehension Strategies, 64J, 64<br>Theme Connection, 81<br>Grammar, Usage, and Mechanics, 81H<br>Listening, Speaking, Viewing, 81I<br>Vocabulary, 81J<br>*Penmanship, 81J | Comprehension and Language<br>  Arts Skills, 14–17<br>Reteach, 16–19<br>Challenge, 14–17<br>Writer's Workbook, 4<br>Spelling and Vocabulary Skills, 14–17<br>Inquiry Journal, 3, 20–21 | Unit 1 Assessment<br>■ Selection Assessment, 14–17<br>■ Spelling Pretest, 32<br>■ Spelling Final Test, 33<br>■ Research Rubrics, 64J<br>*Writing Process Assessment Rubrics, 81J | Lesson 4 |
| Comprehension Strategies, 82J, 82<br>Theme Connection, 93<br>Grammar, Usage, and Mechanics, 93H<br>Listening, Speaking, Viewing, 93I<br>Vocabulary, 93J<br>*Penmanship, 93J | Comprehension and Language<br>  Arts Skills, 18–23<br>Reteach, 20–25<br>Challenge, 18–22<br>Writer's Workbook, 5<br>Spelling and Vocabulary Skills, 18–21<br>Inquiry Journal, 4, 22–23 | Unit 1 Assessment<br>■ Selection Assessment, 18–21<br>■ Spelling Pretest, 34<br>■ Spelling Final Test, 35<br>■ Research Rubrics, 82J<br>*Writing Process Assessment Rubrics, 93J | Lesson 5 |
| Comprehension Strategies, 94J, 94<br>Theme Connection, 111<br>Grammar, Usage, and Mechanics, 111H<br>Listening, Speaking, Viewing, 111I<br>Vocabulary, 111J<br>*Penmanship, 111J | Comprehension and Language<br>  Arts Skills, 24–25<br>Reteach, 26–28<br>Challenge, 23–25<br>Writer's Workbook, 5<br>Spelling and Vocabulary Skills, 22–25<br>Inquiry Journal, 3–4 | Unit 1 Assessment<br>■ Selection Assessment, 22–25<br>■ Spelling Pretest, 36<br>■ Spelling Final Test, 37<br>■ Research Rubrics, 94J<br>*Writing Process Assessment Rubrics, 111J<br><br>End of Unit 1 Assessment, 38–48 | Lesson 6 |

A S S E S S M E N T

*Teacher's Edition* page reference

## Activating Prior Knowledge

Tell students that good readers relate what they know to what they are reading. Students should get into the habit of thinking about an upcoming theme and selections or activities relevant to that theme. As they read the upcoming selections, they should be certain to relate what they already know about friendship to what they are reading. Ask students questions such as the following:

- What do you know about friendship before we read these selections?
- How do you know if someone is a good friend? How can you be a good friend?
- Have you already read any books about friendship?

As students read the selections, they will encounter some of these ideas as well as new ideas. When they read something they already know, encourage them to make a note about this information. When they learn something new, remind them to notice that, too. This will help students learn about friendship as they read the selections. Encourage students to share any stories they have already read about friendship. For English-language learners and others with limited language experience, exploring friendship on the Internet may be helpful.

When students have had some time to compose their thoughts and ideas, call on volunteers to speak. After each student expresses himself or herself, allow a few minutes for questions. As students present their ideas, add them to the Concept/Question Board.

## Read Aloud

Read aloud to the students the story *Amos & Boris*, by William Steig. Prior to reading, provide students with the following background information.

- Whales are mammals that live in the ocean; they are aquatic mammals. Baleen whales have whalebone plates, instead of teeth, that hang down from the roof of the mouth. They feed on small forms of ocean life by swimming with their mouths open or by gulping water.
- Plankton is a term that refers to small organisms that float in both fresh water and sea water. Plankton include some types of algae, bacteria, protozoans, and crustaceans, among other types of animals. They

are the basis of the food chain, providing food for larger animals, such as whales. The plantlike forms of plankton are called phytoplankton; the animal-like forms of plankton are called zooplankton, although some life-forms do not fit neatly into either category. Plankton are nourished directly from the sun and carbon dioxide from the sea. Plankton turn energy from the sun directly into rich chemical components through the process of photosynthesis.

- Explain to students that a *phosphorescent* sea means that the sea has a glowing, greenish quality. Glow-in-the-dark toys contain phosphorescent minerals.
- The Ivory Coast is now officially known as the Republic of Côte d'Ivoire (kōt dēv wär). (The name change occurred in 1986, after this story was written.) The country is located on the western coast of Africa, bordered by the Atlantic ocean.

It is important for you as the teacher to let your students know that you use the comprehension strategies being taught in the program when you read. Thus, as you read "Amos & Boris," make some predictions aloud about the topic of the selection. As you are reading, let students know what questions occur to you, what images pop up in your mind as you are reading, and how points made in the reading relate to information you already have.

Toward the end of the reading, summarize for students. If you cannot summarize the selection well, let students see you go back and reread to fill in the gaps in your summary. One of the most powerful ways to get students to use comprehension strategies is for them to see you using them.

## About the Author/Illustrator

**WILLIAM STEIG** has written a self-illustrated children's book nearly every year since he began in 1968. During this time, he has won both the Caldecott medal and the Newbery Honor Award. Prior to writing children's books, Steig was accomplished as a sculptor and a cartoonist. The latter earned him a reputation for being an observant satirist. Though his cartoons sometimes contain biting witticisms, he maintains a simpler, less political style when writing children's books. Many of Steig's books were adopted as films and filmstrips, including *Amos & Boris*, which he narrated himself.

*Focus Questions* What would it be like to have a friend whom you rarely have the chance to see? What does it feel like to help a friend who is in great need?

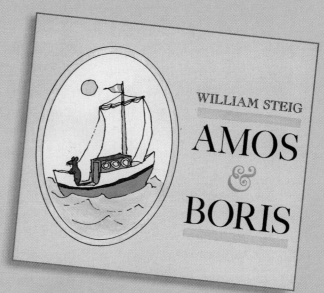

WILLIAM STEIG

AMOS & BORIS

# Amos & Boris

by William Steig

Amos, a mouse, lived by the ocean. He loved the ocean. He loved the smell of sea air. He loved to hear the surf sounds—the bursting breakers, the backwashes with rolling pebbles.

He thought a lot about the ocean, and he wondered about the faraway places on the other side of the water. One day he started building a boat on the beach. He worked on it in the daytime, while at night he studied navigation.

When the boat was finished, he loaded it with cheese, biscuits, acorns, honey, wheat germ, two barrels of fresh water, a compass, a sextant, a telescope, a saw, a hammer and nails and some wood in case repairs should be necessary, a needle and thread for the mending of torn sails, and various other necessities such as bandages and iodine, a yo-yo and playing cards.

On the sixth of September, with a very calm sea, he waited till the high tide had almost reached his boat; then, using his most savage strength, he just managed to push the boat into the water, climb on board, and set sail.

The *Rodent*, for that was the boat's name, proved to be very well made and very well suited to the sea. And Amos, after one miserable day of seasickness, proved to be a natural sailor, very well suited to the ship.

He was enjoying his trip immensely. It was beautiful weather. Day and night he moved up and down, up and down, on waves as big as mountains, and he was full of wonder, full of enterprise, and full of love for life.

One night, in a phosphorescent sea, he marveled at the sight of some whales spouting luminous water; and later, lying on the deck of his boat gazing at the immense, starry sky, the tiny mouse Amos, a little speck of a living thing in the vast living universe, felt thoroughly akin to it all. Overwhelmed by the beauty and mystery of everything, he rolled over and over and right off the deck of his boat and into the sea.

"Help!" he squeaked as he grabbed desperately at the *Rodent.* But it evaded his grasp and went bowling along under full sail, and he never saw it again.

And there he was! Where? In the middle of the immense ocean, a thousand miles from the nearest shore, with no one else in sight as far as the eye could see and not even so much as a stick of driftwood to hold on to. "Should I try to swim home?" Amos wondered. "Or should I just try to stay afloat?" He might swim a mile, but never a thousand. He decided to just keep afloat, treading water and hoping that something—who knows what? —would turn up to save him. But what if a shark, or some big fish, a horse mackerel, turned up? What was he supposed to do to protect himself? He didn't know.

Morning came, as it always does. He was getting terribly tired. He was a very small, very cold, very wet and worried mouse. There was still nothing in sight but the empty sea. Then, as if things weren't bad enough, it began to rain.

At last the rain stopped and the noonday sun gave him a bit of cheer and warmth in the vast loneliness; but his strength was giving out. He began to wonder what it would be like to drown. Would it take very long? Would it feel just awful? Would his soul go to heaven? Would there be other mice there?

As he was asking himself these dreadful questions, a huge head burst through the surface of the water and loomed up over him. It was a whale. "What sort of fish are you?" the whale asked. "You must be one of a kind!"

"I'm not a fish," said Amos. "I'm a mouse, which is a mammal, the highest form of life. I live on land."

"Holy clam and cuttlefish!" said the whale. "I'm a mammal myself, though I live in the sea. Call me Boris," he added.

Amos introduced himself and told Boris how he came to be there in the middle of the ocean. The whale said he would be happy to take Amos to the Ivory Coast of Africa, where he happened to be headed anyway, to attend a meeting of whales from all the seven seas. But Amos said he'd had enough adventure to last him a while. He wanted only to get back home and hoped the whale wouldn't mind going out of his way to take him there.

"Not only would I not mind," said Boris, "I would consider it a privilege. What other whale in all the world ever had the chance to get to know such a strange creature as you! Please climb aboard." And Amos got on Boris's back.

"Are you sure you're a mammal?" Amos asked. "You smell more like a fish." Then Boris the whale went swimming along, with Amos the mouse on his back.

What a relief to be so safe, so secure again! Amos lay down in the sun, and being worn to a frazzle, he was soon asleep.

Then all of a sudden he was in the water again, wide awake, spluttering and splashing about! Boris had forgotten for a moment that he had a passenger on his back and had sounded. When he realized his mistake, he surfaced so quickly that Amos was sent somersaulting, tail over whiskers, high into the air.

Hitting the water hurt. Crazy with rage, Amos screamed and punched Boris until he remembered he owed his life to the whale and quietly climbed on his back. From then on, whenever Boris wanted to sound, he warned Amos in advance and got his okay, and whenever he sounded, Amos took a swim.

Swimming along, sometimes at great speed, sometimes slowly and leisurely, sometimes resting and exchanging ideas, sometimes stopping to sleep, it took them a week to reach Amos's home shore. During that time, they developed a deep admiration for one another. Boris admired the delicacy, the quivering daintiness, the light touch, the small voice, the gemlike radiance of the mouse. Amos admired the bulk, the grandeur, the power, the purpose, the rich voice, and the abounding friendliness of the whale.

They became the closest possible friends. They told each other about their lives, their ambitions. They shared their deepest secrets with each other. The whale was very curious about life on land and was sorry that he could never experience it. Amos was fascinated by the whale's accounts of what went on deep under the sea. Amos sometimes enjoyed running up and down on the whale's back for exercise. When he was hungry, he ate plankton. The only thing he missed was fresh, unsalty water.

The time came to say goodbye. They were at the shore. "I wish we could be friends forever," said Boris. "We *will* be friends forever, but we can't be together. You must live on land and I must live at sea. I'll never forget you, though."

"And you can be sure I'll never forget *you*," said Amos. "I will always be grateful to you for saving my life and I want you to remember that if you ever need my help I'd be more than glad to give it!" How he could ever possibly help Boris, Amos didn't know, but he knew how willing he was.

The whale couldn't take Amos all the way in to land. They said their last goodbye and Amos dived off Boris's back and swam to the sand.

From the top of a cliff he watched Boris spout twice and disappear.

Boris laughed to himself. "How could that little mouse ever help me? Little as he is, he's all heart. I love him, and I'll miss him terribly."

Boris went to the conference off the Ivory Coast of Africa and then went back to a life of whaling about, while Amos returned to his life of mousing around. And they were both happy.

Many years after the incidents just described, when Amos was no longer a very young mouse, and when Boris was no longer a very young whale, there occurred one of the worst storms of the century, Hurricane Yetta; and it just so happened that Boris the whale was flung ashore by a tidal wave and stranded on the very shore where Amos happened to make his home.

It also just so happened that when the storm had cleared up and Boris was lying high and dry on the sand, losing his moisture in the hot sun and needing desperately to be back in the water, Amos came down to the beach to see how much damage Hurricane Yetta had done. Of course Boris and Amos recognized each other at once. I don't have to tell you how these old friends felt at meeting again in this desperate situation. Amos rushed toward Boris. Boris could only look at Amos.

"Amos, help me," said the mountain of a whale to the mote of a mouse. "I think I'll die if I don't get back in the water soon." Amos gazed at Boris in an agony of pity. He realized he had to do something very fast and had to think very fast about what it was he had to do. Suddenly he was gone.

"I'm afraid he won't be able to help me," said Boris to himself. "Much as he wants to do something, what can such a little fellow do?"

Just as Amos had once felt, all alone in the middle of the ocean, Boris felt now, lying alone on the shore. He was sure he would die. And just as he was preparing to die, Amos came racing back with two of the biggest elephants he could find.

Without wasting time, these two goodhearted elephants got to pushing with all their might at Boris's huge body until he began turning over, breaded with sand, and rolling down toward the sea. Amos, standing on the head of one of the elephants, yelled instructions, but no one heard him.

In a few minutes Boris was already in water, with waves washing at him, and he was feeling the wonderful wetness. "You have to be *out* of the sea to really know how good it is to be *in* it," he thought. "That is, if you're a whale." Soon he was able to wiggle and wriggle into deeper water.

He looked back at Amos on the elephant's head. Tears were rolling down the great whale's cheeks. The tiny mouse had tears in his eyes too. "Goodbye, dear friend," squeaked Amos. "Goodbye, dear friend," rumbled Boris, and he disappeared in the waves. They knew they might never meet again. They knew they would never forget each other.

## Discussing the Read Aloud

After you have finished the Read Aloud, ask students the following questions.

- Who are the main characters in this story? (*Amos and Boris*) How do you know they are the main characters? (*The story focuses on their lives.*)
- What did Amos do in the beginning of the story? (*He learned about sailing and built a ship. Then he took it out to sea.*)
- How did Amos and Boris meet? (*They met after Amos fell off his boat. Boris swam up to him and introduced himself. Boris let Amos stay on his back and saved his life.*)
- How did Amos help Boris? (*One day when Boris was grounded on the shore after a storm, Amos got elephants to push Boris back into the sea.*)
- Why was their friendship so special? (*Their friendship was special because on the surface they had nothing at all in common. They each saved the other's life. Their friendship lasted for many years even though they didn't see each other.*)
- Let's review the most important events in the story. What was the first important event? (*Amos and Boris meet.*)

Remind students of some of the questions you asked them to think about before you read the story.

- How do you know if someone is a good friend?
- How can you be a good friend?

Discuss with the class how this Read Aloud is related to the theme Friendship. To stimulate discussion, ask students questions such as the following.

- What did you learn about friendship?
- How does *Amos & Boris* relate to friendship?
- How did *Amos & Boris* change your ideas about friendship?

**Science/Social Studies** SC.G.1.2.2.3.1
**Connection Center**
Refer to the *Science/Social Studies Connection Center* Card 1 for a science activity that students can investigate.

## Concept/Question Board

The Concept/Question Board is a place for students to ask questions and find answers in order to have a better understanding of the unit theme. It is also a place to publish the results of their investigations.

This board could be a standard bulletin board or a large three-sided board placed in the front or to the side of the classroom. The Board will be a permanent place for students to ask questions, post articles or objects, add comments, and so on throughout the study of each unit theme. Students should have easy access to the Concept/Question Board, as they will need to be able to attach items to it on their own and also read what is attached.

Have a large supply of self-stick notepads or index cards and thumbtacks available. Another option is to have students write on paper cut in various shapes that represent each story. For example, you could cut blue construction paper in the shape of a whale to represent the story *Amos & Boris*. Students could write their questions, comments, or theme words on these cutout shapes, which would easily identify the story in the unit.

Ask students to formulate statements about what they know about the unit theme or what they believe to be important about the theme after listening to the Read Aloud. Write these statements and attach them to the Concept side of the Board. Then write any preliminary questions they have about the unit theme and attach those to the Question side of the Board.

Another idea to help students get started is to put up a chart or web that they can add to throughout the unit. For example, you might put up the category *Ways to Keep a Friend Who Moves Away*. As students read the selections in the Friendship unit, they can post examples they find.

As the students progress through the unit, they can refer to the Board

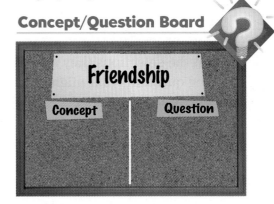

**Concept/Question Board**

Friendship

Concept | Question

to learn which classmates have similar interests. This information can be used to form groups to investigate questions and ideas about the unit theme.

# UNIT | OVERVIEW

## Setting Reading Goals

Good readers regularly set goals when they are reading. Have students examine and share their thoughts on the unit opener in the *Student Anthology,* pages 12–13. Remind them that good readers are always thinking when they read. Also, remind students that good readers browse what they are going to read before reading. Guide their browsing by using the following procedure:

- Turn to the unit opener pages. First, look at the unit title. Ask what the title means and what kinds of selections may be in the unit.

- Look at the illustration on the opener pages. The illustration may answer questions about the title or prompt more questions. Post new questions on the Concept/Question Board.

- Ask students what they are thinking about as they read the unit opener.

- Invite students to browse the selections in the unit. Read the titles and quickly browse each one, looking briefly at the illustrations and the text. Encourage students to look not only at content but also at the genre: Is the selection a story? A poem? Expository text, such as an article? Encourage students to make any observations that interest them.

When students have had sufficient time to browse the unit, encourage them to share their observations. Return to the unit opener on pages 12–13 and use the illustration to help initiate a discussion. Allow them to share whatever comments they have about the illustration.

Tell students that good readers make predictions about what might be in the selections they are about to read. Ask them if they are making predictions about the selections or if they are asking themselves questions about the selections they are about to read. Model asking questions that might have occurred to you as you browsed the selections.

## Inquiry Journal

- After the students have discussed what this unit might be about, have them complete page 1 in their *Inquiry Journal.*

- Share ideas about friendship that they would like to investigate.

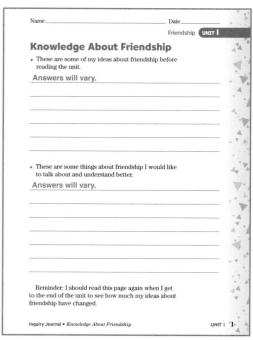

*Inquiry Journal p. 1*

## Professional Resources

Adams, M. J. (1990). *Beginning to read: Thinking and learning about print.* Cambridge, MA: MIT Press.

Adams, M. J. (1990). *Beginning to read: Thinking and Learning about Print: A summary.* Champaign, IL: Center for the Study of Reading.

California State Board of Education. (1998), *Learning to Read.* Sacramento, CA: California State Board of Education.

Honig, B. (1996), *Teaching our children to read.* Thousand Oaks, CA: Corwin Press.

Lehr, F. & Osborn, J. (Eds.) (1994), *Reading, language, and literacy: Instruction for the twenty-first century.* Hillside, NY: Lawrence Eribaum.

National Institute of Education (1985), *Becoming a nation of readers.* Washington, DC: National Institute of Education.

Osborn, J. & Lehr, F. (Eds.) (1998), *Literacy for all: Issues in teaching and learning.* New York: the Guilford Press.

## Home Connection

Each lesson in this program contains a *Home Connection* letter in both English and Spanish. These letters are designed to provide students' families with information about each selection, as well as ideas on how to get families involved in their child's development in reading. Distribute the letter on page 1 of *Home Connection* and encourage students to discuss the theme of Friendship with their families.

Also provided on the *Home Connection* page is a list of the following week's vocabulary and spelling words. Tell parents and students to review and practice these words in preparation for the upcoming week's lessons. This *Home Connection* is also available in Spanish on page 2.

**Home Connection p. 1**

### Research in Reading

#### Joe Campione on Discussion

Students come to understand written language from and through oral language. Discussions that require students, either as part of the class or in a small-group setting, to reflect on their experiences and to communicate their ideas stimulate the cognitive processes that are necessary for knowledge building. Discussions that are tied to reading selections in which students are encouraged to raise questions, offer interpretations, wonder, and challenge, lead to joint construction of meaning and greater comprehension of a selection for all group members.

**Teacher Tip** SETTING READING GOALS
Remind students that good readers regularly set goals when they are reading. Also, make certain students know that they should get into the habit of setting reading goals for themselves, because they should know why they are reading something.

**www.sra4kids.com**
**Web Connection**
Check the Reading link of the SRA Web page for more information on Research in Reading.

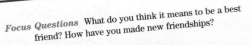

*Focus Questions* What do you think it means to be a best friend? How have you made new friendships?

# Gloria Who Might Be My Best Friend

from *The Stories Julian Tells*
by Ann Cameron
illustrated by Ann Strugnell

If you have a girl for a friend, people find out and tease you. That's why I didn't want a girl for a friend—not until this summer, when I met Gloria. It happened one afternoon when I was walking down the street by myself. My mother was visiting a friend of hers, and Huey was visiting a friend of his. Huey's friend is five and so I think he is too young to play with. And there aren't any kids just my age. I was walking down the street feeling lonely.

14

## Selection Summary

### Genre: Realistic Fiction

This story is realistic fiction, featuring believable characters and a plot that actually could have happened. In Ann Cameron's delightfully upbeat tale, Julian tests his skills at making friends with the new kid on the block—who just happens to be a girl. Julian knows that other boys might make fun of him when they find out, but maybe Gloria will be worth it.

Some of the elements of realistic fiction are:

- The characters behave as people do in real life.
- The setting of the story is a real place or could be a real place.
- The events in the story could happen in real life.

## About the Author

**ANN CAMERON** says that writers are people who capture the positive energy of life, wrap it in paper, and give it, all shimmering and forever bright, to others. Even in third grade, Ann knew she wanted to be one of those people.

*Gloria Who Might Be My Best Friend* received several honors, including the Irma S. and James H. Black Award for Excellence in Children's Literature.

Students can read more about Ann Cameron on page 26 of the ***Student Anthology.***

## About the Illustrator

**ANN STRUGNELL** lives in London, but loves to travel and has visited Spain, Istanbul, and the United States. Strugnell has illustrated many books for children. Drawing on her experiences helps Strugnell to make her artwork interesting.

Students can read more about Ann Strugnell on page 26 of the ***Student Anthology.***

## Inquiry Connections

"Gloria Who Might Be My Best Friend" reminds us all that friendship can bloom anywhere at anytime, with people we never would have supposed would be our friends. Key concepts explored are:

- Friendship can occur between two people who appear to be different, at least on the surface.
- Facing our fears leads to positive results.
- Making assumptions about people based on appearances can be misleading.

Before reading the selection:

- Point out that students may post a question, concept, word, illustration, or object at any time during the course of their unit investigation. Be sure that students include their name or initials on the items they post so that others will know whom to go to if they have an answer or if they wish to collaborate on a related activity.
- Students should feel free to write an answer or a note on someone else's question or to consult the Board for ideas for their own investigations throughout the unit.
- Encourage students to read about friendship at home and to bring in articles or pictures that are good examples to post on the Board.

**Concept/Question Board**

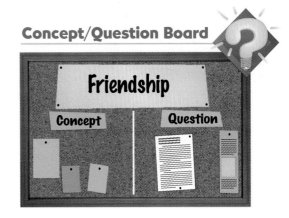

**PROGRAM RESOURCES**

## Leveled Practice

**Reteach**
Pages 2–4

**Challenge**
Pages 2–4

**ELD Workbook**

**Intervention Workbook**

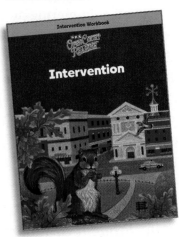

### Decodable Book 11

The Frog Who Wanted to Fly

by Barbara Sieger
illustrated by Kersti Frigell

# Leveled Classroom Library*

Encourage students to read at least 30 minutes daily outside of class. Have them read books in the *Leveled Classroom Library* to support the unit theme and help students develop their vocabulary by reading independently.

### *Alex Is My Friend*

BY MARISABINA RUSSO. GREENWILLOW BROOKS, 1992.

Alex and Ben have been friends since they were little enough to ride in strollers. The friends overcome their differences, even when one is often restricted to a wheelchair. **(Easy)**

### *And to Think That We Thought That We'd Never be Friends*

BY MARY ANN HOBERMAN, CROWN PUBLISHERS, INC., 1999.

Inspired by Dr. Suess' *And to Think That I Saw It on Mulberry Street*, this is a story of how quickly disputes come to an end, and how friendship spreads like wildfire. A friendship started between siblings leads to everyone dancing and playing music in the streets. **(Average)**

### *Best Friends*

BY LORETTA KRUPINSKI. HYPERION, 1998.

Charlotte befriends a Native American girl, Lily, upon moving from her home in Kansas to the Wild West. They communicate through signs and laughter. The unlikely friends are tested when Charlotte learns of the soldiers' plans to drive Lily's tribe off their land. **(Advanced)**

\* These books, which all support the unit theme Friendship, are part of a 36-book *Leveled Classroom Library* available for purchase from SRA/McGraw-Hill.
Note: Teachers should preview any trade books for appropriateness in their classrooms before recommending them to students.

# TECHNOLOGY

## Web Connections

 **www.sra4kids.com**
**Friendship Web Site**

## CD-ROMs

 * **Research Assistant**
**SRA/MCGRAW-HILL, 2002**

 * **Decodable Book Activities**
**SRA/MCGRAW-HILL, 2002**

## Computer Skills

* **Basic Computer Skills**

## Audiocassettes/CDs

 * **Listening Library: Friendship**
**SRA/MCGRAW-HILL, 2002**

 * **Sound/Spelling Card Stories**
**SRA/MCGRAW-HILL, 2002**

Titles preceded by an asterisk (\*) are available through SRA/McGraw-Hill. Other titles can be obtained by contacting the publisher listed with the title.

**LESSON PLANNER**

**Suggested Pacing: 3–5 days**

| | DAY 1 | DAY 2 |
|---|---|---|
| | **DAY 1** | **DAY 2** |

## 1 Preparing to Read

**Materials**
- Student Anthology, Book 1, pp. 14–27
- Decodable Book Activities CD-ROM
- Sound/Spelling Cards 1, 5, 9, 11, 15, 21, 34
- Decodable Book 11
- Lesson Model Videocassette
- Routine Cards, 1, 3, Routines 1–2, 8–9

*Starts Day 1*

**DAY 1**

**Entry Assessment**
- Grade 3 Pretest   *Getting Started*

**Unit Overview**
- Previewing the Unit, pp. 12–13T
- Read Aloud, pp. 13N–13Q   *day before*

**Word Knowledge, pp. 14K–14M**
- /ī/ spelled i_e, _y, igh
- inflectional endings
- review /a/

**About the Words and Sentences, p. 14L**

**DAY 2**

**Word Knowledge**

**Developing Oral Language, p. 14M**

## 2 Reading & Responding

**Materials**
- Student Anthology, Book 1, pp. 14–27
- Program Assessment
- Reading Transparencies 1, 46, 47, 48, 53
- Inquiry Journal, p. 1
- Routine Cards 1–2, Routines 3–6
- Home Connection, p. 2
- Unit 1 Assessment, pp. 2–5
- Writer's Notebook

**DAY 1**

**Build Background, p. 14O**

**Preview and Prepare, pp. 14O–14P**

**Selection Vocabulary, p. 14P**

**Reading Recommendations, p. 14Q**

**Student Anthology, pp. 14–19** [First Read]

✓ **Comprehension Strategies**
- Making Connections, pp. 14, 16
- Predicting, p. 18

**Supporting the Reading, pp. 25C**
- Making Connections

**DAY 2**

**Student Anthology, pp. 20–25** [First Read]

**Comprehension Strategies**
- Summarizing, p. 20
- Predicting, pp. 22, 24

**Discussing Strategy Use, p. 24**

**Discussing the Selection, p. 25A**
- Review Selection
- Complete Discussion

**Meet the Author/Illustrator, p. 26**

✓ **Theme Connections, p. 27**

## Inquiry

**Materials**
- Student Anthology, Book 1, pp. 14–27
- Inquiry Journal, pp. 5–9
- Reading Transparency 2
- Research Assistant CD-ROM

**DAY 1**

**Investigation**
- Investigating Concepts Beyond the Text, p. 27A

**DAY 2**

**Investigation**
- Concept/Question Board, p. 27B

## 3 Language Arts

**Materials**
- Comprehension and Language Arts Skills, pp. 2–3
- Language Arts Handbook, pp. 10, 242
- Language Arts Transparency 38
- Sound/Spelling Card 1
- Spelling and Vocabulary Skills, pp. 2–5
- Student Anthology
- Writer's Workbook, p. 2

**DAY 1**

**Word Analysis**
✓ Spelling: The /a/ Sound Pretest, p. 27F

**Writing Process Strategies**
- Introduction to the Writing Process: Getting Ideas, p. 27F

**English Language Conventions**
- Grammar: Nouns, p. 27F

**DAY 2**

**Word Analysis**
- Spelling: Word Sorting, p. 27G
- Vocabulary: Vocabulary Strategies, p. 27G

**Writing Process Strategies**
- Introduction to the Writing Process: Getting Ideas, p. 27G

**English Language Conventions**
- Grammar: Nouns, p. 27G

| DAY 2 continued | DAY 3 | | |
|---|---|---|---|
| **DAY 3** | **DAY 4** | **DAY 5** | |

---

Ⓟ **Phonics and Fluency, pp. 14M–14N**
- **Review short vowels**

**About the Words and Sentences, p. 14M**

Ⓟ **Phonics and Fluency**
**Developing Oral Language, p. 14N**
**Dictation, p. 14N**

**General Review**

---

**Student Anthology, pp. 14–19** [Second Read]
**Comprehension Skills**
- **Classify and Categorize, pp. 15, 17, 19**

**Social Studies Connection**
- **Maps, p. 25E**

**Student Anthology, pp. 20–25** [Second Read]
**Comprehension Skills**
- **Classify and Categorize, pp. 21, 23, 25**

**Checking Comprehension, p. 25**
**Review Selection Vocabulary, p. 25B**
**Literary Elements, p. 25D**
- **Point of View**

✓**Selection Assessment**
- **"Gloria Who Might Be My Best Friend," pp. 2–5**

**Home Connection, p. 25B**
**Science Connection**
- **Enegy and the Wind, p. 25F**

---

✓**Investigation**
- **Generating Questions to Investigate, p. 27C**

**Supporting the Investigation**
- **Interviewing, p. 27D**

**Investigation**
- **Unit Investigation Continued**
- **Update Concept/Question Board**

---

**Word Analysis**
- **Spelling: The /a/ Sound, p. 27H**
- **Vocabulary:**
  **Vocabulary Strategies, p. 27H**

**Writing Process Strategies**
- **Introduction to the Writing Process: Getting Ideas, p. 27H**

**English Language Conventions**
- **Grammar: Nouns, p. 27H**

**Word Analysis**
- **Spelling: The /a/ Sound, p. 27I**
- **Vocabulary:**
  **Vocabulary Strategies, p. 27I**

**Writing Process Strategies**
- **Introduction to the Writing Process: Getting Ideas, p. 27I**

**English Language Conventions**
✓- **Listening, Speaking, Viewing Listening: Being a Good Listener, p. 27I**

**Word Analysis**
- **Spelling: The /a/ Sound**
✓**Final Test**
- **Vocabulary:**
✓**Vocabulary Strategies, p. 27J**

**Writing Process Strategies**
- **Introduction to the Writing Process: Getting Ideas, p. 27J**

**English Language Conventions**
✓- **Penmanship: Cursive Letters *i* and *t*, p. 27J**

## WORKSHOP

Below are suggestions for differentiating instruction to meet the individual needs of students. These are the same skills shown on the Lesson Planner; however, these pages provide extra practice opportunities or enriching activities to meet the varied needs of students. For Workshop Management Tips, see Appendix.

# Differentiating Instruction

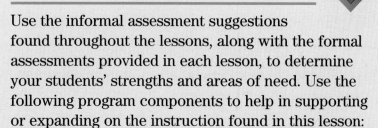

## Small-Group Instruction

Use the informal assessment suggestions found throughout the lessons, along with the formal assessments provided in each lesson, to determine your students' strengths and areas of need. Use the following program components to help in supporting or expanding on the instruction found in this lesson:

***Reteach Workbook*** for use with students who show a basic understanding of the lesson but need a bit more practice to solidify their understanding.

***Intervention Guide*** and ***Intervention Workbook*** for use with students who, even after extra practice, exhibit a lack of understanding of the lesson concepts.

***English-Language Development Guide*** and ***English-Language Development Workbook*** for use with students who need language help.

Have students create small groups to do such things as:

- Discuss questions that arise as they investigate concepts after reading the selection.
- Partner-read to assist those who have problems reading difficult passages or to help develop fluency.

## Independent Activities

### Reading Roundtable

A suggested activity is to have students read other books by Ann Cameron. Teacher model by reading at this time whenever possible.

| | READING | INVESTIGATION ACTIVITIES |
|---|---|---|
| **DAY I** | ■ Record Reaction to Read Aloud in Writer's Notebook<br>■ Browse *Leveled Classroom Library*<br>■ Add vocabulary in Writer's Notebook | ◆ Introduce investigation procedures<br>■ Concept/Question Board<br>■ Record ideas about Friendship in *Inquiry Journal*, p. 1<br>■ Explore OCR Web site (www.sra4kids.com) for Friendship |
| **DAY 2** | ■ Select *Leveled Classroom Library* book for independent reading<br>■ *Listening Library Audiocassette/CD*<br>■ Complete Link to Writing for Supporting the Reading, p. 25C | ■ Concept/Question Board<br>◆ Complete *Inquiry Journal*, p. 5<br>■ Explore OCR Web site (www.sra4kids.com) for Friendship |
| **DAY 3** | ■ Oral reading of selection for fluency<br>■ Record response to selection in Writer's Notebook<br>■ *Listening Library Audiocassette/CD* | ■ Concept/Question Board<br>■ Explore OCR Web site (www.sra4kids.com) for Friendship |
| **DAY 4** | ◆ Partner reading of selection<br>◆ Discuss Theme Connections, p. 27<br>■ Independent reading<br>■◆ Social Studies Connection, p. 25E | ■ Concept/Question Board<br>■ Complete *Inquiry Journal*, p. 6<br>■ Use *Research Assistant* to begin investigation |
| **DAY 5** | ■ Add words to Word Bank<br>■ Complete Independent Practice for Literary Elements, p. 25D<br>■ Reading Roundtable<br>■◆ Science Connection, p. 25F | ■ Concept/Question Board<br>■ Complete *Inquiry Journal*, pp. 7–9 |

◆ **Small-Group Instruction**     ■ **Independent Activities**

| LANGUAGE ARTS | INTERVENTION* | ENGLISH-LANGUAGE LEARNERS** | RETEACH | CHALLENGE |
|---|---|---|---|---|
| **English Language Conventions**<br>■ Complete Nouns, *Comprehension and Language Arts Skills,* pp. 2–3 | **(30 to 45 minutes per day)**<br>◆ Blending, p. 3<br>◆ Preteach "Gloria Who Might Be My Best Friend," pp. 5–6<br>◆ Teach "Intervention Selection One," pp. 6–7<br>◆ Grammar, Usage, and Mechanics, p. 9 | **(30 to 45 minutes per day)**<br>◆ Phonics, p. 2<br>◆ Word Knowledge, Inflectional Endings, p. 4 | | |
| **Word Analysis**<br>◆ Spelling: Word Sort, p. 27G<br>■ Complete Vocabulary: Vocabulary Strategies, *Spelling and Vocabulary Skills,* pp. 2–3 | ◆ Developing Oral Language, p. 3<br>◆ Preteach "Gloria Who Might Be My Best Friend," pp. 5–6<br>◆ Teach Comprehension Strategies, p. 7<br>◆ Reread "Intervention Selection One"<br>◆ Grammar, Usage, and Mechanics, p. 9 | ◆ Selection Vocabulary, p. 7<br>◆ Preteach the Selection, p. 6 | **English Language Conventions**<br>■ Complete Nouns, *Reteach,* p. 4 | **English Language Conventions**<br>■ Complete Nouns, *Challenge,* p. 4 |
| **Word Analysis**<br>■ Complete Spelling: The /a/ Sound, *Spelling and Vocabulary Skills,* p. 4 | ◆ Dictation and Spelling, pp. 3–4<br>◆ Reread "Gloria Who Might Be My Best Friend"<br>◆ Teach "Intervention Selection Two," pp. 7–8<br>◆ Writing Activity, p. 10 | ◆ Word Knowledge, Compound Words, p. 5<br>◆ Dictation and Spelling, p. 5 | **Word Analysis**<br>■ Complete Vocabulary: Vocabulary Strategies, *Reteach,* p. 3 | **Word Analysis**<br>■ Complete Vocabulary: Vocabulary Strategies, *Challenge,* p. 3 |
| **Word Analysis**<br>■ Complete The /a/ Sound, *Spelling and Vocabulary Skills,* p. 5 | ◆ Blending, p. 4<br>◆ Reread "Gloria Who Might Be My Best Friend"<br>◆ Teach Comprehension Strategies, p. 8<br>◆ Reread "Intervention Selection Two"<br>◆ Writing Activity, p. 10 | ◆ Vocabulary Strategies, p. 6 | **Word Analysis**<br>■ Complete Spelling: The /a/ Sound, *Reteach,* p. 2 | **Word Analysis**<br>■ Complete Spelling: The /a/ Sound, *Challenge,* p. 2 |
| **Writing Process Strategies**<br>◆ Seminar: Getting Ideas for an Autobiography, p. 27J<br>**English Language Conventions**<br>■ Penmanship: Practice Letters *i* and *t,* p. 27J | ◆ Developing Oral Language, p. 4<br>◆ Dictation and Spelling, pp. 4–5<br>◆ Repeated Readings/ Fluency Check, p. 8<br>◆ Informal Assessment | ◆ Grammar, Usage, and Mechanics, p. 7 | | |

\* Page numbers refer to *Intervention Guide.*

\*\* Page numbers refer to *English-Language Development Guide.*

 *Florida*

**ASSESSMENT**

# Formal Assessment Options

Use these summative assessments along with your informal observations to assess student progress.

---

**Unit 1 Assessment p. 2**

Name _____ Date _____ Score _____

**UNIT 1** Friendship • Lesson 1

**Gloria Who Might Be My Best Friend**

Read the following questions carefully. Then completely fill in the bubble of each correct answer. You may look back at the story to find the answer to each of the questions.

1. According to Julian, what happens if a boy has a girl for a friend?
   - Ⓐ The boy loses his other friends.
   - ● People find out and tease him.
   - Ⓒ The boy and girl end up fighting.

2. Which of these would be most like a cartwheel because it requires practice?
   - Ⓐ eating breakfast
   - Ⓑ watching a movie
   - ● learning to ski

Read the following questions carefully. Use complete sentences to answer the questions.

3. According to Gloria, what happens if you tell your wish?
   If you tell your wish, the wish won't come true.

4. What does Gloria probably wish about Julian?
   Gloria probably wishes that she and Julian will be friends.

5. When Julian tries a cartwheel, how can you tell that Gloria cares about Julian?
   You can tell Gloria cares because she doesn't laugh at Julian when he tries to do a cartwheel.

2  Unit 1 • Lesson 1      *Gloria Who Might Be My Best Friend* • Unit 1 Assessment

---

**Unit 1 Assessment p. 3**

**Gloria Who Might Be My Best Friend** *(continued)*

6. What interesting thing does Julian show Gloria in her yard?
   Julian shows Gloria a robin's nest with pale blue eggs.

7. What does Julian wish about Gloria?
   Julian wishes that Gloria would stay and be his friend.

8. Why does Julian think his wishes might come true?
   Julian thinks his wishes might come true because there aren't any wishes left on the kite tail.

Read the following questions carefully. Then completely fill in the bubble of each correct answer.

9. Why hasn't Julian met Gloria before?
   - ● Gloria just moved in.
   - Ⓑ Gloria usually stays inside.
   - Ⓒ Gloria is not allowed to play.

10. According to Gloria, what is the best way to make wishes?
    - Ⓐ Make the wishes when you blow out your birthday candles.
    - Ⓑ Make the wishes when you see the first star at night.
    - ● Make the wishes by tying them to the tail of a kite.

Unit 1 Assessment • *Gloria Who Might Be My Best Friend*      Unit 1 • Lesson 1  3

---

**Unit 1 Assessment p. 4**

**Gloria Who Might Be My Best Friend** *(continued)*

Read the questions below. Use complete sentences in your answers.

**Linking to the Concepts** What do you think Julian would say to a person who thinks that boys and girls can't be friends?
Answers will vary. Accept all reasonable answers.

**Personal Response** Who would you rather have as a friend, Julian or Gloria? Why?
Answers will vary. Accept all reasonable answers.

4  Unit 1 • Lesson 1      *Gloria Who Might Be My Best Friend* • Unit 1 Assessment

---

**Unit 1 Assessment p. 5**

**Gloria Who Might Be My Best Friend** *(continued)*

**Vocabulary**

Read the following questions carefully. Then completely fill in the bubble of each correct answer.

1. Julian thinks that when you have a girl for a best friend, people will tease you. **Tease** means
   - Ⓐ be afraid of
   - Ⓑ stay away from
   - ● make fun of

2. There isn't anyone Julian's age, so he feels lonely. To feel **lonely** means to feel
   - Ⓐ like you have nothing to do
   - ● like you have no friends
   - Ⓒ like you have no choice

3. Gloria watched Julian's cartwheel seriously and did not laugh. Another word for **seriously** is
   - ● thoughtfully
   - Ⓑ dishonestly
   - Ⓒ cheerfully

4. Julian shows Gloria his rock collection. A **collection** is a group of things that you
   - Ⓐ make yourself
   - Ⓑ throw away
   - ● put together

5. Julian's neck gets stiff when he watches the kite. In this sentence, **stiff** means
   - Ⓐ a little cold
   - ● a little sore
   - Ⓒ too warm

Unit 1 Assessment • *Gloria Who Might Be My Best Friend*      Unit 1 • Lesson 1  5

---

**Unit 1 Assessment p. 26**

Name _____ Date _____ Score _____

**UNIT 1** Friendship • Lesson 1  *Gloria Who Might Be My Best Friend*

**Spelling Pretest: The /a/ Sound**

Fold this page back on the dotted line. Take the Pretest. Then correct any word you misspelled by crossing out the word and rewriting it next to the incorrect spelling.

1. _____
2. _____
3. _____
4. _____
5. _____
6. _____
7. _____
8. _____
9. _____
10. _____
11. _____
12. _____
13. _____
14. _____
15. _____

1. path
2. lamp
3. damp
4. crash
5. plant
6. math
7. trash
8. stamp
9. hatbox
10. have
11. grass
12. rags
13. back
14. black
15. that

26  Unit 1 • Lesson 1      *Spelling Pretest: The /a/ Sound* • Unit 1 Assessment

---

**Unit 1 Assessment p. 27**

Name _____ Date _____ Score _____

**UNIT 1** Friendship • Lesson 1  *Gloria Who Might Be My Best Friend*

**Spelling Final Test: The /a/ Sound**

Mark the letter next to the underlined word that is misspelled. Focus on the underlined word.

1. Ⓐ It is easy to <u>plant</u> a flower.
   ● A <u>pathe</u> can go into a forest.
   Ⓒ Mowers cut <u>grass</u>.
   Ⓓ Correct as is.

2. ● Tires on cars are <u>blac</u>.
   Ⓑ A saddle fits on a horse's <u>back</u>.
   Ⓗ <u>Add</u> and <u>subtract</u> are <u>math</u> words.
   Ⓙ Correct as is.

3. Ⓐ A sidewalk is a <u>path</u> by a road.
   ● The air feels <u>demp</u> after it rains.
   Ⓒ A <u>stamp</u> is at the post office.
   Ⓓ Correct as is.

4. Ⓕ Torn <u>rags</u> are useful for cleaning.
   ● Some <u>trass</u> can be recycled.
   Ⓗ Oil is a <u>black</u> liquid.
   Ⓙ Correct as is.

5. Ⓐ A <u>hatbox</u> stores hats.
   Ⓑ A computer can <u>crash</u>.
   Ⓒ A <u>plant</u> needs sunlight.
   ● Correct as is.

6. ● A <u>laymp</u> brightens a room.
   Ⓖ The <u>back</u> of a car is the trunk.
   Ⓗ States <u>have</u> governors.
   Ⓙ Correct as is.

Unit 1 Assessment • *Spelling Final Test: The /a/ Sound*      Unit 1 • Lesson 1  27

---

# Informal Comprehension Strategies Rubrics

Use the Informal Comprehension Strategies Rubrics to determine whether or not a student is using any of the strategies listed below. Note the strategies a student is using, instead of the degree to which a student might be using any particular strategy. In addition, encourage the student to tell of any strategies other than the ones being taught that he or she is using.

## Making Connections

- The student activates prior knowledge and related knowledge.
- The student uses prior knowledge to explain something encountered in the text.
- The student connects ideas presented later in the text to ideas presented earlier in the text.
- The student notes ideas in the text that are new or conflict with what he or she thought previously.

## Predicting

- The student makes predictions about the text.
- The student updates predictions during reading, based on information in the text.

## Summarizing

- The student paraphrases the text, reporting main ideas and a summary of what is in the text.
- The student decides which parts of the text are important in his or her summary.
- The student draws conclusions from the text.
- The student makes global interpretations of the text, such as recognizing the genre.

# Research Rubrics

Use the Research Rubrics to assess a student's performance throughout the stages of the investigation for each unit. The rubrics for a given lesson will match the investigation stage for that lesson. In addition, at the end of the unit you can use the rubrics to assess the groups' collaborative work as well as an individual's participation in that group.

During Workshop, assess students using the rubrics below. The rubrics range from 1–4 in most categories, with 1 being the lowest score. Record each student's score on the inside back cover of the ***Inquiry Journal***.

## Formulating Research Questions and Problems

1 With help, identifies things he or she wonders about in relation to a topic.

2 Expresses curiosity about topics; with help, translates this into specific questions.

3 Poses an interesting problem or question for research; with help, refines it into a researchable question.

4 Identifies something he or she genuinely wonders about and translates it into a researchable question.

## Objectives

- Students decode /ī/ spelled i_e, _y, igh.
- Students practice recognizing base words and inflectional endings.
- Students review short vowels.
- Students develop fluency reading words and sentences.

## Materials

- Student Anthology, Book 1, pp. 14–27
- Sound/Spelling Cards 1, 5, 9, 11, 15, 21, 34
- Decodable Book 11
- Decodable Book Activities CD-ROM
- Routine Cards 1, 3, Routines 1–2, 8–9
- Lesson Model Videocassette

## Research in Action
### Blending

Learning to recognize new words by blending together their letters and spelling patterns is one of the most critical steps in becoming a good reader. Follow closely the steps outlined below, at least until the procedure has become well established in your class.

Some students have more difficulty learning to blend than others, so you should not be concerned if only a few students seem to catch on at first. However, the clarity with which you introduce and guide the blending process is extremely important because it will strongly influence the success with which all of your students will learn to blend. Make sure that every student is attempting the blending exercises, even though at this stage many of them can only do it imitatively. You will probably need to lead early blending exercises, but encourage the students to take over as soon as they can.
*(Marilyn J. Adams)*

## WORD KNOWLEDGE

# Word Knowledge

The Word Knowledge activities in Set 1 consolidate what students have learned about reading words. The purpose of the activities is to teach students that they have strategies for figuring out any unfamiliar words they encounter as they read the selection. The entire class participates in these activities before reading the selection.

The Phonics and Fluency exercises in Set 2 provide review and maintenance for students who have used the ***Open Court Reading*** program in Grade 2 and will continue to use it in Grade 3. (It also serves as a general course of phonics instruction for students who have not been exposed to the ***Open Court Reading*** program.)

Use direct teaching when instructing students in word knowledge, phonics and fluency, and developing oral language activities. Use the blending procedure below, without varying from it. That way, students will become accustomed to the routines.

## Blending Procedure

In Grade 3, the focus on blending is for multisyllable words. The focus should be on reading the syllables and blending them. Students should be encouraged to use some of the words in sentences, particularly vocabulary words.

Use the following procedure as you have students read each line of words in this and in subsequent lessons.

- Write the first word on the board. Have students read it. When a new syllable principle is introduced, the first line should be a teaching line for the teacher to model.

- To confirm the response, have a student use each word in a sentence. Asking questions such as *Where? When? Why?* or *How?* will help students extend the sentences both at the beginning and at the end.

- Continue writing the words and have students read them.

- Note any challenging spellings.

- After all words are read, review them with students by pointing to the words in random order for students to read. Discuss About the Words and Sentences and complete Developing Oral Language activities.

- Reading sentences is the logical extension of blending words. This process helps students move from word fluency to sentence fluency. Write each of the sentences that follow the word lines. Have students read each sentence in unison. After students have read the sentence word by word, they should reread the sentence with normal intonation.

- The words in **boldface** are from the selection.

- The blending of syllables should be gradually faded out. Whenever a new syllable concept is introduced, let the instruction focus on that.

Day 1

# Word Knowledge  LA.A.1.2.2.3.1

## Reading the Words and Sentences

■ Display and review **Sound/Spelling Cards 1, 11,** and **34.**

■ Write each word in Reading the Words and Sentences on the board and have students read it together. If they have difficulty reading a word, stop and have them blend the word using whole-word blending. Encourage students to pronounce the words naturally after blending. Because reading sentences helps students move from word fluency to sentence fluency, have them read each sentence in unison, using normal intonation. The words in **boldface** type are from the selection.

| | | | | | |
|---|---|---|---|---|---|
| Line 1: | kite | five | mine | time | | |
| Line 2: | high | might | right | tight | | |
| Line 3: | fly | cry | why | | | |
| Line 4: | like | liked | liking | try | tried | trying |
| Line 5: | happen | happened | happening | | | |
| Line 6: | visit | visited | visiting | | | |
| Line 7: | grass | rags | back | black | that | |
| Sentence 1: | I might try to fly a kite. | | | | | |
| Sentence 2: | Why do you try not to cry? | | | | | |
| Sentence 3: | I don't like to fight. | | | | | |
| Sentence 4: | You can study the clouds if you lie on your back in the grass. | | | | | |

## About the Words and Sentences

■ **Lines 1–3:** The words provide practice with the /ī/ sound spelled *i_e, igh,* and *_y.*

■ **Lines 4–6:** Inflectional endings/syllables are added to base words. Have students identify the base words. Ask students how the endings change the meaning of the base word. Note the syllable changes. Tell students that the inflectional ending *-ing* is its own syllable. Have students read each word again, clapping the syllables in each word.

■ **Line 7:** The words in Line 7 are found in "Gloria Who Might Be My Best Friend" and review the /a/ sound spelled *a*. Have students identify the vowel sound in the words (/a/). Have a volunteer tell why the /k/ sound is spelled ■*ck*. Point out the ■*ck* spelling on **Sound/Spelling Card 11.**

■ **Sentences 1–3:** Ask students to say the words with the /ī/ sound spelled *_y* (*try, fly, why*), *igh* (*might*), and *i_e* (*kite*). Have students identify the pronoun (*I*).

■ **Sentence 4:** Have students point out the words that contain the /a/ sound spelled *a* (*back, grass*).

**WORD KNOWLEDGE**

**Routine Card**
Refer to **Routine 1** for whole-word blending and **Routine 2** for sentence blending.

**Teacher Tip** SYLLABICATION To help students blend words and build fluency, use the syllabication below of the words in the word lines.

| | | | |
|---|---|---|---|
| kite | five | mine | time |
| high | might | right | tight |
| fly | cry | why | like |
| liked | lik•ing | try | tried |
| try•ing | hap•pen | hap•pened | hap•pen•ing |
| vis•it | vis•it•ed | vis•it•ing | grass |
| rags | back | black | that |

## MEETING INDIVIDUAL NEEDS

### ELL Support

For ELD strategies, use the **English-Language Development Guide,** Unit 1, Lesson 1.

### Intervention Support

For intervention strategies, use the **Intervention Guide,** Unit 1, Lesson 1.

**Spelling**
See pages 27E–27J for the corresponding spelling lesson for the /a/ sound.

**Refer to the Lesson Model Videocassette** for instruction on whole-word blending.

Clap syllables, snap or fast, slow, etc.

**PHONICS**

**Teacher Tip** SYLLABICATION To help students blend words and build fluency, use the syllabication below of the words in the word lines.

| | | | | |
|---|---|---|---|---|
| plan•et | Af•ri•ca | prac•tice | eggs | pen•cils |
| clos•et | rob•in | kitch•en | in•side | co•py |
| bot•tom | can•not | up•set | un•til | hun•dred |
| hedge | ridge | dodge | fudge | judge |

**Teacher Tip** It is important to refer to the vowel spelling and not the vowel letter. In the case of short vowels, there is usually only one letter representing the vowel sound. Using the term *vowel spelling* helps students focus on the spelling of the sound rather than on letters which may be misleading.

**Teacher Tip** Remind students that short vowels appear in a green box on the *Sound/Spelling Cards.*

**Teacher Tip** If students do not note the various features of the *Sound/Spelling Cards,* tell them about all the information on these cards: for example, the color bands, the picture, the blanks that are part of the spellings, and so on. *Sound/Spelling Cards* are an important resource for both reading and spelling.

## Developing Oral Language LA.C.1.2.1.3.2

Use direct teaching to review the words. Use one or both of the following activities to help students practice reading the words.

- Have a student choose a word and call out only the line and the position of the word in the line. For example, "Line 3, Word 2." Have the student select a classmate to read the words, saying, for example, "Line 3, Word 2 is *cry.*" Then ask the student to use the word in a sentence.

- Have the students come to the board, continuing to point to and say the word in the word lines. Have them choose a volunteer to use the word in a sentence and extend the sentence. Encourage students to add information at the beginning of the sentence, not just at the end. Students can extend sentences by adding *Who? What? When? Where?* and *How?* statements to the sentences.

## Phonics and Fluency

### Review short vowels

* **Blending**
- Use direct teaching to teach the following words and sentences.
- Display ***Sound/Spelling Cards 1, 5, 9, 15,*** and ***21.***
- Follow the established procedure to have students read the following words and sentences.

| | | | | | |
|---|---|---|---|---|---|
| Line 1: | planet | Africa | practice | eggs | pencils |
| Line 2: | closet | robin | kitchen | inside | copy |
| Line 3: | bottom | cannot | upset | until | hundred |
| Line 4: | hedge | ridge | dodge | fudge | judge |
| Sentence 1: | Anna was upset when she lost her doll. | | | | |
| Sentence 2: | The robin sang a pretty song. | | | | |
| Sentence 3: | The eggs were small and pale blue. | | | | |

* ### About the Words and Sentences

- **Lines 1–3:** Have students identify the short vowel sound in each word. Note that the *e* in *planet* has the /ə/ sound. In *Africa,* the *a* and *i* have short vowel sounds. The final *a* has the /ə/ sound.

- **Line 4:** The words provide practice with the /j/ sound spelled *dge.* Ask students what the green box means *(a short vowel comes before this spelling).* Have students identify the short vowel in each word.

- **Sentences 1–2:** Have students identify words with short vowels. (*Anna, song, upset, doll, robin*)

- **Sentence 3:** This sentence is from the selection. Have students identify the short vowels. (*eggs, and*)

*Day 4*

## Developing Oral Language LA.C.1.2.1.3.2

Use direct teaching to review the words. Use one or both of the following activities to help students practice reading the words.

- Give clues for each of the words in Lines 1–4 and ask students to identify the words. As each word is identified and read, have the students erase it. For example: You use these to write *(pencils)*. I like _____ for breakfast *(eggs)*.
- Say each of the words on the word lines. Have students clap for each syllable. Remind them that there is a vowel sound in every syllable.

## Dictation

Use the following procedures for whole-word and sentence dictation.

- Say the word on the word line, use the word in a sentence, and then repeat the word.
- Have students say the word.
- Have students think about how to segment the word into sounds and write the spellings for each sound. Students should be encouraged to check the *Sound/Spelling Cards.*
- After each line, write (or have a student write) the words on the board.
- Have students proofread. Circle any incorrect words and correct them.
- Say the sentence.
- Dictate one word at a time following the sounds-in-sequence or whole-word dictation, depending upon your students.
- Remind students to use capitals at the beginning of a sentence and end punctuation.
- Write (or have a student write) the sentence on the board.
- Have students proofread.
- Check for spelling.
- Check for capitalization and end punctuation.

Erase the word lines and sentences on the board and have students take out writing paper. Dictate the following words and sentences for students to write.

| | | | |
|---|---|---|---|
| **Line 1:** | packet | empty | picket |
| **Line 2:** | chop | crust | edge |
| **Challenge Word:** | important | | |
| **Sentence:** | The ledge was dusty. | | |

## Building Fluency

*1st 10 books read during getting started.*

***Decodable Books*** are used to help develop fluency for students who need extra practice. The only way to gain fluency is to read. Students will have many opportunities to read, including the ***Student Anthology,*** the ***Leveled Classroom Library,*** and their own reading. The ***Decodable Books*** can be used to practice the phonics and fluency elements being reviewed. Refer to the Appendix for the procedure on using these books. For this lesson, use ***Decodable Book 11,*** *The Frog Who Wanted to Fly.*

**P H O N I C S**

**Routine Card**
Refer to *Routine 8* for the whole-word dictation procedure and *Routine 9* for the sentence dictation procedure.

LA.C.1.2.1.3.2

**Teacher Tip** FLUENCY Gaining a better understanding of the spelling of sounds and structures of words will help students as they encounter unfamiliar words in their reading. By this time in Grade 3 students should be reading approximately 107 words per minute with fluency and expression. As students read, you may notice that some need work in building fluency. During Workshop, have these students select a section of the text (a minimum of 160 words) to read several times in order to build fluency.

Use the *Decodable Book Activities CD-ROM* for activities that support this Phonics lesson.

Refer to the *Lesson Model Videocassette* for instruction on whole-word dictation.

Refer to the *Lesson Model Videocassette* for instruction on reading a *Decodable Book.*

## Objectives

- Students will understand the selection vocabulary before reading, using strategies such as structural cues.
- Students will spell words with the /ī/ sound, the inflectional endings *-ed* and *-ing,* and short vowels.
- Students will use comprehension strategies such as Making Connections, Predicting, and Summarizing to construct meaning from the text and to monitor reading.
- Students will use the comprehension skill Cause and Effect as they read the story the second time.
- Students will discuss personal reactions to the story to begin identifying their own personal reading preferences.

## Materials

- Student Anthology, Book 1, pp. 14–27
- Program Assessment
- Reading Transparencies 1, 46, 47, 48, 53
- Inquiry Journal, p. 1
- Home Connection, p. 2
- Unit 1 Assessment, pp. 2–5
- Routine Cards 1–2, Routines 3–6
- Writer's Notebook

**Routine Card**
Refer to *Routine 4* for the Clues, Problems, and Wonderings procedure.

| Clues | Problems | Wonderings |
|---|---|---|
| The title says "Might Be," maybe Julian isn't sure what will happen. | laughing | Will Julian and Gloria be friends? |

*Reading Transparency 46*

**www.sra4kids.com**
**Web Connection**
Students can use the connections to friendship in the Reading link of the SRA Web page for more background information about friendship.

## Build Background

*Day 1*

### Activate Prior Knowledge

Preteach with students the following questions to help them connect the reading to their own experiences.

- Have you ever moved? If so, what was difficult about it? What was exciting?

### Background Information

The following information may help students to better understand the selection they are about to read.

- Tell students that "Gloria Who Might Be My Best Friend" is realistic fiction. Explain that realistic fiction stories are made-up stories about things that could really happen.
- Explain that this story involves a child whose family relocated to a new city. Some students may not have experience with moving to a new place and not knowing anyone. You might talk about how that could feel.

## Preview and Prepare LA.A.1.2.1.3.1 *Day 1*

### Browse

- Remind students that before they read a selection, they will use a reading strategy called Setting Reading Goals. Explain that setting reading goals will help them to better understand what they read. Explain that to help them set reading goals, they will browse the first page of the selection using the Clues, Problems, and Wonderings procedure.
- Introduce the browsing procedure by having a student read aloud the title. Point out and read the names of the author and illustrators to students. Then have students quickly look over the first page or two of the selection. This allows them to activate prior knowledge relevant to the story. Doing this should also enable them to determine if the selection is fiction or nonfiction. Fiction pieces should not be browsed in their entirety, because browsing might ruin any surprises in the story. After students browse, ask them what they think this story might have to do with friendship.
- Display **Reading Transparency 46,** Clues, Problems, and Wonderings. Under each heading, write in note form rather than in complete sentences, the observations that students generate as they browse. For example, students might list the genre of the selection under Clues; they might note any questions that arise during reading and list unfamiliar words under Problems; they can include statements about things they are curious to find out about as they read under Wonderings. For a full description of setting reading goals and browsing, see the Appendix.
- As students prepare to read the selection, have them browse the Focus Questions on the first page of the selection. Tell them to keep these questions in mind as they read.

## Set Purposes LA.A.1.2.2.3.5

To connect this selection to the theme, tell students as they read to look for characters who show friendship and to note how and why the characters act as they do. Students also should look for clues as to how friendships begin. Encourage students to set additional reading goals based on their clues and wonderings.

## Selection Vocabulary LA.A.1.2.2.3.2  *Day 1*

Students will use a variety of skills, such as context clues, apposition, base words, and other structural clues to figure out the meaning of each vocabulary word. Students will apply these same skills while reading to clarify additional unfamiliar words. After using the skills, students may use dictionaries, or the Glossary if necessary. For example, explain to students that:

■ (base words) We can figure out some words by looking at the word and finding parts that we know. If we take the word *collection*, there are parts we can use to figure out the meaning. We know that the word *collect* means to gather things together. Does anyone know what the suffix *-tion* means? What do you think it might mean, and how would that change the meaning of the base word? (The suffix *-tion* changes the verb *collect* to a noun.) Let's look up the word in the dictionary to be sure we are correct.

■ (apposition) Sometimes the meaning of a word is given in the sentence itself. For example: *The doe, the female deer, was sitting next to the fawn.* In this sentence, we learn that a doe is a female deer.

After figuring out the meaning of each word, have students reread the sentence, substituting the definition for the word in order to see if the sentence still makes sense. Students can write their definitions in their Writer's Notebooks.

Display **Reading Transparency 1** before reading the selection to introduce and discuss the following words and their meanings.

| | |
|---|---|
| **tease:** | to annoy continuously (page 14) |
| **lonely:** | sad from being alone (page 14) |
| **seriously:** | thoughtfully; sincerely (page 16) |
| **collection:** | similar things gathered together to study or to show to others (page 18) |
| **stiff:** | something not easily bent; not flexible (page 24) |
| **probably:** | most likely to happen (page 25) |

Have students read the words in the word box, stopping to blend any words that they have trouble reading. Demonstrate how to decode multisyllabic words by breaking the words into syllables and blending the syllables. Then have students try. If they still have trouble, refer them to the **Sound/Spelling Cards.** If the word is not decodable, give the students the pronunciation.

*make this quick*

*Cover sentences 1st while saying each word. Then read sentences*

*Use on day 1*

**Reading Transparency 1**

**Teacher Tip SELECTION VOCABULARY** To help students decode words, divide them into syllables as shown below. The information following each word tells how students can figure out the meaning of each word.

| | |
|---|---|
| tease | context clues |
| lone·ly | context clues |
| se·ri·ous·ly | context clues |
| col·lec·tion | context clues |
| stiff | context clues |
| prob·a·bly | context clues |

Reading Transparency 47

During Workshop, and after the selection has been read at least once, have students listen to the recording of this lesson's selection on the **Listening Library Audiocassette/CD.** After students have listened, have them discuss their personal preferences of the selections read. Ask them what other things they have listened to and like to listen to on the radio, on audiocassettes, or on CDs.

Have students read the sentences on the transparency to determine the meaning of the underlined word. Each word has two sentences that students will read and from which they should be able to derive the meaning of the underlined word. Remind them to use one or more of the skills they have learned—context clues, word structure, or apposition—to figure out the meaning before using a dictionary. Be sure students explain which skills they are using and how they figured out the meanings of the words. Have students reread the sentence, substituting the definition to see if the sentence makes sense. Have a volunteer create a new sentence using the underlined word.

 You may display **Reading Transparency 47** for additional practice with selection vocabulary. Have students copy the information into their Writer's Notebooks and complete the sentences as they read and become more familiar with the vocabulary words. You may refer to this transparency in subsequent lessons.

## Reading Recommendations          *Day 1*

Students will focus first on reading strategies to develop an overall understanding of the selection. During this initial reading, students will use key reading comprehension strategies (located to the left of the reduced student pages) to monitor their understanding of the selection. Then, students will reread the selection, paying particular attention to specific comprehension skills (found to the right of the reduced student pages) in order to enhance their understanding and appreciation of the text. Therefore, it is suggested that your first reading of the selection focus on developing the reading strategies and your second reading focus on the comprehension skills.

### Oral Reading

Because "Gloria Who Might Be My Best Friend" is the first selection in the book, having students read the story aloud will give you an opportunity to hear and assess how well the students read.

### Using Comprehension Strategies

**Teacher Modeling**

One of the most effective ways to help students use and understand reading strategies is to think aloud. Modeling these strategies and encouraging students to think aloud as they attempt to understand text can demonstrate for everyone in the class how these strategies are put into practice. The most effective models you can offer, however, will be those that come from your own reading experiences. What kinds of things did you yourself think about? What kinds of things gave you problems the first time you read a story? Drawing on such questions and on your students' questions and comments as they read will make both the text and the strategic reading process more meaningful to students. Teacher models are provided with this selection to help you model reading strategies for students.

Comprehension strategy instruction allows students to become aware of how good readers read. Good readers constantly check their understanding as they are reading and ask themselves questions. In addition, skilled readers recognize when they are having problems and stop to use various comprehension strategies to help them make sense of what they are reading.

During the reading of "Gloria Who Might Be My Best Friend," you will model the use of the following reading strategies:

- **Making Connections (Introduction):** Making Connections requires students to activate prior knowledge and connect what they know or have experienced to what they are reading.

- **Predicting (Introduction):** Predicting causes readers to analyze information given about story events and characters in the context of how it may logically connect to the story's conclusion.

- **Summarizing (Introduction):** Summarizing prompts readers to keep track of what they are reading and to focus their minds on important information.

As students read, they should be using a variety of strategies to help them understand the selection. Encourage students to use the strategies listed above as the class reads the story aloud. Do this by stopping at the points indicated by the numbers in the magenta circles on the reduced student page and using a particular strategy. Students can also stop reading periodically to discuss what they have learned and what problems they may be having.

## Building Comprehension Skills

Revisiting or rereading a selection allows students to apply skills that give them a more complete understanding of the text. Some follow-up comprehension skills help readers to organize the information in a selection. Other skills lead students to a deeper understanding of the selection, or to "reading between the lines," as mature readers do. In this selection, students will apply the following comprehension skill:

- **Classify and Categorize (Introduction):** Readers put like things or ideas together in order to make new ideas and information easier to understand.

### Reading with a Purpose

Have students look for ways the story characters demonstrate how to begin a friendship.

**Teacher Tip COMPREHENSION STRATEGIES** Remind students on the second day as they read the story to summarize what they learned from the first day.

## Research in Action
### Decoding and Comprehension

For good readers, recognizing the letters of a word activates knowledge of their spelling patterns, pronunciations, and meanings. At the same time, they use knowledge of context to establish the coherence of the message in the passage being read. In this way, good readers come to recognize the spelling, sound, meaning, and contextual role of a familiar word almost automatically and simultaneously, freeing their attention for critical and reflective thought. Thus, good readers appear to recognize words as wholes because they have developed a thorough and interconnected knowledge of words' spellings, sounds, and meanings. However, to the extent that readers skip or guess at the meaning of unfamiliar words, they limit opportunities for such knowledge to develop.
*(Marilyn Jager Adams)*

**Routine Card**
Refer to *Routine 5* for the procedures on reading the selection.

*(handwritten margin notes:)* While Browsing → use Overhead · Day Chart with Problem Words · Cluess · Question/Concept Board already set up

COMPREHENSION

This selection is broken into two parts. On the first day, read pages 14–19. On the second day, read pages 20–25.

## Comprehension Strategies LA.E.1.2.1.3.3

 First Read

Read the story aloud, taking turns with the students. Model the use of strategies for the students.

*(handwritten note:)* * Can you use tape as 1st read

### Teacher Modeling

**1 Making Connections** *Making connections between what you read and your own experiences is a good way to enjoy and understand a story. I can understand the way that the boy who's telling this story feels. He feels lonely because he doesn't have anyone his own age to play with. I can remember feeling the same way when I didn't have anyone to do something with. I was sad and lonely, and feeling very sorry for myself. As you are reading, be aware of how ideas in the text remind you of things that have happened to you. When you make such connections, tell the class about them.*

*(handwritten margin note:)* scavenger hunt in story

### Word Knowledge

**SCAFFOLDING** The skills students are reviewing in Word Knowledge should help them in reading the story. This lesson focuses on the /ī/ sound/spellings and inflectional endings.

*-ing* added:   walking
                visiting
                feeling

**Teacher Tip** One of the most effective ways to help students to use and understand the behaviors that make successful readers is to make strategic thinking public. Modeling these behaviors for the students shows them how to put the strategies into practice.

### First Reading Recommendation

## ORAL · CHORAL

 Florida

*Focus Questions* What do you think it means to be a best friend? How have you made new friendships?

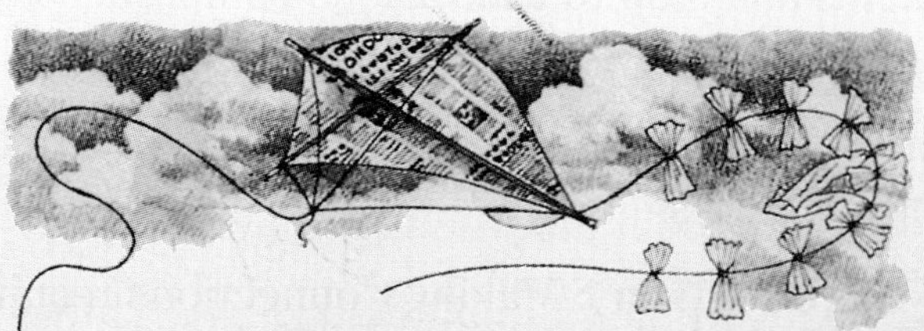

# Gloria Who Might Be My Best Friend

from *The Stories Julian Tells*
by Ann Cameron
*illustrated by Ann Strugnell*

If you have a girl for a friend, people find out and tease you. That's why I didn't want a girl for a friend—not until this summer, when I met Gloria. It happened one afternoon when I was walking down the street by myself. My mother was visiting a friend of hers, and Huey was visiting a friend of his. Huey's friend is five and so I think he is too young to play with. And there aren't any kids just my age. I was walking down the street feeling lonely.  **1**

14

### ✓ Informal Assessment

Observe individual students as they read and use the Teacher Observation Log, found in the *Program Assessment Teacher's Edition,* to record anecdotal information about each student's strengths and weaknesses.

*(handwritten note:)* * Hand up when read a vocabulary word

On the reduced pages above, words that can be found in the *Student Anthology* glossary are underlined in magenta. These words are underlined in the *Teacher's Edition* only. The magenta-encircled numbers appearing beside the text correspond to the Comprehension Strategies numbered in the column to the left.

*more silent + partner reading* **Day 3**

A block from our house I saw a moving van in front of a brown house, and men were carrying in chairs and tables and bookcases and boxes full of I don't know what. I watched for a while, and suddenly I heard a voice right behind me.

"Who are you?"

I turned around and there was a girl in a yellow dress. She looked the same age as me. She had curly hair that was braided into two pigtails with red ribbons at the ends.

"I'm Julian," I said. "Who are you?"

"I'm Gloria," she said. "I come from Newport. Do you know where Newport is?"

I wasn't sure, but I didn't tell Gloria. "It's a town on the ocean," I said.

15

### Word Knowledge

The /ī/ sound:  I
while
right
behind

---

## Comprehension Skills

 Second Read

### Classify and Categorize

Explain to students that putting things that are in some way alike in a group is called *classifying*, or *categorizing*. This technique can help them understand and remember the information they read in a story.

During a second reading of the story, write the heading *Furniture* on the board. Have students search pages 14 and 15 for items that can be classified under this heading. Students should discover all of the items that the moving men carried into the house. As students identify *chairs*, *tables*, and *bookcases*, write the words on the board under the heading *Furniture*.

*Make chart with this heading*

Tell students to look for additional words in the story as they read that can be grouped under different headings or categories, such as *Wishes*.

Tell students that classifying and categorizing items can help them better understand unfamiliar things.

### Skills Trace

**Classify and Categorize**

Introduced in Grade 1.
Scaffolded throughout Grades 2 and 3.

**REINTRODUCED:** Unit 1, Lesson 1
**REINFORCED:** Unit 2, Lesson 1
Unit 3, Lesson 5
Unit 5, Lesson 4
Unit 6, Lesson 5
**TESTED:** Unit 1 Assessment

**Second Reading Recommendation**

**ORAL • SILENT**

**COMPREHENSION**

Day 1

# Comprehension Strategies

**First Read**

## Teacher Modeling

**2 Making Connections** *I read that when Julian didn't do a cartwheel properly, he "looked at Gloria to see if she was laughing." I remember trying to do something in front of a friend and not getting it right. I was afraid that my friend would laugh at me. But instead, my friend helped me learn to do something that I couldn't do before. How has a friend helped you to learn something new? What other connections to the story can you share with the class?*

### Word Knowledge

*-ed* added:  turned
         tried
         looked
         liked

*-ing* added:  laughing
          going

**Teacher Tip** Remind students to stop and ask themselves if they understand what they are reading, and if not, to ask themselves what they can do to figure it out.

**Teacher Tip MAKING CONNECTIONS** Tell students that good readers are active readers, who make connections as they read. Encourage students to make connections as they read and share them with the class.

"Right," Gloria said. "Can you turn a cartwheel?"

She turned sideways herself and did two cartwheels on the grass.

I had never tried a cartwheel before, but I tried to copy Gloria. My hands went down in the grass, my feet went up in the air, and—I fell over.

I looked at Gloria to see if she was laughing at me. If she was laughing at me, I was going to go home and forget about her.

But she just looked at me very seriously and said, "It takes practice," and then I liked her.

"I know where there's a bird's nest in your yard," I said.

16

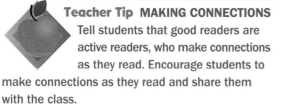

*Florida*

Day 3

"Really?" Gloria said. "There weren't any trees in the yard, or any birds, where I lived before."

I showed her where a robin lives and has eggs. Gloria stood up on a branch and looked in. The eggs were small and pale blue. The mother robin squawked at us, and she and the father robin flew around our heads.

17

## Comprehension Skills

 Second Read

### Classify and Categorize

- Explain to students that classifying objects is a good technique for getting to know more about them, even if they are familiar items.

- Have students identify a group of similar words on page 17 (*trees, birds, robin, eggs,* and *branch*). Invite students to select a heading that fits this category of words. One suggestion is *The Natural World.*

- Another category might be *Things Birds Do* (build nests, squawk, fly).

Have students write the heading that they select in their Writer's Notebooks and add other words that belong under this heading as they encounter them in their reading.

*Things Found in Nature*
*reading an chart*

```
┌─────────────────────────────────────┐
│          Word Knowledge              │
│  -ed ending:    lived                │
│                 squawked             │
└─────────────────────────────────────┘
```

**Teacher Tip** Because this is the first selection, you might draw the students' attention to the illustrations in order to prompt a discussion about the ways that illustrations help us to better understand and enjoy a story.

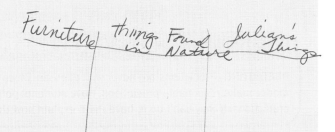

Furniture    things Found    Julian's
            in Nature       Things

COMPREHENSION

**COMPREHENSION**

## Comprehension Strategies

*Day 1*

First Read

### Teacher Modeling

**3** **Predicting** *Good readers often stop to think about what they are reading and then make a prediction about what might happen next based on the clues in the story. As they continue to read, they check to see if their prediction was confirmed. While reading, I learned that Julian told Gloria he wished she would live nearby for a long time. Then Gloria said, "I wish I would too." As I continue to read, I see that Gloria is going to tell Julian the best way to make wishes come true. I wonder if they will try to make their wish that they could stay neighbors come true. Probably, they will try. I wonder if it will work! I'll keep reading in order to find out. Given what the author has told us about the characters so far, what do you think will happen next?*

---

### Word Knowledge

*-ed* ending:     showed

---

**Teacher Tip** Remind students that good readers are active readers, choosing to use the strategies that they have learned. Using these strategies helps the readers understand the story.

---

"They want us to go away," Gloria said. She got down from the branch, and we went around to the front of the house and watched the moving men carry two rugs and a mirror inside.

"Would you like to come over to my house?" I said.

"All right," Gloria said, "if it is all right with my mother." She ran in the house and asked.

It was all right, so Gloria and I went to my house, and I showed her my room and my games and my rock collection, and then I made strawberry Kool-Aid and we sat at the kitchen table and drank it.

18

### MEETING INDIVIDUAL NEEDS

**Intervention**

**PREDICTING** Predictions are never wild guesses. Clues are given in the text that can help the reader make reasonable predictions. Have students point out text clues that lead to their predictions. If they can't do it, have them explain how they made the prediction.

Day 3

"You have a red <u>mustache</u> on your mouth,"
Gloria said.

"You have a red mustache on your mouth, too,"
I said.

Gloria giggled, and we licked off the mustaches
with our tongues.

"I wish you'd live here a long time," I told Gloria.

Gloria said, "I wish I would too.

"I know the best way to make wishes," Gloria said.

"What's that?" I asked.

"First you make a kite. Do you know how to
make one?"

19

## Comprehension Skills

### Classify and Categorize

Remind students that categorizing is a good way to both check comprehension and to add to it.

- Have students look on page 18 for words that describe Julian's things (*room, games, rock collection*). Write these words on the board under the heading *Julian's Things*.

- Another list might be *Things Friends Do Together* (show games to each other, make Kool-Aid together, make kites together).

> ### Word Knowledge
> *-ed* ending:     giggled

**Teacher Tip** Suggest students extend the list of Julian's things by naming other things that Julian might own if he is like them. *(baseball cards, video games, books, etc.)*

**Teacher Tip** Remind students to use context clues, apposition, or word structure to figure out the meaning of difficult words as they are reading.

*make predictions here on first read. What do you think will happen? Predict*

COMPREHENSION

## Comprehension Strategies

*Day 2*

First Read

### Teacher Modeling

**4 Summarizing** *We've read a lot about Gloria and Julian. Let's check to see if we understand what's happened so far. Sometimes it helps to think about what you have read and then to sum it up in your own words. Summarizing helps me to understand what is happening in the story. I know that this is a story about a boy named Julian who never wanted a girl for a friend until he met Gloria. Julian and Gloria meet one day as she is moving into her new house, but he really wasn't very interested because he never wanted a girl as a friend. Let's continue reading, and as we do, remember to summarize what we are reading. Make sure you understand what you have just read. Let me know if you would like to share your summary with the group.*

### Word Knowledge

| | |
|---|---|
| *-ing* ending: | making |
| | planning |

**Teacher Tip** Be sure to encourage all the students to use strategies. Call on various students to share which strategies they are using and to tell how they are using them to figure out the meaning of the text.

**Teacher Tip SUMMARIZING** As students read, have them make up summaries from time to time. This will help them to know whether they understand the selection as well as help them remember it later.

---

"Yes," I said, "I know how." I know how to make good kites because my father taught me. We make them out of two crossed sticks and folded newspaper.

"All right," Gloria said, "that's the first part of making wishes that come true. So let's make a kite."

We went out into the garage and spread out sticks and newspaper and made a kite. I fastened on the kite string and went to the closet and got rags for the tail.

"Do you have some paper and two pencils?" Gloria asked. "Because now we make the wishes."

I didn't know what she was planning, but I went in the house and got pencils and paper. **4**

20

## MEETING INDIVIDUAL NEEDS

### Intervention

As students summarize, write their comments in short note form on the board. Each time they stop to summarize, add to the notes. Encourage students to get in the habit of taking notes to help them remember what they have read.

Day 4

"All right," Gloria said. "Every wish you want to have come true you write on a long thin piece of paper. You don't tell me your wishes, and I don't tell you mine. If you tell, your wishes don't come true. Also, if you look at the other person's wishes, your wishes don't come true."

Gloria sat down on the garage floor again and started writing her wishes. I wanted to see what they were—but I went to the other side of the garage and wrote my own wishes instead. I wrote:

1. I wish the fig tree would be the tallest in town.
2. I wish I'd be a great soccer player.
3. I wish I could ride in an airplane.
4. I wish Gloria would stay here and be my best friend.

21

## Comprehension Skills

Second Read

### Classify and Categorize

Classifying and categorizing are skills students can use to help them understand unfamiliar terms or to find new ways of looking at familiar terms. Give them opportunities to practice using this skill so they can become comfortable enough with it to use it on their own.

- Have students look for words on page 20 that they can add to the heading *Things Needed to Make a Kite (sticks, newspaper, string, rags).*
- Another list could be *How to Make Wishes (make a kite; write wishes on paper; don't tell wishes).*

Have students consider all of the categories discussed so far. Encourage students to think again about how putting related words into groups helps them understand information as they read.

> ### Word Knowledge
> *-ing* ending:     writing

**Teacher Tip** Tell students that good readers keep thinking about the questions that come up about the topic, and they keep coming back to those questions. As they read, tell them to keep the questions on the Concept/Question Board in mind. Have them make notes to themselves in their Writer's Notebooks about which questions seem really important and what information in the selections seems most important. Tell them that good readers always think about what is important in selections, and they try to remember this important information.

COMPREHENSION

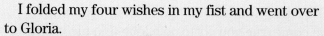

## Comprehension Strategies

**First Read**

### Teacher Modeling

**5 Confirming Predictions** *Earlier, I predicted that Julian and Gloria would try to make their wish that they could remain neighbors and friends come true. Now that I have read more, I know that my prediction was confirmed. That was the fourth wish that he wrote to tie to the kite's tail. But, Gloria is keeping her wishes a secret. I wonder if she will ever tell Julian about the wishes she wrote. I predict that she won't because she is afraid that telling will keep the wishes from coming true. What do you predict? What clues in the text lead you to that prediction?*

---

### Word Knowledge

| | |
|---|---|
| *-ed* ending: | **folded** |
| | **wondered** |
| | **fastened** |

---

**Teacher Tip** Ask students one or more of the following questions to make sure they understand what they are reading: Is anyone confused? Do you need clarification? Can you summarize what you have read so far? Does what you are reading make sense to you?

---

I folded my four wishes in my fist and went over to Gloria.

"How many wishes did you make?" Gloria asked.

"Four," I said. "How many did you make?"

"Two," Gloria said.

I wondered what they were.

"Now we put the wishes on the tail of the kite," Gloria said. "Every time we tie one piece of rag on the tail, we fasten a wish in the knot. You can put yours in first."

I fastened mine in, and then Gloria fastened in hers, and we carried the kite into the yard.

"You hold the tail," I told Gloria, "and I'll pull."

22

*Florida*

Day 4

We ran through the back yard with the kite, passed the garden and the fig tree, and went into the open field beyond our yard.

The kite started to rise. The tail jerked heavily like a long white snake. In a minute the kite passed the roof of my house and was climbing toward the sun.

23

## Comprehension Skills

Second Read

### Classify and Categorize

Remind students that classifying and categorizing is a skill they can use at any time to help them better understand the relationships between items, organize information, or learn about unfamiliar items.

- Students can add to the list *How to Make Wishes (fold up the paper the wishes are on, fasten them to the kite tail)*.
- Another list can be *How to Fly a Kite (one person holds the tail, one person pulls and runs with it)*.

| Word Knowledge |
| --- |
| *-ed* ending:    **passed** |
| **jerked** |

**Teacher Tip** Good readers constantly evaluate their understanding of what they read. Stop often to make sure students are doing this.

Have students close eyes and visualize as you read this page (2nd reading)

## Comprehension Strategies

*Day 2*

 **First Read**

### Teacher Modeling

**6** **Confirming Predictions** *When I tried to predict what Gloria's wishes were, I knew that Julian had wished that they would remain friends. I was pretty sure that Gloria had wished the same thing. Now that I've read the rest of the story, I believe my prediction was confirmed. I still don't know for certain. Gloria is still not telling what her wishes were. But, Julian believes that she made the same wish that he did. I think Julian is right. I did predict that Gloria wouldn't tell Julian what her wishes were, and that prediction was also confirmed. What did you predict Gloria wished? Were your predictions confirmed? What clues did you read in the story that helped you to make your predictions?*

*Day 2*

### Discussing Strategy Use LA.A.1.2.4.3.1

While students are reading the selection, encourage them to share any problems they encountered, and tell what strategies they used to solve them.

- What connections did they make between the reading and what they already know?

- Where did they pause in the reading to summarize?

- What predictions did they make?

These are questions good readers ask after they read a text. After reading, they should always be asking, "What did I find interesting? What is important here?" Later, remind the students again that whenever they conclude a reading, they should ask themselves questions about what was in the text.

#### Word Knowledge

*-ing* ending: **looking**

---

We stood in the open field, looking up at it. I was wishing I would get my wishes.

"I know it's going to work!" Gloria said.

"How do you know?"

"When we take the kite down," Gloria told me, "there shouldn't be one wish in the tail. When the wind takes all your wishes, that's when you know it's going to work."

The kite stayed up for a long time. We both held the string. The kite looked like a tiny black spot in the sun, and my neck got <u>stiff</u> from looking at it.

"Shall we pull it in?" I asked.

"All right," Gloria said.

24

---

 **Teacher Tip** Remind students that "Gloria Who Might Be My Best Friend" is realistic fiction. Everything that occurred in the story could actually have happened.

 **Informal Assessment**

Use the Informal Comprehension Strategies Rubrics on page 14J to determine whether a student is using the strategies being taught.

*Day 4*

We drew the string in more and more until, like a tired bird, the kite fell at our feet.

We looked at the tail. All our wishes were gone. Probably they were still flying higher and higher in the wind.

Maybe I would get to be a good soccer player and have a ride in an airplane and the tallest fig tree in town. And Gloria would be my best friend.

"Gloria," I said, "did you wish we would be friends?"

"You're not supposed to ask me that!" Gloria said.

"I'm sorry," I answered. But inside I was smiling. I guessed one thing Gloria wished for. I was pretty sure we would be friends. **6**

25

### Formal Assessment

See pages 2–5 in **Unit 1 Assessment** to test students' comprehension of "Gloria Who Might Be My Best Friend."

# Comprehension Skills

Second Read

**COMPREHENSION**

## Classify and Categorize

Remind students that classifying and categorizing items can help them better understand those items and the relationships between things. Students can create categories in any way they choose as long as they understand and can explain the connection. Ask students to create a final category of their choosing for items in this story. *(Things Friends Can Share: games, rock collections, kites)*

## Checking Comprehension

Ask students the following questions to check their comprehension of the story.

- Why is Julian worried about being friends with a girl? *(Because people might tease him.)*

- Why does Julian decide he wants to be friends with Gloria? *(Because she is his age and she is nice to him.)*

- How do Julian and Gloria start to become friends? *(They talk to each other. Julian shows Gloria a bird's nest and shares his games and rock collection with her. Gloria shows Julian how to make wishes come true. They make a kite together and make wishes together.)*

Use for "Harding off"

**Teacher Tip FLUENCY** By this time in Grade 3 good readers should be reading approximately 107 words per minute with fluency and expression. The only way to gain this fluency is through practice. Have students reread the selection to you and to each other during Workshop to help build fluency. As students read, you may notice that some need work in building fluency. During Workshop, have these students select a section of the text (a minimum of 160 words) to read several times in order to build fluency.

**Teacher Tip** DISCUSSION When you call on a student, allow him or her a few seconds to consider your question and arrive at an answer.

**Routine Card**
Refer to *Routine 6* for the *handing-off process*.

| Clues | Problems | Wonderings |
|---|---|---|
| The title says "Might Be." Maybe Julian isn't sure what will happen. | laughing | Will Julian and Gloria be friends? |

*Reading Transparency 46*

**www.sra4kids.com**
**Web Connection**
Some students may choose to conduct a computer search for additional books or information about friendship. Invite them to make a list of these books and sources of information to share with classmates and the school librarian. Check the Reading link of the SRA Web page for additional links to theme-related Web sites.

*Day 2*

## Discussing the Selection  LA.E.1.2.1.3.1

Discussion is an integral part of learning. Through discussion, students learn how to express their thoughts and opinions coherently and are exposed to points of view different from their own.

*or 2nd read*

After the first read, the whole group discusses the selection and any personal thoughts, reactions, problems, or questions that it raises. To stimulate discussion, students can ask one another the kinds of questions that good readers ask themselves about a text: *How does it connect to friendship? What have I learned that is new? What did I find interesting? What is important here? What was difficult to understand? Why would someone want to read this?*

**Handing-Off Process**   Seeing you as a contributing member of the group sets a strong example for students. To emphasize that you are part of the group, actively participate in the *handing-off process:* Raise your hand to be called on by the last speaker when you have a contribution to make. Point out unusual and interesting insights verbalized by students so that these insights are recognized and discussed. As the year progresses, students will take more and more responsibility for the discussions of the selections.

Engage students in a discussion to determine whether they have grasped the following ideas:

- why Julian was worried about being friends with Gloria
- why Julian changed his mind
- how Julian and Gloria started becoming friends
- what Gloria probably wished for

During this time, have students return to the clues, problems, and wonderings they noted during browsing to determine whether the clues were borne out by the selection, whether and how their problems were solved, and whether their wonderings were answered or deserve further discussion and investigation. Let the students decide which items deserve further discussion.

Also have students return to the Focus Questions on the first page of the selection. Select a student to read the questions aloud, and have volunteers answer the questions. If students do not know the answers to the questions, have them return to the text to find the answers.

You may wish to review the elements of realistic fiction with the students at this time. Discuss with them how they can tell that "Gloria Who Might Be My Best Friend" is realistic fiction.

Have students break into small groups to discuss what this story tells them about friendship. Groups can then share their ideas with the rest of the class.

*Writer's Notebook*

If they have ever moved to a new place or made a new friend, encourage them to record these events.

*Day 4*

## Review Selection Vocabulary LA.A.1.2.2.3.2

Have students review the definitions of the selection vocabulary words that they wrote in the Vocabulary section of their Writer's Notebooks. Remind them that they discussed the meanings of these words before reading the selection. Have students write sentences for each of the vocabulary words after the definitions in the same section of their Writer's Notebooks. They can use the definitions and the sentences to study for the vocabulary portion of their Lesson Assessments. Have them add to the personal dictionary section of their Writer's Notebooks any other interesting words that they clarified while reading. Encourage students to refer to the selection vocabulary words throughout the unit. The words from the selection are:

| | | |
|---|---|---|
| **tease** | **seriously** | **stiff** |
| **lonely** | **collection** | **probably** |

Create a Word Bank for the students to organize the vocabulary for this unit. Create a Word Bank organized by parts of speech: nouns, verbs, adjectives, and adverbs. Write the words or have the students write the words on cards and then place them under the appropriate part of speech on the Word Bank. Encourage the students to find other words related to the unit theme and add them to the Word Bank. You may also want to encourage students to find synonyms and antonyms for words in the Word Bank and add them as well. A full explanation of the Word Bank can be found in the Appendix.

## Home Connection  ✳ *Homework*

Distribute **Home Connection**, page 3. Encourage students to discuss "Gloria Who Might Be My Best Friend" with their families. Students and their families can try making a kite similar to the one in the story. **Home Connection** is also available in Spanish, page 4.

*Bring in creation to share*

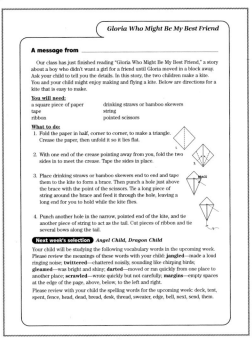

**Home Connection p. 3**

*Homework*

**Teacher Tip** Students may suggest a different method of organizing a Word Bank. Be open to their suggestions.

LA.C.1.2.2.3.1; LA.E.1.2.1.3.3

**Teacher Tip** Have the students choose a book to read from the library relating to the theme. This book should identify their preference in either literary or nonfiction texts. Encourage students to read often from their preferred genre.

*Day 1*

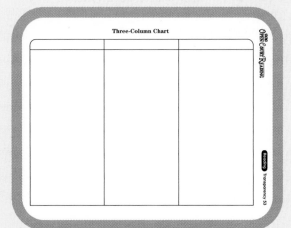

**Reading Transparency 53**

# Supporting the Reading  LA.E.2.2.3.3.1, LA.E.2.2.3.3.2

## Reading Strategy: Making Connections

**Teach** Tell students that connecting what they read to their own experiences helps them better understand what they are reading. Making personal connections also makes reading more interesting.

**Guided Practice** Give students a chance to elaborate on experiences they have had similar to those in the story they have just read. Use a three-column chart on *Reading Transparency 53* to help students connect their experiences to events in the story. In the first column they should list experiences of the story characters. In the second column they should list similar experiences of their own. In the last column they should explain how their experience was the same or different from the character's experience.

Ask students to think about whether the story makes them think anything new about their own experiences. Invite them to share their thoughts with the class. Use the following as an example. *Student response*

| Character's Experience | My Experience | Differences |
|---|---|---|
| Gloria moved to a new town. | I moved one time. | I moved into an apartment building with lots of kids. |
| Julian was afraid to be friends with a girl. | I felt that way before. | I don't have a friend who is a girl. |

**Independent Practice** Remind students that the comprehension strategies they are using in class can be used any time they read. Encourage students to practice using the strategy Making Connections in their reading outside of class.

**Link to Writing** Tell students that keeping a journal is a good way to record connections between stories and personal experiences. Sometimes writing about the connections helps people understand something new. Ask students to write in the Response Journal section of their Writer's Notebooks about one connection in this story.

*Day 4 (optional)*

# Literary Elements

## Point of View

**Teach** Tell students that one of the first things a writer must do in order to write a story is to decide who will tell it. Explain to students that making this decision is something they will also have to do when they write. Tell them that writers have ways of letting the reader know *who is telling the story*. Although an adult, Ann Cameron, wrote this story, she decided to have a child, Julian, tell it. Tell them that this is called the first-person narrative point of view.

Have a volunteer reread the first two pages of the story aloud. Encourage students to explain how they know Julian is telling the story. They will probably point out the *signal* words *I, me, my, we, us,* and so on.

A second way to identify Julian as the storyteller is to notice his own descriptions of his thoughts and feelings, things that only he knows. "I had never tried a cartwheel before" (page 16).

**Guided Practice** The following procedure will help students focus on how Ann Cameron used the first-person narrative point of view:

- Ask a volunteer to find one good example of first-person point of view, tell the page number, and read it aloud to the rest of the group. Allow others to agree or disagree and explain why.
- Repeat the procedure, allowing volunteers to take part and explain their thinking.
- Have students define point of view in their Writer's Notebooks under the section Identifying the Writer's Craft. Also have them include an example for writing a first-person point of view.

**Independent Practice** Ask students to practice using the first-person point of view by using it to write their own one-page story about a problem they have had with a friend. Remind them that main characters will refer to themselves as *I* and will describe their own thoughts and feelings.

*Day 3*

## Social Studies Connection  LA.A.2.2.8.3.1; SS.B.1.2.1.3.1

### Maps

Explain to students that *maps* are drawings that show where places (cities, states, countries, etc.) and things (rivers, mountains, parks, etc.) are located. Symbols and colors are used to show the information on maps. Maps are not always flat like a sheet of paper. A *globe* shows the shape of the world and has a map of the earth around it. When a lot of maps are put together in a book, that book is called an *atlas*.

Point out to students the different features of maps. The *title* tells what place or geographical area the map shows. The *key* of a map explains what each special symbol or color on the map stands for; special symbols often represent rivers, lakes, and parks, for example. Because maps are much smaller than the places they show, the *scale* on a map is included to show how the distance on the map relates to distance on real land. *Direction arrows* show north, south, east, and west; north is usually located toward the top of a map.

Ask students to locate on the United States map the city where they live. Next, ask them to locate Newport, Rhode Island, on the map. Then go over the features of the two areas on the smaller maps and discuss with students the geographical differences between Newport and their own city.

Day 5

# Science Connection

## Energy and the Wind

In "Gloria Who Might Be My Best Friend," Gloria and Julian use energy in different ways. Their bodies create energy as they run with the kite, and the wind creates energy that lifts the kite into the air and carries the wishes into the air. Have the students look up the following objects in a dictionary, encyclopedia, or on the Internet.

- **wind chimes**
- **wind instrument**
- **windmill**
- **wind sail**
- **wind sock**
- **wind tunnel**

Each of these objects requires the energy created by some form of wind in order to work properly. Have the students individually define each of these objects and describe how the wind's energy causes them to work.

You can make this a group project by dividing the class into small groups and assigning one object to each group. Each group could then investigate the object in more detail and create a presentation or a model about how the wind supplies the energy needed for each object to function. Encourage students to use visual aids such as graphs, charts, maps, or photographs, as needed.

**Teacher Tip MATERIALS**
Individual Project:
- ✔ dictionaries
- ✔ encyclopedias
- ✔ Internet
- ✔ paper and pencils

Group Project:
- ✔ dictionaries
- ✔ encyclopedias
- ✔ Internet
- ✔ poster boards
- ✔ colored pencils or markers
- ✔ graph paper
- ✔ cameras

**Teacher Tip PURPOSE** To teach students how energy created by the wind is important to the operation of certain objects.

**Science/Social Studies Connection Center**

Refer to the *Science/Social Studies Connection Center* Card 3 for a science activity that students can investigate.

## Meet the Author *Day 2*

After students read the information about Ann Cameron, discuss the following questions with them.

- Why do you think Ann Cameron believes friends help her to be a better writer? (*Possible answer: She uses memories of her friends and their stories as a resource for ideas.*)

- Ann Cameron was in the third grade when she knew she wanted to be a writer. What kinds of things do you think she wrote about then? (*Answers will vary. Friends, teachers, and school are all common ideas. Help students think of stories in their own lives that they might want to write about.*)

## Meet the Illustrator

After students read the information about Ann Strugnell, discuss the following questions with them.

- How does Ann Strugnell's travel to so many places help make her a better illustrator? (*Possible answer: By seeing so many different places and people, she has more ideas about how to make her drawings special.*)

- Look again at the pictures in "Gloria Who Might Be My Best Friend." In what ways does Ann Strugnell show the children's friendship? (*Possible answer: She shows how the children try to copy each other—like doing a cartwheel. They help one another fly the kite. They look happy flying the kite together.*)

# Gloria Who Might Be My Best Friend

## Meet the Author

**Ann Cameron** was in third grade when she knew she wanted to be a writer. It has been the memories of her friends and the stories they have shared that help her write stories. She says, *"My story will never be exactly like yours. I could never tell yours for you. Your story, if it's really the way you want to tell it, can never be wrong the way an arithmetic answer is wrong; and even if your mother, your father, your teacher, or your best friend doesn't understand it, it's still right for you . . . stories are individual, special, and all different—brand-new thought-flowers blooming in the garden of your head."*

Ann now lives in Guatemala, where the neighborhood children continue to inspire her writing. She is also the supervisor of a local library, where she loves to watch children read and learn.

## Meet the Illustrator

**Ann Strugnell** is a British artist who has illustrated many children's books. She has traveled to faraway places such as Turkey, Spain, and Italy. She has even been to the United States to see New York and Cape Cod. She lives with her husband and illustrates books in the bustling city of London, England. Sometimes she comes to the United States to illustrate books as well.

*Talk about where she's been. Point out on map.*

26

*Day 2* (handwritten)

# Theme Connections

## Within the Selection

Record your answers to the questions below in the Response Journal section of your Writer's Notebook. In small groups, report the ideas you wrote. Discuss your ideas with the rest of the group. Then choose a person to report your group's answers to the class.

- Do you think it was hard for Julian to ask Gloria to be his friend? Why?
- How did the kite help Julian and Gloria become friends?

*use to get started on this* (handwritten)

## Beyond the Selection

- Can you think of a time when you made a new friend?
- Think about what "Gloria Who Might Be My Best Friend" tells you about friendship.
- Add items to the Concept/Question Board about friendship.

27

---

## Theme Connections LA.E.2.2.4.3.1

### Within the Selection

- Julian didn't know that a girl could be a good friend.
- Julian and Gloria showed friendship as they worked together to make a kite that would carry both of their wishes.

### Beyond the Selection

Have groups report and discuss their ideas with the class. As these ideas are stated, have students add them to the Concept/Question Board.

As students complete their discussions, have them sum up what they have learned and tell how they might use this information in further investigations.

### Inquiry Journal

Students should record their ideas and impressions about the selections on page 2 of their *Inquiry Journals.*

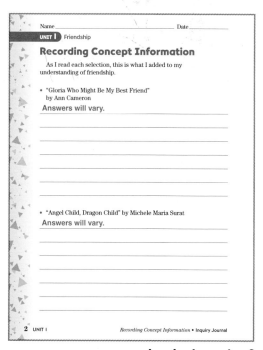

*Inquiry Journal p. 2*

---

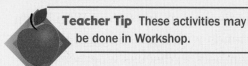

**Teacher Tip** These activities may be done in Workshop.

**Informal Assessment**

This may be a good time to observe students working in small groups and mark your observations in the Teacher Observation Log found in the *Program Assessment Teacher's Edition.*

Day 1

## Objectives

- Students gain a deeper understanding of friendship.
- Students come up with questions about friendship they would like to investigate.
- Students choose an activity with which to explore the concept of friendship.

## Materials

- Student Anthology, Book 1, pp. 14–27
- Inquiry Journal, pp. 5–9
- Reading Transparency 2
- Research Assistant CD-ROM

**INVESTIGATION**

## Investigating Concepts Beyond the Text

The **Open Court Reading** investigation procedure is based on a never-ending, student-driven, recursive cycle. The aim of the investigation is not to come to final conclusions. As with professional researchers, answers to problems, questions, and conjectures may never come. What will come are unexpected findings and more questions.

The steps to follow in the unit investigations are:

- Students decide on a problem or question to investigate.
  *After some discussion of the unit theme, but before students consult investigation resources, students will develop questions that interest them about the theme.*

- Students formulate a conjecture about the problem.
  *A conjecture is a hypothesis that is not based on evidence. It is not expected that students' initial conjectures be well founded, although it is expected that their later conjectures be better founded and thus evolve toward hypotheses.*

- Students revise their conjectures.
  *Students reconsider current conjectures in light of new information. This step is largely a discussion phase. Discussion needs to be focused in ways that will promote revision.*

- Students present their findings.
  *Although this step will most likely occur at the end of a unit, students should understand that the presentation of investigation findings does not mean the investigation has produced final results. Investigations are never-ending and this is a time to present what findings they have made so far.*

The Inquiry portion in each unit of the **Teacher's Edition** will guide you through this recursive process. It will prompt times for discussion, brainstorming, planning, and presenting. It will also offer supplementary activities throughout, which serve to generate questions and discussion for students. It is important to keep in mind, however, that these investigations are student-driven. Specific unit investigation examples are not given so that students are open to pursue their own interests as they seek the answers to their questions.

Explain to students the nature and goals of the unit investigation. For this unit, students will be developing questions and conjectures revolving around the unit theme, Friendship. Start by initiating a whole-class discussion around the theme Friendship.

Include this lesson's selection as part of the discussion. In "Gloria Who Might Be My Best Friend," Julian is afraid to be friends with a girl. Suggest that students form a panel of five or six class members to discuss whether boys and girls in the third grade can really become friends. Individually or in small groups, have them complete **Inquiry Journal,** page 5.

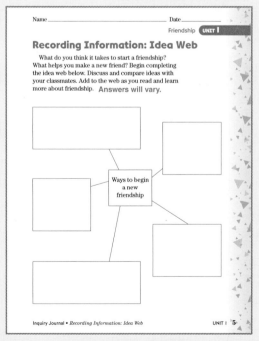

Name _____ Date _____

Friendship **UNIT I**

**Recording Information: Idea Web**

What do you think it takes to start a friendship? What helps you make a new friend? Begin completing the idea web below. Discuss and compare ideas with your classmates. Add to the web as you read and learn more about friendship. **Answers will vary.**

Ways to begin a new friendship

Inquiry Journal • Recording Information: Idea Web    UNIT I    **5**

**Inquiry Journal p. 5**

*Day 2*          *update (revisit at this time)*

# Concept/Question Board

After reading each selection, students should use the Concept/Question Board to do the following:

- Post any questions they asked about a selection before reading that haven't been answered yet.
- Refer to as they formulate statements about concepts that apply to their investigations.
- Post general statements formulated by each collaborative group.
- Continue to post news articles or other items that they find during the unit investigation.
- Read and think about posted questions, articles, or concepts that interest them and provide answers to the questions.

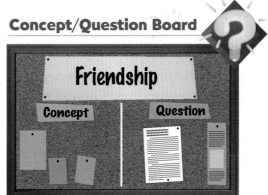

**Concept/Question Board**

Friendship

Concept          Question

## INVESTIGATION

**Teacher Tip** INVESTIGATION ACTIVITIES To assist students in these early investigation activities, continue to provide support by giving them limited choices and modeling the procedure step-by-step. At this point students should be involved in discussions helping them to identify a question or problem or issue that they truly wonder about and wish to understand.

### Research Assistant
The *Research Assistant CD-ROM* can assist students in their investigations.

**Teacher Tip** Although specific investigation examples will not be provided, an outline of a possible unit investigation follows as a model.

Unit Theme: Medicine

✔ Problem or Question: After reading and discussing the Read Aloud, students had many questions. For example: "Do germs have anything to do with medicine?" Students divided into groups based on interest in the questions.

✔ Conjecture: "Doctors invented medicine because of germs."

✔ Needs and Plans: Students decided they needed to consult encyclopedias and books, as well as articles in magazines and on the Internet. They also decided it would be beneficial to have a doctor as a guest speaker. Students planned the investigation on a calendar.

✔ Reevaluate problem or question: Students read articles and perform activities that lead them to a better understanding of their question, "Do germs have anything to do with medicine?"

✔ Revise conjecture: For example, students would revise their initial conjecture from "Doctors invented medicine because of germs" to "Germs can aid in the treatment of some diseases."

✔ Presentation: Students can and should use a variety of ways to present their findings. They should state their original questions and conjectures, the resources they consulted, and how their findings led to a revised conjecture.

✔ Future questions: Students should pose additional questions that would aid in the investigation process of this revised conjecture.

## Unit I Investigation Management

| Lesson I | **Collaborative Investigation**<br>**Introduce the investigation cycle and explain its purpose. Support group discussion and encourage the use of the Concept/Question Board and students' Writer's Notebooks for reflection.**<br>**Supplementary Activities**<br>**Students lead a panel discussion on friendship-related issues.** |
|---|---|
| Lesson 2 | Students can investigate immigration and forming new friendships or other areas of investigation related to friendship. Students should organize into groups based on areas of shared interest. |
| Lesson 3 | Students investigate mending damaged friendships, and student groups should begin forming conjectures. |
| Lesson 4 | Students begin their investigations. Groups can share personal stories, hold a panel discussion, or invite an expert speaker to class. |
| Lesson 5 | Students revise investigation plans as necessary. Groups discuss teammate qualities and invite a coach to class to interview. |
| Lesson 6 | Students wrap up investigations and prepare formal presentations. Students can discuss standing by friends and write a scene or miniplay about a scenario. |

*Day 3*

**Reading Transparency 2**

**Teacher Tip** Remind students that they can use any of the activities performed during the unit to help them come up with their investigation questions, problems, and conjectures. The various activities, readings, and writing projects should generate ideas. Also remind them that the investigation they choose should be one that really interests them. They should be excited about seeking the answers to their questions.

✓ **Formal Assessment**

Use the Research Rubrics on page 14J to assess students' ability to formulate research questions and problems.

**INVESTIGATION**

# Generating Questions to Investigate

Explain that throughout the unit, students may want to write about their investigations or to discuss them with one another. Since this is the first selection in the unit, students will be generating ideas at this stage. They will be generating questions related to friendship.

Have students list the questions that especially interest them in the *Inquiry Journal,* page 6. Tell them that they will look at these questions again as they progress through the unit. These pages will also help them plan their investigation.

Tell students that over the course of the unit, they will produce and publish in some form the results of their investigation. They are free to decide what it is about friendship that they want to investigate, with whom they want to work, and how they want to present their finished product.

Display *Reading Transparency 2* to give students an idea of possible modes of presentation. Remind students that this is just a list of suggestions, and they are free to develop their own ideas.

*Inquiry Journal p. 6*

*Day 4*

# Interviewing

**Teach** Ask students to tell what is meant by interviewing and to talk about any experiences they have had with this process. Interviewing is a special research tool. In an interview, students ask another person questions to get information about a subject or to find out what she or he thinks or feels about something. In an interview, a person is the *source*. Discuss the following rules for conducting an interview.

- Always ask permission to interview a person. Think of *Who? What? When? Where? Why?* and *How?* questions that will help you get the information you need.
- Write down your questions in the order you want to ask them.
- Speak clearly and be polite during the interview.
- Listen carefully to the person's answers.
- Take notes while the person answers your questions. Write down only enough to help you remember what the person said.
- Thank the person for the interview.
- Read your notes as soon after the interview as possible. That way the conversation is still fresh in your mind. Add more notes to help make the information clear.

**Guided Practice** Have students make a list of questions they could use to interview Ann Cameron, the author of "Gloria Who Might Be My Best Friend." Encourage them to ask *Who? What? When? Where? Why?* and *How?* For example, students might ask:

Why did you write this story?

How do you make new friends?

How can you tell if you are going to be good friends with someone?

**Independent Practice** Have students conduct real interviews of family members, staff members, or a guest speaker at school. Have students follow the rules stated above. Record the information and compile results as a reference tool for investigations.

Have students use **Inquiry Journal,** pages 7–9 to help them complete this activity.

*Inquiry Journal p. 7*

**SUPPORTING THE INVESTIGATION**

**Basic Computer Skills**
Encourage students to use *Basic Computer Skills* to learn more about how to use a computer to write a report.

*Homework or workshop ???*

*Inquiry Journal pp. 8–9*

www.sra4kids.com
**Web Connection**
More information about Friendship and links to Web sites concerning friendship can be found at www.sra4kids.com.

## Objectives

**Word Analysis**

**Spelling**
- **The /a/ Sound.** Develop understanding of the /a/ sound spelled *a*.

**Vocabulary**
- **Vocabulary Strategies.** Choose unfamiliar words from "Gloria Who Might Be My Best Friend" and devise strategies for learning the meanings and spellings of those words.

**Writing Process Strategies**
- **Getting Ideas.** Different means by which one may generate ideas for different types of writing will be explored.

**English Language Conventions**

**Grammar, Usage, and Mechanics**
- **Nouns.** Understand what nouns are and the capitalization of proper nouns. Find nouns in "Gloria Who Might Be My Best Friend," and use nouns in writing.

**Listening, Speaking, Viewing**
- **Listening: Being a Good Listener.** Learn the purposes of listening and why each purpose is important.

**Penmanship**
- **Cursive Letters *i* and *t*.** Develop handwriting skills by practicing formation of cursive *i* and *t*.

## Materials

- Language Arts Handbook, pp. 10, 246
- Spelling and Vocabulary Skills, pp. 2–5
- Writer's Workbook, p. 2
- Language Arts Transparency 38
- Comprehension and Language Arts Skills, pp. 2–3
- Student Anthology

## MEETING INDIVIDUAL NEEDS

*Reteach, Challenge, English-Language Development,* and *Intervention* lessons are available to support the language arts instruction in this lesson.

## Research in Action

The purpose of learning to spell is so that writing may become easier, more fluent, more expressive, and more easily read and understood by others. Without writing there would be little purpose in learning to spell. Thus, the proper place for spelling instruction is within the writing program.

(*J. Richard Gentry* and *Jean Wallace Gillet,* Teaching Kids to Spell)

# Language Arts Overview

## Word Analysis

**Spelling** The Spelling activities on the following pages introduce the /a/ sound spelled *a* by developing spelling skills through various strategies.

### Selection Spelling Words

These words from "Gloria Who Might Be My Best Friend" contain the /a/ sound.

gr**a**ss   r**a**gs   b**a**ck   bl**a**ck   th**a**t

**Vocabulary** The Vocabulary activities introduce students to the idea of developing strategies for word analysis. Students are to devise their own strategies for learning the meanings of unfamiliar words.

### Vocabulary Skill Words

These words from "Gloria Who Might Be My Best Friend" may be unfamiliar to students. Students will devise a list of vocabulary words in the Writer's Notebook.

mustache   minute   garage   strawberry   squawked

**Additional Materials:** dictionary

## Writing Process Strategies

The first unit introduces the writing process that students will be practicing as they write throughout the year. To practice, students will be getting ideas for prewriting, drafting, revising, editing/proofreading, and publishing an autobiography.

 **Basic Computer Skills** To introduce students to the computer as a writing tool, have students review computer parts, their functions, basic operation of the computer, and programs and software copyright laws. *Basic Computer Skills* Level 3, Lessons 1–2, teach these basic computer skills. LA.D.2.2.4.3.1

## English Language Conventions

**Grammar, Usage, and Mechanics** **Nouns.** This lesson develops the concept of nouns through reading and writing.

**Listening, Speaking, Viewing** **Listening: Being a Good Listener.** The Listening, Speaking, Viewing lessons are divided into six categories: Listening, Speaking, Language, Viewing, Interacting, and Presenting. In this Listening lesson, students will develop listening and comprehension skills.

**Penmanship** **Cursive Letters *i* and *t*.** This lesson continues the development of cursive handwriting skills. Students learn correct formation of *i* and *t* and then practice writing words from the literature selection that contain those letters.

# DAY 1

| Word Analysis | Writing Process Strategies | English Language Conventions |
|---|---|---|

## Spelling

### Assessment: Pretest

**The /a/ Sound** LA.A.1.2.2.3.1

### Teach

Give students the Pretest found on page 26 of *Unit 1 Assessment* as entry assessment of the spelling pattern. Have them proofread and correct any misspelled words.

### Pretest Sentences

1. **path** When on a nature hike, you should stay on the **path**.
2. **lamp** Sam turned off the **lamp**.
3. **damp** Dew causes **damp** grass.
4. **crash** Wearing a seatbelt can save your life in a car **crash**.
5. **plant** Gardeners **plant** tulip bulbs in the fall.
6. **math** One form of **math** is addition.
7. **trash** A landfill is for **trash**.
8. **stamp** A rare **stamp** can be worth a lot of money.
9. **hatbox** To keep a hat's shape, it is stored in a **hatbox**.
10. **have** I wish we could **have** a dog.
11. **grass** Some people are allergic to **grass**.
12. **rags** Torn **rags** are often used for cleaning and dusting.
13. **back** Rosa Parks would not sit in the **back** of the bus.
14. **black** Ebony is a **black** wood.
15. **that** Hockey is a game **that** is played on ice.

Diagnose any misspellings by determining whether students misspelled the /a/ sound or some other part of the word. Then use the Pretest as a take-home list to study the spellings of words with the /a/ sound.

## Getting Ideas LA.B.1.2.1.3.1

**Introduction to the Writing Process**

### Teach

**Introduce Writing-Process Steps**

Read *Language Arts Handbook,* page 10, to introduce Getting Ideas as an important step in beginning the Writing Process.

**Inspiration**

Teacher Model: *"Sometimes the hardest thing about writing for me is thinking of what to write about. The first thing I do is consider what kind of writing I am going to do. Then I try to think of something I know well. For example, if I am going to write a description, I think about what I am familiar with that I can describe."*

**Brainstorming**

Using description as the type of writing, encourage students to generate ideas they have about what they could describe. Make a list of ideas on the board. Have students write ideas that appeal to them in their Writer's Notebooks.

### Guided Practice

**Getting Ideas**

Have students think of three places, objects, or people they know well enough to describe in detail.

#### The Traits of Writing

Good writers are not born good writers. They learn to be good writers. How? They do it by studying and practicing the traits of good writing. The traits of good writing are certain qualities that make reading it enjoyable. These traits are described below and on the following pages.

**Ideas**

Your ideas should be clear, original, and supported by details. Ideas are the heart of your writing. Good ideas are supported by colorful details that make writing interesting to a reader. Your writing should have a main idea that sends a clear message to the reader. Use accurate details to support your idea.

**Take a Look**

Read this paragraph from *Angel Child, Dragon Child* by Michele Maria Surat.

My sisters skipped through the stone gate two by two. Mother was not there to skip with me. Mother was far away in Vietnam. She could not say, "Ut, my little one, be an Angel Child. Be happy in your new American school."

When you read the paragraph, did you think, "I want to know more about Ut. I like reading about people from other countries"? The author gives enough details to make the reader curious about Ut's culture and care about what happens to her.

10 ▲ The Traits of Writing

*Language Arts Handbook p. 10*

## Grammar, Usage, and Mechanics

**Grammar: Nouns** LA.B.1.2.3.3.4

### Teach

- Use *Language Arts Handbook,* page 246, for the definitions and examples of common and proper nouns.
- Explain that nouns name a person, place, thing, or idea.
- Explain that common nouns name people, places, things, or ideas, but that proper nouns name *specific* people, places, things, or ideas. For example, *dog* is a common noun, while *Spot* is a proper noun.
- Write two columns on the board. Title one *Common Nouns* and the other *Proper Nouns.* Fill in one column and have students fill in the other. Common nouns you could use are *teacher, house,* and *state.* Corresponding proper nouns could be *Mrs. Jones, White House,* and *California.*

### Independent Practice

Use the *Comprehension and Language Arts Skills,* pages 2–3, to identify nouns and name what kind they are.

Name _____ Date _____

UNIT 1 Friendship • Lesson 1 *Gloria Who Might Be My Best Friend*

**Nouns**

Nouns name a person, place, thing, or idea.

| Rule | Example |
|---|---|
| ▶ Some nouns name a person. | ▶ **Eleanor Roosevelt** helped many people. |
| ▶ Some nouns name a place. | ▶ Someday people will travel to **Mars**. |
| ▶ Some nouns name a thing. | ▶ Danny bought his **saxophone** in California. |
| ▶ Some nouns name an idea. | ▶ **Friendship** makes Gloria and Julian happy. |

**Try It!**

Write five nouns that name people or things in your classroom and five nouns that name people or things in your home.

_____  _____
_____  _____
_____  _____
_____  _____

Answers will vary.

2  UNIT 1 • Lesson 1  Comprehension and Language Arts Skills

*Comprehension and Language Arts Skills p. 2*

## DAY 2

| Word Analysis | Writing Process Strategies | English Language Conventions |
|---|---|---|

## Word Analysis

### Spelling

**Word Sorting** LA.A.1.2.2.3.1
- Hold up *Sound/Spelling Card 1*, showing the /a/ sound. Ask the class to say *lamb* and listen to the sound made by the letter *a*.
- **Board Word Sort.** Write *path, with, lamp, stuck, grass, lock, black, late, have,* and *kite* on the board. Write *The /a/ Sound* and *Other Vowel Sounds*. Have the students say each word and sort them under the correct column.

### Vocabulary

**Vocabulary Strategies** LA.A.1.2.3.3.2

#### Teach
- Write *mustache* on the board.
- Ask: Have you heard of this word? How is it used in the story? Does it look like another word you know? Do parts of it look familiar?
- Explain to students that they will encounter many unfamiliar words when reading.

#### Guided Practice
*Spelling and Vocabulary Skills*, page 2, is an introduction for the different strategies used to determine the meaning of a word. Have students complete page 3 as independent practice.

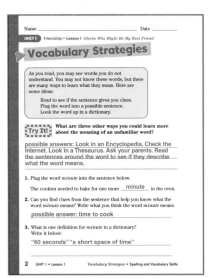

*Spelling and Vocabulary Skills p. 2*

## Writing Process Strategies

**Getting Ideas** LA.B.1.2.1.3.1
**Introduction to the Writing Process**

#### Teach
- **Review** the process students went through for getting ideas for descriptive writing on Day 1.
- Have students brainstorm what they might write about if the task is a newspaper story. Ask them to think about events or people they know that would make a good newspaper story.
- Explain to students that one way to keep track of their ideas is by making a list. Work through **Language Arts Transparency 38,** Lists, with students, making lists of ideas for different tasks.

#### Guided Practice
**Getting Ideas**
Encourage students to make a list of events or people they think would be interesting subjects for news stories in their Writer's Notebooks.

## English Language Conventions

**Grammar, Usage, and Mechanics**
**Grammar: Nouns** LA.B.1.2.3.3.4

#### Teach
- Review common and proper nouns. Remind students that proper nouns are capitalized.
- Write the following sentences on the board and have students identify the common and proper nouns.
  - A girl named Gloria moved from Newport. (Gloria *and* Newport *are proper nouns.*)
  - Kindness and honesty are important to friendship. (Kindness, honesty, *and* friendship *are common nouns.*)
  - Ann Cameron wrote this story and Ann Strugnell did the illustrations. (Ann Cameron *and* Ann Strugnell *are proper nouns.*)
  - A dictionary is a useful book. (Book *and* dictionary *are common nouns.*)

#### Guided Practice in Reading
Ask students to identify the kinds of nouns in the dialogue of "Gloria Who Might Be My Best Friend." Write their answers on the board in the appropriate category.

*students go back into selection for this (look up)*

## DAY 3

| Word Analysis | Writing Process Strategies | English Language Conventions |
|---|---|---|

### Word Analysis

#### Spelling

**The /a/ Sound** LA.A.1.2.2.3.1

**Teach**

- Introduce words with the /a/ sound spelled *a* found in "Gloria Who Might Be My Best Friend." Students should find the five Selection Spelling Words in the story.
- Ask students to think of proper nouns that have the /a/ sound. *(Patrick, Sam, Tammy)*

**Guided Practice**

Have students complete ***Spelling and Vocabulary Skills,*** page 4, to learn strategies for spelling words with the /a/ sound.

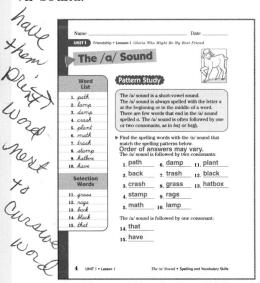

*handwritten: have them print word next to cursive word*

***Spelling and Vocabulary Skills p. 4***

#### Vocabulary (continued)

**Vocabulary Strategies** LA.C.1.2.3.3.1, LA.C.3.2.2.3.1

- Have students write an unfamiliar word in the story on a piece of paper. Separate students into pairs, and have them apply the Ask a Friend strategy by asking one another the definitions for the words. Have students write their partner's suggested definition.
- Compare student definitions to definitions in the dictionary. Discuss how asking a friend can sometimes lead them to a correct definition.

### Writing Process Strategies

#### Getting Ideas LA.B.1.2.1.3.1
**Introduction to the Writing Process**

**Teach**

- **Review** how to make a list to keep track of ideas for writing.
- Ask students to imagine they are going to write a friendly letter. Explain to them that this is a letter usually written to a friend or relative. Discuss what kind of information might be included in a friendly letter.
- Explain to students that another way to get ideas is to ask a friend what they might be interested in reading about in a friendly letter.

**Guided Practice**

**Getting Ideas**

Have students record ideas they have for a friendly letter in their Writer's Notebooks. Then encourage them to record additional ideas they get from asking friends about their ideas.

### English Language Conventions

#### Grammar, Usage, and Mechanics
**Grammar: Nouns** LA.B.1.2.3.3.4

**Teach**

Use ***Language Arts Handbook,*** page 246, to review nouns.

**Guided Practice in Writing**

- Have students write sentences with the following nouns in them: *book, school, airplane, Yellowstone National Park, beach, Florida.* Have some students share their sentences and identify the common and proper nouns.
- Invite students to write about something they think is fun or is important to them. Ask them to use the different kinds of nouns they have learned. Go around the class and have students give examples of nouns from their writing.

 **Informal Assessment**

Check students' work to make sure they are capitalizing proper nouns.

# DAY 4

## Word Analysis

### Spelling

**The /a/ Sound** LA.A.1.2.2.3.1

#### Teach

- Explain that the exercises on page 5 of *Spelling and Vocabulary Skills* are designed to help students learn to use spelling strategies. The Consonant Substitution strategy can help them learn to spell new words using known words.
- Write *damp* on the board. Show students how substituting *c* for *d* in the word helps them learn to spell *camp*.

#### Guided Practice

Have students complete page 5 of *Spelling and Vocabulary Skills* to reinforce the spelling patterns.

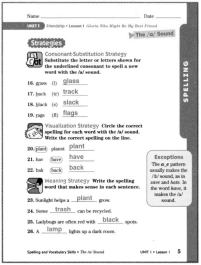

**Spelling and Vocabulary Skills p. 5**

### Vocabulary (continued)

**Vocabulary Strategies** LA.A.1.2.2.3.2

- Ask students to find an unfamiliar word in "Gloria Who Might Be My Best Friend."
- Select one of the students' words and write it on the board or apply the word *fig* from page 23. Ask a student to use the word in a sentence to discover the meaning of the word.

## Writing Process Strategies

### Getting Ideas LA.B.1.2.1.3.1
**Introduction to the Writing Process**

#### Teach

- Review with students that they can get ideas for writing by thinking of things they know about and by asking friends.
- Ask students to imagine they have been asked to write a research report on an animal that lives in their state. Discuss how students might generate ideas for this topic.
- Suggest that a topic such as this might require them to find out more before they can get ideas. For example, they may need to look through nonfiction books or get help searching the Internet to find out what animals live in their state.

#### Guided Practice

**Getting Ideas**

Have students make a list of animals they might be interested in writing a research report on in their Writer's Notebooks. Remind them to think of things they know about, ask a friend, and look through books to get ideas.

## English Language Conventions

### Listening, Speaking, Viewing
**Listening: Being a Good Listener** LA.C.1.2.1.3.1, LA.C.1.2.2.3.1, LA.C.1.2.4.3.1

#### Teach

- In Reading and Responding, we talked about how we listen for answers to help predict what will happen in a story. Now we'll talk more about being a good listener.
- Explain that there are many purposes of listening. We listen for information, to answer questions and solve problems, and for enjoyment.
- Explain why being a good listener is important. People who listen well can answer questions based on what they just heard. Give examples of the different ways that help us to pay attention. (*Sit up tall. Look at the person speaking. Concentrate on what is being said.*)
- Explain that listening well is also a good quality to have in a friend. When friends listen to each other, it shows how much they care about one another, like Gloria and Julian care for each other.

#### Guided Practice

- Read to the class from "Gloria Who Might Be My Best Friend," the two paragraphs where Julian and Gloria write out their wishes. Referring to this section, have the class answer basic plot questions and details to develop their listening comprehension. (*What were some of Julian's wishes? To be a great soccer player; to ride in an airplane; for Gloria to stay and be his best friend.*)
- Ask whether students enjoyed reading the text. Enjoyment is one reason why we listen.

 **Informal Assessment**

Observe students' abilities to recall details from the story. Watch for attentive behavior (*facing the speaker, eye contact, good posture*).

*Make spelling booklets (half sheet) give pretest staple Final test onto Pretest + keep all together for each unit.*

## DAY 5

| Word Analysis | Writing Process Strategies | English Language Conventions |
|---|---|---|

### Word Analysis

#### Spelling

**Assessment: Final Test**

**The /a/ Sound** LA.A.1.2.2.3.1

#### Teach

*or* Repeat the Pretest for this lesson or use the Final Test on page 27 of ***Unit 1 Assessment*** as summative assessment for student understanding of the /a/ sound spelling pattern.

*or dictation etc for post test*

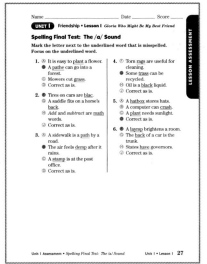

**Unit 1 Assessment p. 27**

#### Guided Practice

Have students categorize any mistakes they made on the Final Test. Are they careless errors? Are they lesson-pattern problems? See if students are spelling the /a/ sound correctly in their assignments.

### Vocabulary LA.B.2.2.1.3.1

 **Informal Assessment**

Explain that the strategies introduced throughout this lesson apply to the Vocabulary sections in Unit 1. Check to see that students are properly thinking of strategies when encountering unfamiliar words. Have students review pages 2 and 3 in *Spelling and Vocabulary Skills.* Ask students to devise a running vocabulary word list in the Writer's Notebook.

### Writing Process Strategies

#### Getting Ideas LA.B.1.2.1.3.1

**Introduction to the Writing Process**

#### Teach

- Review the different ways students can get ideas for a writing project. Remind them that they should always keep in mind what kind of writing they are doing so the ideas will be appropriate.
- Explain to students that an autobiography is a story about one's own life. Encourage a discussion about what kinds of information students think would be important in an autobiography. List these ideas on the board.

#### Guided Practice

**Getting Ideas**

- Have students generate a list of information, dates, events, and other information they would like to include in their autobiography. Encourage them to record these ideas in their Writer's Notebooks.
- Have students fill out their audience and purpose in the ***Writer's Workbook,*** page 2.

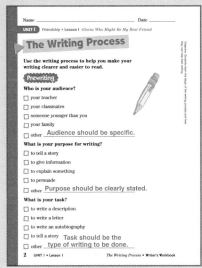

**Writer's Workbook p. 2**

### English Language Conventions

#### Penmanship LA.B.1.2.2

**Cursive Letters *i* and *t***

#### Teach

- **Teacher Model:** Explain that all cursive letters are made of four types of strokes (undercurve, downcurve, overcurve, and slant lines). Draw the curves on the board.

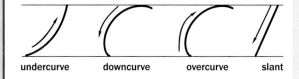

undercurve    downcurve    overcurve    slant

- **Teacher Model:** Introduce lowercase cursive *i* and *t* as undercurve letters.

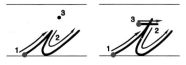

**i**  Starting point, undercurve
Slant down, undercurve to endpoint
Dot exactly above:
small *i*

**t**  Starting point, undercurve
Slant down, undercurve to endpoint
Starting point, straight across:
small *t*

- **Teacher Model:** On the board, write the words *itch, time, like,* and *title* to model proper letter formation.

#### Guided Practice

- Invite students to come to the board to trace the letters *i* and *t.*
- Have students practice writing rows of *i* and *t* in their Writer's Notebooks.
- From "Gloria Who Might Be My Best Friend," ask students to write the words *first, kite,* and *too* to practice letter formation.

 **Informal Assessment**

Check students' handwriting for proper formation of *i* and *t* and that their letters do not "float" between the lines.

# Reading and Language Arts Skills Traces

## Language Arts

### WORD ANALYSIS

**Skills Trace**

**Spelling: The /a/ Sound**

Introduced in Grade 1.
Scaffolded throughout Grades 2–5.
**REINTRODUCED:** Unit 1, Lesson 1, p. 27E
**PRACTICED:** Unit 1, Lesson 1, pp. 27F–27J
*Spelling and Vocabulary Skills,*
pp. 4–5
**TESTED:** Unit 1, Lesson 1, p. 27J
Unit 1 Assessment

**Skills Trace**

**Vocabulary: Vocabulary Strategies**

Introduced in Grade 1.
Scaffolded throughout Grades 2–5.
**REINTRODUCED:** Unit 1, Lesson 1, p. 27E
**PRACTICED:** Unit 1, Lesson 1, pp. 27F–27J
*Spelling and Vocabulary Skills,*
pp. 2–3
**TESTED:** Unit 1 Assessment

### WRITING PROCESS STRATEGIES

**Skills Trace**

**Introduction to the Writing Process: Getting Ideas**

Introduced in Grade K.
Scaffolded throughout Grades 1–6.
**REINTRODUCED:** Unit 1, Lesson 1, p. 27F
**PRACTICED:** Unit 1, Lesson 1, pp. 27G–27J
*Writer's Workbook,* p. 2
**TESTED:** Unit 1 Assessment

### ENGLISH LANGUAGE CONVENTIONS

**Skills Trace**

**Grammar: Nouns**

Introduced in Grade K.
Scaffolded throughout Grades 1–6.
**REINTRODUCED:** Unit 1, Lesson 1, p. 27F
**PRACTICED:** Unit 1, Lesson 1, p. 27G
Unit 1, Lesson 1, p. 27H
*Comprehension and Language Arts Skills,* pp. 2–3
**TESTED:** Unit 1, Lesson 1,
Informal Assessment, p. 27H
Unit 1 Assessment

**Skills Trace**

**Listening, Speaking, Viewing
Listening: Being a Good Listener**

Introduced in Grade K.
Scaffolded throughout Grades 1–5.
**REINTRODUCED:** Unit 1, Lesson 1, p. 27I
**TESTED:** Unit 1, Lesson 1,
Informal Assessment, p. 27I
Unit 1 Assessment

**Skills Trace**

**Penmanship: Cursive Letters *i* and *t***

Introduced in Grade 2.
Scaffolded throughout Grades 3–6.
**REINTRODUCED:** Unit 1, Lesson 1, p. 27J
**TESTED:** Unit 1, Lesson 1,
Informal Assessment, p. 27J

## Reading

### COMPREHENSION

**Skills Trace**

**Classify and Categorize**

Introduced in Grade 1.
Scaffolded throughout Grades 2 and 3.
**REINTRODUCED:** Unit 1, Lesson 1
**REINFORCED:** Unit 2, Lesson 1
Unit 3, Lesson 5
Unit 5, Lesson 4
Unit 6, Lesson 5
**TESTED:** Unit 1 Assessment

# Professional Development: Phonics

## What Is Phonics and Why Is It Important?

As Stahl and his colleagues (1998) point out, it is often difficult to talk about phonics because different people hold different beliefs about what phonics means. Simply put, phonics is the term applied to instructional practices that help children develop an understanding of the *alphabetic principle*—the principle that the symbols they see on a page *(letters, graphemes, letter patterns)* represent the sounds of the language. The alphabetic principle, in turn, is a broad term that enfolds awareness of the sound structure of the language *(phonological awareness)* and knowledge of the shapes and names of letters *(alphabetic knowledge)*.

Understanding the alphabetic principle allows readers to translate words by mapping individual letters to their phonological counterparts. In other words, it helps children understand that printed symbols combine in an ordered fashion to form words, and that words convey the meaning of a text.

Why is phonics instruction important? Skillful reading—reading with fluency and comprehension—depends in no small part on a reader's ability to recognize a printed word quickly and accurately and then link it with its meaning (Adams & Bruck, 1995; Stanovich, 1991).

A wealth of research into what skillful readers do as they read has revealed a great deal about the role of rapid word recognition in reading for meaning. Eye-movement research, for example, shows that skillful readers visually process almost every letter of every word on a page, seldom skipping a word or guessing at what it is. In a fraction of a second—too rapid for readers to be aware of the process—they take in each of the individual letters that make up a word and translate them to speech sounds, using the knowledge they gain to identify the word and determine its meaning (Just & Carpenter, 1987; McConkie, Kerr, Reddix, & Zola, 1988; McConkie & Zola, 1981). The result is that every encounter with a word in print, even an unfamiliar word, increases readers' knowledge of the word's spelling, as well as its spelling-to-meaning relationships (Adams, 1994). Again, the process is instantaneous. It is their ability to translate spellings to sounds to word meanings automatically and effortlessly that allows skillful readers to move smoothly through text (Kucera & Francis, 1967).

However, real reading is *comprehension*, and comprehension of a text depends not on the recognition of its individual words, but on the relationships among those words. Even so, without the ability to obtain meaning from each word, readers would struggle to get the meaning of the entire text. Skillful readers note each word in a sentence and pause briefly at the punctuation mark. At the pause, they construct meaning. If something is amiss, they quickly reread to determine the problem (Just & Carpenter, 1987). Put simply, word recognition is at the core of reading (Daneman, 1991; Stanovich, 1991).

It is hardly surprising, then, that poor reading comprehension is linked closely to poor word recognition skills (Rack, Snowling, & Olson, 1992; Stanovich, 1991; Vellutino, 1991). According to Stanovich (1991), without fluent word recognition, "comprehension processes do not have the raw materials to operate efficiently and understanding of text will be impaired" (page 443).

Therefore, comprehension depends on rapid word recognition, which depends on the ability to map speech sounds to spellings quickly and accurately. By encouraging children to examine every letter of every new word they encounter, and by helping them link speech sounds to the spellings they see on a page, phonics instruction provides children with a powerful strategy to decode written language and to recognize unfamiliar words they encounter as they begin to read independently.

The importance of providing children with this strategy cannot be overstated. How well young children develop the skills necessary to read with fluency and comprehension affects their entire lives profoundly. Indeed, it is overwhelmingly probable that a child who is a poor reader at the end of the first grade will remain a poor reader (Juel, 1988).

*Additional information about phonics as well as resource references can be found in the ***Professional Development Guide: Phonics***.

SELECTION INTRODUCTION

*Focus Questions* What might it be like to be in a new school and in a new country? How would you make friends if you didn't speak the same language as the rest of your classmates?

# Angel Child, Dragon Child

Michele Maria Surat
*illustrated by Vo-Dinh Mai*

My sisters skipped through the stone gate two by two. Mother was not there to skip with me. Mother was far away in Vietnam. She could not say, "Ut, my little one, be an Angel Child. Be happy in your new American school."

I hugged the wall and peeked around the corner.

A boy with fire-colored hair pointed his finger. "Pajamas!" he shouted. "They wore white pajamas to school!" The American children tilted back their long noses, laughing.

28

## Selection Summary

### Genre: Realistic Fiction

When Ut moves to America from Vietnam, she is faced with a strange place and with children who make fun of her. Ut sometimes has to be a brave dragon child, but she desperately wants to be a happy angel child. Ut's life is changed by acts of friendship from people around her.

Some of the elements of realistic fiction are:

- The characters behave as people do in real life.
- The setting of the story is a real place or could be a real place.
- The events in the story could happen in real life.

## About the Author

*Angel Child, Dragon Child* is **MICHELE MARIA SURAT'S** first book for children. It was named Notable Children's Trade Book in the Field of Social Studies, as well as an ALA Booklist Editor's Choice.

Students can read more about Surat on page 44 of the *Student Anthology.*

## About the Illustrator

**VO-DINH MAI** was born in Vietnam, but he left before the war began and studied in France. The illustrator is married to author Helen Coutant and has illustrated books written by her, including *First Snow,* which won a Christopher Award.

Students can read more about Vo-Dinh Mai on page 44 of the *Student Anthology.*

## Inquiry Connections

"Angel Child, Dragon Child" illustrates the challenges involved in cross-cultural friendships. During Ut's first days at school, she experiences alienation and separation. Later, she finds understanding and acceptance. Key concepts explored are:

- Different cultures have different ways of expressing respect and friendship.
- All people, no matter where they come from, share many of the same fears and worries.

Before reading the selection:

- Point out that students may post a question, concept, word, illustration, or object at any time during the course of their unit investigation. Be sure that students include their name or initials on the items they post so that others will know whom to go to if they have an answer or if they wish to collaborate on a related activity.
- Students should feel free to write an answer or a note on someone else's question or to consult the Board for ideas for their own investigations throughout the unit.
- Encourage students to read about friendship at home and to bring in articles or pictures that are good examples to post on the Board.

**Concept/Question Board**

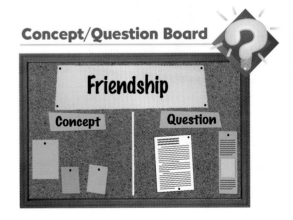

PROGRAM RESOURCES

## Leveled Practice

**Reteach**
Pages 5–9

**Challenge**
Pages 5–8

**ELD Workbook**

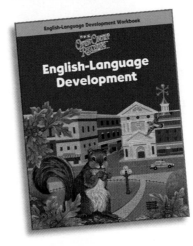

**Intervention Workbook**

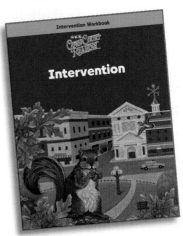

**Decodable Book 12**

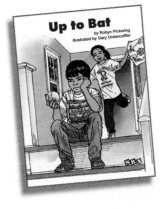

# Leveled Classroom Library*

Encourage students to read at least 30 minutes daily outside of class. Have them read books in the *Leveled Classroom Library* to support the unit theme and help students develop their vocabulary by reading independently.

### *Amigo*

BY BYRD BAYLOR. ALADDIN, 1991.

A poor Mexican boy's only friend is a prairie dog, Amigo. While the boy believes he is taming Amigo as a pet, ironically, it is Amigo who is taming the boy. **(Easy)**

### *Charlotte's Web*

BY E. B. WHITE. HARPERTROPHY, 1952.

This is the classic story of a friendship between a pig and a spider. (Newbery Honor) **(Average)**

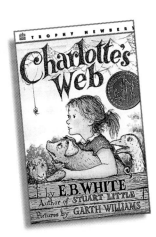

### *The Mountain that loved a Bird*

BY ALICE MCLERRAN. SIMON & SCHUSTER, 1985.

When Joy, a bird, must leave the mountain, Joy makes a promise to the mountain that loves her. Every year, one of her kin will return to the mountain. Joy's kin transform the mountain over time. **(Advanced)**

\* These books, which all support the unit theme Friendship, are part of a 36-book *Leveled Classroom Library* available for purchase from SRA/McGraw-Hill.
Note: Teachers should preview any trade books for appropriateness in their classrooms before recommending them to students.

# TECHNOLOGY

## Web Connections

www.sra4kids.com
**Friendship Web Site**

## CD-ROMs

 **\* Research Assistant**
**SRA/MCGRAW-HILL, 2002**

 **\* Decodable Book Activities**
**SRA/MCGRAW-HILL, 2002**

## Computer Skills

**\* Basic Computer Skills**

## Audiocassettes/CDs

 **\* Listening Library: Friendship**
**SRA/MCGRAW-HILL, 2002**

 **\* Sound/Spelling Card Stories**
**SRA/MCGRAW-HILL, 2002**

Titles preceded by an asterisk (\*) are available through SRA/McGraw-Hill. Other titles can be obtained by contacting the publisher listed with the title.

**LESSON PLANNER**

Suggested Pacing: 3–5 days

| | DAY 1 | DAY 2 |
|---|---|---|
| | **DAY 1** | **DAY 2** |

## 1 Preparing to Read

**Materials**
- Student Anthology, Book 1, pp. 28–47
- Decodable Book Activities CD-ROM
- Decodable Book 12
- Sound/Spelling Card 39
- Lesson Model Videocassette
- Routine Cards 1, 3, Routines 1–2, 8–9

**DAY 1**

Word Knowledge, p. 28K
- plural -s
- inflectional endings
- homographs
- comparative and superlative adjectives
- /e/ spelled e

About the Words and Sentences, pp. 28K–28L

**DAY 2**

Word Knowledge
Developing Oral Language, p. 28L

## 2 Reading & Responding

**Materials**
- Student Anthology, Book 1, pp. 28–47
- Program Assessment
- Reading Transparencies 3, 46, 48, 49
- Inquiry Journal, p. 2
- Home Connection, p. 5
- Unit 1 Assessment, pp. 6–9
- Comprehension and Language Arts Skills, pp. 4–5
- Writer's Notebook
- Routine Cards 1–2, Routines 3–6

**DAY 1**

Build Background, p. 28O
Preview and Prepare, p. 28P
Selection Vocabulary, p. 28P
Reading Recommendations, pp. 28Q–28R
Student Anthology, pp. 28–35 [First Read]
✓Comprehension Strategies
- Asking Questions, pp. 28, 30, 34
- Visualizing, p. 32

**DAY 2**

Student Anthology, pp. 36–43 [First Read]
Comprehension Strategies
- Summarizing, pp. 36, 40, 42
- Visualizing, p. 38
Discussing Strategy Use, p. 42
Discussing the Selection, p. 43A
- Review Selection
- Complete Discussion
Meet the Author/Illustrator, p. 44
✓Theme Connections, p. 45

## Inquiry

**Materials**
- Student Anthology, Book 1, pp. 28–47
- Inquiry Journal, pp. 10–15
- Reading Transparency 2
- Research Assistant CD-ROM

**DAY 1**

Investigation
- Investigating Concepts Beyond the Text, p. 45A

**DAY 2**

Investigation
- Concept/Question Board, p. 45B

## 3 Language Arts

**Materials**
- Comprehension and Language Arts Skills, pp. 4–7
- Language Arts Handbook, pp. 18, 20, 25, 244–245
- Language Arts Transparencies 7–10
- Sound/Spelling Card 5
- Spelling and Vocabulary Skills, pp. 6–9
- Student Anthology
- Writer's Workbook, p. 3

**DAY 1**

Word Analysis
✓- Spelling: The /e/ Sound Pretest, p. 45F
Writing Process Strategies
- Introduction to the Writing Process: Prewriting, p. 45F
English Language Conventions
- Grammar: Pronouns, p. 45F

**DAY 2**

Word Analysis
- Spelling: Word Sorting, p. 45G
- Vocabulary: Context Clues, p. 45G
Writing Process Strategies
- Introduction to the Writing Process: Prewriting, p. 45G
English Language Conventions
- Grammar: Pronouns, p. 45G

| DAY 2 continued | DAY 3 | | |
|---|---|---|---|
| **DAY 3** | **DAY 4** | **DAY 5** | |

---

**Ⓟ Phonics and Fluency, p. 28M**
- Review short vowels
- /m/ spelled -mb
- e spelled ea
- closed syllables

**About the Words and Sentences, p. 28M**

**Ⓟ Phonics and Fluency**

**Developing Oral Language, p. 28N**

**Dictation, p. 28N**

**General Review**

---

**Student Anthology, pp. 28–35** Second Read

**Comprehension Skills**
- Cause and Effect, pp. 29, 31, 33, 35

**Supporting the Reading, pp. 43C–43D**
- Cause and Effect

**Student Anthology, pp. 36–43** Second Read

**Comprehension Skills**
- Cause and Effect, pp. 37, 39, 41, 43

**Checking Comprehension, p. 43**

**Review Selection Vocabulary, p. 43B**

**View Fine Art, p. 43B**

**Literary Elements, p. 43E**
- Plot

✓ **Selection Assessment**
- "Angel Child, Dragon Child," pp. 6–9

**Home Connection, p. 43B**

**Poetry**
- "Janey," pp. 46–47
- Elements of Poetry, p. 47A
  Repetition and Writing
- Listening/Speaking/Viewing, p. 47B
  Presentation: Emphasis

**Social Studies Connection**
- Immigration, p. 43F

---

**Investigation**
- Interviewing, p. 45C

**Supporting the Investigation**
- Choosing Appropriate Sources, p. 45D

**Investigation**
- Unit Investigation Continued
- Update Concept/Question Board

---

**Word Analysis**
- Spelling: The /e/ Sound, p. 45H
- Vocabulary: Context Clues, p. 45H

**Writing Process Strategies**
- Introduction to the Writing Process:
  Prewriting, p. 45H

**English Language Conventions**
- Grammar: Pronouns, p. 45H

**Word Analysis**
- Spelling: The /e/ Sound, p. 45I
- Vocabulary: Context Clues, p. 45I

**Writing Process Strategies**
- Introduction to the Writing Process:
  Prewriting, p. 45I

**English Language Conventions**
- Listening, Speaking, Viewing
✓ Speaking: Speaking Clearly, p. 45I

**Word Analysis**
- Spelling: The /e/ Sound
✓ Final Test
✓ - Vocabulary: Context Clues, p. 45J

**Writing Process Strategies**
- Introduction to the Writing Process:
  Prewriting, p. 45J

**English Language Conventions**
✓ - Penmanship:
  Cursive Letters u and w, p. 45J

Below are suggestions for differentiating instruction to meet the individual needs of students. These are the same skills shown on the Lesson Planner; however, these pages provide extra practice opportunities or enriching activities to meet the varied needs of students. For Workshop Management Tips, see Appendix.

**WORKSHOP**

# Differentiating Instruction

## Small-Group Instruction

Use the informal assessment suggestions found throughout the lessons, along with the formal assessments provided in each lesson, to determine your students' strengths and areas of need. Use the following program components to help in supporting or expanding on the instruction found in this lesson:

***Reteach Workbook*** for use with students who show a basic understanding of the lesson but need a bit more practice to solidify their understanding.

***Intervention Guide*** and ***Intervention Workbook*** for use with students who, even after extra practice, exhibit a lack of understanding of the lesson concepts.

***English-Language Development Guide*** and ***English-Language Development Workbook*** for use with students who need language help.

Have students create small groups to do such things as:

- Discuss books during Reading Roundtable.
- Discuss questions that arise as they investigate concepts after reading the selection.
- Partner-read to assist those who have problems reading difficult passages or to help develop fluency.

## Independent Activities

### Writing Seminar

A suggested activity would be to have students write a personal narrative about friendship. Tell students to request a peer or teacher conference whenever they feel it would benefit their writing.

♦ **Small-Group Instruction**     ■ **Independent Activities**

| | READING | INVESTIGATION ACTIVITIES |
|---|---|---|
| **DAY 1** | ■ Select *Leveled Classroom Library* book for independent reading<br>■ Add vocabulary in Writer's Notebook<br>■ Record response to selection in Writer's Notebook | ■ Concept/Question Board<br>♦ Review presentation methods<br>♦ Complete planning calendars, *Inquiry Journal,* pp. 10–11<br>■ Explore OCR Web site (www.sra4kids.com) for Friendship |
| **DAY 2** | ■ Independent reading<br>■ Oral reading of selection for fluency<br>♦ Discuss Theme Connections, p. 45 | ■ Concept/Question Board<br>■ Use *Research Assistant CD-ROM* to continue investigation |
| **DAY 3** | ♦ Partner reading of selection<br>■ *Listening Library Audiocassette/CD*<br>■ Complete Link to Writing for Supporting the Reading, p. 43D<br>■ Complete *Comprehension and Language Arts Skills,* pp. 4–5 | ■ Concept/Question Board<br>♦ Review Interviewing Skills<br>♦ Complete *Inquiry Journal,* pp. 12–13 |
| **DAY 4** | ■ Independent reading<br>■ Complete Independent Practice for Literary Elements, p. 43E<br>■ Add words to Word Bank | ■ Concept/Question Board<br>■ Complete *Inquiry Journal,* pp. 14–15 |
| **DAY 5** | ■ Reading Roundtable<br>♦ Poetry Activities, pp. 47A–47B<br>■♦ Social Studies Connection, p. 43F | ♦ Continue work on investigation |

| LANGUAGE ARTS | INTERVENTION* | ENGLISH-LANGUAGE LEARNERS** | RETEACH | CHALLENGE |
|---|---|---|---|---|
| **English Language Conventions**<br>■ Complete Pronouns, *Comprehension and Language Arts Skills,* pp. 6–7 | **(30 to 45 minutes per day)**<br>◆ Blending, p. 13<br>◆ Preteach "Angel Child, Dragon Child," pp. 15–16<br>◆ Teach "Intervention Selection One," pp. 16–17<br>◆ Grammar, Usage, and Mechanics, p. 19 | **(30 to 45 minutes per day)**<br>◆ Word Knowledge, Inflectional Endings, p. 8 | | |
| **Word Analysis**<br>◆ Spelling: Word Sort, p. 45G<br>■ Complete Context Clues, *Spelling and Vocabulary Skills,* pp. 6–7 | ◆ Developing Oral Language, p. 13<br>◆ Preteach "Angel Child, Dragon Child," pp. 15–16<br>◆ Teach Comprehension Strategies, p. 17<br>◆ Reread "Intervention Selection One"<br>◆ Grammar, Usage, and Mechanics, p. 19 | ◆ Selection Vocabulary, p. 10<br>◆ Preteach the Selection, p. 10 | **English Language Conventions**<br>■ Complete Pronouns, *Reteach,* p. 9 | **English Language Conventions**<br>■ Complete Pronouns, *Challenge,* p. 8 |
| **Word Analysis**<br>■ Complete Spelling: The /e/ Sound, *Spelling and Vocabulary Skills,* p. 8 | ◆ Dictation and Spelling, pp. 13–14<br>◆ Reread "Angel Child, Dragon Child"<br>◆ Teach "Intervention Selection Two," pp. 17–18<br>◆ Writing Activity, p. 20 | ◆ Word Knowledge, Comparative Adjectives, p. 10<br>◆ Dictation and Spelling, p. 11 | **Reading**<br>◆ Comprehension Skill: Cause and Effect<br>■ Complete *Reteach,* pp. 5–6<br>**Word Analysis**<br>■ Complete Vocabulary: Context Clues, *Reteach,* p. 8 | **Reading**<br>◆ Comprehension Skill: Cause and Effect<br>■ Complete *Challenge,* p. 5<br>**Word Analysis**<br>■ Complete Vocabulary: Context Clues, *Challenge,* p. 7 |
| **Word Analysis**<br>■ Complete The /e/ Sound, *Spelling and Vocabulary Skills,* p. 9 | ◆ Blending, p. 14<br>◆ Reread "Angel Child, Dragon Child"<br>◆ Teach Comprehension Strategies, p. 18<br>◆ Reread "Intervention Selection Two"<br>◆ Writing Activity, p. 20 | ◆ Vocabulary Strategies, p. 12 | **Word Analysis**<br>■ Complete Spelling: The /e/ Sound, *Reteach,* p. 7 | **Word Analysis**<br>■ Complete Spelling: The /e/ Sound, *Challenge,* p. 6 |
| **Writing Process Strategies**<br>◆ Seminar: Prewriting an Autobiography, p. 45J<br>**English Language Conventions**<br>■ Penmanship: Practice Letters *u* and *w,* p. 45J | ◆ Developing Oral Language, p. 14<br>◆ Dictation and Spelling, pp. 14–15<br>◆ Repeated Readings/ Fluency Check, pp. 18–19 | ◆ Grammar, Usage, and Mechanics, p. 13 | | |

\* Page numbers refer to *Intervention Guide.*

\*\* Page numbers refer to *English-Language Development Guide.*

## ASSESSMENT

# Formal Assessment Options

Use these summative assessments along with your informal observations to assess student progress.

---

**Page (p. 6):**

Name _____ Date _____ Score _____

**UNIT I** Friendship • **Lesson 2**

**Angel Child, Dragon Child**

Read the following questions carefully. Then completely fill in the bubble of each correct answer. You may look back at the story to find the answer to each of the questions.

1. Where was Ut born?
   Ⓐ the United States
   Ⓑ Japan
   ● Vietnam

2. Why is Ut lonely at the beginning of the story?
   ● She misses her mother.
   Ⓑ She misses her grandmother.
   Ⓒ She misses her sisters.

Read the following questions carefully. Use complete sentences to answer the questions.

3. How does the rest of the school find out about Ut's mother?
   The rest of the school finds out about Ut's mother when the principal reads Ut's story to them.

4. What will the money from the Vietnam fair be used for?
   The money from the fair will be used to help Ut's mother come to America.

5. When does Ut's mother finally arrive in America?
   Ut's mother finally arrives in America on the last day of school.

6 Unit I • Lesson 2    *Angel Child, Dragon Child* • Unit I Assessment

**Unit 1 Assessment p. 6**

---

**Page (p. 7):**

**Angel Child, Dragon Child** *(continued)*

6. What happened to Ut during her first day at school?
   On Ut's first day of school, the other children teased her.

7. When does Raymond write Ut's story?
   Raymond writes Ut's story when the principal puts Ut and Raymond in a room together after their fight.

8. What does Ut do when she sees that Raymond is crying?
   She pulls on his sleeve and tells him not to cry, and then she gives him a cookie.

Read the following questions carefully. Then completely fill in the bubble of each correct answer.

9. The principal punished Ut and Raymond because
   Ⓐ they were chewing gum
   Ⓑ they didn't do their homework
   ● they were fighting

10. Whose idea is it to have a Vietnamese fair?
    Ⓐ Ut's
    ● Raymond's
    Ⓒ the principal's

Unit I Assessment • *Angel Child, Dragon Child*    Unit I • Lesson 2  **7**

**Unit 1 Assessment p. 7**

---

**Page (p. 8):**

**Angel Child, Dragon Child** *(continued)*

Read the question and statement below. Use complete sentences in your answers.

**Linking to the Concepts** Which character had to learn more about making friends, Raymond or Ut? Why?
Answers will vary. Accept all reasonable answers.

_____

_____

_____

_____

_____

**Personal Response** Suppose you had to move to a new city and go to a new school. What would be most difficult for you?
Answers will vary. Accept all reasonable answers.

_____

_____

_____

_____

_____

_____

_____

**8** Unit I • Lesson 2    *Angel Child, Dragon Child* • Unit I Assessment

**Unit 1 Assessment p. 8**

---

**Page (p. 9):**

**Angel Child, Dragon Child** *(continued)*

**Vocabulary**

Read the following questions carefully. Then completely fill in the bubble of each correct answer.

1. The school bell jangled when it was time for class to start. **Jangled** is another word for
   ● rang
   Ⓑ broke
   Ⓒ sang

2. The children in Ut's class twittered when Ut did not understand the teacher. **Twittered** in this sentence means
   Ⓐ slept
   ● laughed
   Ⓒ played

3. Little Quang's laughing eyes **gleamed** like watermelon seeds. This means that his eyes were
   Ⓐ juicy and sweet
   Ⓑ angry and small
   ● shiny and dark

4. At recess, the red-haired boy darted behind the dumpster. **Darted** means
   Ⓐ waved
   ● ran
   Ⓒ sat

5. Raymond scrawled Ut's words on a piece of paper. In this sentence, **scrawled** means
   ● wrote
   Ⓑ drew
   Ⓒ mapped

Unit I Assessment • *Angel Child, Dragon Child*    Unit I • Lesson 2  **9**

**Unit 1 Assessment p. 9**

---

**Page (p. 28):**

Name _____ Date _____ Score _____

**UNIT I** Friendship • **Lesson 2** *Angel Child, Dragon Child*

**Spelling Pretest: The /e/ Sound**

Fold this page back on the dotted line. Take the Pretest. Then correct any word you misspelled by crossing out the word and rewriting it next to the incorrect spelling.

| | |
|---|---|
| 1. _____ | 1. *deck* |
| 2. _____ | 2. *tent* |
| 3. _____ | 3. *spent* |
| 4. _____ | 4. *fence* |
| 5. _____ | 5. *head* |
| 6. _____ | 6. *dead* |
| 7. _____ | 7. *bread* |
| 8. _____ | 8. *desk* |
| 9. _____ | 9. *thread* |
| 10. _____ | 10. *sweater* |
| 11. _____ | 11. *edge* |
| 12. _____ | 12. *bell* |
| 13. _____ | 13. *next* |
| 14. _____ | 14. *send* |
| 15. _____ | 15. *them* |

**28** Unit I • Lesson 2    *Spelling Pretest: The /e/ Sound* • Unit I Assessment

**Unit 1 Assessment p. 28**

---

**Page (p. 29):**

Name _____ Date _____ Score _____

**UNIT I** Friendship • **Lesson 2** *Angel Child, Dragon Child*

**Spelling Final Test: The /e/ Sound**

Mark the letter next to the underlined word that is misspelled. Focus on the underlined word.

1. Ⓐ She wore a straw hat on her <u>head</u>.
   ● The <u>deac</u> of the ship got wet.
   Ⓒ He <u>spent</u> his last dime.
   Ⓓ Correct as is.

2. ● The <u>fince</u> was made of wood.
   Ⓑ A <u>dead</u> tree must be cut down.
   Ⓗ An apple is on the teacher's <u>desk</u>.
   Ⓙ Correct as is.

3. Ⓐ Yeast helps <u>bread</u> rise.
   Ⓑ He sat <u>next</u> to her on the bus.
   ● The <u>thred</u> is by the needle.
   Ⓓ Correct as is.

4. ● A <u>sweter</u> can be made of cotton.
   Ⓖ Students left after the <u>bell</u>.
   Ⓗ We <u>spent</u> the summer in Texas.
   Ⓙ Correct as is.

5. Ⓐ Neighbors helped <u>them</u> move.
   Ⓑ He was <u>next</u> in line.
   Ⓒ The campers set up their <u>tent</u>.
   ● Correct as is.

6. Ⓕ <u>Dead</u> leaves fall from the trees.
   ● The wheat <u>bred</u> tasted sweet.
   Ⓗ The wool <u>sweater</u> was red.
   Ⓙ Correct as is.

Unit I Assessment • *Spelling Final Test: The /e/ Sound*    Unit I • Lesson 2  **29**

**Unit 1 Assessment p. 29**

---

# Informal Comprehension Strategies Rubrics

Use the Informal Comprehension Strategies Rubrics to determine whether or not a student is using any of the strategies listed below. Note the strategies a student is using, instead of the degree to which a student might be using any particular strategy. In addition, encourage the student to tell of any strategies other than the ones being taught that he or she is using.

## Visualizing

- The student visualizes ideas or scenes described in the text.

## Summarizing

- The student paraphrases the text, reporting main ideas and a summary of what is in the text.
- The student decides which parts of the text are important in his or her summary.
- The student draws conclusions from the text.
- The student makes global interpretations of the text, such as recognizing the genre.

## Asking Questions

- The student asks questions about ideas or facts presented in the text and attempts to answer these questions by reading the text.

# Research Rubrics

Use the Research Rubrics to assess a student's performance throughout the stages of the investigation for each unit. The rubrics for a given lesson will match the investigation stage for that lesson. In addition, at the end of the unit you can use the rubrics to assess the groups' collaborative work as well as an individual's participation in that group.

During Workshop, assess students using the rubrics below. The rubrics range from 1–4 in most categories, with 1 being the lowest score. Record each student's score on the inside back cover of the ***Inquiry Journal***.

## Formulating Research Questions and Problems

1 With help, identifies things he or she wonders about in relation to a topic.

2 Expresses curiosity about topics; with help, translates this into specific questions.

3 Poses an interesting problem or question for research; with help, refines it into a researchable question.

4 Identifies something he or she genuinely wonders about and translates it into a researchable question.

**WORD KNOWLEDGE**

## Objectives

- Students practice recognizing base words and affixes, including comparative and superlative forms.
- Students practice distinguishing between homographs.
- Students practice and review short vowels.
- Students practice recognizing the /m/ sound spelled -mb.
- Students practice recognizing the /e/ sound spelled ea.
- Students practice recognizing closed syllables.
- Students develop fluency reading words and sentences.

## Materials

- Student Anthology, Book 1, pp. 28–47
- Decodable Book Activities CD-ROM
- Decodable Book 12
- Routine Cards 1, 3, Routines 1–2, 8–9
- Sound/Spelling Card 39

**Routine Card**
Refer to *Routine 1* for the whole-word blending procedure and *Routine 2* for the sentence blending procedure.

**Teacher Tip SYLLABICATION** To help students blend words and build fluency, use the syllabication below of the words in the word lines.

| | | | |
|---|---|---|---|
| nos•es | hands | les•sons | cray•ons |
| hooks | seeds | books | words |
| tilt | tilt•ed | tilt•ing | wait |
| wait•ed | wait•ing | bow | bowed |
| bow•ing | curve | curved | curv•ing |
| tack•le | tack•led | tack•ling | small |
| small•er | small•est | tall | tall•er |
| tall•est | them | send | next |
| bell | edge | | |

Refer to the *Lesson Model Videocassette* for instruction on whole-word blending.

## Word Knowledge

### Reading the Words and Sentences

- Display and review *Sound/Spelling Card 39*.

- Write each word in Reading the Words and Sentences on the board and have students read it together. If they have difficulty reading a word, stop and have them blend the word, using whole-word blending. Encourage students to pronounce the word naturally after blending. Because reading sentences helps students to move from word fluency to sentence fluency, have them read each sentence in unison, using normal intonation. The words in **boldface** type are from the selection.

| | | | | | |
|---|---|---|---|---|---|
| Line 1: | noses | hands | lessons | crayons | |
| Line 2: | hooks | seeds | books | words | |
| Line 3: | tilt | tilted | tilting | wait | waited | waiting |
| Line 4: | bow | bowed | bowing | | |
| Line 5: | curve | curved | curving | tackle | tackled | tackling |
| Line 6: | small | smaller | smallest | tall | taller | tallest |
| Line 7: | them | send | next | bell | edge | |

Sentence 1: The American children tilted back their long noses, laughing.
Sentence 2: I stood and bowed.
Sentence 3: Her hands curved over my shoulders.
Sentence 4: Friends like for you to send them letters in the mail.

### About the Words and Sentences   LA.A.1.2.3.3.1

- **Lines 1–2:** The words show plural forms by adding -s. Have the students identify the singular form. Point to the word *noses* and ask what you would have if there was only one *(nose)*. Continue to identify the singular form of each plural.

- **Lines 3–5:** Point out to students that these are all verbs. Have students explain what a verb is. Inflectional endings are added to base words. Ask students how the endings change the meaning of the base word. Line 4 shows the word *bow*, which is a homograph, with the inflectional endings *-ed* and *-ing*. Teach students that homographs are words that are spelled the same but have different meanings and different origins. In the story, the word is pronounced with the /ow/ sound spelled *ow*. Point out *Sound/Spelling Card 39*. Another way to pronounce the word *bow* is bō. When pronounced this way, the word has a different meaning. Line 5 shows inflectional endings added to words that end in silent *e*. Ask students to identify what spelling change took place when *-ed* was added to *curve*. Have students continue with *curving, tackle, tackled,* and *tackling*.

- **Line 6:** These endings are the comparative and superlative forms of adjectives. Ask students to explain how the endings change the meanings of the words and how the words are used to compare things.
- **Line 7:** The words in Line 7 are found in "Angel Child, Dragon Child" and review the /e/ sound spelled *e*.
- **Sentences 1–3:** These sentences are from the story students are about to read. Ask students to identify verb forms with *-ed* and *-ing* endings *(tilted, laughing, bowed, curved)* and the plural forms of words *(children, noses, hands, shoulders)*.
- **Sentence 4:** Have students identify the words in the last sentence that contain the /e/ sound *(send, them, letters)*.

## Developing Oral Language LA.C.1.2.1.3.2

Use direct teaching to review the words. Use one or both of the following activities to help students practice reading the words.

- Have a student choose a word and come to the board to point it out. That student then chooses another student to pronounce that word and use it in a sentence. The student who pronounces and uses the word correctly then goes to the board, chooses a new word, and selects a new student to pronounce it and use it in a sentence. Repeat the process for several more words.
- Have a student come to the board and point to and say a word in the word lines. Have the student use the word in a sentence and then choose a volunteer to extend the sentence. Encourage students to add information at the beginning of the sentence, not just at the end.

**Teacher Tip BLENDING** Assess which students might need extra help during Workshop. Review sound-by-sound blending. Move on to whole-word blending when students are reading with fluency. Specific tips for blending practice are listed in the Appendix.

**Teacher Tip FLUENCY** Gaining a better understanding of the spellings of sounds and structure of words will help students as they encounter unfamiliar words in their reading. By this time in Grade 3 students should be reading approximately 107 words per minute with fluency and expression. As students read, you may notice that some need work in building fluency. During Workshop, have these students select a section of the text (a minimum of 160 words) to read several times in order to build fluency.

**Spelling**
See pages 45E–45J for the corresponding spelling lesson for the /e/ sound.

## MEETING INDIVIDUAL NEEDS

### ELL Support

For ELD strategies, use the *English-Language Development Guide,* Unit 1, Lesson 2.

### Intervention Support

For intervention strategies, use the *Intervention Guide,* Unit 1, Lesson 2.

**PHONICS**

**Teacher Tip** SYLLABICATION To help students blend words and build fluency, use the syllabication of the words below in the word lines.

| | | | |
|---|---|---|---|
| hap•pen | ex•tra | prin•ci•pal | pock•et |
| pup•pet | lamb | numb | thumb |
| crumb | breath | in•stead | mead•ow |
| weath•er | ab•sent | cac•tus | com•mon |
| hel•met | in•sect | | |

**Teacher Tip** Encourage students to just read the words. They should stop and blend only those words that give them problems.

**Teacher Tip** CLOSED SYLLABLES A closed syllable is a syllable in which a single vowel is followed by a consonant, as in *at*, *bat*, and *puppet*. In a closed syllable, the vowel sound is usually short.

# Phonics and Fluency

Review short vowels; /m/ spelled -*mb*;
/e/ spelled *ea*; closed syllables

## Blending

- Use direct teaching to teach the blending lesson.
- Display and review **Sound/Spelling Card 5.**
- Follow the procedure established in Unit 1, Lesson 1, to have students read the following words and sentences. **Boldface** words are found in the selection.

| | | | | | |
|---|---|---|---|---|---|
| Line 1: | happen | extra | **principal** | **pocket** | puppet |
| Line 2: | lamb | numb | thumb | crumb | |
| Line 3: | **breath** | instead | meadow | weather | |
| Line 4: | absent | cactus | common | helmet | insect |
| Sentence 1: | Hannah enjoyed the puppet show. | | | | |
| Sentence 2: | The little lamb was very cute. | | | | |
| Sentence 3: | Instead, they waved their hands and said their lessons one by one. | | | | |

## About the Words and Sentences  LA.A.1.2.2.3.1

- **Line 1:** The words review short vowels. Have students identify the short vowel in each word. Be sure to point out that the *a* in *extra* and the *a* in *principal* have the /ə/ sound.

- **Line 2:** The words practice the -*mb* spelling for the /m/ sound. Point out that this spelling pattern occurs only at the end of words.

- **Line 3:** The words practice short e spelled *ea*.

- **Line 4:** The words practice multisyllabic words with closed syllables. A closed syllable is a syllable in which a single vowel is followed by a consonant, as in *at*, *bat*, and *puppet*. In a closed syllable, the vowel sound is usually short. Review the words and ask students what kind of vowel sound they hear *(short)*. Have students clap each syllable, identify where the word is broken into syllables, and have them tell why.

- **Sentences 1–2:** These sentences review words with short vowels and the /m/ sound spelled -*mb*. Have students identify them *(Hannah, enjoyed, puppet, little, lamb)*.

- **Sentence 3:** This sentence is from the selection. Have students identify words with the /e/ sound. Give the spelling for the /e/ sounds *(instead [ea]; lessons [e])*.

## Developing Oral Language LA.C.1.2.1.3.2

Use direct teaching to review the words. Use one or both of the following activities to help students practice reading the words.

- To review multisyllabic words, have students clap out each syllable as you read words from the word lines.

- Explain that when we see words with more than one syllable, there are some patterns to look for that will help us know if the vowels are long or short. Write the word *napkin* on the board and ask the students to tell you how many vowels are in the word *(2)*. Write a *v* under the *a* and *i*. Then ask the students how many consonants are between the two vowels *(2)*. Write a *c* under the *p* and *k*. Explain to the students that when they see a pattern like this—vccv—they should divide the syllable between the consonants. Teachers should make a slash between the *p* and the *k*. The vowels in this pattern are usually short. Have students practice with other multisyllabic words *(catnip, justice, pencil, basket)*. Have students place the slashes between the consonants. Remind students that they need to look carefully at the consonants for special spellings, such as po/cket.

## Dictation

Following the established procedure in Unit 1, Lesson 1, erase the word lines and sentences on the board and have students take out writing paper. Dictate the following words and sentences for students to write.

| | | | |
|---|---|---|---|
| **Line 1:** | invent | attic | comb |
| **Line 2:** | picnic | signal | cotton |
| **Challenge Word:** | bamboo | | |
| **Sentence:** | The cookies made many crumbs at the picnic. | | |

Have students follow the proper steps for proofreading the dictated words and sentence.

## Building Fluency

***Decodable Books*** are used to help develop fluency for students who need extra practice. The only way to gain fluency is to read. Students will have many opportunities to read, including the ***Student Anthology,*** the ***Leveled Classroom Library,*** and their own reading. The ***Decodable Books*** can be used to practice the phonics and fluency elements being reviewed. Refer to the Appendix for the procedure on using these books. For this lesson, use ***Decodable Book 12,*** *Up to Bat.*

**Up to Bat**
by Robyn Pickering
illustrated by Gary Undercuffler

*Decodable Book 12*

**Routine Card**
Refer to *Routine 8* for the whole-word dictation procedure and *Routine 9* for the sentence dictation procedure.

**Teacher Tip** Explain to students that sometimes closed syllables contain three consonants between two vowels. Syllabication occurs after the digraph.

Use the *Decodable Book Activities CD-ROM* for activities that support this Phonics lesson.

Refer to the *Lesson Model Videocassette* for instruction on whole-word dictation.

Refer to the *Lesson Model Videocassette* for instruction on reading a *Decodable Book.*

## Objectives

- Students will understand the selection vocabulary before reading, using strategies such as suffixes and structural cues.
- Students will spell plurals by adding *-s* with *-ed* and *-ing* endings.
- Students will connect prior knowledge to subjects discussed in text.
- Students will use comprehension strategies such as Self-Questioning, Visualizing, and Summarizing to construct meaning from the text and monitor reading.
- Students will use the comprehension skill Cause and Effect as they read the story the second time.
- Students will discuss personal reactions to the story to begin identifying their own personal reading preferences.

## Materials

- Student Anthology, Book 1, pp. 28–47
- Program Assessment
- Reading Transparencies 3, 4, 46, 48, 49
- Inquiry Journal, p. 2
- Unit 1 Assessment, pp. 6–9
- Home Connection, p. 5
- Comprehension and Language Arts Skills, pp. 4–5
- Routine Cards 1–2, Routines 3–6

## MEETING INDIVIDUAL NEEDS

### ELL Support

For ELD strategies, use the *English-Language Development Guide,* Unit 1, Lesson 2.

### Intervention Support

For intervention strategies, use the *Intervention Guide,* Unit 1, Lesson 2.

**Teacher Tip GENRE: REALISTIC FICTION** Have students record the elements of realistic fiction in the Personal Response section of their Writer's Notebooks.

**www.sra4kids.com**
**Web Connection**
Students can use the connections to friendship in the Reading link of the SRA Web page for more background information about friendship.

# Build Background

## Activate Prior Knowledge

Preteach "Angel Child, Dragon Child" by first determining students' prior knowledge about this selection or about the theme, friendship. Ask questions such as the following:

- What did you learn about friendship from the last story?

- In the last selection, you discussed what it's like to move to a new place. What might it be like to move to a new country? To go to a new school in a new country?

- Remember that the friendship between Gloria and Julian in "Gloria Who Might Be My Best Friend" was unexpected. What other surprising stories about friendship have you personally seen or experienced?

- What questions on the Concept/Question Board might this story answer?

## Background Information LA.E.1.2.4.3.1

The following information may help students understand the selection they are about to read.

- On a world map, help students find the country of Vietnam, in Southeast Asia. Explain that, beginning in 1957, the country was engaged in a civil war in which the United States became involved. Many Vietnamese people fled their country, going to refugee camps or traveling by boat to new places. Many families were separated during this time.

- In the story, *Nguyen* (nōō yen) is the main character's family name. Her given name is *Hoa* (hwä), which means "flower." *Ut* (ōot) is her nickname, an affectionate term for the youngest daughter. Her little brother is named *Quang* (kwäng), and her older sister is named *Chi Hai* (chē hī). Because family ties are very important to Vietnamese people, they put their family name before their given name. Note that this is the case for the story's illustrator, Vo-Dinh Mai (vō din mī).

- Tell students that this selection is realistic fiction. In realistic fiction, characters act in the same way as people do in real life. The events in the story could actually happen.

# Preview and Prepare LA.A.1.2.1.3.1

## Browse

- Demonstrate how to browse. Remind students that good readers browse before they read.

- Have students preview the selection by browsing through the first page or two of the story. This allows them to activate prior knowledge relevant to the story. Fiction pieces should not be browsed in their entirety, because the browsing may ruin the surprise of the story. Discuss with students what they think this story might reveal about friendship.

- Use **Reading Transparency 46,** Clues, Problems, and Wonderings, to note the observations that students generate during browsing, including unfamiliar words or clues about what is going to happen in the story. For example, they might notice that Ut looks sad and wonder why. They might be unfamiliar with the word *trilled.* Note any questions students have about the story, in order to return to them after reading.

- As students prepare to read the selection, have them browse the Focus Questions on the first page of the selection. Tell them to keep these questions in mind as they read.

## Set Purposes LA.A.1.2.2.3.5

Encourage students to set multiple purposes for reading. For example, suggest students consider how Ut might feel, coming to a new country and a new school.

# Selection Vocabulary LA.A.1.2.2.3.2

As students study vocabulary, they will use a variety of skills to determine the meaning of a word. These include context clues, word structure, and apposition. Students will apply these same skills while reading to clarify additional unfamiliar words. Students can write their definitions in their Writer's Notebooks.

Display **Reading Transparency 3** before reading the selection to introduce and discuss the following words and their meanings.

| | |
|---|---|
| **jangled:** | made a loud ringing noise (page 29) |
| **twittered:** | chattered noisily, sounding like chirping birds (page 30) |
| **gleamed:** | was bright and shiny (page 33) |
| **darted:** | moved or ran quickly from one place to another place (page 35) |
| **scrawled:** | wrote quickly but not carefully (page 40) |
| **margins:** | empty spaces at the edge of the page: above, below, to the left and right (page 40) |

Have students read the words in the word box, stopping to blend any words that they have trouble reading. Demonstrate how to decode multisyllabic words by breaking the words into syllables and blending the syllables. Then have students try. If they still have trouble, refer them to the **Sound/Spelling Cards.** If the word is not decodable, give the students the pronunciation.

**Routine Card**
Refer to *Routine 4* for the Clues, Problems, and Wonderings procedure.

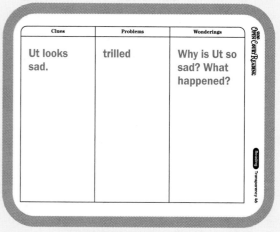

| Clues | Problems | Wonderings |
|---|---|---|
| Ut looks sad. | trilled | Why is Ut so sad? What happened? |

*Reading Transparency 46*

**Routine Card**
Refer to *Routine 3* for the vocabulary procedure.

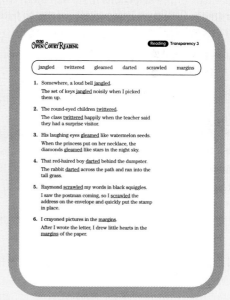

*Reading Transparency 3*

Have students read the sentences on the transparency to determine the meaning of the underlined words. Each word has two sentences that students will read, from which they should be able to derive the meaning of the underlined word. Remind them to use one or more of the skills they have learned—context clues, word structure, or apposition—to figure out the meaning before using a dictionary. Be sure students explain which skills they are using and how they figured out the meaning of the word. Have students reread the sentence, substituting the definition to see if the sentence makes sense. Have a volunteer create a new sentence using the underlined word.

# Reading Recommendations

As in the previous lesson, it is suggested that your first reading of the selection focus on developing the reading strategies found to the left of the reduced student pages. The second reading should focus on the comprehension skills and should be done on another day.

## Oral Reading

This story is a natural for oral reading because of its fluid style and wonderfully descriptive language. Students should read aloud fluently with appropriate expression, vocal patterns, and intonation. Make sure that students attend to punctuation and read in phrases. Tell students to add a sense of feeling or anticipation as they read.

## Using Comprehension Strategies

Comprehension strategy instruction allows students to become aware of how good readers read. Good readers constantly check their understanding as they are reading and ask themselves questions. In addition, skilled readers recognize when they are having problems and stop to use various comprehension strategies to help them make sense of what they are reading. During "Angel Child, Dragon Child," you will model use of the following comprehension strategies.

- **Visualizing (Introduction):** Visualizing requires readers to mentally picture the events or characters in the story, resulting in a more vivid and imaginative understanding of the story.

- **Summarizing** prompts readers to keep track of what they are reading and to focus their minds on important information.

- **Asking Questions (Introduction):** Asking strategic questions helps readers focus attention on what they are reading and engages them in a deeper understanding of themes, concepts, and ideas.

As students read, they should be using a variety of strategies to help them understand the selection. Encourage students to use the strategies listed above as the class reads the story aloud. Do this by stopping at the points indicated by the numbers in the magenta circles on the reduced student page and using a particular strategy. Students can also stop periodically to discuss what they have learned and what problems they may be having.

## Building Comprehension Skills

Revisiting or rereading a selection allows students to apply skills that give them a more complete understanding of the text. Some follow-up comprehension skills help students organize information. Others lead to deeper understanding—to "reading between the lines," as mature readers do.

An extended lesson on the comprehension skill Cause and Effect can be found in the Supporting the Reading section on pages 43C–43D. This lesson is intended to give students extra practice with Cause and Effect. However, it may be used at this time to introduce the comprehension skill to students.

■ **Cause and Effect (Introduction):** Readers identify what causes events to happen or what causes characters to behave in certain ways, which helps readers put together logical explanations in the text.

### Reading with a Purpose

Have students look for ways any of the story characters experience friendship throughout the selection.

## Research in Action
### Visualizing

As they read, good readers envision the action being described in a text. This process heightens their enjoyment of the text and also improves comprehension and long-term memory. Many elementary readers do not visualize sufficiently. As a result, their comprehension suffers. The mental images created while visualizing are a form of interpretation. They reflect the interaction between what the reader receives from the text and what she or he brings to the reading of the text. These images are a type of nonverbal coding that is deeper and more meaningful than the verbal coding that follows from reading the words of the text.
*(Michael Pressley)*

**COMPREHENSION**

This selection is broken into two parts. On the first day, read pages 28–35. On the second day, read pages 36–43.

## Comprehension Strategies LA.E.1.2.1.3.3

**First Read**

Read the story aloud, taking turns with the students. Model the use of strategies for the students.

### Teacher Modeling

**1 Asking and Answering Questions** *Good readers stop and ask themselves questions about what they are reading. Asking questions as you read a story is one way to keep involved with what is happening in the story. I have questions already. I learned from the story that Ut's mother is far away in Vietnam, and Ut has to go to her new American school without her mother there to comfort her. What will Ut's first day at school be like? Will Ut feel shy? Will the other students be nice to her? Will she make friends quickly? As I read, I see that a boy with fire-colored hair pointed at Ut and shouted, "Pajamas! . . . They wore white pajamas to school!" I learned that Ut was already feeling shy and lonely because she "hugged the wall and peeked around the corner." I'll read on and see what happens to Ut. What other questions do you have about the story?*

### Word Knowledge

**SCAFFOLDING:** The skills students are reviewing in Word Knowledge should help them in reading the story. This lesson focuses on plurals and *-ed* and *-ing* endings. These words will be found in boxes similar to this one throughout the selection.

| *-ed* endings: | skipped |
| | hugged |
| | peeked |
| | tilted |

### First Reading Recommendation

## ORAL • CHORAL

*Focus Questions* What might it be like to be in a new school and in a new country? How would you make friends if you didn't speak the same language as the rest of your classmates?

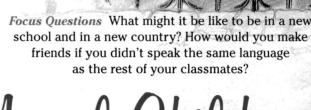

# Angel Child, Dragon Child

Michele Maria Surat
*illustrated by Vo-Dinh Mai*

My sisters skipped through the stone gate two by two. Mother was not there to skip with me. Mother was far away in Vietnam. She could not say, "Ut, my little one, be an Angel Child. Be happy in your new American school." **1**

I hugged the wall and peeked around the corner.

A boy with fire-colored hair pointed his finger. "Pajamas!" he shouted. "They wore white pajamas to school!" The American children tilted back their long noses, laughing.

28

**Informal Assessment**

Observe individual students as they read, and use the Teacher Observation Log, found in the *Program Assessment Teacher's Edition,* to record anecdotal information about each student's strengths and weaknesses.

I turned away. "I want to go home to Father and Little Quang," I said.

Chi Hai's hands curved over my shoulders. "Children stay where parents place them, Ut. We stay."

Somewhere, a loud bell <u>jangled</u>. I lost my sisters in a swirl of rushing children. "Pa-jaa-mas!" they teased.

Inside, the children did not sit together and <u>chant</u> as I was taught. Instead, they waved their hands and said their lessons one by one. I hid my hands, but the teacher called my name. "Nguyen Hoa."

 29

 **Teacher Tip** Encourage students to practice the reading strategies they learned in the last lesson, even as they learn additional strategies.

**Skills Trace**
**Cause and Effect**
Introduced in Grade 1.
Scaffolded throughout Grades 2 and 3.
**REINTRODUCED:** Unit 1, Lesson 2
**REINFORCED:** Unit 1, Lesson 4
Unit 2, Lesson 4
Unit 2, Lesson 5
**TESTED:** Unit 1 Assessment

## Comprehension Skills

### Cause and Effect LA.E.2.2.1.3.1

Explain to students that a *cause-and-effect relationship* exists when one event causes another event to happen. The *cause* is why something happens. The *effect* is what happens. Cause-and-effect relationships are often signaled by *causal indicators*, words such as *because*, *since*, *therefore*, and *so*. As students read, have them think about *why* events are happening in the story.

- On page 28 students learn that Ut is sad because her mother is far away in Vietnam.

Use **Reading Transparency 48** to help students think of causes and effects in the story.

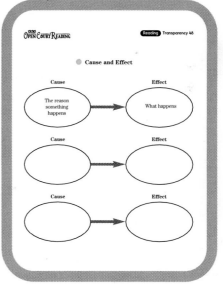

**Reading Transparency 48**

### Word Knowledge
*-ing* ending: rushing

**Second Reading Recommendation**
ORAL • SILENT

**COMPREHENSION**

## COMPREHENSION

## Comprehension Strategies

First Read

### Teacher Modeling

**2 Asking and Answering Questions** *I have another question. Why are the other students in Ut's class laughing at her? I know that she is a new student. I think it is because the other students haven't had a chance to get to know her yet. But I don't think they're being nice to Ut. Why do you think that the other students are treating Ut this way? What do you think of the way they're acting? How would you feel in Ut's place? I would feel sad if someone treated me that way.*

---

### Word Knowledge

**-ed endings:**    **twittered**
                    **poked**

---

**Teacher Tip** Encourage students to ask and answer lots of questions as they read. Remind students that if they are unable to answer a question, reading further in the story might reveal the answer.

---

**Teacher Tip** PRONUNCIATION

| Nguyen | (nōō yen) |
| Hoa | (hwä) |
| Ut | (ōōt) |
| Quang | (kwäng) |
| Chi Hai | (chē hī) |

Hoa is my true name, but I am Ut. Ut is my at-home name—a tender name for smallest daughter.

"Hoa," the teacher said slowly. "Write your name, please." She pressed a chalk-piece to my hand and wrote in the air.

"I not understand," I whispered. The round-eyed children <u>twittered</u>. The red-haired boy poked my back.

30

**COMPREHENSION**

"Stand up, Pajamas!"

I stood and bowed. "*Chao buoi sang*," I said like an Angel Child. The children screeched like bluejays.

I sat down and flipped up my desk top, hiding my angry Dragon face.

Deep in my pocket, I felt Mother's gift—a small wooden matchbox with silvery edges. I took it out and traced the *hoa-phuong* on the lid. When I tapped the tiny drawer, Mother's eyes peeked over the edge.

31

## Comprehension Skills

 Second Read

### Cause and Effect LA.E.2.2.1.3.1

Have students continue to read carefully to find out how one event *(the cause)* helps to make another event *(the effect)* happen. Explain that cause-and-effect relationships are often related to each other. Use the following examples:

- **Cause:** Ut didn't understand the teacher's instruction.
  **Effect:** The red-haired boy poked Ut in the back.
- **Cause:** The red-haired boy poked Ut in the back, and the children laughed at Ut once again.
  **Effect:** Ut was angry and hid her face.

### Word Knowledge

plurals adding -s:  pajamas
blue jays
edges
eyes

 **Teacher Tip** PRONUNCIATION AND DEFINITION

**Chao buoi sang** (chow bwē sung)— Good morning.

**hoa-phung** (hwä fung)—a flower with red blossoms, native to Vietnam.

 **Teacher Tip** Continue to write the cause-and-effect relationships on the transparency, erasing the earlier relationship sets later in the lesson as needed to visually record all of the cause-and-effect relationships.

## MEETING INDIVIDUAL NEEDS

### Intervention

**CAUSE AND EFFECT** If students seem confused about cause and effect, try relating the idea to something physical in the classroom so they can clearly see the relationship at work. For example, drop a heavy book on the floor. What effect does this action have?

## Comprehension Strategies

**First Read**

### Teacher Modeling

**3 Visualizing** *Often, forming mental images or pictures in our heads of what the author is telling us helps us better understand and enjoy the story.*

*In my head, I see Ut looking at her mother's picture. I can almost hear Ut's mother's voice telling her to be brave. I know that Ut's mother is still in Vietnam, but Ut has a picture of her mother in the small wooden matchbox she keeps in her desk. Talking to the picture of her mother makes Ut feel better. I think she's imagining that her mother is with her, and she is thinking of what her mother would say to her if she could be with her. I think Ut misses her mother so much and is so sad that she has closed her mind to the other children's hurtful laughter and is thinking only of her mother now. It is as if Ut can see, hear, and feel her mother there with her. As I think about how Ut feels, I can see Ut, but I can also imagine Ut's mother's picture. Good readers are always getting images in their heads about what they read. If you get a good one, tell the class about it.*

---

### Word Knowledge

*-ed* endings:   whispered
                trilled

---

**Teacher Tip** Remind students to continue looking for answers to questions they might have asked themselves as they continue to read.

"I will keep you safe in here, Mother," I told her. "See? You will just fit beside the crayons."

Her listening face smiled. In my heart, I heard the music of her voice. "Do not be angry, my smallest daughter," she said. "Be my brave little **3** Dragon."

So all day I was brave, even when the children whispered behind their hands and the clock needles ticked slowly. Finally, the bell <u>trilled</u>. Time for home!

32

**COMPREHENSION**

As soon as he saw me, Little Quang crowed, "Ut! Ut! Ut!" His laughing eyes <u>gleamed</u> like watermelon seeds. I dropped my books and slung him on my hip.

There he rode, tugging my hair as I sorted mint leaves and <u>chives</u>. Little Quang strung rice noodles from the cup hooks. Father and I laughed at this happy play.

At night, small brother curled tight beside me. I showed him Mother's lonely face inside the matchbox. Together we prayed, "Keep Mother safe. Send her to us soon." With Mother's picture near, we slept like Angel Children.

In this way, many days passed.

 33

## Comprehension Skills

 Second Read

### Cause and Effect   LA.E.2.2.1.3.1

Remind students that sometimes clue words are used to introduce cause-and-effect relationships.

- Ut imagined her mother's voice telling her to be brave.

- Ut says, "So all day I was brave." *So* is a clue word that helps readers understand that something happened because of what Ut imagined her mother was saying to her. Ut imagined that her mother told her to be brave *(cause)*, so *(causal indicator)* Ut was brave *(effect)*.

Encourage students as they read to look for other causal indicators that will help them understand what happened or why something happened. Discuss these clue words and keep track of them on an overhead transparency.

> **Word Knowledge**
> *-ed* endings:   gleamed
>             dropped
>             passed

 **Teacher Tip** As students read aloud, listen for appropriate pacing, intonation, and expression.

**COMPREHENSION**

## Comprehension Strategies

### Teacher Modeling

**4 Asking Questions** *I'm confused about something. Why does Ut think you can catch snow? Why does she seem to know so little about snow?*

*I think I can figure this out by rereading. It's probably winter. I know that Ut and her sister are from Vietnam. I also know that Vietnam has a tropical climate because I have read other stories about the country. I think that Ut and her sister have never seen snow before. This is probably their first winter in America, and snow is new to them. Remember to keep asking questions and figuring out the answers as you read.*

### Word Knowledge

| | |
|---|---|
| plural *-s:* | feathers |
| | windows |
| | trees |
| | leaves |
| | fingers |
| | snowflakes |
| | kisses |
| | cheeks |
| | disappears |

**Teacher Tip  WAIT TIME** It is important to allow time for students to respond. Although silence can be uncomfortable, don't automatically jump in with more questions or your own response—wait.

**Teacher Tip** Good readers constantly evaluate their understanding of what they read. Stop often to make sure students are doing this.

One day at school, small feathers floated past the frosty windows. "Mother," I whispered, "this is snow. It makes everything soft, even the angry trees with no leaves to make them pretty."

My fingers danced on the desk top while I waited for the bell. When it rang, I rushed out the door.

Outside, snowflakes left wet kisses on my cheeks. "Chi Hai!" I called. "Catch some!"

**4** "It disappears!" she cried.

34

Just as Chi Hai spoke, a snowrock stung her chin. That red-haired boy <u>darted</u> behind the dumpster. He was laughing hard.

I tried, but I could not be a noble Dragon. Before I knew it, I was scooping up snow. My hands burned and my fingers turned red. I threw my snowrock and the laughing stopped.

Suddenly, the boy tackled me! We rolled in the snow, kicking and yelling, until the principal's large hand pinched my shoulder.

"Inside!" he thundered, and he marched us to our classroom.

 35

# COMPREHENSION

## Comprehension Skills

Second Read

### Cause and Effect  LA.E.2.2.1.3.1

Have students continue to identify cause-and-effect relationships. Record their answers on the transparency.

- Under Cause, write *Ut and the red-haired boy fought in the snow.* Encourage students to fill in the information under Effect. *(The principal marched them to a classroom.)*

- Under Effect, write *A snowball hit Chi Hai.* Then encourage students to fill in the information under Cause. *(The red-haired boy threw a snowball at Chi Hai.)*

Encourage students to restate these cause-and-effect relationships using cause-and-effect clue words *(so, since, because,* and *therefore). (For example: The principal marched them to a classroom because Ut and the red-haired boy fought in the snow.)*

> ### Word Knowledge
> *-ing* endings:   laughing
>                    scooping
>                    kicking
>                    yelling

 **Teacher Tip** You may wish to explain to students that sometimes we are aware of an effect but are not sure of the cause. Often when this happens, the cause becomes apparent later.

COMPREHENSION

## Comprehension Strategies

 First Read

### Teacher Modeling

**5** **Summarizing** *A lot has happened in the story so far. Sometimes understanding a story is easier if you think about what you've read and sum up the most important ideas in your own words. Good readers summarize the main ideas of the story as they read. I would begin this summary by saying that Ut is from Vietnam and she is at a new school in America. The other children aren't very nice to Ut, especially a boy named Raymond. Ut misses her mother, who is still in Vietnam. When summarizing, always restate what the author has said in your own words. Summarize only the main ideas and perhaps a very important detail or two. Don't retell the whole story. Let's continue reading, and as we do, remember to summarize what we are reading. Make sure you understand what you have just read. Let me know if you would like to share your summary with the group.*

---

### Word Knowledge

*-ing* endings:    **fighting**

---

**Teacher Tip** Ask students one or more of the following questions to make sure they understand what they are reading: Is anyone confused? Do you need clarification? Can you summarize what you have read so far? Does what you are reading make sense to you?

"We can't have this fighting. You two have to help each other," ordered the principal. He pointed at me. "Hoa, you need to speak to Raymond. Use our words. Tell him about Vietnam." Raymond glared. "And you, Raymond, you must learn to listen. You will write Hoa's story."

36

"But I can't understand her funny words," Raymond <u>whined</u>. "Anyway, I don't have a pencil."

"Use this one, then," said the principal. He slapped down a pencil, turned and slammed the door. His shoes <u>squeegeed</u> down the hall.

"Pajamas!" Raymond hissed. He <u>crinkled</u> his paper and snapped the pencil in two. He hid his head in his arms. How could I tell my story to *him*?

The clock needles blurred before my eyes. No! I *would not* be an Angel Child for this cruel-hearted boy.

But later, across the room, I heard a sniffle. Raymond's shoulders jiggled like Little Quang's when he cried for Mother.

I crept over. Gently, I tugged the sad boy's sleeve. He didn't move. "Raymond," I pleaded, "not cry. I give you cookie."

37

## Comprehension Skills

### Cause and Effect LA.E.2.2.1.3.1

Have students add their observations of causes and effects to the list on the transparency. Help students to notice that one cause can have multiple effects. What are the effects of the principal sending Raymond to the classroom to write Ut's story with her? *(Raymond glared, whined, hissed, crinkled his paper, snapped his pencil, hid his head, sniffed, and cried.)*

Help students to identify cause-and-effect relationships between Raymond's behavior in the classroom and Ut's reaction to Raymond's behavior. Note again that these relationships are interrelated.

- **Cause:** Ut remembered the way that her little brother cried.
- **Effect:** Ut offered Raymond a cookie in order to get him to stop crying.

Remind students that sometimes clue words such as *so* can be used to explain what happened or why something happened in a story. Other cause-and-effect clue words are *because*, *since*, and *therefore*.

> ### Word Knowledge
> **-ed endings:**    **whined**
>                     **turned**
>                     **slammed**
>                     **snapped**
>                     **jiggled**
>                     **pleaded**

**Teacher Tip** Remind students to use context clues, apposition, or word structure to figure out the meaning of difficult words as they are reading.

**COMPREHENSION**

**COMPREHENSION**

## Comprehension Strategies

First Read

### Teacher Modeling

**6** **Visualizing** *I can just imagine what Raymond's face looked like when Ut said his name and offered him a piece of her cookie. I can see the surprise and happiness in his face. He is glad that she is being kind to him. I think he will return the kindness. I can see that both Ut and Raymond look happier and feel better now. Continue to form mental images of the characters and events in the story as we read.*

---

### Word Knowledge

*-ed* endings:    **bounced**
    **answered**

---

**Teacher Tip** Encourage students to think aloud, practicing the strategies they have learned. Tell students that their ideas about the story are very important to the whole class's understanding of the story.

Suddenly, his head bounced up. "Hoa!" he shouted. "You said my name. You didn't use funny words." He broke off a piece of the cookie.

"I say English," I answered proudly. "And you call me Ut. Ut is my at-home name, from Vietnam." **6**

38

"Okay, *Ut*," he mumbled. "But only if you tell me what's in your matchbox."

"My mother," I told him. We giggled and ate the cookie crumbs.

Then Raymond asked, "Why do you need your mother's picture?"

"Mother is far away," I said softly.

"She didn't come with you?"

"So many children in my family," I sighed. "No money for Mother to come."

 39

---

**COMPREHENSION**

## Comprehension Skills

### Cause and Effect LA.E.2.2.1.3.1

Have students continue to look for cause-and-effect relationships in the story. Explain that sometimes we learn about the effect of what happened before we learn about the cause of what happened.

We already know that Ut's mother stayed in Vietnam. Now, we learn the cause—there wasn't enough money to pay her way to come to the United States.

Have students write the following information under the correct headings on the transparency.

- Raymond started talking to Ut *because* she spoke to him in English.

---

**Word Knowledge**

*-ed* endings:  mumbled
asked
sighed

---

**Teacher Tip** COMPREHENSION

Good readers are active readers. They interact with the text as they read by emoting, reacting, responding, and problem solving in their efforts to construct and maintain meaning.

## COMPREHENSION

## Comprehension Strategies

 First Read

### Teacher Modeling

**7 Summarizing** *Now that Raymond and Ut are beginning to be friendly to each other, this is a good time to summarize how their relationship has changed. Raymond was mean to Ut at first, but after they were sent to the principal's office, their relationship changed. Ut felt sorry for Raymond when he started to cry. She started talking to Raymond and even told him about her mother and Vietnam. Let me know if you would like to stop and make another summary.*

---

### Word Knowledge

**plurals with -s:** words
squiggles
pictures

---

**Teacher Tip** If students offer suggestions for the summary, note whether their additions are main points in the story. You may have to remind students to state only the main points of the story when summarizing.

"Wait," said Raymond. He grabbed part of the broken pencil. I handed him a new sheet of paper. "Now tell me about Vietnam," he said.

Raymond <u>scrawled</u> my words in black <u>squiggles</u>. I crayoned pictures in the <u>margins</u>.

When we were ready, Raymond leaned out the door. "Done!" he beamed. He waved the story like a flag.

The principal squeegeed up the hall. "You may go," said the big man.

We dashed through the stone gate together.  **7**

40

The next day, the principal read our story to the whole school. "These girls sailed many oceans to be here. They left behind their home, their friends, and most important of all, their mother. So now . . ."

"Ut's mother needs money for the long boat ride to America!" shouted a familiar voice. Raymond stood on his chair. "And we could have a fair and *earn* the money."

"Young man!" warned the principal.

Raymond slid down in his seat. "We could," he insisted. I hid my eyes. I held my breath. Chi Hai squeezed my hand.

"A special fair! A Vietnamese fair!" my teacher exclaimed. My eyes opened wide.

The principal's eyebrows wiggled like caterpillars. "But who will help with a Vietnamese fair?"

  41

**Science/Social Studies** SS.C.2.2.2.3.1
**Connection Center**

Refer to the *Science/Social Studies Connection Center* Card 4 for a social studies activity that students can investigate.

## Comprehension Skills

 Second Read

### Cause and Effect LA.E.2.2.1.3.1

Identifying causes and effects is an ongoing process. Readers continue noticing effects and identifying their causes throughout a story. Remind students to use causal indicators, such as *so*, *because*, *since*, and *therefore*, to help them understand cause-and-effect relationships. Sometimes students will need to state the effect first.

Have students write the following information under the correct headings on the transparency.

- Raymond suggests having a fair *because* he understands Ut's mother needs money to come to the United States.

- The prinicpal's eyebrows wiggle *because* he is worried about who can help with the fair.

#### Word Knowledge

**plurals with -s:**
girls
friends
eyes
eyebrows
caterpillars

**Teacher Tip** If students do not mention an important cause or story event that is key to understanding a larger issue, you may "drop" that idea into the discussion and then repeat it several times to make sure students incorporate the idea into their thoughts.

COMPREHENSION

COMPREHENSION

## Comprehension Strategies

First Read

### Teacher Modeling

**8** **Summarizing** *I'm glad that I stopped before to summarize. It helped me to understand what happened next. Now, I will summarize the most important events that took place since the principal made Raymond and Ut talk to each other. Raymond wrote Ut's story of her mother in Vietnam. Ut drew pictures to illustrate the story. After the principal read the story to the class, Raymond suggested having a fair to raise money to bring Ut's mother from Vietnam. In the end, Ut was reunited with her mother. Summarizing really helps me to order my thoughts and make sense of the information in the story.*

### Discussing Strategy Use LA.A.1.2.4.3.1

While students are reading the selection, encourage them to share any problems that they encountered and to tell what strategies they used to solve them.

- What questions did they ask as they read?
- Where did they pause in the reading to summarize?
- What did they visualize as they were reading?

These are questions good readers ask after they read a text. After reading, they should always be asking, "What did I find interesting? What is important here?" Later, remind the students again that whenever they conclude a reading, they should ask themselves questions about what was in the text.

**Teacher Tip** BUILDING FLUENCY As students read, you may notice that some need work in building fluency. During Workshop, have these students select a section of the text (a minimum of 160 words) to read several times in order to build fluency.

"Me!" cried Raymond.

"We will!" squealed the children.

"Well, what are we waiting for?" said the principal. And we all clapped for the fair.

On the special day, I wore my white *ao dai* and welcomed everyone to our Vietnamese fair. "*Chao buoi sang,*" I said, bowing like an Angel Child.

"*Chao buoi sang,*" they answered, smiling.

High above our heads, our rainbow dragon floated freely. Below, Chi Hai and her friends sold rice cakes, imperial rolls and <u>sesame</u> cookies. Raymond popped balloons and won three goldfish. He gave one to Little Quang. "Don't eat it," he warned.

By the end of the day, we had just enough money to send to Mother. "When will she come?" I wondered.

42

### Word Knowledge

| *-ed* endings: | squealed | floated |
|---|---|---|
| | clapped | warned |
| | answered | wondered |

 **Informal Assessment**

Use the Informal Comprehension Strategies Rubrics on page 28J to determine whether a student is using the strategies being taught.

Every day, we walked home wondering, "When will Mother come?"

We slid through icy winter. . . .

We splish-splashed through spring rain. . . .

We tiptoed barefoot through the grass, still hoping she would come.

On the last day of school, when I knew the *hoa-phuong* were blossoming in Vietnam, Raymond and I raced home faster than all my sisters. We were the first to see Father and Little Quang at the picture window, and beside them . . .

Mother! **8**

 43

**Teacher Tip FLUENCY** By this time in third grade, good readers should be reading approximately 107 words per minute with fluency and expression. The only way to gain this fluency is through practice. Have students reread the selection to you and to each other during Workshop to help build fluency.

**Formal Assessment**

To assess students' comprehension of "Angel Child, Dragon Child," use pages 6–9 in *Comprehension and Language Arts Skills.*

## Comprehension Skills

Second Read

### Cause and Effect  LA.E.1.2.2.3.2, LA.E.2.2.1.3.1

Remind students that an important cause or a cause-and-effect relationship may not be directly stated in the story. However, students should be able to think about and discuss these relationships after reading the story. Have students identify a cause-and-effect relationship that would explain Ut's character. (*Because Ut's mother was far away, Ut tried especially hard to act the way her mother would have wanted. Ut thought about her mother a lot because Ut missed her so much.*)

### Checking Comprehension

Ask students the following questions to check their comprehension of the story. In addition to the following questions, be sure to revisit any questions students asked when they set purposes before reading.

- How do Raymond and Ut become friends? (*Raymond writes down Ut's story about her life in Vietnam and about coming to the United States without her mother.*)

- How do Ut and the other students in her school become friends? (*The students raise money to pay for Ut's mother to come to the United States by holding a school fair.*)

#### Word Knowledge

*-ing* endings:   wondering
hoping
blossoming

**COMPREHENSION**

**Routine Card**
Refer to *Routine 6* for the *handing-off process.*

| Clues | Problems | Wonderings |
|---|---|---|
| Ut looks sad. | trilled | Why is Ut so sad? What happened? |

**Reading Transparency 46**

**www.sra4kids.com**
**Web Connection**
Some students may choose to conduct a computer search for additional books or information about friendship. Invite them to make a list of these books and sources of information to share with classmates and the school librarian. Check the Reading link of the SRA Web page for additional links to the theme-related Web site.

## MEETING INDIVIDUAL NEEDS

### ELL

Ask English-language learners to share their own experiences of being newcomers to a strange land. Help them compare their experiences with that of the girl in the story, and draw out similarities.

## Discussing the Selection LA.C.1.2.3.3.1; LA.E.1.2.1.3.1

After the first read, the whole group discusses the selection and any personal thoughts, reactions, problems, or questions that it raises. To stimulate discussion, students can ask one another the kinds of questions that good readers ask themselves about a text: *How does it connect to friendship? What have I learned that is new? What did I find interesting? What is important here? What was difficult to understand? Why would someone want to read this?*

**Handing-Off Process** Seeing you as a contributing member of the group sets a strong example for students. To emphasize that you are part of the group, actively participate in the *handing-off process:* Raise your hand to be called on by the last speaker when you have a contribution to make. Point out unusual and interesting insights verbalized by students so that these insights are recognized and discussed. As the year progresses, students will take more and more responsibility for the discussions of the selections.

Engage students in a discussion to determine whether they have grasped the following ideas:

- how Ut must have felt coming to a new school and being far away from her mother
- why Raymond was mean to Ut at first
- how Ut and Raymond started to become friends
- how Ut's classmates showed her friendship

During this time, have the students return to the clues, problems, and wonderings they noted during browsing to determine whether the clues were borne out by the selection, whether and how their problems were solved, and whether their wonderings were answered or deserve further discussion and investigation. Let the students decide which items deserve further discussion.

Also have students return to the Focus Questions on the first page of the selection. Select a student to read the questions aloud, and have volunteers answer the questions. If students do not know the answers to the questions, have them return to the text to find the answers.

You may wish to review the elements of realistic fiction with students at this time. Discuss with them how they can tell that "Angel Child, Dragon Child" is realistic fiction.

Have students break into small groups to discuss what this story tells them about friendship. Groups can then share their ideas with the rest of the class.

Students may wish to record their personal responses to the selection. If they have ever become friends with someone they at one time did not get along with, or with someone who at first seemed totally different from themselves, encourage them to record these events in the Response Journal section of their Writer's Notebooks.

# Review Selection Vocabulary  LA.A.1.2.2.3.2

Have students review the definitions of the selection vocabulary words that they wrote in the Vocabulary section of their Writer's Notebooks. Remind them that they discussed the meanings of these words before reading the selection. Have students write sentences for each of the vocabulary words after the definitions in the same section of their Writer's Notebooks. They can use the definitions and the sentences to study for the vocabulary portion of their Lesson Assessments. Have them add to the personal dictionary section of their Writer's Notebooks any other interesting words that they clarified while reading. Encourage students to refer to the selection vocabulary words throughout the unit. The words from the selection are:

| | | |
|---|---|---|
| **jangled** | **twittered** | **gleamed** |
| **darted** | **scrawled** | **margins** |

Remind students to find words from other resources, from their investigations, and from family discussions and then add them to the Word Bank. They should be organizing words by parts of speech. They may also place synonyms and antonyms in the Word Bank.

**Teacher Tip** Encourage students to write a sentence using these selection words. In order to provide additional help in remembering words, students can write a synonym or an antonym for the word if it is appropriate. Some students may even draw something that helps them to remember the meaning of the word.

# View Fine Art  LA.C.2.2.2.3.1

Have students reflect on the photograph *Children Had Few Toys* on page 63 of the *Student Anthology* and share their thoughts and reactions with the class. Explain that the photograph by William Barnhill is believed to be part of a series taken in North Carolina. His work reflects the daily life of many southerners during the early 1900s. Barnhill's photographs reflect the poverty that remained in rural areas of the South even decades after the Civil War ended. His work also documents the strength of friendship. This photograph portrays a young rural girl lovingly holding her pet chicken.

*Children Had Few Toys.* c. 1914–17. **William Barnhill.** Silver gelatin print. Library of Congress.

*The Good Friends.* c. 1864. **Honoré Daumier.** Pen, brush and ink, conte crayon, watercolor, and charcoal on wove paper. 236 × 303 mm. The Baltimore Museum of Art.

63

*Student Anthology p. 63*

# Home Connection

Distribute *Home Connection,* page 5. Encourage students to discuss "Angel Child, Dragon Child" with their families. Students can participate in a writing activity at home based on the discussion they have. Students may bring their writing in to share with the class. *Home Connection* is also available in Spanish, page 6.

*Angel Child, Dragon Child*

**A message from**

We have just read "Angel Child, Dragon Child." This is the story of a young Vietnamese girl whose mother hasn't yet arrived from Vietnam. Whenever the girl feels lonely, she looks at a picture of her mother that she keeps in a small wooden matchbox. Ask your child to tell you more about the story. Then ask your child to imagine what it would be like to move to another city and not have a friend or to go to another country and leave behind everything that is familiar. What two or three small objects would your child take along in order to feel less lonely? Why would she or he choose to take those objects? Encourage your child to write about each of the objects on this page and bring it to school to share with the class.

**Next week's selection** *The Tree House*

Your child will be studying the following vocabulary words in the upcoming week. Please review the meanings of these words with your child: **magnificent**—great, wonderful; **marvelous**—outstanding; **beautiful**—lovely, pleasing to look at; **peered**—looked; **height**—how tall something is.
Please review with your child the spelling words for the upcoming week: pick, risk, film, grip, brick, give, stitch, finish, trick, live, window, visit, lift, with, into.

*Home Connection p. 5*

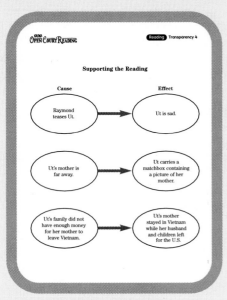

**Reading Transparency 4**

**Teacher Tip** Teach and encourage students to use the Cause-and-Effect skill in all of their readings. Using this skill will aid in their comprehension.

## Supporting the Reading

### Comprehension Skills: Cause and Effect LA.E.2.2.1.3.1

**Teach** Explain to students that identifying causes and effects is an important skill they will use often; understanding *what* and *why* affects nearly every aspect of daily life. Identifying causes and effects in stories helps students become involved with the action and improves their comprehension. Words called *causal indicators* sometimes directly alert readers to these relationships. Even if authors do not use these words, students can use them to express the cause-and-effect relationships they identify. These words include *because, for, since, therefore, so, consequently, reason for, source of, in order that, so that, due to,* and *as a result.*

**Guided Practice** Use *Reading Transparency 4* for identifying causes and effects. Give copies to students. Then have students look back at their Clues, Problems, and Wonderings sheet they filled out before and during their reading of the story. Have students look for answers to their wonderings and then show the cause-and-effect relationships that answer their questions. Have students add other important cause-and-effect relationships they discovered in the story. You may want to make copies of *Reading Transparency 48* for students to use. Model the activity for students. You can use the following as an example.

**Wonderings:**

Why is Ut so sad? What happened?

Why does Ut carry a matchbox with a picture of her mother?

Why is Ut's mother far away?

**Independent Practice** Read through the Focus and Identify sections of *Comprehension and Language Arts Skills,* page 4, with students. Guide students through the Identify portion, and help locate the causal indicators, or clue words. Then have students complete the Practice and Apply portions of *Comprehension and Language Arts Skills,* page 5.

**Link to Writing** Tell students a fun way to start writing a story is to begin with an effect. Then they ask themselves what the cause might be and begin writing a story to explain the situation. Have students invent an effect—either serious or amusing—and exchange it with another student. Then have them write stories to explain the cause of the effect. *(Examples: "And that is how flowers came to be." "And they never ate meatballs again." "And that is why fire engines are red.")*

## MEETING INDIVIDUAL NEEDS

### Reteach

**CAUSE AND EFFECT** Have students who need additional practice with cause and effect complete *Reteach,* pages 5–6.

### Challenge

**CAUSE AND EFFECT** Have students who understand cause and effect complete *Challenge,* page 5.

---

Name _____ Date _____

UNIT I  Friendship • **Lesson 2** *Angel Child, Dragon Child*

### Cause and Effect

**Focus** Writers use causal indicators to help readers notice connections between causes and effects in a story.

▶ A **cause-and-effect relationship** is one in which one event causes another to happen.
▶ **Causal indicators** are words such as *because, therefore,* and *so* that signal a cause-and-effect relationship between two events.
  There was a big snowstorm, *so* the schools were closed.
  **Effect** (What happened?)  Schools were closed.
  **Cause** (Why did it happen?)  There was a big snowstorm.

#### Identify

Draw a line under the causal indicator in each sentence.

1. The lock opened because I used the right key.
2. The tire was flat, so Linda could not ride her bicycle.
3. The birds were singing, therefore I knew it was morning.
4. The first bite of the apple was sour, so Amy threw it away.

4  UNIT I • Lesson 2  Comprehension and Language Arts Skills

---

Name _____ Date _____

UNIT I  Friendship • **Lesson 2** *Angel Child, Dragon Child*

▶ **Cause and Effect**

#### Practice

Read each sentence. Write the effect (what happened) and the cause (why it happened) in each sentence.

5. The eggs cracked because I dropped them on the floor.
  **Effect:** The eggs cracked.
  **Cause:** I dropped them on the floor.

6. The car wouldn't start because Dad was using the wrong key.
  **Effect:** The car wouldn't start.
  **Cause:** Dad was using the wrong key.

#### Apply

Write two sentences that show a cause-and-effect relationship.  Sentences will vary.

7. _____
_____
_____

8. _____
_____
_____

COMPREHENSION

Comprehension and Language Arts Skills  UNIT I • Lesson 2  5

*Comprehension and Language Arts Skills pp. 4–5*

---

### Skills Trace
### Cause and Effect
Introduced in Grade 1.
Scaffolded throughout Grades 2 and 3.
**REINTRODUCED:** Unit 1, Lesson 2
**REINFORCED:** Unit 1, Lesson 4
Unit 2, Lesson 4
Unit 2, Lesson 5
Unit 4, Lesson 2
Unit 4, Lesson 7
Unit 6, Lesson 6
**TESTED:** Unit 1 Assessment

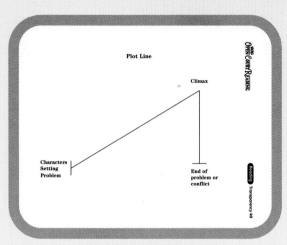

**Reading Transparency 49**

## MEETING INDIVIDUAL NEEDS

### ELL

**PLOT** Encourage English-language learners to relate plots from stories from their own cultures. Lead them to see that basic plot structure is the same for most stories.

### Intervention

**PLOT** Work with a small group of students who are having difficulty with the concept of plot. Help them create a plot line for familiar tales, such as "Little Red Riding Hood" or "The Three Little Pigs."

## Literary Elements LA.A.1.2.1.3.2; LA.E.1.2.2.3.1, LA.E.1.2.2.3.2

### Plot

**Teach** Ask students to explain what a story plot is. If necessary, give them the following information. The happenings or events that occur in a story make up the story's plot. At the beginning of the story, the characters and the problems are identified. The story may include one or more struggles or conflicts leading to the high point, or climax, of the story—the most exciting part. The story usually ends with some sort of solution to the problem. Explain to students that a story is easy to read, follow, and keep track of if it has a well-defined plot. Writing a story is easier if we determine the plot before beginning to write.

Display **Reading Transparency 49.** Explain to students they can use this plot line to show the plot structure of any story they read. Distribute copies of the plot line to students.

**Guided Practice** Ask students to think about the story "Angel Child, Dragon Child," and then write the title above the plot line. Discuss how the plot line for the story should be filled in. This should aid in students' comprehension of the solution or resolution of the story's problem.

**Independent Practice** Have students insert their plot line in their *Writing Folders.* Suggest that they refer to it to plan a problem and solution for their own writing. Also, invite students to fill in a plot line whenever they think it will help them understand the plot of a story. Make copies of the transparency for their use as needed.

# Social Studies Connection LA.C.1.2.5.3.1; SS.B.1.2.3.3.1

## Immigration

In "Angel Child, Dragon Child," students read about the experiences of the character Ut as she adapted to life in a new country. What was life like in Vietnam, the country she left to come to the United States? What are some experiences of real people who have moved here from Vietnam?

Invite small groups of students to focus on one of these two questions and prepare a presentation to share with the class. When conducting research, students should try to capture the perspective of children their own age, if possible. Encyclopedias, Web sites, and nonfiction books about Vietnam and Vietnamese immigrants will help with the investigation. Students should prepare a visual, such as a poster, to accompany their presentation. Students may also invite an expert on Vietnam to come in and talk to the class.

A good way to ensure that students have comprehended a presentation is to have them retell or explain what the speaker said, or ask the speaker questions. They can also connect and relate prior experiences and ideas to those of the speaker.

**Teacher Tip** MATERIALS
✔ paper and pencil for taking notes
✔ reference materials
✔ poster board
✔ colored pencils or markers

**Teacher Tip** PURPOSE To help students understand the major physical and cultural features of Vietnam and to better understand the experiences of those who have come to the United States from Vietnam.

**Teacher Tip** If students decide to invite an expert speaker to class, encourage them to write a formal invitation explaining the nature of the project and the questions they would like to have answered. Contact the speaker to schedule a date and time for the visit. Send a group note or individual notes to thank the speaker after the visit.

## Meet the Author

After students read the information about Michele Maria Surat, discuss the following questions with them.

- Why did Michele Maria Surat think that this was an important story to tell? *(Possible answer: She wants to create a better understanding between Vietnamese and American children.)*

- Michele Maria Surat based this story on one of her students. What kind of teacher do you think she is? *(Possible answer: She seems very kind and understanding. She went out of her way to make life easier for her student. She is also a fair teacher, because she wants people to appreciate each others' cultures.)*

## Meet the Illustrator

After students read about Vo-Dinh Mai, have them answer the following questions.

- Vo-Dinh Mai believes "good illustrations can enrich the mind of a reader, young or old." How do you think his pictures help do this? *(Possible answer: His pictures in this story show the deeper emotions and feelings of the characters. They bring the story to life and give readers a clearer understanding of it.)*

- Vo-Dinh Mai said that the Vietnam War "reinforced his faith in the miracle of life." Why do you think he would want to illustrate this particular story? *(Possible answer: This story is about the love of a child for her mother. It also shows how people can develop an understanding of differences and develop friendships with each other.)*

# Angel Child, Dragon Child

## Meet the Author

**Michele Maria Surat** teaches high school near Washington, D.C., when she is not writing. The tale of Ut, the main character in this story, began when a Vietnamese student came to Surat with tear-filled eyes and shared a photograph of her mother in Vietnam. Surat wanted to tell the story of the brave students she worked with in hopes of creating an understanding between Vietnamese and American children.

## Meet the Illustrator

**Vo-Dinh Mai** is an artist and author from Vietnam. He came to the United States when he was twenty-seven years old. Before that he spent time studying art in Paris, France. In addition to painting, Vo-Dinh loves printmaking from woodcuts. He also loves illustrating books and says, "I believe that good illustrations can enrich the mind of a reader, young or old...."

Vo-Dinh was back in Vietnam during the Vietnam War. He has this to say about how the war affects his art: "If anything, the war between Vietnamese and between Vietnamese and Americans has reinforced my faith in the miracle of life."

44 🌸

# Theme Connections

## Within the Selection

Record your answers to the questions below in the Response Journal section of your Writer's Notebook. In small groups, report the ideas you wrote. Discuss your ideas with the rest of the group. Then choose a person to report your group's answers to the class.

- How did Ut's mother's gift help Ut when she was at a new school without any friends?
- How did Ut and Raymond become friends?
- What did Raymond do to show his friendship for Ut?

## Across Selections

- Ut, like Gloria, has just moved to a new home. What did they both learn about friendship?

## Beyond the Selection

- Think about how "Angel Child, Dragon Child" adds to what you know about friendship.
- Add items to the Concept/Question Board about friendship.

## Theme Connections LA.E.2.2.4.3.1

### Within the Selection

- The picture of Ut's mother reminded Ut that her mother loved her and helped Ut to feel safe in a strange new place.
- After Ut and Raymond were caught fighting, they were forced to listen to one another and became considerate of the other's feelings.
- He had the idea of having a fair to earn money to bring Ut's mother to America.

### Across Selections

- Both Ut and Gloria learned that good friends cooperate and work together.

### Beyond the Selection

Have groups report their ideas to the class. Have students add these ideas to the Concept/Question Board. Have students tell how they might use this in their investigations.

### Inquiry Journal

Students should record their ideas and impressions about the selections on page 2 of their *Inquiry Journals.*

**Informal Assessment**

This may be a good time to observe students working in small groups and to mark your observations in the Teacher Observation Log in the *Program Assessment Teacher's Edition.*

---

Name _____ Date _____
UNIT 1 Friendship

**Recording Concept Information**

As I read each selection, this is what I added to my understanding of friendship.

- "Gloria Who Might Be My Best Friend" by Ann Cameron
Answers will vary.
_____
_____
_____
_____
_____

- "Angel Child, Dragon Child" by Michele Maria Surat
Answers will vary.
_____
_____
_____
_____

2 UNIT 1          *Recording Concept Information • Inquiry Journal*

*Inquiry Journal p. 2*

45

**INVESTIGATION**

### Objectives

- Students gain a deeper understanding of friendship and how to form relationships with people from cultures different from their own.
- Students break into groups based on investigation interests.
- Student groups choose an activity with which to investigate friendship.

### Materials

- Student Anthology, Book 1, pp. 28–47
- Inquiry Journal, pp. 10–15
- Reading Transparency 2
- Research Assistant CD-ROM

---

Name_____ Date_____

**UNIT 1** Friendship

**Project Planning Calendar**

Use the calendar to help schedule your Friendship unit investigation. Fill in the dates. Make sure you mark any days you know you will not be able to work on the investigation. Choose the date on which you will start.

| Sunday | Monday | Tuesday | Wednesday |
|--------|--------|---------|-----------|
|        |        |         |           |
|        |        |         |           |
|        |        |         |           |
|        |        |         |           |
|        |        |         |           |

10 UNIT 1                     *Project Planning Calendar • Inquiry Journal*

---

**Project Planning Calendar** *(continued)*

Then choose the date on which you hope to finish. You may also find it helpful to mark the dates by which you hope to complete different parts of the investigation. Record what you accomplish each day.

| Thursday | Friday | Saturday |
|----------|--------|----------|
|          |        |          |
|          |        |          |
|          |        |          |
|          |        |          |

*Inquiry Journal • Project Planning Calendar*          UNIT 1  **11**

***Inquiry Journal pp. 10–11***

---

LA.C.3.2.2.3.1, LA.C.3.2.5.3.1

## Investigating Concepts Beyond the Text

Using questions students have raised will engage them in activities of their own choosing that allow them to explore friendship more deeply. These investigations may relate to the current selection or to a number of selections, but they must revolve around the concepts.

After the last selection, students began asking questions and became familiar with the different presentation options. If necessary, briefly review with students each item on **Reading Transparency 2** to make sure they understand some of their choices. Students should at this point form into groups based on shared areas of interest. Introduce the schedule you have planned for the investigation projects. Have students record important dates on the calendars in their **Inquiry Journals,** pages 10–11. Conduct a free-floating discussion of questions about the unit theme. As you do, model for students the difference between an investigation topic (for example, germs) and an investigation problem or question (for example, Do germs have anything to do with medicine?). The investigation problems and questions will lead students in determining what the primary objective of their investigation topic will be.

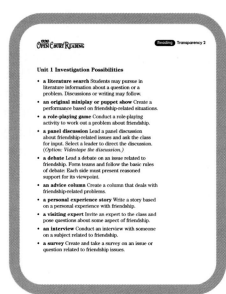

***Reading Transparency 2***

Have students share their investigation questions with the group for discussion. At this time you might suggest the following to get them started. Some students might want to find out, through reading, about famous people who came to the United States from other countries and about their experiences with making friends. They might consider writing about these experiences or making a photo essay to present to the class. If the technology is available, a multimedia presentation is another option. A second choice students might make is to conduct an interview as part of their investigation. Remind them that Raymond listened to and wrote down Ut's story. In this way, he came to know and understand Ut better. Have students talk about people they know in their school or neighborhood who moved to the United States from other countries. These people may be students in their own or in other grades, or teachers, school staff members, family members, or neighbors. Have the students think about how they can find out about the experiences and difficulties these people had trying to form friendships when they first came to this country.

# Concept/Question Board

After reading each selection, students should use the Concept/Question Board to do the following:

- Post any questions they asked about a selection before reading that haven't been answered yet.
- Refer to as they formulate statements about concepts that apply to their investigations.
- Post general statements formulated by each collaborative group.
- Continue to post news articles, or other items that they find during the unit investigation.
- Read and think about posted questions, articles, or concepts that interest them and provide answers to the questions.

**Concept/Question Board**

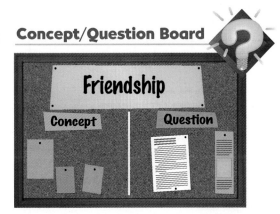

**Friendship**

Concept | Question

**INVESTIGATION**

**Teacher Tip** INVESTIGATION ACTIVITIES To assist students in these early investigation activities, continue to provide support by giving them limited choices and modeling the procedure step by step.

## Research Assistant
The *Research Assistant CD-ROM* assists students in their investigations.

**www.sra4kids.com**
**Web Connection**
More information about Friendship and links to Web sites concerning friendship can be found at www.sra4kids.com.

## Unit I  Investigation Management

| Lesson I | **Collaborative Investigation** Introduce the investigation cycle and explain its purpose. Students can lead a panel discussion on friendship-related issues. |
|---|---|
| Lesson 2 | **Collaborative Investigation** <br> **Students organize into groups based on shared areas of interest.** <br> **Supplementary Activities** <br> **Students can decide to read about famous immigrants to the United States to learn about their experiences making friends, or students can choose to interview someone who has first-hand experience moving to a new country and making friends. Fiction is another rich source of information.** |
| Lesson 3 | Students investigate mending damaged friendships, and groups begin forming conjectures. |
| Lesson 4 | Students begin their investigations. Groups can share personal stories, hold a panel discussion, or invite an expert speaker to class. |
| Lesson 5 | Students revise investigation plans as necessary. Groups discuss teammate qualities and invite a coach to class to interview. |
| Lesson 6 | Students wrap up investigations and prepare formal presentations. Students can discuss standing by friends and write a scene or miniplay about a scenario. |

**INVESTIGATION**

**Teacher Tip** Since this is early in the year, notice how small groups are working together. Offer coaching, if necessary, to help the groups work well together. Encourage each student to freely participate and also to listen attentively to the contributions of others.

**Teacher Tip** When interviewing, remind students that their questions might stimulate sensitive issues, such as the difficulty in making new friends. Remind them to be considerate of the feelings of those people they interview.

## Formal Assessment

Use the Research Rubrics on page 28J to assess students' ability to formulate research questions and problems.

# Interviewing

Explain to students that people can be good sources of information. Interviewing people can be a helpful tool for their investigations. Before students conduct an interview, have them formulate questions. Remind students that they should try to find out how the person they will interview handled being in a strange, new place; what problems arose and how those problems were solved; and how this person made friends here.

Since this is still an early stage in the school year, students might still need extra guidance during this portion of their investigations. Pages 12–13 in their *Inquiry Journals* will help them begin thinking about formulating interview questions. Have students work in small groups to complete the page.

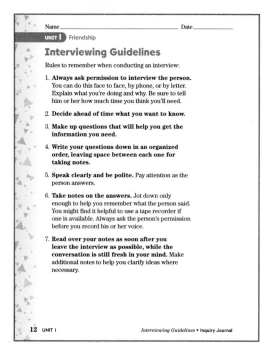

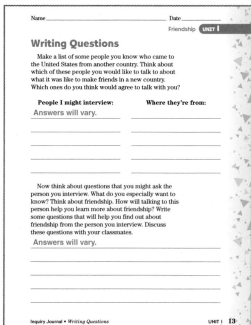

*Inquiry Journal pp. 12–13*

# Choosing Appropriate Sources LA.D.2.2.4.3.1

**Teach** Tell students that there are many ways to find information about a subject of interest. One way to gather information is to ask questions of family members, friends, teachers, and people who are likely to know the subject well. People who specialize in a particular subject or who have first-hand experience in a particular area are said to be *experts* on those subjects. Consulting experts firsthand is often difficult, but looking up information written by experts is easy. List the following sources on the board and discuss each one.

- An *atlas* is a book of maps and related geographical information.
- A *dictionary* contains words and definitions listed in alphabetical order. Students can use dictionaries if they need to find spellings or meanings of words.
- A *thesaurus* contains synonyms and antonyms for words listed in alphabetical order.
- An *encyclopedia* is a set of books that contain information with entries and articles on many subjects.
- Current *magazines* and *newspapers* contain up-to-date information.
- An *expert* can provide valuable first-hand information.
- A *museum* features informative exhibits and experts.
- Web sites on the *Internet* provide information on a wide range of topics. Tell students that not all Web sites are equally reliable. Respected educational sites are the most likely to provide reliable information.

**Guided Practice** For practice identifying appropriate sources, students can use the sample questions and list of sources on pages 14–15 of the ***Inquiry Journal.*** Students can work independently or in small groups to complete the activity.

**Independent Practice** Have students think of a subject that interests them, preferably one related to their investigation in this unit. Students should then consider the best sources for information about that subject. Have them write out a list of specific questions and then note where they are most likely to find the answers.

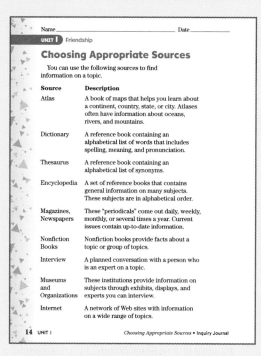

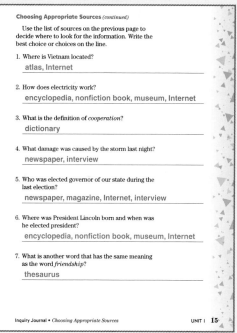

*Inquiry Journal pp. 14–15*

**Teacher Tip** Consider assigning tasks to students so that groups function effectively. For example, students can be assigned tasks to ensure that:

- ✔ everyone has a chance to participate.
- ✔ people stay on task.
- ✔ notes are taken.
- ✔ noise level is appropriate.
- ✔ thoughts and opinions are respected.

## Objectives

**Word Analysis**

**Spelling**
- **The /e/ Sound.** Develop understanding of the /e/ sound spelled *e* and *ea*.

**Vocabulary**
- **Context Clues.** Using words from "Angel Child, Dragon Child," learn to apply Context Clues to discover the meaning of an unknown word.

**Writing Process Strategies**
- **Prewriting.** The focus will be on choosing a topic based on audience and purpose and organizing ideas for writing through the use of graphic organizers.

**English Language Conventions**

**Grammar, Usage, and Mechanics**
- **Pronouns.** Learn what pronouns are, when they are used, and why. Find pronouns in "Angel Child, Dragon Child" and use pronouns in writing.

**Listening, Speaking, Viewing**
- **Speaking: Speaking Clearly.** Practice speaking clearly and at an appropriate volume.

**Penmanship**
- **Cursive Letters *u* and *w*.** Develop handwriting skills by practicing formation of cursive *u* and *w*.

## Materials

- Language Arts Handbook
- Language Arts Transparencies 7–10
- Comprehension and Language Arts Skills, pp. 4–7
- Spelling and Vocabulary Skills, pp. 6–9
- Writer's Workbook, p. 3
- Student Anthology

## MEETING INDIVIDUAL NEEDS

*Reteach, Challenge, English-Language Development,* and *Intervention* lessons are available to support the language arts instruction in this lesson.

## Research in Action

All the evidence we know of indicates that children's main problem with content is in getting access to, and giving order to, the knowledge they have.
(*Carl Bereiter* and *Marlene Scardamalia*, The Psychology of Written Composition)

---

# Language Arts Overview

## Word Analysis

**Spelling** The spelling activities on the following pages introduce the /e/ sound spelled *e* and *ea* by developing spelling skills through various strategies.

### Selection Spelling Words

These words from "Angel Child, Dragon Child" contain the /e/ sound.

th<u>e</u>m     s<u>e</u>nd     n<u>e</u>xt     b<u>e</u>ll     <u>e</u>dge

**Vocabulary** The Vocabulary activities extend the instruction of the Selection Vocabulary from "Angel Child, Dragon Child" to understanding Context Clues. A *context clue* is information from the immediate text that helps identify a word.

### Vocabulary Skill Words

jangled*     chant     thrilled     chives     margins*
*Also Selection Vocabulary*

## Writing Process Strategies

The Writing Process Strategies lesson involves instruction in the prewriting step of the writing process. Special attention is given to choosing a topic and using graphic organizers as a means of organizing ideas for writing. As practice for this skill, students will be prewriting their autobiography.

 **Basic Computer Skills** To introduce students to the computer as a writing tool, teach students how to open a file from the Desktop and open a file using the File menu. *Basic Computer Skills,* Level 3, Lesson 3, teaches these basic computer skills. LA.D.2.2.4.3.1

## English Language Conventions

**Grammar, Usage, and Mechanics** **Pronouns.** This lesson develops the concept of pronouns by teaching how to identify them and how they avoid repetition.

**Listening, Speaking, Viewing** **Speaking: Speaking Clearly.** In this Speaking lesson, students will review the skills important for clear, coherent speech, and will practice speaking in clear sentences and at an appropriate volume.

**Penmanship** **Cursive Letters *u* and *w*.** This lesson continues the development of cursive handwriting skills. Students learn correct formation of *u* and *w* and then practice writing words from the literature selection that contain those letters.

# DAY 1

| Word Analysis | Writing Process Strategies | English Language Conventions |
|---|---|---|

## Word Analysis

### Spelling

**Assessment: Pretest**

The /e/ Sound  LA.A.1.2.2.3.1

**Teach**

Give students the Pretest found on page 28 of *Unit 1 Assessment* as entry assessment for the spelling pattern. Have them proofread and correct any misspelled words.

**Pretest Sentences**

1. **deck**  A ship has a **deck**.
2. **tent**  Campers sleep in a **tent**.
3. **spent**  Money can be **spent**.
4. **fence**  A **fence** surrounds a house.
5. **head**  A CEO is the **head** of a company.
6. **dead**  A dry leaf is **dead**.
7. **bread**  A sandwich is made with **bread**.
8. **desk**  A student studies at a **desk**.
9. **thread**  A **thread** helps you sew.
10. **sweater**  Wearing a **sweater** keeps you warm.
11. **edge**  The **edge** of a knife is sharp.
12. **bell**  A school **bell** rings when class begins.
13. **next**  Red is **next** to orange on a rainbow.
14. **send**  You must buy a stamp to **send** a letter.
15. **them**  If you do not know **them**, they are strangers.

Diagnose any misspellings by determining whether students misspelled the /e/ sound or some other part of the word. Then use the Pretest as a take-home list for students to study the spellings of the /e/ sound.

## Writing Process Strategies

**Prewriting**  LA.B.1.2.1.3.2

**Introduction to the Writing Process**

**Teach**

**Introduce Writing Process Steps**

Read *Language Arts Handbook,* page 18, to introduce prewriting.

**Inspiration**

Teacher Model: *"After I get an idea I want to write about, I have to decide my purpose and who will be reading my writing. Once I decide, I can use a graphic organizer to make sure I get all my thoughts in order."*

**Brainstorming**

- Using description as the type of writing, encourage students to explain what thoughts they would have before they begin to write. Make a list of things they could describe on the board.
- Explain to students that there are many kinds of graphic organizers, depending on the type of writing to be done.
- Work through *Language Arts Transparency 9,* Spatial Order Graphic Organizer.

**Guided Practice**

**Prewriting**

Have students draw and fill in a spatial order graphic organizer.

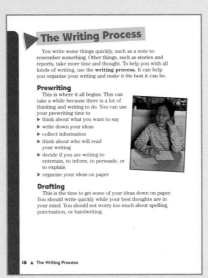

*Language Arts Handbook p. 18*

## English Language Conventions

**Grammar, Usage, and Mechanics**

Grammar: Pronouns  LA.B.1.2.3.3.3

**Teach**

- Explain that a pronoun takes the place of a noun in a sentence. Use the personal pronouns *I, me, you, he, she,* and *we* as examples. Write them on the board.
- Write the following sentence on the board.
  - *Hoa was scared the first day of school because Hoa missed her mother.*

  Then substitute one instance of the name *Hoa* with the appropriate pronoun, to show students how pronouns are used to avoid repetition. *(Hoa was scared the first day of school because she missed her mother.)*
- Use *Language Arts Handbook,* pages 248–249, for the definition and examples of pronouns and how they are used.

**Independent Practice**

Use *Comprehension and Language Arts Skills,* pages 6–7, to practice identifying pronouns.

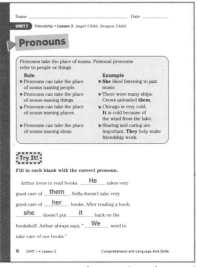

*Comprehension and Language Arts Skills p. 6*

# DAY 2

## Word Analysis

### Spelling

**Word Sorting** LA.A.1.2.2.3.1

- Hold up *Sound/Spelling Card 5*. Ask the class to say *hen* and listen to the /e/ sound made by the letter *e*.
- **Word Sort.** Have students say each spelling word, listening for the /e/ sound, and sort the words under the correct column: 1: /e/ *Sound Spelled* e or 2: /e/ *Sound Spelled* ea.

### Vocabulary

**Context Clues** LA.A.1.2.1.3.1

#### Teach

- Write *strawberry* on the board. Define *context clue* as a word or words near a hard word that help explain the word.
- Explain how clues within a sentence, as on page 7 of *Spelling and Vocabulary Skills*, can help them understand the basic meaning of an unfamiliar word. Read the first sentence and discuss why *strawberry* fits in the context of the sentence. (*A milkshake would not be made from a* mustache, garage, squawked, *or* minute.)

#### Guided Practice

Use *Spelling and Vocabulary Skills*, page 6, to reinforce context clues. Have students complete page 7 as independent practice.

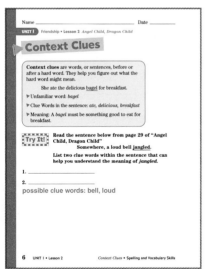

*Spelling and Vocabulary Skills p. 6*

## Writing Process Strategies

### Prewriting LA.B.1.2.1.3.2

**Introduction to the Writing Process**

#### Teach

- **Review** the purpose of using graphic organizers.
- Remind students that there are many types of writing, giving examples such as friendly letters, descriptions, personal narratives, research reports, biographies, and so on.
- Work through *Language Arts Transparency 7*, Time Line Graphic Organizer.
- Ask students what types of writing they would use a time line with to organize their thoughts.

#### Guided Practice

**Prewriting**

Ask students to make a rough time line of things they remember in their lives so far.

## English Language Conventions

### Grammar, Usage, and Mechanics

**Grammar: Pronouns** LA.B.1.2.3.3.3

#### Teach

- **Review** what pronouns do, and why writers and speakers use them.
- Write the following sentences on the board and have students suggest what pronouns can or should replace the second occurrence of the noun.
  - Alaska is the biggest state, but Alaska does not have a big population. (*Change second* Alaska *to* it.)
  - Since Keesha is only five years old, Keesha is not old enough to ride the bus downtown alone. (*Change second* Keesha *to* she.)
  - Horses sleep standing up, but horses lie down when they are sick. (*Change second* horses *to* they.)
  - James ate so much that James got sick and had to lie down. (*Change second* James *to* he.)

#### Guided Practice in Reading

Select two pages of "Angel Child, Dragon Child." Group the students in pairs. Ask each pair to identify the pronouns on each page.

# DAY 3

| Word Analysis | Writing Process Strategies | English Language Conventions |

## Word Analysis

### Spelling

**The /e/ Sound** LA.A.1.2.2.3.1

**Teach**

- Introduce words with the /e/ sound spelled *e* and *ea* by listening for words with the /e/ sound found in "Angel Child, Dragon Child." Students should try to find the five Selection Spelling Words in the story.
- Ask students to find some objects in the room that contain the /e/ sound (*possible answer: desk*).

**Guided Practice**

Have students complete page 8 from **Spelling and Vocabulary Skills** to reinforce the different spelling patterns for the /e/ sound.

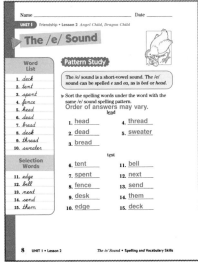

**Spelling and Vocabulary Skills p. 8**

### Vocabulary (continued)

**Context Clues** LA.A.1.2.1.3.1

- Ask students to share the context clues they chose for the words *jangled*, *chant*, and *trilled*.
- Have students share their ideas for discovering the meanings of those words. Ask three students to talk through their reasoning for the meaning of each one of the words.

## Writing Process Strategies

**Prewriting** LA.B.1.2.1.3.2

**Introduction to the Writing Process**

**Teach**

- Ask students what parts are included in a story. They may say characters, setting, and plot. Have them identify these parts in "Gloria Who Might Be My Best Friend" or "Angel Child, Dragon Child."
- Explain to students that a story map is a good graphic organizer to use when prewriting for a story.
- Discuss **Language Arts Transparency 8**, Story Map Graphic Organizer, with students.

**Guided Practice**

**Prewriting**

Have students draw and complete a story map.

## English Language Conventions

### Grammar, Usage, and Mechanics

**Grammar: Pronouns** LA.B.1.2.3.3.3

**Teach**

- Use **Language Arts Handbook**, pages 248–249, to teach about pronouns.
- Invite students to apply pronouns to the people and things in the classroom.

**Guided Practice in Writing**

Ask students to write four sentences, each about something they did with a friend. They should use a different pronoun in each sentence.

 **Informal Assessment**

Check students' work to make sure they are using personal pronouns properly.

# DAY 4

| Word Analysis | Writing Process Strategies | English Language Conventions |
| --- | --- | --- |

## Word Analysis

### Spelling

**The /e/ Sound** LA.A.1.2.2.3.1

#### Teach
- Explain to students that the exercises on page 9 in *Spelling and Vocabulary Skills* are designed to help them become better spellers through the use of strategies.
- Demonstrate the Rhyming strategy and the rationale for this strategy by writing *bend* on the board. Show students that knowing the spelling for *bend* can help them know the spelling for the rhyming words *send*, *mend*, and *lend*.

#### Guided Practice
Have students complete the Spelling Strategies exercises on page 9 of *Spelling and Vocabulary Skills* to reinforce the spelling patterns for the /e/ sound.

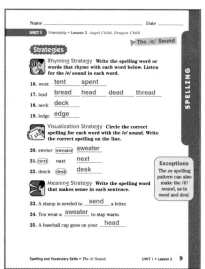

*Spelling and Vocabulary Skills p. 9*

### Vocabulary (continued)

**Context Clues** LA.C.3.2.2.3.1
- Ask the students to share the Context Clue Words they chose for *chives* and *margins*.
- Have students share their ideas for discovering the meanings of those words.

## Writing Process Strategies

### Prewriting  LA.B.1.2.1.3.2
**Introduction to the Writing Process**

#### Teach
- Review audience, purpose, and task as they apply to prewriting.
- Go over *Language Arts Transparency 10,* Chain of Events Graphic Organizer. Discuss for what types of writing this might help them plan. Possible answers include realistic fiction, news story, biography, and so on.

#### Guided Practice
**Prewriting**
Have students draw and complete a chain of events graphic organizer.

## English Language Conventions

### Listening, Speaking, Viewing
**Speaking: Speaking Clearly** LA.C.3.2.1.3.1

#### Teach
- We learned about asking questions in Reading and Responding. Here, we'll learn how speaking clearly is important when we talk to others or ask questions.
- Remind the class how important it is to speak clearly. When we tell others what we are thinking or give directions or explanations, we want to be understood by others.
- We must speak carefully, making sure to say each word slowly, clearly, and loudly enough to be heard, yet not so loudly as to shout. We should finish our sentences and not trail off or turn away before we finish speaking.

#### Guided Practice
- Tell students they are going to read aloud a sentence from either "Angel Child, Dragon Child" or "Janey." Give them a few minutes to find a sentence they want to read.
- Have students take turns reading their sentences aloud. Remind them to speak clearly and loudly enough for others to hear. Ask them to speak more slowly if they are rushing. Gently correct and encourage all efforts.

 **Informal Assessment**

Observe whether students are able to speak clearly at an appropriate rate and volume.

# DAY 5

| Word Analysis | Writing Process Strategies | English Language Conventions |
|---|---|---|

## Word Analysis

### Spelling

#### Assessment: Final Test
**The /e/ Sound** LA.A.1.2.2.3.1

#### Teach
Repeat the Pretest or use the Final Test on page 29 of **Unit 1 Assessment** as summative assessment for student understanding of the /e/ sound spelling patterns.

**Unit 1 Assessment p. 29**

#### Guided Practice
Have students categorize any mistakes they made on the Final Test. Are they careless errors? Are they lesson-pattern problems? Check to see if students correctly spell the /e/ sound in their writing.

### Vocabulary LA.A.1.2.1.3.1

 **Informal Assessment**

Periodically check to see if the students use context clues to help them learn more about unfamiliar words they read. Add any new words to their running list of vocabulary words in the Writer's Notebook.

## Writing Process Strategies

### Prewriting LA.B.1.2.1.3.2
**Introduction to the Writing Process**

#### Teach
- Review **Language Arts Transparency 7** on time lines with students.
- Discuss what information would be appropriate for an autobiography.

#### Independent Practice
**Prewriting**
Have students fill out the information on **Writer's Workbook,** page 3, to be used when they write their autobiographies.

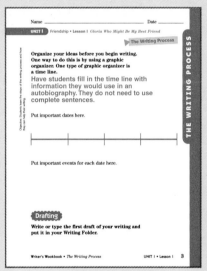

**Writer's Workbook p. 3**

## English Language Conventions

### Penmanship LA.B.1.2.2
**Cursive Letters *u* and *w***

#### Teach
- **Teacher Model:** Tell students that all cursive letters are made of four types of strokes (undercurve, downcurve, overcurve, and slant lines). Draw them on the board.
- Explain to students how important it is for their letters to slant to the right.
- **Teacher Model:** Introduce lowercase cursive *u* and *w* as undercurve letters by demonstrating on the board.

**u** Starting point, undercurve
Slant down, undercurve
Slant down, undercurve:
small *u*

**w** Starting point, undercurve
Slant down, undercurve
Slant down, undercurve,
Small curve to right: small *w*

- **Teacher Model:** Write the words *under, world, snow,* and *mouth* to model proper letter formation and slant.

#### Guided Practice
- Invite students to come to the board and trace the letters *u* and *w*.
- Have students practice writing rows of *u* and *w* in their Writer's Notebooks.
- From "Angel Child, Dragon Child," have students write the words *up, you, words,* and *funny* to practice letter formation.

 **Informal Assessment**

Check students' handwriting for proper slant and that the undercurves in their *u*'s and *w*'s do not "float" between the lines.

## LESSON WRAP-UP

# Reading and Language Arts Skills Traces

## Language Arts

### WORD ANALYSIS

**Skills Trace**

**Spelling: The /e/ Sound**

Introduced in Grade 1.
Scaffolded throughout Grades 2–5.
**REINTRODUCED:** Unit 1, Lesson 2, p. 45E
**PRACTICED:** Unit 1, Lesson 2, pp. 45F–45J
*Spelling and Vocabulary Skills,*
pp. 8–9
**TESTED:** Unit 1, Lesson 2, p. 45J
Unit 1 Assessment

**Skills Trace**

**Vocabulary: Context Clues**

Introduced in Grade 1.
Scaffolded throughout Grades 2–5.
**REINTRODUCED:** Unit 1, Lesson 2, p. 45E
**PRACTICED:** Unit 1, Lesson 2, pp. 45G–45J
*Spelling and Vocabulary Skills,*
pp. 6–7
**TESTED:** Unit 1 Assessment

## Reading

### COMPREHENSION

**Cause and Effect**

Introduced in Grade 1.
Scaffolded throughout Grades 2 and 3.
**REINTRODUCED:** Unit 1, Lesson 2
**REINFORCED:** Unit 1, Lesson 4
Unit 2, Lesson 4
Unit 2, Lesson 5
Unit 4, Lesson 2
Unit 4, Lesson 7
Unit 6, Lesson 6
**TESTED:** Unit 1 Assessment

### WRITING PROCESS STRATEGIES

**Skills Trace**

**Introduction to the Writing Process: Prewriting**

Introduced in Grade K.
Scaffolded throughout Grades 1–6.
**REINTRODUCED:** Unit 1, Lesson 2, p. 45F
**PRACTICED:** Unit 1, Lesson 2, pp. 45G–45J
*Writer's Workbook,* p. 3
**TESTED:** Unit 1 Assessment

### ENGLISH LANGUAGE CONVENTIONS

**Skills Trace**

**Grammar: Pronouns**

Introduced in Grade K.
Scaffolded throughout Grades 1–6.
**REINTRODUCED:** Unit 1, Lesson 2, p. 45F
**PRACTICED:** Unit 1, Lesson 2, p. 45G
Unit 1, Lesson 2, p. 45H
*Comprehension and Language
Arts Skills,* pp. 6–7
**TESTED:** Unit 1, Lesson 2,
Informal Assessment, p. 45H
Unit 1 Assessment

**Skills Trace**

**Listening, Speaking, Viewing
Speaking: Speaking Clearly**

Introduced in Grade K.
Scaffolded throughout Grades 1–5.
**REINTRODUCED:** Unit 1, Lesson 2, p. 45I
**TESTED:** Unit 1, Lesson 2,
Informal Assessment, p. 45I

**Skills Trace**

**Penmanship: Cursive Letters *u* and *w***

Introduced in Grade 2.
Scaffolded throughout Grades 3–6.
**REINTRODUCED:** Unit 1, Lesson 2, p. 45J
**TESTED:** Unit 1, Lesson 2,
Informal Assessment, p. 45J

# Professional Development: Comprehension

## Literal Comprehension

Students' productive, literal comprehension depends in large part on their skill in *decoding*, or word *recognition*, and on the breadth and depth of their *vocabulary knowledge.*

### What Does Research Tell Us About Decoding and Comprehension?

Much research has established that good readers are skillful at decoding words on the basis of graphophonemic, or sound/spelling, cues. To pronounce a word, these readers sound it out, blending the individual sounds represented by the word's letters. Once they have sounded it out, they can recognize what a word means, because most of the words in the materials they read are words that have been in their listening and speaking vocabularies for several years (Gough & Tunmer, 1986). In fact, researchers who have studied decoding make the point emphatically that poor word-level decoding is a critical bottleneck in the comprehension process. When a reader cannot recognize or decode a word, it is impossible for him or her to understand what the word means (Adams, 1990; Pressley, 1998).

Once readers achieve fluency, they seldom sound out words letter by letter as they read. Even when they encounter words they do not know, good readers tend to process them by recognizing common letter chunks, such as prefixes; suffixes; Latin and Greek root words; and rimes (the parts of syllables that follow the initial consonants) such as *-ight*, *-on*, *-ite*, and *-ake* (Ehri, 1992). Thus, good readers do not sound out a word such as *kite* letter by letter; rather, they blend the initial /k/ sound with what they know about the sound of the rime *-ite*. From the time children first learn to read, they are recognizing common letter chunks as wholes and using this knowledge to help them decode (Goswami, 1998).

A lack of skill in decoding words directly affects students' higher order comprehension. This is because word recognition and comprehension compete for attention: The more effort readers require to decode a word, the less attention they have left for comprehension. If readers have to struggle with words, they can easily lose track of meaning. Further, it is the words in a text that constitute the basic data with which the higher-order comprehension processes must work. When readers skip words in a text or fail to understand the words of the text, comprehension suffers (Adams, 1990).

Therefore, it is evident why the primary levels of ***Open Court Reading*** emphasize the development of reading fluency rather than just the sounding out of words. Fluent readers can devote less attention to word recognition and more attention to comprehension. Most teachers have worked with young students who can sound out words—with some effort—but who do not seem to understand or remember any of what they read. All of their attention is consumed by word recognition to the exclusion of comprehension (Gough & Tunmer, 1986; LaBerge & Samuels, 1974).

*Additional information about comprehension as well as resource references can be found in the ***Professional Development Guide: Comprehension.***

## Activating Prior Knowledge LA.E.1.2.5.3.1

- Preteach this lesson by inviting volunteers to talk about what it is like to have a best friend move away.

- Direct students' attention to the illustrations and invite them to discuss how the two friends must feel about each other. How might this poem relate to the unit theme of Friendship? *(It shows a friendship. However, these two friends cannot be together.)* What do the illustrations show about the two girls? *(They look sad because they are apart from each other.)*

## Reading the Poem LA.C.1.2.1.3.1

- Read the poem aloud twice in a voice that reflects the feeling of the girl whose friend Janey has moved away. Encourage students to close their eyes as you read and listen very carefully.

- The poem contains several words and expressions that students might find difficult to understand. Help them to understand the meaning of the words *clinging* (sticking closely), *privet hedge* (a hedge made up of evergreen shrubs), and *stucco* (plaster or cement used to cover outside walls).

Tell students that when reading a poem aloud, they should continue reading until they come to a punctuation mark. Point out that poetry is often written in rhythmic lines but that the reader should not pause at the end of a line unless there is a punctuation mark.

- In the time you designate for Workshop, encourage students to listen to the recording of the poem on the *Listening Library Audiocassette/CD.*

*Focus Questions* What is it like to have a best friend who moves away? What can you do to help keep a friend who moves away?

# Janey

Charlotte Zolotow
*illustrated by Leah Palmer Preiss*

Janey
it's lonely
all day long
since you moved away.

When I walk in the rain
and the leaves are wet
and clinging to the sidewalk
I remember
how we used to walk
home from school
together.

I remember how you had to touch
everything we passed,
the wet leaves
of the <u>privet</u> <u>hedge</u>,
even the <u>stucco</u> part
of the wall.
I only look with my eyes.

I still have the pebble
you found on the
playground.
And I remember how
you skipped flat rocks
into the pond.
Mine just sank.

46

**Teacher Tip** Teach students when reading prose and poetry aloud to do so with fluency, rhythm, and pace, using appropriate intonation and vocal patterns to emphasize important passages of the text being read.

Sometimes when I'm playing
with the other kids
I remember how your voice sounded.
No one else sounds like you.

I remember sometimes
we both talked at once
and when we stopped
we'd said the same thing.
And I remember sitting on the steps
in the sun and not talking
at all.
There is no one else
I can sit with
and not talk.

I remember how
we'd go home for dinner
and I could hardly wait
for dinner to end
to call you.
But sometimes you called me first.

And I remember last Christmas
I half didn't want
to give you your present,
I wanted it so much myself.

You told me later
you half didn't want to give me mine
but when we each opened our present
it was the *same* book.
I think of you every time
I read the stories over again.

When the wind blows
through the trees at night
I remember how we used to
listen together
nights you slept over.

I didn't want you to move away.
You didn't want to either.
Janey
maybe some day
we'll grow up
and live near each other
again.

I wish you hadn't moved away.

47

## Writer's Notebook

Have the students write the following question in their Writer's Notebooks:

- What does this poem teach about friendship?

Then have students write their answers to the question in the response section of their Writer's Notebooks.

## Meet the Poet

Charlotte Zolotow was born in Norfolk, Virginia. She moved to Detroit when she was three years old. Even at that early age, she remembers telling anyone who asked, "I'm going to be an author."

Zolotow has written many picture books and has won several awards. For many of her books, she draws on memories of her own childhood. She has compared the mind of a child with that of a poet: "Their imagery . . . and their freshness fascinate me, and the intensity of their emotions is often greater than [that of] adults."

**Teacher Tip** Continue modeling comprehension strategies for students. For this poem, Making Connections will help students understand what the speaker is communicating. Some students might find visualizing a helpful strategy with this selection.

As the students study poetry, they will learn that there are many elements that make up a poem. Have students look at "Janey" and discuss the following element with them.

## Repetition LA.E.2.2.2.3.1

Explain that the poet emphasizes the poem's message by repeating certain words and phrases. Reread the poem with students and help them identify words and phrases that are repeated *(I remember, moved away)*. What do these repeated words indicate about the poem's message? Sometimes poets use repetition to set the rhythm of a poem as well as to emphasize meaning.

Explain to students that another form of repetition is alliteration. Alliteration is the repetition of the same sound at the beginning of several words in a phrase or sentence. For example:

- Calico cats are cute and cuddly.
- Richie ran rapidly around the racetrack.
- Shelly adopted a Shetland sheepdog from the animal shelter.
- Wilma wed Warren by the waterside.

Locate several poems with examples of alliteration. Have students identify the repeated letters and sounds. Then have students write several sentences of their own using alliteration. Tell them to start with a sentence that uses their own name.

## Writing

Students can respond to poetry by writing poems of their own. Have them think about a time when they or someone they know moved away. Did they leave a special friend behind, or did a special friend leave to move to a new place? What things did they miss about that person? If some students have never had that experience, ask them to think about a special friend they have now. If that friend were to move away, what would they miss about that person? Have students write a poem about their friend and what they would miss if that person moved away. Encourage them to write at least two sentences and to use repetition to emphasize rhythm or important ideas.

# Presentation

## Emphasis  LA.C.3.2.3.3.1; LA.D.2.2.1.3.1

Poetry is a special kind of writing in which the sounds and the meanings of the words are combined to create ideas or feelings. Poets use certain words or phrases to convey an idea or feeling. The way a poem is read can greatly effect its meaning. The reader can emphasize words to make them stand out. The reader can emphasize a word by changing his or her volume, pitch, or speed. Encourage students to read slowly so they can have more noticeable control over their volume, pitch, and speed of reading.

Read the poem again, but this time change the volume of your voice as you read to emphasize a word. Demonstrate how you can read a word more softly or loudly for emphasis. Have students listen carefully to hear which word stands out. Then demonstrate how you can emphasize a word by reading it more slowly or quickly. Have students listen carefully to hear which word stands out.

Have students choose between reciting either "Janey" or their own poem. Tell students to write the poem on a piece of paper. Then have them think about which words they want to emphasize. Tell them to underline or circle the words on their papers for easy identification during their reading. Have the audience identify which words were emphasized and speculate about why the reader chose those words. Finally, remind students to stand up straight with their shoulders back and to look at their audience when they speak.

**LISTENING/SPEAKING/VIEWING**

**Teacher Tip PRESENTATION** Have students think about the point of view of the poem "Janey." Who is talking in the poem? If students recite this poem, have them pretend they are that speaker and recite the poem as that person would say it.

*Focus Questions* What is it like to have a friend be mean to you? How can you make up with a friend when you realize the friendship is more important than whatever caused the fight?

# The Tree House

Lois Lowry
*illustrated by Trina Schart Hyman*

It was a terrific tree house. *Better* than terrific: It was a marvelous, magnificent, one-of-a-kind tree house, with wooden walls painted bright blue. It had two windows, with red shutters on each, and a yellow door with two shiny brass hinges and a small brass bell that rang when you pulled a string. There was a little porch where you could sit with your legs dangling.

Inside were a table, a chair, a small rug with fringe on each end, and two fat pillows so that you could lie on the rug and read.

You reached it by climbing a ladder—a ladder to the best tree house ever. And it belonged to Chrissy.

48

**SELECTION INTRODUCTION**

## Selection Summary

### Genre: Realistic Fiction

Chrissy is thrilled when her grandfather builds her the best tree house she has ever seen. It's not complete, though, until Chrissy hangs a "Keep Out!" sign on the door. Chrissy's friend Leah decides to have a tree house built, too. Each girl spends time alone in her tree house, and they do not speak to each other. Finally, the girls discover that a tree house is best when shared with a friend. Can two girls with two tree houses find a way to share?

Some of the elements of realistic fiction are:

- The characters behave as people do in real life.
- The setting of the story is a real place or could be a real place.
- The events in the story could happen in real life.

## About the Author

"The Tree House," by **Lois Lowry**, is from an anthology of stories called *The Big Book for Peace*, which was named a Notable Children's Trade Book in the Field of Social Studies and an IRA Teacher's Choice. Lowry has also won the Newbery Medal and the International Reading Association Children's Book Award for other works.

Students can read more about Lois Lowry on page 60 of the ***Student Anthology.***

## About the Illustrator

**Trina Schart Hyman** has won numerous awards for her illustrations, including the Caldecott Medal for *St. George and the Dragon.* Her *Little Red Riding Hood* was named a Caldecott Honor Book. When Hyman accepted the Caldecott Medal, she told of her love of books. She said, "When I'm upset or depressed or unhappy, I go to a bookstore for comfort . . . Books and illustrations are part of me: They're not just what I do; they're what I *am.*"

Students can read more about Trina Schart Hyman on page 60 of the ***Student Anthology.***

## Inquiry Connections

In the story, two girls discover that sharing makes a friendship even more special. Below are some key concepts to be explored.

- The pleasure of having things does not compare to the pleasure of having friends.
- Sharing something with a friend increases its worth.
- Sharing is something that true friends do.

Before reading the selection:

- Point out that students may post a question, concept, word, illustration, or object at any time during the course of their unit investigation. Be sure that students include their name or initials on the items they post so that others will know whom to go to if they have an answer or if they wish to collaborate on a related activity.

- Students should feel free to write an answer or a note on someone else's question or to consult the Board for ideas for their own investigations throughout the unit.

- Encourage students to read about friendship at home and to bring in articles or pictures that are good examples to post on the Board.

- Students may have questions about why the tree houses would be a problem. Some students may think they know the answer. Encourage these students to place questions and answers on the Concept/Question Board.

**Concept/Question Board**

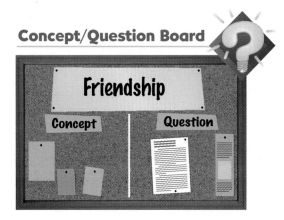

## PROGRAM RESOURCES

## Leveled Practice

**Reteach**
**Pages 10–15**

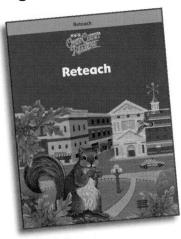

**Challenge**
**Pages 9–13**

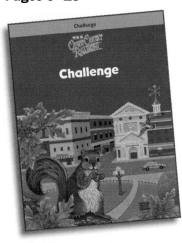

**ELD Workbook**

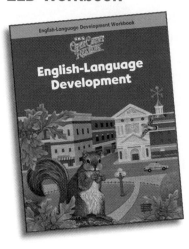

**Intervention Workbook**

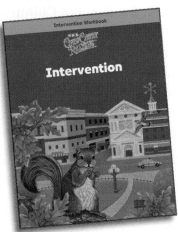

**Decodable Book 13**

## Leveled Classroom Library\*

Encourage students to read at least 30 minutes daily outside of class. Have them read books in the ***Leveled Classroom Library*** to support the unit theme and help students develop their vocabulary by reading independently.

### *Alex Is My Friend*

BY MARISABINA RUSSO. GREENWILLOW BROOKS, 1992.

Alex and Ben have been friends since they were little enough to ride in strollers. The friends overcome their differences, even when one is often restricted to a wheelchair. **(Easy)**

### *And to Think That We Thought That We'd Never be Friends*

BY MARY ANN HOBERMAN, CROWN PUBLISHERS, INC., 1999.

Inspired by Dr. Suess' *And to Think That I Saw It on Mulberry Street*, this is a story of how quickly disputes come to an end, and how friendship spreads like wildfire. A friendship started between siblings leads to everyone dancing and playing music in the streets. **(Average)**

### *Best Friends*

BY LORETTA KRUPINSKI. HYPERION, 1998.

Charlotte befriends a Native American girl, Lily, upon moving from her home in Kansas to the Wild West. They communicate through signs and laughter. The unlikely friends are tested when Charlotte learns of the soldiers' plans to drive Lily's tribe off their land. **(Advanced)**

\* These books, which all support the unit theme Friendship, are part of a 36-book ***Leveled Classroom Library*** available for purchase from SRA/McGraw-Hill. Note: Teachers should preview any trade books for appropriateness in their classrooms before recommending them to students.

# TECHNOLOGY

## Web Connections

  **www.sra4kids.com**
**Friendship Web Site**

## CD-ROMs

 \***Research Assistant**
SRA/MCGRAW-HILL, 2002

 \***Decodable Book Activities**
SRA/MCGRAW-HILL, 2002

## Computer Skills

\* **Basic Computer Skills**

## Audiocassettes/CDs

 \***Listening Library: Friendship**
SRA/MCGRAW-HILL, 2002

 \***Sound/Spelling Card Stories**
SRA/MCGRAW-HILL, 2002

Titles preceded by an asterisk (\*) are available through SRA/McGraw-Hill. Other titles can be obtained by contacting the publisher listed with the title.

**LESSON PLANNER**

| Suggested Pacing: 3–5 days | DAY 1 | DAY 2 |
|---|---|---|
| | **DAY 1** | **DAY 2** |

## 1 Preparing to Read

**Materials**
- Student Anthology, Book 1, pp. 48–61
- Decodable Book Activities CD-ROM
- Sound/Spelling Card 33
- Decodable Book 13
- Lesson Model Videocassette
- Routine Cards 1, 3, Routines 1–2, 8–9

**DAY 1**

**Word Knowledge, p. 48K**
- antonyms
- homophones
- prefix *re-*
- related words
- review /i/

**About the Words and Sentences, pp. 48K–48L**

**DAY 2**

**Word Knowledge**

**Developing Oral Language, p. 48L**

## 2 Reading & Responding

**Materials**
- Student Anthology, Book 1, pp. 48–61
- Program Assessment
- Reading Transparencies 5, 46, 50
- Inquiry Journal, p. 3
- Home Connection, p. 7
- Unit 1 Assessment, pp. 10–13
- Comprehension and Language Arts Skills, pp. 8–9
- Writer's Notebook
- Routine Cards 1–2, Routines 3–6

**DAY 1**

**Build Background, p. 48O**
**Preview and Prepare, pp. 48O–48P**
**Selection Vocabulary, p. 48P**
**Reading Recommendations, pp. 48Q–48R**
**Student Anthology, pp. 48–53** First Read
✓ **Comprehension Strategies**
- **Making Connections, p. 48**
- **Visualizing, p. 50**
- **Asking Questions, p. 52**

**DAY 2**

**Student Anthology, pp. 54–59** First Read
**Comprehension Strategies**
- **Making Connections, pp. 54, 58**
- **Asking Questions, pp. 56, 58**
- **Visualizing, p. 56**

**Discussing Strategy Use, p. 58**
**Discussing the Selection, p. 59A**
- **Review Selection**
- **Complete Discussion**

**Meet the Author/Illustrator, p. 60**
✓ **Theme Connections, p. 61**

## Inquiry

**Materials**
- Student Anthology, Book 1, pp. 48–61
- Inquiry Journal, pp. 16–19
- Research Assistant CD-ROM

**Investigation**
- **Investigating Concepts Beyond the Text: Conjecture and Needs, p. 61A**

**Investigation**
- **Concept/Question Board, p. 61B**

## 3 Language Arts

**Materials**
- Comprehension and Language Arts Skills, pp. 8–13
- Language Arts Handbook, pp. 18, 28, 180, 246
- Language Arts Transparencies 24–25
- Sound/Spelling Card 9
- Spelling and Vocabulary Skills, pp. 10–13
- Student Anthology
- Writer's Workbook, p. 3

**Word Analysis**
- ✓ **Spelling: The /i/ Sound Pretest, p. 61F**

**Writing Process Strategies**
- **Introduction to the Writing Process: Drafting, p. 61F**

**English Language Conventions**
- **Grammar: Verbs, p. 61F**

**Word Analysis**
- **Spelling: Word Sorting, p. 61G**
- **Vocabulary: Word Structure, p. 61G**

**Writing Process Strategies**
- **Introduction to the Writing Process: Drafting, p. 61G**

**English Language Conventions**
- **Grammar: Verbs, p. 61G**

| DAY 2 continued | DAY 3 | |
|---|---|---|
| **DAY 3** | **DAY 4** | **DAY 5** |

| | | |
|---|---|---|
| Ⓟ **Phonics and Fluency, p. 48M**<br>■ /ā/ spelled *a*, *ai_*, *a_e*, *_ay*<br>**About the Words and Sentences,**<br>**p. 48M** | Ⓟ **Phonics and Fluency**<br>**Developing Oral Language, p. 48N**<br>**Dictation, p. 48N** | **General Review** |

| | | |
|---|---|---|
| **Student Anthology, pp. 48–53** Second Read<br>**Comprehension Skills**<br>■ Compare and Contrast, pp. 49, 51, 53<br>**Supporting the Reading, pp. 59C–59D**<br>■ Compare and Contrast | **Student Anthology, pp. 54–59** Second Read<br>**Comprehension Skills**<br>■ Compare and Contrast, pp. 55, 57, 59<br>**Checking Comprehension, p. 59**<br>**Review Selection Vocabulary, p. 59B**<br>**View Fine Art, p. 59B**<br>**Literary Elements, p. 59E**<br>■ Dialogue | ✓ **Selection Assessment**<br>■ "The Tree House," pp. 10–13<br>**Home Connection, p. 59B**<br>**Social Studies Connection**<br>■ City Government, p. 59F |

| | | |
|---|---|---|
| ✓ **Investigation**<br>■ Organizing Investigation, p. 61C | **Supporting the Investigation**<br>■ ABC Order, p. 61D | **Investigation**<br>■ Unit Investigation Continued<br>■ Update Concept/Question Board |

| | | |
|---|---|---|
| **Word Analysis**<br>■ Spelling: The /i/ Sound, p. 61H<br>■ Vocabulary: Word Structure, p. 61H<br>**Writing Process Strategies**<br>■ Introduction to the Writing Process:<br>Drafting, p. 61H<br>**English Language Conventions**<br>■ Grammar: Verbs, p. 61H | **Word Analysis**<br>■ Spelling: The /i/ Sound, p. 61I<br>■ Vocabulary: Word Structure, p. 61I<br>**Writing Process Strategies**<br>■ Introduction to the Writing Process:<br>Drafting, p. 61I<br>**English Language Conventions**<br>✓■ Listening, Speaking, Viewing<br>Language: Changing Our Speech, p. 61I | **Word Analysis**<br>■ Spelling: The /i/ Sound<br>✓ Final Test<br>■ Vocabulary:<br>✓ Word Structure, p. 61J<br>**Writing Process Strategies**<br>■ Introduction to the Writing Process:<br>Drafting, p. 61J<br>**English Language Conventions**<br>✓■ Penmanship:<br>Cursive Letters *r* and *s*, p. 61J |

Below are suggestions for differentiating instruction to meet the individual needs of students. These are the same skills shown on the Lesson Planner; however, these pages provide extra practice opportunities or enriching activities to meet the varied needs of students. For Workshop Management Tips, see Appendix.

**WORKSHOP**

# Differentiating Instruction

## Small-Group Instruction

Use the informal assessment suggestions found throughout the lessons, along with the formal assessments provided in each lesson, to determine your students' strengths and areas of need. Use the following program components to help in supporting or expanding on the instruction found in this lesson:

*Reteach Workbook* for use with students who show a basic understanding of the lesson but need a bit more practice to solidify their understanding.

*Intervention Guide* and *Intervention Workbook* for use with students who, even after extra practice, exhibit a lack of understanding of the lesson concepts.

*English-Language Development Guide* and *English-Language Development Workbook* for use with students who need language help.

## Reading Roundtable

A suggested activity would be to have students read other stories from *The Big Book of Peace*. They may enjoy "The Dream" by Steven Kellogg, an author they will encounter later in Unit 5, or "A Wild Safe Place" by Maurice Sendak.

## Independent Activities

Students can work individually on such things as:

- Inquiry Journal pages
- Challenge
- Writing
- Investigation activities

◆ **Small-Group Instruction**   ■ **Independent Activities**

| | READING | INVESTIGATION ACTIVITIES |
|---|---|---|
| **DAY 1** | ■ Select *Leveled Classroom Library* book for independent reading<br>■ Add vocabulary in Writer's Notebook<br>■ Record response to selection in Writer's Notebook | ■ Concept/Question Board<br>◆ Review investigation conjectures and needs<br>■ Explore OCR Web site (www.sra4kids.com) for Friendship |
| **DAY 2** | ■ Independent reading<br>■ Oral reading of selection for fluency<br>◆ Discuss Theme Connections, p. 61 | ■ Concept/Question Board<br>■ Use *Research Assistant CD-ROM* to continue investigation |
| **DAY 3** | ◆ Partner reading of selection<br>■ *Listening Library Audiocassette/CD*<br>■ Complete Link to Writing for Supporting the Reading, p. 59D<br>■ Complete *Comprehension and Language Arts Skills*, pp. 8–9 | ■ Concept/Question Board<br>◆ Review organizing investigations<br>◆ Complete *Inquiry Journal*, pp. 16–17 |
| **DAY 4** | ■ Independent reading<br>■ Complete Independent Practice for Literary Elements, p. 59E<br>■ Add words to Word Bank | ■ Concept/Question Board<br>■ Complete *Inquiry Journal*, pp. 18–19 |
| **DAY 5** | ■ Reading Roundtable<br>■◆ Social Studies Connection, p. 59F | ◆ Continue work on investigation |

| LANGUAGE ARTS | INTERVENTION* | ENGLISH-LANGUAGE LEARNERS** | RETEACH | CHALLENGE |
|---|---|---|---|---|
| **English Language Conventions**<br>■ Complete Action Verbs, *Comprehension and Language Arts Skills,* pp. 10–11 | **(30 to 45 minutes per day)**<br>◆ Blending, p. 22<br>◆ Preteach "The Tree House," pp. 24–25<br>◆ Teach "Intervention Selection One," pp. 25–26<br>◆ Grammar, Usage, and Mechanics, pp. 28–29 | **(30 to 45 minutes per day)**<br>◆ Word Knowledge, Homophones, p. 14<br>◆ Word Knowledge, Prefix *re-*, p. 14 | | |
| **Word Analysis**<br>◆ Spelling: Word Sort p. 61G<br>■ Complete Word Structure, *Spelling and Vocabulary Skills,* pp. 10–11 | ◆ Developing Oral Language, p. 22<br>◆ Preteach "The Tree House," pp. 24–25<br>◆ Teach Comprehension Strategies, p. 26<br>◆ Reread "Intervention Selection One"<br>◆ Grammar, Usage, and Mechanics, pp. 28–29 | ◆ Selection Vocabulary, p. 16<br>◆ Preteach the Selection, p. 17 | **English Language Conventions**<br>■ Complete Action Verbs, *Reteach,* p. 14 | **English Language Conventions**<br>■ Complete Action Verbs, *Challenge,* p. 12 |
| **Word Analysis**<br>■ Complete Spelling: The /i/ Sound, *Spelling and Vocabulary Skills,* p. 12<br>**Writing Process Strategies**<br>■ Complete Writer's Craft: Topic Sentences, *Comprehension and Language Arts Skills,* pp. 12–13 | ◆ Dictation and Spelling, pp. 22–23<br>◆ Reread "The Tree House"<br>◆ Teach "Intervention Selection Two," pp. 26–27<br>◆ Writing Activity, p. 29 | ◆ Word Knowledge, Plurals, p. 15 | **Reading**<br>◆ Comprehension Skill: Compare and Contrast<br>■ Complete *Reteach,* pp. 10–11<br>**Word Analysis**<br>■ Complete Vocabulary: Word Structure, *Reteach,* p. 13 | **Reading**<br>◆ Comprehension Skill: Compare and Contrast<br>■ Complete *Challenge,* p. 9<br>**Word Analysis**<br>■ Complete Vocabulary: Word Structure, *Challenge,* p. 11 |
| **Word Analysis**<br>■ Complete The /i/ Sound, *Spelling and Vocabulary Skills,* p. 13 | ◆ Blending, p. 23<br>◆ Reread "The Tree House"<br>◆ Teach Comprehension Strategies, p. 27<br>◆ Reread "Intervention Selection Two"<br>◆ Writing Activity, p. 29 | ◆ Word Knowledge, Suffix *-ion,* p. 15 | **Word Analysis**<br>■ Complete Spelling: The /i/ Sound, *Reteach,* p. 12 | **Word Analysis**<br>■ Complete Spelling: The /i/ Sound, *Challenge,* p. 1 |
| **Writing Process Strategies**<br>◆ Seminar: Drafting an Autobiography, p. 61J<br>**English Language Conventions**<br>■ Penmanship: Practice Letters *r* and *s,* p. 61J | ◆ Developing Oral Language, p. 23<br>◆ Dictation and Spelling, p. 24<br>◆ Repeated Readings/ Fluency Check, pp. 27–28<br>◆ Informal Assessment | ◆ Grammar, Usage, and Mechanics, p. 17 | **Writing Process Strategies**<br>■ Complete Writer's Craft: Topic Sentences, *Reteach,* p. 15 | **Writing Process Strategies**<br>■ Complete Writer's Craft: Topic Sentences, *Challenge,* p. 13 |

\* Page numbers refer to *Intervention Guide*.

\*\* Page numbers refer to *English-Language Development Guide*.

**ASSESSMENT**

## Formal Assessment Options

Use these summative assessments along with your informal observations to assess student progress.

---

**LESSON ASSESSMENT**

Name _____ Date _____ Score _____

**UNIT 1** Friendship • Lesson 3

### The Tree House

Read the following questions carefully. Then completely fill in the bubble of each correct answer. You may look back at the story to find the answer to each of the questions.

1. In this story, the girls are alike because
   Ⓐ they both like the same kind of music
   Ⓑ their tree houses are the same
   ● they are stubborn

2. Why does Leah say she hates Chrissy?
   Ⓐ Chrissy won't share her books with Leah.
   Ⓑ Chrissy got Leah into trouble.
   ● Chrissy won't let Leah in her tree house.

Read the following questions carefully. Use complete sentences to answer the questions.

3. What does Leah say they can do to help each other across the bridge?
   Leah says they can each meet halfway, then hold hands.

4. Why does Chrissy say the best part of a tree house is the bridge?
   With a bridge, Chrissy and Leah can share their tree houses.

5. What does Chrissy like about the inside of Leah's tree house?
   Chrissy likes the pictures of beautiful women that cover the walls.

**10** Unit 1 • Lesson 3          *The Tree House • Unit 1 Assessment*

*Unit 1 Assessment p. 10*

---

**The Tree House** (continued)

6. What kind of carpeting is in Chrissy's tree house?
   Chrissy doesn't really have carpeting. She has an old rug.

7. How do the girls change the signs on their tree houses?
   They change their signs to say "Welcome" instead of "Keep Out."

8. What makes Chrissy and Leah start to talk to one another?
   Chrissy asks if Leah has any books she can borrow.

Read the following questions carefully. Then completely fill in the bubble of each correct answer.

9. Who built Leah's tree house?
   Ⓐ her mother
   ● her father
   Ⓒ her grandfather

10. How long did Chrissy and Leah sit in their tree houses, not talking to each other?
   Ⓐ one day
   ● four days
   Ⓒ two weeks

*Unit 1 Assessment • The Tree House*          Unit 1 • Lesson 3  **11**

*Unit 1 Assessment p. 11*

---

**The Tree House** (continued)

Read the question and statement below. Use complete sentences in your answers.

**Linking to the Concepts** Why is sharing important to a friendship?
Answers will vary. Accept all reasonable answers.

**Personal Response** Suppose you had your own tree house. With whom would you like to share it? Why?
Answers will vary. Accept all reasonable answers.

**12** Unit 1 • Lesson 3          *The Tree House • Unit 1 Assessment*

*Unit 1 Assessment p. 12*

---

**The Tree House** (continued)

### Vocabulary

Read the following questions carefully. Then completely fill in the bubble of each correct answer.

1. Chrissy thought her tree house was a marvelous tree house. **Marvelous** means
   Ⓐ grown-up
   Ⓑ strange
   ● wonderful

2. Chrissy also thought her tree house was magnificent. **Magnificent** means
   Ⓐ simple
   ● grand
   Ⓒ cozy

3. Leah thought Chrissy's tree house was beautiful. **Beautiful** means
   Ⓐ scary
   ● lovely
   Ⓒ silly

4. Chrissy peered through her window and saw that Leah was building her own tree house. **Peered** means
   ● looked
   Ⓑ covered
   Ⓒ closed

5. Before putting the board between the two tree houses, Chrissy eyed the height. **Height** is
   Ⓐ how long something is
   Ⓑ how close something is
   ● how high something is

*Unit 1 Assessment • The Tree House*          Unit 1 • Lesson 3  **13**

*Unit 1 Assessment p. 13*

---

Name _____ Date _____ Score _____

**UNIT 1** Friendship • Lesson 3 *The Tree House*

**Spelling Pretest: The /ĭ/ Sound**

Fold this page back on the dotted line. Take the Pretest. Then correct any word you misspelled by crossing out the word and rewriting it next to the incorrect spelling.

| | |
|---|---|
| 1. _____ | 1. *pick* |
| 2. _____ | 2. *risk* |
| 3. _____ | 3. *film* |
| 4. _____ | 4. *grip* |
| 5. _____ | 5. *brick* |
| 6. _____ | 6. *give* |
| 7. _____ | 7. *stitch* |
| 8. _____ | 8. *finish* |
| 9. _____ | 9. *trick* |
| 10. _____ | 10. *live* |
| 11. _____ | 11. *window* |
| 12. _____ | 12. *visit* |
| 13. _____ | 13. *lift* |
| 14. _____ | 14. *with* |
| 15. _____ | 15. *into* |

**30** Unit 1 • Lesson 3          *Spelling Pretest: The /ĭ/ Sound • Unit 1 Assessment*

*Unit 1 Assessment p. 30*

---

Name _____ Date _____ Score _____

**UNIT 1** Friendship • Lesson 3 *The Tree House*

**Spelling Final Test: The /ĭ/ Sound**

Mark the letter next to the underlined word that is misspelled. Focus on the underlined word.

1. Ⓐ A judge can <u>pick</u> the winner.
   Ⓑ The fireplace was made of <u>brick</u>.
   ● Please <u>giv</u> me a gift.
   Ⓓ Correct as is.

2. Ⓕ Soap leaves a <u>film</u> in the bath.
   ● She went to <u>viset</u> her aunt.
   Ⓗ Grapes come <u>with</u> seeds.
   Ⓘ Correct as is.

3. Ⓐ I'll look <u>into</u> going to summer camp.
   ● Which color will you <u>pic</u>?
   Ⓒ She held it with a firm <u>grip</u>.
   Ⓓ Correct as is.

4. Ⓕ A <u>window</u> usually has glass.
   Ⓖ He performed a magic <u>tric</u>.
   Ⓗ An elevator can be called a <u>lift</u>.
   ● Correct as is.

5. Ⓐ A <u>stich</u> was loose in the sweater.
   Ⓑ Koalas <u>live</u> in Australia.
   Ⓒ Runners want to <u>finish</u> the race.
   Ⓓ Correct as is.

6. Ⓕ Order bread <u>with</u> butter.
   Ⓖ The <u>film</u> was boring to watch.
   Ⓗ Climbing the tree was a <u>risk</u>.
   ● Correct as is.

*Unit 1 Assessment • Spelling Final Test: The /ĭ/ Sound*          Unit 1 • Lesson 3  **31**

*Unit 1 Assessment p. 31*

---

# Informal Comprehension Strategies Rubrics

Use the Informal Comprehension Strategies Rubrics to determine whether or not a student is using any of the strategies listed below. Note the strategies a student is using, instead of the degree to which a student might be using any particular strategy. In addition, encourage the student to tell of any strategies other than the ones being taught that he or she is using.

## Asking Questions
- The student asks questions about ideas or facts presented in the text and attempts to answer these questions by reading the text.

## Making Connections
- The student activates prior knowledge and related knowledge.
- The student uses prior knowledge to explain something encountered in text.
- The student connects ideas presented later in the text to ideas presented earlier in the text.
- The student notes ideas in the text that are new or conflict with what he or she thought previously.

## Visualizing
- The student visualizes ideas or scenes described in the text.

# Research Rubrics

Use the Research Rubrics to assess a student's performance throughout the stages of the investigation for each unit. The rubrics for a given lesson will match the investigation stage for that lesson. In addition, at the end of the unit you can use the rubrics to assess the groups' collaborative work as well as an individual's participation in that group.

During Workshop, assess students using the rubrics below. The rubrics range from 1–4 in most categories, with 1 being the lowest score. Record each student's score on the inside back cover of the ***Inquiry Journal***.

## Making Conjectures
1 Offers conjectures that are mainly expressions of fact or opinion. ("I think the Anasazi lived a long time ago." "I think tigers should be protected.")
2 Offers conjectures that partially address the research question. ("I think germs make you sick because they get your body upset." "I think germs make you sick because they multiply really fast.")
3 Offers conjectures that address the research question with guesses. ("I think the Anasazi were wiped out by a meteor.")
4 Offers reasonable conjectures that address the question and that can be improved through further research.

## Objectives

- Students practice recognizing antonyms.
- Students practice recognizing homophones.
- Students practice recognizing word roots and the prefix *re-* and the suffix *-ion,* and how they affect meaning.
- Students practice recognizing groups of related words.
- Students practice and review /ā/ sound spellings.
- Students develop fluency reading words and sentences.
- Students practice recognizing words with the /i/ sound.

## Materials

- Student Anthology, Book 1, pp. 48–61
- Decodable Book Activities CD-ROM
- Sound/Spelling Card 33
- Decodable Book 13
- Routine Cards 1, 3, Routines 1–2, 8–9

**Teacher Tip** SYLLABICATION To help students blend words and build fluency, use the syllabication below of the words in the word lines.

| | | | |
|---|---|---|---|
| out•side | in•side | shin•y | dull |
| beau•ti•ful | ug•ly | o•pen | close |
| down | up | wide | nar•row |
| top | bot•tom | board | bored |
| for | four | no | know |
| hole | whole | hung | re•hung |
| take | re•take | make | re•make |
| trunk | tree | branch•es | wood |
| in•to | with | lift | vis•it |
| win•dow | | | |

## MEETING INDIVIDUAL NEEDS

### ELL Support

For ELD strategies, use the *English-Language Development Guide,* Unit 1, Lesson 3.

### Intervention Support

For intervention strategies, use the *Intervention Guide,* Unit 1, Lesson 3.

**Spelling**
See pages 61E–61J for the corresponding spelling lesson for the /i/ sound.

## Word Knowledge LA.A.1.2.2.3.1, LA.A.1.2.2.3.2, LA.A.1.2.2.3.4

### Reading the Words and Sentences

Write each word in Reading the Words and Sentences on the board and have students read them together. If they have difficulty reading a word, stop and have them blend the word, using whole-word blending. Encourage students to pronounce the word naturally after blending. Because reading sentences helps students to move from word fluency to sentence fluency, have them read each sentence in unison, using normal intonation. The words in **boldface** type are from the selection.

| | | | | | | | | |
|---|---|---|---|---|---|---|---|---|
| Line 1: | outside | inside | shiny | dull | **beautiful** | ugly | | |
| Line 2: | open | close | down | up | wide | narrow | **top** | bottom |
| Line 3: | board | bored | for | four | no | know | **hole** | whole |
| Line 4: | hung | **rehung** | take | retake | make | remake | | |
| Line 5: | trunk | tree | branches | wood | | | | |
| Line 6: | into | with | lift | visit | window | | | |

Sentence 1: The boards were crooked, and the roof had holes where the pieces of wood didn't quite meet.

Sentence 2: Chrissy wondered what Leah had inside her tree house.

Sentence 3: There was a little porch where you could sit with your legs dangling.

Sentence 4: You can get fresh air if you lift open a window.

### About the Words and Sentences

- **Lines 1–2:** Explain to students that the words in Lines 1 and 2 contain pairs of words that are antonyms or opposites. After reading the words, ask the students to identify the antonyms (*outside/inside, shiny/dull, beautiful/ugly, open/close, down/up, wide/narrow, top/bottom*). Ask the students to name some antonyms they know.

- **Line 3:** Explain to students that this line contains words that sound the same but are spelled differently and have different meanings. They are homophones. After reading the words in Line 3, ask students to name some other homophones. (*Possible answers: to/too/two, there/their/they're, here/hear*)

- **Line 4:** The words on Line 4 show verbs with the prefix *re-*. Ask the students what the prefix *re-* means (*again*). Have students read the words and discuss how the meaning of each word changed by adding the prefix.

- **Line 5:** This line shows a group of words that are all related. Ask students to tell you how they are related. (*They are all related to trees.*) Ask them to add their own words to the list. (*Possible answers: leaves, buds, birds, nests, squirrels, forest*)

- **Line 6:** The words in Line 6 are found in "The Tree House" and review the /i/ sound.

- **Sentences 1–3:** These sentences are from the story students are about to read. Ask students to identify a word in Sentence 1 that has a homophone *(hole)*. Have them point to it on the board. Ask a student to tell what the homophone for *hole* would be *(whole)*. Ask for a definition for each word.

- **Sentence 2:** Ask the students to find a word line that has words that are related to "tree house" *(Line 5).*

- **Sentence 3:** Ask the students to identify a word that has an antonym *(little).* Have a student give the antonym *(big).*

- **Sentence 4:** Have students notice the words in the last sentence that contain the /i/ sound spelled *i*.

## Developing Oral Language LA.C.1.2.1.3.2

Use direct teaching to review the words. Use one or both of the following activities to help students practice the words aloud.

- Have a student choose a word and call out only the line and the position of the word in the line. For example, "Line 1, Word 3." Have the student select a classmate to read the words, saying, for example, "Line 1, Word 3 is *shiny.*" Then ask the student to use the word in a sentence.

- Write the following words on the board: *on, dark, happy, asleep, big, soft.* Ask volunteers to say an antonym for each of the words on the board. Have students name other antonym word pairs.

**Routine Card**
Refer to *Routine 1* for the whole-word blending procedure and *Routine 2* for the sentence blending procedure.

**Teacher Tip** FLUENCY Gaining a better understanding of the spellings of sounds and the structure of words will help students as they encounter unfamiliar words in their reading. By this time in Grade 3, students should be reading approximately 107 words per minute with fluency and expression. As students read, you may notice that some need work in building fluency. During Workshop, have these students select a section of the text (a minimum of 160 words) to read several times in order to build fluency.

Refer to the *Lesson Model Videocassette* for instruction on whole-word blending.

**P H O N I C S**

**Teacher Tip** SYLLABICATION To help students blend words and build fluency, use the syllabication below of the words in the word lines.

| a•gent | A•pril | la•dy | a•ble | ta•ble |
|--------|--------|-------|-------|--------|
| bail | hail | nail | frail | snail |
| lake | flake | snake | cup•cake | lo•cate |
| day | say | stay | spray | stray |

**Teacher Tip** Encourage students to just read the words. Stop and blend only those words that give them problems.

**Teacher Tip** Remind students when they see the Vowel-Consonant-Vowel pattern they need to try the long and short vowel sounds to see which makes sense. They should ask themselves if the word sounds right.

# Phonics and Fluency LA.A.1.2.2.3.1

/ā/ spelled *a, ai_, a_e, _ay*

## Blending

- Use direct teaching to teach the blending lessons.
- Display **Sound/Spelling Card 33.**
- Follow the procedure established in Unit 1, Lesson 1, to have students read the following words and sentences. **Boldface** words are found in the selection.

| | | | | | |
|---|---|---|---|---|---|
| Line 1: | agent | April | lady | able | **table** |
| Line 2: | bail | hail | **nail** | frail | snail |
| Line 3: | lake | flake | snake | cupcake | locate |
| Line 4: | day | say | stay | spray | stray |
| Sentence 1: | **Jake will take the cake to the party.** | | | | |
| Sentence 2: | **Gail's birthday is in May.** | | | | |
| Sentence 3: | **My grandpa had paint leftover.** | | | | |

## About the Words and Sentences

- **Line 1:** The words review the /ā/ sound spelled *a*.
- **Line 2:** The words review the /ā/ sound spelled *ai_*. All words end in *ail*. Ask students to name other words that end in *ail*. *(pail, fail, jail, mail)*
- **Line 3:** The words review the /ā/ sound spelled *a_e*. Ask students what the blank in the *a_e* spelling means. *(A consonant belongs in the blank.)*
- **Line 4:** The words review the /ā/ sound spelled *_ay*. Ask students what the blank before the *ay* means. *(A letter always comes before this spelling. This spelling occurs at the end of a word or syllable.)*
- **Sentences 1–2:** These sentences practice the /ā/ sound spellings. Have students identify words with the /ā/ sound spellings *(take, cake, birthday, May, Jake, Gail)*.
- **Sentence 3:** This sentence is from the selection. Have students identify the word with the /ā/ sound spelling *(paint)*. Have students identify the /a/ sound spelling *(ai_)*.

## Developing Oral Language LA.C.1.2.1.3.2

Use direct teaching to review the words. Use one or both of the following activities to help students practice words aloud.

- Say one or more sentences with a word missing and ask students to point to and read words from Lines 1–5 to fill in the blanks. Possible sentences: We eat breakfast at the kitchen _____ *(table)*. My father used a _____ to hang the picture *(nail)*. We adopted a _____ puppy from the humane society *(stray)*. Then have the students repeat the entire sentence.

- Have students reread the words in the word lines, clapping the syllables in each word.

## Dictation

Erase the blending lines and sentences on the board and have students take out writing paper. Dictate the following words and sentences for students to write.

|                   |        |       |      |
|-------------------|--------|-------|------|
| **Line 1:**       | baby   | train | rake |
| **Line 2:**       | play   | bake  | away |
| **Challenge Word:** | ailment | | |
| **Sentence:**     | The students must not be late for the play. | | |

## Building Fluency

***Decodable Books*** are used to help develop fluency for students who need extra practice. The only way to gain fluency is to read. Students will have many opportunities to read, including the ***Student Anthology,*** the ***Leveled Classroom Library,*** and their own reading. The ***Decodable Books*** can be used to practice the phonics and fluency elements being reviewed. Refer to the Appendix for the procedure on using these books. For this lesson, use ***Decodable Book 13,*** *Baking Princess.*

**Baking Princess**
by Barbara Seiger
illustrated by Kersti Frigell

*Decodable Book 13*

**Routine Card** Refer to *Routine 8* for whole-word dictation and *Routine 9* for sentence dictation.

**Teacher Tip** Remind students that long vowel sounds appear in the yellow box on the *Sound Spelling Cards.*

Use the *Decodable Book Activities CD-ROM* for activities that support this Phonics lesson.

Refer to the *Lesson Model Videocassette* for instruction on whole-word dictation.

Refer to the *Lesson Model Videocassette* for instruction on reading a *Decodable Book.*

## Objectives

- Students will understand the selection vocabulary before reading, using strategies such as suffixes and structural cues.
- Students will spell plurals, homophones, words with the affix *re-*, and antonyms.
- Students will connect prior knowledge to subjects discussed in text.
- Students will use comprehension strategies such as Making Connections, Visualizing, and Self-Questioning to construct meaning from the text and monitor reading.
- Students will use the comprehension skill Compare and Contrast as they read the story the second time.
- Students will discuss personal reactions to the story to begin identifying their own personal reading preferences.

## Materials

- Student Anthology, Book 1, pp. 48–63
- Program Assessment
- Reading Transparencies 5, 46, 50
- Inquiry Journal, p. 3
- Routine Cards 1–2, Routines 3–6
- Home Connection, p. 7
- Comprehension and Language Arts Skills, pp. 8–9
- Unit 1 Assessment, pp. 10–13

**Routine Card**
Refer to *Routine 4* for the Clues, Problems, and Wonderings procedure.

| Clues | Problems | Wonderings |
|---|---|---|
| One girl is sitting by herself. | shutters | Why is there a sign that says "Keep Out"? |

**Reading Transparency 46**

 **Teacher Tip** Model browsing for those students who have trouble picking up ideas as they browse.

# Build Background

## Activate Prior Knowledge

Remind students that remembering their own experiences will help them understand the story. Discuss the following with students to find out what they may already know about the selection and have already learned about the theme of Friendship.

- Preteach "The Tree House" by first determining students' prior knowledge about tree houses by asking: "What are tree houses? Who has a tree house?"
- Encourage students to share experiences they have had in tree houses or in other special play "houses."
- Ask students how sharing is a part of friendship and in what ways friends can share. Ask them to think about their own experiences with sharing or times when sharing has been difficult.

## Background Information

The following information may help students understand the selection they are about to read.

- Bring in some pictures or photos of tree houses or play houses, or invite students to bring in photos of their own tree houses or play houses.
- Tell students that this story is realistic fiction. Ask students to tell you some of the characteristics of realistic fiction and to give you examples of stories they have read that are realistic fiction.

# Preview and Prepare LA.A.1.2.1.3.1

## Browse

- Have students preview the selection by browsing through the first page or two of the story. This allows them to activate prior knowledge relevant to the story. Fiction pieces should not be browsed in their entirety, as the browsing may ruin the surprise of the story.
- Have the students search for clues that tell them something about the story. Also, have them look for any problems, such as unfamiliar words or long sentences, that they notice while reading. Use *Reading Transparency 46* to record observations as they browse. For example, a clue to the story that they might mention is that one girl is sitting by herself. For the problems column, students might point out that they are not familiar with the word *shutters*. They might wonder why there is a sign that says "Keep Out." To save time and model note taking, write students' observations as brief notes rather than complete sentences.
- As students prepare to read the selection, have them browse the Focus Questions on the first page of the selection. Tell them to keep these questions in mind as they read.

## Set Purposes LA.A.1.2.2.3.5

Encourage students to set their own purposes for reading. If necessary, suggest that students think about who shows friendship in this story, how they do it, and why they do it. Students should also think about how this story is similar to and different from other stories they have read in this unit.

## Selection Vocabulary LA.A.1.2.2.3.2

As students study vocabulary, they will use a variety of skills to determine the meaning of a word. These include context clues, word structure, and apposition. Students will apply these same skills while reading to clarify additional unfamiliar words. Display **Reading Transparency 5** before reading the selection to introduce and discuss the following words and their meanings. Students can write their definitions in their Writer's Notebooks.

| | |
|---|---|
| **magnificent:** | outstanding (page 48) |
| **marvelous:** | great, wonderful (page 48) |
| **beautiful:** | lovely, pleasing to look at (page 50) |
| **peered:** | looked (page 51) |
| **height:** | how tall something is (page 57) |

Have students read the words in the word box, stopping to blend any words that they have trouble reading. Demonstrate how to decode multisyllabic words by breaking the words into syllables and blending the syllables. Then have students try. If they still have trouble, refer them to the **Sound/Spelling Cards.** If the word is not decodable, give the students the pronunciation.

Have students read the sentences on the transparency to determine the meaning of the underlined words. Each word has two sentences that students will read and from which they should be able to derive the meaning of the underlined word. Remind them to use one or more of the skills they have learned—context clues, word structure, or apposition—to figure out the meaning before using a dictionary. Be sure students explain which skills they are using and how they figured out the meanings of the words. Have students reread the sentence, substituting the definition to see if the sentence makes sense. Have a volunteer create a new sentence using the underlined word.

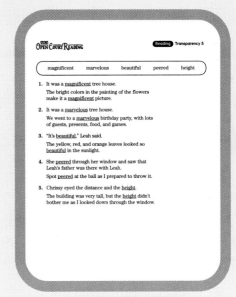

*Reading Transparency 5*

**Teacher Tip SELECTION VOCABULARY** To help students decode words, divide them into syllables as shown below. The information following each word tells how students can figure out the meaning of each word.

| | |
|---|---|
| mag•nif•i•cent | context clues |
| mar•vel•ous | context clues |
| beau•ti•ful | context clues |
| peered | context clues |
| height | apposition |

## MEETING INDIVIDUAL NEEDS

### ELL Support

For ELD strategies, use the **English-Language Development Guide,** Unit 1, Lesson 3.

### Intervention Support

For intervention strategies, use the **Intervention Guide,** Unit 1, Lesson 3.

**Routine Card**
Refer to **Routine 3** for the vocabulary procedure.

**www.sra4kids.com**
**Web Connection**
Students can use the connections to friendship in the Reading link of the SRA Web page for more background information about friendship.

**Routine Card** Refer to *Routine 5* for the procedure on reading the selection.

During Workshop, and after the selection has been read at least once, have students listen to the recording of this lesson's selection on the *Listening Library Audiocassette/CD.* After students have listened, have them discuss their personal preferences of the selections read. Ask them what other things they have listened to and like to listen to on the radio, on audiocassettes, or on CDs.

**Teacher Tip** During Workshop have students find multisyllabic words in their *Anthology* selection and list them under columns for two- or three-syllable words. Have them underline the vowel spellings.

# Reading Recommendations

In your first reading, focus on developing the reading strategies to the left of the reduced student pages. The second reading should focus on the comprehension skills and should be done on another day.

## Oral Reading

"The Tree House" lends itself well to oral reading because of the descriptive passages, strong imagery, and conversational style. Students should read aloud fluently with appropriate expression and intonation. Make sure that students attend to punctuation and read in phrases. Tell students to add a sense of feeling or anticipation as they read.

## Using Comprehension Strategies

Comprehension strategy instruction allows students to become aware of how good readers read. Good readers constantly check their understanding as they read and ask themselves questions. Skilled readers also recognize when they are having problems and stop to use various comprehension strategies to help them make sense of what they are reading.

During the reading of "The Tree House," model the use of the following comprehension strategies:

- **Asking Questions** helps readers focus attention on what they are reading and engages them in deeper understanding of themes, concepts, and ideas.
- **Making Connections** requires readers to activate prior knowledge and connect what they know or have experienced to what they are reading.
- **Visualizing** requires readers to mentally picture the events or characters in the story, resulting in a more vivid and imaginative understanding of the story.

As students read, they should be using a variety of strategies to help them understand the selection. Encourage students to use the strategies listed above as the class reads the story aloud. Do this by stopping at the points indicated by the numbers in the magenta circles on the reduced student page and using a particular strategy. Students can also stop reading periodically to discuss what they have learned and what problems they may be having.

## Building Comprehension Skills

Revisiting or rereading a selection allows students to apply skills that give them a more complete understanding of the text. Some follow-up comprehension skills help students organize information. Others lead to deeper understanding—to "reading between the lines," as mature readers do.

An extended lesson on the comprehension skill Compare and Contrast can be found in the Supporting the Reading section on pages 59C–59D. This lesson is intended to give students extra practice with Compare and Contrast. However, it may be used at this time to introduce the comprehension skill to students.

- **Compare and Contrast (Introduction):** Readers distinguish differences and similarities between two or more ideas, characters, settings, or events.

## Reading with a Purpose

Have students look for ways any of the story characters show friendship throughout the selection.

### Research in Action
### Metacognition

Helping students to become aware of how they comprehend is an important part of comprehension instruction. *Cognition* refers to functions of the mind, such as remembering, focusing attention, and processing information. *Metacognition* refers to our awareness of our cognition—it is thinking about thinking. When it is applied to reading, the term *metacognitive awareness* means that readers are aware of what they do when they read, what to do when they encounter difficulties, and how to select strategies to accomplish their purposes for reading. *(Ann L. Brown)*

**Teacher Tip COMPREHENSION STRATEGIES** Remind students as they read the story on the second day to summarize what they learned from the first day.

**COMPREHENSION**

This selection is broken into two parts. On the first day, read pages 48–53. On the second day, read pages 54–59.

## Comprehension Strategies  LA.E.1.2.1.3.3

**First Read**

Read the story aloud, taking turns with the students. Model the use of strategies for the students.

### Teacher Modeling

**❶ Making Connections** *Good readers pay attention to things in the story that remind them of their own experiences or of knowledge that they already have. These connections can help you understand what you are reading. I have a connection with this story. I always wanted to have a tree house like Chrissy's. I can imagine how excited she is to have it. Have you ever been in a tree house? What kind of tree house would you like? Be sure to let the class know when you make connections to the story.*

### Word Knowledge

**SCAFFOLDING:** The skills students are reviewing in Word Knowledge should help them in reading the story. This lesson focuses on antonyms, homophones, and the prefix *re-*. Words with these spellings will be found in boxes similar to this one throughout the selection.

**antonyms:**  **marvelous** (terrible)
 **bright** (dull)
 **small** (large)

**Teacher Tip** Remind students that the things they wonder about as they read can be valid topics for further research or investigation.

### First Reading Recommendation

## ORAL · CHORAL

*Focus Questions*  What is it like to have a friend be mean to you? How can you make up with a friend when you realize the friendship is more important than whatever caused the fight?

# The Tree House

Lois Lowry

*illustrated by Trina Schart Hyman*

t was a terrific tree house. *Better* than terrific: It was a <u>marvelous</u>, <u>magnificent</u>, one-of-a-kind tree house, with wooden walls painted bright blue. It had two windows, with red <u>shutters</u> on each, and a yellow door with two shiny brass <u>hinges</u> and a small brass bell that rang when you pulled a string. There was a little porch where you could sit with your legs <u>dangling</u>. **❶**

Inside were a table, a chair, a small rug with fringe on each end, and two fat pillows so that you could lie on the rug and read.

You reached it by climbing a ladder——a ladder to the best tree house ever. And it belonged to Chrissy.

48

**Informal Assessment**

Observe individual students as they read and use the Teacher Observation Log, found in the *Program Assessment Teacher's Edition,* to record anecdotal information about each student's strengths and weaknesses.

Theme: **Friendship**

"It's all mine, isn't it?" she had asked her grandfather after he built the house for her. "Just mine, and nobody else's?"

Grandpa was washing his paintbrush. He nodded. "I built it just for you," he said.

So Chrissy used her markers and made a sign. CHRISSY'S HOUSE, the sign said. KEEP OUT! She tacked it to the door. Then she took her favorite books into the tree house, curled up on the pillows, and began to read.

"Chrissy?" The voice came from the next yard, from just across the fence.

Chrissy got up and looked through the tree house window. "Hi, Leah," she said to the girl who lived next door. "How do you like my tree house, now that it's all done?"

49

## Comprehension Skills  LA.A.2.2.7.3.1; LA.E.1.2.3.3.2

**Second Read**

### Compare and Contrast

Remind students that writers often make comparisons and contrasts to help readers form pictures in their minds. Explain to students that when they compare, they find parts that are alike, and when they contrast, they find parts that are different.

- On page 48, there is a description of the tree house. Have students compare the tree house to a regular house. (*The tree house has windows, a door, and a porch, much like a regular house.*)

- Page 48 describes the interior of the tree house. Have students contrast the interior of the tree house to that of a regular house. (*one small room only, unlike a regular house*)

Help students realize that they should compare and contrast to help them better understand people and items in the story.

---

### Word Knowledge

**homophones:**   **for** (four)
        **I** (eye)
        **made** (maid)

### Skills Trace
### Compare and Contrast
Introduced in Grade 1.
Scaffolded throughout Grades 2 and 3.
**REINTRODUCED:** Unit 1, Lesson 3
**REINFORCED:** Unit 3, Lesson 4
        Unit 6, Lesson 1
**TESTED:** Unit 1 Assessment

**Second Reading Recommendation**

ORAL • **SILENT**

COMPREHENSION

COMPREHENSION

## Comprehension Strategies

First Read

### Teacher Modeling

**2 Visualizing** *Good readers often form mental images in their minds as they read as a way to picture what the writer is saying. This makes the story more enjoyable and also helps you put information from the story in order. I want to take a moment and visualize Chrissy's tree house. The author has revealed a lot about how it looks, so I can easily picture the blue walls, red shutters, and yellow brass hinges, along with all the interior decorations that Chrissy has added. What do you picture the inside of the tree house to look like? I picture Chrissy's tree house to be very neat inside. What do you see? What do you think Chrissy saw as she watched Leah's father start to work? What do you see as you visualize him working?*

### Word Knowledge

homophones:   **two** (to, too)
              **see** (sea)

**Teacher Tip** Remind students that different readers may picture the same scene quite differently, and this is fine. Every reader responds to a story in his or her own way.

---

"It's beautiful," Leah said. "What do you have inside?"

"A table and two chairs and a rug and some pillows," Chrissy told her. "And some secret stuff," she added, though she didn't have secret stuff, really. She *planned* to.

"Can I come up and see?" Leah asked.

"No," Chrissy said. "It's just for me. That's why I made the sign."

Leah stood silently for a moment. Then she said, "I hate you, Chrissy."

"I hate you, too," Chrissy replied. She went back to the pillows and opened her book again.

50

## MEETING INDIVIDUAL NEEDS

### ELL

The strategies for responding to text help English-language learners contribute to class discussions because the strategies draw on personal experience and understanding.

A short time later, she heard voices in the next yard. She <u>peered</u> through her window and saw that Leah's father was there with Leah. They had a wheelbarrow full of old boards, and a jar of nails. As Chrissy watched from her window, she saw Leah's father prop an old ladder against the trunk of the tree on the other side of the fence. Then, after he <u>jiggled</u> the ladder and made certain it was steady,

**2** he climbed up, carrying a board, and began to nail it into place where the branches came together.

51

## Comprehension Skills LA.A.2.2.7.3.1; LA.E.1.2.2.3.1

COMPREHENSION

### Compare and Contrast

Point out to students that this part of the story tells how both Chrissy and Leah feel. Have students compare the girls' feelings toward each other and note that they appear to be the same. What other comparisons or contrasts can students make?

- *On page 50, the girls say that they hate each other.*
- *Chrissy's grandfather built a nice, fancy tree house for her. Leah's father is going to build one with old boards. It probably won't be as fancy as Chrissy's.*

Have Chrissy and Leah's feelings changed since the beginning of the story? What might have brought about this change? Remind students that comparing and contrasting information during reading leads to a better understanding of what happens in the story.

### Word Knowledge

antonyms:     **inside** (outside)
                       **up** (down)

COMPREHENSION

## Comprehension Strategies

First Read

### Teacher Modeling

**3 Asking Questions** *Good readers wonder as they read and ask themselves questions constantly about what they are reading. I often wonder about why certain characters behave as they do. Chrissy and Leah are not getting along. It is too bad that they cannot be friends and share both tree houses. I wonder why they can't. I wonder what it will take to get them to be friends. As we read, keep asking yourself questions and trying to find the answers. Let the class know when you have a question or an answer to somebody else's question.*

---

### Word Knowledge

**homophones:** **week** (weak)
            **new** (knew)
            **one** (won)

---

**Teacher Tip** An absence of questions does not necessarily indicate that students understand what they are reading. Be especially alert to students who never seem to ask questions. They may need extra help on an individual basis.

---

**Teacher Tip** Remind students to use context clues, apposition, or word structure to figure out the meaning of difficult words as they are reading.

He was making Leah a tree house. Chrissy laughed to herself. Leah's father was at home because he had lost his job. She knew they didn't have extra money now for things like paint and brass hinges. And Leah's tree house would never be as good as hers. Never in a million years. Chrissy went back to her book and turned the pages while the hammering continued.

That evening, after supper, Chrissy stood beside the fence and looked up at Leah's finished house. She laughed aloud.

It had taken a week for Grandpa to finish building her beautiful tree house. Grandpa had used new wooden boards from the lumberyard. But Leah's had been completed in a day, and Chrissy could see that it was made from the stack of old weathered boards that had been in the corner of Leah's yard. Only one board remained there now; the others had become the tree house.

52

The house had walls and a porch and a door and two windows, but it had no shutters and no paint and no door bell. The boards were crooked, and the roof had holes where the pieces of wood didn't quite meet.

Even the sign wasn't as good, because Leah had done hers with crayons instead of marking pens. But its message was the same. LEAH'S HOUSE, it said. KEEP OUT.

Leah's head appeared in the window of her tree house.

"Your house is not as nice as mine," Chrissy told her.

"Not on the outside," Leah said. "But inside, it's better."

**3** Chrissy wondered what Leah had inside her tree house. But she didn't ask.

53

## COMPREHENSION

### Comprehension Skills LA.A.2.2.7.3.1; LA.E.1.2.3.3.2

Second Read

#### Compare and Contrast

Tell students that Chrissy compares the two tree houses to see how they are the same and how they are different. Tell students that often, when there are lots of things to compare and contrast, a chart is helpful for organizing the information. Have students complete the following chart. Students may wish to add other similarities and differences. If you like, you can record your observations on a transparency or on the board.

| *Chrissy's and Leah's Tree Houses* | |
|---|---|
| *Chrissy* | *Leah* |
| **Kind of Boards** | |
| *new* | *old* |
| **Number of Windows** | |
| *2* | *2* |
| **Signs** | |
| *made with marking pens* | *made with crayons* |
| **Time to Build** | |
| *1 week* | *1 day* |

#### Word Knowledge
**homophones:**  **no** (know)
 **meet** (meat)

**Teacher Tip** As students read aloud, listen for appropriate pacing, intonation, and expression.

**COMPREHENSION**

## Comprehension Strategies

First Read

### Teacher Modeling

**4 Making Connections**

*I remember one time when my friend and I were mad at each other. We acted a lot like Chrissy and Leah. We didn't talk to each other, but then we started to feel lonely. It wasn't nice being mad at each other. I'm glad we started talking again, just like Chrissy and Leah. What experiences have you had that are similar to that of Chrissy and Leah?*

---

### Word Knowledge

**antonyms:**  **appeared** (disappeared)
**down** (up)

---

**Teacher Tip** One of the most effective ways to help students use and understand the behaviors that are successful for good readers is to make strategic thinking public. Modeling these behaviors and encouraging students to think aloud as they attempt to understand text can demonstrate for the class how these behaviors are put into practice.

---

**Teacher Tip COMPREHENSION**
Good readers are active readers. They interact with the text as they read by emoting, reacting, responding, and problem solving in their efforts to construct and maintain meaning.

---

**4**

For several days the two girls didn't speak to each other. They sat alone in their tree houses. By the fourth day, Chrissy had finished all her books and had read some of them twice. She went to her window and called across the fence to Leah.

"Do you have any books I can borrow?" she asked, when Leah's head appeared.

"No. Our car's broken so we can't go to the library."

"You don't have any books at *all?*"

Leah shook her head.

Chrissy sat back down. She wondered what it would be like to be in a tree house with no books at all. She wondered what Leah was doing in there.

Finally she called across the fence again. "Would you like to borrow some of mine?" she asked. And Leah said yes.

So Chrissy climbed down, stood at the fence, and handed two books over to Leah, who had climbed down her ladder, too.

54

55

## Comprehension Skills  LA.A.2.2.7.3.1; LA.E.1.2.3.3.1

### Compare and Contrast

Point out to students that the two girls now have something in common. They both seem to want to share. Have students locate the question about sharing that each girl asks.

- Page 54, second paragraph: *"Do you have any books I can borrow?"*
- Page 54, seventh paragraph: *"Would you like to borrow some of mine?"*

Have students continue to add to the chart.

**Teacher Tip** Good readers constantly evaluate their understanding of what they read. Stop often to make sure students are doing this.

**Teacher Tip** Tell students that good readers keep thinking about the questions that come up about the topic, and they keep coming back to those questions. As they read, tell them to keep the questions on the Concept/Question Board in mind. Have them make notes to themselves in the Response Journal section of their Writer's Notebooks about which questions seem most important. Tell them that good readers always think about what is important in selections, and they try to remember this important information.

COMPREHENSION

## Comprehension Strategies

First Read

### Teacher Modeling

**5 Answering Questions** *As I continued to read, I think I found an answer to my previous question. I wondered what it would take to reunite Chrissy and Leah. I think I have found my answer. Chrissy and Leah are starting to share things from their tree houses, like the books and the bananas. I think they will continue to share things and will realize that they like being friends.*

**6 Visualizing** *I'm trying to form a mental picture of the bridge between Chrissy's and Leah's tree houses. I don't think the bridge is too far off the ground or it would be dangerous, but it must be as high off the ground as the top of the fence because Leah says it will go across the top of the fence. What do you imagine the bridge to look like? Remember to tell the class when you form a good mental picture of the characters or events in the story.*

---

### Word Knowledge

**prefix re-:**    returned

---

**Teacher Tip** Ask students one or more of the following questions to make sure they understand what they are reading: Is anyone confused? Do you need clarification? Can you summarize what you have read so far? Does what you are reading make sense to you?

"I have some bananas," Leah told her. "Do you want one?" Chrissy nodded, and Leah climbed up and returned with a banana to pass across the fence.  **5**

Back in her own tree house, Chrissy peeled and ate the banana. Then she called to Leah again.

"Do you have a wastebasket in your house? I don't want to mess up my carpeting with this banana peel."

Leah, looking through her window, nodded. So Chrissy climbed down, and Leah climbed down, and Chrissy handed the banana peel across the fence.

Both girls climbed back into their houses. Chrissy sat alone and admired her fringed rug for a moment, then leafed through her books again, wondering what Leah was doing. She called through her window.

"Leah?"

Leah looked out. "What?"

"I could come visit you if you want," Chrissy said.

Leah didn't answer.

"Or you could come visit me," Chrissy added.

"Your sign says KEEP OUT," Leah pointed out. "So does mine."

"Well," Chrissy suggested, "we could change them."

56

Leah nodded. Each girl removed her sign and crossed out the words KEEP OUT. They wrote WELCOME instead. They rehung their signs.

"You know what, Chrissy?" Leah said. "We could use that wide board in the corner of my yard. It would go from your porch to my porch, over the top of the fence. Then we could visit each other by walking across the board." **6**

Chrissy eyed the distance and the <u>height</u>. "What if we fell?"

"It's not very high," Leah pointed out. "And if we each came out halfway and held hands, we could help each other across."

They climbed down their ladders. The wide board was heavy, but when each girl took an end they were able to lift it into place. In a few minutes they had made a bridge between the houses, over the top of the fence.

57

# COMPREHENSION

## Comprehension Skills
LA.A.2.2.7.3.1; LA.E.1.2.3.3.3  **Second Read**

### Compare and Contrast

Explain to students that at the end of the story, the signs on the tree houses are different from what they were at the beginning of the story. Ask students to explain how the purpose of the signs in this story changed from the beginning of the story to the end. Ask students to find the text that describes the signs and compare the message each sign conveys. See page 59.

■ KEEP OUT *(beginning of the story)*

■ WELCOME *(end of the story)*

What other things do Chrissy and Leah have in common now? *(both have Welcome signs, both like bananas, both like books, both have a tree house connected by a bridge)*

---

### Word Knowledge

prefix *re-:*    removed
             rehung

---

**Teacher Tip** If you observe persistent omissions or confusion in the use of strategies, focus on problem areas and model those strategies, prompting students often to use them also.

---

**Teacher Tip** Encourage students to differentiate between characters' actions and their thoughts and feelings. Ensure that they recognize how the two are different but related.

**COMPREHENSION**

## Comprehension Strategies

### Teacher Modeling

**7 Making Connections** *I enjoy sharing things with my friends, just as Chrissy and Leah do in this part of the story. Since I know about the nice feelings that go with sharing, I can understand how the two girls feel at the end of the story.*

### Teacher Modeling

**8 Asking and Answering Questions** *What does Chrissy mean when she says the best part is the bridge? I think she means that sharing makes the tree houses even more fun. I think Chrissy and Leah have realized that their friendship is the most important thing of all.*

### Discussing Strategy Use  LA.A.1.2.4.3.1

While students are reading the selection, encourage them to share any problems they encounter and to tell what strategies they use to solve them.

- What connections did they make between the reading and what they already know?

- What questions did they ask as they read?

- What did they visualize as they were reading?

These are questions good readers ask after they read a text. After reading, they should always be asking, "What did I find interesting? What is important here?" Later, remind the students again that whenever they conclude a reading, they should ask themselves questions about what was in the text.

---

### Word Knowledge
**antonyms:**  **wide** (narrow)
**women** (men)
**new** (old)
**better** (worse)

---

Chrissy stepped from her tree house porch onto the wide board, reached for Leah's waiting hand, and walked across. She entered Leah's tree house and looked around.

There was no rug, and the only books were her own that Leah had borrowed. But there was a bowl of fruit, a wastebasket, and curtains at the windows. The walls were covered with portraits of beautiful women—the most beautiful women Chrissy had ever seen.

"I like your art collection, Leah," Chrissy said.

"They're left over from where my mom works," Leah explained. "She works at a beauty parlor, and they get pictures of all the new hairstyles. These are last year's."

"You can't tell. They look brand new."

"My house isn't as nice as yours," Leah added. "I said it was better inside, but it isn't, really."

58

---

"I don't really have carpeting," Chrissy admitted. "Only an old rug. And I don't have curtains, or a single picture on my walls."

"I could let you have one of my pictures. Two, even. You can have the blonde shag and the auburn blunt cut."

"My grandpa had paint left over. He could paint the outside of your house so we'd match. But I'm afraid we don't have another door bell." **7**

"Now that my sign says WELCOME, I don't think I need a door bell," Leah said.

"I don't really hate you, Leah," Chrissy said.

"I don't really hate you, either," Leah replied.

They sat together on Leah's porch and looked around happily.

"What do you think is the best part of a tree house, Chrissy?" Leah asked.

Chrissy thought. She looked over at her own house, with its shutters and brass hinges. She looked around at Leah's, with its bowl of bright apples and its yellow curtains.

"The *very* best part," she said finally, "is the bridge." **8**

59

COMPREHENSION

## Comprehension Skills LA.E.1.2.3.3.1

 **Second Read**

### Compare and Contrast

Remind students that comparing and contrasting items is a skill they can use in everyday life and in their reading outside of class. Understanding similarities and differences and being able to explain them improves student comprehension. Words that students can use to express similarities and differences include *like, as, although, similarly, different from, same, too, in contrast, but,* and *on the other hand.* Invite students to summarize similarities and differences of characters in this story. *(Chrissy and Leah both like to read, and they both have tree houses. On the other hand, Chrissy's tree house is fancier than Leah's. But both of them like to share.)*

### Checking Comprehension

- In what ways are Chrissy and Leah alike? *(They are about the same age; they both have tree houses; they are both competitive.)*

- In what ways are the girls different? *(Chrissy has a fancier tree house.)*

- Why is the bridge important to the friends? *(It provides a way for the two girls to get together and helps to solve their differences.)*

### Word Knowledge

| | |
|---|---|
| antonyms: | **old** (new) |
| | **outside** (inside) |
| | **happily** (unhappily) |
| | **best** (worst) |

 **Teacher Tip FLUENCY** By this time in third grade, good readers should be reading approximately 107 words per minute with fluency and expression. The only way to gain this fluency is through practice. Have students reread the selection to you and to each other during Workshop to help build fluency.

**Formal Assessment**

See pages 10–13 in *Unit 1 Assessment* to test students' comprehension of "The Tree House."

**Teacher Tip** DISCUSSION In order for the *handing-off process* to work effectively, a seating arrangement that allows students to face one another is essential. A circle or semicircle is effective.

**Routine Card**
Refer to *Routine 6* for the *handing-off process*.

**www.sra4kids.com**
**Web Connection**
Some students may choose to conduct a computer search for additional books or information about friendship. Invite them to make a list of these books and sources of information to share with classmates and the school librarian. Check the Reading link of the SRA Web page for additional links to theme-related Web sites.

| Clues | Problems | Wonderings |
|---|---|---|
| One girl is sitting by herself. | shutters | Why is there a sign that says "Keep Out"? |

*Reading Transparency 46*

## Discussing the Selection LA.C.1.2.3.3.1; LA.E.1.2.1.3.1

After the first read, the whole group discusses the selection and any personal thoughts, reactions, problems, or questions that it raises. To stimulate discussion, students can ask one another the kinds of questions that good readers ask themselves about a text: *How does it connect to friendship? What have I learned that is new? What did I find interesting? What is important here? What was difficult to understand? Why would someone want to read this?*

**Handing-Off Process** Seeing you as a contributing member of the group sets a strong example for students. To emphasize that you are part of the group, actively participate in the *handing-off process*: Raise your hand to be called on by the last speaker when you have a contribution to make. Point out unusual and interesting insights verbalized by students so that these insights are recognized and discussed. As the year progresses, students will take more and more responsibility for the discussions of the selections.

Engage students in a discussion to determine whether they have grasped the following ideas:

- why Chrissy and Leah stopped talking to each other
- how they started talking to each other again
- how they found a way to share with each other
- how sharing made the tree houses better

During this time, have students return to the clues, problems, and wonderings they noted during browsing to determine whether the clues were borne out by the selection, whether and how their problems were solved, and whether their wonderings were answered or deserve further discussion and investigation. Let the students decide which items deserve further discussion.

Also have students return to the Focus Questions on the first page of the selection. Select a student to read the questions aloud, and have volunteers answer the questions. If students do not know the answers to the questions, have them return to the text to find the answers.

You may wish to review the elements of realistic fiction with students at this time. Discuss with them how they can tell that "The Tree House" is realistic fiction.

Have students break into small groups to discuss what this story tells them about how important sharing is in friendship. Groups can discuss their ideas with the rest of the class.

Students may wish to record their personal responses to the selection. If they have ever had an argument and made up with a friend, or experienced how sharing can make friendship more fun, encourage them to record these events.

## Review Selection Vocabulary LA.A.1.2.2.3.2

Have students review the definitions of the selection vocabulary words that they wrote in the Vocabulary section of their Writer's Notebooks. Remind them that they discussed the meanings of these words before reading the selection. Have students write sentences for each of the vocabulary words after the definitions in the same section of their Writer's Notebooks. They can use the definitions and the sentences to study for the vocabulary portion of their Lesson Assessments. Have them add to the personal dictionary section of their Writer's Notebooks any other interesting words that they clarified while reading. Encourage students to refer to the selection vocabulary words throughout the unit. The words from the selection are:

**magnificent     marvelous     beautiful     peered     height**

Remind students to find words from other resources, from their activities, and from family discussions and add them to the Word Bank. Students may also place synonyms and antonyms in the Word Bank.

## View Fine Art LA.C.2.2.2.3.1

Have students reflect on the painting *The Good Friends* on page 63 of the *Student Anthology* and share their thoughts and reactions with the class. Explain that the painting by Honoré Daumier features the gestures and facial expressions of two old friends. Ask students to react to the expressions and gestures of the two friends and explain what they imagine the relationship to be like. Do the two friends share with each other? Have they ever had an argument? Have they been friends a long time? Ask students to explain their reactions.

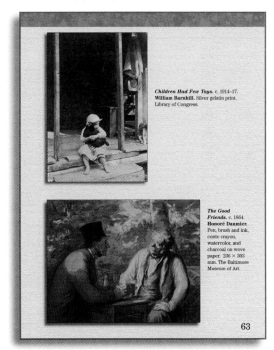

*Children Had Few Toys.* c. 1914–17. **William Barnhill.** Silver gelatin print. Library of Congress.

*The Good Friends.* c. 1864. **Honoré Daumier.** Pen, brush and ink, conté crayon, watercolor, and charcoal on wove paper. 236 × 303 mm. The Baltimore Museum of Art.

63

*Student Anthology p. 63*

## Home Connection

Distribute *Home Connection,* page 7. Encourage students to discuss "The Tree House" with their families. With a family member, students will learn how to make banana pops—a tasty treat inspired by this selection. *Home Connection* is also available in Spanish, page 8.

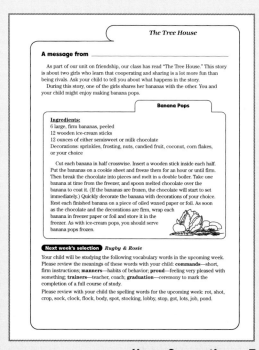

*Home Connection p. 7*

*Reading Transparency 50*

**Teacher Tip** Teach students that using the skill Compare and Contrast will benefit them in both reading and writing.

## Supporting the Reading  LA.A.2.2.7.3.1; LA.E.1.2.3.3.2, LA.E.1.2.3.3.3

### Comprehension Skills: Compare and Contrast

**Teach** Tell students that comparing and contrasting helps them understand the similarities and differences between people, places, things, or events. Sometimes similarities and differences are not directly pointed out as such by a writer, but they become apparent through description.

**Guided Practice** Use the two-column chart on *Reading Transparency 50* to help students list similarities and differences. Label the chart columns: *Chrissy's Tree House* and *Leah's Tree House.* Have students reread the descriptions of the tree houses and record information in the chart. You may use the following as an example to get started. After the list is complete, have students identify the information as either a similarity or a difference.

| Chrissy's Tree House | Leah's Tree House |
|---|---|
| built in one week | built in one day |

**Independent Practice** Read through the Focus and Identify sections of *Comprehension and Language Arts Skills,* page 8, with students. Guide students through the Identify portion, and help them come up with examples found in the story. Then have students complete the Practice and Apply portions of *Comprehension and Language Arts Skills,* page 9.

**Link to Writing** Tell students that comparing and contrasting is a good way to improve comprehension and also to help make decisions. Have students write about the similarities and differences between two things of interest to them. Perhaps they are wondering which sports game is their favorite and can write about the similarities and differences between two sports. They can also compare things such as seasons of the year, types of pets, or different places to live *(apartment, house, country, town).*

## Meeting Individual Needs

### Reteach

**COMPARE AND CONTRAST** Have students who need additional practice with Compare and Contrast complete *Reteach,* pages 10–11.

### Challenge

**COMPARE AND CONTRAST** Have students who understand Compare and Contrast complete *Challenge,* page 9.

**Skills Trace**
Compare and Contrast
Introduced in Grade 1.
Scaffolded throughout Grades 2 and 3.
**REINTRODUCED:** Unit 1, Lesson 3
**REINFORCED:** Unit 3, Lesson 4
Unit 6, Lesson 1
**TESTED:** Unit 1 Assessment

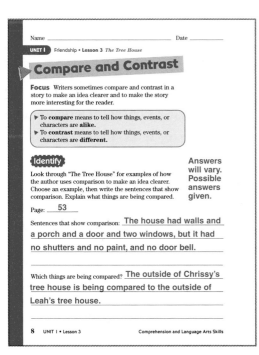

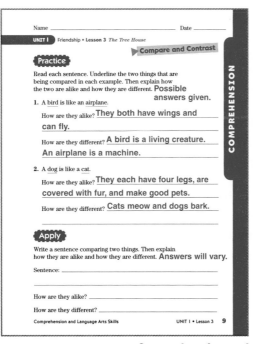

*Comprehension and Language Arts Skills pp. 8–9*

## Literary Elements    LA.E.1.2.2.3.3

### Dialogue

**Teach** Teach students that *dialogue* is conversation between characters and that a character's exact words are enclosed in quotation marks.

Tell students that writers use informal language in dialogue so characters sound natural and talk the way people really talk. Writers also use dialogue to add humor to a story.

To make dialogue sound natural, writers sometimes use contractions and slang, include pauses or incomplete thoughts, and sometimes spell words the way a character might pronounce them.

Explain to students that an author can share information about setting, plot, and characters' feelings through a character's words.

**Guided Practice** Have students find and read aloud examples of dialogue from "The Tree House." Have them identify clues that the words are spoken by a character. Encourage students to discuss what a character's dialogue indicates about the character. Have students write the definition of dialogue in their Writer's Notebooks under the section Identifying the Writer's Craft. Also have them include examples of dialogue from the current selection.

**Independent Practice** Have students write a narrative from a previous conversation they had with a friend. Tell them to be sure to use quotation marks to indicate when characters are speaking.

## Social Studies Connection SS.A.2.2.4.3.1

### City Government

In "The Tree House," Chrissy and Leah had an argument and quit talking to each other for several days. Sometimes neighbors in a community also have disagreements over issues such as property, taxes, or transportation, to name a few.

Allow individuals or small groups to search in the library or on the Internet to find out how city government is organized, where citizens can address local concerns, and how neighbors can resolve disputes. Have each group of students make a poster or overhead transparency showing the information they learned about city government. Then students can share their information with the class.

**Teacher Tip  MATERIALS**
- ✔ poster boards
- ✔ colored pencils or markers
- ✔ overhead transparencies and markers

**Teacher Tip  PURPOSE**  To help make students aware of city government and established practices for resolving local issues.

## Meet the Author

After students read about Lois Lowry, have them answer the following questions:

- Lois Lowry was four when she decided that she would like to write stories, but she didn't write her first children's book until she was forty. What does this tell you about her desire to be a writer? *(Possible answer: She really wanted to do it. She set a goal and worked hard for it.)*

- Lois Lowry has published many children's stories. Based on the story you just read, why do you think she's been so successful? *(Possible answer: Answers will vary. She is a good story teller and bases some of her stories on her real life. She likes to talk about friendship.)*

## Meet the Illustrator

After students read about Trina Schart Hyman, have them answer the following questions:

- Why do you think Trina Schart Hyman uses people from her life in her drawings? Do you think the children in the pictures in this story are people she knows? *(Possible answer: It might be easier to draw what you see every day. She cares about these people and wants to preserve their memories.)*

- Why do you think Trina Schart Hyman kept trying when she received so many rejections for her drawings? *(Possible answer: She was determined to be a successful artist. She believed in herself.)*

# The Tree House

## Meet the Author

**Lois Lowry** was born in Honolulu, Hawaii. Her father was in the army, so the family lived in many different places. She even attended junior high school in Tokyo, Japan. Lowry taught herself to read before she was four years old when she realized that letters made sounds, sounds made words, words made sentences, and sentences made stories. She was so excited by her discovery that she says, *"It was then that I decided that one day I would write books."* She wrote her first children's book when she was forty years old, in honor of her sister Helen who died of cancer. Since then she has published many children's stories, some of them based upon the lives of her own children.

## Meet the Illustrator

**Trina Schart Hyman** worked many years before she became a famous children's illustrator. She started drawing when she was young and went on 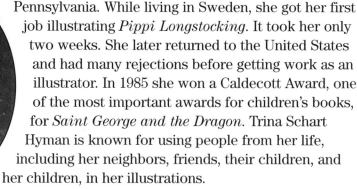 to art schools in her hometown of Philadelphia, Pennsylvania. While living in Sweden, she got her first job illustrating *Pippi Longstocking*. It took her only two weeks. She later returned to the United States and had many rejections before getting work as an illustrator. In 1985 she won a Caldecott Award, one of the most important awards for children's books, for *Saint George and the Dragon*. Trina Schart Hyman is known for using people from her life, including her neighbors, friends, their children, and her children, in her illustrations.

60

# Theme Connections

## Within the Selection

Record your answers to the questions below in the Response Journal section of your Writer's Notebook. In small groups, report the ideas you wrote. Discuss your ideas with the rest of the group. Then choose a person to report your group's answers to the class.

- How did Chrissy's tree house hurt her friendship with Leah?
- Why did Chrissy and Leah decide to change their signs from **KEEP OUT** to **WELCOME?**

## Across Selections

- How is this story like the other stories you have read?
- How is Chrissy different than Julian from "Gloria Who Might Be My Best Friend"?

## Beyond the Selection

- Did you ever have an argument with a friend? Did the story give you any ideas about how to make up with a friend?
- Think about how "The Tree House" adds to what you know about friendship.
- Add items to the Concept/Question Board about friendship.

61

## Theme Connections  LA.E.2.2.4.3.1

### Within the Selection

- When Chrissy told Leah to **KEEP OUT,** Leah's feelings were hurt and both girls began saying mean things to each other.
- Chrissy and Leah both realized that they were lonely and bored without a friend.

### Across Selections

- The characters have all become friends in the end.
- Julian decided to seek out a friendship as soon as he saw Gloria. At first, Chrissy wanted to keep her tree house and all of its belongings to herself.

### Beyond the Selection

Have groups report their ideas to the class and add these ideas to the Concept/Question Board. Have students tell how they might use this in their investigations.

### Inquiry Journal

Students should record their ideas and impressions about the selections on page 3 of their *Inquiry Journals.*

Recording Concept Information *(continued)*
- "The Tree House" by Lois Lowry
Answers will vary.

- "Rugby & Rosie" by Nan Parson Rossiter
Answers will vary.

Inquiry Journal • *Recording Concept Information*          UNIT 1  **3**

*Inquiry Journal p. 3*

**Teacher Tip** These activities may be done in Workshop.

**Informal Assessment**

This may be a good time to observe students working in small groups and to mark your observations in the Teacher Observation Log, found in the *Program Assessment Teacher's Edition.*

**INVESTIGATION**

## Objectives

- Students gain a deeper understanding of friendship.
- Students form conjectures and share them with the group.
- Students divide up the work for the investigations and create a plan for getting the work done and presenting the investigation.

## Materials

- Student Anthology, Book 1, pp. 48–63
- Research Assistant CD-ROM
- Inquiry Journal, pp. 16–19

## Investigating Concepts Beyond the Text: Conjecture and Needs LA.C.3.2.2.3.1

Real investigation is motivated by more than a general interest or curiosity about a topic. It is motivated by a problem or by questions. Students might still need some help formulating their investigation questions. Once they have formed their questions, the next step is to form a conjecture. The Conjecture Phase provides an opportunity for the students to think about a hypothesis related to their investigation questions. As students share their conjectures, record them on the board or on a transparency.

Help students identify their information needs. Questions they should be asking themselves are, "What information do I need to answer my question?" and, "How will that information affect my conjecture?" Students' investigations should be focused on coming to a deeper understanding of friendship.

If students still need some guidance in choosing their investigations, you can offer the following suggestion. Some students may want to engage in some role-playing. Point out that Chrissy and Leah became friends again when they "mended fences." Explain that this expression means to mend or repair a friendship. When two people mend fences, they take steps to fix what is wrong between them. Encourage students to share their thoughts about mending fences through sharing. Small groups can role-play good ways to repair damaged friendships. After the role-play, students should discuss their ideas about ways to mend a friendship.

# Concept/Question Board

After reading each selection, students should use the Concept/Question Board to do the following:

- Post any questions they asked about a selection before reading that have not yet been answered.

- Refer to as they formulate statements about concepts that apply to their investigations.

- Post general statements formulated by each collaborative group.

- Continue to post news articles or other items that they find during the unit investigation.

- Read and think about posted questions, articles, or concepts that interest them and provide answers to the questions.

**Concept/Question Board**

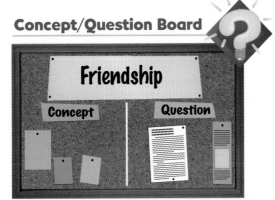

Friendship

Concept     Question

**INVESTIGATION**

**Teacher Tip INVESTIGATION ACTIVITIES** To assist students with the role-play, encourage them to think about a time when a friendship was not working. What caused the friendship to break apart? What could have been done to repair the problem? Thinking of personal experiences will guide students in this activity.

## Research Assistant
The *Research Assistant CD-ROM* assists students in their investigations.

**www.sra4kids.com**
**Web Connection**
More information about Friendship and links to Web sites concerning friendship can be found at www.sra4kids.com.

# Unit I Investigation Management

| Lesson I | **Collaborative Investigation**<br>Introduce the investigation cycle and explain its purpose. Students can lead a panel discussion on friendship-related issues. |
|---|---|
| Lesson 2 | **Collaborative Investigation**<br>Students organize into groups based on shared areas of interest. |
| Lesson 3 | **Collaborative Investigation**<br>**Student groups form conjectures to direct initial investigations.**<br>**Supplementary Activities**<br>**Students can participate in role-playing to explore ways to mend damaged friendships.** |
| Lesson 4 | Students begin their investigations. Groups can share personal stories, hold a panel discussion, or invite an expert speaker to class. |
| Lesson 5 | Students revise investigation plans as necessary. Groups discuss teammate qualities and invite a coach to class to interview. |
| Lesson 6 | Students wrap up investigations and prepare formal presentations. Students can discuss standing by friends and write a scene or miniplay about a scenario. |

**INVESTIGATION**

**Teacher Tip** Encourage students to use the Concept/Question Board frequently. Remind them that they can ask and answer questions as well as post objects or items related to the theme or selection.

### Formal Assessment

Use the Research Rubrics on page 48J to assess students' ability to make conjectures.

## Organizing Investigation LA.C.3.2.2.3.1

As students check the Concept/Question Board and participate in activities such as role-playing, questions may come up that they would like to think more about. Explain to students that creating a plan for their investigation will help them organize tasks and information or discoveries.

Tell students that they will continue to ask more questions throughout the Research Cycle—that is the nature of investigation. Having a plan can help students organize the investigation for new questions as they arise and incorporate them into their investigations. Have student groups work on pages 16–17 of the *Inquiry Journal,* and tell them they may have to revisit these pages as their investigations continue.

Name _____ Date _____

**UNIT I** Friendship

**Planning Investigation**

How can you investigate friendship further? You may have already started working on a survey to investigate what people look for in a friend. Write down some other ways you can find out more about friendship.

**Answers will vary.**

_____

_____

_____

As you investigate friendship, you will want to keep a list of things you need to do. Check off each item as you complete it. Here is the start of a list of things you might want to remember to do. Add to it as you become more sure about what route your investigation will take. **Answers will vary.**

| Things to Do | Completed |
|---|---|
| talk to friends | |
| talk to adults | |
| find and use books from bibliographies | |
| | |
| | |

16 UNIT I          *Planning Investigation • Inquiry Journal*

**Planning Investigation** *(continued)*

What ideas do you have for investigating and writing about friendship? What ideas about friendship would you like to explore further? Write your thoughts here. If you don't have many ideas right now, that's okay. You will probably think of more ideas as you read the rest of the stories in the unit. Add to this list each time you get a new idea.

**Answers will vary.**

_____

_____

_____

_____

Now think of ways you can present your information to the rest of the class. Remember, you don't have to present a written report. You may choose to prepare a poster, a speech, a video, whatever you think would be the best way to present new information to your classmates. List your ideas about how to present your project. Add to this list as you read and investigate and come up with new ideas.

**Answers will vary.**

_____

_____

_____

_____

*Inquiry Journal • Planning Investigation*          UNIT I 17

*Inquiry Journal pp. 16–17*

# ABC Order

**Teach** Ask students if they know what is meant by ABC, or alphabetical order. If necessary, tell students that it means listing information in the same order as the letters of the alphabet.

Explain to students that many times the information they need is arranged in ABC order. Ask students to tell what sources they know that list information in ABC order. (These might include *dictionaries, thesauruses, encyclopedias, indexes, glossaries,* and *phone books.*)

Tell students the following rules for putting information in ABC order:

1. When words start with different letters, use the first letter of each word to put the words in ABC order.
   **buddy     friend     pal**

2. When the words start with the same first letter, use the next letter that is different in each word to put the words in alphabetical order.
   **s<u>o</u>ggy     s<u>p</u>oiled     s<u>t</u>oop**

3. If the first word of a title is *a, an,* or *the,* do not use that word. Instead, use the first letter of the second word.
   **"The <u>B</u>oy Who Didn't Believe in Spring"**
   **"A <u>C</u>loak for the Dreamer"**
   **"The <u>T</u>ree House"**

4. When you look up or list names, use the first letter of the person's last name.
   **Ann <u>C</u>ameron**
   **Peter <u>G</u>olenboch**
   **Lois <u>L</u>owry**

**Guided Practice** Have students look through reference books to reinforce the idea that information is listed in ABC order. Then put students' names in ABC order by having them line up in front of the classroom.

**Independent Practice** Have students rearrange the following list of words to put them in ABC order:

| | | | |
|---|---|---|---|
| **vanilla** | **apple** | **peach** | **strawberry** |
| **blueberry** | **cinnamon** | **pineapple** | **chocolate** |

For more practice with ABC order, have students complete the *Inquiry Journal,* pages 18–19.

Name_____ Date_____

UNIT 1  Friendship

## ABC Order

ABC order, or alphabetical order, is a good way to organize lists. Look at the first letter of each word and arrange the words in ABC order. If the first letters are the same, use the letter that follows them: **stem, stick, stump.**

Use the lines below to write down the first names of all of the students in your class. Then on the next page, write the list of names in ABC order.

Answers will vary.

18  UNIT 1                ABC Order • Inquiry Journal

ABC Order *(continued)*

Names in ABC order:
Answers will vary.

Inquiry Journal • *ABC Order*                UNIT 1  **19**

*Inquiry Journal pp. 18–19*

## Objectives

**Word Analysis**

**Spelling**
- **The /i/ Sound.** Develop understanding of the /i/ sound spelled *i*.

**Vocabulary**
- **Word Structure.** Using words from "The Tree House," learn to apply Word Structure to discover the meaning of an unknown word.

**Writing Process Strategies**
- **Drafting.** Using the chosen topic and graphic organizer from the prewriting step, students will put their ideas into sentences.

**English Language Conventions**

**Grammar, Usage, and Mechanics**
- **Verbs.** This lesson defines verbs and distinguishes action verbs from state-of-being verbs. Find action and state-of-being verbs in "The Tree House" and use them in writing.

**Listening, Speaking, Viewing**
- **Language: Changing Our Speech.** Learn differences among vocabulary, speech topics, and voice volume when speaking at home and at school.

**Penmanship**
- **Cursive Letters *r* and *s*.** Develop handwriting skills by practicing formation of cursive *r* and *s*.

## Materials

- Language Arts Handbook
- Comprehension and Language Arts Skills, pp. 8–13
- Writer's Workbook, p. 3
- Language Arts Transparencies 24–25
- Student Anthology
- Writing Folder
- Spelling and Vocabulary Skills, pp. 10–13
- Sound/Spelling Card 9
- High-Frequency Flash Cards

## MEETING INDIVIDUAL NEEDS

*Reteach, Challenge, English-Language Development,* and *Intervention* lessons are available to support the language arts instruction in this lesson.

## Research in Action

. . . We should habitually encourage students to look at spelling patterns and vocabulary items that we want them to learn. We should write the words of interest on the board or point to them on the page. *(Marilyn Adams, Beginning to Read: Thinking and Learning About Print)*

**OVERVIEW**

# Language Arts Overview

## Word Analysis

**Spelling** The Spelling activities on the following pages introduce the /i/ sound spelled *i* by developing spelling skills through various strategies.

### Selection Spelling Words

These words from "The Tree House" contain the /i/ sound.

l**i**ttle   l**i**ft   w**i**th   v**i**s**i**t   w**i**ndow

**Vocabulary** The Vocabulary activities introduce word structure. The *structure* of a word refers to the parts, or morphemes, of the word. Breaking apart a word into its roots, prefixes, suffixes, endings, and base words can help identify the known parts of a word. Understanding the structural patterns can help the reader gain an understanding of the meaning of the word.

### Vocabulary Skill Words

shutters   hinges   markers   belonged   paintbrush

**Additional Materials:** dictionary

## Writing Process Strategies

The Writing Process Strategies lesson involves instruction in the drafting step of the writing process. The focus of the drafting step is to use the foundation established during prewriting to get one's thoughts down on paper quickly. As practice for this skill, students will draft their autobiographies.

**Basic Computer Skills** To introduce students to the computer as a writing tool, teach students how to use the Help feature to find information about how to use computer programs. *Basic Computer Skills*, Level 3, Lesson 4, teaches these basic computer skills. LA.D.2.2.4.3.1

## English Language Conventions

**Grammar, Usage, and Mechanics** **Verbs.** Understand action and state-of-being verbs, and that some state-of-being verbs are linking verbs. Apply that understanding to their autobiographies.

**Listening, Speaking, Viewing** **Language: Changing Our Speech.** In this language lesson, students will review how language usage varies for different situations and audiences.

**Penmanship** **Cursive Letters *r* and *s*.** This lesson continues the development of cursive handwriting skills. Students learn correct formation of *r* and *s* and then practice writing words from the literature selection that contain those letters.

# DAY I

## Word Analysis

### Spelling

#### Assessment: Pretest

**The /i/ Sound** LA.A.1.2.2.3.1

#### Teach

Give students the Pretest found on page 30 of *Unit 1 Assessment* as entry assessment of the spelling pattern. Have them proofread and correct any misspelled words.

**Pretest Sentences**

1. **pick** A farmer has a **pick** for hay.
2. **risk** Jumping off rocks is a **risk**.
3. **film** You put **film** in a camera.
4. **grip** You **grip** a rope during tug-of-war.
5. **brick** Some houses are made of **brick**.
6. **give** Many charities **give** food to the hungry.
7. **stitch** Each **stitch** in a quilt should be straight.
8. **finish** Contestants run to **finish** a marathon.
9. **trick** A magic **trick** can be amazing.
10. **live** Many people **live** in apartments.
11. **window** Stained glass fits into a **window**.
12. **visit** Some people take trips to **visit** their families.
13. **lift** A heavy book is hard to **lift**.
14. **with** The winner of a contest often smiles **with** pride.
15. **into** Keys fit **into** locks.

Diagnose any misspellings by determining whether students misspelled the /i/ sound or some other part of the word. Then use the Pretest as a take-home list to study spellings of the /i/ sound.

## Writing Process Strategies

### Drafting LA.B.1.2.2.3.5
Introduction to the Writing Process

#### Teach

**Introduce Writing Process Steps**
Read *Language Arts Handbook,* page 28, to introduce the drafting step of the writing process.

**Inspiration**
Teacher Model: *"I am glad I did so much work on my graphic organizer. Now, all I have to do is to put my ideas into sentences. Of course, I have to keep my audience in mind so I can write as though I am talking to my readers."*

### Guided Practice

**Drafting**
Put students into groups and have them draft a paragraph from notes on getting ideas and prewriting from their Writer's Notebooks.

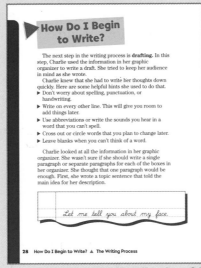

*Language Arts Handbook p. 28*

## English Language Conventions

### Grammar, Usage, and Mechanics
**Grammar: Verbs** LA.B.1.2.3.3.3

#### Teach

- Explain that verbs show the actions, condition, or state of being of the subject of a sentence. Explain that action verbs can be seen or unseen.
- Create a chart on the board of action and state-of-being verbs. Some action verbs to use are *run, read,* and *forget.* Some state-of-being verbs to use are *am, is,* and *are.*
- Explain that some state-of-being verbs can also be linking verbs. Write these sentences on the board.
  - I am a teacher. (Am *is the linking verb; it links the noun* teacher *to the subject* I.)
  - They are both very tall. (Are *is the linking verb; it links the adjective* tall *to the subject* they.)
- Use *Language Arts Handbook,* page 250, for the definition and examples of verbs.

### Independent Practice
Use *Comprehension and Language Arts Skills,* pages 10–11, to reinforce what verbs do and practice identifying action and state-of-being verbs.

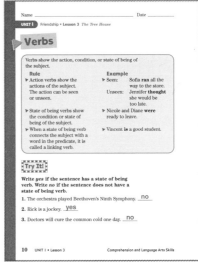

*Comprehension and Language Arts Skills p. 10*

# DAY 2

| Word Analysis | Writing Process Strategies | English Language Conventions |
| --- | --- | --- |

## Word Analysis

### Spelling

**Word Sorting** LA.A.1.2.2.3.1

- Hold up **Sound/Spelling Card 9**. Have the class say the word *pig* and notice the /i/ sound made by the letter *i*.
- **Word Sort.** Find **High-Frequency Word Flash Cards** of *give, best, this, day, did, ride, saw, his, when,* and *in*. Write *Words with the /i/ Sound* and *Words with Other Vowel Sounds* as two columns. Have students sort the words under the correct column.

### Vocabulary

**Word Structure** LA.A.1.2.2.3.4

#### Teach

- Write *shutters* on the board. Explain how a word's *structure* can be broken into parts.
- Underline *shut* in *shutters*. Ask what *shut* means. ("to close") Circle *er* in *shutters*. Explain that *er* makes a word mean "something that can _____ ."
- Circle the *s*. Explain that *s* added to a word makes it mean "more than one."

#### Guided Practice

Use **Spelling and Vocabulary Skills,** page 10, to reinforce word structure. Ask students to complete page 11 as independent practice.

*Spelling and Vocabulary Skills p. 10*

## Writing Process Strategies

**Drafting** LA.B.1.2.2.3.5
**Introduction to the Writing Process**

### Teach

- **Review** the drafting step of the writing process.
- Go over **Language Arts Transparency 24,** Word Choice, with students.
- Remind students that even though they are getting their thoughts down quickly, they must keep word choice in mind. As they are drafting, they may realize that the word they thought of is not the one they really want.
- Encourage students to circle words they want to change so they remember to think about it later. The important thing for students is to keep the writing flow going.

### Guided Practice

**Drafting**
Encourage students to make word banks by listing words for given categories, such as Ways to Move, Kinds of Pets, Positive Adjectives, and so on.

## English Language Conventions

**Grammar, Usage, and Mechanics**
**Grammar: Verbs** LA.B.1.2.3.3.3

### Teach

- Review what verbs do, and discuss the difference between action and state-of-being verbs.
- Write the following sentences on the board. Ask students to identify action and state-of-being verbs.
  • I am happy because we moved to New York City. (*Am is a state-of-being verb. Moved is an action verb.*)
  • We packed last month. I was sad at first. (*Was is a state-of-being verb. Packed is an action verb.*)
  • New York City is full of fun places to go. We visited the Statue of Liberty last weekend. (*Is is a state-of-being verb. Visited is an action verb.*)
  • Our family rents an apartment next to Central Park. (*Rents is an action verb.*)
  • My dad runs with our dogs in the park every morning. (*Runs is an action verb.*)
  • My dogs are my only friends in New York, until I make new ones. (*Are is a state-of-being verb. Make is an action verb.*)

### Guided Practice in Reading

Read a section of "The Tree House" aloud as the students follow along. Ask students to identify three action verbs and three state-of-being verbs from the section you have read.

# DAY 3

| Word Analysis | Writing Process Strategies | English Language Conventions |
|---|---|---|

## Word Analysis

### Spelling

**The /i/ Sound** LA.A.1.2.2.3.1; LA.B.2.2.2.3.1

#### Teach
Introduce words with the /i/ sound spelled *i* found in "The Tree House." Students should try to put the five Selection Spelling Words in alphabetical order.

#### Guided Practice
Have students complete page 12 from *Spelling and Vocabulary Skills* to begin to learn strategies for spelling words with the /i/ sound.

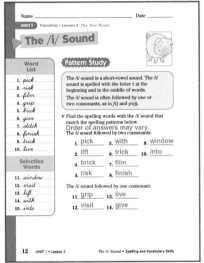

**Spelling and Vocabulary Skills p. 12**

### Vocabulary (continued)

**Word Structure** LA.A.1.2.2.3.4
- Write *shutters, hinges, belonged, markers,* and *paintbrush* on the board.
- As on Day 2, underline *shut* in *shutters.* Ask students to come to the board and underline the words found within the Selection Words. As a class, discuss the underlined words. Point out that the word *paintbrush* is made with two complete words, making it a *compound word.*

## Writing Process Strategies

**Drafting** LA.B.1.2.2.3.5
**Introduction to the Writing Process**

#### Teach
Review *Language Arts Handbook,* page 18, on drafting.

Writer's Craft
**Topic Sentence**
- Introduce the idea of a topic sentence by asking students what they think a topic sentence is.
- Ask them what they think a paragraph with this topic sentence will be about: *My name is Alex.* Accept answers indicating that students are aware that the rest of the paragraph will tell about Alex.
- Read *Language Arts Handbook,* page 182, on topic sentences.
- Read *Comprehension and Language Arts Skills,* pages 12–13, on topic sentences.

#### Guided Practice

**Drafting**
Provide opportunities for students to practice drafting their writing.

## English Language Conventions

**Grammar, Usage, and Mechanics**
**Grammar: Verbs** LA.B.1.2.3.3.3; LA.D.1.2.2.3.1

#### Teach
Use *Language Arts Handbook,* page 250, to review action and state-of-being verbs.

#### Guided Practice in Writing
- Have students make lists of all of the action and state-of-being verbs they can think of. Have them share their lists, writing them on the board as they read them out loud.
- Have students write two sentences about their life that include at least one action verb and one state-of-being verb. Have some students share their sentences and identify the action and state-of-being verbs they used.

**Informal Assessment**

Check to make sure students can identify state-of-being and action verbs in their own writing.

# DAY 4

## Word Analysis

### Spelling

**The /i/ Sound**   LA.A.1.2.2.3.1

#### Teach
Explain to students that the exercises in the **Spelling and Vocabulary Skills** are designed to help them become better spellers. The Meaning strategy helps them become familiar with the meanings of words they know how to spell.

#### Guided Practice
Have students complete the exercises on page 13 of **Spelling and Vocabulary Skills** to reinforce the spelling patterns for the /i/ sound.

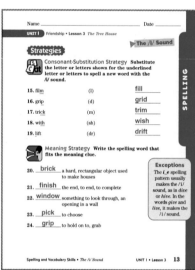

**Spelling and Vocabulary Skills p. 13**

### Vocabulary (continued)

**Word Structure**   LA.A.1.2.2.3.4
- Write *hinges* and *markers* on the board.
- Circle *er* in *markers*. Remind students how *er* adds "something that can ____" meaning to a word. Ask a student to give a general meaning for *marker*. *(possible definition: "something that can mark")*
- Circle the *s* in *hinges* and *markers*. Remind students that *s* makes a word mean "more than one." Have students discuss what *hinges* and *markers* mean. *("things that hinge" and "things that make marks")*

## Writing Process Strategies

**Drafting** LA.B.1.2.2.3.5, LA.B.2.2.6.3.7
**Introduction to the Writing Process**

#### Teach
- Discuss **Language Arts Transparency 25,** Sentence Fluency, with students.
- Explain that sentence fluency is a mixture of short and long sentences that make your writing flow and easier to read.
- Provide examples of sentence fluency from "The Tree House."
- Ask students to notice the use of different sentence lengths in "The Tree House."

#### Guided Practice
**Drafting**
Encourage students to look through any writing they may have for situations in which they could improve their writing by varying the sentence lengths. Students should use a variety of sentence structures to present ideas.

## English Language Conventions

**Listening, Speaking, Viewing**
**Language: Changing Our Speech**   LA.D.1.2.2.3.1

#### Teach
- In Reading and Responding we discussed how to compare and contrast. Here we will compare and contrast how we speak in different situations.
- Explain that the way we speak at home with our family or friends may not be appropriate for school. When something is not *appropriate*, it is not suitable or fitting to a situation.
- At home or at school, we may use different words, or vocabulary, to tell different stories or to talk about different topics.

#### Guided Practice
- In "The Tree House," what kinds of things do Chrissy and Leah say to one another that would not be appropriate to say at school? *(Chrissy brags about her tree house. The girls tell each other that they hate one another.)*
- Ask how the students would speak differently if they were giving a presentation to everyone in their grade compared to telling their friends something during lunch. *(Presentation: use complete sentences; speak clearly; no joking around. At lunch: not as formal; less serious topics.)*

 **Informal Assessment**

Observe whether students understand that the language they use should vary according to the situation or setting they are in.

# DAY 5

| Word Analysis | Writing Process Strategies | English Language Conventions |

## Word Analysis

### Spelling

**Assessment: Final Test**

**The /i/ Sound** LA.A.1.2.2.3.1

#### Teach

Repeat the Pretest for this lesson or use the Final Test on page 31 of *Unit 1 Assessment* as summative assessment for student understanding of the /i/ sound spelling pattern.

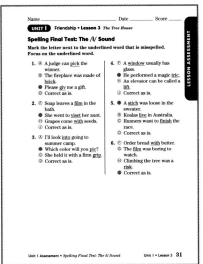
***Unit 1 Assessment, p. 31***

#### Guided Practice

Have students categorize any mistakes they made on the Final Test. Are they careless errors? Are they lesson-pattern problems? Check student assignments to see if they are correctly spelling words with the /i/ sound.

### Vocabulary LA.A.1.2.2.3.4

**Informal Assessment**

Periodically check to see if students are properly using word structure to understand the meanings of unfamiliar words in their reading assignments. Have students add any new words to the running vocabulary word list in the Writer's Notebook.

## Writing Process Strategies

### Drafting LA.B.1.2.2.3.5
**Introduction to the Writing Process**

#### Teach

- Have students look over their time lines for their autobiographies. Discuss how these will be helpful as they write the first draft of their autobiographies. Explain that they will help them keep their dates in the right order.
- Review with students the purpose of writing a topic sentence before they begin the drafting step. Explain that the topic sentence lets their readers know the subject of their writing.

#### Guided Practice
**Drafting**
- Read *Writer's Workbook*, page 3, on drafting.
- Encourage students to write a draft of their autobiographies using information from their time lines. Tell students that they will revise, edit, and do a clean copy of their writing later.

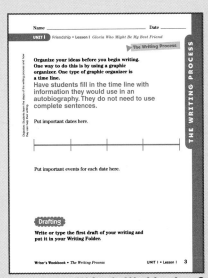
***Writer's Workbook p. 3***

## English Language Conventions

### Penmanship
**Cursive Letters *r* and *s***

#### Teach

- **Teacher Model:** Remind students that all cursive letters are made of four types of strokes (undercurve, overcurve, downcurve, and slant lines). Draw them on the board.
- **Teacher Model:** Introduce lowercase cursive *r* and *s* as undercurve letters.

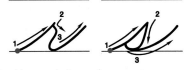

*r*   Starting point, undercurve
     Slant right
     Slant down, undercurve: small *r*

*s*   Starting point, undercurve
     Curve down and back
     Undercurve: small *s*

- **Teacher Model:** On the board, write the words *snake, slurp, rabbit,* and *run* to model proper letter formation and slant by drawing slanted lines through the letters.

#### Guided Practice
- Invite students to come to the board and trace the letters *r* and *s*.
- Have students practice writing rows of *r* and *s* in their Writer's Notebooks.
- From "The Tree House," have students write the words *terrific, tree, was,* and *house* in their Writer's Notebooks to practice letter formation.

**Informal Assessment**

Check students' handwriting for proper slant and that their undercurves rest on the baseline. The letters should not "float" between the lines.

**LESSON WRAP-UP**

# Reading and Language Arts Skills Traces

## Language Arts

### WORD ANALYSIS

**Skills Trace**

**Spelling: The /i/ Sound**
Introduced in Grade 1.
Scaffolded throughout Grades 2–5.
**REINTRODUCED:** Unit 1, Lesson 3, p. 61E
**PRACTICED:** Unit 1, Lesson 3, pp. 61F–61J
*Spelling and Vocabulary Skills,*
pp. 12–13
**TESTED:** Unit 1, Lesson 3, p. 61J
Unit 1 Assessment

**Skills Trace**

**Vocabulary: Word Structure**
Introduced in Grade 1.
Scaffolded throughout Grades 2–5.
**REINTRODUCED:** Unit 1, Lesson 3, p. 61E
**PRACTICED:** Unit 1, Lesson 3, pp. 61F–61J
*Spelling and Vocabulary Skills,*
pp. 10–11
**TESTED:** Unit 1 Assessment

## Reading

### COMPREHENSION

**Skills Trace**

**Compare and Contrast**
Introduced in Grade 1.
Scaffolded throughout Grades 2 and 3.
**REINTRODUCED:** Unit 1, Lesson 3
**REINFORCED:** Unit 3, Lesson 4
Unit 6, Lesson 1
**TESTED:** Unit 1 Assessment

### WRITING PROCESS STRATEGIES

**Skills Trace**

**Introduction to the Writing Process**
Introduced in Grade K.
Scaffolded throughout Grades 1–6.
**REINTRODUCED:** Unit 1, Lesson 3, p. 61F
**PRACTICED:** Unit 1, Lesson 3, pp. 61G–61J
*Writer's Workbook,* p. 3
**TESTED:** Unit 1 Assessment

### ENGLISH LANGUAGE CONVENTIONS

**Skills Trace**

**Grammar: Verbs—Action,
State of Being, and Linking**
Introduced in Grade K.
Scaffolded throughout Grades 1–6.
**REINTRODUCED:** Unit 1, Lesson 3, p. 61F
**PRACTICED:** Unit 1, Lesson 3, p. 61G
Unit 1, Lesson 3, p. 61H
*Comprehension and Language
Arts Skills,* pp. 10–11
**TESTED:** Unit 1, Lesson 3,
Informal Assessment, p. 61H
Unit 1 Assessment

**Skills Trace**

**Listening, Speaking, Viewing
Language: Changing Our Speech**
Introduced in Grade K.
Scaffolded throughout Grades 1–6.
**REINTRODUCED:** Unit 1, Lesson 3, p. 61I
**TESTED:** Unit 1, Lesson 3,
Informal Assessment, p. 61I

**Skills Trace**

**Penmanship: Cursive Letters *r* and *s***
Introduced in Grade 3.
Scaffolded throughout Grades 4–6.
**INTRODUCED:** Unit 1, Lesson 3, p. 61J
**TESTED:** Unit 1, Lesson 3,
Informal Assessment, p. 61J

# Professional Development: Inquiry

## How Does the Inquiry/Investigation Procedure Differ from Conventional Research Instruction?

In conventional elementary school classrooms, *research* generally means having students collect information and prepare a paper. They conduct their research by following a procedure that usually involves a series of steps such as the following: (1) select a topic, (2) narrow the topic, (3) collect materials, (4) take notes, (5) organize notes, (6) make an outline, (7) write the paper, and (8) present the paper.

Topic selection usually means choosing from a list of topics suggested or directed by the teacher. The remainder of the steps usually requires students to locate encyclopedia entries or articles easily found in a library or on the Internet—then write down information from them (Schack, 1993).

Although this procedure may result in the preparation of an adequate paper, it does not constitute *research* in any meaningful or useful sense. Indeed, it gives students a distorted and depressing idea of what real research is all about.

Ample evidence exists that elementary school students *can* do descriptive, historical, and experimental research that seeks answers to real questions or solutions to real problems (Schack, 1993). To do this kind of work, however, students need a better research procedure than the one provided by the traditional approach.

The inquiry/investigation procedure is based on the assumption that students *can* do research that will result in the construction of deeper knowledge. The procedure presents research as a never-ending, recursive cycle. Like real-world researchers, students produce their own questions, develop ideas or conjectures about why

something is the way it is, then pursue the answers. The answers, as for real researchers, may never come. What will come are more questions. Developing the questions, pursuing the answers, developing conjectures, revising ideas, and setting off on new avenues of research and exploration are the stuff of which strong, deep knowledge and expertise are made. The web of knowledge expands in ways that no teacher or student can predict easily.

Translated into instruction, the inquiry/investigation procedure provides enough structure that students do not get lost or bogged down as they explore concepts, while it preserves the open-ended character of real research, which can lead to unexpected findings and to questions that students did not consider originally. To do this, the procedure follows these important principles (Bereiter & Scardamalia, 1993):

- Research focuses on problems, not topics.
- Conjectures guide the research rather than the reverse.
- New information is gathered to test and revise conjectures.
- Discussion, constant feedback, and constructive criticism are important in all phases of the research, especially in the revising of problems and conjectures.
- The cycle of true research is essentially endless, although findings are presented from time to time; new findings give rise to new problems and conjectures, and thus to new cycles of research.

*Additional information about inquiry and investigation as well as resource references can be found in the ***Professional Development Guide: Inquiry and Investigation.***

## Viewing the Theme Through Fine Art

Students can use the artworks on these pages to explore the unit theme Friendship in images rather than words. Encourage them to talk about their impressions of the artworks and how each one might relate to the unit theme Friendship.

Below is background information about each of the artworks. Share with students whatever you feel is appropriate. You may also wish to encourage students to find out more about artists and artistic styles that interest them.

### *Conjunction*

**ROMARE BEARDEN** (1912–1988) often combines torn papers and photos with painted areas to create "a variety of contrary images into one unified expression." Born in Charlotte, North Carolina, he moved at the age of three to Harlem, New York, where he was exposed to many artists, writers, and musicians who regularly visited his home during the Harlem Renaissance. In college he studied math, working his way through as an illustrator and cartoonist. It was at the age of 21 that Bearden decided to pursue a career in art. He studied in both New York and Paris, where he was influenced by the modern painters of his time.

***Conjunction*** is a print which, like his paintings, portrays his subjects at odd angles; the right figure is shown with feet and head in profile, while the body is frontally displayed. Much of his work is about the African-American experience; however, he was also inspired by the works of Homer, and by religion and music, particularly jazz.

# Fine Art · Friendship

***Conjunction.*** 1971. **Romare Bearden.** Piquette. ©Romare Bearden Foundation/Licensed by VAGA, New York, NY.

62

*Children Had Few Toys.* c. 1914–17. **William Barnhill.** Silver gelatin print. Library of Congress.

*The Good Friends.* c. 1864. **Honoré Daumier.** Pen, brush and ink, conte crayon, watercolor, and charcoal on wove paper. 236 × 303 mm. The Baltimore Museum of Art.

63

## Children Had Few Toys

**WILLIAM BARNHILL** was an American photographer. Little is known about him, but it is believed this photo was taken as part of a series on North Carolina. His work is unusual because he documented a way of life for so many southerners during the 1910s. Most photographers took portraits that were more lucrative.

*Children Had Few Toys* portrays a young rural girl lovingly holding her pet chicken. In the South, poverty was a common malady after the Civil War, especially in rural areas where unemployment was high. Barnhill not only documented the poverty of the South, but also the strength of friendship.

## The Good Friends

**HONORÉ DAUMIER** (1808–1879) was a French artist known for his caricatures, exaggerating the characteristics of the common people of Paris. He was adept at capturing the subtleties of changing facial expressions and gestures of men and women as they went about their daily routines. As a painter, sculptor, and caricaturist, he often portrayed individuals alone in a crowd.

*The Good Friends* shows two elderly gentleman enjoying an afternoon conversation and drink together. Like many of Daumier's caricatures, this drawing captures the gestures of the figures and facial expressions. However, it was very rare for him to portray the friendship between two people as he did here.

*Focus Questions* What is it like to have a pet as a best friend? What would it be like to lose a friend, even if it were for a good reason?

# Rugby & Rosie

by Nan Parson Rossiter

Rugby is my dog. He is a chocolate Labrador, and we have had him for as long as I can remember.

He walks with me to the school-bus stop in the morning, and he meets me there when I get home. He follows me around when I do my chores, and he sleeps beside my bed at night. He is my best friend.

We used to do everything together—just the two of us.

Then Rosie came.

64

## Selection Summary

### Genre: Realistic Fiction

"Rugby & Rosie" takes a look at the bonds that develop between people and pets and between pets living in the same home. This realistic story highlights the emotions that accompany new relationships and growing attachments. Sometimes, however, friends must let go, even if ties between them are strong, so that each one can follow their path in life.

Some of the elements of realistic fiction are:

- The characters behave as people do in real life.
- The setting of the story is a real place or could be a real place.
- The events in the story could happen in real life.

## About the Author/Illustrator

**NAN PARSON ROSSITER** received an *American Bookseller* "Pick of the Lists" for "Rugby & Rosie." She has worked as an illustrator since graduating from the Rhode Island School of Design in 1986. In her second book, "The Way Home," Rossiter continues to explore the theme of letting go of a loved animal. In this story, a farm family adopts an injured goose and her mate. Eventually, the geese must be set free.

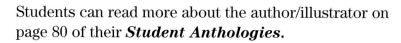

Students can read more about the author/illustrator on page 80 of their ***Student Anthologies.***

## Inquiry Connections

This story explores the dynamics of how relationships begin and grow and also allows readers to think about times when letting go is necessary. Key concepts explored are:

■ Pets can teach people lessons about friendship.

■ Friends keep each other company and enjoy spending time together.

■ Sometimes friends must separate and learn to say good-bye.

■ Even when someone is sad over a relationship that has changed or ended, a new one can begin to grow.

Before reading the selection:

■ Point out that students may post a question, concept, word, illustration, or object at any time during the course of their unit investigations. Be sure that students include their names or initials on the items they post so that others will know whom to go to if they have an answer or if they wish to collaborate on a related activity.

■ Students should feel free to write an answer or a note on someone else's question or to consult the Board for ideas for their own investigations throughout the unit.

■ Encourage students to read about friendship at home and to bring in articles or pictures that are good examples to post on the Board.

**Concept/Question Board**

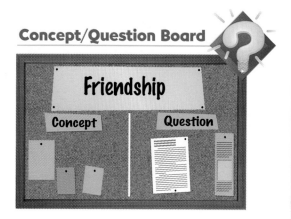

**PROGRAM RESOURCES**

## Leveled Practice

**Reteach**
Pages 16–19

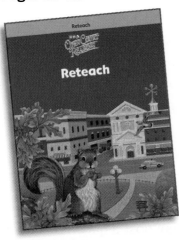

**Challenge**
Pages 14–17

**ELD Workbook**

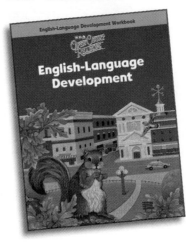

**Intervention Workbook**

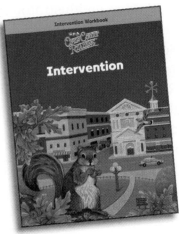

**Decodable Book 14**

# Leveled Classroom Library*

Encourage students to read at least 30 minutes daily outside of class. Have them read books in the *Leveled Classroom Library* to support the unit theme and help students develop their vocabulary by reading independently.

### *Alex Is My Friend*

BY MARISABINA RUSSO. GREENWILLOW BROOKS, 1992.

Alex and Ben have been friends since they were little enough to ride in strollers. The friends overcome their differences, even when one is often restricted to a wheelchair. **(Easy)**

### *Charlotte's Web*

BY E. B. WHITE. HARPERTROPHY, 1952.

This is the classic story of a friendship between a pig and a spider. (Newbery Honor) **(Average)**

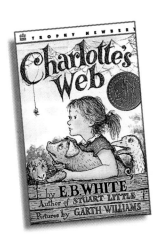

### *The Mountain that loved a Bird*

BY ALICE MCLERRAN. SIMON & SCHUSTER, 1985.

When Joy, a bird, must leave the mountain, Joy makes a promise to the mountain that loves her. Every year, one of her kin will return to the mountain. Joy's kin transform the mountain over time. **(Advanced)**

* These books, which all support the unit theme Friendship, are part of a 36-book *Leveled Classroom Library* available for purchase from SRA/McGraw-Hill. Note: Teachers should preview any trade books for appropriateness in their classrooms before recommending them to students.

# TECHNOLOGY

## Web Connections

**www.sra4kids.com**

**Friendship Web Site**

## CD-ROMs

* **Research Assistant**
  SRA/MCGRAW-HILL, 2002

* **Decodable Book Activities**
  SRA/MCGRAW-HILL, 2002

## Computer Skills

* **Basic Computer Skills**

## Audiocassettes/CDs

* **Listening Library: Friendship**
  SRA/MCGRAW-HILL, 2002

* **Sound/Spelling Card Stories**
  SRA/MCGRAW-HILL, 2002

Titles preceded by an asterisk (*) are available through SRA/McGraw-Hill. Other titles can be obtained by contacting the publisher listed with the title.

| | | DAY 1 | DAY 2 |
|---|---|---|---|
| Suggested Pacing: 3–5 days | | DAY 1 | DAY 2 |

**LESSON PLANNER**

## 1 Preparing to Read

**Materials**
- Student Anthology, Book 1, pp. 64–81
- Decodable Book Activities CD-ROM
- Sound/Spelling Card 37
- Decodable Book 14
- Routine Cards 1, 3, Routines 1–2, 8–9

**DAY 1**

**Word Knowledge, p. 64K**
- suffixes *-ly, -ed, -ing*
- contractions
- /o/

**About the Words and Sentences, p. 64K**

**DAY 2**

**Developing Oral Language, p. 64L**

## 2 Reading & Responding

**Materials**
- Student Anthology, Book 1, pp. 64–81
- Program Assessment
- Reading Transparencies 4, 6, 46, 50
- Inquiry Journal, p. 3
- Home Connection, p. 9
- Unit 1 Assessment, pp. 14–17
- Writer's Notebook
- Routine Cards 1–2, Routines 3–6

**DAY 1**

**Build Background, p. 64O**
**Preview and Prepare, pp. 64O–64P**
**Selection Vocabulary, p. 64P**
**Reading Recommendations, pp. 64Q–64R**
**Student Anthology, pp. 64–70** First Read
✓**Comprehension Strategies**
- Making Connections, pp. 68, 70
- Asking Questions, pp. 64, 66

**Supporting the Reading, p. 79C**
- Predicting

**DAY 2**

**Student Anthology, pp. 71–79** First Read
**Comprehension Strategies**
- Predicting, pp. 72, 76, 78
- Asking Questions, p. 74
- Making Connections, p. 78

**Discussing Strategy Use, p. 78**
**Discussing the Selection, p. 79A**
- Review Selection
- Complete Discussion

**Meet the Author/Illustrator, p. 80**
✓**Theme Connections, p. 81**

## Inquiry

**Materials**
- Student Anthology, Book 1, pp. 64–81
- Inquiry Journal, pp. 20–21
- Research Assistant CD-ROM

**DAY 1**

**Investigation**
- Investigating Concepts Beyond the Text: Needs and Plans, p. 81A

**DAY 2**

**Investigation**
- Concept/Question Board, p. 81B

## 3 Language Arts

**Materials**
- Student Anthology, Book 1, pp. 64–81
- Comprehension and Language Arts Skills, pp. 14–17
- Language Arts Handbook, pp. 10–15, 19, 24, 34, 36–37
- Language Arts Transparencies 17–21
- Sound/Spelling Card 15
- Spelling and Vocabulary Skills, pp. 14–17
- Writer's Workbook, p. 4

**DAY 1**

**Word Analysis**
✓- Spelling: The /o/ Sound Pretest, p. 81F

**Writing Process Strategies**
- Introduction to the Writing Process: Revising, p. 81F

**English Language Conventions**
- Grammar: Verbs, p. 81F

**DAY 2**

**Word Analysis**
- Spelling: Word Sorting, p. 81G
- Vocabulary: Dictionary Strategy, p. 81G

**Writing Process Strategies**
- Introduction to the Writing Process: Revising, p. 81G

**English Language Conventions**
- Grammar: Verbs, p. 81G

| DAY 2 continued | DAY 3 | |
|---|---|---|
| **DAY 3** | **DAY 4** | **DAY 5** |
| Ⓟ **Phonics and Fluency, p. 64M**<br>■ Review /ē/ spelled e, *ea*, *e_e*, *_y*, *ee*, *_ie_*<br>**About the Words and Sentences, p. 64M** | **Developing Oral Language, p. 64N**<br>**Dictation, p. 64N** | **Review Word Knowledge and Phonics** |
| **Student Anthology, pp. 64–70** Second Read<br>**Comprehension Skills**<br>■ Cause and Effect, pp. 65, 67, 69<br>**Science Connection**<br>■ Guide Dogs, p. 79E | **Student Anthology, pp. 71–79** Second Read<br>**Comprehension Skills**<br>■ Cause and Effect, pp. 71, 73, 75, 77, 79<br>**Checking Comprehension, p. 79**<br>**Review Selection Vocabulary, p. 79B**<br>**Literary Elements, p. 79D**<br>■ Characterization: Analyzing Character Traits | ✓ **Selection Assessment**<br>■ "Rugby & Rosie," pp. 14–17<br>**Home Connection, p. 79B**<br>**Social Studies Connection**<br>■ Helping Those in Need, p. 79F |
| ✓**Investigation**<br>■ Investigating the Theme, p. 81C | **Supporting the Investigation**<br>■ Following Directions, p. 81D | **Investigation**<br>■ Unit Investigation Continued<br>■ Update Concept/Question Board |
| **Word Analysis**<br>■ Spelling: The /o/ Sound, p. 81H<br>■ Vocabulary: Dictionary Strategy, p. 81H<br>**Writing Process Strategies**<br>■ Introduction to the Writing Process: Revising, p. 81H<br>**English Language Conventions**<br>■ Grammar: Verbs, p. 81H | **Word Analysis**<br>■ Spelling: The /o/ Sound, p. 81I<br>■ Vocabulary: Dictionary Strategy, p. 81I<br>**Writing Process Strategies**<br>■ Introduction to the Writing Process: Revising, p. 81I<br>**English Language Conventions**<br>■ Listening, Speaking, Viewing<br>✓ Viewing: Learning from Pictures, p. 81I | **Word Analysis**<br>✓■ Spelling: The /o/ Sound Final Test<br>✓■ Vocabulary: Dictionary Strategy, p. 81J<br>**Writing Process Strategies**<br>■ Introduction to the Writing Process: Revising, p. 81J<br>**English Language Conventions**<br>✓■ Penmanship: Cursive Letters *p* and *j*, p. 81J |

Below are suggestions for differentiating instruction to meet the individual needs of students. These are the same skills shown on the Lesson Planner; however, these pages provide extra practice opportunities or enriching activities to meet the varied needs of students. For Workshop Management Tips, see Appendix.

## WORKSHOP

# Differentiating Instruction

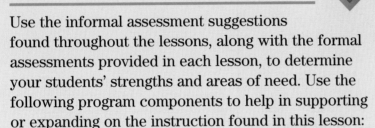

## Small-Group Instruction

Use the informal assessment suggestions found throughout the lessons, along with the formal assessments provided in each lesson, to determine your students' strengths and areas of need. Use the following program components to help in supporting or expanding on the instruction found in this lesson:

*Reteach Workbook* for use with students who show a basic understanding of the lesson but need a bit more practice to solidify their understanding.

*Intervention Guide* and *Intervention Workbook* for use with students who, even after extra practice, exhibit a lack of understanding of the lesson concepts.

*English-Language Development Guide* and *English-Language Development Workbook* for use with students who need language help.

## Independent Activities

Students can work individually on such things as:

- Inquiry Journal pages
- Independent reading
- Challenge
- Investigation activities

### Writing Seminar

A suggested activity would be to have students write about a friendship they have, or would like to have, with a pet. You may want to have students share their stories with the class.

◆ **Small-Group Instruction**    ■ **Independent Activities**

| | READING | INVESTIGATION ACTIVITIES |
|---|---|---|
| **DAY 1** | ■ Select *Leveled Classroom Library* book for independent reading<br>■ *Listening Library Audiocassette/CD*<br>■ Add vocabulary in Writer's Notebook<br>■ Oral reading of selection for fluency | ■ Concept/Question Board<br>■ Explore OCR Web site (www.sra4kids.com) for Friendship<br>◆ Needs and Plans, p. 81A |
| **DAY 2** | ■ Independent reading<br>◆ Discuss Theme Connections, p. 81<br>■ Record response to selection in Writer's Notebook<br>■ Complete Link to Writing for Supporting the Reading, p. 79C | ■ Concept/Question Board<br>■ Use *Research Assistant CD-ROM* to continue investigation |
| **DAY 3** | ■ Independent reading<br>■ *Listening Library Audiocassette/CD*<br>◆ Partner reading of selection<br>■◆ Science Connection, p. 79E | ■ Concept/Question Board<br>◆ Investigating the Theme, p. 81C<br>■ Record theme concepts in *Inquiry Journal,* p. 20 |
| **DAY 4** | ■ Independent reading<br>■ Complete Independent Practice for Literary Elements, p. 79D<br>■ Add words to Word Bank | ■ Concept/Question Board<br>◆ Complete Independent Practice for Supporting the Investigation, p. 81D |
| **DAY 5** | ■ Reading Roundtable<br>■◆ Social Studies Connection, p. 79F | ◆ Continue work on investigation<br>■ Additional practice for "Following Directions," *Inquiry Journal,* p. 21 |

| LANGUAGE ARTS | INTERVENTION* | ENGLISH-LANGUAGE LEARNERS** | RETEACH | CHALLENGE |
|---|---|---|---|---|
| **English Language Conventions**<br>■ Complete Main Verbs and Verb Phrases, *Comprehension and Language Arts Skills,* pp. 14–15 | **(30 to 45 minutes per day)**<br>◆ Blending, p. 31<br>◆ Preteach "Rugby and Rosie," pp. 33–34<br>◆ Teach "Intervention Selection One," pp. 34–35<br>◆ Grammar, Usage, and Mechanics, p. 37 | **(30 to 45 minutes per day)**<br>◆ Word Knowledge, Suffix *-ly*, p. 18<br>◆ Word Knowledge, Descriptive Words, p. 18 | | |
| **Word Analysis**<br>◆ Spelling: Word Sort, p. 81G<br>■ Complete Dictionary Strategy, *Spelling and Vocabulary Skills,* pp. 14–15 | ◆ Developing Oral Language, p. 31<br>◆ Preteach "Rugby and Rosie," pp. 33–34<br>◆ Teach Comprehension Strategies, p. 35<br>◆ Reread "Intervention Selection One"<br>◆ Grammar, Usage, and Mechanics, p. 37 | ◆ Selection Vocabulary, p. 20<br>◆ Preteach the Selection, p. 20 | **English Language Conventions**<br>■ Complete Main Verbs and Verb Phrases, *Reteach,* p. 18 | **English Language Conventions**<br>■ Complete Main Verbs and Verb Phrases, *Challenge,* p. 16 |
| **Word Analysis**<br>■ Complete Spelling: The /o/ Sound, *Spelling and Vocabulary Skills,* p. 16 | ◆ Dictation and Spelling, pp. 31–32<br>◆ Reread "Rugby and Rosie"<br>◆ Teach "Intervention Selection Two," pp. 35–36<br>◆ Writing Activity, p. 38 | ◆ Word Knowledge, /ē/, p. 19 | **Word Analysis**<br>■ Complete Vocabulary: Dictionary Strategy, *Reteach,* p. 17 | **Word Analysis**<br>■ Complete Vocabulary: Dictionary Strategy, *Challenge,* p. 15 |
| **Word Analysis**<br>■ Complete The /o/ Sound, *Spelling and Vocabulary Skills,* p. 17<br>**Writing Process Strategies**<br>■ Complete Writer's Craft: Sentence Variety, *Comprehension and Language Arts Skills,* pp. 16–17 | ◆ Blending, p. 32<br>◆ Reread "Rugby and Rosie"<br>◆ Teach Comprehension Strategies, p. 36<br>◆ Reread "Intervention Selection Two"<br>◆ Writing Activity, p. 38 | ◆ Dictation and Spelling, p. 19 | **Word Analysis**<br>■ Complete Spelling: The /o/ Sound, *Reteach,* p. 16 | **Word Analysis**<br>■ Complete Spelling: The /o/ Sound, *Challenge,* p. 14 |
| **Writing Process Strategies**<br>◆ Seminar: Revise an Autobiography, p. 81J<br>**English Language Conventions**<br>■ Penmanship: Practice Letters *p* and *j*, p. 81J | ◆ Developing Oral Language, p. 32<br>◆ Dictation and Spelling, pp. 33–34<br>◆ Repeated Readings/ Fluency Check, p. 36 | ◆ Grammar, Usage, and Mechanics, p. 21 | **Writing Process Strategies**<br>■ Complete Writer's Craft: Sentence Variety, *Reteach,* p. 19 | **Writing Process Strategies**<br>■ Complete Writer's Craft: Sentence Variety, *Challenge,* p. 17 |

\* Page numbers refer to *Intervention Guide*.

\*\* Page numbers refer to *English-Language Development Guide*.

 *Florida*

ASSESSMENT

## Formal Assessment Options

Use these summative assessments along with your informal observations to assess student progress.

---

**Unit 1 Assessment p. 14**

Name _____ Date _____ Score _____

LESSON ASSESSMENT

**UNIT 1** Friendship • Lesson 4

### Rugby & Rosie

Read the following questions carefully. Then completely fill in the bubble of each correct answer. You may look back at the story to find the answer to each of the questions.

1. Why does Rugby ignore Rosie at first?
   Ⓐ Rosie is not very friendly to him.
   ● He is used to being the only dog.
   Ⓒ He knows Rosie will not stay long.

2. Which of these best describes the new puppy?
   ● full of energy
   Ⓑ quiet and calm
   Ⓒ cute but naughty

Read the following questions carefully. Use complete sentences to answer the questions.

3. What kind of a learner was Rosie?
   She was a fast learner.

4. Why didn't Rugby meet the boy at the bus stop one day?
   He was asleep on the porch with Rosie.

5. What kind of trips did the family take Rosie on?
   They took her to places where she would later have to take her visually impaired owner.

14  Unit 1 • Lesson 4     Rugby & Rosie • Unit 1 Assessment

---

**Unit 1 Assessment p. 15**

**Rugby & Rosie** (continued)

6. How did the boy know that Rugby missed Rosie?
   Rugby whined and moped when she was gone.

7. How did Rosie behave at the graduation?
   She was calm, proud, and did not leave her new owner.

8. How did Rugby react to the new puppy at the end of the story?
   He welcomed the new puppy and kissed him on his nose.

Read the following questions carefully. Then completely fill in the bubble of each correct answer.

9. After living with the boy's family one year, Rosie
   Ⓐ decided to stay there
   ● went to a special school
   Ⓒ became a dog trainer

10. Who did the boy get to meet at Rosie's graduation?
    ● Rosie's new owner
    Ⓑ Rosie's parents
    Ⓒ Rosie's teacher

Unit 1 Assessment • Rugby & Rosie     Unit 1 • Lesson 4  15

---

**Unit 1 Assessment p. 16**

**Rugby & Rosie** (continued)

Read the question and statement below. Use complete sentences in your answers.

**Linking to the Concepts** What lessons can be learned about fun ways to help others by reading this story?
Answers will vary. Accept all reasonable answers.

**Personal Response** Write about a time when you wanted to help someone, so you gave away something that was very special to you.
Answers will vary. Accept all reasonable answers.

16  Unit 1 • Lesson 4     Rugby & Rosie • Unit 1 Assessment

---

**Unit 1 Assessment p. 17**

**Rugby & Rosie** (continued)

### Vocabulary

Read the following questions carefully. Then completely fill in the bubble of each correct answer.

1. Dad showed how to teach Rosie simple commands. A **command** is when you
   Ⓐ give a dog a special treat
   Ⓑ take a dog for a long walk
   ● tell a dog to do something

2. The family worked together to teach Rosie good manners. **Manners** are
   Ⓐ where you live
   ● how you behave
   Ⓒ who you know

3. Standing with her new owner, Rosie looked proud. To feel **proud** means to feel
   Ⓐ tired from working too hard
   Ⓑ sad about how things change
   ● good about what you have done

4. Rosie's trainers said that Rosie was doing well at school. A **trainer** is most like a
   Ⓐ student
   ● teacher
   Ⓒ runner

5. Rugby received special permission to go to Rosie's graduation. A **graduation** is
   ● a ceremony held when school is finished
   Ⓑ a time when school starts again
   Ⓒ a place to take classes

Unit 1 Assessment • Rugby & Rosie     Unit 1 • Lesson 4  17

---

**Unit 1 Assessment p. 32**

Name _____ Date _____ Score _____

**UNIT 1** Friendship • Lesson 4  Rugby and Rosie

### Spelling Pretest: The /o/ Sound

Fold this page back on the dotted line. Take the Pretest. Then correct any word you misspelled by crossing out the word and rewriting it next to the incorrect spelling.

| | |
|---|---|
| 1. _____ | 1. *rot* |
| 2. _____ | 2. *shot* |
| 3. _____ | 3. *crop* |
| 4. _____ | 4. *sock* |
| 5. _____ | 5. *clock* |
| 6. _____ | 6. *flock* |
| 7. _____ | 7. *body* |
| 8. _____ | 8. *spot* |
| 9. _____ | 9. *stocking* |
| 10. _____ | 10. *lobby* |
| 11. _____ | 11. *stop* |
| 12. _____ | 12. *got* |
| 13. _____ | 13. *lots* |
| 14. _____ | 14. *job* |
| 15. _____ | 15. *pond* |

32  Unit 1 • Lesson 4     Spelling Pretest: The /o/ Sound • Unit 1 Assessment

---

**Unit 1 Assessment p. 33**

Name _____ Date _____ Score _____

**UNIT 1** Friendship • Lesson 4  Rugby and Rosie

### Spelling Final Test: The /o/ Sound

Mark the letter next to the underlined word that is misspelled. Focus on the underlined word.

1. Ⓐ A swan can be found in a pond.
   ● A boddy is covered with skin.
   Ⓒ Fingernails do not stop growing.
   Ⓓ Correct as is.

2. ● A camera shaut is a photograph.
   Ⓑ A silk sock is very smooth.
   Ⓒ Guests can be found in a lobby.
   Ⓓ Correct as is.

3. Ⓐ A flock of birds can fill the sky.
   Ⓑ One body of water is the sea.
   ● America gat its freedom in 1776.
   Ⓓ Correct as is.

4. ● A stain is a dirty sput on clothes.
   Ⓑ There are lots of fish in an ocean.
   Ⓒ Cars stop at red lights.
   Ⓓ Correct as is.

5. Ⓐ Corn is grown as a crop.
   Ⓑ Blood flows through the body.
   Ⓒ A clock has two hands.
   ● Correct as is.

6. Ⓕ A wool sock is warm.
   Ⓖ You can spot a star at night.
   ● A hotel loby is often crowded.
   Ⓒ Correct as is.

Unit 1 Assessment • Spelling Final Test: The /o/ Sound     Unit 1 • Lesson 4  33

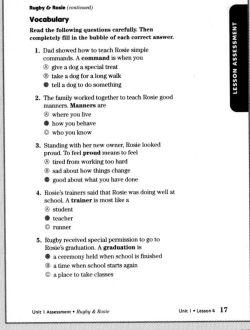

# Informal Comprehension Strategies Rubrics

## Asking Questions

- The student asks questions about ideas or facts presented in the text and attempts to answer these questions by reading the text.

## Making Connections

- The student activates prior knowledge and related knowledge.
- The student uses prior knowledge to explain something encountered in the text.
- The student connects ideas presented later in the text to ideas presented earlier in the text.
- The student notes ideas in the text that are new or conflict with what he or she thought previously.

## Predicting

- The student makes predictions about the text.
- The student updates predictions during reading, based on information in the text.

# Research Rubrics

Use the Research Rubrics to assess a student's performance throughout the stages of the investigation for each unit. The rubrics for a given lesson will match the investigation stage for that lesson. In addition, at the end of the unit you can use the rubrics to assess the groups' collaborative work as well as an individual's participation in that group.

During Workshop, assess students using the rubrics below. The rubrics range from 1–4 in most categories, with 1 being the lowest score. Record each student's score on the inside back cover of the *Inquiry Journal*.

## Recognizing Information Needs

**1** Identifies topics about which more needs to be learned. ("I need to learn more about the brain.")

**2** Identifies information needs that are relevant though not essential to the research question. ("To understand how Leeuwenhoek invented the microscope, I need to know what size germs are.")

**3** Identifies questions that are deeper than the one originally asked. (Original question: "How does the heart work?" Deeper question: "Why does blood need to circulate?")

## Objectives

- Students practice recognizing base words and the suffixes *-ly, -ed,* and *-ing,* necessary spelling changes they require, and how they affect meaning.
- Students practice recognizing irregular past tense verbs.
- Students practice spelling words with the /o/ sound.
- Students practice recognizing contractions.
- Students practice recognizing difficult words from the story.
- Students develop fluency reading words and sentences.

## Materials

- Student Anthology, Book 1, pp. 64–81
- Decodable Book Activities CD-ROM
- Sound/Spelling Card 37
- Decodable Book 14
- Routine Cards 1, 3, Routines 1–2, 8–9

**Teacher Tip** **SYLLABICATION** To help students blend words and build fluency, use the syllabication below of the words in the word lines.

| | | | |
|---|---|---|---|
| ea•ger•ly | tight•ly | friend•ly | wig•gly |
| squig•gly | licked | trot•ted | wagged |
| turned | moped | chas•ing | rac•ing |
| pleas•ing | leav•ing | hav•ing | know |
| knew | make | made | think |
| thought | kneel | knelt | was•n't |
| he'd | did•n't | would•n't | could•n't |
| she's | cho•co•late | res•tau•rant | tongues |
| es•pec•ial•ly | | pa•tient | pond |
| job | lots | got | stop |

**Routine Card**
Refer to *Routine 1* for the whole-word blending procedure and *Routine 2* for the sentence blending procedure.

Refer to the *Lesson Model Videocassette* for instruction on whole-word blending.

## Word Knowledge

### Reading the Words and Sentences

- Write each word in Reading the Words and Sentences on the board and have students read them together. If they have difficulty reading a word, stop and have them blend the word using whole-word blending. Encourage students to pronounce the word naturally after blending. Because reading sentences helps students to move from word fluency to sentence fluency, have them read each sentence in unison, using normal intonation. The words in **boldface** type are from the selection.

| | | | | | | |
|---|---|---|---|---|---|---|
| Line 1: | eagerly | tightly | friendly | wiggly | squiggly | |
| Line 2: | licked | trotted | wagged | turned | moped | |
| Line 3: | chasing | racing | pleasing | leaving | having | |
| Line 4: | know knew make | made | think thought | kneel | knelt | |
| Line 5: | wasn't | he'd | didn't | wouldn't | couldn't | she's |
| Line 6: | chocolate | restaurant tongues | especially | patient | | |
| Line 7: | pond | job | lots | got | stop | |
| Sentence 1: | She leaned forward eagerly and licked Rugby right on the nose. | | | | | |
| Sentence 2: | He made it very clear he wasn't interested in being friends. | | | | | |
| Sentence 3: | Day after day, Rugby just moped around and wouldn't play with us. | | | | | |
| Sentence 4: | A pond is a habitat for lots of animals. | | | | | |

### About the Words and Sentences

- **Line 1:** All of the words on Line 1 end in the suffix *-ly.* Explain that when the suffix *-ly* is added to a word the word becomes an adverb. Ask the students to define *adverb (a word that modifies a verb, an adjective, or another adverb).* Have the students identify the base word and ask if any spelling changes were necessary *(wiggle/wiggly, squiggle/squiggly).*

- **Line 2:** These words have the suffix *-ed.* Notice that some words have a double consonant added before the suffix. Have the students identify the base words and identify why the consonants at the end of the words *trot* and *wag* double. *(The final consonant doubles when it is a consonant-vowel-consonant word and a suffix is being added).*

- **Line 3:** These words have the suffix *-ing* added to them. Ask the students to identify the base word and spell it. Write the base word on the board *(chase/chasing).* Ask the students to tell what happens when you have a base word that ends in *e* and you want to add an ending *(drop the* e *and add the ending).* Continue until all words on Line 3 have been discussed.

- **Line 4:** Tell students these are irregular past tense verbs. To make many verbs past tense, you often only need to add *-ed*. With these verbs, the spellings of the past tense change form. Ask students to give the past tense of the following verbs: run *(ran)*; tell *(told)*; throw *(threw)*; drink *(drank)*; hang *(hung)*; buy *(bought)*; spend *(spent)*.

- **Line 5:** These words are contractions. Have a student tell what a contraction is *(a word made with components of two words to signify those words)*. Ask the students to identify the two words that form each contraction. Ask the students to identify the punctuation mark used in each contraction *(apostrophe)*. Ask what the purpose of the apostrophe is *(takes the place of omitted letters)*.

- **Line 6:** These are challenging words from the selection. Allowing students to read these words here will help them avoid having to stop during reading to decode. After reading each word here, have students clap the syllables. Also, have students give a definition for each word.

- **Line 7:** The words in Line 7 are found in "Rugby & Rosie" and review the /o/ sound spelled *o*.

- **Sentences 1–3:** These sentences are from the story the students are about to read. Ask the students to identify the words with a suffix. Have students underline the suffix in each word *(lean<u>ed</u>, eager<u>ly</u>, lick<u>ed</u>, interest<u>ed</u>, be<u>ing</u>, friend<u>s</u>, mop<u>ed</u>)*. Ask the students to identify the contractions and tell what two words form the contractions *(wasn't/was not, wouldn't/would not)*. Ask if anyone can identify the irregular past tense verb *(made)*.

- **Sentence 4:** Have students identify the words in the last sentence that contain the /o/ sound spelled *o (pond, lots)*.

## Developing Oral Language LA.C.1.2.1.3.2

To review the words, do one or both of the following activities. Use these activities to help students practice the words aloud.

- Have a student choose two words from the word lines on the board and use them in a sentence. For example, "He <u>wasn't</u> <u>chasing</u> the cat." Have another student create a new sentence using the original words, plus a new word from the list; for example, "Since Fido <u>wasn't</u> <u>chasing</u> the cat, he sat and <u>licked</u> his sore paw."

- Have students come to the board, point to, and say a word in the word lines. Have them choose a volunteer to use the word in a sentence and extend the sentence. Encourage students to add information at the beginning of the sentence, not just at the end.

**Teacher Tip** FLUENCY Gaining a better understanding of the spellings of sounds and structure of words will help students as they encounter unfamiliar words in their reading. By this time in Grade 3 students should be reading approximately 107 words per minute with fluency and expression. As students read, you may notice that some need work in building fluency. During Workshop, have these students select a section of the text (a minimum of 160 words) to read several times in order to build fluency.

### MEETING INDIVIDUAL NEEDS

**ELL Support**

For ELD strategies, use the *English-Language Development Guide,* Unit 1, Lesson 4.

**Intervention Support**

For intervention strategies, use the *Intervention Guide,* Unit 1, Lesson 4.

**Spelling**
See pages 81E–81J for the corresponding spelling lesson for the /o/ sound.

**PHONICS**

**Teacher Tip** SYLLABICATION To help students blend words and build fluency, use the syllabication below of the words in the word lines.

| | | | | |
|---|---|---|---|---|
| e•ven | ce•dar | se•cret | lean | ea•ger |
| clear | eve | com•pete | ath•lete | Rug•by |
| fun•ny | cit•y | fam•i•ly | meet | sleep |
| greet | de•gree | brief | grief | chief |

**Teacher Tip** Encourage students to read the words. Stop and blend only those words that give them problems.

# Phonics and Fluency

Review /ē/ spelled e, ea, e_e, _y, ee, _ie_

## Blending

- Use direct teaching to teach the blending lesson.
- Display **Sound/Spelling Card 37.**
- Follow the established procedure to have students read the following words and sentences. **Boldface** words are found in the selection.

| | | | | | |
|---|---|---|---|---|---|
| Line 1: | even | cedar | secret | lean | eager |
| Line 2: | **clear** | eve | compete | athlete | **Rugby** |
| Line 3: | funny | city | **family** | meet | sleep |
| Line 4: | **greet** | degree | brief | grief | chief |
| Sentence 1: | Jean wants a puppy for her birthday. | | | | |
| Sentence 2: | She will eat only one piece of cake. | | | | |
| Sentence 3: | Sometimes the three of us went swimming in a nearby pond. | | | | |

## About the Words and Sentences

- **Line 1:** The words practice the /ē/ sound spelled e and ea.
- **Line 2:** The words practice the /ē/ sound spelled ea, e_e, and _y.
- **Line 3:** The words practice the /ē/ sound spelled _y and ee.
- **Line 4:** The words practice the /ē/ sound spelled ee and _ie_.
- **Sentences 1–2:** These sentences contain words with the /ē/ sound. Have students identify the words with the /ē/ sound. (Jean, puppy, she, eat, only, piece) and tell which spelling is used in the word (Jean/ea, puppy/y, she/e, eat/ea, piece/ie).
- **Sentence 3:** This sentence is from the selection. Have students identify the words with an /ē/ sound (three, nearby) and tell which spelling for the /ē/ sound is used in the word.

## Developing Oral Language  LA.C.1.2.1.3.1

- Point to a word on the word line. Have a volunteer use that word in a sentence. Have another volunteer extend the sentence by adding to either the beginning or the ending of the original sentence. Continue with other words on the word lines.

- As you say the words on the word lines, have students clap for each syllable. As you go, underline the long e spellings. After clapping the syllables, have students use the words in a sentence.

## Dictation

Erase the blending lines and sentences on the board and have students take out writing paper. Dictate the following words and sentences for students to write.

| | | | |
|---|---|---|---|
| **Line 1:** | zebra | theme | happy |
| **Line 2:** | story | sweet | field |
| **Challenge Word:** | ecology | | |
| **Sentence:** | The students must complete the test before going to recess. | | |

- Have the students follow proper procedures for proofreading the dictated words and sentence.

## Building Fluency

***Decodable Books*** are used to help develop fluency for students who need extra practice. The only way to gain fluency is to read. Students will have many opportunities to read, including the ***Student Anthology,*** the ***Leveled Classroom Library,*** and their own reading. The ***Decodable Books*** can be used to practice the phonics and fluency elements being reviewed. Refer to the Appendix for the procedure on using these books. For this lesson, use ***Decodable Book 14,*** *City Girl.*

**City Girl**
by Dennis Anderson
illustrated by Meryl Henderson

*Decodable Book 14*

**Routine Card**
Refer to *Routine 8* for the whole-word dictation procedure and *Routine 9* for the sentence dictation procedure.

 **R**esearch in Action
**Decoding and Comprehension**

A lack of skill in decoding words directly affects students' higher order comprehension. This is because word recognition and comprehension compete for attention: The more effort readers require to decode a word, the less attention they have left for comprehension. If readers have to struggle with words, they can easily lose track of meaning. *(Michael Pressley)*

 Refer to the *Lesson Model Videocassette* for instruction on whole-word dictation.

Use the *Decodable Book Activities CD-ROM* for activities that support this Phonics lesson.

 Refer to the *Lesson Model Videocassette* for instruction on reading a *Decodable Book.*

| Clues | Problems | Wonderings |
|---|---|---|
| Rugby is a dog. Is Rosie a dog too? | Labrador | How do Rugby and Rosie meet? |

*Reading Transparency 46*

## Build Background

### Activate Prior Knowledge

Discuss the following with students to find out what they may already know about the selection and have already learned about the theme of Friendship.

- Preteach "Rugby & Rosie" by first determining students' prior knowledge about living with pets by asking, "Have any of you ever lived with a dog? Does anyone you know live with a dog? Have you ever played with a dog? Do you or someone you know live with two dogs? How do the dogs act around each other? Do they play together?"

- Discuss what actions people must perform to care for pets. How do people train dogs? *(through repetitive practice and rewards for good behavior)*

- Ask students how they would feel if they had to give up a pet. How would they feel if they knew their pet was going to help someone who really needed it?

- Ask students to think about whether animals can teach people anything about friendship. If so, ask them for examples.

### Background Information

The following information may help students understand the selection they are about to read.

- Some dogs go through intense special training to become guide dogs for blind persons. Before the dogs are accepted into the strict programs, however, they spend the first year of their lives with temporary families.

- The temporary family's job is to expose the puppy to many different environments, such as cars, grocery stores, parks, and city streets. These experiences help the puppy adapt to busy, noisy places.

- Since 1929, 11,000 guide dogs have been trained in the United States and Canada. The guide dogs allow their owners independence, increased mobility, protection, and companionship.

- Tell students that this story is realistic fiction. Ask students to tell you some of the characteristics of realistic fiction and to give you examples of stories they have read that are realistic fiction.

## Preview and Prepare LA.A.1.2.1.3.1

### Browse

- Have a student read aloud the title and the name of the author/illustrator. Demonstrate how to browse. Then have students preview the selection by browsing through the first page or two of the story. This allows students to activate prior knowledge relevant to the selection. Discuss what they think this story might have to do with friendship.

- Have the students search for clues that tell them something about the story. Also, have them look for any problems, such as unfamiliar words or long

sentences, that they notice while reading. Use *Reading Transparency 46* to record their observations as they browse. For example, a student might notice that Rugby is a dog and guess that Rosie might also be a dog. For the Problems column, students might point out that they are unfamiliar with the word *Labrador.* They might wonder how Rugby and Rosie meet. To save time and to model note taking, write students' observations as brief notes rather than as complete sentences.

■ As students prepare to read the selection, have them browse the Focus Questions on the first page of the selection. Tell them to keep these questions in mind as the selection is read.

## Set Purposes LA.A.1.2.2.3.5

Encourage students to set their own purposes for reading this selection. As they read, have students think about who experiences friendship in this story, how they experience friendship, and why they experience friendship.

## Selection Vocabulary LA.A.1.2.2.3.2

As students study vocabulary, they will use a variety of skills to determine the meaning of a word. These include context clues, word structure, and apposition. Students will apply these same skills while reading to clarify additional unfamiliar words. Students can write their definitions in their Writer's Notebooks.

Display *Reading Transparency 6* before reading the selection to introduce and discuss the following words and their meanings.

| | |
|---|---|
| **commands:** | short, firm instructions (page 71) |
| **manners:** | habits of behavior (page 71) |
| **proud:** | feeling very pleased with something (page 72) |
| **trainers:** | teacher, coach (page 76) |
| **graduation:** | ceremony to mark the completion of a full course of study (page 76) |

Have students read the words in the word box, stopping to blend any words that they have trouble reading. Demonstrate how to decode multisyllabic words by breaking the words into syllables and blending the syllables. Then have the students try. If they still have trouble, refer them to the *Sound/Spelling Cards.* If the word is not decodable, give the students the pronunciation.

Have students read the sentences on the transparency to determine the meaning of the underlined words. Each word has two sentences that students will read and from which they should be able to derive the meaning of the underlined word. Remind them to use one or more of the skills they have learned—context clues, word structure, or apposition—to figure out the meaning before using a dictionary. Be sure students explain which skills they are using and how they figured out the meanings of the words. Have students reread the sentence, substituting the definition to see if the sentence makes sense. Have a volunteer create a new sentence using the underlined word.

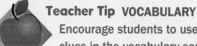

**Teacher Tip VOCABULARY** Encourage students to use context clues in the vocabulary sentences to figure out what the vocabulary words mean. The sentence for the word *trainer* is a good example to use for this purpose.

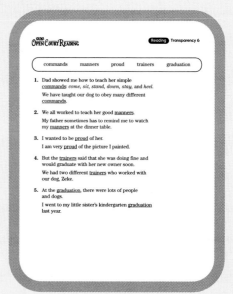

**Reading Transparency 6**

**Teacher Tip SELECTION VOCABULARY** To help students decode words, divide them into syllables when you are saying them, as shown below. The information following each word tells how students can figure out the meaning of each word. When writing words on the board, do not divide them into syllables.

| | |
|---|---|
| com•mands | context clues |
| man•ners | context clues |
| proud | context clues |
| train•ers | context clues |
| grad•u•a•tion | apposition |

**Routine Card**
Refer to *Routine 3* for the vocabulary procedure.

During Workshop, and after the selection has been read at least once, have students listen to the recording of this lesson's selection on the *Listening Library Audiocassette/CD.* After students have listened, have them discuss their personal preferences of the selections read. Ask them what other things they have listened to and like to listen to on the radio, on audiocassettes, or on CDs.

**Teacher Tip COMPREHENSION STRATEGIES** Refer to the Comprehension Strategies poster as the class reads the selection. As students are reading, ask them, "Which of the strategies listed on the poster might be good to use at this point in the selection?"

**Teacher Tip** Review point of view and ensure that students know the point of view used by the current author. *(first-person)*

**www.sra4kids.com**
**Web Connection**
Students can use the connections to friendship in the Reading Link of the SRA Web page for more information about friendship.

**Routine Card**
Refer to *Routine 5* for the procedure on reading the selection.

# Reading Recommendations

## Oral Reading

Oral reading should work well with this story because of its conversational style. The story is told in the voice of a child about the same age as the students. Students should read aloud fluently with appropriate expression and intonation. Make sure that students attend to punctuation and read in phrases. Tell students to add a sense of feeling or anticipation as they read.

Have students make use of the comprehension strategies listed on the next page to help them understand the selection. Have them stop reading periodically or wait until they have completed the selection to discuss the reading strategies. After the students have finished reading the selection, use the Discussing the Selection questions on page 79A to see if they understand what they have read.

## Using Comprehension Strategies

Comprehension strategy instruction allows students to become aware of how good readers read. Good readers constantly check their understanding as they are reading and ask themselves questions. In addition, skilled readers recognize when they are having problems and stop to use various comprehension strategies to help them make sense of what they are reading.

During the reading of "Rugby & Rosie," model and prompt the use of the following comprehension strategies.

- **Asking Questions** helps readers focus attention on what they are reading and engages them in deeper understanding of themes, concepts, and ideas.
- **Making Connections** requires readers to activate prior knowledge and connect what they know or have experienced to what they are reading.
- **Predicting** causes readers to analyze information given about story events and characters in the context of how it may logically connect to the story's conclusion.

An extended lesson on the comprehension strategy Predicting can be found in the Supporting the Reading section on page 79C. This lesson is intended to give students extra practice with Predicting. However, it may be used at this time to introduce the comprehension strategy to students.

As students read, they should be using a variety of strategies to help them understand the selection. Encourage students to use the strategies listed above as the class reads the story aloud. Do this by stopping at the points indicated by the numbers in the magenta circles on the reduced student page and using a particular strategy. Students can also stop reading periodically to discuss what they have learned and what problems they may be having.

## Building Comprehension Skills

Revisiting or rereading a selection allows students to apply skills that give them a more complete understanding of the text. Some follow-up comprehension skills help students organize information. Other skills lead to deeper understanding—to "reading between the lines," as mature readers do. In this selection, students will apply the following comprehension skill:

- **Cause and Effect** helps readers identify what causes events to happen or what caused characters to behave in certain ways, which helps readers put together logical explanations in the text.

### Reading with a Purpose

Have students look for ways the story characters show friendship or learn something new about friendship. What techniques does the author employ to communicate this information? *(She tells the story from the point of view of the boy so that we can see what he learned and how his understanding changed.)*

## Research in Action
### Comprehension Strategy Use

In general, good readers use a variety of strategies to construct meaning as they read. However, not all good readers use the same strategies; they tend to develop and practice those strategies that are most useful to them. Further, good readers are flexible in their strategy use: They switch from strategy to strategy as they read, and they use different kinds of strategies with different kinds of texts. *(Michael Pressley)*

**Teacher Tip** Ensure that students understand that events that happen in the "outside" physical world can be caused by thoughts and feelings occurring in the "internal" mental world and vice versa.

This selection is broken into two parts. On the first day, read pages 64–70. On the second day, read pages 71–77.

## Comprehension Strategies

First Read

Read the story aloud, taking turns with the students. Model the use of strategies for the students.

### Teacher Modeling

**1 Asking Questions** *Good readers stop and ask themselves questions about what they are reading. Asking questions as you read a story is one way to keep involved with what is happening in the story. I have questions already. I learned that Rugby is a Labrador, but I'm not sure what that word means. I wonder if it's a type of dog. The story says, "Then Rosie came." Who is Rosie? Why is she going there? I want to read more to find out what happens next. Who else has questions about the story?*

---

### Word Knowledge

**SCAFFOLDING** The skills students are reviewing in Word Knowledge should help them in reading the story. This lesson focuses on the inflectional endings *-ly, -ed,* and *-ing,* irregular past tense verbs, and contractions.

**-ing ending:**    **morning**

---

**Teacher Tip  USING STRATEGIES**
Although Asking Questions is the strategy being modeled, encourage students to use any strategy they have learned as they read the story.

---

### First Reading Recommendation

## ORAL • CHORAL

---

*Focus Questions* What is it like to have a pet as a best friend? What would it be like to lose a friend, even if it were for a good reason?

# Rugby & Rosie
by Nan Parson Rossiter

Rugby is my dog. He is a chocolate Labrador, and we have had him for as long as I can remember. **1**

He walks with me to the school-bus stop in the morning, and he meets me there when I get home. He follows me around when I do my <u>chores</u>, and he sleeps beside my bed at night. He is my best friend.

We used to do everything together—just the two of us.

Then Rosie came.

64

 **Informal Assessment**

Observe individual students as they read, and use the Teacher Observation Log, found in the *Program Assessment Teacher's Edition,* to record anecdotal information about each student's strengths and weaknesses.

One fall day, my dad brought home a little yellow puppy. Her name was Rosie. She was so cute that I loved her right away. But she wasn't an <u>ordinary</u> puppy. She was coming to live with my family for only a year.

Then Rosie would be old enough to go to a special school. There she would learn how to be a guide dog for a blind person. She and her new owner would always be together. They would be best friends. Just like Rugby and me.

65

## Comprehension Skills

Second Read

**COMPREHENSION**

### Cause and Effect LA.E.2.2.1.3.1 FCAT

During a second reading of the story tell students that looking for causes and effects will help improve their understanding of the story. They have already identified causes and effects before, so they should have some practice identifying these relationships. Remind students that sometimes these relationships are not directly pointed out by writers or indicated by clue words. Have students look for implied causes and effects in the story.

- She was so cute *(cause)*. I loved her right away *(effect)*.
- She will be old enough to go *(cause)*. She will go to a special school *(effect)*.

Use an overhead transparency to help students think of causes and effects in the story.

> ### Word Knowledge
> **irregular past tense verbs:** was

### Skills Trace
**Cause and Effect**
Introduced in Grade 1.
Scaffolded throughout Grades 2 and 3.
**REINTRODUCED:** Unit 1, Lesson 2
**REINFORCED:** Unit 1, Lesson 4
Unit 2, Lesson 4
Unit 2, Lesson 5
Unit 4, Lesson 2
**TESTED:** Unit 1 Assessment

**Second Reading Recommendation**

ORAL • **SILENT**

COMPREHENSION

## Comprehension Strategies

 First Read

### Teacher Modeling

**2** **Asking Questions** *I have another question. Why did Rugby turn away? Doesn't he like Rosie? Why not? Maybe he is just feeling shy, or maybe he needs time to get used to her. I'll read on to find out more.*

---

### Word Knowledge

**irregular past tense verbs:**    **knew**
                                                 **did**
                                                 **gave**
                                                 **was**
                                                 **thought**

---

 **Teacher Tip  QUESTIONS** Encourage students to ask and answer lots of questions as they read. Remind students that if they are unable to answer a question, reading further in the story might reveal the answer.

---

**Teacher Tip** Tell students that good readers keep thinking about the questions that come up about the topic, and they keep coming back to those questions. As they read, tell them to keep the questions on the Concept/Question Board in mind. Have them make notes to themselves in the Response Journal section of their Writer's Notebooks about which questions seem most important. Tell them that good readers always think about what is important in selections, and they try to remember this important information.

---

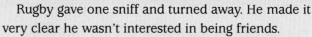

I knew all this before Rosie came, but Rugby didn't. I held the puppy out to him to see how he would greet **2** Rosie. She leaned forward eagerly and licked Rugby right on the nose.

Rugby gave one sniff and turned away. He made it very clear he wasn't interested in being friends.

"Come on, Rugby," I said. "She wants to play with you." And it was true. Rosie did want to play. But Rugby wasn't in the <u>mood</u>.

My mom and dad told me to be <u>patient</u> with Rugby, that he'd get used to having another dog around the house. But I wasn't sure. He looked so sad. Maybe he thought I didn't love him anymore, which wasn't true!

66

COMPREHENSION

Rosie fit in with the family right away. She was so friendly and always wanted to play. She would chase after anything and then run back. She loved everyone in the family—even Rugby! But he still wasn't friendly. Day after day, Rugby just moped around and wouldn't play with us.

That didn't bother Rosie one bit. She thought Rugby was the greatest. She trotted along after him, ran between his legs, tripped him, jumped on him, and barked at him.

Rugby did his best to ignore her.

But Rosie just wouldn't give up.

67

## Comprehension Skills

Second Read

### Cause and Effect LA.E.2.2.1.3.1 FCAT

Have students continue to read carefully to find out how one event *(the cause)* creates another event *(the effect)*. Remind students that these relationships are not always directly indicated. Students must ask themselves *what* happened to identify cause, and *why* it happened to identify effect.

- **Cause:** Maybe Rugby thought the boy didn't love him anymore.
  **Effect:** Rugby looked sad.
- **Cause:** Rosie was so friendly and always wanted to play.
  **Effect:** She fit in with the family right away.

### Word Knowledge

*-ed* endings:　loved
　　　　　　moped
　　　　　　trotted
　　　　　　jumped
　　　　　　barked

**Teacher Tip** CAUSE AND EFFECT
Continue to write the cause-and-effect relationships on the transparency, erasing the earlier relationship sets later in the lesson, as needed, to visually record all of the cause-and-effect relationships.

**Teacher Tip** Explore with the students how internal feelings are caused by external events.

COMPREHENSION

## Comprehension Strategies

First Read

### Teacher Modeling

 **Making Connections** *Good readers make connections between what they are reading and what they already know from past experience or from previous reading. I think I can understand how the boy in the story feels here. He must be very happy to see Rugby. He must be especially happy to see him getting along with Rosie. I know what it's like to feel worried about something and then find out everything is all right. Who else has connections to the selection that they would like to share?*

---

### Word Knowledge

**-ed endings:**  worried
curled
looked
wagged
yawned
stretched
settled

---

**Teacher Tip STRATEGIES** Remind students to use all the reading strategies they have learned so far in order to better understand and appreciate the story.

---

Then one day, Rugby was not waiting at the school-bus stop. I was worried. He *always* met me at the bus stop.

I ran home—and there I found Rugby asleep on the porch. Curled up in a little ball next to him was Rosie. "Rugby!" I said. They both looked up at me and wagged their tails. Rosie yawned and stretched and settled back down against Rugby's side.

68

COMPREHENSION

From then on, Rugby and Rosie were always together. They romped and played and chased the falling leaves. And they *both* waited for me at the bus stop.

69

## Comprehension Skills

Second Read

### Cause and Effect  LA.E.2.2.1.3.1 FCAT

Have students continue to identify cause-and-effect relationships. Record their answers on the transparency.

- Under Effect write *The boy was worried.* Encourage students to fill in the information under Cause. *(Rugby was not waiting for him at the bus stop.)*

- Under Effect write *Rugby was not at the bus stop.* Students should give you the information to put under Cause. *(He was sleeping next to Rosie.)*

Explain to students that causes and effects often occur in a chain. Point out how the above examples are all related in a chain of causes and effects.

> ### Word Knowledge
> *-ing* endings:    falling

 **Teacher Tip  CAUSE AND EFFECT**
You may wish to explain to students that sometimes we are aware of an effect but are not sure of the cause. Often when this happens, the cause becomes apparent later.

COMPREHENSION

## Comprehension Strategies

**First Read**

### Teacher Modeling

**4 Making Connections** *I think I know how he feels here. When you know that someone you like to spend time with has to leave, you feel a little sad even though they are still here. Then you have to try not to think about that time and have fun anyway. I think the boy in the story probably does think about when Rosie will have to leave, even though he tries not to. Who else has a connection with the selection here?*

### Word Knowledge

irregular past tense verbs:    **came**
                               **were**
                               **had**
                               **felt**
                               **did**

**Teacher Tip STRATEGIES** Encourage students to think aloud, practicing the strategies they have learned. Tell students that their ideas about the story are very important to the whole class's understanding of the story.

**Teacher Tip COMPREHENSION** Good readers are active readers. They interact with the text as they read by emoting, reacting, responding, and problem solving in their efforts to construct and maintain meaning.

Rosie was getting bigger. But she was still a puppy with lots of energy. Poor old Rugby tried his best to keep up! Soon winter came, and the three of us were racing and chasing through the new snow. We had so much fun together!

Sometimes it felt as if Rosie had always been with us—and always would be. I

**4** didn't want to think about the day when she would have to leave.

70

Rosie was old enough now for short lessons. Dad showed me how to teach her simple commands: *come, sit, stand, down, stay,* and *heel.*

We all worked to teach her good manners. A dog who begged for food at the table or jumped up on people would not make a good guide dog.

Rosie learned fast. Dad said that she was very smart and loved to please people. But she would have to pass many tests before she could become a guide dog.

71

## COMPREHENSION

## Comprehension Skills

**Second Read**

### Cause and Effect  LA.E.2.2.1.3.1 FCAT

Have students continue to look for cause-and-effect relationships in the story. Remind them that certain words, called causal indicators, can be used to show cause-and-effect relationships. These words include *so, because, since,* and *therefore.* Even if the writer does not use these words in the selection, students can use the words to explain the relationships. Have them practice using these words in sentences they make up from the information on the transparency.

- *Dad showed me how to teach Rosie simple commands* (effect) *because she was old enough now* (cause).

- *A dog that jumped on people would not make a good guide dog* (cause); *therefore, we all worked to teach her good manners* (effect).

| Word Knowledge |
| --- |
| *-ed* endings:     showed |
| worked |
| begged |
| learned |
| loved |

**COMPREHENSION**

## Comprehension Strategies

### Teacher Modeling

**5** **Predicting** *Good readers make predictions about what will probably happen later on in the selection. Then they read to see if their predictions are right. Sometimes as they read and learn more, they change their predictions. I'm going to make a prediction right now that Rosie will pass the tests. She seems like a good dog, and the family is trying to train her. She should do well on the tests. Who else has a different prediction?*

### Word Knowledge

contractions:    couldn't
                 didn't

**Teacher Tip USING STRATEGIES** Be sure to encourage all the students to use strategies. Call on various students to share which strategies they are using and to tell how they are using them to figure out the meaning of the text.

**Teacher Tip** Remind students to use context clues, apposition, or word structure to figure out the meaning of difficult words as they are reading.

I asked Dad what would happen if Rosie didn't pass the tests. He said that she couldn't be a guide dog, but she could still be a good pet. Then we would be able to keep her. **5**

Now I didn't know what to think. I wanted Rosie to do well. I wanted to be <u>proud</u> of her. And I wanted her to help a blind person someday. I knew how important that was. But it was getting harder and harder to think of Rosie going away. And how could I explain it to Rugby? He loved Rosie as much as I did. Now the three of us were best friends.

72

When spring came, my family started taking Rosie
on trips. We wanted her to be used to cars and buses
and to the places where she would have to take her
blind owner, like the bank and the store. We even took
her to a restaurant. Of course, Rugby couldn't come
with us. He always looked a little sad when Rosie got
to go somewhere he couldn't go. And I knew he would
be waiting for us when we got home.

Rosie would jump out of the car, and the two of
them would race off, barking and playing and jumping.
Later, they would come home in time for dinner,
muddy and wet, with their tongues hanging out.

73

# Comprehension Skills

**Second Read**

## Cause and Effect   LA.E.2.2.1.3.1 FCAT

Have students continue to add to the
transparency their observations of
causes and effects. Help students
identify cause-and-effect relationships
between the boy's conflicting feelings.

- Cause: He wants to be proud of Rosie.
  Effect: He wants her to do well on
  the tests.
- Cause: He loved Rosie.
  Effect: It was hard to think of her
  going away.

---

### Word Knowledge

*-ing* endings:   **taking**
  **waiting**
  **barking**
  **playing**
  **jumping**

---

**Teacher Tip** CAUSE AND EFFECT
Continue to encourage students to
use clue words as they restate cause-
and-effect relationships.

**COMPREHENSION**

COMPREHENSION

## Comprehension Strategies

First Read

### Teacher Modeling

**6 Asking Questions** *I have more questions now. I wonder if a lot of time has passed quickly here. Is it fall already? It must be, because the boy says, "When that day did come, I tried to be brave." Now I wonder what's going to happen next. Will Rosie pass the tests? Why does the story say she's not coming back? Does that mean she passes the tests and goes to the special school? I'll read more to find out. Who else has other questions?*

### Word Knowledge

| | |
|---|---|
| irregular past tense verbs: | **was** |
| | **went** |
| | **threw** |

**Teacher Tip** Help students to understand that each person's response to a text is a very individual matter and that no two people will respond in exactly the same way. Encourage students to respect each other's contributions.

Soon summer came. The days were long and hot. Rosie was almost full grown. She was a beautiful dog. She and Rugby liked to sleep in the cool shade together. Sometimes the three of us went swimming in a nearby pond. Rugby and Rosie loved to fetch sticks and tennis balls that I threw into the water.

It was a wonderful summer, and I wanted it to last forever.

74

**COMPREHENSION**

I knew that when fall came, it would be time for **6** Rosie to go. When that day did come, I tried to be brave. Rugby and I stood and watched as Dad opened the car door for Rosie to jump in. Rugby wasn't upset. He didn't know that Rosie wasn't coming back. But I was so sad. I took Rugby on a long walk and tried not to think about Rosie. It was just like old times, before she came—when there were just the two of us.

When Dad came home, Rugby was waiting, his tail wagging. But, of course, Rosie wasn't in the car. Rugby looked all over for her. He whined. I wanted to explain everything, but I knew he couldn't understand. Instead, I buried my face in his neck and whispered, "She's gone, and I miss her, too."

75

## Comprehension Skills

 Second Read

**Cause and Effect** LA.E.2.2.1.3.1 FCAT

Have students continue to read carefully to find out how one event causes another. Encourage them to look for chains of causes and effects throughout the selection.

- Cause: Rugby did not know Rosie wasn't coming back.
  Effect: He was not upset.
- Cause: Rosie did not come back.
  Effect: Rugby looked all over for her.

---

**Word Knowledge**

contractions:   wasn't
                didn't

---

**Research in Action**

By the time students are in Grade 3, most students understand that including both events in the outside physical world and thoughts and feelings that occur in the inside mental world make stories more interesting and more realistic. *(Anne McKeough)*

COMPREHENSION

## Comprehension Strategies

**First Read**

### Teacher Modeling

**7 Predicting** *Good readers check their predictions when they read. Earlier I predicted that Rosie would pass the tests. I see now that she passed the tests and is doing well with her new training. I have another prediction now. I predict that Rosie will make her new owner very happy. Who else has a prediction?*

---

### Word Knowledge

**-ly endings:**     especially
                     hardly

---

**Teacher Tip  WAIT TIME** Make sure to allow students enough time to respond. Although silence can be uncomfortable, don't automatically jump in with your own response—wait.

---

**Writer's Craft**

**Sentence Variety**
Point out the writer's use of sentences of different lengths. Explain that students should do this in their own writing so that it is easier to read. If all of the sentences are long or short, their writing won't flow, and it will sound awkward. See Writer's Craft, page 81l.

We all missed Rosie very much, especially Rugby. Her trainers called several times. At first, I hoped that Rosie wasn't doing well. Then she could come back to live with us. But the trainers said that she was doing fine and would graduate with her new owner soon. That made me feel so mixed-up. I didn't want to think about Rosie with a new owner, but I knew how important Rosie would be to a person who needed her. Could that person love her as much as Rugby and I had?

I wanted to go to the graduation and see Rosie again. Then I had a great idea. I asked Dad if we could take Rugby, too. I knew how he'd missed Rosie—after all, they'd been best friends.  **7**

We got special permission for Rugby to go to the graduation. I could hardly wait.

76

At the graduation, there were lots of people and dogs. Rugby spotted Rosie right away. She was in her guide-dog harness, standing beside her new owner. She seemed so calm, and we thought she looked so proud. Rugby bounded over to her, pulling me along. The two dogs greeted each other nose to nose, tails wagging. But Rosie would not leave her owner's side. She was a working dog now with an important job to do.

77

## Comprehension Skills

### Cause and Effect  LA.E.2.2.1.3.1 FCAT

Identifying causes and effects is an ongoing process. Readers should continue noticing effects and identifying their causes throughout a story. Remind students to use causal indicators to help them understand these relationships. Sometimes students will need to state the effect first.

- *The boy wanted to see Rosie again* (cause) <u>*so he asked his Dad if he could take Rugby to the graduation*</u> (effect).

- *Rosie would not leave her owner's side* (effect) <u>*because she had an important job to do*</u> (cause).

### Word Knowledge

*-ing* endings:     standing
                  pulling
                  wagging
                  working

**COMPREHENSION**

COMPREHENSION

## Comprehension Strategies

 First Read

### Teacher Modeling

**8 Confirm Predictions** *I see now that my earlier prediction was confirmed. Rosie did make her new owner very happy. Has anyone else's prediction been confirmed?*

### Teacher Modeling

**9 Making Connections**

*I understand how he feels here. Sometimes I feel happy and nervous at the same time, like when I'm looking forward to something new. I see how he feels okay about Rosie because she has a good home with someone who will really love and appreciate her. Now he's excited about a new puppy. I felt that way when we got a puppy last year.*

### Discussing Strategy Use LA.A.1.2.4.3.1

After students read the selection, encourage them to share any problems they encountered and to tell what strategies they used.

- What connections did they make between the reading and what they already know?
- What questions did they ask as they read?
- On what basis did they make and confirm predictions?
- How did they make, confirm, and revise predictions as they read?
- What predictions did they make?

These are questions good readers ask after they read a text. After reading, they should always be asking, "What did I find interesting? What is important here?" Later, remind the students again that whenever they conclude a reading, they should ask themselves questions about what was in the text.

Her owner talked to us for a while. She told us how grateful she was to have Rosie and what a wonderful dog she was. And she thanked us for taking good care of her while she was a puppy. **8**

When it was time to go, we said good-bye to Rosie. Poor Rugby. On the way home in the car, I tried to make him feel better. I talked to him and patted him. I told him that her new owner loved her and would take good care of her.

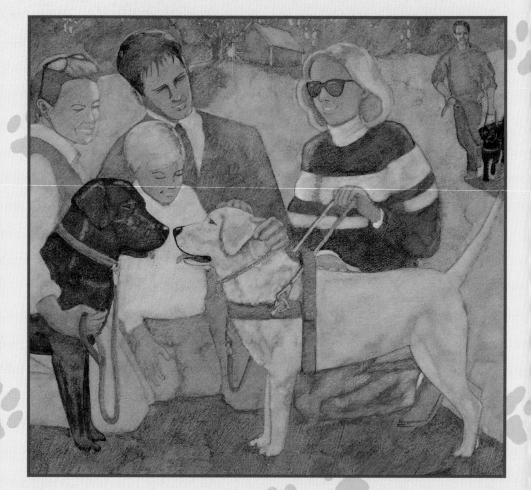

78

 **Informal Assessment**

Use the Informal Comprehension Strategies Rubrics on page 64J to determine whether a student is using the strategies being taught.

 **Teacher Tip** BUILDING FLUENCY
As students read, you may notice that some need work in building fluency. During Workshop, have these students select a section of the text (a minimum of 160 words) to read several times in order to build fluency.

The next morning, Rugby was still moping around when my dad left in the car. I was excited—and nervous, too.

I knew where my dad was going.

When the car came back, I was waiting with Rugby. Dad got out. He had a wiggly little puppy in his arms. I knew I was holding on to Rugby too tightly—wishing, hoping. I wanted him to know that, because we had all loved Rosie so much, we had decided we would help raise another puppy that would be ours for a year.

Dad knelt down in front of Rugby. "Rugby," he said, "this is Blue."

And Rugby leaned forward and licked that little puppy right on the nose.

79

## COMPREHENSION

## Comprehension Skills

 Second Read

### Cause and Effect LA.E.2.2.1.3.1 FCAT

Remind students that identifying cause-and-effect relationships can help them better understand the selections they read. Encourage them to think about and discuss these relationships after reading this selection. *(At first Rugby didn't like Rosie, maybe because he was jealous. Then he liked her because she was fun to play with. The boy felt sad sometimes because he knew Rosie would leave one day. In the end, he wasn't sad anymore since he knew she was going to help someone who needed her.)*

### Checking Comprehension

Ask students the following questions to check their comprehension of the selection.

- How do the characters in this selection show friendship? *(The boy and Rugby are friends because they play together, and the boy is careful with Rugby's feelings. Rugby and Rosie are friends too because they play together and keep each other company. Rugby misses her when she leaves.)*

- Why did the boy have mixed feelings about Rosie leaving? *(He wanted Rosie to help someone who needed her, but he knew he would miss her.)*

- How can you tell the boy has learned to accept Rosie's new life? *(He is excited about the new puppy they are keeping.)*

 **Teacher Tip FLUENCY** By this time in third grade, good readers should be reading approximately 107 words per minute with fluency and expression. The only way to gain this fluency is through practice. Have students reread the selection to you and to each other during Workshop to help build fluency.

**Formal Assessment**

See pages 14–17 in *Unit 1 Assessment* to test students' comprehension of "Rugby & Rosie."

 **Routine Card**
Refer to *Routine 6* for the *handing-off process.*

| Clues | Problems | Wonderings |
|---|---|---|
| Rugby is a dog. Is Rosie a dog too? | Labrador | How do Rugby and Rosie meet? |

**Reading Transparency 46**

 **www.sra4kids.com**
**Web Connection**
Some students may choose to conduct a computer search for additional books or information about friendship. Invite them to make a list of these books and sources of information to share with classmates and the school librarian. Check the Reading link of the SRA Web page for additional links to the theme-related Web site.

## Discussing the Selection  LA.C.1.2.3.3.1

 After the first read, the whole group discusses the selection and any personal thoughts, reactions, problems, or questions that it raises. To stimulate discussion, students can ask one another the kinds of questions that good readers ask themselves about a text: *How does the selection connect to the theme of Friendship? What did I find interesting? What is important here? What was difficult to understand? Why would someone want to read this?*

**Handing-off Process**   Seeing you as a contributing member of the group sets a strong example for students. To emphasize that you are part of the group, actively participate in the *handing-off process*: Raise your hand to be called on by the last speaker when you have a contribution to make. Point out unusual and interesting insights verbalized by students so that these insights are recognized and discussed. As the year progresses, students will take more and more responsibility for the discussions of the selections.

Engage students in a discussion to determine whether they have grasped the following ideas:

- how pets can teach people about friendship
- how friendships can begin even after a rough start
- how friends sometimes have to say good-bye

During this time, have students return to the clues, problems, and wonderings they noted during browsing to determine whether the clues were borne out by the selection, whether and how their problems were solved, and whether their wonderings were answered or deserve further discussion and investigation. Let the students decide which items deserve further discussion.

Also, have students return to the Focus Questions on the first page of the selection. Select a student to read the questions aloud, and have volunteers answer the questions. If students do not know the answers to the questions, have them return to the text to find the answers.

You may wish to review the elements of realistic fiction with the students at this time. Discuss with them how they can tell "Rugby & Rosie" is realistic fiction.

 Have students break into small groups to discuss what this story tells them about how important sharing is in friendship. Groups can discuss their ideas with the rest of the class.

 Students may wish to record their personal responses to the selection. If they have ever had a special pet or have ever learned something about friendship from a pet, encourage them to write about their experiences.

# Review Selection Vocabulary

Have students review the definitions of the selection vocabulary words that they wrote in the Vocabulary section of their Writer's Notebooks. Remind them that they discussed the meanings of these words before reading the selection. Have students write sentences for each of the vocabulary words after the definitions in the same section of their Writer's Notebooks. They can use the definitions and the sentences to study for the vocabulary portion of their Lesson Assessments. Also, have them add any other interesting words that they clarified while reading to the Personal Dictionary section of their Writer's Notebooks. Encourage students to refer to the selection vocabulary words throughout the unit. The words from the selection are:

| | | |
|---|---|---|
| **commands** | **proud** | **graduation** |
| **manners** | **trainers** | |

If you created a Word Bank of key words related to the theme Friendship, remind students to find words from other resources, from their activities, and from family discussions and add them to the Word Bank. Students may also place synonyms and antonyms in the Word Bank, or organize words by parts of speech.

# Home Connection

Distribute **Home Connection,** page 9. Encourage students to discuss "Rugby & Rosie" with their families. **Home Connection** is also available in Spanish, page 10.

*Rugby & Rosie*

**A message from** _____

Our class has just read "Rugby & Rosie." In this story, a new puppy comes to live with Rugby's family, but only for one year. Rugby is the family dog. The family will spend one year training the puppy and exposing it to different types of environments. At the end of the year, if the puppy passes the tests, it will go on to take special training to become a guide dog for a blind person. The boy in the story is happy to have a puppy to play with him and Rugby, but the boy worries that he will miss the new puppy when she is gone. As for Rugby, he takes some time to get used to the puppy. Ask your child to tell you more about the story and how the friendship grew, what lessons pets can teach us about friendship, and how friends sometimes have to let go.

Ask your child if he or she has ever taken some time to build a new friendship with someone. Was that difficult? If so, why? What kinds of things can people do together to begin a friendship? Ask your child to write about their suggestions here. Encourage your child to explain how the activities he or she suggests can help friendship grow.

**Next week's selection**  *Teammates*

Your child will be studying the following vocabulary words in the upcoming week. Please review the meanings of these words with your child: **exist**—to be around; **extraordinary**—remarkable; very special; **apathetic**—not interested; not caring; **intimidate**—to make someone feel bad by hurting their feelings; **experiment**—a test used to discover something; **humiliations**—things that cause someone to be embarrassed.

Please review with your child the spelling words for the upcoming week: dusk, blush, crust, thump, shut, dump, scrub, pump, buff, buzz, but, just, bus, upon, much.

*Home Connection p. 9*

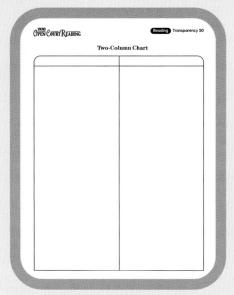

**Reading Transparency 50**

Teacher Tip **CONFIRMING PREDICTIONS** Remind students that good readers continuously make predictions as they read. They also confirm their predictions and update them as they go along.

## Supporting the Reading

### Comprehension Strategies: Predicting  LA.A.1.2.1.3.1

**Teach**  Tell students that making predictions while they read engages them in the story, helps them pay attention to details, and improves their comprehension. Predictions should be based on information in the text plus their own experiences. Then after they make a prediction, they keep reading to see if they are right. Sometimes further reading provides more information even before students find out whether their prediction was right. They should continue to revise predictions as they obtain more information.

**Guided Practice**  Have students reflect on the predictions they made as they were reading "Rugby & Rosie." Use **Reading Transparency 50** to provide them with a two-column chart where they can write their predictions and tell whether they were confirmed.

**Independent Practice**  Encourage students to practice using this strategy in their own personal reading. Tell them they can even make quick notes of their predictions and check to see if they are confirmed.

**Link to Writing**  Have students write out the predictions they made as they read "Rugby & Rosie." Ask them to include an explanation of why they made those predictions, any key words or illustrations that helped them arrive at their predictions, and whether the predictions were correct. Students can then exchange papers to compare and discuss the predictions they made.

| My Prediction | What Happened |
|---|---|
| I predicted that Rugby would be happy to play with a new puppy. | My prediction was not confirmed. Rugby ignored Rosie when she first arrived. |

# Literary Elements

## Characterization: Analyzing Character Traits  LA.E.1.2.3.3.1, LA.E.1.2.2.3.3

**Teach** Tell students that in most stories, characters go through some changes because of experiences they have. Characterization is the way a writer reveals what the characters in a story are like—by telling what they do, say, think, and feel. Invite students to describe characters they have read about that seemed particularly real or interesting. After some discussion, point out that good writers do not simply state that a character is caring, selfish, brave, or absent-minded. Readers are able to identify a character's traits or how a character changes by paying attention to the kinds of words authors use when describing a character's actions or speech.

**Guided Practice** Invite a volunteer to summarize what experience the boy and Rugby have in "Rugby & Rosie." *(A puppy comes to live with them for a year.)* Ask students to describe how the boy's actions and feelings are different at the beginning of the story and at the end of the story. Also have them explain how Rugby's actions have changed.

## Independent Practice

- Ask students to label one side of a sheet of paper *Beginning* and the other side *Ending*. Ask them to think of things the boy does or says at the beginning of the story that show how he feels about the puppy. Tell students to record these examples on the side of paper labeled *Beginning*. Encourage students to tell what kind of person they think the boy is, based on these observations.

- Then, ask students to think of things the boy does or says at the end of the story that show how he feels about the puppy leaving. Have students record these examples on the second side, labeled *Ending*.

- Next, ask students to write a conclusion that answers the question, "How did the boy change?"

- They can do the same exercise for Rugby if they choose.

**Teacher Tip** MATERIALS
- ✔ poster boards
- ✔ colored pencils or markers

**Teacher Tip** PURPOSE To help students understand more about the animal world in general and dogs in particular.

**Teacher Tip** You may want to invite a guide dog trainer or a blind person and guide dog to visit the class.

# Science Connection LA.C.1.2.1.3.1; SC.F.1.2.3.3.1; SC.H.3.2.1.3.2

## Guide Dogs

In "Rugby & Rosie," Rosie is trained to be a guide for a blind person. Why are dogs especially well suited to the task of being trained as guides for blind people? What abilities and characteristics of dogs make them good candidates for this role? What are the differences between the larger animal group, of which dogs are a part, and other animal groups, such as birds, fish, reptiles, and amphibians?

Ask small groups of students to look in the encyclopedia or other reference books in the library or conduct an Internet search to learn the answers to these and other questions about dogs and other vertebrate animals. Have each group create a visual to explain an aspect of answers to one of the questions listed above. Students should use this time to create a presentation that showcases their talents. They may wish to present their findings as a skit or song. Encourage students to present their findings in a creative manner. Invite groups to present their information to the class.

# Social Studies Connection SS.C.2.2.2.3.1

## Helping Those in Need

The story "Rugby & Rosie" should raise questions about the importance and significance of helping those in need. In "Rugby & Rosie," Rugby's family helped by raising and training a puppy that would eventually become a guide dog for a blind person. As students probably observed, this was not an easy task for the family. The family spent much time with Rosie and it was very difficult for them all to say good-bye. However, the service they were providing was more important.

Discuss with the students acts of generosity. Explain how sometimes people perform single acts of generosity, or in this case, perform deeds that require a more long-term commitment. Brainstorm a list of the different ways people can be generous to those in need. This list may include donating money to organizations that help toward cures for diseases, the homeless, animal shelters, and so forth. It should also include ways people, including students, can use their time to help those in need. This list might include volunteering in kitchens that feed the homeless, delivering meals to the elderly, volunteering in schools and animal shelters, and so on.

Have the students create a poster which displays the many different ways people can demonstrate acts of generosity. They can draw pictures or cut pictures from magazines of people performing acts of generosity. For a more extensive investigation, you might have students investigate some of the various organizations that support those in need and have groups present their findings. You may want to invite local leaders of various charitable organizations into the classroom to hold discussions and answer questions. Students could conduct interview sessions and include their findings in their presentations.

**Teacher Tip MATERIALS**
- poster boards
- colored pencils or markers, magazines

**Teacher Tip PURPOSE** To help students understand the role each citizen plays in helping those in need.

**Science/Social Studies Connection Center**
SS.C.2.2.2.3.1
Refer to the *Science/Social Studies Connection Center* Card 5 for a social studies activity that students can investigate.

## Meet the Author/Illustrator

After students read the information about Nan Parson Rossiter, discuss the following questions with them.

- Why do you think Rossiter hasn't raised guide dog puppies? *(Possible answer: She knows it would be difficult to let them go after a year. Maybe she thinks she would grow too attached to the puppies.)*

- Why might Rossiter want to write about the topic of saying good-bye in two books? *(Possible answer: Students encounter situations like these often. Rossiter understands it is an important and difficult topic. She also respects those who do raise guide dogs, and she probably feels they deserve to have a story written about them.)*

- How is the "sad song of the Canada geese" like the main idea in "Rugby & Rosie"? *(Possible answer: When the geese honk, they are leaving. It is the same theme of saying good-bye to animals. Maybe she feels sad when they leave every year.)*

## Meet the Author/Illustrator

**Nan Parson Rossiter** focuses her stories on the pain of saying good-bye to loved ones. Her stories are special because the loved ones are animals. In *Rugby & Rosie* and *The Way Home*, the main characters must learn to let go of an animal that has been in their care. Rossiter never raised a guide dog, but she respects those who do. She understands the time, love, and heartbreak that is a part of such a worthwhile endeavor. Rossiter has a chocolate retriever named Briar. She lives in Connecticut with her husband and children. Each fall she loves the sad song of the Canada geese as they migrate south.

80

# Theme Connections

## Within the Selection

Record your answers to the questions below in the Response Journal section of your Writer's Notebook. In small groups, report the ideas you wrote. Discuss your ideas with the rest of the group. Then choose a person to report your group's answers to the class.

- Rubgy and his boy are best friends. What happens to their friendship when Rosie comes to live with the family?
- Rosie left the family after only a year to learn how to be a guide dog. Why did the boy in the story sometimes wish that Rosie wasn't doing well with her trainers?

## Across Selections

- How is this story different than the other stories you have read?
- Compare how the boy in this story and Chrissy and Leah in "The Tree House" showed friendship by giving something away.

## Beyond the Selection

- Think about how "Rugby & Rosie" adds to what you know about friendship.
- Add items to the Concept/Question Board about friendship.

81

# Theme Connections

## Within the Selection

- Rugby doesn't want to share his boy with Rosie, but once he gets to know the puppy, all three become best friends.
- The boy knew that Rosie was being trained for a job, but he still missed her and wanted her to live with him.

## Across Selections

- Rugby and Rosie are animals who show friendship.
- The boy gave Rosie to a new owner who needed a guide dog. Chrissy gave Leah paint, and Leah gave Chrissy pictures.

## Beyond the Selection

Have groups discuss their ideas with the class. Have students add these ideas to the Concept/Question Board. Have students sum up what they have learned and tell how they might use this in investigations.

## Inquiry Journal

Students should record their ideas and impressions about the selections on page 3 of their **Inquiry Journals.**

 **Informal Assessment**

This may be a good time to observe students working in small groups and to mark your observations in the Teacher Observation Log found in the **Program Assessment Teacher's Edition.**

Recording Concept Information *(continued)*

- "The Tree House" by Lois Lowry
  Answers will vary.

- "Rugby & Rosie" by Nan Parson Rossiter
  Answers will vary.

Inquiry Journal • *Recording Concept Information*          UNIT I  **3**

*Inquiry Journal p. 3*

## Objectives

- Students gain a deeper understanding of friendship.
- Students discuss investigation needs and make plans.
- Students begin their investigations.

## Materials

- Student Anthology, Book 1, pp. 64–81
- Research Assistant CD-ROM
- Inquiry Journal, pp. 20–21

**Teacher Tip** You may find it beneficial to read aloud to students from books they or you have found related to their questions.

**INVESTIGATION**

LA.C.1.2.3.3.1, LA.C.3.2.2.3.1, LA.C.3.2.5.3.1

# Investigating Concepts Beyond the Text: Needs and Plans

Now that students have organized into groups and formed conjectures, they are ready to enter the needs and plans phase. This phase provides an opportunity for the students to gather information and revise problems.

Provide time for the investigation groups to meet and identify knowledge needs related to their conjectures. Help those students who are having difficulty. Within the investigation groups, students should make individual job assignments. Then meet with the groups to help them refine their plans. Questions students should focus on are: *What information do I need to find or figure out to help answer my problem? How will it affect my conjecture?*

Have the groups meet to discuss questions or ideas they might have about the selection they have just read. Does the selection tell them something about friendship that they hadn't thought of before? Does the story make them wonder about something? After reading "Rugby & Rosie," students may wish to learn more about guide dogs and providing temporary homes for them. Students might also wish to hold a panel discussion to investigate friendships between people and pets. Students may wish to share personal experience stories or invite an expert speaker to class.

# Concept/Question Board

After reading each selection, students should use the Concept/Question Board to do the following:

- Post any questions they asked about a selection before reading that have not yet been answered.
- Refer to as they formulate statements about concepts that apply to their investigations.
- Post general statements formulated by each collaborative group.
- Continue to post news articles or other items that they find during the unit investigation.
- Read and think about posted questions, articles, or concepts that interest them and provide answers to the questions.

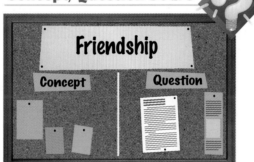

**Concept/Question Board**

Friendship

Concept          Question

**INVESTIGATION**

**Teacher Tip** PANEL DISCUSSION
Tell students that introducing thought-provoking questions keeps a discussion interesting. Some questions they might ask are: *Can people really have friendships with pets? Why or why not? In what ways are pets good friends for people? What is your definition of friendship?*

**Teacher Tip** CONCEPT/QUESTION
BOARD Remind students that when working on a unit, they will have questions that they will want to have answered. New questions will arise as the unit proceeds. Tell them that good readers continue to generate questions as they get deeper into a topic.

**Research Assistant**
The *Research Assistant CD-ROM* can assist students in their investigations.

## Unit 1   Investigation Management

| Lesson 1 | **Collaborative Investigation**<br>Introduce the investigation cycle and explain its purpose. Students can lead a panel discussion on friendship-related issues. |
|---|---|
| Lesson 2 | Students can investigate immigration and forming new friendships or other areas of investigation related to friendship. Students should organize into groups based on areas of shared interest. |
| Lesson 3 | Students investigate mending damaged friendships, and groups begin forming conjectures. |
| Lesson 4 | **Collaborative Investigation**<br>**Students begin the needs and plans phase and begin investigations.**<br>**Supplementary Activities**<br>**Students share personal stories, hold a panel discussion, or invite an expert speaker to class.** |
| Lesson 5 | Students revise investigation plans as necessary. Groups discuss teammate qualities and invite a coach to class to interview. |
| Lesson 6 | Students wrap up investigations and prepare formal presentations. Students can discuss standing by friends and write a scene or miniplay about a scenario. |

**INVESTIGATION**

**Teacher Tip** WRITER'S NOTEBOOK
While students are investigating Friendship and the other themes in "Rugby & Rosie," have them review and elaborate on the ideas they have written in their Writer's Notebooks.

**Teacher Tip** Remind students that their investigations are ongoing. The unit investigations are not performed to find final conclusions or come to final decisions regarding any one topic. Instead, they are designed to stimulate further thinking and investigation, lasting past the end of a unit or the end of the school year.

### Formal Assessment

Use the Research Rubrics on page 64J to assess students' ability to recognize information needs.

# Investigating the Theme

Explain that throughout this unit on Friendship, the goal of investigation is to come to a deeper understanding of some aspect of the theme. Students might wish to re-examine personal experiences of their own or talk to others as they investigate this topic.

Remind students that by the end of the unit they will need to produce and publish in some form the results of their investigation. They are free to decide how they want to present their finished product.

Have students list the questions or problems that especially interest them in their *Inquiry Journals,* page 20. Tell them that they will look at these questions again as they meet with their groups to discuss their findings and refine their searches.

*Inquiry Journal p. 20*

# Following Directions LA.B.1.2.1.3.2, LA.B.2.2.3.3.1

**Teach** Lead students in playing a game that depends upon following directions exactly, such as Simon Says or Red Light, Green Light. Discuss with students the importance of following directions in playing the game.

Have students list everyday events during which they are required to read or listen to directions. Point out that most directions follow a logical sequence of steps that makes them easy to follow. Include in your discussion the consequences of not following directions.

**Guided Practice** Organize students into pairs. Give each student a different drawing of geometric figures, such as two intersecting rectangles, an octagon with a triangle on top, and so on. Tell students not to show the figures to their partners. Have each student give his or her partner directions on how to draw the secret figure. Once the drawing is complete, the partners compare it to the original figure. Have them discuss which directions were effective and which were not.

**Independent Practice** Ask students to think about a simple game they enjoy playing with friends. Then, have them write the directions. Ask volunteers to read the directions aloud for a pair or small group to follow.

For more practice with following directions, have students complete *Inquiry Journal,* page 21.

**Teacher Tip** You might want to have students practice following multistep written directions at this time. You can do this by bringing a new game into the classroom and having the students read the directions before playing.

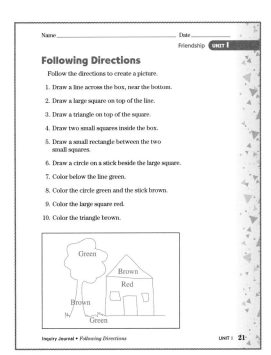

*Inquiry Journal p. 21*

OVERVIEW

## Objectives

### Word Analysis

**Spelling**
- **The /o/ Sound.** Develop an understanding of the /o/ sound.

**Vocabulary**
- **Dictionary Strategy.** Using words from "Rugby & Rosie," learn to apply the dictionary to discover the meaning or meanings of an unfamiliar word.

### Writing Process Strategies
- **Revising.** By rereading their draft and looking for certain problems, students will improve their writing during the revising step of the writing process.

### English Language Conventions

**Grammar, Usage, and Mechanics**
- **Verbs.** This lesson defines verb phrases, main verbs, and helping verbs. Find verb phrases in "Rugby & Rosie" and identify the main and helping verbs. Use verb phrases in writing.

**Listening, Speaking, Viewing**
- **Viewing: Learning from Pictures.** Learn to interpret themes and ideas presented in images.

**Penmanship**
- **Cursive Letters p and j.** Develop handwriting skills by practicing formation of cursive p and j.

## Materials

- Language Arts Handbook
- Comprehension and Language Arts Skills, pp. 14–17
- Sound/Spelling Card 15
- Writer's Workbook, p. 4
- Language Arts Transparencies 17–21
- Student Anthology
- Spelling and Vocabulary Skills, pp. 14–17

## MEETING INDIVIDUAL NEEDS

*Reteach, Challenge, English-Language Development,* and *Intervention* lessons are available to support the language arts instruction in this lesson.

## Research in Action

*Give Students Something Concrete to Talk About. . . . give the students something to do—moving things, underlining, searching, etc.— and then discuss what they are doing as they do it.*
*(Carl Bereiter* and *Marlene Scardamalia,* The Psychology of Written Composition)

# Language Arts Overview

## Word Analysis

**Spelling** The Spelling activities on the following pages introduce the /o/ sound spelled *o* by developing spelling skills through various strategies.

### Selection Spelling Words

These words from "Rugby & Rosie" contain the /o/ sound spelled *o*.

st<u>o</u>p   g<u>o</u>t   l<u>o</u>ts   j<u>o</u>b   p<u>o</u>nd

**Vocabulary** The Vocabulary activities extend the instruction of the Vocabulary Skill Words from "Rugby & Rosie" to recognize the dictionary as a valuable resource for finding the many definitions, forms, and origins of a single word.

### Vocabulary Skill Words

**chocolate   Labrador   ordinary   manners\*   graduation\***
*\*Also Selection Vocabulary*

**Additional Materials:** dictionary

## Writing Process Strategies

The Writing Process Strategies lesson involves instruction in the revising step of the writing process. Students will revise by adding copy, deleting copy, consolidating, rearranging, clarifying, and using the traits of good writing. As practice for this skill, students will revise their autobiographies.

 To introduce students to the computer as a writing tool, teach students how to use the Find feature to locate and open a file. *Basic Computer Skills,* Level 3, Lesson 5, teaches these basic computer skills. LA.D.2.2.4.3.1

## English Language Conventions

**Grammar, Usage, and Mechanics** **Verbs.** Understand verb phrases, main verbs, and helping verbs, through reading and writing.

**Listening, Speaking, Viewing** **Viewing: Learning from Pictures.** In this Viewing lesson, students will further develop their skills for interpreting images.

**Penmanship** **Cursive Letters p and j.** This lesson continues the development of cursive handwriting skills. Students learn correct formation of *p* and *j* and then practice writing words from the literature selection that contain those letters.

# DAY 1

| Word Analysis | Writing Process Strategies | English Language Conventions |
|---|---|---|

## Spelling

### Assessment: Pretest

**The /o/ Sound** LA.A.1.2.2.3.1

### Teach

Give students the Pretest found on page 32 of *Unit 1 Assessment* as entry assessment of the spelling pattern. Have them proofread and correct any misspelled words.

### Pretest Sentences

1. **rot** A banana peel can **rot**.
2. **shot** The flu **shot** is a vaccine.
3. **crop** Cotton is a type of **crop**.
4. **sock** A **sock** goes on your foot.
5. **clock** At 2:00 A.M., a **clock** chimes twice.
6. **flock** A group of birds can be called a **flock**.
7. **body** The human **body** is made of cells.
8. **spot** A freckle is a **spot** on your skin.
9. **stocking** A **stocking** can be made of wool.
10. **lobby** The entrance to a hotel is called a **lobby**.
11. **stop** A **stop** sign is an octagon.
12. **got** She **got** into her car to drive to the store.
13. **lots** Cookies are made with **lots** of sugar.
14. **job** The **job** of a governor is to govern the people.
15. **pond** Water lilies grow best in a **pond**.

Diagnose any misspellings by determining whether students misspelled the /o/ sound or some other part of the word. Then use the Pretest as a take-home list to study the spellings of words with the /o/ sound.

## Revising LA.B.1.2.2.3.4, LA.B.1.2.2.3.6

### Introduction to the Writing Process

### Teach

**Introduce Writing Process Steps**

■ Read *Language Arts Handbook,* page 19, to introduce the revising step of the writing process.
■ Discuss *Language Arts Transparency 17,* Revising: Adding Copy.
■ Model how additional information can be helpful by saying "*I am a teacher*" and asking students what could be added to give more information. Accept answers such as telling what grade level you teach, adding adjectives to describe you, and so on.

### Inspiration

Teacher Model: "*Even though I did my best drafting, I know there are many ways to improve my writing. I reread it many times, looking for different ways to improve what I want to say to my audience. I also like to get someone else's reaction to it.*"

## Guided Practice

### Revising

Have students revise a piece of writing from their *Writing Folders.*

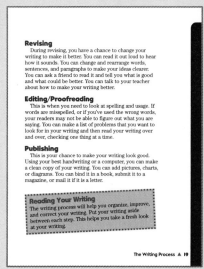

*Language Arts Handbook p. 19*

## Grammar, Usage, and Mechanics

**Grammar: Verbs** LA.B.1.2.3.3.4

### Teach

■ Use *Language Arts Handbook,* page 250, for the definition and examples of verb phrases, main verbs, and helping verbs.
■ Explain what a verb phrase, main verb, and helping verb are.
■ Write these sentences on the board as examples of verb phrases. Show students what the verb phrases, main verbs, and helping verbs are.
• I am going to eat a sandwich for lunch. (Am going to eat *is the verb phrase;* eat *is the main verb;* am *and* going *are the helping verbs.*)
• Marjorie told Thomas he could borrow her book. (Could borrow *is the verb phrase;* borrow *is the main verb;* could *is the helping verb.*)

### Independent Practice

Use *Comprehension and Language Arts Skills,* pages 14–15, to reinforce what verbs do and to practice identifying verb phrases, main verbs, and helping verbs.

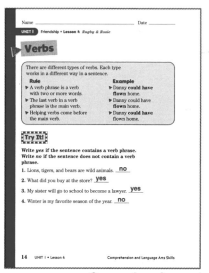

*Comprehension and Language Arts Skills p. 14*

# DAY 2

## Word Analysis

### Spelling

**Word Sorting** LA.A.1.2.2.3.1
- Hold up **Sound/Spelling Card 15.** Ask the class to say the word *fox* and listen to the /o/ sound.
- **Board Word Sort.** Write on the board: *out, with, blob, stuck, jaw, lock, black, bottle, slot,* and *hot.* Write *The /o/ Sound* and *Other Vowel Sounds.* Have the students sort the words under the correct heading.

### Vocabulary

**Using a Dictionary** LA.A.1.2.4.3.1

#### Teach
- Write *patient* from page 66 of "Rugby & Rosie" on the board.
- Explain that context clues and word structure do not always help find a word's meaning.
- Help a student find a dictionary and look for words beginning with the letter *p*. Help the student find *patient* in the dictionary and read the definition.

#### Guided Practice
Use **Spelling and Vocabulary Skills,** page 14, to teach students how to use a dictionary. Ask students to complete page 15 as independent practice.

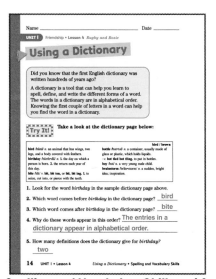

*Spelling and Vocabulary Skills p. 14*

## Writing Process Strategies

### Revising LA.B.1.2.2.3.4, LA.B.1.2.2.3.6
**Introduction to the Writing Process**

#### Teach
**Introduce The Traits of Writing**
- Read **Language Arts Handbook,** pages 10–15, to introduce the traits of writing. Discuss with students how these traits will help during the revising step of the writing process.
- Introduce sentence lifting as a revising strategy. See the Appendix for more information.
- Discuss **Language Arts Transparency 18,** Revising: Deleting Copy.

#### Guided Practice
**Revising**
Have students look at a piece of writing from their **Writing Folders** to check for information that does not belong. Have them put a box around information they think strays off the topic.

## English Language Conventions

### Grammar, Usage, and Mechanics
**Grammar: Verbs** LA.B.1.2.3.3.4

#### Teach
- Review what verbs do, and discuss verb phrases, main verbs, and helping verbs.
- Write the following sentences on the board. Ask students to identify the verb phrases, main verbs, and helping verbs.
  - I could go to the zoo. (Could go *is the verb phrase;* go *is the main verb;* could *is the helping verb.*)
  - You should buy that sweater. (Should buy *is the verb phrase;* buy *is the main verb;* should *is the helping verb.*)
  - We were planning on leaving tomorrow. (Were planning on leaving *is the verb phrase;* leaving *is the main verb;* were *and* planning *are the helping verbs.*)
  - We might have won the prize, but we won't know until Monday. (Might have won *and* won't know *are verb phrases;* won *and* know *are main verbs;* might have *and* won't *are helping verbs.*)

#### Guided Practice in Reading
Read a section of "Rugby & Rosie" aloud as the students follow along. Ask students to identify a verb phrase, then the main verb and helping verb.

# DAY 3

| **Word Analysis** | **Writing Process Strategies** | **English Language Conventions** |
| --- | --- | --- |

## Spelling

**The /o/ Sound** LA.A.1.2.2.3.1

### Teach
Introduce words with the /o/ sound spelled *o* found in "Rugby & Rosie." Ask students to think of names that contain the /o/ sound. *(Tom, Bob)*

### Guided Practice
Have students complete page 16 of *Spelling and Vocabulary Skills* to begin to learn strategies for spelling words with /o/ sound.

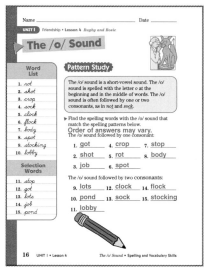

**Spelling and Vocabulary Skills p. 16**

## Vocabulary (continued)

**Using a Dictionary** LA.A.1.2.4.3.1

- Write *manners* from page 71 of "Rugby & Rosie" on the board.
- Write *manner* on the board next to *manners*.
- Ask students how they would find this word in a dictionary. *(Find the* m *section, look under* ma, *find* man, *find* manner.)
- Have a student read the definitions in the dictionary.

## Revising LA.B.1.2.2.3.4, LA.B.1.2.2.3.6
**Introduction to the Writing Process**

### Teach
- Review the strategies for revising covered on Days 1 and 2. Explain to students that today they will learn about another revising strategy—putting similar information together.
- Discuss *Language Arts Transparency 19,* Revising: Consolidating, with students. Consolidating, or combining sentences, is taking out the extra words from short, choppy sentences and combining them.
- Discuss how consolidating information enables the reader to better connect the information and contributes to fluency.

### Guided Practice
**Revising**
Have students look at a piece of their writing from their *Writing Folders* to check for information that can be consolidated. Suggest that they use a colored marker or crayon to underline text that they think can be consolidated.

## Grammar, Usage, and Mechanics
**Grammar: Verbs** LA.B.1.2.3.3.4

### Teach
Use *Language Arts Handbook,* page 250, to review verb phrases, main verbs, and helping verbs.

### Guided Practice in Writing
Have students write a sentence that includes a verb phrase. Have some of them share their sentences and identify their verb phrases.

 **Informal Assessment**

Check to make sure students can identify verb phrases, main verbs, and helping verbs in their own writing.

# DAY 4

| Word Analysis | Writing Process Strategies | English Language Conventions |
|---|---|---|

## Word Analysis

### Spelling

**The /o/ Sound** LA.A.1.2.2.3.1

#### Teach

Explain to students that the exercises on page 17 of **Spelling and Vocabulary Skills** are designed to help them learn to become better spellers. The Rhyming strategy can help them learn to recognize similar spellings in words that sound alike, as in the words *rock* and *sock*.

#### Guided Practice

Have students complete the exercises on page 17 of **Spelling and Vocabulary Skills** to reinforce the spelling patterns for the /o/ sound.

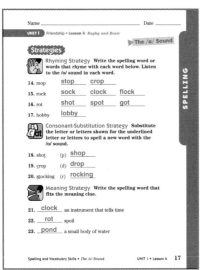

**Spelling and Vocabulary Skills p. 17**

### Vocabulary (continued)

**Using a Dictionary** LA.A.1.2.4.3.1

- Write *graduation* from page 76 of "Rugby & Rosie" on the board.
- Ask a student to find *graduation* in the dictionary and read its definition.
- Ask a student to explain the meaning of the word *graduation* as it is found in "Rugby & Rosie" on page 77. *(the special occasion, or ceremony, when a dog has become a guide dog)*

## Writing Process Strategies

**Revising** LA.B.1.2.2.3.4, LA.B.1.2.2.3.6
**Introduction to the Writing Process**

#### Teach

- **Troubleshooting**
  - Words, sentences, or paragraphs that are out of order
  - A weak beginning and ending
  - Ideas that are not clear, original, and supported with details

Writer's Craft
 **Sentence Variety**

- Introduce the concept of sentence variety by writing the following sentences on the board:
  *I am a teacher. I teach third grade. I love to teach. We learn new things. I enjoy my students.*
  Ask students if they can think of ways to make these sentences more interesting. Encourage students to use sentences of different lengths by combining ideas.
- Read **Language Arts Handbook,** page 34, on sentence variety.
- Read **Comprehension and Language Arts Skills,** pages 16–17, on sentence variety.
- Review peer conferencing with students using **Language Arts Handbook,** pages 36–37.
- Discuss **Language Arts Transparency 20,** Revising: Rearranging.

#### Guided Practice
**Revising**
Encourage students to have a group discussion about a book they have recently read to practice good conferencing behaviors.

## English Language Conventions

**Listening, Speaking, Viewing**
**Viewing: Learning from Pictures** LA.C.2.2.1.3.1

#### Teach

- Explain to the class that developing our viewing skills is important. We need to be able to look at a picture or a work of art and identify what its main idea is.
- While pictures have meaning alone, they can also add to the meanings of words. We can learn more about a story when we pay attention to both the words and pictures.

#### Guided Practice

- Discuss what kind of information we learn from the pictures in "Rugby & Rosie." *(what the two dogs look like; how close they are)*
- Discuss how the pictures combine with the words to make the story more powerful. *(We felt bad when Rosie left Rugby, especially when we saw the pictures and saw how close they were.)*
- Ask how our understanding of the story would be different if there were no pictures.

### Informal Assessment

Observe whether or not students were able to find the main ideas in the illustrations from the text. Students should understand the importance of viewing skills in interpreting literature.

# DAY 5

## Word Analysis

### Spelling

#### Assessment: Final Test
**The /o/ Sound** LA.A.1.2.2.3.1

#### Teach
Repeat the Pretest or use the Standardized Test on page 33 of *Unit 1 Assessment* as summative assessment for student understanding of the /o/ sound spelling pattern.

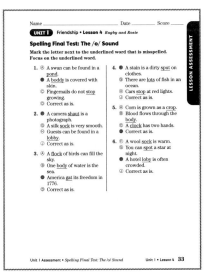

*Unit 1 Assessment p. 33*

#### Guided Practice
Have students categorize any mistakes they made on the Final Test. Are they careless errors? Are they lesson-pattern problems? See if students are spelling the /o/ sound correctly in their writing.

### Vocabulary LA.A.1.2.4.3.1

#### Informal Assessment

Ask the students to find an unfamiliar word in "Rugby & Rosie." Have the class look up the word in a dictionary and find the various definitions. Then have students discuss their own definitions for the word as it is found in the text (*possible words:* ignore, romped, commands). Check to see if students are having difficulty finding words in the dictionary. Have students add any new words to the word list in their Writer's Notebooks.

## Writing Process Strategies

### Revising LA.B.1.2.2.3.4, LA.B.1.2.2.3.6
**Introduction to the Writing Process**

#### Teach
- Review revising by adding copy, deleting copy, consolidating, rearranging, and peer conferencing with students, using your own work.
- Discuss *Language Arts Transparency 21*, Revising: Clarifying, with students.
- Remind students that their goal in writing should be to communicate with their audience. Help them to see how clarifying information helps the reader.

#### Independent Practice
**Revising**
Have students use the checklist and suggestions in the *Writer's Workbook,* page 4, to revise their autobiographies.

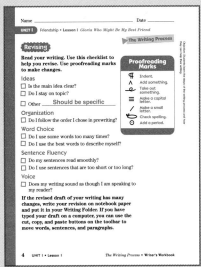

*Writer's Workbook p. 4*

## English Language Conventions

### Penmanship
**Cursive Letters *p* and *j***

#### Teach
- **Teacher Model:** Explain to students that cursive letters are made of four strokes (undercurve, downcurve, overcurve, and slant lines). Draw them on the board.
- **Teacher Model:** On the board, introduce lowercase cursive *p* and *j* as undercurve letters.

**p**
Starting point, undercurve
Slant, loop back
Overcurve
Curve back, undercurve: small *p*

**j**
Starting point, undercurve
Slant down
Loop back
Overcurve to endpoint
Dot exactly above: small *j*

- On the board, write the words *puppy, play, jump,* and *pajamas* to model proper letter formation and slant.

#### Guided Practice
- Invite students to come to the board to trace the letters *p* and *j*.
- Have students practice writing rows of *p* and *j* in their Writer's Notebooks.
- Have students write the words *tripped, jumped, ignore,* and *her* from "Rugby & Rosie" to practice letter formation.

#### Informal Assessment

Check students' handwriting to see if all their loops are closed below the baseline and for proper slant.

## LESSON WRAP-UP

# Reading and Language Arts Skills Traces

## Language Arts

### WORD ANALYSIS

**Skills Trace**

**Spelling: The /o/ Sound**
Introduced in Grade 1.
Scaffolded throughout Grades 2–5.
**REINTRODUCED:** Unit 1, Lesson 4, p. 81E
**PRACTICED:** Unit 1, Lesson 4, pp. 81F–81J
*Spelling and Vocabulary Skills,*
pp. 16–17
**TESTED:** Unit 1, Lesson 4, p. 81J
Unit 1 Assessment

**Skills Trace**

**Vocabulary: Dictionary Strategy**
Introduced in Grade 1.
Scaffolded throughout Grades 2–5.
**REINTRODUCED:** Unit 1, Lesson 4, p. 81E
**PRACTICED:** Unit 1, Lesson 4, pp. 81F–81J
*Spelling and Vocabulary Skills,*
pp. 14–15
**TESTED:** Unit 1 Assessment

## Reading

### COMPREHENSION

**Skills Trace**

**Cause and Effect**
Introduced in Grade 1.
Scaffolded throughout Grades 2 and 3.
**REINTRODUCED:** Unit 1, Lesson 2
**REINFORCED:** Unit 1, Lesson 4
Unit 2, Lesson 4
Unit 2, Lesson 5
Unit 4, Lesson 2
Unit 4, Lesson 7
Unit 6, Lesson 6
**TESTED:** Unit 1 Assessment

### WRITING PROCESS STRATEGIES

**Skills Trace**

**Introduction to the Writing Process: Revising**
Introduced in Grade K.
Scaffolded throughout Grades 1–6.
**REINTRODUCED:** Unit 1, Lesson 4, p. 81F
**PRACTICED:** Unit 1, Lesson 4, pp. 81G–81J
*Writer's Workbook,* p. 4
**TESTED:** Unit 1 Assessment

### ENGLISH LANGUAGE CONVENTIONS

**Skills Trace**

**Grammar: Verbs—Verb Phrase, Main Verb, and Helping Verb**
Introduced in Grade K.
Scaffolded throughout Grades 1–6.
**REINTRODUCED:** Unit 1, Lesson 4, p. 81F
**PRACTICED:** Unit 1, Lesson 4, p. 81G
Unit 1, Lesson 4, p. 81H
*Comprehension and Language Arts Skills,* pp. 14–15
**TESTED:** Unit 1, Lesson 4,
Informal Assessment, p. 81H
Unit 1 Assessment

**Skills Trace**

**Listening, Speaking, Viewing Viewing: Learning From Pictures**
Introduced in Grade 1.
Scaffolded throughout Grades 2–6.
**REINTRODUCED:** Unit 1, Lesson 4, p. 81I
**TESTED:** Unit 1, Lesson 4,
Informal Assessment, p. 81I

**Skills Trace**

**Penmanship: Cursive Letters *p* and *j***
Introduced in Grade 3.
Scaffolded throughout Grades 4–6.
**INTRODUCED:** Unit 1, Lesson 4, p. 81J
**TESTED:** Unit 1, Lesson 4,
Informal Assessment, p. 81J

# Professional Development: Writing

## Becoming Real Writers: What It's All About

The writing classroom is changing, and adjusting to this change is one of many challenges facing today's teachers. Instruction now encourages the expression of ideas and feelings, the development of fluency, the building of knowledge, the sharing of learning, and the development of confidence and self-esteem. ***Open Court Reading*** sees every child as a writer and an author. This program provides not only opportunities for independent writing in every lesson, but also for feedback in teacher and peer writing conferences and in Seminar, where authors interact with peers while reading and discussing each other's writing.

What has caused this change in writing instruction? Much of our insight comes from our growing understanding of what good writers do. They have ownership of their work and are actively involved in the process from start to finish. The same should be true for the young authors in our classrooms.

### What Do Successful Writers Do?

Writers spend time thinking about and planning their topics. They choose their own topics from a number of sources including their interests; what they care about, dream about, or have experienced; and what they have yet to learn. Writers consider their audience and develop and conduct research, if necessary, before they ever begin writing.

- Writers draft or put their ideas into words. They get their ideas down on paper, often in a rough form.
- Writers revise and revisit their work. They take another look to see if it makes sense and to see if it says what they want it to say. They check to be sure the meaning is clear for the reader.
- Writers edit their work. Good writers recognize the importance of writing conventions—grammar, mechanics, and spelling—that allow the reader to understand and enjoy published works.

- Writers go public with their works. They publish their work in books, newspapers, magazines, anthologies, and so on.

Writing is a recursive process as authors move back and forth through writing activities—from planning to drafting to revising and back—to create their final pieces. It is a process of thinking, experimenting, and evaluating.

All writers need feedback throughout the writing process. They need reactions to ideas, drafts, and revisions before it is too late to make changes. ***Open Court Reading's*** writing conferences and Seminar support young authors and provide opportunities for feedback about work in progress.

### How Can We Create Environments That Nurture Our Young Authors?

- Inspire even our youngest students to communicate, even if it is only through drawings and invented spellings.
- Set aside blocks of time each day for writing—time in which students can think about ideas, read about their topics, draft, reflect upon, and publish their pieces.
- Provide opportunities for students to experiment with different types of writing, to take risks, to learn from their mistakes, and to get reactions from others throughout the process.
- Provide constructive feedback to help students recognize and solve problems, to grow in their understanding, and to become independent writers.

*Additional information about writing as well as resource references can be found in the ***Professional Development Guide: Writing***.

**SELECTION INTRODUCTION**

Focus Questions Why must we sometimes show courage in order to keep a friend? Why is working together toward a common goal important to friendships?

## Teammates

Peter Golenbock
illustrated by Paul Bacon

EBBETS FIELD

Jackie Robinson

Pee Wee Reese

*Jackie Robinson was more than just my teammate. He had a tremendous amount of talent, ability, and dedication. Jackie set a standard for future generations of ball players. He was a winner. Jackie Robinson was also a man.*

—PEE WEE REESE
October 31, 1989

82

## Selection Summary

### Genre: Biography

"Teammates" shows the courage of three men: Jackie Robinson, who became the first African-American baseball player in the major leagues; Branch Rickey, who hired Robinson to play for the Brooklyn Dodgers, and Pee Wee Reese, who befriended Robinson and risked the rejection of his teammates and fans. This inspirational story sets an emotional scene as it relates how Jackie Robinson blazed the trail for African-American athletes in major league baseball.

Some elements of biography include:

- A biography is written about one person's life by someone else.
- A biography contains a variety of important information about the person's life. The story tells how the person talks, feels, and thinks about things.
- A biography may span a person's whole life or it may tell about an important part of a person's life. An account of a person's entire life is almost always told chronologically, or in the order in which the events happened in time.
- A biography often tells about the most important things that happened in a person's life.

# About the Author

**PETER GOLENBOCK,** a former sports columnist, has co-authored many stories about sports figures and has written several best-selling books for adults. *Teammates*, his first children's book, was awarded the Redbook Children's Picturebook Award and named a Notable Children's Trade Book for Social Studies. When Golenbock was 12, he met Jackie Robinson and remembers the ballplayer as a big man with "great presence."

Students can read more about Peter Golenbock on page 92 of the *Student Anthology.*

# About the Illustrator

**PAUL BACON** has illustrated many books. Additionally, he is well known for book jacket design, which is considered a specialized talent. He has received awards from the Society of Illustrators, the Art Directors Club, and the Type Directors Club.

Students can read more about Paul Bacon on page 92 of the *Student Anthology.*

# Inquiry Connections

This selection describes a courageous friendship between three men who stood up for what they believed in and faced the prejudices of the times. The key concepts to be explored are:

- True friends are interested in what a person is like on the inside, not on the outside.
- Friends stand up for each other.
- Courageous acts come in many different forms.
- Make your own decisions about who is your friend; don't let others make those decisions for you.

Before reading the selection:

- Point out that students may post a question, concept, word, illustration, or object at any time during the course of their unit investigation. Be sure that students include their names or initials on the items they post so that others will know whom to go to if they have an answer or if they wish to collaborate on a related activity.
- Students should feel free to write an answer or a note on someone else's question or to consult the Board for ideas for their own investigations throughout the unit.
- Encourage students to read about friendship at home and to bring in articles or pictures that are good examples to post on the Board.

**Concept/Question Board**

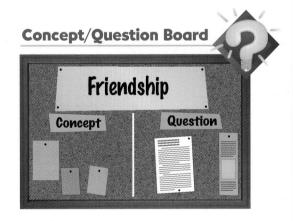

## Leveled Practice

**Reteach**
Pages 20–25

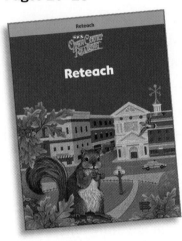

**Challenge**
Pages 18–22

**ELD Workbook**

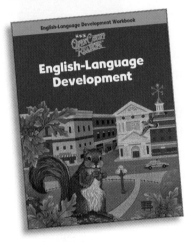

**Intervention Workbook**

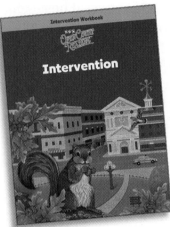

**Decodable Book 15**

## Leveled Classroom Library*

Encourage students to read at least 30 minutes daily outside of class. Have them read books in the **Leveled Classroom Library** to support the unit theme and help students develop their vocabulary by reading independently.

### Amigo

BY BYRD BAYLOR. ALADDIN, 1991.

A poor Mexican boy's only friend is a prairie dog, Amigo. While the boy believes he is taming Amigo as a pet, ironically, it is Amigo who is taming the boy. **(Easy)**

### And to Think That We Thought That We'd Never be Friends

BY MARY ANN HOBERMAN, CROWN PUBLISHERS, INC., 1999.

Inspired by Dr. Suess' *And to Think That I Saw It on Mulberry Street*, this is a story of how quickly disputes come to an end, and how friendship spreads like wildfire. A friendship started between siblings leads to everyone dancing and playing music in the streets. **(Average)**

### Best Friends

BY LORETTA KRUPINSKI. HYPERION, 1998.

Charlotte befriends a Native American girl, Lily, upon moving from her home in Kansas to the Wild West. They communicate through signs and laughter. The unlikely friends are tested when Charlotte learns of the soldiers' plans to drive Lily's tribe off their land. **(Advanced)**

* These books, which all support the unit theme Friendship, are part of a 36-book **Leveled Classroom Library** available for purchase from SRA/McGraw-Hill. Note: Teachers should preview any trade books for appropriateness in their classrooms before recommending them to students.

# TECHNOLOGY

## Web Connections

 www.sra4kids.com
**Friendship Web Site**

## CD-ROMs

 * **Research Assistant**
SRA/MCGRAW-HILL, 2002

 * **Decodable Book Activities**
SRA/MCGRAW-HILL, 2002

## Computer Skills

* **Basic Computer Skills**

## Audiocassettes/CDs

 * **Listening Library: Friendship**
SRA/MCGRAW-HILL, 2002

 * **Sound/Spelling Card Stories**
SRA/MCGRAW-HILL, 2002

Titles preceded by an asterisk (✱) are available through SRA/McGraw-Hill. Other titles can be obtained by contacting the publisher listed with the title.

**LESSON PLANNER**

| Suggested Pacing: 3–5 days | DAY 1 | DAY 2 |
|---|---|---|
| | **DAY 1** | **DAY 2** |

## 1 Preparing to Read

**Materials**
- Student Anthology, Book 1, pp. 82–93
- Decodable Book Activities CD-ROM
- Sound/Spelling Card 34
- Decodable Book 15
- Routine Cards 1, 3, Routines 1–2, 8–9

**DAY 1**

**Word Knowledge, p. 82K**
- suffix *-tion*
- prefixes and suffixes
- frequently misspelled words
- plural forms of nouns that end in -y
- /u/

**About the Words and Sentences, p. 82K**

**DAY 2**

**Developing Oral Language, p. 82L**

## 2 Reading & Responding

**Materials**
- Student Anthology, Book 1, pp. 82–93
- Program Assessment
- Reading Transparencies 7, 46, 51
- Inquiry Journal, p. 4
- Home Connection, p. 11
- Unit 1 Assessment, pp. 18–21
- Comprehension and Language Arts Skills, pp. 18–19
- Writer's Notebook
- Writing Folders
- Routine Cards 1–2, Routines 3–6

**DAY 1**

**Build Background, p. 82O**
**Preview and Prepare, pp. 82O–83P**
**Selection Vocabulary, p. 82P**
**Reading Recommendation, pp. 82Q–82R**

**DAY 2**

**Student Anthology, pp. 82–91** [First Read]
✓ **Comprehension Strategies**
- Monitoring and Clarifying, pp. 82, 86, 88
- Predicting, pp. 84, 86, 90
- Summarizing, p. 90

**Discussing Strategy Use, p. 90**
**Discussing the Selection, p. 91A**
- Review Selection
- Complete Discussion

## Inquiry

**Materials**
- Student Anthology, Book 1, pp. 82–93
- Inquiry Journal, pp. 22–23
- Research Assistant CD-ROM

**DAY 1**

**Investigation**
- Investigating Concepts Beyond the Text: Revising Conjectures, p. 93A

**DAY 2**

**Investigation**
- Concept/Question Board, p. 93B

## 3 Language Arts

**Materials**
- Student Anthology, Book 1, pp. 82–93
- Comprehension and Language Arts Skills, pp. 18–23
- Language Arts Handbook, pp. 19, 31, 38–39, 41, 255
- Language Arts Transparencies 27–31
- Sound/Spelling Card 21
- Spelling and Vocabulary Skills, pp. 18–21
- Student Anthology
- Writer's Workbook, p. 5

**DAY 1**

**Word Analysis**
✓ Spelling: The /u/ Sound Pretest, p. 93F

**Writing Process Strategies**
- Introduction to the Writing Process: Editing/Proofreading, p. 93F

**English Language Conventions**
- Grammar: Sentences, p. 93F

**DAY 2**

**Word Analysis**
- Spelling: Word Sorting, p. 93G
- Vocabulary: Thesaurus Strategy, p. 93G

**Writing Process Strategies**
- Introduction to the Writing Process: Editing/Proofreading, p. 93G

**English Language Conventions**
- Grammar: Sentences, p. 93G

Ⓟ **Phonics** ✓ **Informal Assessment Available** ✓ **Formal Assessment Available**

| DAY 2 continued | DAY 3 | |
|---|---|---|
| **DAY 3** | **DAY 4** | **DAY 5** |
| **Ⓟ Phonics and Fluency, p. 82M**<br>■ Review /ī/ spelled *i, _y, i_e, _ie, igh*<br>**About the Words and Sentences, p. 82M** | **Developing Oral Language, p. 82N**<br>**Dictation, p. 82N** | **Review Word Knowledge** |
| **Student Anthology, pp. 82–91** Second Read<br>**Comprehension Skills**<br>■ Main Idea and Supporting Details, pp. 83, 85, 87, 89, 91<br>**Checking Comprehension, p. 91**<br>**Supporting the Reading, pp. 91C–91D**<br>■ Main Idea and Supporting Details | **Student Anthology**<br>■ Meet the Author/Illustrator, p. 92<br>✓ ■ Theme Connections, p. 93<br>**Review Selection Vocabulary, p. 91B**<br>**View Fine Art, p. 91B**<br>**Literary Elements, p. 91E**<br>■ Characteristics of Nonfiction | ✓ **Selection Assessment**<br>■ "Teammates," pp. 18–21<br>**Home Connection, p. 91B**<br>**Social Studies Connection**<br>■ American Heroes, p. 91F |
| ✓**Investigation**<br>■ Revising Investigations, p. 93C | **Supporting the Investigation, p. 93D**<br>■ Parts of a Book | **Investigation**<br>■ Unit Investigation Continued<br>■ Update Concept/Question Board |
| **Word Analysis**<br>■ Spelling: The /u/ Sound, p. 93H<br>■ Vocabulary: Thesaurus Strategy, p. 93H<br>**Writing Process Strategies**<br>■ Introduction to the Writing Process: Editing/Proofreading, p. 93H<br>**English Language Conventions**<br>■ Grammar: Sentences, p. 93H | **Word Analysis**<br>■ Spelling: The /u/ Sound, p. 93I<br>■ Vocabulary: Thesaurus Strategy, p. 93I<br>**Writing Process Strategies**<br>■ Introduction to the Writing Process: Editing/Proofreading, p. 93I<br>**English Language Conventions**<br>✓ ■ Listening, Speaking, Viewing Interacting: Using Gestures, p. 93I | **Word Analysis**<br>✓ ■ Spelling: The /u/ Sound, p. 93J Final Test<br>✓ ■ Vocabulary: Thesaurus Strategy, p. 93J<br>**Writing Process Strategies**<br>■ Introduction to the Writing Process: Editing/Proofreading, p. 93J<br>**English Language Conventions**<br>✓ ■ Penmanship: Cursive Letters *a, c,* and *d*, p. 93J |

Below are suggestions for differentiating instruction to meet the individual needs of students. These are the same skills shown on the Lesson Planner; however, these pages provide extra practice opportunities or enriching activities to meet the varied needs of students. For Workshop Management Tips, see Appendix.

**WORKSHOP**

# Differentiating Instruction

## Small-Group Instruction

Use the informal assessment suggestions found throughout the lessons, along with the formal assessments provided in each lesson, to determine your students' strengths and areas of need. Use the following program components to help in supporting or expanding on the instruction found in this lesson:

***Reteach Workbook*** for use with students who show a basic understanding of the lesson but need a bit more practice to solidify their understanding.

***Intervention Guide*** and ***Intervention Workbook*** for use with students who, even after extra practice, exhibit a lack of understanding of the lesson concepts.

***English-Language Development Guide*** and ***English-Language Development Workbook*** for use with students who need language help.

## Reading Roundtable

A suggested activity would be to have students read other biographies. Have them compare similarities they find in biographies.

## Independent Activities

Students can work individually on such things as:

- Inquiry Journal pages
- Challenge
- Writing
- Investigation activities

| | READING | INVESTIGATION ACTIVITIES |
|---|---|---|
| **DAY 1** | ■ Select *Leveled Classroom Library* book for independent reading<br>■ *Listening Library Audiocassette/CD*<br>■ Add vocabulary in Writer's Notebook | ■ Concept/Question Board<br>■ Explore OCR Web site (www.sra4kids.com) for Friendship<br>◆ Revising Conjectures, p. 93A |
| **DAY 2** | ■ Independent reading<br>■ Oral reading of selection for fluency | ■ Concept/Question Board<br>■ Use *Research Assistant CD-ROM* to continue investigation |
| **DAY 3** | ■ Independent reading<br>◆ Partner reading of selection<br>■ Record response to selection in Writer's Notebook<br>■ Complete Link to Writing for Supporting the Reading, p. 91D | ■ Concept/Question Board<br>◆ Revising Investigations, p. 93C<br>■ Complete *Inquiry Journal*, pp. 22–23 |
| **DAY 4** | ■ Independent reading<br>◆ Discuss Theme Connections, p. 93<br>■ Add words to Word Bank<br>■ Complete Independent Practice for Literary Elements, p. 91E | ■ Concept/Question Board<br>◆ Complete Independent Practice for Supporting the Investigation, p. 93D |
| **DAY 5** | ■ Reading Roundtable<br>■ ◆ Social Studies Connection, p. 91F | ◆ Continue work on investigation<br>■ Supporting the Reading, complete *Inquiry Journal*, pp. 24–25 |

◆ **Small-Group Instruction**    ■ **Independent Activities**

| LANGUAGE ARTS | INTERVENTION* | ENGLISH-LANGUAGE LEARNERS** | RETEACH | CHALLENGE |
|---|---|---|---|---|
| **English Language Conventions**<br>■ Complete Types of Sentences, *Comprehension and Language Arts Skills,* pp. 20–21 | **(30 to 45 minutes per day)**<br>◆ Blending, p. 40<br>◆ Preteach "Teammates," pp. 42–43<br>◆ Teach "Intervention Selection One," pp. 43–44<br>◆ Grammar, Usage, and Mechanics, pp. 46–47 | **(30 to 45 minutes per day)**<br>◆ Word Knowledge, Suffix *-tion,* p. 22<br>◆ Word Knowledge, Prefixes and Suffixes, p. 22 | **English Language Conventions**<br>■ Complete Types of Sentences, *Reteach,* p. 24 | **English Language Conventions**<br>■ Complete Types of Sentences, *Challenge,* p. 21 |
| **Word Analysis**<br>■ Complete Thesaurus Strategy, *Spelling and Vocabulary Skills,* pp. 18–19<br>**Writing Process Strategies**<br>■ Complete Writer's Craft: *Comprehension and Language Arts Skills,* pp. 22–23 | ◆ Developing Oral Language, p. 40<br>◆ Preteach "Teammates," pp. 42–43<br>◆ Teach Comprehension Strategies, p. 44<br>◆ Reread "Intervention Selection One"<br>◆ Grammar, Usage, and Mechanics, pp. 46–47 | ◆ Activate Prior Knowledge, p. 24<br>◆ Selection Vocabulary, p. 25<br>◆ Preteach the Selection, p. 25 | ◆ Supporting the Reading: Main Idea and Supporting Details<br>**Word Analysis**<br>■ Complete Vocabulary: Thesaurus Strategy, *Reteach,* p. 23 | **Word Analysis**<br>■ Complete Vocabulary: Thesaurus Strategy, *Challenge,* p. 20<br>◆ Supporting the Reading: Main Idea and Supporting Details |
| **Word Analysis**<br>■ Complete Spelling: The /u/ Sound, *Spelling and Vocabulary Skills,* p. 20 | ◆ Dictation and Spelling, pp. 40–41<br>◆ Reread "Teammates"<br>◆ Teach "Intervention Selection Two," pp. 44–45<br>◆ Writing Activity, p. 47 | ◆ Word Knowledge, Plurals, p. 23<br>◆ Dictation and Spelling, p. 24 | ■ Complete *Reteach,* pp. 20–21<br>**Word Analysis**<br>■ Complete Spelling: The /u/ Sound, *Reteach,* p. 22 | **Word Analysis**<br>■ Complete Spelling: The /u/ Sound, *Challenge,* p. 19<br>■ Complete *Challenge,* p. 18 |
| **Word Analysis**<br>■ Complete The /u/ Sound, *Spelling and Vocabulary Skills,* p. 21 | ◆ Blending, p. 41<br>◆ Reread "Teammates"<br>◆ Teach Comprehension Strategies, p. 45<br>◆ Reread "Intervention Selection Two"<br>◆ Writing Activity, p. 47 | ◆ Vocabulary Strategies, p. 25 | **Writing Process Strategies**<br>■ Complete Writer's Craft: Staying on Topic, *Reteach,* p. 25 | **Writing Process Strategies**<br>■ Complete Writer's Craft: Staying on Topic, *Challenge,* p. 22 |
| **Writing Process Strategies**<br>◆ Seminar: Edit/Proofread an Autobiography, p. 93J<br>**English Language Conventions**<br>■ Penmanship: Practice Letters *a, c,* and *d,* p. 93J | ◆ Developing Oral Language, p. 41<br>◆ Dictation and Spelling, pp. 41–42<br>◆ Repeated Readings/ Fluency Check, p. 45 | ◆ Grammar, Usage, and Mechanics, p. 26 | | |

* Page numbers refer to *Intervention Guide.*
** Page numbers refer to *English-Language Development Guide.*

ASSESSMENT

# Formal Assessment Options

Use these summative assessments along with your informal observations to assess student progress.

---

## Unit 1 Assessment p. 18

Name _____ Date _____ Score _____

**UNIT 1** Survival • Lesson 5

### Teammates

Read the following questions carefully. Then completely fill in the bubble of each correct answer. You may look back at the story to find the answer to each of the questions.

1. What were the two baseball leagues in this story called?
   - Ⓐ the Major Leagues and the Minor Leagues
   - Ⓑ the National Leagues and the American Leagues
   - ● the Negro Leagues and the Major Leagues

2. What is this story mostly about?
   - Ⓐ which Major League team was the best
   - Ⓑ why Jackie Robinson was a good player
   - ● how black players entered the Major Leagues

Read the following questions carefully. Use complete sentences to answer the questions.

3. Why did Jackie Robinson promise not to fight back?
   Jackie knew that if he fought back, other black players would be kept out of the Major Leagues.

4. Why did Pee Wee Reese stand beside Jackie Robinson?
   Pee Wee Reese stood beside Jackie Robinson because Jackie was Pee Wee's teammate.

5. Why did the players in the Negro Leagues carry their own food?
   The players carried their own food because some restaurants would not serve them.

18 Unit 1 • Lesson 5 — Teammates • Unit 1 Assessment

---

## Unit 1 Assessment p. 19

**Teammates** *(continued)*

6. Who was Branch Rickey?
   Branch Rickey was the general manager of the Brooklyn Dodgers.

7. Why did Branch Rickey hire Jackie Robinson?
   Branch Rickey hired Jackie Robinson because Branch wanted the best players.

8. What is the hiring of Jackie Robinson known as?
   The hiring of Jackie Robinson is known as "the great experiment."

Read the following questions carefully. Then completely fill in the bubble of each correct answer.

9. Who was Pee Wee Reese?
   - ● the Dodger shortstop
   - Ⓑ the bus driver
   - Ⓒ the pitcher

10. Which word best describes Pee Wee Reese?
    - ● loyal
    - Ⓑ jealous
    - Ⓒ angry

Unit 1 Assessment • Teammates — Unit 1 • Lesson 5 19

---

## Unit 1 Assessment p. 20

**Teammates** *(continued)*

Read the question and statement below. Use complete sentences in your answers.

**Linking to the Concepts** How does Pee Wee Reese prove he is a true friend?
Answers will vary. Accept all reasonable answers.

**Personal Response** Tell about a time when you had to stick up for a friend.
Answers will vary. Accept all reasonable answers.

20 Unit 1 • Lesson 5 — Teammates • Unit 1 Assessment

---

## Unit 1 Assessment p. 21

**Teammates** *(continued)*

### Vocabulary

Read the following questions carefully. Then completely fill in the bubble of each correct answer.

1. The Negro Leagues **no longer exist**. This means that they
   - Ⓐ will not be remembered
   - Ⓑ did not really happen
   - ● are not around anymore

2. The Negro Leagues had extraordinary players, and adoring fans. **Extraordinary** means
   - ● amazing
   - Ⓑ unknown
   - Ⓒ awkward

3. Many people were apathetic about racial problems. If you are **apathetic** about something, you
   - Ⓐ have not heard about it
   - ● do not care about it
   - Ⓒ refuse to ignore it

4. Branch Rickey wanted a ball player that people could not intimidate. In this sentence, **intimidate** means to
   - Ⓐ praise
   - Ⓑ enjoy
   - ● annoy

5. Branch Rickey and Jackie Robinson started something that became known as "the great experiment." An **experiment** is something you
   - ● try out
   - Ⓑ give up on
   - Ⓒ look for

Unit 1 Assessment • Teammates — Unit 1 • Lesson 5 21

---

## Unit 1 Assessment p. 34

Name _____ Date _____ Score _____

**UNIT 1** Friendship • Lesson 5 *Teammates*

### Spelling Pretest: The /u/ Sound

Fold this page back on the dotted line. Take the Pretest. Then correct any word you misspelled by crossing out the word and rewriting it next to the incorrect spelling.

| | |
|---|---|
| 1. _____ | 1. *dusk* |
| 2. _____ | 2. *blush* |
| 3. _____ | 3. *crust* |
| 4. _____ | 4. *thump* |
| 5. _____ | 5. *shut* |
| 6. _____ | 6. *dump* |
| 7. _____ | 7. *scrub* |
| 8. _____ | 8. *pump* |
| 9. _____ | 9. *buff* |
| 10. _____ | 10. *buzz* |
| 11. _____ | 11. *but* |
| 12. _____ | 12. *just* |
| 13. _____ | 13. *bus* |
| 14. _____ | 14. *upon* |
| 15. _____ | 15. *much* |

34 Unit 1 • Lesson 5 — Spelling Pretest: The /u/ Sound • Unit 1 Assessment

---

## Unit 1 Assessment p. 35

Name _____ Date _____ Score _____

**UNIT 1** Friendship • Lesson 5 *Teammates*

### Spelling Final Test: The /u/ Sound

Mark the letter next to the underlined word that is misspelled. Focus on the underlined word.

1. Ⓐ <u>Much</u> of Earth is water.
   Ⓑ Computers rely <u>upon</u> electricity.
   ● A <u>buss</u> can carry many people.
   Ⓓ Correct as is.

2. Ⓕ You <u>pump</u> water from a well.
   ● The sun sets at <u>dusc</u>.
   Ⓗ Eyes <u>shut</u> when blinking.
   Ⓙ Correct as is.

3. Ⓐ Women put <u>blush</u> on their faces.
   Ⓑ A school <u>bus</u> is usually yellow.
   Ⓒ We <u>buff</u> the car after we wax it.
   ● Correct as is.

4. Ⓕ Doctors <u>scrub</u> their hands clean.
   ● Earth's <u>krust</u> has layers.
   Ⓗ Do not <u>dump</u> trash on highways.
   Ⓙ Correct as is.

5. Ⓐ Bees <u>buz</u> around flowers.
   Ⓑ Spiders have <u>just</u> eight legs.
   Ⓒ A gasoline <u>pump</u> provides fuel.
   ● Correct as is.

6. ● There is <u>jest</u> one planet Mars.
   Ⓑ Dentists know <u>much</u> about teeth.
   Ⓗ The sky at <u>dusk</u> can look pink.
   Ⓙ Correct as is.

Unit 1 Assessment • Spelling Final Test: The /u/ Sound — Unit 1 • Lesson 5 35

---

Florida

# Informal Comprehension Strategies Rubrics

## Predicting

- The student makes predictions about the text.
- The student updates predictions during reading, based on information in the text.

## Summarizing

- The student paraphrases the text, reporting main ideas and a summary of what is in the text.
- The student decides which parts of the text are important in his or her summary.
- The student draws conclusions from the text.
- The student makes global interpretations of the text, such as recognizing the genre.

## Monitoring and Clarifying

- The student notes characteristics of the text, such as whether it is difficult to read or whether some sections are more challenging or more important than others.
- The student shows awareness of whether he or she understands the text and takes appropriate action, such as rereading, in order to understand the text better.
- The student rereads to reconsider something presented earlier in the text.
- The student recognizes problems during reading, such as a loss of concentration, unfamiliar vocabulary, or lack of sufficient background knowledge to comprehend the text.

# Research Rubrics

Use the Research Rubrics to assess a student's performance throughout the stages of the investigation for each unit. The rubrics for a given lesson will match the investigation stage for that lesson. In addition, at the end of the unit you can use the rubrics to assess the groups' collaborative work as well as an individual's participation in that group.

During Workshop, assess students using the rubrics below. The rubrics range from 1–4 in most categories, with 1 being the lowest score. Record each student's score on the inside back cover of the ***Inquiry Journal***.

## Finding Needed Information

**1** Collects information loosely related to topic.

**2** Collects information clearly related to topic.

**3** Collects information helpful in advancing on a research problem.

**4** Collects problem-relevant information from varied sources and notices inconsistencies and missing pieces.

**5** Collects useful information, paying attention to the reliability of sources and reviewing information critically.

## Objectives

- Students practice recognizing word roots and suffixes, including *-tion, un-,* and *-ly.*
- Students practice recognizing frequently misspelled words.
- Students practice spelling words with the /u/ sound.
- Students develop fluency reading words and sentences.

## Materials

- Student Anthology, Book 1, pp. 82–93
- Decodable Book Activities CD-ROM
- Decodable Book 15
- Routine Cards 1, 3, Routines 1–2, 8–9
- Sound/Spelling Card 34

**Teacher Tip SYLLABICATION** To help students blend words and build fluency, use the syllabication below of the words in the word lines.

| | | |
|---|---|---|
| ded•i•cate | ded•i•ca•tion | |
| seg•re•gate | seg•re•ga•tion | |
| in•tim•i•date | in•tim•i•da•tion | |
| hu•mil•i•ate | hu•mil•i•a•tion | |
| fair | un•fair | un•fair•ly |
| e•qual•ly | un•e•qual | un•e•qual•ly |
| e•qual | league | op•po•nent |
| ra•cial | dif•fi•cul•ties | vic•tor•ies |
| wor•ries | much | u•pon |
| bus | just | but |

**Routine Card**

Refer to *Routine 1* for the whole-word blending procedure and *Routine 2* for the sentence blending procedure.

**Teacher Tip** You may need to define some of the words from the board for students, because some of these words may be difficult or unfamiliar.

Refer to the *Lesson Model Videocassette* for instruction on whole-word blending.

**WORD KNOWLEDGE**

# Word Knowledge

## Reading the Words and Sentences

Use direct teaching to teach this blending lesson.

■ Write each word in Reading the Words and Sentences on the board and have students read them together. If they have difficulty reading a word, stop and have them blend the word using whole-word blending. Encourage students to pronounce the word naturally after blending. Because reading sentences helps students to move from word fluency to sentence fluency, have them read each sentence in unison, using normal intonation. The words in **boldface** type are from the selection.

| | | | | | |
|---|---|---|---|---|---|
| Line 1: | dedicate | **dedication** | segregate | **segregation** | |
| Line 2: | **intimidate** | intimidation | humiliate | **humiliation** | |
| Line 3: | fair | **unfair** | unfairly | | |
| Line 4: | **equally** | unequal | unequally | equal | |
| Line 5: | **league** | opponent | **racial** | | |
| Line 6: | **difficulties** | victories | worries | | |
| Line 7: | **much** | upon | bus | just | but |

**Sentence 1:** He thought segregation was unfair and wanted to give everyone, regardless of race or creed, an opportunity to compete equally on ballfields across America.

**Sentence 2:** Despite all the difficulties, Jackie Robinson didn't give up.

**Sentence 3:** Many Americans knew that racial prejudice was wrong, but few dared to challenge openly the way things were.

**Sentence 4:** A bus fare does not cost much for just a short ride.

## About the Words and Sentences

■ **Lines 1 and 2:** Have the students look at the words *dedicate, segregate, intimidate,* and *humiliate.* Ask them how the spelling changed when the suffix *-tion* was added *(dropped the* e*).* Remind the students that the suffix *-tion* means "act or process."

■ **Lines 3 and 4:** Have students identify the base word, the prefix, and the suffix in each word. Have students give a definition of the base word and tell how the meaning changed when the prefix and/or suffix was added.

■ **Line 5:** These words are frequently misspelled. Review correct spellings with students. Discuss why they think many people misspell the words. Have students identify the elements in each word.

■ **Line 6:** This line contains the plural forms of nouns that end in *y.* Have the students identify the base word in each word. Write the base word on the board and have students explain what spelling change takes place when you add an ending to a word ending with *y (change* y *to* i *and add the ending).*

■ **Line 7:** The words in Line 7 are found in "Teammates" and review the /u/ sound spelled *u.*

- **Sentences 1–3:** These sentences are from the story students are about to read. Have the students identify and circle the words with a prefix *(unfair)* and suffixes *(segregation, equally, openly)*. Have them point to the word that is frequently misspelled *(racial)*.
- **Sentence 4:** Have students identify the words in the last sentence that contain the /u/ sound spelled *u (bus, much, just)*.

## Developing Oral Language  LA.C.1.2.1.3.2

Use direct teaching to review the words. Use one or both of the following activities to help students practice reading the words.

- Have one student choose a line of words from the board and point to a word in that line. Then have the student choose a classmate to read the word and give a brief definition.
- Choose one of the lines for students to focus on. Have a volunteer choose a word and use it in a sentence to begin a story. Have another volunteer continue the story by supplying a sentence that uses another word from the line. Continue until all the words are used.

**Teacher Tip FLUENCY** Have students browse the selection for words with affixes and inflectional endings.

**Spelling** See pages 93E–93J for the corresponding lesson for the /u/ sound.

**Teacher Tip FLUENCY** Gaining a better understanding of the spellings of sounds and structure of words will help students as they encounter unfamiliar words in their reading. By this time in Grade 3 students should be reading approximately 107 words per minute with fluency and expression. As students read, you may notice that some need work in building fluency. During Workshop, have these students select a section of the text (a minimum of 160 words) to read several times in order to build fluency.

### MEETING INDIVIDUAL NEEDS

**ELL Support**

For ELD strategies, use the *English-Language Development Guide,* Unit 1, Lesson 5.

**Intervention Support**

For intervention strategies, use the *Intervention Guide,* Unit 1, Lesson 5.

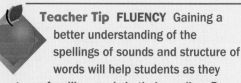

**Teacher Tip SYLLABICATION** To help students blend words and build fluency, use the syllabication below of the words in the word lines.

| | | | | |
|---|---|---|---|---|
| ti•ny | pi•lot | gi•ant | spi•der | sky |
| dry | de•ny | ap•ply | time | in•side |
| de•spite | si•lence | Chi•na | pie | lie |
| high | fight | might | night | fright |

# Phonics and Fluency

Review /ī/ spelled *i, _y, i_e, _ie, igh*

## Blending

■ Follow the established procedure to have students read the following words and sentences. **Boldface** words are found in the selection.

■ Display *Sound/Spelling Card 34.*

| | | | | | |
|---|---|---|---|---|---|
| Line 1: | tiny | pilot | giant | spider | sky |
| Line 2: | dry | deny | apply | time | inside |
| Line 3: | despite | silence | China | pie | lie |
| Line 4: | high | fight | might | night | fright |
| Sentence 1: | When the moon is full, the sky is bright at night. | | | | |
| Sentence 2: | Kyra likes to ride her bike. | | | | |
| Sentence 3: | **His worst pain was inside.** | | | | |

## About the Words and Sentences

■ **Line 1:** The words practice the /ī/ sound spelled *i* and *_y.*

■ **Line 2:** The words practice the /ī/ sound spelled *_y* and *i_e.* Point out the /ə/ sound in *apply.* Be sure the students understand that the /ə/ sound is an alternate sound for a vowel. Have the students say the word *apply* and clap the syllables. Ask the students to listen as you clap *(clap lightly on the first syllable and loudly on the second syllable)*. Tell the students that the unstressed syllable has the /ə/ sound.

■ **Line 3:** The words practice the /ī/ sound spelled *i_e* and *_ie.* Point out the /ī/ sound in *China.* Ask students to clap the syllables, clapping lightly on the unstressed syllables.

■ **Line 4:** The words practice the /ī/ sound spelled *igh.*

■ **Sentences 1–2:** These sentences contain words with long i spellings. Have students identify the words *(sky, bright, night, Kyra, likes, ride, bike).* Have students identify the spellings of the /ī/ sound.

■ **Sentence 3:** This sentence is from the selection. Have students identify the words with the /ī/ sound *(inside).*

## Developing Oral Language LA.C.1.2.2.3.1

To review the words, do one or both of the following activities. Use these activities to help students practice words aloud.

- Have individual students touch a word on the board, say it, underline it, and then use it in a sentence. Have other students extend the sentences by asking such questions as *Who? What? When? Where? Why?* or *How?*

- Give clues for each of the words in the word lines and have individual students say each word and then circle it. Possible clues: This person flies a plane *(pilot)*; an insect *(spider)*; the opposite of day *(night)*.

## Dictation

Erase the blending lines and sentences on the board and have students take out writing paper. Dictate the following words and sentences for students to write.

|                   |          |          |       |
|-------------------|----------|----------|-------|
| **Line 1:**       | title    | July     | drive |
| **Line 2:**       | tie      | bright   | lion  |
| **Challenge Word:** | diagram |          |       |
| **Sentence:**     | Tyler rode his bike nine miles. | | |

## Building Fluency

*Decodable Books* are used to help develop fluency for students who need extra practice. The only way to gain fluency is to read. Students will have many opportunities to read, including the *Student Anthology,* the *Leveled Classroom Library,* and their own reading. The *Decodable Books* can be used to practice the phonics and fluency elements being reviewed. Refer to the Appendix for the procedure on using these books. For this lesson, use *Decodable Book 15, The Prince's Foolish Wish.*

The Prince's Foolish Wish

by Laura Edwards
illustrated by Linda Kelen

*Decodable Book 15*

**P H O N I C S**

**Teacher Tip** BLENDING Remind students who are intimidated by large words to start by blending the syllables. Remind students that each syllable in a word contains only one vowel sound. They should identify vowel sounds first, blend each syllable, then blend the syllables together.

**Routine Card**
Refer to *Routine 8* for whole-word dictation and *Routine 9* for sentence dictation.

Use the *Decodable Book Activities CD-ROM* for activities that support this Phonics lesson.

Refer to the *Lesson Model Videocassette* for instruction on whole-word blending.

Refer to the *Lesson Model Videocassette* for instruction on reading a *Decodable Book.*

## Objectives

- Students will understand the selection vocabulary before reading, using strategies such as suffixes and structural cues.
- Students will spell words with the affixes *-tion, un-,* and *-ly,* and change *y* to *-ies.*
- Students will connect prior knowledge to subjects discussed in the text.
- Students will use comprehension strategies such as Clarifying, Predicting, and Summarizing to construct meaning from the text and monitor reading.
- Students will use the comprehension skill Main Idea and Details as they read the story the second time.
- Students will discuss personal reactions to the story to begin identifying their own personal reading preferences.

## Materials

- Student Anthology, Book 1, pp. 82–93
- Program Assessment
- Reading Transparencies 7, 46, 51
- Inquiry Journal, p. 4
- Unit 1 Assessment, pp. 18–21
- Routine Cards 1–2, Routines 3–6
- Home Connection, p. 11
- Comprehension and Language Arts Skills, pp. 18–19
- Writing Folder

---

**Teacher Tip** GENRE: BIOGRAPHY
Have students record the elements of biography in the Literary Elements and Genre section of their Writer's Notebooks.

---

**Teacher Tip** Highlight the differences between a biography and an autobiography.

---

| Clues | Problems | Wonderings |
|---|---|---|
| real people true story | segregation | What was it like to be the first African-American major league baseball player? |

*Reading Transparency 46*

# Build Background

## Activate Prior Knowledge

Many students will probably be eager to comment on the subject of baseball teams, baseball cards, and special players. Encourage students to share what they know with the class. Remind them to keep what they already know about baseball in mind as they read so that they can connect it to what they are reading.

- Before reading, remind students to check the Concept/Question Board to refresh their memories about what they learned about friendship from the previous selections in the unit, and to see if there are any questions that this story might answer.
- Ask students to tell you what they know about baseball. Ask them if they know who Jackie Robinson is. *(first African-American to play major league baseball)*
- Ask students to discuss whether courage is sometimes necessary in friendship. If so, when?

## Background Information  LA.E.1.2.4.3.1

The following information may help students to better understand the selection they are about to read.

- Remind students that a biography is the true story about someone's life. A biography can be about the person's entire life or a part of it and is written by someone else. An autobiography is when a person writes their own story about their life.
- Tell students that "Teammates" is a biography. This true story tells about the courage of Jackie Robinson and others connected to the Brooklyn Dodgers when he became the first African-American baseball player on a major league team.
- This selection deals with the issues of segregation and prejudice. Some of your students may not be aware of what segregation is and how it affected people.

# Preview and Prepare  LA.A.1.2.1.3.1

## Browse

- Because this is a biography, you may wish to have students preview the selection by browsing the entire story. Encourage students to discuss what they noticed during browsing. Some may be familiar with the story of Jackie Robinson. Others may comment on the illustration of baseball cards or on the unusual names of some characters.
- Use *Reading Transparency 46* to write the observations that students generate during browsing. These might include unfamiliar words or clues as to what is going to happen in the selection. Students will return to these observations after reading. To save time and to model note taking, write students' observations as brief notes rather than as complete sentences.

■ As students prepare to read the selection, have them browse the Focus Questions on the first page of the selection. Tell them to keep these questions in mind as the selection is read.

## Set Purposes  LA.A.1.2.2.3.5

Encourage students to set their own multiple purposes for reading. If necessary, prompt students to think about who experiences friendship in this selection, how they experience it, and why they experience it. Also have students think about what is special about the teammates in the selection. You may also have students think about how the theme of the selection piques their curiosity or connects to their personal interests. In addition, they might compare the way that friendship is presented in this selection with the other stories in this unit.

## Selection Vocabulary  LA.A.1.2.3.3.1

As students study vocabulary, they will use a variety of skills to determine the meaning of a word. These include context clues, word structure, and apposition. Students will apply these same skills while reading to clarify additional unfamiliar words.

Display **Reading Transparency 7** before reading the selection to introduce and discuss the following words and their meanings.

| | |
|---|---|
| **exist:** | to be around (page 83) |
| **extraordinary:** | remarkable; very special (page 83) |
| **apathetic:** | not interested; does not care (page 85) |
| **intimidate:** | to make someone feel bad by hurting their feelings (page 86) |
| **experiment:** | a test used to discover something (page 86) |
| **humiliations:** | things that cause someone to be embarrassed (page 87) |

Have students read the words in the word box, stopping to blend any words that they have trouble reading. Demonstrate how to decode multisyllabic words by breaking the words into syllables and blending the syllables. Then have students try. If they still have trouble, refer them to the **Sound/Spelling Cards.** If the word is not decodable, give the students the pronunciation.

Have students read the sentences on the transparency to determine the meaning of the underlined words. Each word has two sentences that students will read, from which they should be able to derive the meaning of the underlined word. Remind them to use one or more of the skills they have learned—context clues, word structure, or apposition—to figure out the meaning before using a dictionary. Be sure students explain which skills they are using and how they figured out the meanings of the words. Have students reread the sentence, substituting the definition to see if the sentence makes sense. Have a volunteer create a new sentence using the underlined word.

**Teacher Tip** SELECTION VOCABULARY To help students decode words, divide them into syllables when you are saying them, as shown below. The information following each word tells how students can figure out the meaning of each word. When writing words on the board, do not divide them into syllables.

| | |
|---|---|
| ex • ist | context clues |
| ex • traor • di • nar • y | context clues |
| ap • a • the • tic | context clues |
| in • tim • i • date | context clue |
| ex • per • i • ment | context clues |
| hu • mil • i • a • tions | context clues |

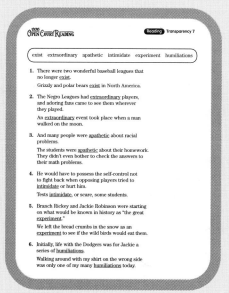

**Reading Transparency 7**

## MEETING INDIVIDUAL NEEDS

### ELL Support

For ELD strategies, use the **English-Language Development Guide,** Unit 1, Lesson 5.

### Intervention Support

For intervention strategies, use the **Intervention Guide,** Unit 1, Lesson 5.

**Routine Card**
Refer to **Routine 3** for the vocabulary procedure.

During Workshop, and after the selection has been read at least once, have students listen to the recording of this lesson's selection on the *Listening Library Audiocassette/CD.* After students have listened, have them discuss their personal preferences of the selections read. Ask them what other things they have listened to and like to listen to on the radio, on audiocassettes, or on CDs.

 **Teacher Tip DECODING** Students should use decoding skills to figure out unfamiliar words. Often, students will know the meaning of the word once they have read it.

 **Teacher Tip** Have students think about how Pee Wee's and Jackie's adult friendship differs from childhood friendships.

 **Routine Card**
Refer to *Routine 5* for the procedure on reading the selection.

# Reading Recommendations

## Oral Reading

Oral reading is recommended, since many terms and concepts in "Teammates" may be unfamiliar to some students.

Your first reading of the selection focuses on developing the comprehension strategies found to the left of the reduced student pages. The second reading should focus on developing the comprehension skills found to the right of the reduced pages. Rereading should be done on another day.

Have students make use of the comprehension strategies listed below to help them understand the selection. Have them stop reading periodically or wait until they have completed the selection to discuss the reading strategies. After the students have finished reading the selection, use the Discussing the Selection questions on page 91A to see if they understand what they have read.

## Using Comprehension Strategies

Comprehension strategy instruction allows students to become aware of how good readers read. Good readers constantly check their understanding as they are reading and ask themselves questions. In addition, skilled readers recognize when they are having problems and stop to use various comprehension strategies to help them make sense of what they are reading.

During the reading of "Teammates" model the following reading strategies:

- **Predicting** causes readers to analyze information given about story events and characters in the context of how it may logically connect to the story's conclusion.

- **Summarizing** prompts readers to keep track of what they are reading and to focus their minds on important information.

- **Monitoring and Clarifying (Introduction):** Monitoring and Clarifying takes different forms, including clarifying the meaning of words and clarifying difficult ideas or passages. In order to clarify meanings, students can use context, use structural analysis, use apposition, reread the text, use charts or graphic organizers, or use resources outside of the text.

As students read, they should be using a variety of strategies to help them understand the selection. Encourage students to use the strategies listed above as the class reads the story aloud. Do this by stopping at the points indicated by the numbers in the magenta circles on the reduced student page and using a particular strategy. Students can also stop reading periodically to discuss what they have learned and what problems they may be having.

## Building Comprehension Skills

Revisiting or rereading a selection allows students to apply skills that give them a more complete understanding of the text. Some follow-up comprehension skills help students organize information. Others lead to deeper understanding—to "reading between the lines," as mature readers do.

An extended lesson on the comprehension skill Main Idea and Details can be found in the Supporting the Reading section page 91C. This lesson is intended to give students extra practice with Main Idea and Details. However, it may be used at this time to introduce the comprehension skill to students.

- **Main Idea and Details (Introduction):** Readers identify relevant information in a text, including main ideas and the relationships among ideas.

### Reading with a Purpose

Have students look for ways any of the story characters learn about friendship throughout the selection.

## Research in Action

Remember to discuss with students difficulties that occurred during reading. While problems that arise during reading should be addressed as they occur, it is important to reflect on the problems and how they were solved. After reading, have students identify the difficulties. Probe with questions that foster metacognition, or thinking about thinking, such as: *What did you find difficult here? How did you try to figure it out? Did that work? What else might work?* (Michael Pressley)

**Teacher Tip COMPREHENSION STRATEGIES** Students' own think alouds are always preferred to the teacher's. Encourage students to model for one another when they work out problems or as they come up with ideas when they read.

**Teacher Tip COMPREHENSION STRATEGIES** Remind students as they read the story on the second day to summarize what they learned from the first day.

## COMPREHENSION

Read pages 82–91.

## Comprehension Strategies

First Read

Read the story aloud, taking turns with the students. Model the use of strategies for the students.

### Teacher Modeling

**1** **Monitoring and Clarifying** *I'm confused. Maybe stopping to think about what is confusing me will help. This story starts with the words "Once upon a time." Those words are usually a clue that the story is make-believe. However, this story contains photographs of people. I think these are real people whom I could look up in an encyclopedia. There must be a reason the author chooses to begin this way. Maybe it's because it's about the past. If I continue reading, I'll probably find out.*

### Teacher Modeling

**2** **Monitoring and Clarifying** *I'm not sure what segregation means. I'll read a little further to see if I can figure it out. Oh, I see—I think it means "keeping people separated." Does that make sense to you?*

---

### Word Knowledge

**SCAFFOLDING** The skills students are reviewing in Word Knowledge should help them in reading the story. This lesson focuses on the affixes *-tion, un-,* and *-ly,* and changing *-y* to *-ies.*

**dedication**

---

**Teacher Tip  CLARIFICATION**
Encourage students to clarify unfamiliar words or concepts as they read. If students don't ask for clarification and you think there are things that they may not understand, prompt them to ask for clarification.

---

### First Reading Recommendation

## ORAL · CHORAL

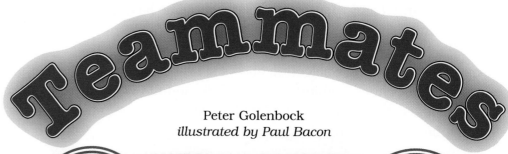

*Focus Questions*  Why must we sometimes show courage in order to keep a friend? Why is working together toward a common goal important to friendships?

# Teammates

Peter Golenbock
illustrated by Paul Bacon

Jackie Robinson                Pee Wee Reese

*Jackie Robinson was more than just my teammate.
He had a tremendous amount of talent, ability, and dedication.
Jackie set a standard for future generations of ball players.
He was a winner. Jackie Robinson was also a man.*

—PEE WEE REESE
*October 31, 1989*

82

---

**Teacher Tip  PHONICS** Check to see that students are using all the sound/spellings they've learned to decode words, and not just the sound/spellings introduced in this lesson.

**Informal Assessment**

Observe individual students as they read, and use the Teacher Observation Log, found in the ***Program Assessment Teacher's Edition,*** to record anecdotal information about each student's strengths and weaknesses.

Once upon a time in America, when automobiles were black and looked like tanks and laundry was white and hung on clotheslines to dry, there were two wonderful baseball leagues that no longer exist. They were called the Negro Leagues. ❶

The Negro Leagues had extraordinary players, and adoring fans came to see them wherever they played. They were heroes, but players in the Negro Leagues didn't make much money and their lives on the road were hard.

Laws against segregation didn't exist in the 1940s. In many places in this country, black people were not allowed to go to the same schools and churches as white people. They couldn't sit in the front of a bus or trolley car. They couldn't drink from the same drinking fountains that white people drank from. ❷

Satchel Paige

83

## Comprehension Skills

 Second Read

COMPREHENSION

### Main Idea and Supporting Details LA.A.2.2.1.3.1

Explain to students that they will better understand a paragraph if they locate the main, or most important, idea in it. The rest of the paragraph provides details that support, or tell more about, the main idea.

- Direct students to the first sentence in the third paragraph on page 83. Point out that this is the main idea of the paragraph. The other sentences give more details.

- **Main Idea:** There were no laws against segregation in the 1940s.

- **Details:** African-Americans could not go to church or school with white people. They could not sit in the front of buses or trolleys. They could not drink from drinking fountains used by whites.

Discuss that finding main ideas will help them remember the most important information in a selection.

> ### Word Knowledge
> *-tion* endings: segregation

### ◆ Skills Trace ◆
**Main Idea and Supporting Details**
Introduced in Grade 1.
Scaffolded throughout Grades 2 and 3.
**REINTRODUCED:** Unit 1, Lesson 5
**REINFORCED:** Unit 4, Lesson 3
Unit 5, Lesson 6
Unit 6, Lesson 6
**TESTED:** Unit 1 Assessment

### Second Reading Recommendation

ORAL • **SILENT**

**COMPREHENSION**

## Comprehension Strategies

### Teacher Modeling

**③ Predicting** *Predicting what will happen next in a story helps readers to think seriously about what they are reading. Predictions are not wild guesses; rather, predictions should be based on information in the story. After reading that Branch Rickey wanted the best players on his team regardless of their skin color, I predict that his team will soon have players other than white players, but that would not have been easy because of the way things were in America at the time. As I continue reading, I'll check to see if my prediction is confirmed. As we continue reading, see if you can predict what is going to happen next. Maybe some of you will share your predictions with us.*

---

### Word Knowledge

compound word:    baseball

---

**Teacher Tip** Tell students that good readers keep thinking about the questions that come up about the topic, and they keep coming back to those questions. As they read, tell them to keep the questions on the Concept/Question Board in mind. Have them make notes to themselves in the Response Journal section of their Writer's Notebooks about which questions seem most important. Tell them that good readers always think about what is important in selections, and they try to remember this important information.

Back then, many hotels didn't rent rooms to black people, so the Negro League players slept in their cars. Many towns had no restaurants that would serve them, so they often had to eat meals that they could buy and carry with them.

Life was very different for the players in the Major Leagues. They were the leagues for white players. Compared to the Negro League players, white players were very well paid. They stayed in good hotels and ate in fine restaurants. Their pictures were put on baseball cards and the best players became famous all over the world.

84

Branch Rickey

Many Americans knew that racial prejudice was wrong, but few dared to challenge openly the way things were. And many people were apathetic about racial problems. Some feared that it could be dangerous to object. Vigilante groups, like the Ku Klux Klan, reacted violently against those who tried to change the way blacks were treated.

The general manager of the Brooklyn Dodgers baseball team was a man by the name of Branch Rickey. He was not afraid of change. He wanted to treat the Dodger fans to the best players he could find, regardless of the color of their skin. He thought segregation was unfair and wanted to give everyone, regardless of race or creed, an opportunity to compete equally on ballfields ❸ across America.

85

## MEETING INDIVIDUAL NEEDS

### Intervention

**MAIN IDEA** If students are confused about main ideas, write a paragraph that contains no clearly stated main idea, and have the students tell what they think the paragraph is about. Then write that idea in the paragraph.

## Comprehension Skills

### Main Idea and Supporting Details LA.A.2.2.1.3.1

The main idea of a paragraph is often found in the first sentence, called the topic sentence.

- **Main Idea:** White baseball players' lives were different from those of African-American baseball players. (page 84, paragraph 2)
- **Details:** White players were well paid. They stayed in good hotels and ate at fine restaurants. They had their pictures on baseball cards. They were world famous.

---

**Word Knowledge**

*-ly* endings:  openly
  violently
  equally

---

**Teacher Tip ENCOURAGING IDEAS** Encourage students to think aloud. Tell students that their ideas about the selection are very important to the whole class's understanding of the main idea of the selection.

COMPREHENSION

## Comprehension Strategies

### Teacher Modeling

**4 Confirming Predictions** *Part of the process of predicting what will happen in a story is to check as you continue to read to see if your prediction was correct. I see that my prediction was confirmed. Rickey's all-white baseball team has changed, and an African-American player, Jackie Robinson, has joined the team. I still don't know how he will be treated. I guess I need to keep reading. Have your predictions been confirmed? Sometimes new information in the story prompts me to change my predictions. Who wants to modify their predictions or to make new predictions?*

### Teacher Modeling

**5 Monitoring and Clarifying**

*I'm confused. What is the meaning of "the great experiment"? This isn't usually what I think of when I think of an experiment. But I guess it is sort of like an experiment, because when you experiment, you try something new to see what will happen. Branch Rickey is trying something new to see how baseball fans will respond. There are a lot of unfamiliar words in this story. Who sees a word, phrase, or idea from the story that they would like to have clarified?*

---

**Word Knowledge**

*-ly* endings:    **successfully**

---

**Teacher Tip  USING STRATEGY** As students read the story aloud, stop and ask questions about the reading strategies they might be using. Encourage students to use their own language to describe what they are thinking.

---

To do this, the Dodgers needed one special man. Branch Rickey <u>launched</u> a search for him. He was looking for a star player in the Negro Leagues who would be able to compete successfully <u>despite</u> threats on his life or attempts to injure him. He would have to <u>possess</u> the self-control not to fight back when opposing players tried to <u>intimidate</u> or hurt him. If this man <u>disgraced</u> himself on the field, Rickey knew, his opponents would use it as an excuse to keep blacks out of Major League baseball for many more years.

Rickey thought Jackie Robinson might be just the man.

Jackie rode the train to Brooklyn to meet Mr. Rickey. When Mr. Rickey told him, "I want a man with the courage not to fight back," Jackie Robinson replied, "If you take this <u>gamble</u>, I will do my best to **4** perform." They shook hands. Branch Rickey and Jackie Robinson were starting on what would be known in history as "the great <u>experiment</u>." **5**

Branch Rickey and Jackie Robinson.

86

At spring training with the Dodgers, Jackie was mobbed by blacks, young and old, as if he were a savior. He was the first black player to try out for a Major League team. If he succeeded, they knew, others would follow.

Initially, life with the Dodgers was for Jackie a series of humiliations. The players on his team who came from the South, men who had been taught to avoid black people since childhood, moved to another table whenever he sat down next to them. Many opposing players were cruel to him, calling him nasty names from their dugouts. A few tried to hurt him with their spiked shoes. Pitchers aimed at his head. And he received threats on his life, both from individuals and from organizations like the Ku Klux Klan.

87

## Comprehension Skills

Second Read

### Main Idea and Supporting Details LA.A.2.2.1.3.1

Explain to students that asking "What is this paragraph mostly about?" can help them find the main idea. A detail sentence would not answer the question. Encourage them to ask themselves this question as they continue to read.

- **Main Idea** (page 87): Jackie had problems when he started to play with the Dodgers.

- **Details:** Some players on his team didn't want to sit by him. Players on opposing teams called him names and tried to hurt him with the spikes on their shoes. Pitchers threw balls at his head. People and organizations threatened his life.

> ### Word Knowledge
> *-tion* endings:  humiliations
>  organizations

COMPREHENSION

## Comprehension Strategies

First Read

### Teacher Modeling

**6 Monitoring and Clarifying**

*I don't understand what the phrase "on the road" means. I'll think about it and try to make sense of what I've read. The story says that Jackie Robinson had to live by himself "on the road." I'll read the whole sentence to see if I can clarify what "on the road" means. It probably doesn't mean that Jackie Robinson built a house in the middle of the road. The rest of the sentence tells about the players staying in hotels in towns where they played ball. I guess "on the road" means "while traveling." This story is expository text that is written to inform the reader, and it is full of information. Stopping to clarify often helps me to understand the story better.*

---

### Word Knowledge

*y → ies:* **difficulties**

---

**Teacher Tip** Assure students that remembering other things as they read, wondering about what they read, and experiencing emotions as they read are natural responses to reading.

---

**Teacher Tip** Remind students to use context clues, apposition, or word structure to figure out the meaning of difficult words as they are reading.

---

Team photo of the 1947 Brooklyn Dodgers.

Despite all the difficulties, Jackie Robinson didn't give up. He made the Brooklyn Dodgers team.

But making the Dodgers was only the beginning. Jackie had to face abuse and hostility throughout the season, from April through September. His worst pain was inside. Often he felt very alone. On the road he had to

**6** live by himself, because only the white players were allowed in the hotels in towns where the team played.

The whole time Pee Wee Reese, the Dodger shortstop, was growing up in Louisville, Kentucky, he had rarely even seen a black person, unless it was in the back of a bus. Most of his friends and relatives hated the idea of his playing on the same field as a black man. In addition, Pee Wee Reese had more to lose than the other players when Jackie joined the team.

Jackie Robinson.

88

---

## MEETING INDIVIDUAL NEEDS

### Intervention

Provide help as needed in stating questions, suggesting words such as *Who? What? When? Where? How?* and *Why?* By asking open-ended questions and by asking important questions, students are encouraged to explore the possibilities for learning in the text and to connect the meaning of the text to the world and their own lives.

Jackie had been a shortstop, and everyone thought that Jackie would take Pee Wee's job. Lesser men might have felt anger toward Jackie, but Pee Wee was different. He told himself, "If he's good enough to take my job, he deserves it."

When his Southern teammates <u>circulated</u> a <u>petition</u> to throw Jackie off the team and asked him to sign it, Pee Wee <u>responded</u>, "I don't care if this man is black, blue or striped"—and refused to sign. "He can play and he can help us win," he told the others. "That's what counts."

Very early in the season, the Dodgers traveled west to Ohio to play the Cincinnati Reds. Cincinnati is near Pee Wee's hometown of Louisville.

89

## Comprehension Skills

### Main Idea and Supporting Details LA.A.2.2.1.3.1

Tell students that main ideas are not always stated in the first sentence of a paragraph. Sometimes they are implied, and sometimes they appear after the first sentence.

- **Main Idea** (page 89, paragraph 1): Pee Wee was different from some other people.
- **Details:** He did not feel anger thinking that Jackie could take his position. Pee Wee thought if Jackie was good enough to do that, he deserved the position.

> ### Word Knowledge
> **compound words:**     **shortstop**
>                         **teammates**

**Teacher Tip COMPREHENSION**
Good readers are active readers. They interact with the text as they read by emoting, reacting, responding, and problem solving in their efforts to construct and maintain meaning.

COMPREHENSION

COMPREHENSION

## Comprehension Strategies

### Teacher Modeling

**7** **Predicting** *When I read "Pee Wee decided to take a stand," I predicted that the baseball player was going to do something to help Jackie. What I already knew about Pee Wee and his feelings helped me make this prediction. When I read this page, I found out that my prediction was correct. Pee Wee stood next to Jackie and put his arm around his teammate.*

### Teacher Modeling

**8** **Summarizing** *I've learned a lot of new information from this story. This seems like a good place to summarize what I've learned. First, Branch Rickey wanted the best players, no matter what color their skin was. Then he hired Jackie Robinson, the first African-American ball player to play on a white team. Who would like to help me finish summarizing the story?*

### Discussing Strategy Use LA.A.1.2.4.3.1

After students have read the selection, encourage them to share any problems they encountered and to tell what strategies they used to solve them.

- How did they clarify confusing passages?
- Where did they pause in the reading to summarize?
- On what basis did they make and confirm predictions?

These are questions good readers ask after they read a text. After reading, they should always be asking, "What did I find interesting? What is important here?" Later, remind the students again that whenever they conclude a reading, they should ask themselves questions about what was in the text.

The Reds played in a small ballpark where the fans sat close to the field. The players could almost feel the breath of the fans on the backs of their necks. Many who came that day screamed terrible, hateful things at Jackie when the Dodgers were on the field.

More than anything else, Pee Wee Reese believed in doing what was right. When he heard the fans yelling at Jackie, Pee Wee decided to take a stand. **7**

With his head high, Pee Wee walked directly from his shortstop position to where Jackie was playing first base. The <u>taunts</u> and shouting of the fans were ringing in Pee Wee's ears. It saddened him, because he knew it could have been his friends and neighbors. Pee Wee's legs felt heavy, but he knew what he had to do.

As he walked toward Jackie wearing the gray Dodger uniform, he looked into his teammate's bold, pained eyes. The first baseman had done nothing to <u>provoke</u> the hostility except that he <u>sought</u> to be treated as an equal. Jackie was <u>grim</u> with anger. Pee Wee smiled broadly as he reached Jackie. Jackie smiled back.

90

 **Informal Assessment**
Use the Informal Comprehension Strategies Rubrics on page 82J to determine whether a student is using the strategies being taught.

 **Teacher Tip** BUILDING FLUENCY
As students read, you may notice that some need work in building fluency. During Workshop, have these students select a section of the text (a minimum of 160 words) to read several times in order to build fluency.

Stopping beside Jackie, Pee Wee put his arm around Jackie's shoulders. An <u>audible</u> gasp rose up from the crowd when they saw what Pee Wee had done. Then there was silence.

Outlined on a sea of green grass stood these two great athletes, one black, one white, both wearing the same team uniform.

**(8)** "I am standing by him," Pee Wee Reese said to the world. "This man is my teammate."

91

**COMPREHENSION**

## Comprehension Skills

Second Read

### Main Idea and Supporting Details LA.A.2.2.1.3.1; LA.E.1.2.4.3.1

Remind students that main ideas are not always directly stated. Students must look at all the details in a paragraph and decide which main idea the details support. Most of the time, however, the main idea is stated near the beginning of a paragraph. Have students state the main idea and details of the last paragraph on page 90. *(Main Idea: Pee Wee wanted to show his support for Jackie. Details: Jackie was grim with anger. Jackie and Pee Wee smiled at each other as Pee Wee approached.)*

### Checking Comprehension LA.E.2.2.5.3.1

Ask students the following questions to check their comprehension of the story.

- How did Branch Rickey, Jackie Robinson, and Pee Wee Reese show their courage in this story? *(Branch Rickey hired a black player. Jackie Robinson didn't fight back. Pee Wee Reese stood up for his teammate.)*

- What was the result of "the great experiment"? *(African-American baseball players got to play on formerly all-white teams.)*

- What is the main idea of the story? *(Segregation is unfair in baseball and everywhere else.)*

**Teacher Tip** FLUENCY By this time in third grade, good readers should be reading approximately 107 words per minute with fluency and expression. The only way to gain this fluency is through practice. Have students reread the selection to you and to each other during Workshop to help build fluency.

## MEETING INDIVIDUAL NEEDS

 **Formal Assessment**

See pages 18–21 in *Unit 1 Assessment* to test students' comprehension of "Teammates."

### ELL

**NATIONAL PRIDE** Ask English-language learners if they come from a country where baseball is popular, and to name any major league players who also came from there.

**Teacher Tip RESPONDING** Help students to see that they are responsible for carrying the discussion. After a question is asked, always wait for students to respond. Students will come to understand that discussion is their responsibility.

**Routine Card**
Refer to *Routine 6* for the *handing-off process.*

| Clues | Problems | Wonderings |
|---|---|---|
| real people true story | segregation | What was it like to be the first African-American major league baseball player? |

**Reading Transparency 46**

**www.sra4kids.com**
**Web Connection**
Some students may choose to conduct a computer search for additional books or information about friendship. Invite them to make a list of these books and sources of information to share with classmates and the school librarian. Check the Reading link of the SRA Web page for additional links to the theme-related Web site.

## Discussing the Selection LA.C.1.2.3.3.1; LA.E.1.2.1.3.2

After the first read, the whole group discusses the selection and any personal thoughts, reactions, problems, or questions that it raises. To stimulate discussion, students can ask one another the kinds of questions that good readers ask themselves about a text: *What did I find interesting? What is important here? What was difficult to understand? Why would someone want to read this? How does this selection connect to the theme of Friendship?*

**Handing-Off Process** Seeing you as a contributing member of the group sets a strong example for students. To emphasize that you are part of the group, actively participate in the *handing-off process:* Raise your hand to be called on by the last speaker when you have a contribution to make. Point out unusual and interesting insights verbalized by students so that these insights are recognized and discussed. As the year progresses, students will take more and more responsibility for the discussions of the selections.

Engage students in a discussion to determine whether they have grasped the following ideas:

- how the people in the text showed courage
- how their actions changed American history
- what is the importance of being teammates
- how segregation affected this country and the relationships between people

During this time, have students return to the clues, problems, and wonderings they noted during browsing to determine whether the clues were borne out by the selection, whether and how their problems were solved, and whether their wonderings were answered or deserve further discussion and investigation. Let the students decide which items deserve further discussion.

Also, have students return to the Focus Questions on the first page of the selection. Select a student to read the questions aloud, and have volunteers answer the questions. If students do not know the answers to the questions, have them return to the text to find the answers.

You may wish to review the elements of a biography with the students at this time. Discuss with them how they can tell "Teammates" is a biography.

Have students break into small groups to discuss what this story tells them about how important sharing is in friendship. Groups can discuss their ideas with the rest of the class.

If students have ever experienced a time when friendship required courage or some type of difficult choice, encourage them to record this event.

## eview Selection Vocabulary LA.A.1.2.2.3.2

ave students review the definitions of the selection vocabulary words that they ote in the Vocabulary section of their Writer's Notebooks. Remind them that ey discussed the meanings of these words before reading the selection. Have udents write sentences for each of the vocabulary words after the definitions in e same section of their Writer's Notebooks. They can use the definitions and e sentences to study for the vocabulary portion of their Lesson Assessments. ave them add any other interesting words that they clarified while reading to e personal dictionary section of their Writer's Notebooks. Encourage students refer to the selection vocabulary words throughout the unit. The words from e selection are:

**Teacher Tip** Encourage students to write a sentence using these words. In order to provide additional help in remembering words, students can write a synonym or an antonym for the word if it is appropriate. Some students may even draw something that helps them to remember the meaning of the word.

| | | |
|---|---|---|
| **exist** | **extraordinary** | **apathetic** |
| **intimidate** | **experiment** | **humiliations** |

you created a Word Bank of key words related to the theme Friendship, remind udents to find words from other resources, from their activities, and from mily discussions and add them to the Word Bank. Organize the words according parts of speech.

## iew Fine Art LA.C.2.2.2.3.1

ave students reflect on the painting *onjunction* on page 62 of the *tudent Anthology* and share their oughts and reactions with the class. xplain that the print by Romare earden portrays his subjects at odd gles; the right figure is shown with et and head in profile, while the body frontally displayed. Much of the tist's work is about the African-merican experience; however, he was so inspired by the works of Homer, ligion, and music, particularly jazz. e artist grew up in Harlem, New ork, during the early 1900s, during an a called the Harlem Renaissance.

*Conjunction.* 1971. **Romare Bearden.** Piquette. ©Romare Bearden Foundation/Licensed by VAGA, New York, NY.

62

***Student Anthology p. 62***

## ome Connection

istribute ***Home Connection,*** page 11. Encourage students to discuss eammates" with their families. A Spanish version of this letter appears on ge 12.

---

*Teammates*

**A message from**

Our class has just finished a selection called "Teammates," about the friendship between the baseball players Jackie Robinson and Pee Wee Reese. It tells about the courage of Jackie Robinson, the first African American to play Major League baseball. It also tells about Pee Wee Reese, who had the courage to stand up for his teammate.

You can increase your child's understanding of the difficult issues raised in this article by discussing it with him or her. Ask your child to tell you about the events described in the article. Then ask what he or she thinks prejudice is and how a person decides what is right and what is wrong. Encourage your child to write his or her thoughts and feelings about these issues on this page, and bring it to school to share with the class.

_____
_____
_____
_____
_____
_____
_____

**Next week's selection** *The Legend of Damon and Pythias*

Your child will be studying the following vocabulary words in the upcoming week. Please review the meanings of these words with your child: **tyrant**—a harsh, unjust ruler; **rebel**—to resist a ruler's power; **appointed**—to name officially; **traitor**—someone who betrays another's trust; **honorable**—deserving of honor or respect.

Please review with your child the spelling words for the upcoming week: brand, candy, plan, hobby, best, read, us, top, jump, send, tell, prison, last, robbers, struggle.

***Home Connection p. 11***

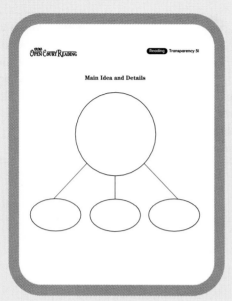

**Reading Transparency 51**

Teacher Tip Tell students that this skill will help them with the Summarizing strategy. Once students have discerned the Main Idea and Details, they can easily move through a quick summary.

## Supporting the Reading

### Comprehension Skills: Main Idea and Details  LA.A.2.2.1.3.1

**Teach** Tell students that identifying the main idea and supporting details of paragraphs helps readers understand the important points in a text.

Sometimes main ideas are implied. In these cases, students should use their prior knowledge of a topic to help them decide what is more and less important in a text.

**Guided Practice** Use an idea map to help students identify the main ideas and details from "Teammates." In the main circle have students list a main idea from the story. *(Pee Wee stood up for his teammate in front of a stadium of people.)* In the surrounding circles, have students list supporting information. *(Jackie, Pee Wee, and Branch created baseball history. Jackie was the first major league African-American player. Pee Wee was a true friend to Jackie.)* Use **Reading Transparency 51** to record their suggestions. Have students refer to the selection when responding.

**Independent Practice** Read through the Focus and Identify sections of *Comprehension and Language Arts Skills,* page 18, with students. Guide them through the Identify portion, and help them come up with examples found in the story. Then have students complete the Practice and Apply portions of *Comprehension and Language Arts Skills,* pages 18–19.

**Link to Writing** Have students write out main-idea statements first. Next have them add supporting information to create a paragraph. Then have them copy the details without the main-idea statement, and trade papers with a classmate. Students should try to identify the main ideas of the paragraphs and create the missing main-idea statements.

### MEETING INDIVIDUAL NEEDS

**Reteach**

**MAIN IDEA AND SUPPORTING DETAILS** Have students who need additional practice with Main Idea and Supporting Details complete *Reteach,* pages 20–21.

**Challenge**

**MAIN IDEA AND SUPPORTING DETAILS** Have advanced students who understand Main Idea and Supporting Details complete *Challenge,* page 8.

**Skills Trace**
Main Idea and Supporting Details
Introduced in Grade 1.
Scaffolded throughout Grades 2 and 3.
**REINTRODUCED:** Unit 1, Lesson 5
**REINFORCED:** Unit 4, Lesson 3
Unit 5, Lesson 6
Unit 6, Lesson 6
**TESTED:** Unit 1 Assessment

---

Name _____ Date _____

**UNIT I** Friendship • **Lesson 5** *Teammates*

## Main Idea and Details

**Focus** The **main idea** is what the story or paragraph is mostly about. **Details** or **reasons** help tell more about the main idea.

▸ Often the main idea will be in the first or last sentence in a paragraph.
▸ Details or reasons provide readers with information that helps them understand the story and support the main idea.

**Identify**

Look through "Teammates" for main-idea sentences that are followed by details. Write two examples and then list the details that tell more about the main idea. Answers will vary. Possible answers given.

Page: __84__

Main idea: Life was different for players in the Major Leagues.

Details about the main idea: Players in the Major Leagues were paid better, stayed in nice hotels, and ate well. They were on baseball cards.

Page: _____

Main idea: _____

Details about the main idea: _____

18 UNIT I • Lesson 5       Comprehension and Language Arts Skills

---

Name _____ Date _____

**UNIT I** Friendship • **Lesson 5** *Teammates*

◥ Main Idea and Details

**Practice**

Read each list of details. Then write a main idea to fit each list.

to cool off        to build sand castles
to swim            to have fun in the sun

1. The main idea: why we go to the beach

get presents       blow out the candles
play games         sing a special song

2. The main idea: what we do at a birthday party

**Apply**

Write one main-idea sentence and two detail sentences about a topic. Answers will vary.

Main idea sentence: _____

_____

Detail sentence: _____

Detail sentence: _____

Comprehension and Language Arts Skills       UNIT I • Lesson 5   19

COMPREHENSION

*Comprehension and Language Arts Skills pp. 18–19*

**Teacher Tip** Extend the lesson on nonfiction to encompass media pieces. Ask the students to identify television shows, movies, or newspaper articles that could be classified as nonfiction. Ask them how they know when a movie is about a real event or person and when it is a fictional story.

## Literary Elements

### Characteristics of Nonfiction  LA.E.1.2.1.3.2

**Teach**  Ask students to explain what *nonfiction* means. If necessary, give them the following information:

Nonfiction is about real things and people (as opposed to *fiction*, which can be realistic but is made up). Some different types of nonfiction include expository texts, which give information about a subject; biographies, written by authors about the lifetime of someone other than himself or herself; autobiographies, stories of the lifetime of the person writing the book; news articles; reference books; and persuasive or opinion texts.

**Guided Practice**  Write the word *nonfiction* on the board. Read aloud a page or two from "Teammates," and ask students to listen for clues that let them know this is a nonfiction text. *(Factual historical events described, dates and places given, information is verifiable through other sources.)*

**Independent Practice**  Ask students to look in the **Writing Folder** for a nonfiction piece they have written. Have them identify the characteristics that make it nonfiction. Ask them to identify what type of nonfiction the piece is.

Have students write a short nonfiction piece about a current event, a favorite hobby, or a past experience with friendship.

# Social Studies Connection SS.A.1.2.2.3.1

## American Heroes

Explain to students that primary sources are original, first-hand sources. Examples include a direct interview with an eyewitness, a diary or journal, or lab reports from an experiment. Secondary sources gather information from primary sources and other secondary sources. Although they can be reliable, they are not first-hand accounts of information. Ask small groups of students to gather information using secondary and, if possible, primary sources, about an American hero who fought for civil rights. It may be necessary to explain to the students that people have not always been treated as equals. Explain that discrimination occurs not only across races, but sexes, religions, and other sociological classes. Ask the students who Dr. Martin Luther King, Jr. was. Explain that Dr. King is an excellent example of a civil rights hero. Brainstorm other ideas to give the class examples of heroes they can research. Students can create a visual and share their information with the class. They may wish to create a skit based on their information.

**Teacher Tip MATERIALS**
✔ library resources
✔ poster boards
✔ colored pencils or markers

**Teacher Tip PURPOSE** To help students understand more about using primary and secondary sources and to take a deeper look at American heroes of civil rights.

## Meet the Author

After students read about Peter Golenbock, have them answer the following questions.

- Why do you think Peter Golenbock decided to write a children's book when he had already written several well-known books for adults? *(Possible answer: He wanted to share his knowledge about sports with children because he remembered how much sports meant to him as a child.)*

- Why do you think Peter Golenbock picked Jackie Robinson and Pee Wee Reese to be the subjects of his first children's book? *(Possible answer: This story is not just about baseball history. It's about people standing up for what they believe in, even if what they believe in is not popular.)*

## Meet the Illustrator

After students read about Paul Bacon, have them answer the following questions.

- Look back at the pictures in "Teammates." Paul Bacon tells a story with his drawings. What do you notice about the people's faces? *(Possible answer: They show lots of emotion. You can see humor, hate, and understanding—all without even reading the story.)*

- Paul Bacon is famous for designing book jackets. Why do you think he chose the first picture for the cover of his story? *(Possible answer: It shows the connection between the two friends united by a common sport.)*

## Meet the Author

**Peter Golenbock** is a sportswriter who especially loves baseball. He remembers going to the World Series in 1956 with his uncle and afterward meeting Jackie Robinson. He says, *"I was 12 years old, and I'll never forget being struck by how large he was."* Throughout his career Peter Golenbock has had the opportunity to meet many famous players and to hear the stories they tell about the game's history. He has even written biographies about some of the players he has talked to. He is the author of many well-known books about sports, but this book was the first one he wrote for children.

## Meet the Illustrator

**Paul Bacon** is an award-winning illustrator and famous designer of book jackets. He lives in Clintondale, New York, with his wife.

92

# Theme Connections

## Within the Selection

 Record your answers to the questions below in the Response Journal section of your Writer's Notebook. In small groups, report the ideas you wrote. Discuss your ideas with the rest of the group. Then choose a person to report your group's answers to the class.

- Jackie Robinson, the first African American player in the Major Leagues, was not always treated kindly. How did Pee Wee Reese show Jackie his friendship?
- Why was Pee Wee's friendship so important?

## Across Selections

- What other stories have you read that show friendships like Jackie's and Pee Wee's?
- How is this story like "Gloria Who Might Be My Best Friend"?

## Beyond the Selection

- Think about how "Teammates" adds to what you know about friendship.
- Add items to the Concept/Question Board about friendship.

93

 **Informal Assessment**

This may be a good time to observe students working in small groups and to mark your observations in the Teacher Observation Log found in the *Program Assessment Teacher's Edition.*

## Theme Connections LA.E.2.2.4.3.2

### Within the Selection

- Pee Wee Reese stood up for Jackie Robinson when he was being taunted, and called Jackie his teammate.
- Many people did not want Jackie to play for the Dodgers. Having a friend on the team meant that he was not alone.

### Across Selections

- Students cite previous unit selections.
- Gloria and Julian were not expected to be friends because they were different.

### Beyond the Selection

Have groups report their ideas to the class. Have students add these ideas to the Concept/Question Board. Students should tell how they might use what they have learned in their investigations.

### Inquiry Journal

Students should record their ideas and impressions about the selections on page 4 of their *Inquiry Journals.*

Recording Concept Information *(continued)*

- "Teammates" by Peter Golenbock
Answers will vary.

- "The Legend of Damon and Pythias" adapted by Fan Kissen
Answers will vary.

4 UNIT I  *Recording Concept Information • Inquiry Journal*

*Inquiry Journal p. 4*

### Objectives

- Students gain a deeper understanding of friendship.
- Students make informal presentations to the group.
- Students revise investigation plans as necessary.

### Materials

- Student Anthology, Book 1, pp. 82–93
- Inquiry Journal, pp. 22–23
- Research Assistant CD-ROM

**Teacher Tip** Remind students of the importance of sticking to their project schedules while being flexible to change. Encourage the students' changes of interest while keeping them on task.

# Investigating Concepts Beyond the Text: Revising Conjectures LA.C.1.2.3.3.1, LA.C.3.2.2.3.1, LA.C.3.2.5.3.1

Students up to this point have raised questions, formed groups based on areas of interest, formed conjectures, drawn up plans for their investigation of friendship, have begun gathering information, and have begun to reevaluate questions. Students can now meet to discuss their progress and revise their plans as necessary.

Throughout the remaining time, meet with each group to arrange schedules and update calendars, discuss problems that students are encountering in their investigations, hear preliminary presentations and discussions of interesting findings, and arrange more formal presentations of students' investigations. As students progress, meet informally with them during Workshop. During these individual conferences, you might ask questions such as the following: *What did you look up? What are you finding out? What else might you need to find out? Can you give me more details about that fact or idea? How does this information help you? What does this information tell you that you didn't already know? How might you present this information?*

After reading this selection, groups may wish to engage in the following activities. "Teammates" illustrated the special bond that existed between Jackie and Pee Wee through their participation together on a team. Students probably have some ideas about team spirit and the qualities they consider important in a teammate. Ask them to think about what a coach or a group leader might look for in members of a team. The students might like to invite a school or community coach to speak to the class. Have them plan two or three questions to ask the coach about managing a group of friends and teammates. After the students have conducted their interview, allow time for them to discuss ideas, adding any important new information to the Concept/Question Board.

# Concept/Question Board

After reading each selection, students should use the Concept/Question Board to do the following:

- Post any questions they asked about a selection before reading that haven't been answered yet.
- Refer to as they formulate statements about concepts that apply to their investigations.
- Post general statements formulated by each collaborative group.
- Continue to post news articles or other items that they find during the unit investigation.
- Read and think about posted questions, articles, or concepts that interest them and provide answers to the questions.

**INVESTIGATION**

### Research Assistant

The *Research Assistant CD-ROM* can assist students with their investigations.

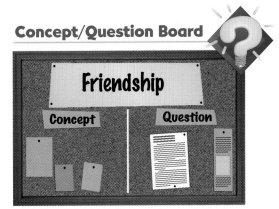

**Concept/Question Board**

Friendship

Concept     Question

## Unit I  Investigation Management

| | |
|---|---|
| **Lesson 1** | Introduce the investigation cycle and explain its purpose. Students can hold a panel discussion to discuss friendship-related issues. |
| **Lesson 2** | Students can investigate immigration and forming new friendships or other areas of investigation related to friendship. Students should organize into groups based on shared areas of interest. |
| **Lesson 3** | Students investigate mending damaged friendships, and groups begin forming conjectures. |
| **Lesson 4** | Students begin their investigations. They can also share personal stories, hold a panel discussion, or invite an expert speaker to class. |
| **Lesson 5** | **Collaborative Investigation**<br>**Students revise investigation plans as necessary.**<br><br>**Supplementary Activities**<br>**Groups discuss teammate qualities and invite a coach to class to interview.** |
| **Lesson 6** | Students prepare formal presentations. Groups discuss standing up for a friend and might write a scene or miniplay about it. |

Encourage students to use *Basic Computer Skills* to learn more about how to use a computer to write a report.

### Formal Assessment

Use the Research Rubrics on page 82J to assess students' ability to find needed information.

**INVESTIGATION**

# Revising Investigations

Explain that throughout this unit on Friendship, the goal of investigation is to come to a deeper understanding of some aspect of the theme. Students might wish to re-examine personal experiences of their own or talk to others as they investigate this topic.

As student groups meet to share information, have them refer to pages 22–23 of their *Inquiry Journals.* Students will bring in the results of their investigations, re-evaluate the group plan, and revise it as necessary. Tell them to continue to refer to their investigation questions and conjectures as they progress. Students should be in the final stages of preparation for their presentations.

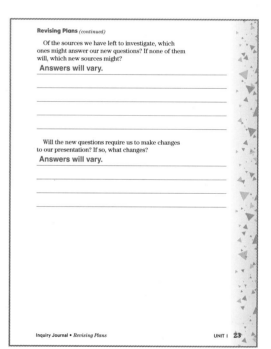

*Inquiry Journal pp. 22–23*

# Parts of a Book LA.A.1.2.1.3.1

**Teach** Tell students that books have parts other than the main part in which the author tells a story or gives information. Ask students to tell what other parts they know. Record their responses on the board. If necessary, add the following items to the list and define:

**Title page**—gives the title of the book, the name of the author or editor, and the name of the publisher.

**Copyright page**—comes after the title page. It gives the publisher's name and the place and year in which the book was published.

**Table of contents**—a list, in order of appearance, of the units, chapters, or stories in the book, with the page number on which each begins.

**Glossary**—an alphabetical list of new words that are used in the book, along with their definitions.

**Bibliography**—an alphabetical list of books in which the author of the book found information.

**Index**—an alphabetical list of names, places, and topics covered in the book, with the numbers of the pages on which they are mentioned.

**Guided Practice** Write the various book parts on small index cards so each student has one. Distribute the cards.

Read aloud the following questions. Tell students that if they have the answer to the question written on their card, they are to hold up the card.

- Where would I find the definition for a word in the book? *(glossary)*
- Where would I find what page Chapter 2 starts on? *(table of contents)*
- Where would I find who published the book? *(title page and copyright page)*
- Where would I look to find which page or pages give information about a specific topic? *(index)*

Have students exchange cards and continue the activity, giving specific examples from the book you are using.

**Independent Practice** Encourage students to select a nonfiction book or a textbook. Let them skim through the book to find or identify its various parts. Invite students to tell about and discuss any differences they find among the books.

For more practice on this topic, have students complete ***Inquiry Journal,*** pages 24–25.

## SUPPORTING THE INVESTIGATION

## MEETING INDIVIDUAL NEEDS

### Intervention

**PARTS OF A BOOK** Work with small groups of students who are having difficulty using the parts of a book. Spend time with just one part, such as the index, asking students to locate page numbers about different topics.

### Challenge

**PARTS OF A BOOK** Invite small groups of advanced students to create posters to demonstrate how to use the parts of a book.

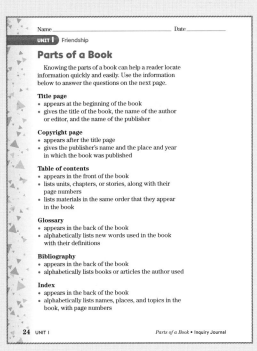

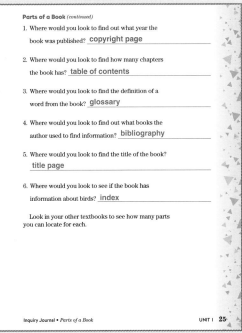

*Inquiry Journal pp. 24–25*

## Objectives

**Word Analysis**

**Spelling**
- **The /u/ Sound.** Develop an understanding of the /u/ sound spelled *u*.

**Vocabulary**
- **Thesaurus Strategy.** Using words from "Teammates," learn to apply the thesaurus to discover the meaning or meanings of an unfamiliar word through words with similar meanings, known as *synonyms*.

**Writing Process Strategies**
- **Editing/Proofreading.** Proofreading and editing for conventions will be presented in this lesson.

**English Language Conventions**

**Grammar, Usage, and Mechanics**
- **Sentences.** Understand the four different types of sentences, the correct punctuation for each kind of sentence, and capitalization of the first letter of the first word of a sentence. Identify types of sentences in "Teammates."

**Listening, Speaking, Viewing**
- **Interacting: Using Gestures.** Discuss the function and usage of gestures.

**Penmanship**
- **Cursive Letters *a, c,* and *d*.** Develop handwriting skills by practicing formation of cursive *a, c,* and *d*.

### Materials

- Language Arts Handbook
- Comprehension and Language Arts Skills, pp. 18–23
- Language Arts Transparencies 27–31
- Writer's Workbook, p. 5
- Student Anthology
- Spelling and Vocabulary Skills, pp. 18–21
- Sound/Spelling Card 21

## MEETING INDIVIDUAL NEEDS

*Reteach, Challenge, English-Language Development,* and *Intervention* lessons are available to support the language arts instruction in this lesson.

## Research in Action

Editing is one of the harder parts of writing. Writers generally have trouble spotting surface errors in their own work…. Asking students to edit one another's papers in class is an effective way to help them improve the quality of their papers…. *(James D. Williams,* Preparing to Teach Writing: Research, Theory, and Practice)

# Language Arts Overview

## Word Analysis

**Spelling** The Spelling activities on the following pages introduce the /u/ sound spelled *u* by developing spelling skills through various strategies.

### Selection Spelling Words

These words from "Teammates" contain the /u/ sound.

b**u**t    j**u**st    b**u**s    **u**pon    m**u**ch

**Vocabulary** The Vocabulary activities extend the instruction of the Vocabulary Skill Words from "Teammates" to recognize the thesaurus as a valuable resource for finding the various synonyms and antonyms that relate to a single word.

### Vocabulary Skill Words

**extraordinary\***    **segregation**    **apathetic\***    **hostility**    **taunts**
*\*Also Selection Vocabulary*

**Additional Materials:** dictionary, thesaurus

## Writing Process Strategies

The Writing Process Strategies lesson involves instruction in following the conventions of grammar, usage, spelling, and punctuation during the editing/proofreading step of the writing process. As practice for this skill, students will edit/proofread their autobiographies.

 **Basic Computer Skills** To introduce students to the computer as a writing tool, teach students how to resize and move windows, and work with more than one window at a time. *Basic Computer Skills,* Level 3, Lesson 6, teaches these basic computer skills. LA.D.2.2.4.3.1

## English Language Conventions

**Grammar, Usage, and Mechanics** **Sentences.** This lesson defines a sentence and explains what it includes. It also covers types of sentences, end punctuation, and capitalization, through writing a friendly letter. This reconfirms the conventions developed in the Writing Process Strategies lesson.

**Listening, Speaking, Viewing** **Interacting: Using Gestures.** In this Interacting lesson, students will develop their understanding and use of gestures as a way to communicate without words.

**Penmanship** **Cursive Letters *a, c,* and *d*.** This lesson continues the development of cursive handwriting skills. Students learn correct formation of *a, c,* and *d* and then practice writing words from the literature selection that contain those letters.

# DAY I

| **Word Analysis** | **Writing Process Strategies** | **English Language Conventions** |

## Word Analysis

### Spelling

**Assessment: Pretest**

**The /u/ Sound** LA.A.1.2.2.3.1

### Teach

Give students the Pretest found on page 34 of *Unit 1 Assessment* as entry assessment of the spelling pattern. Have them proofread and correct any misspelled words.

**Pretest Sentences**

1. **dusk** At **dusk,** the sun sets in the west.
2. **blush** A person might **blush** if he or she gets embarrassed.
3. **crust** The **crust** of a pie should not get too brown.
4. **thump** The **thump** in your chest is your heartbeat.
5. **shut** You should **shut** a door to keep out insects.
6. **dump** Garbage is collected at a **dump**.
7. **scrub** Cinderella had to **scrub** the dirty floor.
8. **pump** You **pump** gas into your car at a gas station.
9. **buff** People **buff** wax off cars.
10. **buzz** Bees **buzz** around flowers in a garden.
11. **but** Flowers should be smelled, **but** not eaten.
12. **just** Most puppies **just** want to play.
13. **bus** A **bus** can take you all around a city.
14. **upon** Weather forecasters rely **upon** radar.
15. **much** A desert does not get **much** rain.

Diagnose any misspellings by determining whether students misspelled the /u/ sound or some other part of the word. Then use the Pretest as a take-home list to study the spellings of words with the /u/ sound.

## Writing Process Strategies

### Editing/Proofreading LA.B.1.2.2.3.1, LA.B.1.2.2.3.7

**Introduction to the Writing Process**

### Teach

**Introduce Writing Process Steps**

- Read *Language Arts Handbook,* pages 19 and 38, to introduce the editing/proofreading step of the writing process.
- Discuss with students *Language Arts Transparency 27,* Conventions: Grammar.
- Discuss with students *Language Arts Transparency 31,* Proofreader's Marks.

**Inspiration**

Teacher Model: *"I know that a paper with a lot of spelling and punctuation mistakes is difficult to read. I will take time to look over my writing and make sure I have made any needed corrections."*

**Brainstorming**

Ask students what kinds of mistakes they make when they are writing. List their answers on the board. Then ask them to think of a plan they could use to check their writing for these errors.

### Guided Practice

**Editing/Proofreading**

Have students look at a paper from their *Writing Folders* for spelling errors and mark them with proofreader's marks.

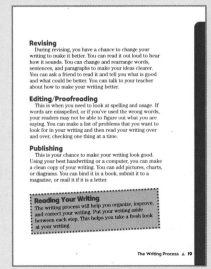

*Language Arts Handbook p. 19*

## English Language Conventions

### Grammar, Usage, and Mechanics

**Grammar: Sentences** LA.B.1.2.3.3.2

### Teach

- Use *Language Arts Handbook,* page 259, for definitions and examples of kinds of sentences.
- Explain that a sentence is a group of words that makes a complete thought about something and that every complete sentence includes a subject and predicate. Write these sentences on the board. Point out the subjects and predicates and that the first letter of the first word in a sentence is capitalized.
  - *Rain is falling.* (Rain *is the subject; the predicate is* is falling; *it tells what the rain is doing.*)
  - *Riley is the tallest in the class.* (The subject is Riley; *the predicate is* is the tallest; *it tells what Riley is.)*
- Explain that every sentence has end punctuation. Declarative and imperative end in a period; interrogative end with a question mark; exclamatory end with an exclamation point.

### Independent Practice

Use *Comprehension and Language Arts Skills,* pages 20–21, to practice identifying types of sentences.

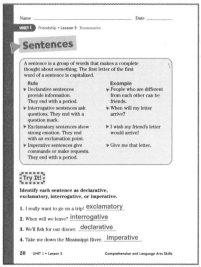

*Comprehension and Language Arts Skills pp. 20–21*

# DAY 2

## Word Analysis

### Spelling

**Word Sorting** LA.A.1.2.2.3.1

- Hold up *Sound/Spelling Card 21.* Ask the class to say *tug* and listen to the /u/ sound.
- **Board Word Sort.** Write on the board: *upon, butter, cup, utter, slug, ugly, bug, funny, stuck,* and *luck.* Write 1: *Words with* u *at the Beginning* and 2: *Words with* u *in the Middle* as two columns. Have the students sort the words under the correct column.

### Vocabulary

**Using a Thesaurus** LA.A.1.2.4.3.1

#### Teach

Write *thesaurus* on the board. Explain that a *thesaurus* is a resource book that gives *synonyms* for words, not definitions like a dictionary. Define a *synonym* as a word that has nearly the same meaning as another word.

#### Guided Practice

Use *Spelling and Vocabulary Skills,* page 18, to teach students how to use a thesaurus. Ask students to complete page 19 as independent practice.

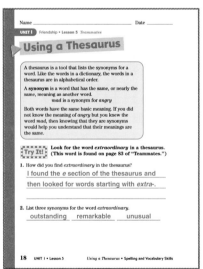

*Spelling and Vocabulary Skills p. 18*

## Writing Process Strategies

### Editing/Proofreading  LA.B.1.2.2.3.1, LA.B.1.2.2.3.7
**Introduction to the Writing Process**

#### Teach

- Discuss with students *Language Arts Transparency 28,* Conventions: Grammar and Punctuation. Discuss how changing these kinds of mistakes improves one's writing.

Writer's Craft
   **Staying on Topic**

- Read the following sentence to students and ask them to tell you which information doesn't belong.
  - *I went to a movie the other day. It was very scary, but I like scary movies. I used to live in Seattle. I was afraid to go outside when the movie was over.*

  Discuss how the information about living in Seattle did not fit with the rest of your story. Explain to students that they should look for information that does not go with their topic sentence when they are revising.
- Read *Language Arts Handbook,* pages 31 and 183, on staying on topic.
- Read *Comprehension and Language Arts Skills,* pages 22–23, on staying on topic.
- Remind students to check for conventions as well, while making sure they are staying on topic.

#### Guided Practice
**Editing Checklist**

- Review the editing checklist on *Language Arts Handbook,* page 39. Discuss how a checklist can enable a writer to stay organized during the editing/proofreading process.
- Have students use the grammar and punctuation conventions from *Language Arts Transparency 28* to check a piece of writing from their *Writing Folders.*

## English Language Conventions

### Grammar, Usage, and Mechanics
**Grammar: Sentences** LA.B.1.2.3.3.2

#### Teach

- Review the four types of sentences.
- Write the following sentences on the board. Ask students to identify the type. Point out the end punctuation and initial capitalization.
  - Why were people mean to Jackie Robinson? *(interrogative)*
  - Wow, look at the size of that bird! *(exclamatory)*
  - Stop that! *(imperative)*
  - Friday is my favorite day of the week. *(declarative)*
  - Have you been to the doctor? *(interrogative)*
  - The sun is 93 million miles away. *(declarative)*

#### Guided Practice in Reading

- Have students identify two declarative sentences in "Teammates." Have students choose a declarative sentence from the story and change it to an interrogative sentence. *(Change "I am standing by him," Pee Wee Reese said to the world. "This man is my teammate." to "Why am I standing by him?" Pee Wee Reese asked the world. "This man is my teammate.")*
- Ask students to find a sentence that can be changed to become exclamatory. *(Change "This man is my teammate." to "This man is my teammate!")* Have students share their sentences.

# DAY 3

| Word Analysis | Writing Process Strategies | English Language Conventions |
|---|---|---|

## Word Analysis

### Spelling

**The /u/ Sound** LA.A.1.2.2.3.1

#### Teach
- Introduce words with the /u/ sound spelled *u* found in "Teammates." Students should try to find the five selection spelling words in the story.
- Ask students to think of foods that contain the /u/ sound. (*butter, cupcake*)

#### Guided Practice
Have students complete page 20 from the **Spelling and Vocabulary Skills** to begin to learn strategies for spelling words with the /u/ sound.

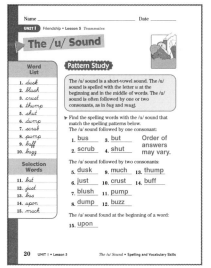

*Spelling and Vocabulary Skills p. 20*

### Vocabulary (continued)

**Using a Thesaurus** LA.A.1.2.4.3.1
- Write *taunts* from page 90 of "Teammates" on the board. Write *taunt* next to *taunts*.
- Have a student read some of the synonyms they can find for *taunt* in a thesaurus (*ridicule, heckle, hound*) and discuss the meaning of the word *taunts* (*bothers, bullies*).

## Writing Process Strategies

### Editing/Proofreading LA.B.1.2.2.3.1, LA.B.1.2.2.3.7
**Introduction to the Writing Process**

#### Teach
- Discuss with students **Language Arts Transparency 29,** Conventions: Grammar, Punctuation, Capitalization. Ask students to generate a list of conventions that can be added to the list from Day 2.
- Review editing on **Writer's Workbook,** page 5. Ask students to compare it to the **Language Arts Handbook** checklist on page 39 that was discussed on Day 2. Discuss what students consider appropriate or important to add to the **Writer's Workbook** checklist.

#### Guided Practice
**Editing/Proofreading**
Encourage students to check a piece of their writing for grammar and punctuation conventions discussed on **Language Arts Transparency 29.**

## English Language Conventions

### Grammar, Usage, and Mechanics

**Grammar: Sentences** LA.B.1.2.3.3.2

#### Teach
Use **Language Arts Handbook,** page 257, to review sentences.

#### Guided Practice in Writing
- Have students write one of each kind of sentence: exclamatory, declarative, interrogative, imperative. Have some students share their sentences with the class.
- Explain to students that using the four types of sentences when writing a friendly letter can make their writing more interesting to their reader.

**Informal Assessment**

Check to make sure students can identify the four types of sentences: interrogative, declarative, imperative, and exclamatory. Check students' work to make sure they are using the correct end punctuation.

# DAY 4

| Word Analysis | Writing Process Strategies | English Language Conventions |
| --- | --- | --- |

## Word Analysis

### Spelling

**The /u/ sound** LA.A.1.2.2.3.1

**Teach**

- Explain that exercises in *Spelling and Vocabulary Skills* are designed to help students become familiar with the correct spelling of a word.
- Demonstrate the Visualization strategy by writing *much* and *mech* on the board. Explain how the misspelled word looks "wrong" compared to the correct spelling.

**Guided Practice**

Have students complete the exercises on page 21 of *Spelling and Vocabulary Skills* to reinforce the spelling patterns for the /u/ sound.

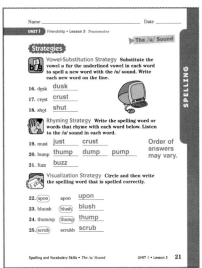

**Spelling and Vocabulary Skills p. 21**

### Vocabulary (continued)

**Using a Thesaurus** LA.A.1.2.4.3.1

- Write *humiliation* from "Teammates" on the board.
- Ask a student to find *humiliation* in the thesaurus and read two of the synonyms given. *(disgrace, discredit)*
- Ask another student, applying the synonyms, to define the meaning of the word *humiliation* as it is found in "Teammates."

## Writing Process Strategies

### Editing/Proofreading LA.B.1.2.2.3.1, LA.B.1.2.2.3.7
**Introduction to the Writing Process**

**Teach**

- Discuss *Language Arts Transparency 30*, Conventions: Grammar, Punctuation, Capitalization, and Spelling, with students. Ask them how these conventions relate to their own writing.
- Ask students to list conventions from today's lesson that can be added to the list from Days 2 and 3. Record their suggestions.
- If computers are available to students, encourage them to edit their work using the available spelling and grammar tools. Remind them that this is not a substitute for their own editing, but an additional aid.
- For more information on editing on a computer, see *Language Arts Handbook,* page 41.

**Guided Practice**

**Editing/Proofreading**

Provide time for students to practice editing on the computer so they will become proficient with the tools available.

## English Language Conventions

### Listening, Speaking, Viewing

**Interacting: Using Gestures** LA.C.1.2.4.3.1, LA.C.3.2.4.3.1

**Teach**

- In Reading and Responding, we discussed Predicting and Clarifying. When people use gestures, we have to predict and clarify what they are trying to tell us.
- Explain how we can communicate without words. Making eye contact is one skill of a good listener. When we look directly at a speaker, the speaker knows that we are paying close attention to his or her words.
- Explain what a gesture is. A gesture is a movement of part of your body, like a hand, an arm, or an eye, that expresses an idea. We can say "hello" to a friend by waving our hand. When we speak to a person or an audience, we can capture their attention by using gestures when we speak. Gestures and eye contact grab the audience's attention.

**Guided Practice**

- Discuss the text, "Teammates." Do the students know what kind of gestures baseball players and other athletes use to communicate with each other? *(A coach may hold up one finger to tell the pitcher what kind of pitch to throw or move his arm in a circular motion to tell a base runner to run the whole way around the bases.)*
- Ask what other gestures athletes use, and ask for demonstrations. *(hurry up, stop, stretch, dribble a basketball, ski faster, pedal faster)*
- What kind of gestures do we use in the classroom? *(Raising our hand to ask a question.)*

 **Informal Assessment**

Observe whether students understand what gestures are and how they and making eye contact help in communicating.

# DAY 5

| Word Analysis | Writing Process Strategies | English Language Conventions |

## Word Analysis

### Spelling

#### Assessment: Final Test
**The /u/ Sound** LA.A.1.2.2.3.1

#### Teach
Repeat the Pretest or use the Final Test on page 35 of *Unit 1 Assessment* as summative assessment for student understanding of the /u/ sound spelling patterns.

***Unit 1 Assessment p. 35***

#### Guided Practice
Have students categorize any mistakes they made on the Final Test. Are they careless errors? Are they lesson-pattern problems? Check to see if students correctly spell the /u/ sound in their writing.

### Vocabulary LA.A.1.2.4.3.1

#### Informal Assessment
Ask students to find an unfamiliar word in "Teammates" *(possible word: audible)*. Have the class look up the word in a thesaurus and find its synonyms. Check to see if students are having difficulty using a thesaurus. Have students discuss their own definitions for the word as it is found in the text. Have students add any new words to the word list in their Writer's Notebooks.

## Writing Process Strategies

### Editing/Proofreading LA.B.1.2.2.3.1, LA.B.1.2.2.3.7
Introduction to the Writing Process

#### Teach
- Review with students all the conventions discussed this week. Clarify anything students are uncertain about.
- Encourage students to mention anything else they think should be considered.
- Discuss what students consider appropriate or important to add to the *Writer's Workbook* checklist.
- Ask students to provide helpful hints they use or know of to make editing/proofreading more efficient. They may mention reading your paper for one convention at a time, using a checklist, editing on a computer, or peer conferencing.

#### Guided Practice
**Editing/Proofreading**
- Refer to the Grammar, Usage, and Mechanics lesson, page 93F, on types of sentences. Have students check their use of prepositions and prepositional phrases in their work.
- Have students use the editing checklist on *Writer's Workbook,* page 5, as they proofread and edit their autobiographies. Encourage them to use proofreader's marks.

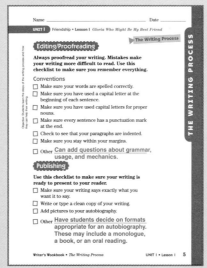

***Writer's Workbook p. 5***

## English Language Conventions

### Penmanship LA.B.1.2.2
**Cursive Letters *a*, *c*, and *d***

#### Teach
- **Teacher Model:** Tell students that cursive letters are made of four types of strokes (undercurve, downcurve, overcurve, and slant lines). Draw them on the board.
- **Teacher Model:** On the board, introduce lowercase cursive *a*, *c*, and *d* as downcurve letters.

**a** Starting point, downcurve
Undercurve to starting point
Slant down, undercurve: small *a*

**c** Starting point, downcurve
Undercurve: small *c*

**d** Starting point, downcurve
Undercurve past starting point
Slant down, undercurve: small *d*

- **Teacher Model:** On the board, write the words *many, dad, card, case,* and *friend* to model proper letter formation and slant.

#### Guided Practice
- Invite students to come to the board to trace the letters *a*, *c*, and *d*.
- Have students practice writing rows of *a*, *c*, and *d* in their Writer's Notebooks.
- From "Teammates," have students write the words *once, black, was, dry,* and *clothes* in their Writer's Notebooks to practice letter formation.

#### Informal Assessment
Check students' handwriting for proper slant.

# Reading and Language Arts Skills Traces

## Language Arts

### WORD ANALYSIS

**Skills Trace**

**Spelling: The /u/ Sound**
Introduced in Grade 1.
Scaffolded throughout Grades 2–5.
**REINTRODUCED:** Unit 1, Lesson 5, p. 93E
**PRACTICED:** Unit 1, Lesson 5, pp. 93F–93J
*Spelling and Vocabulary Skills,*
pp. 20–21
**TESTED:** Unit 1, Lesson 5, p. 93J
Unit 1 Assessment

**Skills Trace**

**Vocabulary: Dictionary Strategy**
Introduced in Grade 1.
Scaffolded throughout Grades 2–5.
**REINTRODUCED:** Unit 1, Lesson 5, p. 93E
**PRACTICED:** Unit 1, Lesson 5, pp. 93F–93J
*Spelling and Vocabulary Skills,*
pp. 18–19
**TESTED:** Unit 1 Assessment

## Reading

### COMPREHENSION

**Skills Trace**

**Main Idea and Supporting Details**
Introduced in Grade 1.
Scaffolded throughout Grades 2 and 3.
**REINTRODUCED:** Unit 1, Lesson 5
**REINFORCED:** Unit 4, Lesson 3
Unit 5, Lesson 6
Unit 6, Lesson 6
**TESTED:** Unit 1 Assessment

### WRITING PROCESS STRATEGIES

**Skills Trace**

**Introduction to the Writing Process:**
**Editing/Proofreading**
Introduced in Grade K.
Scaffolded throughout Grades 1–6.
**REINTRODUCED:** Unit 1, Lesson 5, p. 93F
**PRACTICED:** Unit 1, Lesson 5, pp. 93G–93J
*Writer's Workbook,* p. 5
**TESTED:** Unit 1 Assessment

### ENGLISH LANGUAGE CONVENTIONS

**Skills Trace**

**Grammar: Sentences—4 Types,**
**End Punctuation, Capitalization**
Introduced in Grade K.
Scaffolded throughout Grades 1–6.
**REINTRODUCED:** Unit 1, Lesson 5, p. 93F
**PRACTICED:** Unit 1, Lesson 5, p. 93G
Unit 1, Lesson 5, p. 93H
*Comprehension and Language*
*Arts Skills,* pp. 20–21
**TESTED:** Unit 1, Lesson 5,
Informal Assessment, p. 93H
Unit 1 Assessment

**Skills Trace**

**Listening, Speaking, Viewing**
**Interacting: Using Gestures**
Introduced in Grade K.
Scaffolded throughout Grades 1–6.
**REINTRODUCED:** Unit 1, Lesson 5, p. 93I
**TESTED:** Unit 1, Lesson 5,
Informal Assessment, p. 93I

**Skills Trace**

**Penmanship:**
**Cursive Letters *a*, *c*, and *d***
Introduced in Grade 2 (*a* and *d*) and Grade 3 (*c*).
Scaffolded throughout Grades 3–6 and
Grades 4–6.
**INTRODUCED:** Unit 1, Lesson 5, p. 93J
**TESTED:** Unit 1, Lesson 5,
Informal Assessment, p. 93J

# Professional Development: Assessment

## The Changing Face of Reading Assessment

Reading assessment has moved away from being based predominantly on multiple-choice items and toward requiring students to be more active, or *constructive*, in responding. Formal, standardized assessment, while retaining an important role in education, is being supplemented by teacher observations, samples of students' work, and other activities that can be used to infer achievement and reading progress. The new, or *alternative*, forms of assessment are called by several names, including *authentic* assessment and *performance-based* assessment. Whatever the name, the idea behind alternative assessment is that testing should be an integral part of instruction, not the end purpose of learning (Reichel, 1994). Alternative assessments include portfolio assignments, written responses to reading, oral fluency or miscue analysis, word reading, cloze passages, and a variety of other assessments that are useful in guiding instruction and showing how well students can read (Pearson, DeStefano, & García, 1998; Tierney, Carter, & Desai, 1991).

One reason for the shift in reading assessment is that traditional, standardized tests provide relatively little instructional guidance (García & Pearson, 1994; Shepard, 1989; Stallman & Pearson, 1990). Although alternative assessments have shortcomings that prevent their widespread use for accountability purposes, they provide a great deal of meaningful instructional guidance (Pearson et al., 1998). A second reason for the shift is a new concept of reading. The traditional perspective of reading was more or less that students either did or did not read and comprehend what they read. Recent views of reading interpret reading as a more dynamic act that includes a variety of skills and active processing by the reader (Anderson & Pearson, 1984; Rumelhart, 1985).

One of the greatest advantages of alternative assessments is that students actually may learn in the process of engaging in assessment. From taking a traditional multiple-choice comprehension test, students may learn little more than surface knowledge of a passage (Winograd, Paris, & Bridge, 1991). An alternative assessment that involves having a student write or tell about a passage that she or he has read, engage in reading-related investigations, or make a presentation about the reading often creates highly motivating learning opportunities and gives the teacher great insights into a student's ability.

Another advantage of alternative assessment is that students have more time to respond than they do when they take a standardized test. Not surprisingly, a significant difference often appears between some students' standardized test scores and their scores on an alternative assessment.

Assessment, whether traditional or alternative, is only a sample of behavior from which conclusions can be drawn and generalizations made. In the case of a traditional test, the behavior sample is a single event that occurs in a relatively short duration of time. In alternative assessment, the sample is drawn over a longer time period and involves complex thinking, problem solving, and continuous feedback (Wiggins, 1993). Students:

- construct responses instead of choosing one correct answer.
- solve a problem or apply principles instead of responding to text by choosing an answer, usually from four options, that is "more correct" than the others.
- apply several skills at once, rather than depending on an isolated skill.

Although alternative assessments have enjoyed increasing popularity, their widespread use has been limited by a number of factors. They are difficult to score and are highly susceptible to subjective interpretation. The time and effort involved mean they cost more to develop and to score. They lack the rigor of traditional assessments. Finally, for certain students, alternative assessments may be just as unfair as traditional assessments. For example, students who are good at presenting their ideas may be overrated when compared to students who comprehend what they read just as well but cannot present their ideas as clearly as other students (Mehrens, 1992; Pearson et al., 1998).

*Focus Questions* What would be a true test of friendship?
What would you be willing to give up for a friend?

THE
# LEGEND OF DAMON AND PYTHIAS

adapted as a play by Fan Kissen
illustrated by Fabricio Vanden Broeck

CAST

Damon
Pythias
Soldier
King
Mother
First Robber

Second Robber
First Voice
Second Voice
Third Voice
Announcer
Narrator

SOUNDS

*Iron door open and shut*       *Key in lock*

94

**SELECTION INTRODUCTION**

## Selection Summary

### Genre: Myth

In this fresh rendering of "The Legend of Damon and Pythias," adapted as a play, readers can appreciate the eloquence of the formal language and have the opportunity to use their own voices and gestures to capture the plot and characters found in this touching and enlightening story.

Some elements of a myth include:

- A myth may explain how something in nature looks or works—for example, why the spider spins a web.

- A myth may explain why people behave in certain ways—for example, why people are hopeful even though bad things happen.

- A myth often includes gods and goddesses who interact with humans.

## About the Author

**FAN KISSEN** is most widely known for her radio program series, *Tales from the Four Winds*, for which she won educational radio awards. Many of her plays were written in the same style as her radio programs, including instructions for announcers and sound effects. Kissen's career began as an elementary school teacher in New York City.

Students can read more about Fan Kissen on page 110 of the *Student Anthology.*

## About the Illustrator

**FABRICIO VANDEN BROECK** was born in Mexico City. He is an editor and a children's book illustrator. Broeck studied in Switzerland under the supervision of a well-known artist. His accomplishments extend beyond the Mexican borders. His works have appeared in numerous exhibits in Mexico and abroad. A leading Mexican newspaper also publishes his illustrations.

Students can read more about Fabricio Vanden Broeck on page 110 of the *Student Anthology.*

## Inquiry Connections

This myth illustrates the ideas that trust and loyalty are the best qualities of true friendship. In the tradition of a myth, this selection explains aspects of the customs and ideals of a society. Because Damon and Pythias are willing to make a noble sacrifice for each other, they have come to stand for true friendship. Key concepts explored are:

- Sometimes friendship requires some sacrifice.
- True friends are loyal to each other because they trust each other.
- True friendship is too strong to be ruined by people who try to disrupt it.

Before reading the selection:

- Point out that students may post a question, concept, word, illustration, or object at any time during the course of their unit investigation. Be sure that students include their names or initials on the items they post, so that others will know whom to go to if they have an answer or if they wish to collaborate on a related activity.
- Students should feel free to write an answer or a note on someone else's question or to consult the Board for ideas for their own investigations throughout the unit.
- Encourage students to read about friendship at home and to bring in articles or pictures that are good examples to post on the Board.

**Concept/Question Board**

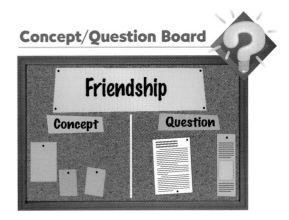

PROGRAM RESOURCES

## Leveled Practice

**Reteach**
**Pages 26–28**

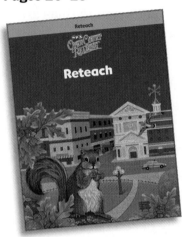

**Challenge**
**Pages 23–25**

**ELD Workbook**

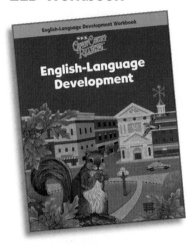

**Intervention Workbook**

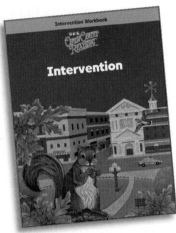

### Decodable Book 16

## Leveled Classroom Library*

Encourage students to read at least 30 minutes daily outside of class. Have them read books in the *Leveled Classroom Library* to support the unit theme and help students develop their vocabulary by reading independently.

### *Amigo*

BY BYRD BAYLOR. ALADDIN, 1991.

A poor Mexican boy's only friend is a prairie dog, Amigo. While the boy believes he is taming Amigo as a pet, ironically, it is Amigo who is taming the boy. **(Easy)**

### *Charlotte's Web*

BY E. B. WHITE. HARPERTROPHY, 1952.

This is the classic story of a friendship between a pig and a spider. (Newbery Honor) **(Average)**

### *The Mountain that loved a Bird*

BY ALICE MCLERRAN. SIMON & SCHUSTER, 1985.

When Joy, a bird, must leave the mountain, Joy makes a promise to the mountain that loves her. Every year, one of her kin will return to the mountain. Joy's kin transform the mountain over time. **(Advanced)**

✳ These books, which all support the unit theme Friendship, are part of a 36-book *Leveled Classroom Library* available for purchase from SRA/McGraw-Hill.
Note: Teachers should preview any trade books for appropriateness in their classrooms before recommending them to students.

# TECHNOLOGY

## Web Connections

www.sra4kids.com
**Friendship Web Site**

## CD-ROMs

✳**Research Assistant**
SRA/MCGRAW-HILL, 2002

✳**Decodable Book Activities**
SRA/MCGRAW-HILL, 2002

## Computer Skills

✳ **Basic Computer Skills**

## Audiocassettes/CDs

✳**Listening Library: Friendship**
SRA/MCGRAW-HILL, 2002

✳**Sound/Spelling Card Stories**
SRA/MCGRAW-HILL, 2002

Titles preceded by an asterisk (✳) are available through SRA/McGraw-Hill. Other titles can be obtained by contacting the publisher listed with the title.

**Suggested Pacing: 3–5 days**

| | DAY 1 | DAY 2 |
|---|---|---|
| | **DAY 1** | **DAY 2** |

## LESSON PLANNER

### 1 Preparing to Read

**Materials**
- Student Anthology, Book 1, pp. 94–111
- Decodable Book Activities CD-ROM
- Sound/Spelling Cards 3, 35
- Decodable Book 16
- Routine Cards 1, 3, Routines 1–2, 8–9

**DAY 1**

**Word Knowledge, p. 94K**
- Inflectional endings and suffixes added to root words
- /k/
- nouns
- short vowels

**About the Words and Sentences, p. 94K–94L**

**DAY 2**

**Developing Oral Language, p. 94L**

---

### 2 Reading & Responding

**Materials**
- Student Anthology, Book 1, pp. 94–111
- Program Assessment
- Reading Transparencies 8, 9, 46, 50, 52
- Inquiry Journal, p. 4
- Home Connection, p. 13
- Unit 1 Assessment, pp. 22–25
- Writer's Notebook
- Routine Cards 1–2, Routines 3–6

**DAY 1**

**Build Background, p. 94O**
**Preview and Prepare, pp. 94O–94P**
**Selection Vocabulary, p. 94P**
**Reading Recommendations, p. 94Q**
**Student Anthology, pp. 94–100** First Read
✓ **Comprehension Strategies**
- Monitoring and Adjusting Reading Speed, pp. 94, 96
- Asking Questions, pp. 96, 98, 100

**Supporting the Reading, p. 109C**
- Asking Questions

**DAY 2**

**Student Anthology, pp. 101–109** First Read
**Comprehension Strategies**
- Asking Questions, pp. 102, 106
- Summarizing, pp. 102, 108
- Monitoring and Adjusting Reading Speed, p. 104

**Discussing Strategy Use, p. 108**
**Discussing the Selection, p. 109A**
- Review Selection
- Complete Discussion

**Meet the Author/Illustrator, p. 110**
✓ **Theme Connections, p. 111**

---

### Inquiry

**Materials**
- Student Anthology, Book 1, pp. 94–111
- Research Assistant CD-ROM

**DAY 1**

**Investigation**
- Investigating Concepts Beyond the Text, p. 111A

**DAY 2**

**Investigation**
- Concept/Question Board, p. 111B

---

### 3 Language Arts

**Materials**
- Student Anthology, Book 1, pp. 94–111
- Comprehension and Language Arts Skills, pp. 24–25
- Language Arts Handbook, pp. 42–45, 196–197, 242, 244–247, 255
- Language Arts Transparencies 2, 33
- Sound/Spelling Cards 1, 5, 9, 15, 21
- Spelling and Vocabulary Skills, pp. 22–25
- Writer's Workbook, p. 5
- Spelling Software

**DAY 1**

**Word Analysis**
✓ Spelling: Short Vowel Sounds Pretest, p. 111F

**Writing Process Strategies**
- Introduction to the Writing Process: Publishing, p. 111F

**English Language Conventions**
- Grammar: Review, p. 111F

**DAY 2**

**Word Analysis**
- Spelling: Sound Sorting, p. 111G
- Vocabulary: Word Mapping, p. 111G

**Writing Process Strategies**
- Introduction to the Writing Process: Publishing, p. 111G

**English Language Conventions**
- Grammar: Review, p. 111G

---

| DAY 2 continued | DAY 3 | |
|---|---|---|
| **DAY 3** | **DAY 4** | **DAY 5** |

**DAY 3**

(P) **Phonics and Fluency, p. 94M**
- Review the /ō/ sound spelled o, _ow, o_e, oa_, _oe

**About the Words and Sentences, p. 94M**

**DAY 4**

**Developing Oral Language, p. 94N**
**Dictation, p. 94N**

**DAY 5**

**Review Word Knowledge and Phonics**

---

**DAY 3**

**Student Anthology, pp. 94–100** [Second Read]
**Comprehension Skills**
- Sequence, pp. 95, 97, 99

**Social Studies Connection**
- Greek Drama, p. 109E

**DAY 4**

**Student Anthology, pp. 101–109** [Second Read]
**Comprehension Skills**
- Sequence, pp. 101, 103, 105, 107, 109

**Checking Comprehension, p. 109**
**Review Selection Vocabulary, p. 109B**
**Literary Elements, p. 109D**
- Features of a Play

**DAY 5**

✔ **Selection Assessment**
- "The Legend of Damon and Pythias," pp. 22–25

**Home Connection, p. 109B**
**Science Connection**
- Stars and Constellations, p. 109F

---

**DAY 3**

✔ **Investigation**
- Presentations and Proposal Questions, p. 111C

**DAY 4**

**Supporting the Investigation**
- ABC Order, p. 111D

**DAY 5**

**Investigation**
- Unit Investigation Continued
- Update Concept/Question Board, p. 111B

---

**DAY 3**

**Word Analysis**
- Spelling: Short Vowel Sounds, p. 111H
- Vocabulary: Word Grouping, p. 111H

**Writing Process Strategies**
- Introduction to the Writing Process: Publishing, p. 111H

**English Language Conventions**
- Grammar: Review, p. 111H

**DAY 4**

**Word Analysis**
- Spelling: Short Vowel Sounds, p. 111I
- Vocabulary: Comparisons, p. 111I

**Writing Process Strategies**
- Introduction to the Writing Process: Publishing, p. 111I

**English Language Conventions**
- ✔ Listening, Speaking, Viewing Presenting: Sharing Information, p. 111I

**DAY 5**

**Word Analysis**
- ✔ Spelling: Short Vowel Sounds Final Test Unit 1 Assessment, p. 42
- ✔ Vocabulary: Word Maps, p. 111J Unit 1 Assessment, p. 43

**Writing Process Strategies**
- Introduction to the Writing Process: Publishing, p. 111J

**English Language Conventions**
- ✔ Penmanship: Cursive Letters q, g, and o, p. 111J

Below are suggestions for differentiating instruction to meet the individual needs of students. These are the same skills shown on the Lesson Planner; however, these pages provide extra practice opportunities or enriching activities to meet the varied needs of students. For Workshop Management Tips, see Appendix.

**WORKSHOP**

# Differentiating Instruction

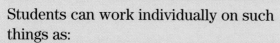

## Small-Group Instruction

Use the informal assessment suggestions found throughout the lessons, along with the formal assessments provided in each lesson, to determine your students' strengths and areas of need. Use the following program components to help in supporting or expanding on the instruction found in this lesson:

**Reteach Workbook** for use with students who show a basic understanding of the lesson but need a bit more practice to solidify their understanding.

**Intervention Guide** and **Intervention Workbook** for use with students who, even after extra practice, exhibit a lack of understanding of the lesson concepts.

**English-Language Development Guide** and **English-Language Development Workbook** for use with students who need language help.

### Theater Seminar

A suggested activity would be to have students perform this play, taking turns playing the roles.

## Independent Activities

Students can work individually on such things as:

- Inquiry Journal pages
- Independent reading
- Challenge
- Writing
- Investigation activities

| | READING | INVESTIGATION ACTIVITIES |
|---|---|---|
| **DAY 1** | ■ Select *Leveled Classroom Library* book for independent reading<br>■ Add vocabulary in Writer's Notebook<br>■ Complete Link to Writing for Supporting the Reading, p. 109C | ■ Concept/Question Board<br>■ Explore OCR Web site (www.sra4kids.com) for Friendship<br>◆ Investigating Concepts Beyond the Text, p. 111A |
| **DAY 2** | ■ Independent reading<br>■ Oral reading of selection for fluency<br>◆ Discuss Theme Connections, p. 111 | ■ Concept/Question Board<br>■ Use *Research Assistant CD-ROM* to continue investigation |
| **DAY 3** | ■ Independent reading<br>■ Record response to selection in Writer's Notebook<br>■◆ Social Studies Connection, p. 109E | ■ Concept/Question Board<br>◆ Presentations and Proposal Questions, p. 111C |
| **DAY 4** | ■ Independent reading<br>◆ Partner reading of selection<br>■ Add words to Word Bank<br>■ Complete Independent Practice for Literary Elements, p. 109D | ■ Concept/Question Board<br>◆ Complete Independent Practice for Supporting the Investigation, p. 111D |
| **DAY 5** | ■ Reading Roundtable<br>■◆ Science Connection, p. 109F<br>■ *Listening Library Audiocassette/CD* | ◆ Final preparations for presentations<br>◆ Record responses to investigations |

◆ **Small-Group Instruction**      ■ **Independent Activities**

| LANGUAGE ARTS | INTERVENTION* | ENGLISH-LANGUAGE LEARNERS** | RETEACH | CHALLENGE |
|---|---|---|---|---|
| **English Language Conventions**<br>■ Complete Review, *Comprehension and Language Arts Skills,* pp. 24–25 | **(30 to 45 minutes per day)**<br>◆ Blending, p. 50<br>◆ Preteach "The Legend of Damon and Pythias," pp. 52–53<br>◆ Teach "Intervention Selection One," pp. 53–54<br>◆ Grammar, Usage, and Mechanics, pp. 56–57 | **(30 to 45 minutes per day)**<br>◆ Word Knowledge, Suffix -*ment*, p. 27<br>◆ Activate Prior Knowledge, p. 28 | **English Language Conventions**<br>■ Complete Review, *Reteach,* p. 28 | **English Language Conventions**<br>■ Complete Review, *Challenge,* p. 25 |
| **Word Analysis**<br>◆ Spelling: Word Sort, p. 111G<br>■ Complete Vocabulary Strategies, *Spelling and Vocabulary Skills,* pp. 22–23 | ◆ Developing Oral Language, p. 50<br>◆ Preteach "The Legend of Damon and Pythias," pp. 52–53<br>◆ Teach Comprehension Strategies, p. 54<br>◆ Reread "Intervention Selection One"<br>◆ Grammar, Usage, and Mechanics, pp. 56–57 | ◆ Selection Vocabulary, p. 29<br>◆ Preteach the Selection, p. 29 | **Word Analysis**<br>■ Complete Vocabulary: Vocabulary Strategies, *Reteach,* p. 27 | ◆ Literary Elements, p. 109D<br>**Word Analysis**<br>■ Complete Vocabulary: Vocabulary Strategies, *Challenge,* p. 24 |
| **Word Analysis**<br>■ Complete Spelling: Review Short Vowel Sounds, *Spelling and Vocabulary Skills,* p. 24 | ◆ Dictation and Spelling, pp. 50–51<br>◆ Reread "The Legend of Damon and Pythias"<br>◆ Teach "Intervention Selection Two," pp. 54–55<br>◆ Writing Activity, p. 58 | ◆ Phonics and Fluency, /ō/, p. 27<br>◆ Dictation and Spelling, p. 28 | **Word Analysis**<br>■ Complete Spelling: Review Short Vowel Sounds, *Reteach* | **Word Analysis**<br>■ Complete Spelling: Review Short Vowel Sounds, *Challenge,* p. 23 |
| **Word Analysis**<br>■ Complete Review Short Vowel Sounds, *Spelling and Vocabulary Skills,* p. 25 | ◆ Blending, p. 51<br>◆ Reread "The Legend of Damon and Pythias"<br>◆ Teach Comprehension Strategies, p. 55<br>◆ Reread "Intervention Selection Two"<br>◆ Writing Activity, p. 58 | ◆ Vocabulary Strategies, p. 30 | | ◆ Supporting the Investigation, p. 111D |
| **Writing Process Strategies**<br>◆ Seminar: Publishing an Autobiography, p. 111J<br>**English Language Conventions**<br>■ Penmanship: Practice Letters *q, g,* and *o,* p. 111J | ◆ Developing Oral Language, p. 51<br>◆ Dictation and Spelling, pp. 51–52<br>◆ Repeated Readings/ Fluency Check, pp. 55–56<br>◆ Informal Assessment | ◆ Grammar, Usage, and Mechanics, p. 30 | | |

\* Page numbers refer to *Intervention Guide*.

\*\* Page numbers refer to *English-Language Development Guide*.

 *Florida*

## Formal Assessment Options

Use these summative assessments along with your informal observations to assess student progress.

---

**Unit 1 Assessment p. 22**

Name _____ Date _____ Score _____

**UNIT I** Friendship • Lesson 6

### The Legend of Damon and Pythias

Read the following questions carefully. Then completely fill in the bubble of each correct answer. You may look back at the story to find the answer to each of the questions.

1. What does Pythias do before he is thrown into jail?
   Ⓐ He ignores the king's laws.
   Ⓑ He turns people against the king.
   ● He speaks against the king's laws.

2. Who comes to visit Pythias in prison?
   ● a friend
   Ⓑ a soldier
   Ⓒ the king

Read the following questions carefully. Use complete sentences to answer the questions.

3. What does Damon offer to do for Pythias?
   He offers to stay in prison while Pythias says goodbye to his family.

4. Why does the king agree to lock up Damon and let Pythias go?
   He wants to test their friendship.

5. Why don't the robbers believe Pythias's story?
   They don't believe anyone would go back to prison to die. They also don't think anyone would die for a friend.

22 Unit I • Lesson 6     The Legend of Damon and Pythias • Unit I Assessment

---

**Unit 1 Assessment p. 23**

The Legend of Damon and Pythias *(continued)*

6. Just before Damon is about to die, how does he feel about Pythias?
   He still believes in him and is happy to die for him.

7. Why does the king let both men go free at the end?
   He can not kill anyone with such a true friendship.

8. What does the king want more than anything?
   He wants a real friend like Damon or Pythias.

Read the following questions carefully. Then completely fill in the bubble of each correct answer.

9. When Damon is led into the square, the crowd is angry with
   ● the king
   Ⓑ Damon
   Ⓒ Pythias

10. In all, how long was Pythias gone?
    Ⓐ one week
    ● two weeks
    Ⓒ three weeks

Unit I Assessment • The Legend of Damon and Pythias     Unit I • Lesson 6  23

---

**Unit 1 Assessment p. 24**

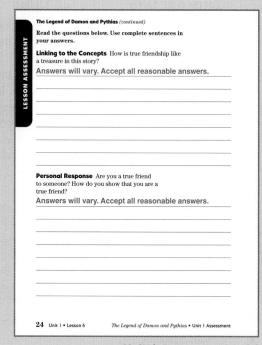

The Legend of Damon and Pythias *(continued)*

Read the questions below. Use complete sentences in your answers.

**Linking to the Concepts** How is true friendship like a treasure in this story?
Answers will vary. Accept all reasonable answers.

**Personal Response** Are you a true friend to someone? How do you show that you are a true friend?
Answers will vary. Accept all reasonable answers.

24 Unit I • Lesson 6     The Legend of Damon and Pythias • Unit I Assessment

---

**Unit 1 Assessment p. 25**

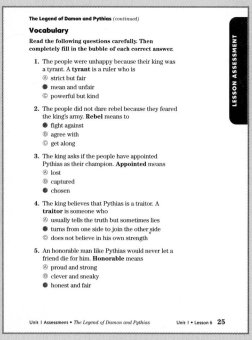

The Legend of Damon and Pythias *(continued)*

### Vocabulary

Read the following questions carefully. Then completely fill in the bubble of each correct answer.

1. The people were unhappy because their king was a **tyrant**. A **tyrant** is a ruler who is
   Ⓐ strict but fair
   ● mean and unfair
   Ⓒ powerful but kind

2. The people did not dare rebel because they feared the king's army. **Rebel** means to
   ● fight against
   Ⓑ agree with
   Ⓒ get along

3. The king asks if the people have appointed Pythias as their champion. **Appointed** means
   Ⓐ lost
   Ⓑ captured
   ● chosen

4. The king believes that Pythias is a traitor. A **traitor** is someone who
   Ⓐ usually tells the truth but sometimes lies
   ● turns from one side to join the other side
   Ⓒ does not believe in his own strength

5. An honorable man like Pythias would never let a friend die for him. **Honorable** means
   Ⓐ proud and strong
   Ⓑ clever and sneaky
   ● honest and fair

Unit I Assessment • The Legend of Damon and Pythias     Unit I • Lesson 6  25

---

**Unit 1 Assessment p. 36**

Name _____ Date _____ Score _____

**UNIT I** Friendship • Lesson 6  *The Legend of Damon and Pythias*

### Spelling Pretest: Short Vowel Sounds

Fold this page back on the dotted line. Take the Pretest. Then correct any word you misspelled by crossing out the word and rewriting it next to the incorrect spelling.

| | | |
|---|---|---|
| 1. _____ | 1. | *brand* |
| 2. _____ | 2. | *candy* |
| 3. _____ | 3. | *plan* |
| 4. _____ | 4. | *hobby* |
| 5. _____ | 5. | *best* |
| 6. _____ | 6. | *read* |
| 7. _____ | 7. | *us* |
| 8. _____ | 8. | *top* |
| 9. _____ | 9. | *jump* |
| 10. _____ | 10. | *send* |
| 11. _____ | 11. | *tell* |
| 12. _____ | 12. | *prison* |
| 13. _____ | 13. | *last* |
| 14. _____ | 14. | *robbers* |
| 15. _____ | 15. | *struggle* |

36 Unit I • Lesson 6     Spelling Pretest: Short Vowel Sounds • Unit I Assessment

---

**Unit 1 Assessment p. 37**

Name _____ Date _____ Score _____

**UNIT I** Friendship • Lesson 6  *The Legend of Damon and Pythias*

### Spelling Final Test: Short Vowel Sounds

Mark the letter next to the underlined word that is misspelled. Focus on the underlined word.

1. ● Cowboys <u>brend</u> cattle.
   Ⓑ Chocolate is a type of <u>candy</u>.
   Ⓒ Painting is a fun <u>hobby</u>.
   Ⓓ Correct as is.

2. Ⓕ The <u>best</u> apples are firm and tart.
   ● Books are meant to be <u>reed</u>.
   Ⓗ A cherry goes on <u>top</u> of a sundae.
   Ⓙ Correct as is.

3. Ⓐ My grandparents <u>send</u> me cards for holidays.
   Ⓑ You should not <u>tell</u> lies.
   ● Criminals go to <u>preson</u>.
   Ⓓ Correct as is.

4. Ⓕ People that steal are <u>robbers</u>.
   ● He read the book's <u>lest</u> chapter.
   Ⓗ Storytellers <u>tell</u> stories.
   Ⓙ Correct as is.

5. Ⓐ People <u>struggle</u> to untie knots.
   Ⓑ A <u>prison</u> is a sad place.
   Ⓒ Sewing is a <u>hobby</u>.
   Ⓓ Correct as is.

6. ● Do not <u>jemp</u> on a bed.
   Ⓖ A schedule is a <u>plan</u>.
   Ⓗ I'll <u>send</u> you a note.
   Ⓙ Correct as is.

Unit I Assessment • Spelling Final Test: Short Vowel Sounds     Unit I • Lesson 6  37

---

*Florida*

# Informal Comprehension Strategies Rubrics

## Asking Questions

- The student asks questions about ideas or facts presented in the text and attempts to answer these questions by reading the text.

## Monitoring and Adjusting Reading Speed

The student changes reading speed in reaction to the text, exhibiting such behavior as

- Skimming parts of the text that are not important or relevant.
- Purposely reading more slowly because of difficulty in comprehending the text.

# Research Rubrics

Use the Research Rubrics to assess a student's performance throughout the stages of the investigation for each unit. The rubrics for a given lesson will match the investigation stage for that lesson. In addition, at the end of the unit you can use the rubrics to assess the groups' collaborative work as well as an individual's participation in that group.

During Workshop, assess students using the rubrics below. The rubrics range from 1–4 in most categories, with 1 being the lowest score. Record each student's score on the inside back cover of the *Inquiry Journal*.

## Communicating Research Progress and Results

(This rubric may apply to oral, written, or multimedia reports.)

**1** Reporting is sparse and fragmentary.

**2** Report is factual; communicates findings but not the thinking behind them.

**3** Report provides a good picture of the research problem, of how original conjectures were modified in light of new information, and of difficulties and unresolved issues.

**4** A report that not only interests and informs the audience but also draws helpful commentary from them.

## Overall Assessment of Research

**1** A collection of facts related in miscellaneous ways to a topic.

**2** An organized collection of facts relevant to the research problem.

**3** A thoughtful effort to tackle a research problem, with some indication of progress toward solving it.

**4** Significant progress on a challenging problem of understanding.

## Objectives

- Students practice recognizing inflectional endings and suffixes and how they change meaning when added to base words.
- Students practice recognizing when the letter *c* makes the /k/ sound.
- Students practice recognizing vivid nouns that refer to groups of people.
- Students practice recognizing short vowel sounds.
- Students develop fluency reading words and sentences.

## Materials

- Student Anthology, Book 1, pp. 94–111
- Decodable Book Activities CD-ROM
- Decodable Book 16
- Routine Cards 1, 3, Routines 1–2, 8–9
- Sound/Spelling Cards 3, 35

**Teacher Tip** SYLLABICATION To help students blend words and build fluency, use the syllabication below of the words in the word lines.

| | | |
|---|---|---|
| a•ston•ish | a•ston•ished | a•ston•ish•ment |
| pun•ish | pun•ish•ing | pun•ish•ment |
| ap•point | ap•point•ed | ap•point•ment |
| coun•try | coins | cried |
| could | crowd | call |
| cru•el | ty•rant | cham•pi•on |
| pris•on•er | trai•tor | strug•gle |
| rob•bers | last | pris•on      tell |

**Routine Card**
Refer to *Routine 1* for the whole-word blending procedure and *Routine 2* for the sentence blending procedure.

## MEETING INDIVIDUAL NEEDS

### ELL Support

For ELD strategies, use the *English-Language Development Guide*, Unit 1, Lesson 6.

### Intervention Support

For intervention strategies, use the *Intervention Guide*, Unit 1, Lesson 6.

**Spelling**
See pages 111E–111J for the corresponding spelling lesson reviewing the short vowel sounds.

## Word Knowledge LA.A.1.2.2.3.1

### Reading the Words and Sentences

Use direct teaching to teach this blending lesson.

- Display **Sound/Spelling Card 3.**
- Write each word in Reading the Words and Sentences on the board and have students read them together. If they have difficulty reading a word, stop and have them blend the word using whole-word blending. Encourage students to pronounce the word naturally after blending. Because reading sentences helps students to move from word fluency to sentence fluency, have them read each sentence in unison, using normal intonation. The words in **boldface** type are from the selection.

| | |
|---|---|
| Line 1: | astonish **astonished** astonishment |
| Line 2: | punish punishing **punishment** |
| Line 3: | appoint **appointed** appointment |
| Line 4: | **country coins cried could crowd call cruel** |
| Line 5: | **tyrant champion prisoner traitor** |
| Line 6: | **struggle robbers last prison tell** |
| Sentence 1: | When Damon heard that his friend Pythias had been thrown into prison, and the severe punishment that was to follow, he was heartbroken. |
| Sentence 2: | I'll tell him that if you do not return by the appointed day, he may kill me, in your place. |
| Sentence 3: | The King of that country was a cruel tyrant. |
| Sentence 4: | When robbers get caught stealing, they go to prison. |

### About the Words and Sentences

- **Lines 1–3:** These lines illustrate how adding inflectional endings and suffixes to base words results in new words. After reading each line, have students circle the suffixes. Ask what adding the inflectional ending *-ed* to a word means (*in the past*) and what adding the suffix *-ment* to a word means (*the act or process of*). Discuss how the endings change the meanings of the words in each line.

- **Line 4:** These words illustrate the /k/ sound for the letter *c*. Point out that *c* usually makes the /k/ sound when it is followed by the vowel *a*, *o*, or *u* or any consonant except *h*. After reading the words, have students explain why the *c* is hard in each word.

- **Line 5:** These words identify types of people. Have students use each word in a sentence. Clarify the meanings of any words the students do not know. Remind them to use vivid, descriptive nouns such as these to make their own writing more descriptive.

- **Line 6:** The words in Line 6 are found in "The Legend of Damon and Pythias" and review the short vowel sounds /a/, /e/, /i/, /o/, and /u/.

- **Sentences 1–3:** These sentences are from the story students are about to read. Ask students to identify words with inflectional endings or suffixes *(punishment, appointed)*. Have them point to the words that have the /k/ sound *(country)*. Ask them to identify and point to a word that is a vivid noun and is a type of person *(tyrant)*.

- **Sentence 4:** Have students identify the words in the last sentence that contain short vowel sounds.

## Developing Oral Language LA.C.1.2.1.3.2

To review the words, do one or both of the following activities. Use these activities to help students practice reading the words.

- Point to the words from Line 4. You may also consider listing other words with the hard *c* sound. Have a student choose and point to a word. Then select another student to pronounce that word and use it in a sentence. The student who pronounces and uses the word correctly then goes to the board, chooses a new word, and selects a new student to pronounce it and use it in a sentence. Repeat the process.

- Choose one of the lines for students to focus on. Have a volunteer choose a word and use it in a sentence to begin a story. Have another volunteer continue the story by supplying a sentence that uses another word from the line. Continue until all the words are used.

**WORD KNOWLEDGE**

**Teacher Tip** FLUENCY Gaining a better understanding of the spellings of sounds and structure of words will help students as they encounter unfamiliar words in their reading. By this time in Grade 3 students should be reading approximately 107 words per minute with fluency and expression. As students read, you may notice that some need work in building fluency. During Workshop, have these students select a section of the text (a minimum of 160 words) to read several times in order to build fluency.

**Teacher Tip** BROWSE Have students browse the selection for other hard and soft consonant sounds. Ask them to generalize about the rules for pronunciation.

Refer to the *Lesson Model Videocassette* for instruction on whole-word blending.

**PHONICS**

**Teacher Tip SYLLABICATION** To help students blend words and build fluency, use the syllabication below of the words in the word lines.

| | | | |
|---|---|---|---|
| a•go | o•pen | on•ly | mo•ment |
| crow | flow | stow | win•dow |
| home | throne | a•lone | broke |
| oak | goat | toast | coach |
| ap•proach | doe | foe | woe |

## Phonics and Fluency

Review /ō/ spelled o, _ow, o_e, oa_, _oe

### Blending

Follow the established procedure to have students read the following words and sentences. **Boldface** words are found in the selection.

- Display *Sound/Spelling Card 35*.

| | | | | | |
|---|---|---|---|---|---|
| Line 1: | **ago** | open | **only** | moment | crow |
| Line 2: | flow | stow | window | **home** | **throne** |
| Line 3: | **alone** | **broke** | oak | goat | toast |
| Line 4: | coach | approach | doe | foe | woe |
| Sentence 1: | Tomorrow we will reach our goal. | | | | |
| Sentence 2: | We will see the ocean when we get to the coast. | | | | |
| Sentence 3: | One day a soldier overheard Pythias speaking against a new law the King had proclaimed. | | | | |

### About the Words and Sentences

- **Line 1:** The words practice the /ō/ sound spelled *o* and *_ow*.
- **Line 2:** The words practice the /ō/ sound spelled *_ow* and *o_e*.
- **Line 3:** The words practice the /ō/ sound spelled *o_e* and *_oa_*.
- **Line 4:** The words practice the /ō/ sound spelled *_oa_* and *_oe*.
- **Sentences 1–2:** The sentences have words with the /ō/ sound spellings. Have students identify these words *(tomorrow, goal, ocean, coast)*. Have students tell which spelling is used in each word.
- **Sentence 3:** This sentence is from the selection. Have students identify the words with the /ō/ sound spellings *(soldier, overheard, proclaimed)*.

## Developing Oral Language  LA.C.1.2.2.3.1

To review the words, do one or both of the following activities. Use these activities to help students practice reading the words.

- Read each of the words on the word lines. As you teach each word, have students clap out the syllables. Underline the long vowel spellings as you go.

- Have students give clue words for words on the word lines. For example: I had this for breakfast. Then have volunteers use the words in sentences. Ask other students to extend the sentences by adding a *Who? What? When? Why? Where?* or *How?* statement at the beginning or end of the sentences or by adding adjectives and adverbs.

## Dictation

Erase the blending lines and sentences on the board and have students take out writing paper. Dictate the following words and sentences for students to write.

|  |  |  |  |
|---|---|---|---|
| **Line 1:** | piano | elbow | globe |
| **Line 2:** | toad | throat | toe |
| **Challenge Word:** | oatmeal |  |  |
| **Sentence:** | Do you want tomato or potato soup for lunch? |  |  |

## Building Fluency

***Decodable Books*** are used to help develop fluency for students who need extra practice. The only way to gain fluency is to read. Students will have many opportunities to read, including the ***Student Anthology,*** the ***Leveled Classroom Library,*** and their own reading. The ***Decodable Books*** can be used to practice the phonics and fluency elements being reviewed. Refer to the Appendix for the procedure on using these books. For this lesson, use ***Decodable Book 16,*** *Rose, the Brave.*

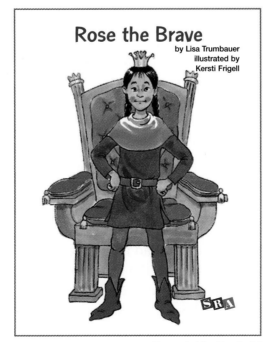

Rose the Brave
by Lisa Trumbauer
illustrated by Kersti Frigell

***Decodable Book 16***

**Teacher Tip** PROOFREADING
Remind students that whether they are writing on the board or on paper, they should proofread their work.

Use the ***Decodable Book Activities CD-ROM*** for activities that support this Phonics lesson.

Refer to the ***Lesson Model Videocassette*** for instruction on whole-word dictation.

**Routine Card**
Refer to ***Routine 8*** for the whole-word dictation procedure and ***Routine 9*** for the sentence dictation procedure.

Refer to the ***Lesson Model Videocassette*** for instruction on reading a ***Decodable Book.***

*Florida*

## Objectives

- Students will understand the selection vocabulary before reading, using strategies such as suffixes and structural cues.
- Students will spell words with the inflectional endings *-ed, -ment,* and *-ing,* and words that begin with hard *c.*
- Students will connect prior knowledge to subjects discussed in text.
- Students will use comprehension strategies such as Self-Questioning, Clarifying, and Summarizing to construct meaning from the text and monitor reading.
- Students will use the comprehension skill sequence as they read the story the second time.
- Students will discuss personal reactions to the story to begin identifying their own personal reading preferences.

## Materials

- Student Anthology, Book 1, pp. 94–111
- Program Assessment
- Reading Transparencies 8, 9, 46, 50, 52
- Inquiry Journal, p. 4
- Home Connection, p. 13
- Unit 1 Assessment, pp. 22–25
- Routine Cards 1–2, Routines 3–6

## MEETING INDIVIDUAL NEEDS

### ELL Support

For ELD strategies, use the *English-Language Development Guide,* Unit 1, Lesson 6.

### Intervention Support

For intervention strategies, use the *Intervention Guide,* Unit 1, Lesson 6.

**www.sra4kids.com**
**Web Connection**
Students can use the connections to friendship in the Reading link of the SRA Web page for more information about friendship.

**Routine Card**
Refer to *Routine 4* for the Clues, Problems, and Wonderings procedure.

# Build Background

## Activate Prior Knowledge

Discuss the following with students to find out what they may already know about the selection and have already learned about the theme of friendship.

- Preteach "The Legend of Damon and Pythias," by first determining students' prior knowledge by asking, "What stories do you know of that show trust and loyalty between true friends?"
- Ask students if they have read any other myths, such as the stories of Hercules or other legendary heroes.
- Ask students for examples of true friendship. What sorts of actions indicate trust and loyalty between friends?
- Discuss reading drama by asking, "How is reading a play different from other types of reading? What are the characteristics of plays?"

## Background Information   LA.E.1.2.4.3.1

The following information may help students understand the selection they are about to read.

- Point out to students that the selection they will be reading is a play. Plays are meant to be performed live with actors, costumes, and stage sets. As students read, they will notice that the names of the characters who are speaking appear in the margin, followed by his or her lines (words).
- Point out to students that the story takes place in ancient Sicily, an island off the coast of Italy. Invite them to find Sicily on a map or a globe. The way people dressed was different from the way we dress today. As they read, the students may notice other differences between the way the characters lived and the way people live today.
- Inform students this story is based on a famous Greek myth. Explain that myths are often remembered and passed down because the characters in them demonstrate qualities that people admire. While some myths and legends are fictional, many of them are based on actual events or real people. You may wish to have the students find out more about the real people in this legend. Tell them that Damon and Pythias were real people who lived more than two thousand years ago.

# Preview and Prepare

## Browse   LA.A.1.2.1.3.1

- Have a student read aloud the title and the name of the author/illustrator. Have students preview the selection by browsing through the first page or two of the story making sure not to give away any surprises the story contains. Discuss what they think this play might have to do with friendship.

- Have the students search for clues that tell them something about the story. Also, have them look for any problems, such as unfamiliar words, they notice while reading. Use **Reading Transparency 46** to record their observations as they browse. For example, a student might notice that one character seems to be in trouble with the king.

- As students prepare to read the selection, have them browse the Focus Questions on the first page of the selection. Tell them to keep these questions in mind as the selection is read.

For the Problems column, students might point out they are unfamiliar with the word *narrator.* They might wonder how Damon and Pythias became such role models of true friendship. To save time and to model note taking, write students' observations as brief notes rather than as complete sentences.

## Set Purposes LA.A.1.2.2.3.5

Encourage students to set their own purposes for reading this selection. As they read, have students think about who shows friendship in this story, how they show friendship, and why they show friendship. Remind them to think about finding answers to the clues, problems, and wonderings they noted during browsing.

## Selection Vocabulary LA.A.1.2.3.3.1

As students study vocabulary, they will use a variety of skills to determine the meaning of a word. These include context clues, word structure, and apposition. Students will apply these same skills while reading to clarify unfamiliar words.

Display **Reading Transparency 8** before reading the selection to introduce and discuss the following words and their meanings:

| | |
|---|---|
| **tyrant:** | a harsh, unjust ruler (page 96) |
| **rebel:** | to resist a ruler's power (page 96) |
| **appointed:** | to name officially (page 97) |
| **traitor:** | someone who betrays another's trust (page 101) |
| **honorable:** | deserving of honor or respect (page 103) |

Have students read the words in the word box, stopping to blend any words that they have trouble reading. Demonstrate how to decode multisyllabic words by breaking the words into syllables and blending the syllables. Then have the students try. If they still have trouble, refer them to the **Sound/Spelling Cards.** If the word is not decodable, give the students the pronunciation.

Have students read the sentences on the transparency to determine the meaning of the underlined word. Each word has two sentences that students will read, from which they should be able to derive the meaning of the underlined word. Remind them to use one or more of the skills they have learned to figure out the meaning before using a dictionary. Be sure students explain which skills they are using and how they figured out the meanings of the words. Have students reread the sentence, substituting the definition to see if the sentence makes sense. Have a volunteer create a new sentence using the underlined word.

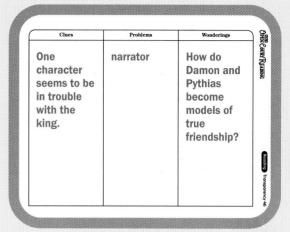

| Clues | Problems | Wonderings |
|---|---|---|
| One character seems to be in trouble with the king. | narrator | How do Damon and Pythias become models of true friendship? |

**Reading Transparency 46**

**Routine Card**
Refer to **Routine 3** for the vocabulary procedure.

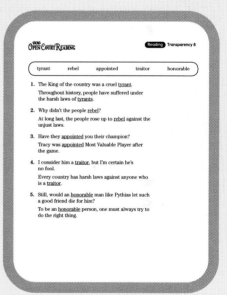

**Reading Transparency 8**

**Teacher Tip SELECTION VOCABULARY** To help students decode words, divide them into syllables when you are saying them, as shown below. The information following each word tells how students can figure out the meaning of each word. When writing words on the board, do not divide them into syllables.

| | |
|---|---|
| **ty•rant** | context clues |
| **re•bel** | context clues |
| **ap•poin•ted** | context clues |
| **trai•tor** | context clues |
| **hon•or•a•ble** | apposition |

During Workshop, and after the selection has been read at least once, have students listen to the recording of this lesson's selection on the *Listening Library Audiocassette/CD.* After students have listened, have them discuss their personal preferences of the selections read. Ask them what other things they have listened to and like to listen to on the radio, on audiocassettes, or on CDs.

**Routine Card**
Refer to *Routine 5* for the procedure on reading the selection.

**Teacher Tip COMPREHENSION STRATEGIES** Remind students as they read the story on the second day to summarize what they learned from the first day.

# Reading Recommendations

## Oral Reading

Have students decide how they want to read the selection. Since the story is told through dialogue in the form of a play, oral reading is recommended. You may wish to assign character parts to students for reading.

Have students make use of the comprehension strategies listed below to help them understand the selection. Have them stop reading periodically or wait until they have completed the selection to discuss the reading strategies. After the students have finished reading the selection, use the Discussing the Selection questions on page 109A to see if they understand what they have read.

## Using Comprehension Strategies

Comprehension strategy instruction allows students to become aware of how good readers read. Good readers constantly check their understanding as they are reading and ask themselves questions. In addition, skilled readers recognize when they are having problems and stop to use various comprehension strategies to help them make sense of what they are reading.

An extended lesson on the comprehension strategy Asking Questions can be found in the Supporting the Reading section on page 109C. This lesson is intended to give students extra practice with Asking Questions. However, it may be used at this time to introduce the comprehension strategy to students.

During the first reading of "The Legend of Damon and Pythias," teacher model the use of the following comprehension strategies:

- **Asking Questions** helps readers focus attention on what they are reading and engages them in a deeper understanding of themes, concepts, and ideas.

- **Monitoring and Adjusting Reading Speed (Introduction):** Sometimes it is necessary for readers to slow down and reread in order to obtain all of the information.

- **Summarizing** prompts readers to keep track of what they are reading and to focus their minds on important information.

As students read, they should be using a variety of strategies to help them understand the selection. Encourage students to use the strategies listed above as the class reads the story aloud. Do this by stopping at the points indicated by the numbers in the magenta circles on the reduced student page and using a particular strategy. Students can also stop reading periodically to discuss what they have learned and what problems they may be having.

## Building Comprehension Skills

Revisiting or rereading a selection allows students to apply skills that give them a more complete understanding of the text. Some follow-up comprehension skills help students organize information. Others lead to deeper understanding—to "reading between the lines," as mature readers do.

- **Sequence (Introduction):** Readers place events in the time order in which they occur in the story.

### Reading with a Purpose

Have students look for ways the story characters show friendship or learn something new about friendship.

## Research in Action

Students who set their own goals for reading with a greater sense of engagement notice more than students whose goals are set for them by the teacher or the reading program. The purpose of initial browsing is to help think about what they will be reading and to build a sense of anticipation for the reading they will do. As students progress, they will browse—noticing titles, headings, and first sentences in paragraphs. Model often how you browse.
*(Michael Pressley)*

**Teacher Tip** A creative approach to the second reading of the selection is to read it straight through like a performance. Complete the strategies on the first read so that the performance read is uninterrupted. Be sure to teach the comprehension skills after the performance.

This selection is broken into two parts. On the first day, read pages 94–100. On the second day, read pages 102–107.

## Comprehension Strategies

First Read

Read the story aloud, taking turns with the students. Model the use of strategies for the students.

### Teacher Modeling

**1 Monitoring and Adjusting Reading Speed** *The format of the story is a bit harder to read. There are new elements, like stage directions, that are unlike the previous selections. I'd better slow down my reading speed so that I can clarify who is speaking, who the narrator is, and what is happening.*

### Word Knowledge

**SCAFFOLDING** The skills students are reviewing in Word Knowledge should help them in reading the story. This lesson focuses on inflectional endings, the suffix *-ment,* and words that begin with hard *c.*

*-ed* **endings:**     adapted

**Teacher Tip PRONUNCIATION**
Pythias is pronounced pith´ ē əs.

**First Reading Recommendation**

## ORAL · CHORAL

*Focus Questions* What would be a true test of friendship? What would you be willing to give up for a friend?

# THE LEGEND OF DAMON AND PYTHIAS

adapted as a play by Fan Kissen
*illustrated by Fabricio Vanden Broeck*

## CAST

| | |
|---|---|
| Damon | Second Robber |
| Pythias | First Voice |
| Soldier | Second Voice |
| King | Third Voice |
| Mother | Announcer |
| First Robber | Narrator |

## SOUNDS

*Iron door open and shut*     *Key in lock*

94

**Informal Assessment**

Observe individual students as they read, and use the Teacher Observation Log, found in the *Program Assessment Teacher's Edition,* to record anecdotal information about each student's strengths and weaknesses.

ANNOUNCER: Hello, listeners! It's story time again. Today's story is about the strong friendship between two men. Listen, and you'll hear how one of these men was ready to give up his life for his friend's sake.

MUSIC: (*Up full and out*)

NARRATOR: Long, long ago there lived on the island of Sicily two young men named Damon and Pythias. They were known far and wide for the strong friendship each had for the other. Their names have come down to our own times to mean true friendship. You may hear it said of two persons:

FIRST VOICE: Those two? Why, they're like Damon and Pythias!

95

---

## Comprehension Skills

 Second Read

### Sequence LA.A.2.2.1.3.1

Tell students that looking for the sequence, or order of events, will help improve their understanding of the selection. Tell students to look for clues that tell them in what order events happen. They should periodically place plot events in sequential order. Ask them to look for clues of sequential order on these two pages.

■ The announcer says, "Listen, and you'll hear . . . ." The action is about to start.

■ The first statement of the narrator says, "Long, long ago there lived . . . Damon and Pythias." The narrator begins to tell the action of the story.

Use ***Reading Transparency 52*** to help identify sequence in the story.

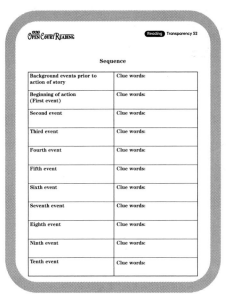

***Reading Transparency 52***

**Second Reading Recommendation**

### ORAL • SILENT

---

### Word Knowledge

*-ed* endings:    lived

---

**Skills Trace**

**Sequence**

Introduced in Grade 1.
Scaffolded throughout Grades 2 and 3.

| | |
|---|---|
| **REINTRODUCED:** | Unit 1, Lesson 6 |
| **REINFORCED:** | Unit 4, Lesson 6 |
| | Unit 5, Lesson 1 |
| **TESTED:** | Unit 1 Assessment |

**COMPREHENSION**

## Comprehension Strategies

First Read

### Teacher Modeling

**2 Monitoring and Adjusting Reading Speed** *I wonder about something else. I see a First Voice and a Second Voice. I'm not sure what this means. I'll slow down my reading to make sure I understand what is happening. I see. Those parts are just for random voices from the crowd. They don't belong to a major character.*

**3 Asking Questions** *I see that Pythias is a brave person. But I have some questions. If the King is so cruel, won't he punish Pythias for disagreeing with him? What will happen to Pythias? I'll read on to find out.*

### Word Knowledge

hard c:     country
            cruel
            come

 **Teacher Tip** ASKING QUESTIONS
Inform students that they should keep asking questions and trying to answer them as they read.

**Teacher Tip** Tell students that good readers keep thinking about the questions that come up about the topic, and they keep coming back to those questions. As they read, tell them to keep the questions on the Concept/Question Board in mind. Have them make notes to themselves in the Response Journal section of their Writer's Notebooks about which questions seem most important. Tell them that good readers always think about what is important in selections, and they try to remember this important information.

**NARRATOR:** The King of that country was a cruel tyrant. He made cruel laws, and he showed no mercy toward anyone who broke his laws. Now, you might very well wonder:

**SECOND VOICE:** Why didn't the people rebel? **2**

**NARRATOR:** Well, the people didn't dare rebel, because they feared the King's great and powerful army. No one dared say a word against the King or his laws—except Damon and Pythias. One day a soldier overheard Pythias speaking against a new law the King had proclaimed.

**SOLDIER:** Ho, there! Who are you, that dares to speak so about our King?

**PYTHIAS:** (*Unafraid*) I am called Pythias. **3**

**SOLDIER:** Don't you know it is a crime to speak against the King or his laws? You are under arrest! Come and tell this opinion of yours to the King's face!

**MUSIC:** (*A few short bars in and out*)

96

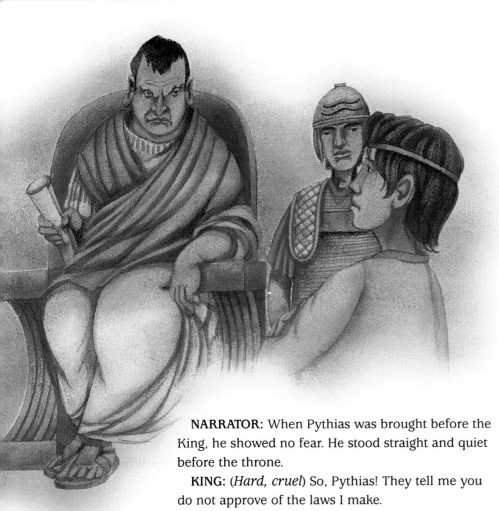

NARRATOR: When Pythias was brought before the King, he showed no fear. He stood straight and quiet before the throne.

KING: (*Hard, cruel*) So, Pythias! They tell me you do not approve of the laws I make.

PYTHIAS: I am not alone, your Majesty, in thinking your laws are cruel. But you rule the people with such an iron hand that they dare not complain.

KING: (*Angry*) But *you* have the daring to complain *for* them! Have they <u>appointed</u> you their <u>champion</u>?

PYTHIAS: No, your Majesty. I speak for myself alone. I have no wish to make trouble for anyone. But I am not afraid to tell you that the people are suffering under your rule. They want to have a voice in making the laws for themselves. You do not allow them to speak up for themselves.

97

## Comprehension Skills

 Second Read

### Sequence  LA.A.2.2.1.3.1

Tell students to keep track of the order of events as they read. Record their answers for the class as they read the story a second time. Point out that clue words, called time-order words, can sometimes help them understand the order of events. These words include *first, second, last, earlier, later, now, then, next, after,* and *finally,* among others. What is the order of events on these two pages?

- First: A soldier overheard Pythias complaining about the new law.
- Next: The soldier arrested Pythias.
- Then: The King was angry with Pythias.

> **Word Knowledge**
> hard *c:*    cruel
>              complain

 **Teacher Tip  SEQUENCE** Tell students that they can use time-order words to retell the order of events in their own words. Using the words will help them have a clear idea of sequence.

 **Teacher Tip** Remind students to use context clues, apposition, or word structure to figure out the meaning of difficult words as they are reading.

**COMPREHENSION**

## Comprehension Strategies

First Read

### Teacher Modeling

**4** **Asking Questions**  *I don't understand something. Why is the King so angry with Pythias? Why is the punishment so harsh? Maybe if I read more, I'll find answers to those questions.*

**5** **Asking Questions**  *How will Pythias be able to take care of his family? Will Damon try to help him in some way?*

> ### Word Knowledge
> *-ing* endings:   calling
>                         speaking

**Teacher Tip  USING STRATEGIES**
Remind students to use all the reading strategies they have learned so far in order to better understand and appreciate the story.

**Teacher Tip  COMPREHENSION**
Good readers are active readers. They interact with the text as they read by emoting, reacting, responding, and problem solving in their efforts to construct and maintain meaning.

**KING:** In other words, you are calling me a tyrant! Well, you shall learn for yourself how a tyrant treats a rebel! Soldier! Throw this man into prison! **4**

**SOLDIER:** At once, your Majesty! Don't try to <u>resist</u>, Pythias!

**PYTHIAS:** I know better than to try to resist a soldier of the King! And for how long am I to remain in prison, your Majesty, merely for speaking out for the people?

**KING:** (*Cruel*) Not for very long, Pythias. Two weeks from today at noon, you shall be put to death in the public square, as an example to anyone else who may dare to question my laws or acts. Off to prison with him, soldier!

**MUSIC:** (*In briefly and out*)

98

**NARRATOR:** When Damon heard that his friend Pythias had been thrown into prison, and the <u>severe</u> punishment that was to follow, he was heartbroken. He rushed to the prison and persuaded the guard to let him speak to his friend.

**DAMON:** Oh, Pythias! How terrible to find you here! I wish I could do something to save you!

**PYTHIAS:** Nothing can save me, Damon, my dear friend. I am prepared to die. But there is one thought that troubles me greatly.

**DAMON:** What is it? I will do anything to help you.

**PYTHIAS:** I'm worried about what will happen to my mother and my sister when I'm gone.

**DAMON:** I'll take care of them, Pythias, as if they were my own mother and sister.

**PYTHIAS:** Thank you, Damon. I have money to leave them. But there are other things I must <u>arrange</u>. If only I could go to see them before I die! But they live two days' <u>journey</u> from here, you know.

99

## Comprehension Skills

Second Read

### Sequence LA.A.2.2.1.3.1

Have students continue to identify the sequence of events using time-order words to retell events. Record their answers on the transparency.

- Next: The King throws Pythias in jail and sentences him to die.
- Then: Damon went to see Pythias in prison.

**Word Knowledge**

*-ment* **endings:**          **punishment**

COMPREHENSION

COMPREHENSION

## Comprehension Strategies

 First Read

### Teacher Modeling

**6 Asking Questions** *I have one answer now. I see that Pythias could take care of his family if Damon could take his place in jail. But now I have another question. Will the King allow them to trade places? Why would he? Who else has questions?*

---

### Word Knowledge

*-ed* endings: appointed

---

**Teacher Tip** THINKING ALOUD
Encourage students to think aloud, practicing the strategies they have learned. Tell students that their ideas about the story are very important to the whole class's understanding of the story.

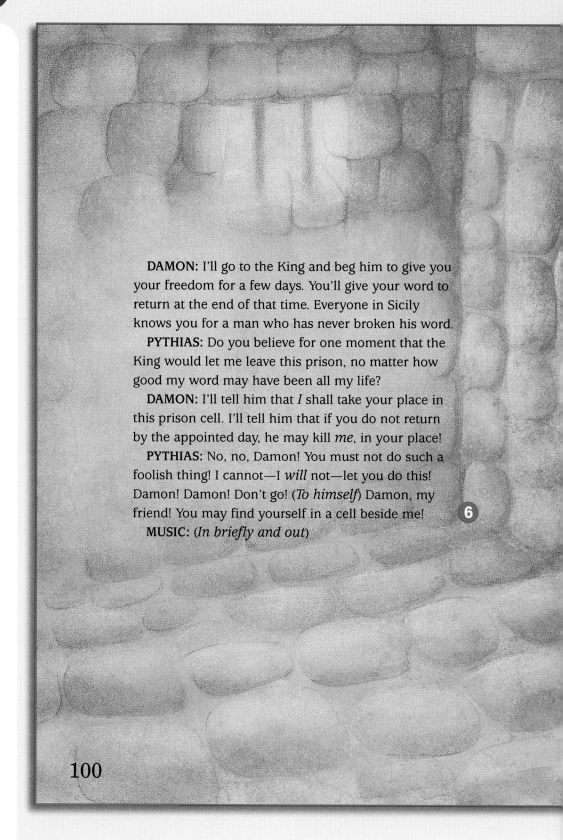

**DAMON:** I'll go to the King and beg him to give you your freedom for a few days. You'll give your word to return at the end of that time. Everyone in Sicily knows you for a man who has never broken his word.

**PYTHIAS:** Do you believe for one moment that the King would let me leave this prison, no matter how good my word may have been all my life?

**DAMON:** I'll tell him that *I* shall take your place in this prison cell. I'll tell him that if you do not return by the appointed day, he may kill *me*, in your place!

**PYTHIAS:** No, no, Damon! You must not do such a foolish thing! I cannot—I *will* not—let you do this! Damon! Damon! Don't go! (*To himself*) Damon, my friend! You may find yourself in a cell beside me! **6**

**MUSIC:** (*In briefly and out*)

100

DAMON: (*Begging*) Your Majesty! I beg of you! Let Pythias go home for a few days to bid farewell to his mother and sister. He gives his word that he will return at your appointed time. Everyone knows that his word can be trusted.

KING: In ordinary business affairs—perhaps. But he is now a man under sentence of death. To free him even for a few days would strain his honesty—*any* man's honesty—too far. Pythias would never return here! I consider him a traitor, but I'm certain he's no fool.

DAMON: Your Majesty! I will take his place in the prison until he comes back. If he does not return, then you may take *my* life in his place.

101

## Comprehension Skills

### Sequence LA.A.2.2.1.3.1

Have students continue to look for the sequence of events in the selection. Remind them that certain words, called time-order words, can be used to show sequence. Even if the writer does not use these words in the selection, students can use the words to explain sequence. Have them practice using these words in sentences they make up from the information on the transparency.

- Next, Damon offered to take the place of Pythias in prison.
- Finally, Pythias agreed to let Damon ask the King for permission.
- Then Damon tells the King he can take Damon's life in place of his friend if he does not return.

### Word Knowledge

| -*ed* endings: | appointed |
|---|---|
| | trusted |

COMPREHENSION

COMPREHENSION

## Comprehension Strategies

First Read

### Teacher Modeling

**7 Answering Questions** *Now I have some more answers to my questions. The King is going to let Damon stay in place of Pythias. The King is allowing the exchange because he is curious to see if a friend could really be loyal enough to come back and save his friend. Will he come back?*

**8 Summarizing** *Good readers summarize story events as they read. This looks like a good place to stop and summarize all that's happened. Let's see, first, Pythias was thrown in prison and sentenced to die for speaking against a new law. Then Damon offered to take the place of Pythias so he could take care of his family. Now Damon is waiting in prison for Pythias to return and will die if Pythias does not come back in time.*

---

### Word Knowledge

*-ing* endings:    offering
                   willing

---

🍎 **Teacher Tip  USING STRATEGIES**
Be sure to encourage all the students to use strategies. Call on various students to share which strategies they are using and to tell how they are using them to figure out the meaning of the text.

---

KING: (*Astonished*) What did you say, Damon?
DAMON: I'm so certain of Pythias that I am offering to die in his place if he fails to return on time.
KING: I can't believe you mean it!
DAMON: I do mean it, your Majesty.
KING: You make me very <u>curious</u>, Damon, so curious that I'm willing to put you and Pythias to the test. This exchange of prisoners will be made. But Pythias must be back two weeks from today, at noon.
DAMON: Thank you, your Majesty!
KING: The order with my official seal shall go by your own hand, Damon. But I warn you, if your friend **7** does not return on time, you shall surely die in his place! I shall show no mercy.

102

**MUSIC:** (*In briefly and out*)

**NARRATOR:** Pythias did not like the King's <u>bargain</u> with Damon. He did not like to leave his friend in prison, with the chance that he might lose his life if something went wrong. But at last Damon persuaded him to leave, and Pythias set out for his home. More than a week went by. The day set for the death sentence drew near. Pythias did not return. Everyone in the city knew of the condition on which the King had permitted Pythias to go home. Everywhere people met, the talk was sure to turn to the two friends. **8**

**FIRST VOICE:** Do you suppose Pythias will come back?

**SECOND VOICE:** Why should he stick his head under the King's axe, once he's escaped?

**THIRD VOICE:** Still, would an <u>honorable</u> man like Pythias let such a good friend die for him?

103

## Comprehension Skills

### Sequence LA.A.2.2.1.3.1

Have students continue to add to the transparency the events of the selection in sequential order. As the transparency fills, you may have to add more boxes or create a second copy to continue filling in.

- Next: The King agrees to let Damon stay in place of Pythias.
- Then: Pythias left to take care of his family.
- Next: Pythias did not return after a week.

> ### Word Knowledge
> *-ed* endings:      persuaded

COMPREHENSION

## Comprehension Strategies

**First Read**

### Teacher Modeling

**9** **Monitoring and Adjusting Reading Speed** *I see a word I don't understand: mocking. I can't tell what it means from looking at the words around it. Maybe I should slow down my reading to see if I understand the whole passage and then figure out the word. I see the crowd is making fun of Damon in a mean way. But the King doesn't say the word; it is part of the stage directions. I think "mocking" is the way the actor is supposed to read the King's line.*

---

### Word Knowledge

*-ing* endings:   **telling**
                  **killing**

---

**Teacher Tip** Help students to understand that each person's response to a text is a very individual matter and that no two people will respond in exactly the same way. Encourage students to respect each other's contributions.

---

**FIRST VOICE:** There's no telling what a man will do when it's a question of his own life against another's.

**SECOND VOICE:** But if Pythias doesn't come back before the time is up, he will be killing his friend.

**THIRD VOICE:** Well, there's still a few days' time. I, for one, am certain that Pythias *will* return in time.

**SECOND VOICE:** And *I* am just as certain that he will *not*. Friendship is friendship, but a man's own life is something stronger, *I* say!

104

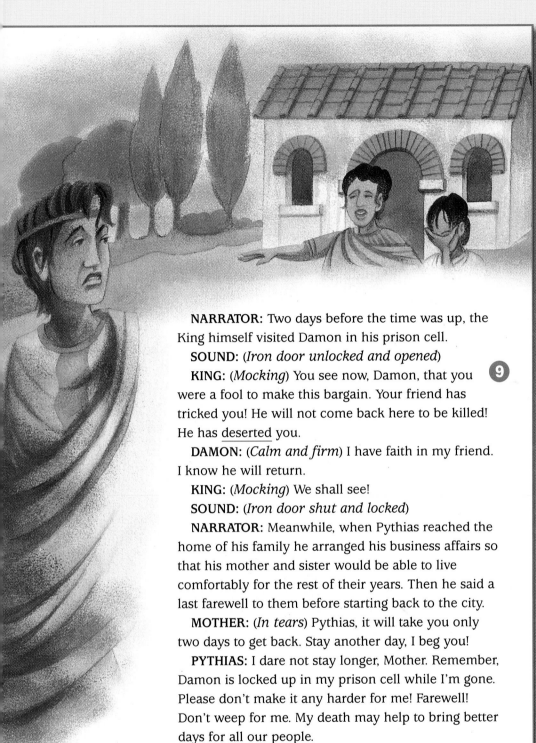

NARRATOR: Two days before the time was up, the King himself visited Damon in his prison cell.

SOUND: (*Iron door unlocked and opened*)

KING: (*Mocking*) You see now, Damon, that you were a fool to make this bargain. Your friend has tricked you! He will not come back here to be killed! He has <u>deserted</u> you.

DAMON: (*Calm and firm*) I have faith in my friend. I know he will return.

KING: (*Mocking*) We shall see!

SOUND: (*Iron door shut and locked*)

NARRATOR: Meanwhile, when Pythias reached the home of his family he arranged his business affairs so that his mother and sister would be able to live comfortably for the rest of their years. Then he said a last farewell to them before starting back to the city.

MOTHER: (*In tears*) Pythias, it will take you only two days to get back. Stay another day, I beg you!

PYTHIAS: I dare not stay longer, Mother. Remember, Damon is locked up in my prison cell while I'm gone. Please don't make it any harder for me! Farewell! Don't weep for me. My death may help to bring better days for all our people.

105

## Comprehension Skills

### Sequence LA.A.2.2.1.3.1

Have students continue to read carefully to place selection events in order. Encourage them to continue using time-order words as they retell events.

- Next: the King visits Damon to mock him because Pythias has not returned.
- Then: Damon does not lose faith in his friend.
- Next: Pythias leaves his family to return and save Damon's life.

#### Word Knowledge
hard *c*:     come
          calm

**Teacher Tip** Ensure that students understand that events occur in the outside physical worlds and the internal mental worlds of the characters.

## Comprehension Strategies

 First Read

### Teacher Modeling

**⑩ Asking Questions** *I see that Pythias did leave his family to come back and save Damon. That answers one of my questions. But will the robbers prevent him from returning? Does anyone else have questions here?*

---

### Word Knowledge

**-ed endings:**  walked

---

 **Teacher Tip** **WAIT TIME** Make sure to allow students enough time to respond. Although silence can be uncomfortable, don't automatically jump in with your own response—wait.

---

**NARRATOR:** So Pythias began his journey in plenty of time. But bad luck struck him on the very first day. At twilight, as he walked along a lonely stretch of woodland, a rough voice called:

**FIRST ROBBER:** Not so fast there, young man! Stop!

**PYTHIAS:** (*Startled*) Oh! What is it? What do you want?

**SECOND ROBBER:** Your money bags.

**PYTHIAS:** My money bags? I have only this small bag of coins. I shall need them for some favors, perhaps, before I die.

**FIRST ROBBER:** What do you mean, before you die? We don't mean to kill you, only take your money.

**PYTHIAS:** I'll give you my money, only don't delay me any longer. I am to die by the King's order three days from now. If I don't return to prison on time, my friend must die in my place.

**FIRST ROBBER:** A likely story! What man would be fool enough to go back to prison, ready to die.

**SECOND ROBBER:** And what man would be fool enough to die *for* you?

**FIRST ROBBER:** We'll take your money, all right. And we'll tie you up while we get away.

**PYTHIAS:** (*Begging*) No! No! I must get back to free **⑩** my friend! (*Fade*) I must go back!

106

NARRATOR: But the two robbers took Pythias's money, tied him to a tree, and went off as fast as they could. Pythias struggled to free himself. He cried out for help as loud as he could, for a long time. But no one traveled through that lonesome woodland after dark. The sun had been up for many hours before he finally managed to free himself from the ropes that had tied him to the tree. He lay on the ground, hardly able to breathe.

MUSIC: (*In briefly and out*)

NARRATOR: After a while Pythias got to his feet. Weak and dizzy from hunger and thirst and his struggle to free himself, he set off again. Day and night he traveled without stopping, desperately trying to reach the city in time to save Damon's life.

MUSIC: (*Up and out*)

107

## Comprehension Skills

**Second Read**

### Sequence LA.A.2.2.1.3.1

Identifying sequence in a story is an ongoing process. Readers should continue noticing events and time-order words and placing events in order.

- Next: Pythias is tied up by robbers and can't return to save Damon.
- Then: Pythias freed himself from the ropes and rushed to return to the city in time.

### Word Knowledge

**-ed endings:**  struggled
traveled
managed

**COMPREHENSION**

## Comprehension Strategies

 First Read

### Teacher Modeling

**11** **Summarizing** *I want to stop here and make sure I have kept track of everything that's happened. After Pythias took care of his family, he left in plenty of time to save Damon, but he was detained. Damon was just about to be killed, and now Pythias has arrived to save the life of his friend who was willing to die in his place. The people are happy to see this strong friendship and want to see them both freed.*

### Discussing Strategy Use LA.A.1.2.4.3.1

After students read the selection, encourage them to share any problems encountered and to tell what strategies they used.

- How did they clarify confusing passages?

- What questions did they ask as they read?

- Where did they pause in the reading to summarize?

These are questions good readers ask after they read a text. After reading, they should always be asking, "What did I find interesting? What is important here?" Later, remind the students again that whenever they conclude a reading, they should ask themselves questions about what was in the text.

**Science/Social Studies Connection Center**
SC.E.2.2.1.3.1
Refer to the *Science/Social Studies Connection Center* Card 7 for a science activity that students can investigate.

108

NARRATOR: On the last day, half an hour before noon, Damon's hands were tied behind his back and he was taken into the public square. The people muttered angrily as Damon was led in by the jailer. Then the King entered and seated himself on a high platform.

SOUND: (*Crowd voices in and hold under single voices*)

SOLDIER: (*Loud*) Long live the King!

FIRST VOICE: (*Low*) The longer he lives, the more miserable our lives will be!

KING: (*Loud, mocking*) Well, Damon, your lifetime is nearly up. Where is your good friend Pythias now?

DAMON: (*Firm*) I have faith in my friend. If he has not returned, I'm certain it is through no fault of his own.

KING: (*Mocking*) The sun is almost overhead. The shadow is almost at the noon mark. And still your friend has not returned to give you back your life!

DAMON: (*Quiet*) I am ready, and happy, to die in his place.

KING: (*Harsh*) And you shall, Damon! Jailer, lead the prisoner to the—

SOUND: (*Crowd voices up to a roar, then under*)

FIRST VOICE: (*Over noise*) Look! It's Pythias!

SECOND VOICE: (*Over noise*) Pythias has come back!

PYTHIAS: (*Breathless*) Let me through! Damon!

DAMON: Pythias!

PYTHIAS: Thank the gods I'm not too late!

DAMON: (*Quiet, sincere*) I would have died for you gladly, my friend.

CROWD VOICES: (*Loud, demanding*) Set them free! Set them both free!

 **Teacher Tip BUILDING FLUENCY**
As students read, you may notice that some need work in building fluency. During Workshop, have these students select a section of the text (a minimum of 160 words) to read several times in order to build fluency.

 **Informal Assessment**

Use the Informal Comprehension Strategies Rubrics on page 94J to determine whether a student is using the strategies being taught.

**KING:** (*Loud*) People of the city! (*Crowd voices out*) Never in all my life have I seen such faith and friendship, such <u>loyalty</u> between men. There are many among you who call me harsh and cruel. But I cannot kill *any* man who proves such strong and true friendship for another. Damon and Pythias, I set you both free. (*Roar of approval from crowd*) I am King. I command a great army. I have stores of gold and precious jewels. But I would give all my money and power for one friend like Damon or Pythias.

**SOUND:** (*Roar of approval from crowd up briefly and out*)

**MUSIC:** (*Up and out*)

109

**Formal Assessment**

See pages 22–25 in *Unit 1 Assessment* to test students' comprehension of "The Legend of Damon and Pythias."

**COMPREHENSION**

## Comprehension Skills

Second Read

### Sequence  LA.A.2.2.1.3.1

Remind students that identifying the sequence of events can help them better understand the selections they read. Encourage them to think about and discuss the order of events after reading this selection.

- Next: Damon was about to die because Pythias had not yet returned.
- Then: Damon returned just in time.
- Finally: The King was so moved by their loyalty that he set them both free.

### Checking Comprehension  LA.E.1.2.3.3.3, LA.E.2.2.4.3.1

Ask students the following questions to check their comprehension of the selection.

- How do the characters in this selection show friendship? (*Damon stayed in prison so Pythias could take care of his family. Pythias returned to the city to be killed, even after he was free, so his friend wouldn't have to die.*)
- Why were the friends able to stay so loyal to each other? (*Because they trusted each other. They each knew the other was an honorable person.*)
- Why did the King set them both free? (*Because he had never seen such true friendship. He knew it would be wrong to kill such an honorable person.*)

**Teacher Tip  FLUENCY** By this time in third grade, good readers should be reading approximately 107 words per minute with fluency and expression. The only way to gain this fluency is through practice. Have students reread the selection to you and to each other during Workshop to help build fluency.

**Routine Card**
Refer to *Routine 6* for the *handing-off process.*

| Clues | Problems | Wonderings |
|-------|----------|------------|
| One character seems to be in trouble with the king. | narrator | How do Damon and Pythias become models of true friendship? |

OPEN COURT READING
Reading Transparency 46

**Reading Transparency 46**

**www.sra4kids.com**
**Web Connection**
Some students may choose to conduct a computer search for additional books or information about friendship. Invite them to make a list of these books and sources of information to share with classmates and the school librarian. Check the Reading link of the SRA Web page for additional links to the theme-related Web site.

# Discussing the Selection LA.C.1.2.3.3.1, LA.C.3.2.2.3.1; LA.E.1.2.1.3.1

After the first read, the whole group discusses the selection and any personal thoughts, reactions, problems, or questions that it raises. To stimulate discussion, students can ask one another the kinds of questions that good readers ask themselves about a text: *What did I find interesting about this play? What is important here? What was difficult to understand? Why would someone want to read this? How does the selection connect to the theme of Friendship?*

**Handing-Off Process**   Seeing you as a contributing member of the group sets a strong example for students. To emphasize that you are part of the group, actively participate in the *handing-off process*: Raise your hand to be called on by the last speaker when you have a contribution to make. Point out unusual and interesting insights verbalized by students so that these insights are recognized and discussed. As the year progresses, students will take more and more responsibility for the discussions of the selections.

Engage students in a discussion to determine whether they have grasped the following ideas:

- how the King's ideas change by the end of the story and why they changed.
- how students feel about the King's actions and about the actions of Damon and Pythias.
- why the friends were willing to sacrifice so much for each other.

During this time, have students return to the clues, problems, and wonderings they noted during browsing to determine whether the clues were borne out by the selection, whether and how their problems were solved, and whether their wonderings were answered or deserve further discussion and investigation. Let the students decide which items deserve further discussion.

Also, have students return to the Focus Questions on the first page of the selection. Select a student to read the questions aloud, and have volunteers answer the questions. If students do not know the answers to the questions, have them return to the text to find the answers.

You may wish to review the elements of a myth with the students at this time. Discuss with them how they can tell "The Legend of Damon and Pythias" is a myth.

Have students break into small groups to discuss what this story tells them about how important sharing is in friendship. Groups can discuss their ideas with the rest of the class.

*Writer's Notebook*   If they have ever had a special friendship with someone or if they have ever witnessed a situation between two people who demonstrated great trust and loyalty, encourage them to record those events.

# Review Selection Vocabulary

Have students review the definitions of the selection vocabulary words that they wrote in the Vocabulary section of their Writer's Notebooks. Remind them that they discussed the meanings of these words before reading the selection. Have students write sentences for each of the vocabulary words after the definitions in the same section of their Writer's Notebooks. They can use the definitions and the sentences to study for the vocabulary portion of their Lesson Assessments. Have them add to the personal dictionary section of their Writer's Notebooks any other interesting words that they clarified while reading. Encourage students to refer to the selection vocabulary words throughout the unit. The words from the selection are:

**tyrant      appointed      rebel      traitor      honorable**

If you created a Word Bank of key words related to the theme Friendship, remind students to find words from other resources, from their activities, and from family discussions and add them to the Word Bank. Students may also place synonyms and antonyms in the Word Bank, or organize words by parts of speech.

# Home Connection

Distribute **Home Connection,** page 13. Encourage students to discuss "The Legend of Damon and Pythias" with their families. Students will have the opportunity to read library books about other legendary figures with their families. **Home Connection** is also available in Spanish, page 14.

*Home Connection p. 13*

**Reading Transparency 50**

**Teacher Tip  ASKING QUESTIONS**
Inform students that they should keep asking questions and trying to answer them as they read.

## Supporting the Reading  LA.C.3.2.2.3.1

### Comprehension Strategies: Asking Questions

**Teach**  Tell students that asking strategic questions helps them focus their attention on important points. Asking questions also leads students to a deeper understanding of themes, concepts and ideas in texts.

**Guided Practice**  Have students reflect on the wonderings they recorded before reading the play. In a two-column chart, such as *Reading Transparency 50,* have them record in the first column those questions and others they asked themselves during the reading. In the second column, have them record the answers they found by reading more of the play. You can start by displaying the following example:

| My Questions | Answers |
|---|---|
| Why was the King so angry with Pythias? | The King was angry because he considered Pythias to be a traitor. |

**Independent Practice**  Encourage students to practice using this strategy in their own personal reading. Tell them to record questions in the Wonderings column of the Clues, Problems, Wonderings chart and look for answers as they read.

**Link to Writing**  Have students write the play in narrative form, using the dialogue as a guide. Afterwards, invite students to exchange their stories and compare their versions of the play.

# Literary Elements LA.C.1.2.1.3.1; LA.E.1.2.1.3.1

## Features of a Play

**Teach** Ask students to tell you what they know about plays. Tell them that although they can be read and enjoyed, plays are meant to be performed. The writer of a play tells the story through the words and actions of the characters, with actors portraying the characters.

When writing a play, the writer includes directions for the actors and others involved in producing the play. These directions tell how the stage is to look, when music should be used, and what props are needed. The writer's directions also tell the actors where to move and how to speak in order to show each character's feelings.

**Guided Practice** Show *Reading Transparency 9* to students and discuss the features of a play. Allow students to identify those features in the play they have just read. Discuss any other elements of a play that students have noticed, as well as any questions they have about the play format.

**Independent Practice** Identify the parts of a play and put them to use in a classroom production of "The Legend of Damon and Pythias."

*Reading Transparency 9*

## MEETING INDIVIDUAL NEEDS

### Challenge

Have advanced learners create, write, and perform a play of their own for the class.

**Teacher Tip** Be sure students use clear and specific vocabulary to communicate ideas and establish the tone.

 **Teacher Tip MATERIALS**
- ✔ poster board
- ✔ colored pencils or markers
- ✔ sheets
- ✔ simple masks made in the style of Greek theater (Make masks from cardboard and string, or papier-mâché, if time allows.)

 **Teacher Tip PURPOSE** To make students aware of the significant achievements in Greek art, particularly drama, and its contribution to modern theater.

## Social Studies Connection

### Greek Drama

"The Legend of Damon and Pythias" is a modern adaptation of an ancient Greek legend. Perhaps the writer of this version chose to write a play because he knows that modern drama has its roots in ancient Greek drama.

Allow groups of students to do library research to find out when drama began. They should be able to identify the major features of Greek theater and describe what productions looked like. Groups can create a visual aid, including objects, photographs, and charts, to accompany their findings and give a presentation to the class.

Some aspects of Greek drama your students might investigate are the following:

- Modern drama has its roots in Greece, 6th century BC, as part of the worship of Dionysus.
- The chorus danced and chanted during worship.
- The chant was called *tragos*, which is the origin of the word *tragedy*.
- Ceremonies evolved into drama contests.
- Eventually, actors separated from the chorus, but the chorus remained a feature of Greek drama.
- At first, actors and spectators were only men.
- The hut behind the acting area for changing masks and costumes was called the *skene*.
- The actors wore exaggerated masks.

# Science Connection SC.E.1.2.1.3.1, SC.E.1.2.3.3.1, SC.E.2.2.1.3.1

## Stars and Constellations

In "The Legend of Damon and Pythias," the King warns Damon of his impending deadline saying, "The sun is almost overhead. The shadow is almost at the noon mark." Ask the students what the King means by this. Explain that one can tell time from looking at the sun and the shadow it casts. To demonstrate, ask for volunteers to move the ball around the light, mimicking Earth's rotation around the sun. Placing the construction paper on the floor, mark the placement of different shadows. Explain that the shadow created by an object blocking the sun creates, what the King called, the noon mark shadow.

Next, explain that the sun is a star, just like the other stars in the night sky. And just like the sun telling the time of day, Ancient Greeks could tell the time of year by the movement of the stars. The Ancient Greek astronomers grouped the stars into constellations. Have the students break into groups and research a constellation, using resources such as encyclopedias, the Internet, reference books, or other teachers. You might want to put the names of constellations in a hat to be drawn or on the board for the students to choose. The group's goal is to find out what their constellation looks like and cut out stars, paste them onto paper, then draw the figure the Greeks believed the constellation looked like. While the students conduct their research, ask them to find out when their constellation can be seen in the night sky. Invite groups to present their pictures and information to the class.

**Teacher Tip MATERIALS**
- ✔ lamp
- ✔ ball
- ✔ white poster board
- ✔ colored construction paper
- ✔ scissors
- ✔ glue
- ✔ colored pencils or markers

**Teacher Tip PURPOSE** To help students understand the movement of the sun and other stars in the night sky.

**Teacher Tip** Make sure the students know what the constellation is supposed to resemble. Here is a list of some highly visible, well-known constellations:

| | |
|---|---|
| Andromeda: | the Princess |
| Cetus: | the Whale |
| Draco: | the Dragon |
| Gemini: | the Twins |
| Hercules | |
| Leo: | the Lion |
| Orion: | the Hunter |
| Pisces: | the Fish |
| The Pleiades: | the Seven Sisters |
| Ursa Major: | the Great Bear |

### Science/Social Studies Connection Center

Refer to the *Science/Social Studies Connection Center* Card 6 for a science activity that students can investigate.

## Meet the Author

After students read the information about Fan Kissen, discuss the following questions with them.

- Why do you think Fan Kissen writes her plays like her radio shows? *(Possible answer: She likes to use music and sound effects for added effect in her plays as well as in her radio shows.)*

- How might Kissen's travels have influenced her writing? *(Possible answer: She has learned folk tales and legends, like Damon and Pythias, from all over the world. She can write both American legends and those from other cultures.)*

## Meet the Illustrator

After students read the information about Fabricio Vanden Broeck, discuss the following questions with them.

- How might studying art in two different continents have helped Broeck's illustrations? *(Possible answer: He has experienced different cultures and countries. This helps him draw different types of people and lifestyles.)*

- Why do you think Broeck is able to be successful as a children's book illustrator and a newspaper illustrator? *(Possible answer: Both books and newspapers need illustrations to help tell stories.)*

# THE LEGEND OF DAMON AND PYTHIAS

## Meet the Author

**Fan Kissen** writes plays for eight to ten year olds. These plays often tell folktales and legends, such as the Greek myth of Damon and Pythias. She writes her plays in the same style as one would write a radio show, by including announcers, sound effects, and background music. She has received many awards for her successful radio series, *Tales from the Four Winds*. Kissen has traveled to South America, Europe, and the Near East. She speaks French, German, and a little Italian.

## Meet the Illustrator

**Fabricio Vanden Broeck** was born in Mexico City. He went on to study art in Mexico and Europe. His illustrations have appeared in children's books, exhibits, and newspapers. Displays of Broeck's work have been shown around the world. In the United States, his illustrations have appeared in the famous newspaper, *The New York Times*.

110

# Theme Connections

## Within the Selection

 Record your answers to the questions below in the Response Journal section of your Writer's Notebook. In small groups, report the ideas you wrote. Discuss your ideas with the rest of the group. Then choose a person to report your group's answers to the class.

- What did Damon do to show his friendship for Pythias?
- How did the friendship of Damon and Pythias save their lives?

## Across Selections

- How is this story different from the other stories you have read?
- How are Damon and Pythias like the other friends you have read about? How are they different?

## Beyond the Selection

- Think about how "The Legend of Damon and Pythias" adds to what you know about friendship.
- Add items to the Concept/Question Board about friendship.

111

# Theme Connections

## Within the Selection

- Damon took Pythias's place in jail so that Pythias could see his family.
- The King could not kill anyone who had shown such true friendship.

## Across Selections

- "The Legend of Damon and Pythias" is a story written as a play.
- Damon and Pythias cared about each other. They were in a position, however, to make a much bigger sacrifice for their friendship than the other friends had to make.

## Beyond the Selection

Have groups report their ideas to the class. Have students add these ideas to the Concept/Question Board. Have students sum up what they have learned and tell how they might use this in their investigations.

## Inquiry Journal

Students should record their ideas and impressions about the selections on page 4 of their *Inquiry Journals*.

Recording Concept Information *(continued)*

- "Teammates" by Peter Golenbock

  Answers will vary.

- "The Legend of Damon and Pythias" adapted by Fan Kissen

  Answers will vary.

4  UNIT I          *Recording Concept Information • Inquiry Journal*

*Inquiry Journal p. 4*

 **Teacher Tip** These activities may be done during Workshop.

**Informal Assessment**

This may be a good time to observe students working in small groups and to mark your observations in the Teacher Observation Log found in the *Program Assessment Teacher's Edition.*

## Objectives

- Students gain a deeper understanding of friendship.
- Students make final revisions to investigation plans.
- Students prepare and present presentations of investigation results.

## Materials

- Student Anthology, Book 1, pp. 94–111
- Research Assistant CD-ROM

**INVESTIGATION**

LA.C.3.2.2.3.1, LA.C.3.2.5.3.1

# Investigating Concepts Beyond the Text

At this point, students should be concluding their investigations. Groups that are giving presentations should begin putting them together, although some revision might be necessary before the final presentation.

As the unit comes to an end, you might consider providing additional class time for the students to finish their investigations, completing the visual and written portions of their projects. Arrange ample time for formal presentations, spreading them out over several days.

Remind students of the recursive nature of investigations. Students should be continually raising new questions and forming new conjectures. Even as the unit concludes and presentations are taking place, students should be discussing the theme.

Even though the formal investigation is concluding, students may want to further investigate this topic. Have the groups meet to discuss questions or ideas they might have about the selection they have just read. Does the selection tell them something about friendship that they hadn't thought of before? Does the selection make them wonder about something? After reading "The Legend of Damon and Pythias," students might wish to discuss situations in which they would stand by a trusted friend. Groups can then plan a scene to illustrate such a situation. They might consider turning the scene into a miniplay, including a cast list; a description of the setting; stage directions; comments from the narrator, if needed, to explain the situation; and dialogue.

# Concept/Question Board

After reading each selection, students should use the Concept/Question Board to do the following:

- Post any questions they asked about a selection before reading that haven't been answered yet.
- Refer to as they formulate statements about concepts that apply to their investigations.
- Post general statements formulated by each collaborative group.
- Continue to post news articles or other items that they find during the unit investigation.
- Read and think about posted questions, articles, or concepts that interest them and provide answers to the questions.

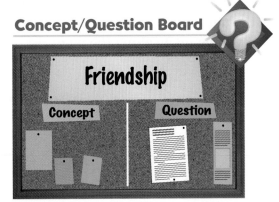

**Concept/Question Board**

Friendship

Concept    Question

**INVESTIGATION**

**Teacher Tip** If students' investigations have been going well, they will be eager for a chance to share their findings and not so eager to hear how others are doing. If you have students who are anxious to share information, let them report briefly to remove that pressure. Then return to the larger group and refocus discussion.

## Research Assistant

The *Research Assistant CD-ROM* can assist students with their investigations.

## Unit I  Investigation Management

| Lesson I | Introduce the investigation cycle and explain its purpose. Students can hold a panel discussion to discuss friendship-related issues. |
|---|---|
| Lesson 2 | Students can investigate immigration and forming new friendships or other areas of investigation related to friendship. Students should organize into groups based on shared areas of interest. |
| Lesson 3 | Students investigate mending damaged friendships, and groups begin forming conjectures. |
| Lesson 4 | Students begin their investigations. Groups can share personal stories, hold a panel discussion, or invite an expert speaker to class. |
| Lesson 5 | Students revise investigation plans as necessary. Groups discuss teammate qualities and invite a coach to class to interview. |
| Lesson 6 | **Collaborative Investigation** <br> **Students wrap up investigations and prepare formal presentations.** <br><br> **Supplementary Activities** <br> **Students discuss standing by friends and write a scene or miniplay about a scenario.** |

**Informal Assessment**

Observe and assess students during their oral presentations. Record your observations in the Teacher Observation Log found in the *Program Assessment Teacher's Edition.*

 **Formal Assessment**

Use the Research Rubrics on page 94J to assess students' ability to communicate research progress and results. Also, use this rubric to assess students' overall research.

# Presentations and Proposed Questions

Now that students have been investigating the concept of friendship for several weeks, they may have new insights they would like to discuss with others or record for themselves. Looking over the entries they've made in their *Inquiry Journals* will show them how far they've come in their investigations.

As students are concluding their investigations, remind them to look at questions and ideas they had at the beginning of the unit. Have those ideas changed? If so, in what ways have they changed? What do they know now that they didn't know before?

Have students propose new questions and form new conjectures based on their readings, activities, and investigations of this unit's theme. Encourage students to pursue these questions on their own if they desire. Remind them of the never-ending nature of research and investigation and of the discoveries that will be made along the way.

# ABC Order

**Teach** Ask students what they remember about ABC order. To review the importance of understanding ABC order, ask students to tell what sources of information are written in alphabetical order *(dictionaries, encyclopedias, indexes, glossaries, and phone books)*.

**Guided Practice** Write the following words on the board. Ask how the words are alike. Have students write three more words on their own papers to add to the list. Have students write the list from the board and their words in alphabetical order.

| | |
|---|---|
| baseball | bowling |
| swimming | basketball |
| tennis | soccer |
| sailing | |

**Independent Practice** As students are wrapping up projects, they need to keep track of tasks and information. Have them create a chart of group members' names placed in ABC order. Then, next to names, students can list the remaining tasks each group member has left to perform.

SUPPORTING THE INVESTIGATION

## MEETING INDIVIDUAL NEEDS

### Challenge

**ALPHABETICAL ORDER** Ask students to choose a category and write ten words that belong in that category. Have them exchange lists with a friend. Each student puts the friend's words in alphabetical order.

**Teacher Tip** Provide a visual alphabet on students' desks or in a place in the room that all students can see.

## Objectives

**Word Analysis**

**Spelling**
- **Review of Short Vowel Sounds.** Review understanding of spelling patterns for short vowel sounds.

**Vocabulary**
- **Vocabulary Strategies.** Using words from "The Legend of Damon and Pythias," learn to apply Word Mapping, Grouping, and Comparisons to fully recognize the meaning of a word.

**Writing Process Strategies**
- **Publishing.** Presenting final writing will be covered in this lesson.

**English Language Conventions**

**Grammar, Usage, and Mechanics**
- **Skills Review.** Display knowledge and understanding of nouns, pronouns, verbs, and sentences learned in Lessons 1–5.

**Listening, Speaking, Viewing**
- **Presenting: Sharing Information.** Develop presentation skills through paraphrasing and presenting information to the class.

**Penmanship**
- **Cursive Letters *q, g,* and *o*.** Develop handwriting skills by practicing formation of cursive *q, g,* and *o*.

## Materials
- Language Arts Handbook
- Comprehension and Language Arts Skills, pp. 24–25
- Spelling and Vocabulary Skills, pp. 22–25
- Writer's Workbook, p. 5
- Language Arts Transparencies 2, 33
- Student Anthology
- Sound/Spelling Cards 1, 5, 9, 15, 21

## MEETING INDIVIDUAL NEEDS

*Reteach, Challenge, English-Language Development,* and *Intervention* lessons are available to support the language arts instruction in this lesson.

## Research in Action

*Publishing* is used in composition to refer to the act of making a finished paper public.... Making a paper public may involve simply sharing it aloud with other students or posting it on a bulletin board or some other place where people can read the work....
*(James D. Williams,* Preparing to Teach Writing: Research, Theory, and Practice)

**OVERVIEW**

# Language Arts Overview

## Word Analysis

**Spelling** The Spelling activities on the following pages review the /a/, /e/, /i/, /o/, and /u/ sounds by developing spelling skills through various strategies.

### Selection Spelling Words

These words from "The Legend of Damon and Pythias" contain short vowel sounds.

str**u**ggle    r**o**bbers    l**a**st    pr**i**son    t**e**ll

**Vocabulary** The Vocabulary activities introduce how word mapping, word grouping, and word comparisons can help students develop word consciousness.

### Vocabulary Skill Words

**tyrant*    champion    traitor*    astonished    mocking**
*\*Also Selection Vocabulary*

## Writing Process Strategies

The Writing Process Strategies lesson involves instruction in publishing the writers' final copy, including choosing the best presentation, or ways to showcase the writing. As practice for this skill, students will publish their autobiographies.

**Basic Computer Skills** To reinforce basic computer skills, you might want to help students toggle between open documents, access the Help feature, and use the Find feature to find files on the computer. *Basic Computer Skills,* Level 3, Lessons 3–6, teach these basic computer skills. LA.D.2.2.4.3.1

## English Language Conventions

**Grammar, Usage, and Mechanics** **Review.** This lesson reviews the skills learned in Lessons 1–5.

**Listening, Speaking, Viewing** **Presenting: Sharing Information.** In this Presenting lesson, students will develop presentation skills through paraphrasing ideas they tell to one another and sharing information with the class.

**Penmanship** **Cursive Letters *q, g,* and *o*.** This lesson continues the development of cursive handwriting skills by having students learn correct formation of *q, g,* and *o*. Students then practice writing words from the literature selection that contain those letters.

# DAY 1

## Word Analysis

### Spelling LA.B.1.2.2.3.7

**Assessment: Pretest**

**Short Vowel Sounds** LA.A.1.2.2.3.1

#### Teach

Give students the Pretest found on page 36 of *Unit 1 Assessment* as entry assessment of the spelling pattern. Have them proofread and correct any misspelled words.

#### Pretest Sentences

1. **brand** Many people like a certain **brand** of toothpaste.
2. **candy** Most **candy** is sweet.
3. **plan** My sister will **plan** the party.
4. **hobby** Quilting is a **hobby**.
5. **best** A blue ribbon goes to the **best** entry in a contest.
6. **read** Have you **read** this book?
7. **us** Electricity helps **us** use computers and lamps.
8. **top** There are high altitudes at the **top** of a mountain.
9. **jump** Can you **jump** very high?
10. **send** We **send** postcards from the beach.
11. **tell** Books **tell** stories.
12. **prison** A **prison** sentence is the length of time to serve.
13. **last** The finale is the **last** song.
14. **robbers** Stealing is a crime committed by **robbers**.
15. **struggle** The **struggle** for freedom led to the Civil War.

Diagnose any misspellings by determining whether students misspelled the short vowel sound or some other part of the word. Then use the Pretest as a take-home list to study the spellings of words with short vowel sounds.

## Writing Process Strategies

### Publishing LA.B.1.2.3.3.5

**Introduction to the Writing Process**

#### Teach

**Introduce Writing Process Steps**
Read *Language Arts Handbook,* pages 42–43, to introduce the publishing step of the writing process.

**Inspiration**
Teacher Model: *"I have worked very hard on my writing. Now I want to make sure it looks good so people will want to read it."*

**Brainstorming**
Discuss ways different kinds of writing can be published and presented. For example, stories can be illustrated and bound into books; letters can be mailed; charts or tables can be added to reports; news stories can be printed in a local or school newspaper. Ask students to think of ways that an autobiography can be presented.

### Guided Practice

**Publishing**
- Have students list different ideas for presentation.
- Have students look over their autobiographies and make notes of ideas they have for publishing.

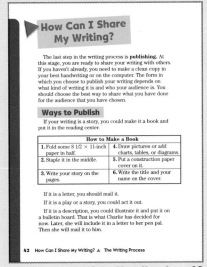

*Language Arts Handbook p. 42*

## English Language Conventions

### Grammar, Usage, and Mechanics

**Grammar Review** LA.B.1.2.3.3.2, LA.B.1.2.3.3.3, LA.B.1.2.3.3.4

#### Teach

- Remind students that they will use all of the different skills introduced in this unit throughout the year in their writing.
  - Lesson 1, Nouns: Make sure students know a noun is a person, place, thing, or idea. Reference *Language Arts Handbook,* pages 246–247.
  - Lesson 2, Pronouns: Make sure students know that pronouns take the place of nouns. Reference *Language Arts Handbook,* pages 248–249.
  - Lesson 3, Verbs: Make sure students know what a verb is. Reference *Language Arts Handbook,* page 250.
  - Lesson 4, Verbs: Make sure students can recognize a verb phrase. Reference *Language Arts Handbook,* page 250.
  - Lesson 5, Sentences: Make sure students understand how sentences are formed. Reference *Language Arts Handbook,* page 257.

### Independent Practice

Have students complete *Comprehension and Language Arts Skills,* pages 24–25, which review all the skills in the unit.

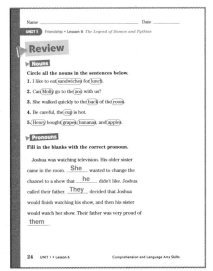

*Comprehension and Language Arts Skills p. 24*

# DAY 2

## Word Analysis

### Spelling

**Sound Sorting** LA.A.1.2.2.3.1
**Word Sort.** Write /a/, /e/, /i/, /o/, and /u/ on five sheets of paper. Tape the sheets around the room. Say each spelling word and have the class point to the word's vowel sound.

### Vocabulary

**Word Mapping** LA.A.2.2.5.3.1

#### Teach
- Write *tyrant* in a box. Explain that a *word map* will help them visualize this word. Ask students to find a synonym for *tyrant* in a thesaurus. (*dictator, oppressor, absolute ruler*)
- Label the left side *Synonyms*. Write three synonyms in boxes, connected to the center box.
- Label the right side *Related Words*. Have students look for context clues that relate to the word (*cruel laws, no mercy, feared*). Write three related words in boxes connected to the center box.

#### Guided Practice
Use **Spelling and Vocabulary Skills,** page 22, to reinforce the concept of word mapping. Have students complete page 23 as independent practice.

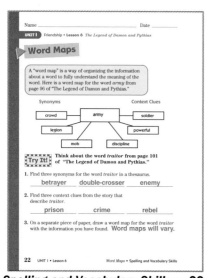

***Spelling and Vocabulary Skills p. 22***

## Writing Process Strategies

### Publishing LA.B.1.2.3.3.5
**Introduction to the Writing Process**

#### Teach
- Discuss **Language Arts Transparency 2,** Models of Good Writing: Personal Essay, with students.
- Discuss with students how this information can help them with their autobiographies.

#### Guided Practice
**Publishing**
Encourage students to look for time-order words in the **Leveled Classroom Library** selections or for situations in which such words should be inserted in their own writing.

## English Language Conventions

### Grammar, Usage, and Mechanics
**Skills Review** LA.B.1.2.3.3.2, LA.B.1.2.3.3.3, LA.B.1.2.3.3.4

#### Teach
- Review nouns by having the students tell you nouns they know and writing them on the board.
- Review pronouns by writing the following sentences on the board and calling on students to change the noun to a pronoun.
  - Kelly has a cat. (***She** has a cat.*)
  - I told Min he could go, but Min didn't want to go. (*I told Min he could go, but **he** didn't want to go.*)
- Review action and state-of-being verbs by writing the following verbs on the board and asking the students to identify them as action verbs or state-of-being verbs.
  - *eat* (action); *be* (state-of-being); *want* (action); *read* (action); *play* (action)
- Review verb phrases, main verbs, and helping verbs orally, referencing **Language Arts Handbook,** page 250.
- Review the four types of sentences orally, using the **Language Arts Handbook,** page 259, as reference.

### Guided Practice in Reading
Ask students to find a proper noun; common noun; pronoun; action verb; state-of-being verb; verb phrase, including the main verb and helping verb(s); and the four types of sentences in "The Legend of Damon and Pythias."

# DAY 3

| Word Analysis | Writing Process Strategies | English Language Conventions |
|---|---|---|

## Word Analysis

### Spelling

**Short Vowel Sounds**  LA.A.1.2.2.3.1

#### Teach
Have students complete the Spelling Bee activity for Unit 1 on the **Spelling CD-ROM.**

#### Guided Practice
Have students complete page 24 from **Spelling and Vocabulary Skills** to reinforce the spelling patterns for short vowel sounds.

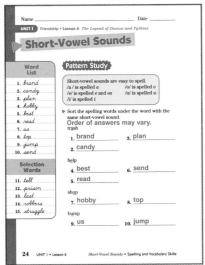

*Spelling and Vocabulary Skills p. 24*

### Vocabulary (continued)

**Word Grouping**  LA.A.2.2.5.3.1

- Explain that *word grouping* is similar to word mapping. Grouping a word is relating it to other words in the same category.
- Write *champion* from page 97 of "The Legend of Damon and Pythias" in a box. To the right, write *What* and to the left of the box, write *Examples.*
- Have students write three synonyms for what *champion* means in three connected boxes. (*support, endorse, superior*)
- Have the class write three examples of a champion within the story in boxes under Examples (*Damon, Pythias, friend*).

## Writing Process Strategies

### Publishing  LA.B.1.2.3.3.5
**Introduction to the Writing Process**

#### Teach
- Review with students ideas of visuals that can be added to different kinds of writing as discussed on **Language Arts Handbook,** pages 44–45.
- Discuss which would work best for their autobiographies.
- Encourage students to think about what they can add to an autobiography.

#### Guided Practice
**Publishing**
Have students write down ideas for photographs, charts, or diagrams (such as a family tree) that they could add to a piece of writing in their **Writing Folders.**

## English Language Conventions

### Grammar, Usage, and Mechanics
**Skills Review**  LA.B.1.2.3.3.2, LA.B.1.2.3.3.3, LA.B.1.2.3.3.4

#### Teach
Write sentences on the board to review the skills learned in this unit.
- Nouns and pronouns
  - The house was cold. (*Noun naming a place is* house.)
  - Happiness should be shared. (*Noun naming an idea is* happiness.)
  - Walter and Michael are neighbors. They live across the street from each other. (*Pronoun is* they; *proper nouns are* Walter *and* Michael.)
- Verbs
  - Mia visited her grandmother in Florida. (*Action verb is* visited.)
  - Blue whales are the largest mammals in the world. (*State-of-being verb is* are.)
  - I will go to the store. (*Verb phrase is* will go; *main verb is* go; *helping verb is* will.)
- Sentence types and end punctuation
  - Why is that on the top shelf? (*interrogative*)
  - Watch out, it's going to fall! (*exclamatory*)
  - I want to get it down. (*declarative*)
  - Get it down for me. (*imperative*)

### Guided Practice in Writing
Ask students to write a story about a time when they were a good friend, which they will include in their autobiographies.

 **Informal Assessment**

Make sure students are using nouns, pronouns, verbs, and the four types of sentences correctly in their writing.

# DAY 4

| Word Analysis | Writing Process Strategies | English Language Conventions |
| --- | --- | --- |

## Spelling

**Short Vowel Sounds** LA.A.1.2.2.3.1

### Teach
Explain that the exercises on page 25 in **Spelling and Vocabulary Skills** are designed to help them learn to look for the correct spelling of short vowel sounds.

### Guided Practice
Have students complete the exercises on page 25 of **Spelling and Vocabulary Skills** to reinforce the spelling patterns for the short vowel sounds.

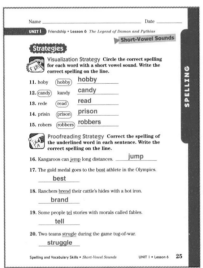

**Spelling and Vocabulary Skills p. 25**

## Vocabulary (continued)

**Comparisons** LA.A.2.2.7.3.1

- Explain to students that showing *comparisons* between words will help them learn more about a word. Write the comparison "apples : fruit as ring : _____." Explain that the ( : ) symbol stands for "*is to*" or "*are to*," meaning "apples *are to* fruit." Since apples are a type of fruit, then a ring is a type of what? *(jewelry)*
- Write *foolish* from page 100 of "The Legend of Damon and Pythias" on the board. Then add the ":" symbol and *smart*. Ask the class to think of comparisons that could fit this example. *(wet:dry)*

## Publishing LA.B.1.2.3.3.5
### Introduction to the Writing Process

### Teach
- Review the publishing step of the writing process. Remind students that not every piece of writing will be published. Review the considerations one should make in determining whether or not to publish a piece. For a more thorough review, reread **Language Arts Handbook,** pages 42–43.
- Model your decision about publishing your autobiography. *"I think my autobiography is interesting, and it is a story I want to share with others. I am going to include a time line so my readers can get a quick idea of events in my life. I am also going to include photos."*

### Guided Practice
**Publishing**
Remind students that clean copies, charts, diagrams, and art can all be added if they write their autobiographies on the computer. Encourage students to practice using these tools on the computer.

## Listening, Speaking, Viewing
**Presenting: Sharing Information** LA.C.1.2.5.3.1, LA.C.3.2.2.3.1

### Teach
- Explain that when we make a presentation we share information or ideas with a group of people. We should speak clearly so that everyone understands what is being presented.
- Explain that those who listen to a presentation also have an important role. They need to pay attention and listen carefully in order to get the most information from the speaker. They also need to pay attention so that if they have a question, they are able to ask it clearly.
- Explain that paraphrasing is similar to summarizing. Students should listen for the main points so they can tell them to others.

### Guided Practice
- Have students sit with a partner and spend five minutes finding out two things the other person likes to do during the summer. *(swimming, playing outside, going to camp)*
- Next, have students paraphrase what they learned about the other person's summer interests, and have them present the information to the rest of the class.
- Remind students to speak clearly and to make eye contact when they present what they have learned.

 **Informal Assessment**

Observe whether students understand paraphrasing, are able to listen to others, and can paraphrase information.

# DAY 5

| Word Analysis | Writing Process Strategies | English Language Conventions |

## Word Analysis

### Spelling

#### Assessment: Final Test

**Short Vowel Sounds** LA.A.1.2.2.3.1

#### Teach
Repeat the Pretest or use the Final Test on page 37 of *Unit 1 Assessment* as summative assessment for student understanding of short vowel sound spelling patterns.

**Unit 1 Assessment p. 37**

#### Guided Practice
Have students categorize any mistakes they made on the Final Test. Are they careless errors? Are they lesson-pattern problems? Check student writing assignments to see if they are correctly spelling words with short vowel sounds.

### Vocabulary LA.A.2.2.5.3.1

#### Informal Assessment

Ask the students to find *persuaded* in "The Legend of Damon and Pythias" on page 99. Have the class create a word map to determine the meaning of *persuade (argue, convince, get* and *let, do anything, do something)*. See if students understand what a word map is and how it is organized. Have students add any new words to their running list in their Writer's Notebooks.

## Writing Process Strategies

### Publishing LA.B.1.2.3.3.5
**Introduction to the Writing Process**

#### Teach
Discuss *Language Arts Transparency 33*, Presentation: Personal Essay, with students.

#### Independent Practice
**Publishing**
Have students use the checklist in the *Writer's Workbook,* page 5, to help them publish their autobiographies.

#### Formal Assessment

**ASSESSMENT RUBRICS** Share the rubrics with students before they begin the assignment to give them a foundation from which to work.
Total Point Value: 10
1. There is a list of possible ideas. (1 point)
2. Audience and purpose are clear. (1 point)
3. A graphic organizer shows prewriting ideas. (1 point)
4. A draft uses ideas from the graphic organizer. (2 points)
5. The draft is revised by adding copy, deleting copy, rearranging copy, or combining copy. (2 points)
6. The writing has been edited for spelling. (1 point)
7. A neat, correct, final copy is presented. (2 points)

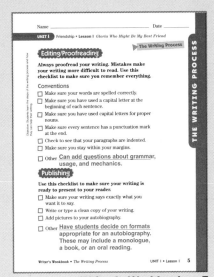

**Writer's Workbook p. 5**

## English Language Conventions

### Penmanship LA.B.1.2.2
**Cursive Letters *q*, *g*, and *o***

#### Teach
■ **Teacher Model:** On the board, introduce lowercase cursive *q*, *g*, and *o* as downcurve letters.

**q** Starting point, downcurve
Undercurve to starting point
Slant down and loop forward
Undercurve: small *q*

**g** Starting point, downcurve
Undercurve to starting point
Slant down and loop back
Overcurve: small *g*

**o** Starting point, downcurve
Undercurve
Small curve to right: small *o*

■ **Teacher Model:** On the board, write the words *queen, quiet, gate, soon,* and *sag* to model proper letter formation and slant.

#### Guided Practice
■ Invite students to come to the board and trace *q*, *g*, and *o*.
■ Have students practice writing rows of *q*, *g*, and *o* in their Writer's Notebooks.
■ From "The Legend of Damon and Pythias," have students write the words *king, great, army, of,* and *gold* to practice letter formation.

#### Informal Assessment

Check students' handwriting for legible loops below the baseline and proper slant.

**LESSON WRAP-UP**

# Reading and Language Arts Skills Traces

## Language Arts

### WORD ANALYSIS

**Skills Trace**

**Spelling: Short Vowel Sounds**

Introduced in Grade 1.
Scaffolded throughout Grades 2–5.
**REINTRODUCED:** Unit 1, Lesson 6, p. 111E
**PRACTICED:** Unit 1, Lesson 6,
pp. 111F–111J
*Spelling and Vocabulary Skills,*
pp. 24–25
**TESTED:** Unit 1, Lesson 6, p. 111J
Unit 1 Assessment

**Skills Trace**

**Vocabulary: Dictionary Strategy**

Introduced in Grade 1.
Scaffolded throughout Grades 3–5.
**REINTRODUCED:** Unit 1, Lesson 6, p. 111E
**PRACTICED:** Unit 1, Lesson 6,
pp. 111F–111J
*Spelling and Vocabulary Skills,*
pp. 22–23
**TESTED:** Unit 1 Assessment

### WRITING PROCESS STRATEGIES

**Skills Trace**

**Introduction to the Writing Process: Publishing**

Introduced in Grade K.
Scaffolded throughout Grades 1–6.
**REINTRODUCED:** Unit 1, Lesson 6, p. 111F
**PRACTICED:** Unit 1, Lesson 6,
pp. 111G–111J
*Writer's Workbook,* p. 5
**TESTED:** Unit 1 Assessment

### ENGLISH LANGUAGE CONVENTIONS

**Skills Trace**

**Listening, Speaking, Viewing Presenting: Sharing Information**

Introduced in Grade K.
Scaffolded throughout Grades 1–6.
**REINTRODUCED:** Unit 1, Lesson 6, p. 113I
**TESTED:** Unit 1, Lesson 6,
Informal Assessment, p. 113I

**Skills Trace**

**Penmanship: Cursive Letters *q*, *g*, and *o***

Introduced in Grade 2 (*q* and *g*) and Grade 3 (*o*).
Scaffolded throughout Grades 3–6 and 4–6.
**REINTRODUCED:** Unit 1, Lesson 6, p. 111J
**TESTED:** Unit 1, Lesson 6,
Informal Assessment, p. 111J

## Reading

### COMPREHENSION

**Skills Trace**

**Sequence**

Introduced in Grade 1.
Scaffolded throughout Grades 2 and 3.
**REINTRODUCED:** Unit 1, Lesson 6
**REINFORCED:** Unit 4, Lesson 6
Unit 5, Lesson 1
Unit 5, Lesson 7
**TESTED:** Unit 1 Assessment

# Professional Development: Phonics

## Phonological and Phonemic Awareness

Before children can map sounds to spellings proficiently, they must possess an awareness of the workings of spoken language—*phonological awareness*—and, in particular, of the individual sounds in spoken words—*phonemic awareness*.

- *Phonological awareness* is an umbrella term that encompasses phonemic awareness. It is the ability to think about and manipulate the sounds of language separately from their meaning. Specific features of phonological awareness include an understanding that words can rhyme; that sentences are made up of words; and that words have syllables, can begin or end with the same sound, and are made up of individual sounds, or phonemes, that can be put together or taken apart to make new words.

- *Phonemic awareness* is the conscious understanding that spoken words are made up of individual and separable sounds—phonemes. It involves the ability to play with and manipulate these sounds in order to put together and take apart spoken language. Phonemic awareness seems to depend on a child's ability to focus on the sounds (as opposed to the meanings) of words.

- A *phoneme* is the smallest unit of speech that conveys a distinction in meaning (for example, the word *sat* contains three phonemes, /s/ /a/ /t/, and differs by one phoneme from each of the spoken words *sad*, *sap*, *hat*, *mat*, and *sit*).

### What Does Research Tell Us about Phonological Awareness?

At school entry, the level of a child's phonological awareness appears to be a strong indicator of the success that child will experience in learning to read (Stanovich, 1986). In fact, children who become successful readers invariably have phonemic awareness, whereas those who lack it invariably have difficulty in hearing and distinguishing individual phonemes (Tunmer & Nesdale, 1985). Children's ability to attend to and manipulate phonemes strongly correlates with their reading success

all the way through their school years (Calfee, Lindamood, & Lindamood, 1973). Good readers can recognize phonemes quickly, accurately, and automatically and can put them together to make words and phrases quickly, accurately, and automatically. Children without this ability find it difficult to read single words, much less sentences, paragraphs, or entire texts (Bradley & Bryant, 1983; Juel, 1991; Stanovich, 1994; Tunmer & Nesdale, 1985).

Given this, it is alarming that 25 percent of middle-class first-grade students do not possess phonemic awareness. The percentage is even higher for children who come to school from literacy-poor homes (Adams, 1990). These figures are understandable. Becoming aware of phonemes is not easy. They are not defined distinctly by their sounds, but rather by their manner of articulation. As words are said, sounds are coarticulated. As language is listened to and spoken, attention is focused on the meaning of a word, not on its individual sounds. Why bother at all, then, to teach children to attend to sounds in words? The answer is because letters represent sounds, and children must learn to think of words as having sounds as well as meaning if they are to understand the alphabetic principle and, thus, become successful readers (Stahl & Murray, 1998).

The good news is that phonemic awareness *can be taught* (Ball & Blachman, 1991; Lundberg, Frost, & Peterson, 1988; Williams, 1980). Indeed, 15 minutes per day of direct instruction throughout the school year can significantly help kindergarten children develop important phonological analysis skills (Cunningham, 1991). For first-grade students, 15 minutes or so of instruction each day for two or three months should be sufficient. For second-grade and older students, phonemic awareness instruction should be necessary only for students who have difficulty recognizing words or who do not read at grade level (CORE, 1999).

*Additional information about phonics as well as resource references can be found in the ***Professional Development Guide: Phonics.***

**INVESTIGATION WRAP-UP**

## Review the Concepts

After all of the groups have presented their findings, lead students in a large group discussion about the unit activity. Ask students which part of the investigations they enjoyed the most. Which part was the most challenging? What part of their investigations can they use in their everyday lives? Review with students the following key concepts:

- Friends can be people whom we never expected to be our friends.
- People can become friends after they learn to understand each other.
- Damaged friendships can be mended.
- Sometimes pets can be our best friends.
- Sometimes friendship takes courage.
- True friends are loyal to each other and can trust each other.

### Tips for Reviewing the Concepts

- If necessary, remind students of the questions they raised throughout the unit and ask them to discuss each one.
- As always, students' ideas should determine the discussion.
- Remind students that they can continue to investigate friendship even though they have completed the unit.

Have students refer to page 1 of the *Inquiry Journal* to remind themselves of what their ideas about friendship were when the unit began, and also of what they expected to learn from the unit. Ask them to describe the new ideas they have acquired and the new information they have learned.

## Evaluating the Unit

- Have students conduct an evaluation of the unit selections, identifying those selections they found most and least interesting.
- Have students evaluate the different activities throughout this unit. Which activities did they find the most enjoyable and informative?
- Ask students to evaluate the overall unit. Have them answer questions such as the following: How well did the unit cover the theme? Which selections added something new to your knowledge of friendship?
- Have students suggest ideas related to friendship to explore further, possibly beginning with any questions left on the Concept/Question Board.

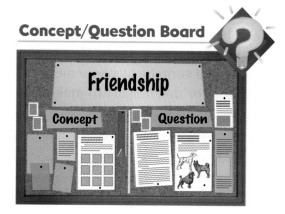

**Concept/Question Board**

Friendship

Concept        Question

---

Name_____ Date_____
Friendship **UNIT I**

**Knowledge About Friendship**

- These are some of my ideas about friendship before reading the unit.
Answers will vary.

_____
_____
_____
_____

- These are some things about friendship I would like to talk about and understand better.
Answers will vary.

_____
_____
_____
_____
_____

Reminder: I should read this page again when I get to the end of the unit to see how much my ideas about friendship have changed.

Inquiry Journal • *Knowledge About Friendship*        UNIT I **1**

*Inquiry Journal p. 1*

# Evaluating Group Participation

Have students in their small groups discuss the unit activity. Encourage them to talk about the importance of teamwork. Have the groups consider the following questions: What things did we do well as a team? What things could we do better next time? Why is teamwork important?

Throughout this unit investigation into Friendship, you have been informally assessing student progress. Go over your notes to see who has been contributing to the group's investigation, and how students have helped each other during this process. Talk with each group to get their feedback about how they felt working as a team. Use your observation notes and feedback from the group to assess the groups.

## Research Rubrics

### Collaborative Group Work

(this rubric is applied to groups, not individuals)

1 Group members work on separate tasks with little interaction.

2 Work-related decisions are made by the group, but there is little interaction related to ideas.

3 Information and ideas are shared, but there is little discussion concerned with advancing understanding.

4 The group clearly progresses in its thinking beyond where individual students could have gone.

### Participation in Collaborative Inquiry

(this rubric is applied to individual students)

1 Does not contribute ideas or information to team or class.

2 Makes contributions to Concept/Question Board or class discussions when specifically called upon to do so.

3 Occasionally contributes ideas or information to other students' inquiries.

4 Takes an active interest in the success of the whole class's knowledge-building effort.

## Progress Assessment

### Self-Evaluation

Give students the opportunity to evaluate their personal learning experiences during this unit by completing *Inquiry Journal,* pages 26–27. The students could also complete the self-evaluation questions on the *Research Assistant CD-ROM*.

Name _____ Date _____

**UNIT I** Friendship

**Unit Wrap-Up**

- How did you like this unit?
  - ☐ I really enjoyed it.   ☐ I liked it.
  - ☐ I liked some of it.   ☐ I didn't like it.
- How would you rate the difficulty of the unit?
  - ☐ easy   ☐ medium   ☐ hard
- How would you rate your performance during this unit?
  - ☐ I learned a lot about friendship.
  - ☐ I learned some new things about friendship.
  - ☐ I didn't learn much about friendship.
- Why did you choose these ratings?
  Answers will vary.

- What was the most interesting thing you learned about friendship?
  Answers will vary.

- Is there anything else about friendship that you would like to learn? If so, what?
  Answers will vary.

26 UNIT I    *Unit Wrap-Up • Inquiry Journal*

**Unit Wrap-Up** *(continued)*

- What did you learn about friendship that you didn't know before reading this unit?
  Answers will vary.

- What did you learn about yourself as a learner?
  Answers will vary.

- What do you need to work on to improve your skills as a learner?
  Answers will vary.

- What resources (books, films, magazines, interviews, other) did you use on your own during this unit? Which of these were the most helpful? Why?
  Answers will vary.

*Inquiry Journal • Unit Wrap-Up*    UNIT I   27

*Inquiry Journal pp. 26–27*

# UNIT | WRAP-UP

ASSESSMENT

*Pick and choose assessments. Can't do all!*

## Formal Assessment

Use these summative assessments along with your informal observations to assess student mastery.

---

**Unit 1 Assessment p. 38**

Name _____ Date _____ Score _____

**UNIT 1** Friendship

### Connecting Unit Selections

Read the following questions carefully. Then answer each one in complete sentences. You may want to refer back to the stories.

1. How is "The Legend of Damon and Pythias" like "Rugby & Rosie"?
In both stories, people made sacrifices. Damon and Pythias were willing to sacrifice themselves for their friends. The family was willing to give up Rosie so she could serve as a guide dog for a visually impaired person.

2. In "Teammates" and "Angel Child, Dragon Child," people from different races help one another. Why is this an important type of friendship?
People from different races sometimes don't know each other well. Friendship can help people get to know one another better.

38 · Connecting Unit Selections · Unit 1 Assessment

---

**Unit 1 Assessment p. 39**

### Connecting Unit Selections (continued)

3. How is "The Tree House" different from "Gloria Who Might Be My Best Friend"?
In "Gloria Who Might Be My Best Friend," the characters are friends at the beginning of the story. In "The Tree House," the girls become friends toward the end of the story.

4. How is "Rugby & Rosie" different from the other stories in the unit?
It shows a friendship between animals and humans.

Unit 1 Assessment · Connecting Unit Selections   39

---

**Unit 1 Assessment p. 40**

Name _____ Date _____ Score _____

**UNIT 1** Friendship

### Comprehension Assessment

Read the following selection and questions carefully. Then completely fill in the bubble of each correct answer.

**Lewis and Clark**

Camping is fun, but it's also a little challenging. There is the long car ride, cooking your own food, and no showering. Imagine a camping trip that lasts a year and a half. President Thomas Jefferson sent Meriwether Lewis on such a trip in 1804. Jefferson wanted to learn more about the West. Lewis knew that going to the West would be the chance of a lifetime. He also knew he could not make the trip alone.

Lewis asked William Clark to join him, and Clark agreed. Clark had been in the army with Lewis. Lewis was a captain, and Clark was an officer under Lewis. The two men became fast friends. As they planned the trip, Lewis and Clark made a private pact. Both of them would lead. From then on, Captain Lewis called his friend "Captain Clark."

The two worked closely together. They trained a group of strong men to go with them. They gathered food, medicine, and supplies. They also packed gifts for the Native Americans they would meet.

At last, the group set off. The trip was 8,000 miles of pure adventure. Lewis collected unusual plants and animals to send back to the president. Clark made maps of the new lands, using the stars as guides.

It was a long, difficult journey. The freezing winter, raging waters, and lack of food made Lewis and Clark's friendship even stronger. The trip was a total success, and would be forever known as the Lewis and Clark Expedition.

40   Comprehension Assessment · Unit 1 Assessment

---

**Unit 1 Assessment p. 41**

### Comprehension Assessment (continued)

1. What is this story mostly about?
Ⓐ an unusual person
Ⓑ an interesting place
● an important journey

2. Why did Lewis ask Clark to go West with him?
● Lewis needed Clark's help.
Ⓑ Clark was Lewis's only friend.
Ⓒ Clark was an army captain.

3. What was sent back to President Jefferson?
Ⓐ gifts from Native Americans
● unusual plants and animals
Ⓒ pictures of what they found

Read the following questions carefully. Use complete sentences to answer the questions.

4. Why did Lewis call Clark "Captain Clark"?
Lewis called him Captain Clark to show they were both leading the trip.

5. How far did Lewis and Clark travel?
They traveled 8,000 miles.

Unit 1 Assessment · Comprehension Assessment   41

---

**Unit 1 Assessment p. 42**

Name _____ Date _____ Score _____

**UNIT 1** Friendship

### Spelling Assessment

Read each line carefully. Look for the underlined word that is misspelled. Then completely fill in the bubble of the line where the word is misspelled. If no word is misspelled, fill in the bubble of the line marked "Correct as is."

1. Ⓐ Canned goods can last for years.
● Campers sleep in a teant.
Ⓒ Leopards have lots of spots.
Ⓓ Correct as is.

2. Ⓕ A loaf of bread can be sliced.
Ⓖ A saddle fits on a horse's back.
● People pic apples from trees.
Ⓙ Correct as is.

3. ● Sheep gather in a floch.
Ⓑ It is kind to give to others.
Ⓒ Letters can be sent by mail.
Ⓓ Correct as is.

4. Ⓕ Sponges are used to scrub dishes.
Ⓖ A pie krust should be flaky.
Ⓗ A vaccination is a type of shot.
Ⓙ Correct as is.

5. Ⓐ Most candy contains sugar.
Ⓑ A computer can crash.
Ⓒ A finale is the last song.
Ⓓ Correct as is.

6. Ⓕ A laymp brightens a room.
Ⓖ Tourists visit different places.
Ⓗ A bell is an instrument.
Ⓙ Correct as is.

42   Spelling Assessment · Unit 1 Assessment

---

**Unit 1 Assessment p. 43**

Name _____ Date _____ Score _____

**UNIT 1** Friendship

### Vocabulary Assessment

Look at each underlined vocabulary word. Choose the answer that best completes each sentence.

**SAMPLE** A garage is a place for ____.
Ⓐ dogs
Ⓑ flowers
● cars
Ⓓ papers

1. A margin is the blank part around a ____.
Ⓐ lamp
● page
Ⓒ tree
Ⓓ chair

2. A house has shutters around the ____.
● window
Ⓖ roof
Ⓗ lawn
Ⓙ pool

3. A Labrador is a type of ____.
Ⓐ room
Ⓑ paper
Ⓒ school
● dog

4. Something that is extraordinary is ____.
Ⓕ plain
Ⓖ dull
● amazing
Ⓙ boring

5. A tyrant is a ____.
Ⓐ kind servant
● cruel ruler
Ⓒ bold hero
Ⓓ sad uncle

Unit 1 Assessment · Vocabulary Assessment   43

---

1110   Unit 1   *Florida*

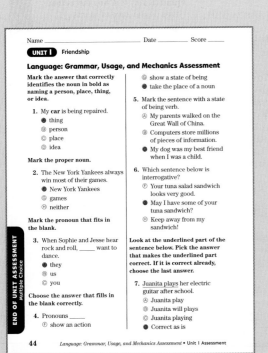

**Unit 1 Assessment p. 44**

Name _____ Date _____ Score _____

**UNIT 1** Friendship

**Language: Grammar, Usage, and Mechanics Assessment**

Mark the answer that correctly identifies the noun in bold as naming a person, place, thing, or idea.

1. My **car** is being repaired.
   Ⓐ thing
   Ⓑ person
   Ⓒ place
   Ⓓ idea

Mark the proper noun.

2. The New York Yankees always win most of their games.
   Ⓕ New York Yankees
   Ⓖ games
   Ⓗ neither

Mark the pronoun that fits in the blank.

3. When Sophie and Jesse hear rock and roll, _____ want to dance.
   Ⓐ they
   Ⓑ us
   Ⓒ you

Choose the answer that fills in the blank correctly.

4. Pronouns _____
   Ⓕ show an action

   Ⓖ show a state of being
   Ⓗ take the place of a noun

5. Mark the sentence with a state of being verb.
   Ⓐ My parents walked on the Great Wall of China.
   Ⓑ Computers store millions of pieces of information.
   Ⓒ My dog was my best friend when I was a child.

6. Which sentence below is interrogative?
   Ⓕ Your tuna salad sandwich looks very good.
   Ⓖ May I have some of your tuna sandwich?
   Ⓗ Keep away from my sandwich!

Look at the underlined part of the sentence below. Pick the answer that makes the underlined part correct. If it is correct already, choose the last answer.

7. Juanita plays her electric guitar after school.
   Ⓐ Juanita play
   Ⓑ Juanita will plays
   Ⓒ Juanita playing
   Ⓓ Correct as is

44  Language: Grammar, Usage, and Mechanics Assessment • Unit 1 Assessment

END OF UNIT ASSESSMENT — Multiple Choice

---

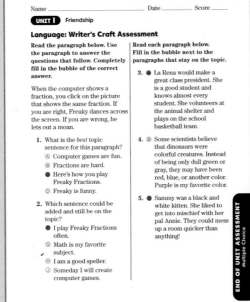

**Unit 1 Assessment p. 45**

Name _____ Date _____ Score _____

**UNIT 1** Friendship

**Language: Writer's Craft Assessment**

Read the paragraph below. Use the paragraph to answer the questions that follow. Completely fill in the bubble of the correct answer.

When the computer shows a fraction, you click on the picture that shows the same fraction. If you are right, Freaky dances across the screen. If you are wrong, he lets out a moan.

1. What is the *best* topic sentence for this paragraph?
   Ⓐ Computer games are fun.
   Ⓑ Fractions are hard.
   Ⓒ Here's how you play Freaky Fractions.
   Ⓓ Freaky is funny.

2. Which sentence could be added and still be on the topic?
   Ⓕ I play Freaky Fractions often.
   Ⓖ Math is my favorite subject.
   Ⓗ I am a good speller.
   Ⓘ Someday I will create computer games.

Read each paragraph below. Fill in the bubble next to the paragraphs that stay on the topic.

3. Ⓐ La Rena would make a great class president. She is a good student and knows almost every student. She volunteers at the animal shelter and plays on the school basketball team.

4. Ⓑ Some scientists believe that dinosaurs were colorful creatures. Instead of being only dull green or gray, they may have been red, blue, or another color. Purple is my favorite color.

5. Ⓒ Sammy was a black and white kitten. She liked to get into mischief with her pal Annie. They could mess up a room quicker than anything!

Unit 1 Assessment • Language: Writer's Craft Assessment  45

END OF UNIT ASSESSMENT — Multiple Choice

---

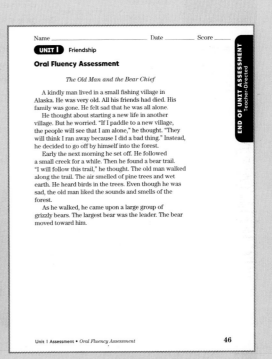

**Unit 1 Assessment p. 46**

Name _____ Date _____ Score _____

**UNIT 1** Friendship

**Oral Fluency Assessment**

*The Old Man and the Bear Chief*

A kindly man lived in a small fishing village in Alaska. He was very old. All his friends had died. His family was gone. He felt sad that he was all alone.

He thought about starting a new life in another village. But he worried. "If I paddle to a new village, the people will see that I am alone," he thought. "They will think I ran away because I did a bad thing." Instead, he decided to go off by himself into the forest.

Early the next morning he set off. He followed a small creek for a while. Then he found a bear trail. "I will follow this trail," he thought. The old man walked along the trail. The air smelled of pine trees and wet earth. He heard birds in the trees. Even though he was sad, the old man liked the sounds and smells of the forest.

As he walked, he came upon a large group of grizzly bears. The largest bear was the leader. The bear moved toward him.

Unit 1 Assessment • Oral Fluency Assessment  46

END OF UNIT ASSESSMENT — Teacher-Directed

---

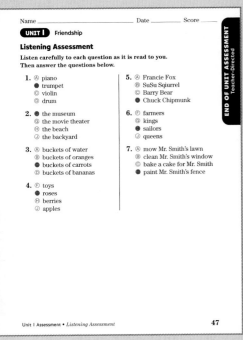

**Unit 1 Assessment p. 47**

Name _____ Date _____ Score _____

**UNIT 1** Friendship

**Listening Assessment**

Listen carefully to each question as it is read to you. Then answer the questions below.

1. Ⓐ piano
   Ⓑ trumpet
   Ⓒ violin
   Ⓓ drum

2. Ⓔ the museum
   Ⓕ the movie theater
   Ⓖ the beach
   Ⓗ the backyard

3. Ⓐ buckets of water
   Ⓑ buckets of oranges
   Ⓒ buckets of carrots
   Ⓓ buckets of bananas

4. Ⓕ toys
   Ⓖ roses
   Ⓗ berries
   Ⓘ apples

5. Ⓐ Francie Fox
   Ⓑ SuSu Squirrel
   Ⓒ Barry Bear
   Ⓓ Chuck Chipmunk

6. Ⓕ farmers
   Ⓖ kings
   Ⓗ sailors
   Ⓘ queens

7. Ⓐ mow Mr. Smith's lawn
   Ⓑ clean Mr. Smith's window
   Ⓒ bake a cake for Mr. Smith
   Ⓓ paint Mr. Smith's fence

Unit 1 Assessment • Listening Assessment  47

END OF UNIT ASSESSMENT — Teacher-Directed

---

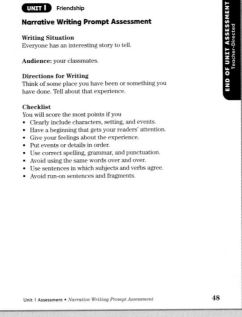

**Unit 1 Assessment p. 48**

Name _____ Date _____ Score _____

**UNIT 1** Friendship

**Narrative Writing Prompt Assessment**

**Writing Situation**
Everyone has an interesting story to tell.

**Audience:** your classmates.

**Directions for Writing**
Think of some place you have been or something you have done. Tell about that experience.

**Checklist**
You will score the most points if you
- Clearly include characters, setting, and events.
- Have a beginning that gets your readers' attention.
- Give your feelings about the experience.
- Put events or details in order.
- Use correct spelling, grammar, and punctuation.
- Avoid using the same words over and over.
- Use sentences in which subjects and verbs agree.
- Avoid run-on sentences and fragments.

Unit 1 Assessment • Narrative Writing Prompt Assessment  48

END OF UNIT ASSESSMENT — Teacher-Directed

---

## Also included:

- **Writing Rubrics (Four Point and Six Point)**
- **Writing Portfolio Assessment and Rubrics**
- **Directions for Listening Assessment**
- **Teacher's Record of Oral Fluency**
- **Formal Assessment Record**

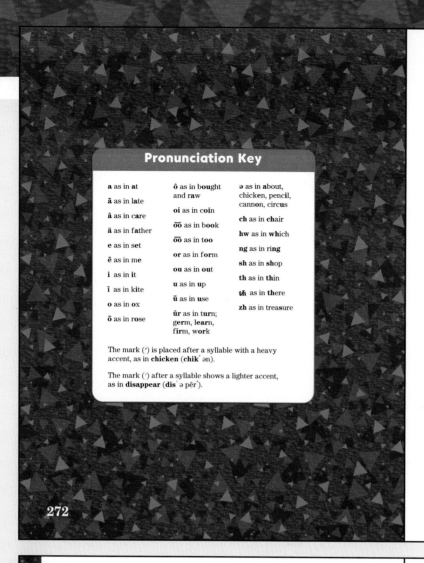

## Pronunciation Key

| | | |
|---|---|---|
| **a** as in **at** | **ô** as in **bought** and **raw** | **ə** as in **about**, **chicken**, **pencil**, **cannon**, **circus** |
| **ā** as in **late** | | |
| **â** as in **care** | **oi** as in **coin** | |
| **ä** as in **father** | **o͝o** as in **book** | **ch** as in **chair** |
| **e** as in **set** | **o͞o** as in **too** | **hw** as in **which** |
| **ē** as in **me** | **or** as in **form** | **ng** as in **ring** |
| **i** as in **it** | **ou** as in **out** | **sh** as in **shop** |
| **ī** as in **kite** | **u** as in **up** | **th** as in **thin** |
| **o** as in **ox** | **ū** as in **use** | **th** as in **there** |
| **ō** as in **rose** | **ûr** as in **turn**; **germ**, **learn**, **firm**, **work** | **zh** as in **treasure** |

The mark (´) is placed after a syllable with a heavy accent, as in **chicken** (**chik´** ən).

The mark (ˊ) after a syllable shows a lighter accent, as in **disappear** (**dis´** ə pēr´).

# Glossary

## A

**abandon** (ə ban´ dən) *v.* To leave empty.

**absorb** (ab sorb´) *v.* To soak up.

**abundantly** (ə bun´ dənt lē) *adv.* With more than enough; richly; well.

**abuse** (ə būs´) *n.* Unkind or cruel words or actions.

**adapt** (ə dapt´) *v.* To fit in.

**adequate** (ad´ i kwit) *adj.* As much as needed; enough.

**adorn** (ə dorn´) *v.* To decorate.

**ailanthus tree** (ā lan´ thəs trē´) *n.* A wide-spreading tree with long leaves and thick clusters of flowers.

**alarm** (ə lärm´) *n.* Sudden fear; a sense of danger.

**alert** (ə lûrt´) *v.* To warn or make aware of.

**amber** (am´ bər) *n.* A yellowish-brown color.

**amethyst** (am´ ə thist) *n.* A purple color.

**anxiously** (angk´ shəs lē) *adv.* With a worried or uneasy feeling.

**ao dai** (ow zī) *n. Vietnamese.* A garment worn by females in Vietnam, usually for special occasions.

**apathetic** (ap´ ə thet´ ik) *adj.* Not interested; not caring about something.

**aphid** (ā´ fid) *n.* A tiny insect that lives on the juice of plants.

**appoint** (ə point´) *v.* To name officially.

**appreciate** (ə prē´ shē āt´) *v.* To understand the nature of.

**arctic** (ärk´ tik) *adj.* Having to do with the area around the North Pole.

**arrange** (ə rānj´) *v.* To take steps to make something happen.

**astonish** (ə stä´ nish) *v.* To surprise or amaze.

**auburn** (ô´ bərn) *adj.* Reddish-brown.

**audible** (ô´ də bəl) *adj.* Loud enough to be heard.

## B

**bandit** (ban´ dit) *n.* A robber; a thief.

---

banister                                                                                    cavity

Pronunciation Key: **at**; **lāte**; **câre**; **fäther**; **set**; **mē**; **it**; **kīte**; **ox**; **rōse**; **ô** in **bought**; **coin**; **bo͝ok**; **to͞o**; **form**; **out**; **up**; **ūse**; **tûrn**; **ə** sound in **about**, **chicken**, **pencil**, **cannon**, **circus**; **chair**; **hw** in **which**; **ring**; **shop**; **thin**; **there**; **zh** in **treasure**.

**banister** (ban´ ə stər) *n.* The railing on a staircase.

**barbed** (bärbd) *adj.* With a sharp point.

**bargain** (bär´ gən) *n.* A deal or agreement between two people or parties.

**beautiful** (bū´ ti fəl) *adj.* Lovely; pleasing to look at.

**beckon** (bek´ ən) *v.* To invite someone by waving.

**binoculars** (bə no´ kyə lərz) *n.* A device to help see objects that are far away.

**biologist** (bī ol´ ə jist) *n.* A person who studies plants and animals.

**blossom** (blä´ səm) *v.* To bloom; to produce flowers.

**blunt** (blunt) *adj.* Having a dull or thick edge.

**bolster** (bōl´ stər) *v.* To support; to make stronger.

**border** (bor´ dər) *v.* To touch at the edge or boundary.

**bow** (bō´) *n.* A wooden rod with horsehair stretched from end to end used in playing a stringed instrument.

**Braille** (brāl) *n.* A system of printing with raised dots that stand for letters. Blind people read Braille by touching the dots.

**bridle** (brīd´ l) *n.* The part of a horse's harness that goes over its head.

**buck** (bək) *n.* A male deer.

**burdock** (bûr´ dok) *n.* A weed with coarse, broad leaves and prickly heads or burs.

**burglar** (bər´ glər) *n.* A person who steals; a thief.

**burrow** (bər´ō´) *v.* To make a snug, warm place, usually deep and narrow, like a tunnel that a rabbit or gopher digs.

**burst** (bərst´) *v.* To be filled and overflowing with strong emotion.

## C

**camouflage** (kam´ ə fläzh´) *v.* To disguise; to hide.

**cartwheel** (kärt´ hwēl´) *n.* A jump made by landing on the hands and then the feet, turning like a wheel.

**carve** (kärv´) *v.* To cut carefully.

**cast** (kast) *v.* To throw.

**catnip** (kat´ nip) *n.* A spicy-smelling plant that cats like.

**cavity** (kav´ i tē) *n.* A small hole; a hollow.

---

champion                                                                                    crinkle

**champion** (cham´ pē ən) *n.* 1. A person who stands up for a cause or for others. 2. One who wins first place.

**chant** (chant) *v.* To sing or repeat words as a group.

**chao buoi sang** (chow bwē sung) *Vietnamese.* Good morning.

**chisel** (chiz´ əl) *v.* To cut with a metal tool.

chisel

**chive** (chīv) *n.* A small plant related to leeks and onions.

**chore** (chor) *n.* A small job.

**circulate** (sûr´ kyə lāt´) *v.* To pass around.

**clamor** (klam´ ər) *n.* A loud, lengthy noise.

**cloak** (klōk) *n.* A loose-fitting coat that is worn over the shoulders.

**clutch** (kluch) *n.* A group of eggs to be hatched.

**collection** (kə lek´ shən) *n.* An assortment of similar things gathered together to study or to show to others.

**colonel** (kûr´ nl) *n.* An officer in the army, marines, or air force.

**command** (kə mand´) *v.* To order. —*n.* A short, firm instruction.

**commute** (kə myo͞ot´) *v.* To travel between two places every day.

**compete** (kəm pēt´) *v.* To try to win by striving against another person or people.

**complex** (kom´ pleks) *n.* A group of related things.

**concrete** (kän´ krēt´) *n.* A strong building material that hardens as it dries. —*adj.* Made of concrete.

**content** (kən tent´) *adj.* Satisfied; pleased.

**controversial** (kon´ trə vûr´ shəl) *adj.* Causing arguments or different opinions.

**corkscrew** (kork´ skro͞o´) *v.* To move by turning back and forth or twisting.

**courtyard** (kort´ yärd´) *n.* An open area with walls around it that is next to a large building.

**cozy** (kō´ zē) *adj.* Warm and comfortable.

**cranny** (kran´ ē) *n.* A slit; a narrow opening.

**creed** (krēd) *n.* The statement of a person's belief or faith.

**crevice** (krev´ is) *n.* A crack.

**crinkle** (kring´ kəl) *v.* To wrinkle.

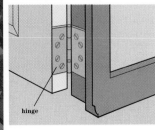

**Pronunciation Key: at; lāte; câre; fäther; set; mē; it; kīte; ox; rōse; ô in bought; coin; bŏŏk; tōō; form; out; up; ūse; tûrn; ə sound in about, chicken, pencil, cannon, circus; chair; hw in which; ring; shop; thin; <i>th</i>ere; zh in treasure.**

**crop** (kräp) *n.* A plant grown for food or to sell to make money.

**cubism** (kū′ biz əm) *n.* A style of painting in which the picture is formed by cubes or square shapes.

**curious** (kyur′ ē əs) *adj.* Interested in knowing.

### D

**dahlia** (dal′ yə) *n.* A plant with showy, bright-colored flowers.

**dangle** (dang′ gəl) *v.* To hang down loosely.

**dart** (därt) *v.* To move or run quickly from one place to another.

**debris** (də brē′) *n.* Rubbish; trash.

**decorate** (de′ kə rāt) *v.* To add ornamentation; to adorn or make beautiful.

**delighted** (di lī′ təd) *adj.* Very happy; pleased.

**depression** (di presh′ ən) *n.* 1. A shallow hole or a dent. 2. A period of time when business is slow and people are out of work.

**desert** (di zərt′) *v.* To leave or abandon.

**design** (di zīn′) *n.* A plan for putting something together.

**desire** (di zīr′) *v.* To have a strong wish for.

**despite** (di spīt′) *prep.* In spite of; regardless of.

**diagonal** (dī a′ gə nəl) *n.* A line connecting two opposite angles on a four-sided shape.

**discard** (di skärd′) *v.* To throw away.

**disgrace** (dis grās′) *v.* To act badly; to shame.

**dither** (di<i>th</i>′ ər) *n.* An upset, confused feeling.

**doe** (dō) *n.* A female deer.

**dollop** (dol′ əp) *n.* A blob of something; a small amount of something.

**dweller** (dwel′ ər) *n.* Someone who lives in a certain place.

**dwelling** (dwel′ ing) *n.* A place to live.

### E

**emperor** (em′ pər ər) *n.* A man who rules an empire.

**encourage** (en kûr′ ij) *v.* To urge or inspire someone to do something.

**enormous** (i nor′ məs) *adj.* Very large; huge or massive.

**environment** (en vī′ rən mənt) *n.* Everything surrounding a plant, animal, or person.

276

**exercise** (ek′ sər sīz′) *n.* A physical activity for the sake of fitness.

**exhaust** (ig zôst′) *n.* The gases and smoke from a car that go into the air.

**exist** (ig zist′) *v.* To be or to continue to be.

**experiment** (ik sper′ ə mənt) *n.* A test used to discover something.

**exploration** (ek′ splə rā′ shən) *n.* The act of searching or looking closely at a new area.

**extraordinary** (ik stror′ dn er′ ē) *adj.* Rare; not ordinary.

### F

**fabric** (fa′ brik) *n.* Material used to make clothing.

**falcon** (fôl′ kən) *n.* A powerful bird of prey.

**fashion** (fa′ shən) *v.* To create.

**faze** (fāz) *v.* To bother.

**finery** (fīn′ rē) *n.* Fancy or dressy clothing.

**flat** (flat) *n.* A musical note that sounds one-half tone lower than it usually does.

**flatter** (flat′ ər) *adj.* More flat. —*v.* To compliment.

**flimsy** (flim′ zē) *adj.* Weak; slight; breakable.

**flourish** (flûr′ ish) *v.* To grow well; to succeed.

**ford** (ford) *v.* To cross a river or stream.

**forklift** (for′ klift) *n.* A small truck with a lifting device on the front so that things can be easily picked up and moved.

**fragrant** (frā′ grənt) *adj.* Sweet-smelling.

**freight** (frāt) *n.* Products and materials that are transported by trains, boats, or planes.

### G

**gamble** (gam′ bəl) *n.* A risk; a chance.

**garment** (gär′ mənt) *n.* An item of clothing.

**gleam** (glēm) *v.* To be bright and shiny.

**Gothic** (goth′ ik) *adj.* A style of art that uses much detail and decoration.

**graduation** (gra′ jə wā′ shən) *n.* A ceremony to mark the completion of a full course of study.

**graze** (grāz) *v.* To eat or feed on grasses.

**greasewood** (grēs′ wŏŏd) *n.* A woody plant that grows in the dry West.

**grim** (grim) *adj.* Stern; harsh.

**gutter** (gut′ ər) *n.* A curved path or trough for carrying off rainwater.

277

**Pronunciation Key: at; lāte; câre; fäther; set; mē; it; kīte; ox; rōse; ô in bought; coin; bŏŏk; tōō; form; out; up; ūse; tûrn; ə sound in about, chicken, pencil, cannon, circus; chair; hw in which; ring; shop; thin; <i>th</i>ere; zh in treasure.**

### H

**habitat** (hab′ i tat′) *n.* The natural surroundings of a plant or animal.

**haunch** (hônch) *n.* The hip and the thickest part of the thigh.

**hedge** (hej) *n.* A row of bushes used as a fence.

**height** (hīt) *n.* The distance from the top to the bottom of something.

**hexagon** (hek′ sə gän′) *n.* A six-sided shape with six angles.

**hinge** (hinj) *n.* A metal joint that attaches a door to its frame and lets the door move.

hinge

**hoa-phuong** (hwä fung) *n.* *Vietnamese.* A tropical flower in Vietnam that has groups of red blossoms.

**honorable** (ä′ nər ə bəl) *adj.* Deserving of honor or respect.

**hoof** (hŏŏf) *n.* A hard covering on the feet of animals such as horses and cows.

**hostility** (ho stil′ i tē) *n.* Unfriendliness; willingness to fight.

**hover** (huv′ ər) *v.* To hang in the air near something.

**humiliation** (hū mil′ ē ā′ shən) *n.* An action or event that hurts someone's pride.

### I

**imagination** (i maj′ ə nā′ shən) *n.* The ability to create new ideas in one's mind.

**imitate** (im′ i tāt′) *v.* To copy.

**immature** (im′ ə chŏŏr′) *adj.* Not fully grown.

**inconvenient** (in′ kən vē′ nyənt) *adj.* Causing difficulty.

**initially** (i nish′ əl lē) *adv.* At first.

**intersection** (in′ tər sek′ shən) *n.* The place where two streets cross each other.

278

**intruder** (in trōō′ dər) *n.* Someone who enters a place against the owner's will.

**island** (ī′ lənd) *n.* 1. A piece of land surrounded by water. 2. Anything surrounded by something else.

**intimidate** (in tim′ i dāt′) *v.* To threaten; to try to scare.

### J

**jangle** (jang′ gəl) *v.* To make a harsh sound, like two pieces of metal hitting each other.

**jiggle** (jig′ əl) *v.* To move back and forth quickly.

**jostle** (jos′ əl) *v.* To bump into.

**journey** (jər′ nē) *n.* A trip.

### K

**kip** (kip) *n.* A nap; sleep.

### L

**laboratory** (la′ bə rə tôr′ ē) *n.* A place where science studies and experiments are done.

**launch** (lônch) *v.* To begin.

**lollop** (lä′ ləp) *v.* To move in a slow, lazy way.

**lonely** (lōn′ lē) *adj.* Sad from being alone.

**loom** (lōōm) *n.* A machine that weaves thread into cloth.

**loyalty** (loi′ əl tē′) *n.* The quality of being faithful to a person or cause.

### M

**magnificent** (mag ni′ fə sənt) *adj.* Of grand character and beauty; wonderful.

**manners** (ma′ nərz) *n.* Habits of behavior.

**margin** (mär′ jin) *n.* The blank edge of a paper.

**marvelous** (märv′ ə ləs) *adj.* Outstanding.

**mayor** (mā′ ər) *n.* The chief elected official of a city.

**metallic** (mə tal′ ik) *adj.* As if made of metal.

**microscope** (mī′ krə skōp′) *n.* An instrument that makes small things look larger.

**migrate** (mī′ grāt) *v.* To move from colder to warmer lands and back again.

**miniature** (min′ ē ə chər) *adj.* Tiny; very small.

**molt** (mōlt) *v.* To lose or shed hair, feathers, or a shell.

279

Pronunciation Key: **at**; l**ā**te; c**â**re; f**ä**ther; set; m**ē**; **it**; k**ī**te; **ox**; r**ō**se; **ô** in b**ou**ght; c**oi**n; b**oo̅**k; t**oo̅**; f**or**m; **out**; **up**; **ū**se; t**ûr**n; **ə** sound in about, chicken, pencil, cannon, circus; **ch**air; **hw** in **wh**ich; r**ing**; **sh**op; **th**in; **th**ere; **zh** in treasure.

**monument** (mon′ yə mənt) *n.* Anything built to honor a person or event.

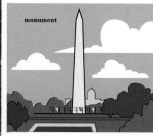
monument

**mood** (mo̅o̅d) *n.* A general state of mind.

**mottled** (mot′ ld) *adj.* Spotted or blotched with different colors.

**mound** (mound) *n.* A pile or heap of something.

**mustache** (mus′ tash) *n.* Hair grown on the upper lip.

## N

**nervous** (nər′ vəs) *adj.* Moving in an excited or jumpy way.

**nest** (nest) *v.* To build a home. —*n.* A shelter made by animals; a home.

**nestling** (nest′ ling) *n.* A bird too young to leave the nest.

**nibble** (ni′ bəl) *v.* To take small bites.

**nimbly** (nim′ blē) *adv.* Quickly and easily.

**nook** (no̅o̅k) *n.* A small, hidden place.

## O

**observation** (ob′ zûr vā′ shən) *n.* The act of studying or noticing.

**observe** (əb zûrv′) *v.* To see; to look at.

**occasion** (ə kā′ zhən) *n.* An event.

**ocotillo** (ō′ kə tēl′ yō) *n.* A desert bush with sharp spines.

**opportunity** (op′ ər to̅o̅′ ni tē) *n.* A good chance.

**ordinary** (ôr′ dən er′ ē) *adj.* The usual kind.

**organization** (or′ gə nə zā′ shən) *n.* A group of people who join together for one purpose; a club.

**originality** (ə rij′ ə nal′ i tē) *n.* Newness; freshness.

**originally** (ə rij′ ə nl ē) *adv.* At first; in the beginning.

**outfit** (out′ fit′) *n.* A group of people with a common purpose or belief.

**overpass** (ō′ vər pas′) *n.* A road that crosses above another road.

overpass

## P

**parachute** (par′ ə sho̅o̅t′) *n.* An umbrella-shaped object that helps other objects float down slowly from heights.

**parade** (pə rād′) *v.* To march in an orderly fashion.

**parasite** (par′ ə sīt′) *n.* An animal that lives and feeds on another animal.

**patch** (pach) *n.* A small area.

**particular** (pər tik′ yə lər) *adj.* Only; special.

**patient** (pā′ shənt) *adj.* Calmly putting up with something difficult.

**passageway** (pas′ ij wā′) *n.* A narrow place to walk between two buildings.

**pattern** (pat′ ərn) *n.* The way in which things are placed.

**peer** (pēr) *v.* To look.

**peregrine** (per′i grin) *n.* A type of falcon that catches other birds in flight.

**period** (pēr′ ē əd) *n.* An amount of time.

**permission** (pər mi′ shən) *n.* Consent that allows one to do something.

**petition** (pə tish′ ən) *n.* A written request to someone in charge, signed by those who agree.

**petroleum jelly** (pe′ trō′ lē əm jel′ ē) *n.* A greasy, sticky substance used to coat things.

**plantain** (plan′ tin) *n.* A weed that has large leaves and long spikes with small flowers.

**plaster** (plas′ tər) *n.* A substance like cement that is used to make walls and ceilings.

**plume** (plo̅o̅m) *n.* A long feather.

**poet** (pō′ ət) *n.* A person who writes or composes poems.

**pollution** (pə lo̅o̅′ shən) *n.* Harmful or dirty material added to the air, water, or soil.

**population** (pä′ pyə lā′ shən) *n.* A count of how many in a group.

**porcupine** (por′ kyə pīne) *n.* An animal with stiff pointy hairs.

**portion** (por′ shən) *n.* A part.

**possess** (pə zes′) *v.* To have; to own.

Pronunciation Key: **at**; l**ā**te; c**â**re; f**ä**ther; set; m**ē**; **it**; k**ī**te; **ox**; r**ō**se; **ô** in b**ou**ght; c**oi**n; b**oo̅**k; t**oo̅**; f**or**m; **out**; **up**; **ū**se; t**ûr**n; **ə** sound in about, chicken, pencil, cannon, circus; **ch**air; **hw** in **wh**ich; r**ing**; **sh**op; **th**in; **th**ere; **zh** in treasure.

**post** (pōst) *n.* A position that one is appointed to.

**pottery** (pot′ ə rē) *n.* Bowls, pots, plates, and other objects shaped from moist clay and hardened by heat.

**practical** (prak′ ti kəl) *adj.* Useful.

**prejudice** (prej′ ə dis) *n.* Unfairness; an opinion formed without knowing the facts.

**prickly** (prik′ lē) *adj.* Full of sharp points that stick or sting.

**privet** (priv′ it) *n.* A shrub related to the lilac bush and the olive tree. It has small white flowers and smooth, dark fruit; all parts are poisonous.

**probably** (prä′ bə blē) *adv.* Most likely to happen.

**procession** (prə se′ shən) *n.* A group of people that moves along in a formal manner.

**proclaim** (prō klām′) *v.* To declare; to announce officially.

**proper** (pro′ pər) *adj.* Acceptable.

**protest** (prō′ test) *n.* A statement against something.

**proud** (proud) *adj.* Feeling very pleased with something.

**provoke** (prə vōk′) *v.* To cause.

## Q

**Queen Anne's lace** (kwēn′ anz′ lās′) *n.* A wild form of the carrot plant with lacy white flowers.

**quill** (kwil) *n.* The stiff pointy hairs on a porcupine.

## R

**racial** (rā′ shəl) *adj.* Having to do with a race of people.

**rebel** (ri bəl′) *v.* To resist a ruler's power.

**rectangle** (rek′ tan′ gəl) *n.* A four-sided shape with four right angles.

**regardless** (ri gärd′ lis) *adv.* Without concern for.

**relocate** (rē lō′ kāt′) *v.* To move to a different place.

**rescue** (res′ kū) *v.* To save from harm or danger.

**resist** (ri zist′) *v.* To fight against.

**respond** (ri spond′) *v.* To answer.

**responsibility** (ri spon′ sə bil′ i tē) *n.* A duty; a job.

**rotate** (rō′ tāt′) *v.* To move as though going around in a circle.

**routine** (ro̅o̅ tēn′) *n.* The same actions done over and over.

**royal** (roi′ əl) *adj.* Owned by a king or a queen.

## S

**scenery** (sē′ nə rē) *n.* The painted pictures and objects used on stage in a play.

**scholar** (sko′ lər) *n.* A person who has learned a great deal about a subject.

**scrawl** (skrôl) *v.* To write in a fast, messy way. —*n.* A scribble.

**sculpt** (skulpt) *v.* To make a figure, statue, or design by carving wood or stone or by forming clay.

**sculpture** (skulp′ chər) *n.* A figure, statue, or design carved out of something solid.

**segregation** (seg′ ri gā′ shən) *n.* Keeping different races of people apart from each other.

**seldom** (sel′ dəm) *adv.* Rarely; not often.

**sensitive** (sen′ si tiv) *adj.* Able to feel things well.

**seriously** (sir′ ē əs lē) *adv.* Thoughtfully, sincerely.

**sesame** (ses′ ə mē) *n.* The seed of an Asian plant which is used to add flavor to food.

**severe** (sə vir′) *adj.* Harsh or extreme.

**sewer** (so̅o̅′ ər) *n.* An underground pipe that carries dirty water away from buildings.

**shades** (shādz) *n.* Sunglasses.

**shadowed** (sha′ dōd) *adj.* Covered in shadow; partially hidden.

**shallow** (shal′ ō) *adj.* Being close to the bottom; not deep.

**sharp** (shärp) *n.* A musical note that sounds one-half tone higher than it usually does. —*adj.* 1. Clear. 2. Keen.

**shock** (shok) *v.* To surprise and upset at the same time.

**shutter** (shut′ ər) *n.* A doorlike cover that opens and closes over a window.

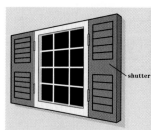
shutter

**skyscraper** (skī′ skrā′ pər) *n.* A very tall building found in a city.

**slope** (slōp) *n.* An upward or downward slant.

**smokestack** (smōk′ stak′) *n.* A large, tall chimney from which smoke is released.

**soar** (sor) *v.* To fly at a great height.

ANTHOLOGY GLOSSARY

**Pronunciation Key: at; lāte; câre; fäther; set; mē; it; kīte; ox; rōse; ô in bought; coin; bŏŏk; tōō; form; out; up; ūse; tûrn; ə sound in about, chicken, pencil, cannon, circus; chair; hw in which; ring; shop; thin; ther̶e; zh in treasure.**

**solemnly** (so′ ləm lē) *adv.* In a serious way.

**solution** (sə lōō′ shən) *n.* A way to solve a problem.

**sought** (sôt) *v.* Past tense of **seek:** To look for.

**species** (spē′ shēz) *n.* An animal family; a kind of animal.

**splinter** (splin′ tər) *n.* A small sharp piece of wood broken off from a larger piece.

**squeegee** (skwē′ jē) *v.* To make a squeaking sound by rubbing as if using a squeegee, which is a rubber-edged tool for removing excess water from windows.

**squiggle** (skwig′ əl) *n.* A line that is curved or wavy.

**stalk** (stôk) *n.* The stem of a plant.

**starve** (stärv) *v.* To die from hunger.

**statue** (stach′ ōō) *n.* A carved figure of a person or an animal.

**sternly** (stûrn′ lē) *adv.* In a strict or harsh way.

**stiff** (stif) *adj.* Something not easily bent; not flexible.

**stitch** (stich) *n.* A tight loop of thread holding two pieces of cloth together.

**stout** (stout) *adj.* Sturdy; strong.

**stucco** (stuk′ ō) *n.* Plaster that covers outside walls.

**sturdy** (stər′ dē) *adj.* Solidly built.

**style** (stīl) *n.* The way something is done.

**subject** (səb′ jikt) *n.* A person who is ruled over.

**suburb** (sub′ ûrb) *n.* A town on the outer edge of a larger city.

**suitable** (sōō′ tə bəl) *adj.* Fitting; right.

**sycamore** (sik′ ə mor′) *n.* A shade tree; a buttonwood tree.

## T

**taunt** (tônt) *n.* Spoken words that make fun of someone in a mean way.

**tease** (tēz) *v.* To annoy continuously.

**temperature** (tem′ pər ə chər) *n.* The hotness or coldness of a thing.

**territory** (ter′ ə tor′ ē) *n.* An area of land.

**toil** (toi′ əl) *v.* To work hard.

**trace** (trās) *v.* To form carefully; to sketch.

**trainer** (trā′ nər) *n.* Teacher, coach.

284

**traitor** (trā′ tər) *n.* Someone who betrays another's trust.

**triangle** (trī′ an′ gəl) *n.* A three-sided shape with three angles.

**trestle** (tres′ əl) *n.* A framework that holds up train tracks above a river or above the ground.

trestle

**trill** (tril) *v.* To make a vibrating sound, like the sound some birds make.

**tundra** (tun′ drə) *n.* In the arctic regions, a flat plain with no trees.

**twitter** (twi′ tər) *v.* To chatter noisily; to sound like chirping birds.

**tyrant** (tī′ rənt) *n.* A harsh, unjust ruler.

## U

**urban** (ûr′ bən) *adj.* In a city.

## V

**vacant** (vā′ kənt) *adj.* Empty.

**vigilante** (vij′ ə lan′ tē) *n.* A person who acts as if he or she is the law.

**violently** (vī′ ə lənt lē) *adv.* With destructive force.

**visible** (viz′ ə bəl) *adj.* Able to be seen.

## W

**wardrobe** (wor′ drōb′) *n.* A collection of clothes.

**warehouse** (war′ hous′) *n.* A building where products and materials are stored.

**whine** (hwīn) *v.* To talk in a complaining, annoying voice.

**wilderness** (wil′ dər nəs) *n.* A wild, natural area that has not been developed or occupied by people.

**windswept** (wind′ swept′) *adj.* Blown by wind constantly.

285

# Program Appendix

# Program Appendix

The Program Appendix includes a step-by-step explanation of procedures for research-based, effective practices in reading instruction that are repeatedly used throughout *SRA/Open Court Reading*. These practices may also be used in other instructional materials.

## Table of Contents

# Reading Materials and Techniques

Different reading materials and techniques are appropriate at different stages of reading development. The purpose of this section is to discuss different types of reading materials and how they may be used most effectively.

## Reading Big Books

### Purpose

Many students come from homes where they are read to often, but a significant number of other students have not had this valuable experience. Big Books (Levels K and 1) offer all students crucial opportunities to confirm and expand their knowledge about print and reading. They are especially useful for shared reading experiences in the early grades.

The benefits of reading Big Books include engaging even nonreaders in:

- unlocking the books' messages.
- developing print awareness.
- participating in good reading behaviors.
- observing what a good reader does: remarking on the illustrations and the title, asking questions about the content and what might happen, making predictions, and clarifying words and ideas.
- promoting the insight that a given word is spelled the same way every time it occurs as high-frequency words are pointed out.
- reinforcing the correspondence between spoken and written words and spelling patterns.
- enjoying the illustrations and connecting them to the text to help students learn to explore books for enjoyment and information.
- interpreting and responding to literature and expository text before they can read themselves.

### Procedure for Reading Big Books

During the first reading of the Big Books, you will model reading behaviors and comprehension strategies similar to those that will later be taught formally. During the second reading, you will address print awareness and teach comprehension skills such as classifying and categorizing or sequencing, which help the reader organize information. In addition, you will teach skills such as making inferences and drawing conclusions, which help the reader focus on the deeper meaning of the text. At first, teachers should expect to do all of the reading but should not prevent students from trying to read on their own or from reading words they already know.

- **Activate Prior Knowledge.** Read the title of the selection and the author's and illustrator's names. At the beginning of each Big Book, read the title of the book and discuss what the whole book is about before going on to reading the first selection.
- **Discuss Prior Knowledge.** Initiate a brief discussion of any prior knowledge the students have that might help them understand the selection.
- **Browse the Selection.** Ask students to tell what they think the story might be about just from looking at the illustrations. This conversation should be brief so that the students can move on to a prereading discussion of print awareness.

> *Big Books offer all students crucial opportunities to confirm and expand their knowledge about print and reading.*

- **Develop Print Awareness.** The focus of browsing the Big Books is to develop awareness of print. Urge students to tell what words or letters they recognize rather than what they expect the selection to be about.

  To develop print awareness, have students look through the selection page by page and comment on whatever they notice in the text. Some students may know some of the words, while others may only recognize specific letters or sounds. The key is to get the students to look at the print separately from the illustrations even before they have heard the actual text content. This process isolates print awareness so that it is not influenced by content. It also gives you a clearer idea of what your students do or do not know about print.
- **Read Aloud.** Read the selection aloud expressively. The reading enables the students simply to hear and enjoy the text as it is read through once. With this reading, you will model behaviors and comprehension strategies that all students will need to develop to become successful readers—for example, asking questions; clarifying unfamiliar words, first by using the pictures and later by using context; or predicting what might happen next.
- **Reread.** Read the selection expressively again. During the second reading of the stories, you will focus on teaching comprehension skills. Also, to develop print awareness, point to each word as it is read, thus demonstrating that text proceeds from left to right and from top to bottom and helping advance the idea that words are individual spoken and written units. Invite the students to identify the rhyming words in a poem or chime in on repetitive parts of text as you point to the words. Or students can read with you on this second reading, depending on the text.
- **Discuss Print.** Return to print awareness by encouraging discussion of anything the students noticed about the words. Young students should begin to realize that you are reading separate words that are separated by spaces. Later, students will begin to see that each word is made up of a group of letters. The students should be encouraged to discuss anything related to the print. For example, you might ask students to point to a word or count the number of words on a line. Or you might connect the words to the illustrations by pointing to a word and saying it and then asking the students to find a picture of that word.
- **Responding.** Responding to a selection is a way of insuring comprehension. Invite students to tell about the story by asking them what they like about the poem or story or calling on a student to explain in his or her own words what the poem or story tells about. Call on others to add to the telling as needed. For nonfiction selections, this discussion might include asking students what they learned about the topic and what they thought was most interesting.

### Tips for Using Big Books

- Make sure the entire group is able to see the book clearly while you are reading.
- If some students are able to read or predict words, encourage them to do so during the rereading.
- Encourage students to present and use their knowledge of print.
- Allow students to look at the Big Books whenever they wish.
- Provide small versions of the Big Books for students to browse through and try to read at their leisure.
- The reader of the Big Book should try to be part of the collaborative group of learners rather than the leader.

# Using the Pre-Decodable Books

## Purpose

**Pre-Decodable Books** play an important role in students' early literacy development by providing them with meaningful "reading" experiences before they are actually reading on their own and by expanding their awareness of the forms and uses of print. By following along as you read aloud a **Pre-Decodable Book,** students learn about the left-to-right and top-to-bottom progression of print on a page, the clues that indicate the beginnings and endings of sentences, the connections between pictures and words, and important book conventions, such as front and back covers, authors' and illustrators' names, title pages, and page numbers.

The **Pre-Decodable Books** provide students with opportunities to apply their growing knowledge of letter names, shapes, and sounds, and to become familiar with individual words.

Through retelling the story in a **Pre-Decodable Book,** predicting or wondering about what will happen, and asking and responding to questions about the book, students not only learn about the relationship between spoken and written language, they learn to think about what they have read.

## About the Pre-Decodable Books

Each **Pre-Decodable Book** contains a story that engages students' interest as it provides them with opportunities to practice what they are learning in their lessons. These "Pre-Decodable" stories each contain several high-frequency words that most students already have in their spoken vocabularies and that are a basic part of all meaningful stories. Learning to identify high-frequency words quickly, accurately, and effortlessly is a critical part of students' development as fluent, independent readers. The inside back cover of each **Pre-Decodable Book** contains a list of high-frequency words.

## How to Read the Pre-Decodable Books

- Before reading a **Pre-Decodable Book,** take time to familiarize students with any new **high-frequency words** in the book and to review previously introduced words. To reinforce the idea that it is important to know these words because they are used so often in print, always point out the words in context. For example, focus students' attention on the words in Big Book selections or on signs and posters around the classroom.
- Give each student a copy of the book. Tell students that you will read the book together. Hold up your book. Read the title. If the title has a rebus picture, point to it and tell the students what it is. Then point to the word beneath it and explain that the picture represents that word. Point to and read the names of the author and illustrator, reminding students that an author writes a book and an illustrator draws the pictures. Page through the book, pointing to and naming the rebus pictures. Have the students say the name of each rebus. To avoid confusion, always *tell* them the *exact* word that a rebus represents. *Don't encourage them to guess at its meaning.*
- Allow students time to browse through the book on their own, commenting on what they see in the illustrations and making predictions about what they think the book will be about. Encourage them to comment on anything special they notice about the story, the illustrations, or the words in the book.
- Help the students to find page 3. Read the book aloud without stopping. As you read, move your hand beneath the words to show the progression of print. Pause at each rebus as you say the word it represents, pointing first to the rebus, then to the word beneath it.
- Reread the book. This time, ask the students to point to and read the high-frequency words.
- Tell the students to follow along in their books as you read the story again. Read the title aloud, and then have the students read it with you. Reread page 3. Point to each rebus picture and ask a volunteer to "read" it. Point to the word beneath the picture and remind students that the picture shows what the word is. Continue through each page of the book, calling on volunteers to "read" and stopping as necessary to clarify and help students with words.
- After reading, answer any questions the students might have about the book. Encourage them to discuss the illustrations and to explain what is happening in each one.

# Reading Decodables and Building Fluency

## Purpose

The most urgent task of early reading instruction is to make written thoughts intelligible to students. This requires a balanced approach that includes systematic instruction in phonics as well as experiences with authentic literature. Thus, from the very beginning, *Open Court Reading* includes the reading of literature. At the beginning of first grade, when students are learning phonics and blending as a tool to access words, the teacher reads aloud. During this time students are working on using comprehension strategies and skills and discussing stories. As students learn the code and blend words, recognize critical sight words, and develop some level of fluency, they take more responsibility for the actual reading of the text.

This program has a systematic instruction in phonics that allows the students to begin reading independently. This instruction is supported by *Open Court Reading* Decodable Books.

## Practice

The *Open Court Reading* Decodable Books are designed to help the students apply, review, and reinforce their expanding knowledge of sound/spelling correspondences. Each story supports instruction in new phonic elements and incorporates elements and words that have been learned earlier. There are eight page and sixteen page Decodable Books. Grade K has eight-page Decodable Books. In Grade 1 the eight-page books focus on the new element introduced in the lesson, while the sixteen-page books review and reinforce the elements that have been taught since the last sixteen-page book. They review sounds from several lessons and provide additional reading practice. Grades 2–3 have eight-page Decodable Books in Getting Started, and sixteen-page books in the first 4–5 units of the grade level. The primary purpose is to provide practice reading the words. It is important that the students also attach meaning to what they are reading. Questions are often included in the *Teacher's Edition* to check both understanding and attention to words.

### Fluency

Fluency is the effortless ability to read or access words with seemingly little attention to decoding. It also involves grouping words into meaningful units and using expression appropriately. Fluency is critical but not sufficient for comprehension.

To become proficient readers who fully understand what they read, the whole process of decoding must become as automatic as possible. The students need to be so familiar with the

## Reading Materials and Techniques (continued)

sound/spellings and with the most common nondecodable sight words that they automatically process the letters or spellings and expend most of their energy on comprehending the meaning of the text.

While fluency begins in first grade, many students will continue to need practice in building fluency in second and third grades. Initially, students can use the *Open Court Reading* **Decodable Books** in grades 2 and 3, but fluency practice should include using materials from actual literature the students are reading.

## Procedure

### Preparing to Read

- Introduce and write on the board any nondecodable high-frequency or story words introduced or reviewed in the story. Tell the students how to pronounce any newly introduced high-frequency words. Then point to each new word and have the students say it. Have them read any previously introduced sight word in the Word Bank list. All of the *Open Court Reading* **Decodable Books** contain high-frequency words that may not be decodable. For example, the word *said* is a very common high-frequency word that is not decodable. Including words like *said* makes the language of the story flow smoothly and naturally. The students need to be able to recognize these words quickly and smoothly.

- Read the title. At the beginning of the year, you may need to read the title of the book to the students, but as the year goes on, you should have a student read it whenever possible. The sixteen-page *Open Court Reading* **Decodable Books** contain two related chapters, each using the same sounds and spellings. In such cases, read the title of the **Decodable** book, and then point out the two individual chapter titles. Have volunteers read the title of the chapter you are about to read.

- Browse the story. Have the students look through the story, commenting on whatever they notice in the text or illustrations and telling what they think the story will tell them.

### Reading the Story

After this browsing, the students will read the story a page at a time. Again, these books are designed to support the learning of sounds and spellings. The focus should not be on comprehension. Students should understand what they are reading, and they should feel free to discuss anything in the story that interests them. Any areas of confusion are discussed and clarified as they arise, as described below.

- Have the students read a page to themselves. Then call on one student to read the page aloud, or have the whole group read it aloud.

- If a student has difficulty with a word that can be blended, help her or him blend the word. Remind the student to check the **Sound/Spelling Cards** for help. If a word cannot be blended using the sound/spellings learned so far, pronounce the word for the student.

- If a student has trouble with a word or sentence, have the reader call on a classmate for help, and then continue reading after the word or sentence has been clarified. After something on a page has been clarified or discussed, have that page reread by a different student before moving on to the next page.

- Repeat this procedure for each page.

- Reread the story twice more, calling on different students to read or reading it in unison. These readings should go more quickly, with fewer stops for clarification.

### Responding to the Story

Once the story has been read aloud a few times, have the students respond as follows:

- Ask the students what hard words they found in the story and how they figured them out. They may mention high-frequency words they didn't recognize, words they had to blend, and words whose meanings they did not know.

- Invite the students to tell about the story, retelling it in their own words, describing what they liked about it, or citing what they found interesting or surprising. Specific suggestions to use are listed in the *Teacher's Edition.*

- Questions are provided in the *Teacher's Edition.* They are designed to focus the students' attention on the words and not just the pictures. The questions require answers that cannot be guessed by looking at the pictures alone, such as a name, a bit of dialogue, or an action or object that is not pictured. Have the students point to the words, phrases, or sentences that answer the questions.

### Building Fluency

Buiding fluency is essential to gaining strong comprehension. The more fluent the students become, the more they can attend to the critical business of understanding the text. Opportunities for students to build fluency may include:

- Have students "partner read" the most recent *Open Court Reading* **Decodable Book** twice, taking turns reading a page at a time. The partners should switch the second time through so they are reading different pages from the ones they read the first time. If there is time left, the partners should choose any of the previously read stories to read together. Use this time for diagnosis, having one student at a time read with you.

- Making sure that the *Open Court Reading* **Decodable Books** are readily available in the classroom.

- Reading **Decodable Books** with as many students as possible one at a time.

- Reminding the students that they may read with partners during Workshop.

The only way the students can become fluent readers is to read as much and as often as possible.

# Reading the Student Anthologies

## Purpose

Reading is a complex process that requires students not only to decode what they read but also to understand and respond to it. The purpose of this section is to help you identify various reading behaviors used by good readers and to encourage those behaviors in your students.

## Reading Behaviors and Comprehension Strategies

There are four basic behaviors that good readers engage in during reading. These behaviors include the application of certain comprehension strategies, which are modeled while reading the Student Anthology (Levels 1–6).

### Setting Reading Goals and Expectations

Good readers set reading goals and expectations before they begin reading. This behavior involves a variety of strategies that will help students prepare to read the text.

- **Activate prior knowledge.** When good readers approach a new text, they consider what they already know about the subject or what their experiences have been in reading similar material.
- **Browse the text.** To get an idea of what to expect from a text, good readers look at the title and the illustrations. They may look for potential problems, such as difficult words. When browsing a unit, have students glance quickly at each selection, looking briefly at the illustrations and the print. Have them tell what they think they might be learning about as they read the unit.
- **Decide what they expect from the text.** When reading for pleasure, good readers anticipate enjoying the story or the language. When reading to learn something, they ask themselves what they expect to find out.

### Responding to Text

Good readers are active readers. They interact with text by using the following strategies:

- **Making connections.** Good readers make connections between what they read and what they already know. They pay attention to elements in the text that remind them of their own experiences.
- **Visualizing, or picturing.** Good readers visualize what is happening in the text. They form mental images as they read. They picture the setting, the characters, and the action in a story. When reading expository text, good

readers picture the objects, processes, or events described. Visualizing helps readers understand descriptions of complex activities or processes.

- **Asking questions.** Good readers ask questions that may prepare them for what they will learn. If their questions are not answered in the text, they may try to find answers elsewhere and thus add even more to their store of knowledge.
- **Predicting.** Good readers predict what will happen next. When reading fiction, they make predictions about what they are reading and then confirm or revise those predictions as they go.
- **Thinking about how the text makes you feel.** Well-written fiction touches readers' emotions; it sparks ideas.

### Checking Understanding

One of the most important behaviors good readers exhibit is the refusal to continue reading when something fails to make sense. Good readers continually assess their understanding of the text with strategies such as:

- **Interpreting.** As they read, good readers make inferences that help them understand and appreciate what they are reading.
- **Summing up.** Good readers sum up to check their understanding as they read. Sometimes they reread to fill in gaps in their understanding.
- **Monitoring and adjusting reading speed.** Good readers monitor their understanding of what they read. They slow down as they come to difficult words and passages. They speed up as they read easier passages.

### Monitoring and Clarifying Unfamiliar Words and Passages

- **Apply decoding skills** to sound out unknown words.
- **Determine what is unclear** to find the source of the confusion.
- **Apply context clues** in text and illustrations to figure out the meanings of words or passages.
- **Reread the passage** to make sure the passage makes sense.
- **Check a dictionary or the glossary** to understand the meanings of words not clarified by clues or rereading.

## Procedures

### Modeling and Thinking Aloud

Modeling and encouraging students to think aloud as they attempt to understand text can demonstrate for everyone how reading behaviors are put into practice. The most effective models will be those that come from your own reading. Using questions such as the following, as well as your students' questions and comments, will

make both the text and the strategic reading process more meaningful to students.

- What kinds of things did you wonder about?
- What kinds of things surprised you?
- What new information did you learn?
- What was confusing until you reread or read further?

Model comprehension strategies in a natural way, and choose questions and comments that fit the text you are reading. Present a variety of ways to respond to text.

- Pose questions that you really do wonder about.
- Identify with characters by comparing them with yourself.
- React emotionally by showing joy, sadness, amusement, or surprise.
- Show empathy with or sympathy for characters.
- Relate the text to something that has happened to you or to something you already know.
- Show interest in the text ideas.
- Question the meaning or clarity of the author's words and ideas.

### Encouraging Students' Responses and Use of Strategies

Most students will typically remain silent as they try to figure out an unfamiliar word or a confusing passage. Encourage students to identify specifically what they are having difficulty with. Once the problem has been identified, ask the students to suggest a strategy for dealing with the problem. Remind students to:

- Treat problems encountered in text as interesting learning opportunities.
- Think out loud about text challenges.
- Help each other build meaning. Rather than tell what a word is, students should tell how they figured out the meanings of challenging words and passages.
- Consider reading a selection again with a partner after reading it once alone. Partner reading provides valuable practice in reading for fluency.
- Make as many connections as they can between what they are reading and what they already know.
- Visualize to clarify meanings or enjoy descriptions.
- Ask questions about what they are reading.
- Notice how the text makes them feel.

## Reading Materials and Techniques (continued)

# Reading Techniques

## Reading Aloud

### Purpose

Adults read a variety of materials aloud to students. These include Big Books, picture books, and novels. Research has shown that students who are read to are more likely to develop the skills they need to read successfully on their own.

In every grade level of **Open Court Reading** there are opportunities for teachers to read aloud to students. At the beginning of each unit is a Read-Aloud selection tied to the unit theme. This Read-Aloud selection allows students the opportunity to think about the unit theme before reading selections on their own.

Reading aloud at any age serves multiple purposes. Reading aloud:

- Provokes students' curiosity about text.
- Conveys an awareness that text has meaning.
- Demonstrates the various reasons for reading text (to find out about the world around them, to learn useful new information and new skills, or simply for pleasure).
- Exposes students to the "language of literature," which is more complex than the language they ordinarily use and hear.
- Provides an opportunity to teach the problem-solving strategies that good readers employ. As the students observe you interacting with the text, expressing your own enthusiasm, and modeling your thinking aloud, they perceive these as valid responses and begin to respond to text in similar ways.

### Procedures

The following set of general procedures for reading aloud is designed to help you maximize the effectiveness of Read-Aloud sessions.

- **Read-aloud sessions.** Set aside time each day to read aloud.
- **Introduce the story.** Tell the students that you are going to read a story aloud to them. Tell its title and briefly comment on the topic. To allow the students to anticipate what will happen in the story, be careful not to summarize.
- **Activate prior knowledge.** Ask whether anyone has already heard the story. If so, ask them to see if this version is the same as the one they have heard. If not, activate prior knowledge by saying, "First, let's talk a little about _____." If the story is being read in two (or more) parts, before reading the second part, ask the students to recall the first part.
- **Before reading.** Invite students to interrupt your reading if there are any words they do not

understand or ideas they find puzzling. Throughout the reading, encourage them to do this.

- **Read the story expressively.** Occasionally react verbally to the story by showing surprise, asking questions, giving an opinion, expressing pleasure, or predicting events. Think-aloud suggestions are outlined below.
- **Use Comprehension Strategies.** While reading aloud to the students, model the use of comprehension strategies in a natural, authentic way. Remember to try to present a variety of ways to respond to text. These include visualizing, asking questions, predicting, making connections, clarifying, and summarizing.
- **Retell.** When you have finished reading the story, call on volunteers to retell it.
- **Discuss.** After reading, discuss with the students their own reactions: how the story reminded them of things that have happened to them, what they thought of the story, and what they liked best about the story.
- **Reread.** You may wish to reread the selection on subsequent occasions focusing the discussion on the unit theme.

### Think-Aloud Responses

The following options for modeling thinking aloud will be useful for reading any story aloud. Choose responses that are most appropriate for the selection you are reading.

- **React emotionally** by showing joy, sadness, amusement, or surprise.
- **Ask questions** about ideas in the text. This should be done when there are points or ideas that you really do wonder about.
- **Identify with characters** by comparing them to yourself.
- **Show empathy with or sympathy for** characters.
- **Relate the text to something** you already know or something that has happened to you.
- **Show interest** in the text ideas.
- **Question the meaning and/or clarity** of the author's words and ideas.

### Questions to Help Students Respond

At reasonable stopping points in reading, ask the students general questions in order to get them to express their own ideas and to focus their attention on the text.

- What do you already know about this?
- What seems really important here? Why do you think so?
- Was there anything that you didn't understand? What?
- What did you like best about this?
- What new ideas did you learn from this?
- What does this make you wonder about?

# Reading Roundtable

## Purpose

Adult readers discuss their reading, give opinions on it, and recommend books to each other. Reading Roundtable, an activity students may choose to participate in during **Workshop**, provides the same opportunity for students in the classroom. Sessions can be small or large. During Reading Roundtable, students share the reading they do on their own. They can discuss a book they have all read, or one person can review a book for the others and answer questions from the group.

During Reading Roundtable, students can discuss and review a variety of books:

- Full-length versions of Anthology selections.
- Classroom Library selections.
- Books that students learn about when discussing authors and illustrators.
- Books related to the investigations of unit concepts can be shared with others who might want to read them.
- Interesting articles from magazines, newspapers, and other sources.

## Procedures

### Encouraging Reading

- Read aloud to your students regularly. You can read Classroom Library selections or full-length versions of Student Anthology selections.
- Provide a time each day for students to read silently. This time can be as short as 10–15 minutes but should be strictly observed. You should stop what you are doing and read. Students should be allowed to choose their own reading materials during this time and record their reactions in the Response Journal section of their Writer's Notebook.
- Establish a classroom library and reading center with books from the school or local library or ask for donations of books from students, parents, and community members.
- Take your students to the school library or to the public library.

### Conducting a Reading Roundtable

- When a student reviews a book others have not read, he or she can use some of the sentence starters to tell about the book. These may include, "This book is about . . . , I chose this book because. . . , What I really like/don't like about this book is . . . " and so on.
- When several students read the same book and discuss it during Reading Roundtable, they can use discussion starters. If the book is from the Classroom Library, they can discuss how it relates to the unit concepts.

# Introducing Sounds and Letters

## Purpose

In *SRA/Open Court Reading*, students learn to relate sounds to letters in Kindergarten through the use of thirty-one **Alphabet Sound Cards** (Level K). In the upper grade levels, **Sound Spelling Cards** (Levels 1–3) are used to relate sounds and spellings. The purpose of the **Alphabet Sound Cards** is to remind the students of the sounds of the English language and their letter correspondences. These cards are a resource for the students to use to remember sound-letter associations for both reading and writing.

Each card contains the capital and small letter, and a picture that shows the sound being produced. For instance, the **Monkey** card introduces the /m/ sound and shows a monkey looking at bananas and saying /m/ /m/ /m/. The name of the picture on each card contains the target sound at the beginning of the word for the consonants and in the middle for most of the vowels. Vowel letters are printed in red and consonants are printed in black. In addition, the picture associates a sound with an action. This action-sound association is introduced through a short, interactive story found in the *Teacher's Edition* in which the pictured object or character "makes" the sound of the letter. Long vowels are represented by a tall—or "long"—picture of the letters themselves, rather than by a picture for action-sound association.

## Procedures

- Display the cards 1–26 with the picture sides to the wall. Initially post the first twenty-six cards in alphabetical order so that only the alphabet letters show. The short vowel cards may be posted as they are introduced later. As you introduce the letter sound, you will turn the card to show the picture and the letter on the other side. Once the cards are posted, do not change their positions so that the students can locate the cards quickly.
- Before turning a card, point to the letter. Ask students to tell what they know about the letter. For example, they are likely to know its name and possibly its sound if the letter is one they have already worked with.

- Turn the card and show the picture. Tell the students the name of the card, and explain that it will help them to remember the sound the letter makes.
- Read the story that goes with the letter. Read it expressively, emphasizing the words with the target sound and the isolated sound when it occurs. Have the students join in to produce the sound.
- Repeat the story a few times, encouraging all students to say the sound along with you.
- Follow the story with the cards for the target sound. (These are listed within the lessons.)
- Name each picture, and have students listen for the target sound at the beginning of the word. Ask students to repeat the words and the sound.
- For every letter sound, a listening activity follows the introduction of the cards. Lead the students in the "Listening for the Sound" activity to reinforce the letter sound.
- To link the sound and the letter, demonstrate how to form the uppercase and lowercase letter by writing on the board or on an overhead transparency. The students practice forming the letter and saying the sound as they write.

### Alphabet Sound Cards

The pictures and letters on the **Alphabet Sound Cards (Wall Cards)** also appear on the small sets of **Alphabet Sound Cards (Individual)**. The Teacher's Edition specifically suggests that you use the **Individual Alphabet Sound Cards** for some activities. You may also use the small cards for review and for small-group reteaching and practice sessions. Have sets of the cards available for the students to use during **Workshop** either alone or with partners. Add each small card to the Activity Center after you have taught the lesson in which the corresponding **Alphabet Sound Card** is introduced. Here are some suggestions for activities using the **Alphabet Sound Cards**:

1. **Saying sounds from pictures.** The leader flashes pictures as the others say the sound each picture represents.
2. **Saying sounds.** The leader flashes the letters on the cards as the others say the sound that the letters represent.

3. **Naming words from pictures.** The leader flashes pictures. The others say the sound, and then say a word beginning with that sound.
4. **Writing letters from the pictures.** Working alone, a student looks at a picture and then writes the letter for the sound that picture represents.

### Tips

- Throughout the beginning lessons, help students remember that vowels are special by reminding them that vowels sometimes say their names in words. For example, the picture of the *a* on the long *a* **Alphabet Sound Card** is long because the long *a* says its name. The short *a* **Alphabet Sound Card** pictures the lamb, because the lamb makes the short *a* sound, and you can hear the sound in the word, *lamb*. In the later lessons, students will use both sets of cards to help them remember that the vowels have both a short and a long sound.
- From the very beginning, encourage students to use the **Alphabet Sound Cards** as a resource to help them with their work.
- Mastery of letter recognition is the goal students should reach so that they will be prepared to link each letter with its associated sound. If students have not yet mastered the names of the letters, it is important to work with them individually in **Workshop**, or at other times during the day.
- The *Kk* card is a little tricky. A camera makes the /k/ sound when it clicks, and the word *camera* begins with the /k/ sound. However, the word *camera* is not spelled with a *k*. While you need not dwell on this, be aware that some students may be confused by the fact that the *Cc* and *Kk* cards have the same picture.
- The picture on the *Qq* card depicts ducks, *quacking ducks*. Make sure that the students consistently call them *quacking ducks*, not *ducks*, and that they focus on the /kw/ sound.

# The Alphabetic Principle: How the Alphabet Works

## The Alphabetic Principle

### Purpose

A major emphasis in the kindergarten program is on letter recognition and attending to sounds. Students need to learn the alphabetic principle: that letters work together in a systematic way to connect spoken language to written words. This understanding is the foundation for reading. Students are not expected to master letter/sound correspondence at the beginning of kindergarten, nor are they expected to blend sounds into words themselves. They are only expected to become an "expert" on their Special Letter as they learn how the alphabet works. Through this introduction to the alphabetic principle, the students will have the basic understanding required to work through the alphabet letter by letter, attaching sounds to each.

Key concepts of the Alphabetic Principle include:

- A limited number of letters combine in different ways to make many different words.
- Words are composed of sounds and letters represent those sounds.
- Anything that can be pronounced can be spelled.
- Letters and sounds can be used to identify words.
- Meaning can be obtained by using letters and sounds to figure out words.

### Procedures for Kindergarten

The following steps can be used for introducing letters and sounds in Kindergarten. These steps may be adapted for students at other grades if they do not understand the alphabetic principle. The tone of these activities should be informal, fun, and fast-paced. The purpose of these activities is to familiarize the students with how the alphabet works by having them participate in group play with letters and sounds.

#### Introducing Letters

- Reinforce the idea that anything that can be pronounced can be spelled with the letters of the alphabet.
- Tell the students that you can spell any word. Have them give you words to spell.
- Write the words on the board, and show students that the words contain the letters displayed on the **Alphabet Sound Cards**.
- Have students help you spell the words by pointing to letters as you say them and then write them.
- Encourage students to spell each word letter by letter.

#### Letter Expert Groups

- Have **Letter Cards** (Levels K and 1) available for the following set of letters: *b, d, f, h, l, m, n, p, s, t*. You will need two or three cards for each letter. (You will not need the **Alphabet Sound Cards** until later.)
- You will be the letter expert for the vowels.
- Divide the class into groups of two or three and assign each group a letter. Give each student the appropriate **Letter Card**.
- Tell the students that they are now in their Letter Expert groups and that they are going to become experts on their Special Letter's name, shape, and sound.

> *Students need to learn the alphabetic principle: that letters work together in a systematic way to connect spoken language to written words. This understanding is the foundation for reading.*

#### Making Words

- Begin each lesson with a rehearsal of each group's letter name.
- Demonstrate how letters work by writing a word in large letters on the board.
- Tell the students the experts for each letter in the word should hold up their **Letter Cards** and name the letter. One member of the group should stand in front of their letter on the board.
- Continue until all letters in the word are accounted for. Remember that you are responsible for the vowels.
- Demonstrate that you can make different words by changing a letter or by changing the letter order.

#### Identifying Sounds in Words

- Use the **Alphabet Sound Cards** to demonstrate that every letter has at least one sound.
- Give each student the **Alphabet Sound Card** for his or her Special Letter.
- Point out the pictures on the cards. Explain that each card has a picture of something that makes the letter's sound. The picture will help them remember the sound.
- Tell each group the sound for its letter. (Remember, you are the expert for the vowels.)

- Quickly have each group rehearse its letter's name and sound.
- Write a word on the board in large letters. Say the word first sound-by-sound and then blend the word.
- For each letter/sound in the word, have one student from each Letter Expert group come forward, stand in front of the appropriate letter, and hold their cards. Although only one member of the group may come forward with the **Letter Card** or **Alphabet Sound Card**, all students in a Special Letter group should say the name and/or sound of their letter when it occurs in words.
- Say the word again, pointing to the **Alphabet Sound Cards**.
- Ask students who are not already standing to help you hold the vowel cards.
- Vary the activity by changing one letter sound and having an expert for that letter come forward.
- End the activity for each word by saying the sounds in the words one by one and then saying the entire word. Encourage the students to participate.

### Tips

- Remind the students to use the picture on the **Alphabet Sound Card** for their Special Letter to help them remember the letter's sound. The students are expected only to "master" their own Special Letter and share the information with their classmates. At this point in the year, they are not expected to blend and read the words by themselves. These are group activities in which you work with the students to help them gain insight into the alphabet.
- Have students note that what they learn about the letters and words applies to the words they work with in Big Book selections.
- Occasionally, have students find their special letters in a Big Book selection. Play some of the letter replacement and rearrangement games with words encountered in the Big Books.

# Developing the Alphabetic Principle

## Purpose

The following activities are extended to provide kindergarten students with a more thorough understanding of how sounds "work" in words. In this group of exercises, the students are introduced to specific letter/sound correspondences, consonants and short vowels. The students have previously been introduced to vowels and their special characteristics. This understanding is extended by introducing students to the convention that a vowel has a short sound in addition to its long sound. With this information and a carefully structured set of activities, the students can begin to explore and understand the alphabetic principle in a straightforward and thorough manner. The students not only listen for sounds in specified positions in words; they also link sounds to their corresponding letters. The activities in this group of lessons lay the groundwork for students to work their way through the entire alphabet as they learn letter-sound associations and to understand the purpose and the value of this learning.

Move the students quickly through these activities. Do not wait for all the students to master each letter/sound correspondence before going on. The students will have more opportunities to achieve mastery. The goal of these activities is for the students to obtain a basic understanding of the alphabetic principle.

## Procedures

### Introducing Consonant Letters and Sounds

- Point to the **Alphabet Sound Card** and name the letter.
- Point to the picture. Tell the students the sound of the letter and how the picture helps them to remember the sound. Repeat the sound several times.
- Tell the students you will read them the short story or an alliterative sentence to help them remember the sound of the letter. Read the story several times, emphasizing the words with the target sound. Have the students join in and say the sound.
- After introducing and reviewing a letter/sound correspondence, summarize the information on the **Alphabet Sound Card**.

### Generating Words with the Target Sound

- Brainstorm to create a list of words that begin with the target sound. Write the words on the board or on a chart. Include any of the students' names that begin with the target sound.
- Play the *I'm Thinking of Something That Starts With* game. Begin with the target sound and add clues until the students guess the word. If the students guess a word that does not begin with the target sound, emphasize the beginning sound and ask if the word begins with the target sound.
- Silly Sentences. Make silly sentences with the students that include many words with the target sound. Encourage the students to participate by extending the sentences: *Mary mopes. Mary mopes on Monday. Mary and Michael mope on Monday in Miami.*

### Listening for Initial Sounds

- Give each student a **Letter Card** for the target sound, /s/.
- Point to the picture on the **Alphabet Sound Card**, and have the students give the sound, /s/.
- Tell the students to listen for the first sound in each word you say. If it is /s/, they should hold up their *s* cards. Establish a signal so that the students know when to respond.
- Read a list of words, some beginning with /s/, some beginning with other sounds.

### Listening for Final Sounds

The procedure for listening for the final sound of a word is the same as that for listening for the initial sound. The students may need to be reminded throughout the activity to pay attention to the *final* sound.

- Read a list of words, some ending with the target sound and some ending with other sounds. Avoid words that begin with the target sound.

### Linking the Sound to the Letter

- **Word Pairs (initial sounds).** Write pairs of words on the board. One of each pair should begin with the target sound. Say the word beginning with the target sound, and ask the students to identify it. Remind them to listen for the target sound at the beginning of the word, to think about which letter makes that sound, and to find the word that begins with that letter. For example,
  Target sound: /s/
  Word pair: *fit sit*
  Which word is *sit*?

- **Word Pairs (final sounds).** Follow the same procedure used for initial sounds, and direct the students to think about the sound that they hear at the end of the word. Since it is often more difficult for the students to attend to the ending sound, you may need to lead them through several pairs of words. Remind the students to listen for the target sound and to think about which letter makes that sound.

- **Writing Letters.** Using either of the handwriting systems outlined in the Program Appendix of *SRA/Open Court Reading*, or the system in use at your school, have students practice writing uppercase and lowercase letters. Remind the students about the letter sound, and have them repeat it.

### Comparing Initial Consonant Sounds

This activity is exactly like **Listening for Initial Sounds** except that the students must discriminate between two sounds. They are given **Letter Cards** for both sounds and must hold up the appropriate card when they hear the sound.

### Comparing Final Consonant Sounds

This activity is exactly like listening for final sounds except that the students must discriminate between two sounds. They are given **Letter Cards** for both sounds and must hold up the appropriate card when they hear the sound.

### Linking the Consonant Sound to the Letter

In this activity to help students link sounds and letters, the students will make words either by adding initial consonants to selected word parts or by adding a different final consonant to a consonant-vowel-consonant combination.

## The Alphabetic Principle: How the Alphabet Works (continued)

### Introducing Short Vowel Sounds

■ Tell the students that the vowels are printed in red to remind them that they are special letters. (They are not special because they are printed in red.) They are special because they have more than one sound, and every word must have a vowel sound.

■ Point to the long *Aa* **Alphabet Sound Card,** and remind the students that this letter is called a *vowel*. Vowels sometimes say their names in words: for example, *say, day, tray*. This vowel sound is called long *a*.

■ Have the students repeat the sound.

■ Sometimes vowels say different sounds. Point to the picture of the lamb on the short *Aa* card, and tell students that *a* also makes the sound heard in the middle of *lamb*. This is the short *a*. Read the short vowel story to help the students remember the short *a*.

■ Have all the students join in saying /a/ /a/ /a/.

### Listening for Short Vowel Sounds Versus Long Vowel Sounds

■ Tell the students that you will read words with long *a* and short *a*. Review the two sounds.

■ Give the students a signal to indicate when they hear the vowel sound. You may want one signal for short *a*, such as scrunching down, and another for long *a*, such as stretching up tall.

■ Continue with lists of words such as: *add, back, aid, tan, bake, tame*.

### Linking the Vowel Sound to the Letter

■ Writing Letters. Have students practice writing the letter and review the sound of the letter.

■ In this activity to help students link sounds and letters, the students will make words either by adding initial consonants to selected word parts or by adding a different final consonant to a consonant-vowel-consonant combination. Change the beginning of the word or the word ending, but retain the vowel sound to make new words:

| | | | |
|---|---|---|---|
| *at* | *hat* | *mat* | *pat* |
| *ap* | *map* | *tap* | *sap* |
| *am* | *Sam* | *Pam* | *ham* |

### Comparing Short Vowel Sounds

This activity requires students to discriminate between short vowel sounds in the middle of words. Review the vowel sounds.

■ Say a word, and have the students repeat it. Establish a signal to indicate whether they hear short *a* or short *o* in the middle of the word. For example, they can hold up the appropriate **Letter Card** when they hear a sound. Sample words: *cap, cot, rat, rot, rack, rock*.

### Linking the Sound to the Letter

■ In this activity write a word on the board, and help the students say it.

■ Change the word by changing the vowel. Help the students say the new word, for example, *map, mop; hot, hat; pot, pat*.

■ For a variation of this activity, write the pairs of words, and simply have the students say which word is the target word. For example, the students see *tap* and *top*. Ask which word *top* is, directing the students' attention to the vowel.

### Tips

■ Lead and model the exercises as necessary until the students begin to catch on and can participate with confidence.

■ To keep the students focused on the various activities, have them tell you the task for each activity. For example, after telling the students to listen for final sounds, ask the students what they will be listening for.

■ Actively involve the students by giving them opportunities to tell what they know rather than supplying the information for them. Do they know the letter name? Do they know the sound? Can they think of words that begin with the sound?

■ Keeping the students focused on the idea that they are learning about sounds and letters so they can read these books themselves makes the lessons more relevant for the students.

The basic purpose of providing structured practice in phonemic awareness is to help the students hear and understand the sounds from which words are made. Before students can be expected to understand the sound/symbol correspondence that forms the base of written English, they need to have a strong working knowledge of the sound relationships that make up the spoken language. This understanding of spoken language lays the foundation for the transition to written language.

Phonemic awareness activities provide the students with easy practice in discriminating the sounds that make up words. Phonemic awareness consists of quick, gamelike activities designed to help students understand that speech is made up of distinct, identifiable sounds. The playful nature of the activities makes them appealing and engaging, while giving the students practice and support for learning about language. Once the students begin reading and writing, this experience with manipulating sounds will help them use what they know about sounds and letters to sound out and spell unfamiliar words when they read and write.

The two main formats for teaching phonemic awareness are oral blending and segmentation. These are supported by occasional discrimination activities and general wordplay. Oral blending encourages students to combine sounds to make words. Segmentation, conversely, requires them to isolate sounds from words. Other activities support discrimination, or recognition, of particular sounds. Sometimes simple songs, rhymes, or games engage students in wordplay. In these, the students manipulate words in a variety of ways. From these playful activities, the students derive serious knowledge about language.

As the students progress through different phonemic awareness activities, they will become proficient at listening for and reproducing the sounds they hear. It is essential for their progression to phonics and reading that they are able to hear the sounds and the patterns used to make up recognizable words. The phonemic awareness activities support the phonics instruction, but the activities are oral and do not focus on sound/spelling correspondences. Because the students are not expected to read the words they are experimenting with, any consonant and vowel sounds may be used, even if the students have not been formally taught the sound and its spellings.

## Oral Blending

### Purpose

In oral blending, the students are led through a progression of activities designed to help them hear how sounds are put together to make words.

Until students develop an awareness of the component parts of words, they have no tools with which to decode words or put letters together to form words. Oral blending helps students master these component parts of words, from syllables down to single sounds, or phonemes. Oral blending is not to be confused with the formal blending of specific sounds whose spellings the students will be taught through phonics instruction. Oral blending does not depend on the recognition of written words; it focuses instead on hearing the sounds.

Oral blending focuses on hearing sounds through a sequence that introduces the most easily distinguished word parts and then systematically moves to sound blending that contains all the challenges of phonic decoding (except letter recognition). This sequence provides support for the least-prepared student—one who comes to school with no concept of words or sounds within

words. At the same time, the lively pace and playful nature of oral blending activities hold the interest of students who already have some familiarity with words and letters.

Oral blending prepares students for phonics instruction by developing an awareness of the separate sounds that make up speech. Oral blending activities then continue in concert with phonics instruction to reinforce and extend new learning. And, because these activities involve simply listening to and reproducing sounds, oral blending need not be restricted to the sounds students have been or will be taught in phonics.

The tone of the activities should be playful and informal and should move quickly. Although these activities will provide information about student progress, they are not diagnostic tools. Do not expect mastery. Those students who have not caught on will be helped more by varied experiences than by more drilling on the same activity.

### Procedures

Following is a description of the progression of oral blending activities.

### Syllable Blending

Syllables are easier to distinguish than individual sounds (phonemes), so students can quickly experience success in forming meaningful words. Tell the students that you are going to say some words in two parts. Tell them to listen carefully so that they can discover what the words are. Read each word, pronouncing each part distinctly with a definite pause between syllables broken by. . . . The lists of words that follow are arranged in sequence from easy to harder. They cover different types of cues. At any point where they fit in the sequence, include multisyllable names of students in the class.

### Model

**TEACHER:** *dino . . . saur. What's the word?*
**STUDENTS:** *dinosaur*

### Example Words

- First part of the word cues the whole word:
  *vita . . . min    vaca . . . tion*
  *hippopot . . . amus    ambu . . . lance*
- Two distinct words easily combined:
  *butter. . . fly    straw. . . berry*
  *surf . . . board   basket . . . ball*

## Phonemic Awareness (continued)

- Two distinct words, but first word could cue the wrong ending:
  *tooth . . . ache   tooth . . . paste*
  *water . . . fall   water . . . melon*
- First part, consonant + vowel, not enough to guess whole word:
  *re . . . member   re . . . frigerator*
  *bi . . . cycle   bi . . . ology*
- Identifying clues in second part:
  *light . . . ning   sub . . . ject   in . . . sect*
- Last part, consonant + vowel sound, carries essential information:
  *yester . . . day   rain . . . bow*
  *noi . . . sy   pota . . . to*
- Changing the final part changes the word:
  *start . . . ing   start . . . er   start. . . ed*

### Initial Consonant Sounds

Initial consonant blending prepares students for consonant replacement activities that will come later. Tell the students that you will ask them to put some sounds together to make words. Pronounce each word part distinctly, and make a definite pause at the breaks indicated. When a letter is surrounded by slash marks, pronounce the letter's sound, not its name. When you see /s/, for example, you will say "ssss," not "ess." The words that follow are arranged from easy to harder. At any point where they fit in the sequence, include names of students in the class.

#### Model

**TEACHER:** /t/ . . . iger. What's the word?
**STUDENTS:** tiger

#### Example Words

- Separated consonant blend, with rest of word giving strong cue to word identity:
  */b/ . . . roccoli   /k/ . . . racker*
  */f/ . . . lashlight   /k/ . . . reature*
- Held consonant that is easy for students to hear, with rest of word giving strong cue:
  */s/ . . . innamon   /l/ . . . adybug*
  */s/ . . . eventeen   /n/ . . . ewspaper*
- Stop consonant that is harder for students to hear preceding vowel, with rest of word giving strong cue:
  */t/ . . . adpole   /p/ . . . iggybank*
  */d/ . . . ragonfly   /b/ . . . arbecue*
- Single-syllable words and words in which the second part gives a weaker cue:
  */s/ . . . ing   /l/ . . . augh   /v/ . . . ase*

### Final Consonant Sounds

In this phase of oral blending, the last sound in the word is separated.

#### Model

**TEACHER:** cabba . . . /j/. What's the word?
**STUDENTS:** cabbage

#### Example Words

- Words that are easily recognized even before the final consonant is pronounced:
  *bubblegu . . . /m/   Columbu . . . /s/*
  *crocodi . . . /l/   submari . . . /n/*
- Multisyllable words that need the final consonant for recognition:
  *colle . . . /j/ (college)   come . . . /t/ (comet)*
- Single-syllable words:
  *sa . . . /d/   gra . . . /s/   snai . . . /l/*

### Initial Consonant Sound Replacement

This level of oral blending further develops awareness of initial consonant sounds. The activity begins with a common word, then quickly changes its initial consonant sound. Most of the words produced are nonsense words, which helps keep the focus on the sounds in the word. Note that the words are written on the board, but the students are not expected to read them. The writing is to help the students see that when the sounds change, the letters change, and vice versa.

#### Model

**TEACHER:** [Writes word on board.] This word is *magazine*. What is it?
**STUDENTS:** *magazine*
**TEACHER:** Now I'm going to change it. [Erases initial consonant.] Now it doesn't start with /m/, it's going to start with /b/. What's the new word?
**STUDENTS:** *bagazine*
**TEACHER:** That's right . . . [Writes b where m had been.] It's *bagazine*. Now I'm going to change it again. . . .

Repeat with different consonant sounds. Then do the same with other words, such as: *remember, Saturday, tomorrow, lotion,* and *million*. Continue with single-syllable words, such as: *take, big, boot, cot, seat, look, tap, ride,* and *late*. There are two stages in using written letters:

- The replacement letter is not written until *after* the new "word" has been identified.
- Later, the replacement letter is written *at the same time* the change in the initial phoneme is announced. For example, the teacher erases *d* and writes *m* while saying, "Now it doesn't start with /d/, it starts with /m/."

You may wish to alter the procedure when the consonants used have already been introduced in phonics by writing the replacement letter and having students sound out the new word. Feel free to switch between the two procedures within a single exercise. If the students are not responding orally to written spellings that have been introduced in phonics, don't force it. Proceed by saying the word before writing the letter, and wait until another time to move on to writing before pronouncing.

### One-Syllable Words

The students now begin blending individual phonemes to form words. This important step can be continued well into the year. Continued repetitions of this activity will help the students realize how they can use the sound/spellings they are learning to read and write real words.

At first, the blended words are presented in a story context that helps the students identify the words. They soon recognize that they are actually decoding meaningful words. However, the context must not be so strong that the students can guess the word without listening to the phonemic cues. Any vowel sounds and irregularly spelled words may be used, since there is no writing involved.

#### Model

**TEACHER:** *When I looked out the window, I saw a /l/ /ī/ /t/. What did I see?*
**STUDENTS:** *A light.*
**TEACHER:** *Yes, I saw a light. At first I thought it was the /m/ /o͞o/ /n/. What did I think it was?*
**STUDENTS:** *The moon.*
**TEACHER:** *But it didn't really look like the moon. Suddenly I thought, maybe it's a space /sh/ /i/ /p/. What did I think it might be?*
**STUDENTS:** *A space ship!*

Once the students are familiar with this phase of oral blending, they can move to blending one-syllable words without the story context.

#### Example Words

- CVC (consonant/vowel/consonant) words beginning with easily blended consonant sounds (/sh/, /h/, /r/, /v/, /s/, /n/, /z/, /f/, /l/, /m/):
  *nip   nap*
- CVC words beginning with any consonant:
  *ten   bug   lip*
- Add CCVC words:
  *flap   step*
- Add CVCC words:
  *most   band   went*
- Add CCVCC words:
  *stamp   grand   scuffs*

### Final Consonant Sound Replacement

Final consonant sounds are typically more difficult for students to use than initial consonants.

- Begin with multisyllable words, and move to one-syllable words.
- As with initial consonants, first write the changed consonant after students have pronounced the new word.
- Then write the consonant as they pronounce it.
- For sound/spellings introduced in phonics instruction, write the new consonant spelling, and have students identify and pronounce it.

*Model*

TEACHER: *[Writes word on board.] This word is* teapot. *What is it?*

STUDENTS: *teapot*

TEACHER: *Now I'm going to change it. [Erases final consonant.] Now it doesn't end with /t/, it ends with /p/. What's the word now?*

STUDENTS: *teapop*

TEACHER: *That's right . . . [Writes p where t had been.] It's* teapop. *Now I'm going to change it again. . . .*

*Example Words*

- Words that are easily recognized even before the final consonant is pronounced:
  *picnic picnit picnis picnil picnid*
  *airplane airplate airplabe airplafe*

- Multisyllable words that need the final consonant for recognition:
  *muffin muffil muffim muffip muffit*
  *amaze amate amake amale amade*

- Single-syllable words:
  *neat nean neap neam neaj nead neaf*
  *broom broot brood broof broop broon*

### Initial Vowel Replacement

Up to now, oral blending has concentrated on consonant sounds because they are easier to hear than vowels. As you move to vowel play, remember that the focus is still on the sounds, not the spellings. Use any vowel sounds.

*Model*

TEACHER: *[Writes word on board.] This word is* elephant. *What is it?*

STUDENTS: *elephant*

TEACHER: *Now I'm going to change it. [Erases initial vowel.] Now it doesn't start with /e/, it starts with /a/. What's the word now?*

STUDENTS: *alephant*

TEACHER: *That's right . . . [Writes a where e had been.] It's* alephant. *Now I'm going to change it again. . . .*

*Example Words*

- Multisyllable words:
  *angry ingry oongry ungry engry*
  *ivy avy oovy evy ovy oivy*

- One-syllable words:
  *ink ank oonk unk onk oink*
  *add odd idd oudd edd udd*

# Segmentation

## Purpose

Segmentation and oral blending complement each other: Oral blending puts sounds together to make words, while segmentation separates words into sounds. Oral blending will provide valuable support for decoding when students begin reading independently.

## Procedure

### Syllables

The earliest segmentation activities focus on syllables, which are easier to distinguish than individual sounds, or phonemes. Start with students' names, then use other words. As with the oral blending activities, remember to move quickly through these activities. Do not hold the class back waiting for all students to catch on. Individual progress will vary, but drilling on one activity is less helpful than going on to others. Return to the same activity often. Frequent repetition is very beneficial and allows students additional opportunities to catch on.

- Say, for example, "Let's clap out Amanda's name. A-man-da."

- Have the students clap and say the syllables along with you. Count the claps.

- Tell the students that these word parts are called *syllables.* Don't try to explain; the idea will develop with practice. Once you have provided the term, simply say, "How many syllables?" after the students clap and count.

- Mix one-syllable and multisyllable words:
  *fantastic tambourine good*
  *imaginary stand afraid*

### Comparative Length of Words

Unlike most phonemic awareness activities, this one involves writing on the board or on an overhead transparency. Remember, though, that the students are not expected to read what is written. They are merely noticing that words that take longer to say generally look longer when written.

- Start with students' names. Choose two names, one short and one long, with the same first initial (for example, *Joe* and *Jonathan*).

- Write the two names on the board, one above the other, so that the difference is obvious.

- Tell the students that one name is *Jonathan* and one is *Joe.* Have them pronounce and clap each name. Then, have them tell which written word they think says *Joe.*

- Move your finger under each name as they clap and say it, syllable by syllable.

- Repeat with other pairs of names and words, such as: *tea/telephone, cat/caterpillar,*

*butterfly/bug.* Be sure not to give false clues. For example, sometimes write the longer word on top, sometimes the shorter one; sometimes ask for the shorter word, sometimes the longer; sometimes ask for the top word, sometimes the bottom; sometimes point to a word and ask the students to name it, and sometimes name the word and ask the students to point to it.

### Listen for Individual Sounds

Activities using a puppet help the students listen for individual sounds in words. Use any puppet you have on hand. When you introduce the puppet, tell the students that it likes to play word games. Each new activity begins with the teacher speaking to and for the puppet until the students determine the pattern. Next, students either speak for the puppet or correct the puppet. To make sure all the students are participating, alternate randomly between having the whole group or individuals respond. The activities focus on particular parts of words, according to the following sequence:

1. **Repeating last part of word.** Use words beginning with easy-to-hear consonants, such as *f, l, m, n, r, s,* and *z.* The puppet repeats only the rime, the part of the syllable after the initial consonant.

*Model*

TEACHER: *farm*

PUPPET: *arm*

Once the pattern is established, the students respond for the puppet.

TEACHER: *rope*

STUDENTS: *ope*

*Example Words*

Use words such as the following: *mine . . . ine soup . . . oup feet . . . eet*

2. **Restoring initial phonemes.** Now the students correct the puppet. Be sure to acknowledge the correction.

*Model*

TEACHER: *lake*

PUPPET: *ake*

TEACHER: *No, lllake. You forgot the /l/.*

TEACHER: *real*

PUPPET: *eal*

TEACHER: *What did the puppet leave off?*

STUDENTS: */r/. It's supposed to be real.*

TEACHER: *That's right. The word is real.*

*Example Words*

Use words such as the following:

*look . . . ook mouse . . . ouse sand . . . and*

3. **Segmenting initial consonants.** The puppet pronounces only the initial consonant.

*Model*

TEACHER:  *pay*

PUPPET:  */p/*

*Example Words*

Use words such as the following:

*moon . . . /m/    nose . . . /n/    bell . . . /b/*

4. **Restoring final consonants.** The students correct the puppet. Prompt if necessary: *"What's the word? What did the puppet leave off?"*

*Model*

TEACHER:  *run*

PUPPET:  *ru*

STUDENTS:  *It's run! You left off the /n/.*

TEACHER:  *That's right. The word is* run.

*Example Words*

Use words such as the following:

*meet. . . mee    cool . . . coo    boot. . . boo*

5. **Isolating final consonants.** The puppet pronounces only the final consonant.

*Model*

TEACHER:  *green*

PUPPET:  */n/*

*Example Words*

Use words such as the following:

*glass . . . /s/    boom . . . /m/    mice . . . /s/*

6. **Segmenting initial consonant blends.** The sounds in blends are emphasized.

*Model*

TEACHER:  *clap*

PUPPET:  *lap*

Next have students correct the puppet.

TEACHER:  *stain*

PUPPET:  *tain*

STUDENTS:  *It's stain! You left off the /s/.*

TEACHER:  *That's right. The word is* stain.

*Example Words*

Use words such as the following:

*blaze . . . laze    draw . . . raw    proud . . . roud*

# Discrimination

## Purpose

Discrimination activities help students focus on particular sounds in words.

**Listening for long vowel sounds** is the earliest discrimination activity. Vowel sounds are necessary for decoding, but young students do not hear them easily. This is evident in students' invented spellings, where vowels are often omitted. Early in the year, the students listen for long vowel sounds, which are more easily distinguished than short vowel sounds:

- Explain to the students that vowels are special, because sometimes they say their names in words.
- Tell the students which vowel sound to listen for.
- Have them repeat the sound when they hear it in a word. For example, if the target vowel sound is long e, the students will say long e when you say *leaf* but they should not respond when you say *loaf*.
- Initially the students should listen for one long vowel sound at a time. Later they can listen for two vowel sounds. All **Example Words**, however, should contain one of the target vowels.

## Procedure

**Listening for short vowel sounds** discrimination activities should be done once the short vowels /a/ and /i/ have been introduced. Short vowels are very useful in reading. They are generally more regular in spelling than long vowels, and they appear in many short, simple words. However, their sounds are less easily distinguished than those of long vowels. Thus, the activities focus only on /a/ and /i/. All the words provided have one or the other of these sounds. Either have the students repeat the sound of a specified vowel, or vary the activity as follows: Write an *a* on one side of the board and an *i* on the other. Ask the students to point to the *a* when they hear a word with the /a/ sound and point to the *i* when they hear a word with the /i/ sound. Use words such as the following:

| | | | | |
|---|---|---|---|---|
| *bat* | *mat* | *sat* | *sit* | *spit* |
| *pit* | *pat* | *pan* | *pin* | *spin* |

**Consonant sounds in multisyllable words.** Discriminating these sounds helps students attend to consonant sounds in the middle of words.

- Say the word *rib*, and have the students repeat it. Ask where they hear the /b/ in *rib*.
- Then say *ribbon* and ask the students where they hear the /b/ in *ribbon*.
- Tell the students that you will say some words and they will repeat each word.
- After they repeat each word, ask what consonant sound they hear in the middle of that word. Use words such as the following:

| | | |
|---|---|---|
| *famous* | *message* | *picky* |
| *jogger* | *flavor* | *zipper* |

# Phonemic Play

## Purpose

Wordplay activities help the students focus on and manipulate sounds, thus supporting the idea that words are made of specific sounds that can be taken apart, put together, or changed to make new words. Through wordplay, students gain important knowledge about language.

## Procedure

**Producing rhymes.** Many phonemic play activities focus on producing rhymes. A familiar or easily learned rhyme or song is introduced, and the students are encouraged to substitute words or sounds. An example is "*Willaby Wallaby Woo,*" in which students change the rhyming words in the couplet "*Willaby Wallaby Woo/An elephant sat on you*" so that the second line ends with a student's name and the first line ends with a rhyme beginning with W (for example, "*Willaby Wallaby Wissy/An elephant sat on Missy*").

**Generate alliterative words.** Students can also say as many words as they can think of that begin with a given consonant sound. This is a valuable complement to discrimination activities in which the teacher produces the words and the students identify them.

The purpose of phonics instruction is to teach students the association between the sounds of the language and the written symbols—spellings—that have been chosen to represent those sounds.

As with all alphabetic languages, English has a limited number of symbols—twenty-six—that are combined and recombined to make the written language. These written symbols are a visual representation of the speech sounds we use to communicate. This is simply a code. The faster the students learn the code and how it works, the faster the whole world of reading opens to them.

Students are introduced to the sounds and spellings of English in a very systematic, sequential manner. This allows them to continually build on what they learned the day before. As each sound/symbol relationship is introduced, students learn about and practice with words containing the target sound/spelling and then reinforce their learning through the use of engaging text specifically written for this purpose.

It can be very difficult for students to hear the individual sounds, or phonemes, that make up words. When phonics instruction is explicit—students are told the sounds associated with the different written symbols—there is no guesswork involved. They know that this sound /b/ is spelled *b*. Therefore, students in an SRA/Open Court Reading classroom spend time learning to discriminate individual speech sounds, and then they learn the spellings of those sounds. This systematic, explicit approach affords students the very best chance for early and continuing success.

## Sound/Spelling Cards

### Purpose

The purpose of the **Sound/Spelling Cards** (Levels 1–3) is to remind the students of the sounds of English and their spellings. The name of the picture on each card contains the target sound at the beginning for the consonants and in the middle for most vowels. In addition, the picture associates a sound with an action. This association is introduced through an interactive story in which the pictured object or character "makes" the sound. These cards are a resource for the students to use to remember sound/spelling associations for both reading and writing.

### Procedure

#### Posting the Cards

Initially, post the first twenty-six cards with the picture to the wall so that only the alphabet letters on the backs show. As you introduce each card, you will turn it to show the picture and the spellings on the front of the card. If, however, most of your students already have some knowledge of the letters—this is a second- or third-grade classroom and students are reviewing what they learned the year before—you may want to go ahead and place the cards with the picture and the spellings facing forward to provide support as they begin writing. Make sure that the cards are positioned so that you can touch them with your hand or with a pointer when you refer to them and so that all of the students can see them easily. The cards should be placed where the students can readily see them during reading and writing.

### Special Devices

- Vowel spellings are printed in red to draw attention to them. Consonants are printed in black. The blank line in a spelling indicates that a letter will take the place of the blank in a word. For example, the replacement of the blank with *t* in the spelling *a_e* makes the word *ate*. The blank lines may also indicate the position of a spelling in a word or a syllable. The blank in *h_* for example, means that the spelling occurs at the beginning of a word or a syllable.

- The blanks in *_ie_* indicate that the *ie* spelling comes in the middle of a word or a syllable, while the blank in *_oy* shows that the *oy* spelling comes at the end of a word or a syllable. Uses of blanks in specific spellings are in the lessons. Please note now, however, that when you write a spelling of a sound on the board or an overhead transparency, you should include the blanks.

- The color of the background behind the spellings also has a meaning. Consonants have a white background. The colors behind vowel spellings are pronunciation clues. Short vowel spellings have a green background, which corresponds to the green box that appears before some consonant spellings. Thus, before *ck* or *x* you will see a green box, which indicates that a short vowel always precedes that spelling. Long vowel spellings have a yellow background; other vowel spellings, such as r-controlled vowels and diphthongs, have a blue background. The color code reinforces the idea that vowels are special and have different pronunciations.

### Introducing the Sound/Spelling Cards

In first grade, each sound and spelling is introduced by using a see/hear/say/write sequence. In grades two and three the same sequence is used in the review of the cards.

1. **See:** Students see the spelling or spellings on the **Sound/Spelling Card** and the board or an overhead transparency.

2. **Hear:** Students hear the sound used in words and in isolation in the story. The sound is, of course, related to the picture (and the action) shown on the **Sound/Spelling Card.**

3. **Say:** Students say the sound.

4. **Write:** Students write the spelling(s) for the sound.

There are a number of important points to remember about this technique.

- The first item written on the board or an overhead transparency is the spelling of the sound being introduced. This gives the spelling a special emphasis in the mind of the student. It is the "see" part of the sequence.

- One of the causes of blending failure is the failure to teach sounds thoroughly during introduction of the **Sound/Spelling Card** and during initial sounding and blending. To help ensure success for all students, make certain that every student is able to see the board or screen.

- After you present the sound and spelling, have several students go to the board to write the spelling. Have them say the sound as they write the spelling. After they have written the spelling of the sound, give them a chance to proofread their own work. Then give the other

## Explicit, Systematic Phonics (continued)

**PROGRAM APPENDIX**

students the opportunity to help with proofreading by noting what is good about the spelling and then suggesting how to make it better.

### Sample Lesson, Using the Letter m and the Sound /m/

- Point to the **Sound/Spelling Card 13 Monkey** and have students tell you whether it is a vowel or a consonant. Have them tell the name of the card. If they do not know it, tell them it is Monkey. Point to the *monkey* in the picture and say the word monkey, emphasizing the initial consonant sound—*mmmonkey*.

- Point to the spelling *m*. Tell students that /m/ is spelled *m*.

- If you wish, make up an alliterative sentence about the Monkey, or use the alliterative story that accompanies the card. (In first grade this story is printed on the page on which the card is introduced and in the Appendix. In grades two and three, the cards are printed in the Appendix of the *Teacher's Edition.*) For example, *When Muzzie the monkey munches bananas, the sound she makes is /mmmmmm/.*

- If students had **SRA/Open Court Reading** before, you can ask them if they learned an action such as rubbing their tummies to help them remember the sound. If your students don't have an action they associate with the cards already, make some up with your students. They will have fun, and it will be another way for them to remember the sound/spelling relationships.

- Write *m* on the board or on an overhead transparency and say the sound. Write the letter again and ask the students to say the sound with you as they write the letter on slates, on paper, or with their index finger on a surface. Repeat this activity several times.

- Have the students listen for words beginning with /m/, indicating by some signal, such as thumbs-up or thumbs-down, whether they hear the /m/ sound and saying /m/ when they hear it in a word. Repeat with the sound in various positions in words. Encourage students to tell you and the class words with /m/ at the beginning and end as well as in the middle of words.

- Check students' learning by pointing to the card. Have students identify the sound, name the spelling, and discuss how the card can help them remember the sound.

### Individual Sound/Spelling Cards

Use the **Individual Sound/Spelling Cards** for review and for small-group reteaching and practice sessions. Students can use them alone or with partners. Here are some suggestions for activities using the **Individual Sound/Spelling Cards**:

1. **Saying sounds from pictures.** The leader flashes pictures as the others say the sound each picture represents.

2. **Saying sounds.** The leader flashes the spellings on the cards as the others say the sound that the spellings represent.

> *The faster the students learn the code and how it works, the faster the whole world of reading opens to them.*

3. **Naming spellings from pictures.** The leader flashes pictures. The others name the card, say the sound, and then name as many spellings as they can.

4. **Writing spellings from the pictures.** Working alone, a student looks at a picture and then writes as many spellings for that **Sound/Spelling Card** as he or she can remember.

5. **Saying words from pictures.** The leader presents a series of pictures. The others form words by blending the sounds represented.

# Blending

## Purpose

The purpose of blending is to teach the students a strategy for figuring out unfamiliar words. Initially, students will be blending sound by sound. Ultimately, the students will sound and blend only those words that they cannot read. Eventually, the blending process will become quick and comfortable for them.

## Procedure

Learning the sounds and their spellings is only the first step in learning to read and write. The second step is learning to blend the sounds into words.

### Blending Techniques

Blending lines are written on the board or an overhead transparency as the students watch and participate. The lines and sentences should not be written out before class begins. It is through the sound-by-sound blending of the words and the sentences that the students learn the blending process.

### Sound-by-Sound Blending

- Write the spelling of the first sound in the word. Point to the spelling, and say the sound.

- Have the students say the sound with you as you say the sound again. Write the spelling of the next sound. Point to the spelling, and say the sound. Have the students say the sound with you as you say the sound again. After you have written the vowel spelling, blend through the vowel (unless the vowel is the first letter of the word), making the blending motion—a smooth sweeping of the hand beneath the sounds, linking them from left to right, for example, *ba*. As you make the blending motion, make sure that your hand is under the letter that corresponds to the sound you are saying at the moment.

- Have the students blend through the vowel. Write the spelling of the next sound. Point to the spelling and say the sound. Have the students say the sound with you as you touch the letter and say the sound again.

- Continue as described above through the word. After pronouncing the final sound in the word, make the blending motion from left to right under the word as you blend the sounds. Then have the students blend the word. Let them be the first to pronounce the word normally.

- Ask a student to read the word again and use it in a sentence. Ask another student to extend the sentence—that is, make it longer by giving more information. Help the student by asking an appropriate question about the sentence, using, for example, *How? When? Where?* or *Why?* Continue blending the rest of the words.

## Whole-Word Blending

Once students are comfortable with sound-by-sound blending, they are ready for whole-word blending.

- Write the whole word to be blended on the board or an overhead transparency.
- Ask the students to blend the sounds as you point to them.
- Then have the students say the whole word.
- Ask the students to use the word in a sentence and then to extend the sentence.
- When all of the words have been blended, point to words randomly and ask individuals to read them.

## Blending Syllables

In reading the **Student Anthologies,** students will often encounter multisyllabic words. Some students are intimidated by long words, yet many multisyllabic words are easily read by reading and blending the syllables rather than the individual sounds. Following a set of rules for syllables is difficult since so many of the rules have exceptions. Students need to remember that each syllable in a word contains one vowel sound.

- Have students identify the vowel sounds in the word.
- Have students blend the first syllable sound by sound if necessary or read the first syllable.
- Handle the remaining syllables the same way.
- Have students blend the syllables together to read the word.

## Blending Sentences

Blending sentences is the logical extension of blending words. Blending sentences helps students develop fluency, which is critical to comprehension. Encourage students to reread sentences with phrasing and natural intonation.

- Write the sentence on the board or on a transparency, underlining any high-frequency sight words—words that the students cannot decode either because they are irregular or because they contain sounds or spellings that the students have not yet learned or reviewed. If the students have not read these words before, write the words on the board or an overhead transparency and introduce them before writing the sentence. These words should not be blended but read as whole words.

## Building for Success

A primary cause of students' blending failure is their failure to understand how to use the **Sound/Spelling Cards.** Students need to practice sounds and spellings when the **Sound/Spelling Cards** are introduced and during initial blending. They also need to understand that if they are not sure of how to pronounce a spelling, they can check the cards.

Early blending may be frustrating. You must lead the group almost constantly. Soon, however, leaders in the group will take over. Watch to see whether any students are having trouble during the blending. Include them in small-group instruction sessions. At that time you may want to use the vowel-first procedure described below to reteach blending lines.

## Extra Help

In working with small groups during **Workshop,** you may want to use some of the following suggestions to support students who need help with blending.

## Vowel-First Blending

Vowel-first blending is an alternative to sound-by-sound and whole-word blending for students who need special help. Used in small-group sessions, this technique helps students who have difficulty with the other two types of blending to focus on the most important part of each word, the vowels, and to do only one thing at a time. These students are not expected to say a sound and blend it with another at virtually the same time. The steps to use in vowel-first blending follow:

> ***Blending is the heart of phonics instruction and the key strategy students must learn to open the world of written language.***

1. Across the board or on an overhead transparency, write the vowel spelling in each of the words in the line. For a short vowel, the line may look like this:
   a    a    a
   For a long vowel, the line may look like this:
   ee   ea   ea
2. Point to the spelling as the students say the sound for the spelling.
3. Begin blending around the vowels. In front of the first vowel spelling, add the spelling for the beginning sound of the word. Make the blending motion, and have the students blend through the vowel, adding a blank to indicate that the word is still incomplete. Repeat this procedure for each partial word in the line until the line looks like this:
   ma__  sa__     pa__
   see__  mea__    tea__
4. Have the students blend the partial word again as you make the blending motion and then add the spelling for the ending sound.

5. Make the blending motion, and have the students blend the completed word—for example, *mat* or *seed*.
6. Ask a student to repeat the word and use it in a sentence. Then have another student extend the sentence.
7. Repeat steps 4, 5, and 6 for each word in the line, which might look like this:
   *mat   sad    pan*
   or
   *seed   meat   team*

## Tips

- In the early lessons, do blending with as much direction and dialogue as is necessary for success. Reduce your directions to a minimum as soon as possible. You have made good progress when you no longer have to say, "Sound—Sound—Blend," because the students automatically sound and blend as you write.
- Unless the line is used to introduce or to reinforce a spelling pattern, always ask a student to use a word in a sentence and then to extend the sentence immediately after you've developed the word. If the line is used to introduce or to reinforce a spelling pattern, however, ask the students to give sentences at the end of the line. Students will naturally extend sentences by adding phrases to the ends of the sentences. Encourage them to add phrases at the beginning or in the middle of the sentence.
- Use the vowel-first procedure in small group preteaching or reteaching sessions with students who are having a lot of trouble with blending. Remember that you must adapt the blending lines in the lessons to the vowel-first method.
- The sight words in the sentences cannot be blended. The students must approach them as sight words to be memorized. If students are having problems reading sight words, tell them the words.
- Cue marks written over the vowels may help students.
  - ✓ Straight line cue for long vowels
    EXAMPLES: *āpe, mē, fīne, sō, ūse*
  - ✓ Curved line cue for short vowels
    EXAMPLES: *căt, pĕt, wĭn, hŏt, tŭg*
  - ✓ Tent cue for variations of a and o
    EXAMPLES: *âll, ôff*
  - ✓ Dot cue for schwa sound with multiple-syllable words
    EXAMPLES: *saläd, planet, pencil, wagon*

## Explicit, Systematic Phonics (continued)

# Dictation and Spelling

## Purpose

The purpose of dictation is to teach the students to spell words based on the sounds and spellings. In addition, learning dictation gives students a new strategy for reflecting on the sounds they hear in words to help them with their own writing.

As the students learn that sounds and spellings are connected to form words and that words form sentences, they begin to learn the standard spellings that will enable others to read their writing. As students learn to encode correctly, they develop their visual memory for words (spelling ability) and hence increase their writing fluency. Reinforcing the association between sounds and spellings and words through dictation gives students a spelling strategy that provides support and reassurance for writing independently. Reflecting on the sounds they hear in words will help students develop writing fluency as they apply the strategy to writing unfamiliar words.

A dictation activity is a learning experience; it is not a test. The students should be encouraged to ask for as much help as they need. The proofreading techniques are an integral part of dictation. Students' errors lead to self-correction and, if need be, to reteaching. The dictation activities must not become a frustrating ordeal. The students should receive reinforcement and feedback.

There are two kinds of dictation: Sounds-in-Sequence Dictation and Whole-Word Dictation. The two types differ mainly in the amount of help they give the students in spelling the words. The instructions vary for each type.

## Procedure

### Sounds-in-Sequence Dictation

Sounds-in-Sequence Dictation gives the students the opportunity to spell words sound by sound, left to right, checking the spelling of each sound as they write. (Many students write words as they think they hear and say the words, not as the words are actually pronounced or written.)

- Pronounce the first word to be spelled. Use the word in a sentence and say the word again (word/sentence/word). Have students say the word.
- Tell students to think about the sounds they hear in the word. Ask, "What's the first sound in the word?"
- Have students say the sound.
- Point to the **Sound/Spelling Card**, and direct the students to check the card. Ask what the spelling is. The students should say the spelling and then write it.

- Proceed in this manner until the word is complete.
- Proofread. You can write the word on the board as a model, or have a student do it. Check the work by referring to the **Sound/Spelling Cards**. If a word is misspelled, have the students circle the word and write it correctly, either above the word or next to it.

### Whole-Word Dictation

Whole-Word Dictation gives the students the opportunity to practice this spelling strategy with less help from the teacher.

- Pronounce the word, use the word in a sentence, and then repeat the word (word/sentence/word). Have the students repeat the word. Tell the students to think about the word. Remind the students to check the **Sound/Spelling Cards** for spellings and to write the word.
- Proofread. Write or have a volunteer write the word on the board as a model. Check the word by referring to the **Sound/Spelling Cards**.

### Sentence Dictation

**Writing dictated sentences**. Help students apply this spelling strategy to writing sentences. Dictation supports the development of fluent and independent writing. Dictation of a sentence will also help the students apply conventions of written language, such as capitalization and punctuation.

- Say the complete sentence aloud.
- Dictate one word at a time following the procedure for Sounds-in-Sequence Dictation.

Continue this procedure for the rest of the words in the sentence. Remind the students to put a period at the end. Then proofread the sentence, sound by sound, or word by word. When sentences contain sight words, the sight words should be dictated as whole words, not sound by sound. As the students learn to write more independently, the whole sentence can be dictated word by word.

### Proofreading

Whenever the students write, whether at the board or on paper, they should proofread their work. Proofreading is an important technique because it allows the students to learn by self-correction and it gives them an immediate second chance for success. It is the same skill students will use as they proofread their writing. Students should proofread by circling—not by erasing—each error. After they circle an error, they should write the correction beside the circle. This type of correction allows you and the students to see the error as well as the correct form. Students also can see what needs to be changed and how they have made their own work better.

You may want to have students use a colored pencil to circle and write in the correction. This will make it easier for them to see the changes.

### Procedure for Proofreading

- Have a student write the word or sentence on the board or on an overhead transparency.
- Have students tell what is good.
- Have students identify anything that can be made better.
- If there is a mistake, have the student circle it and write it correctly.
- Have the rest of the class proofread their own work.

### The Word Building Game

The major reason for developing writing alongside reading is that reading and writing are complementary communicative processes. Decoding requires that students blend the phonemes together into familiar cohesive words. Spelling requires that students segment familiar cohesive words into separate phonemes. Both help students develop an understanding of how the alphabetic principle works.

The Word Building game gives the students a chance to exercise their segmentation abilities and to practice using the sounds and spellings they are learning. The game is a fast-paced activity in which the students spell related sets of words with the teacher's guidance. (Each successive word in the list differs from the previous one by one sound.)

For the Word Building game, the students use their **Individual Letter Cards** (Levels K and 1) to build the words. (As an alternative they can use pencil and paper.) You will be writing at the board.

Give the students the appropriate **Letter Cards**. For example, if the list for the Word Building game is *am*, *at*, *mat*, they will need their *a*, *m*, and *t* **Letter Cards**.

- Say the first word, such as *am*. (Use it in a sentence if you wish.) Have the students repeat the word. Say the word slowly, sound by sound. Tell the students to look at the **Sound/Spelling Cards** to find the letters that spell the sounds. Touch the first sound's card, in this case the Lamb card, and have students say the sound. Continue the process with the second sound. Write the word on the board while the students use their **Letter Cards** to spell it. Have students compare their words with your word, make changes as needed, and then blend and read the word with you.
- The students will then change the first word to make a different word. Say the next word in the list, (*at*). Segment the sounds of the word, and have students find the **Sound/Spelling Cards** that correspond. Write the new word (*at*) under the first word (*am*) on the board and have the students change their cards to spell the new word. Have them compare their words to yours and make changes as needed. Blend and read the word with the students. Continue in a like manner through the word list.

# Spelling and Vocabulary Strategies

## Spelling Strategies

### Spelling

Many people find English difficult, because English sound/spelling patterns seem to have a million exceptions. The key to becoming a good speller, however, is not just memorization. The key is recognizing and internalizing English spelling patterns. Some people do this naturally as they read and develop large vocabularies. They intuitively recognize spelling patterns and apply them appropriately. Others need explicit and direct teaching of vocabulary and spelling strategies and spelling patterns before they develop spelling consciousness.

### Purpose

Spelling is a fundamental skill in written communication. Although a writer may have wonderful ideas, he or she may find it difficult to communicate those ideas without spelling skills. Learning to spell requires much exposure to text and writing. For many it requires a methodical presentation of English spelling patterns.

### English Spelling Patterns

A basic understanding of English spelling patterns will help provide efficient and effective spelling instruction. Just as the goal of phonics instruction is to enable students to read fluently, the goal of spelling instruction is to enable students to write fluently so they can concentrate on ideas rather than spelling.

- **Sound Patterns** Many words are spelled the way they sound. Most consonants and short vowels are very regular. Once a student learns the sound/spelling relationships, he or she has the key to spelling many words.
- **Structural Patterns** Structural patterns are employed when adding endings to words. Examples of structural patterns include doubling the final consonant, adding –s or –es to form plurals, and dropping the final e before adding –ing, -ed, -er, or –est. Often these structural patterns are very regular in their application. Many students have little trouble learning these patterns.
- **Meaning Patterns** Many spelling patterns in English are *morphological*; in other words, the meaning relationship is maintained regardless of how a sound may change. Prefixes, suffixes, and root words that retain their spellings regardless of how they are pronounced are further examples of meaning patterns.
- **Foreign Language Patterns** Many English words are derived from foreign words and retain those language patterns. For example, *kindergarten* (German), *boulevard* (French), and *ballet* (French from Italian) are foreign language patterns at work in English.

### Developmental Stages of Spelling

The most important finding in spelling research in the past thirty years is that students learn to spell in a predictable developmental sequence, much as they learn to read. It appears to take the average student three to six years to progress through the developmental stages and emerge as a fairly competent, mature speller.

**Prephonemic** The first stage is the *prephonemic* stage, characterized by random letters arranged either in continuous lines or in word-like clusters. Only the writer can "read" it, and it may be "read" differently on different days.

**Semiphonemic** As emergent readers learn that letters stand for sounds, they use particular letters specifically to represent the initial consonant sound and sometimes a few other very salient sounds. This marks the discovery of *phonemic awareness* that letters represent speech sounds in writing.

**Phonemic** When students can represent most of the sounds they hear in words, they have entered the *phonemic* stage of spelling. They spell what they hear, using everything they know about letter sounds, letter names, and familiar words. Many remedial spellers never develop beyond this stage and spell a word the way it sounds whenever they encounter a word they can't spell.

**Transitional or Within Word Pattern** As they are exposed to more difficult words, students discover that not all words are spelled as they sound. They learn that they must include silent letters, spell past tenses with –ed, include a vowel even in unstressed syllables, and remember how words look. The *transitional* stage represents the transition from primarily phonemic strategies to rule-bound spelling.

**Derivational** The *derivational* stage occurs as transitional spellers accumulate a large spelling vocabulary and gain control over affixes, contractions, homophones and other meaning patterns. They discover that related or derived forms of words share spelling features even if they do not sound the same. As spellers gain control over these subtle word features and spell most words correctly, they become conventional spellers.

### Procedures

The spelling lessons are organized around different spelling patterns, beginning with phonetic spelling patterns and progressing to other types of spelling patterns in a logical sequence. Word lists including words from the literature selection focus on the particular patterns in each lesson. In general, the sound patterns occur in the first units at each grade, followed by structural patterns, meaning patterns, and foreign language patterns in the upper grade levels.

- As you begin each new spelling lesson, have students identify the spelling pattern and how it is like and different from other patterns.
- Give the pretest to help students focus on the lesson pattern.
- Have students proofread their own pretests immediately after the test, crossing out any misspellings and writing the correct spelling.
- Have them diagnose whether the errors they made were in the lesson pattern or in another part of the word. Help students determine where they made errors and what type of pattern they should work on to correct them.
- As students work through the spelling pages from the *Spelling and Vocabulary Skills* book, encourage them to practice the different spelling strategies in the exercises.

#### Sound Pattern Strategies

✓ **Pronunciation Strategy** As students encounter an unknown word, have them say the word carefully to hear each sound. Encourage them to check the **Sound/Spelling Cards.** Then have them spell each sound. (/s/ + /i/ + /t/: *sit*)

✓ **Consonant Substitution** Have students switch consonants. The vowel spelling usually remains the same. *(bat, hat, rat, flat, splat)*

✓ **Vowel Substitution** Have students switch vowels. The consonant spellings usually remain the same. (CVC: *hit, hat, hut, hot;* CVCV: *mane, mine;* CVVC: *boat, beat, bait, beet*)

✓ **Rhyming Word Strategy** Have students think of rhyming words and the rimes that spell a particular sound. Often the sound will be spelled the same way in another word. *(cub, tub, rub)*

#### Structural Pattern Strategies

✓ **Conventions Strategy** Have students learn the rule and exceptions for adding endings to words (dropping *y*, dropping *e*, doubling the final consonant, and so on).

✓ **Proofreading Strategy** Many spelling errors occur because of simple mistakes. Have students check their writing carefully and specifically for spelling.

✓ **Visualization Strategy** Have students think about how a word looks. Sometimes words "look" wrong because a wrong spelling pattern has been written. Have them double-check the spelling of any word that looks wrong.

#### Meaning Pattern Strategies

✓ **Family Strategy** When students are not sure of a spelling, have them think of how words from the same base word family are spelled. *(critic, criticize, critical; sign, signal, signature)*

## Spelling and Vocabulary Strategies (continued)

✓ **Meaning Strategy** Have students determine a homophone's meaning to make sure they are using the right word. Knowing prefixes, suffixes, and base words will also help.

✓ **Compound Word Strategy** Tell students to break a compound apart and spell each word. Compounds may not follow conventions rules for adding endings. (*homework, nonetheless*)

✓ **Foreign Language Strategy** Have students think of foreign language spellings that are different from English spelling patterns. (*ballet, boulevard, sauerkraut*)

✓ **Dictionary Strategy** Ask students to look up the word in a dictionary to make sure their spelling is correct. If they do not know how to spell a word, have them try a few different spellings and look them up to see which one is correct. (*fotograph, photograph*) This develops a spelling consciousness.

Use the Final Test to determine understanding of the lesson spelling pattern and to identify any other spelling pattern problems. Encourage student understanding of spelling patterns and use of spelling strategies in all their writing to help transfer spelling skills to writing.

# Vocabulary Strategies

## Purpose

Strong vocabulary skills are correlated to achievement throughout school. The purpose of vocabulary strategy instruction is to teach students a range of strategies for learning, remembering, and incorporating unknown vocabulary words into their existing reading, writing, speaking, and listening vocabularies.

## Procedures

The selection vocabulary instruction in the first and second part of the lesson focuses on teaching specific vocabulary necessary for understanding the literature selection more completely. The weekly vocabulary instruction in the Language Arts part of each lesson is geared toward teaching vocabulary skills and strategies to build and secure vocabulary through word relationships or develop vocabulary strategies for unknown words.

### General Strategies

There is no question that having students read and reading to students are effective vocabulary instructional strategies. Most word learning occurs through exposure to words in listening and reading. Multiple exposures to words, particularly when students hear, see, say, and write words, is also effective. Word play, including meaning and dictionary games, helps to develop a word consciousness as well.

## Vocabulary Skills and Strategies

**Word Relationships** People effectively learn new words by relating them to words they already know. An understanding of different word relationships enables students to quickly and efficiently secure new vocabulary. The weekly vocabulary lessons are organized around these types of word groups. Word relationships include:

- **Antonyms** Words with opposite or nearly opposite meanings. (*hot/cold*)
- **Synonyms** Words with similar meanings. (*cup, mug, glass*)
- **Multiple Meanings** Words that have more than one meaning. (*run, dressing, bowl*)
- **Shades of Meaning** Words that express degrees of a concept or quality. (*like, love, worship*)
- **Levels of Specificity** Words that describe at different levels of precision. (*living thing, plant, flower, daffodil*)
- **Analogies** Pairs of words that have the same relationship. (*ball is to baseball as puck is to hockey*)
- **Compound Words** Words comprised of two or more words. (*daylight*)
- **Homographs** Words that are spelled the same but have different meanings and come from different root words. (*bear, count*)
- **Homophones** Words that sound the same but have different spellings and meanings. (*mane/main, to/two/too*)
- **Base Word Families** Words that have the same base word. (*care, careless, careful, uncaring, carefree*)
- **Prefixes** An affix attached before a base word that changes the meaning of the word. (*misspell*)
- **Suffixes** An affix attached to the end of a base word that changes the meaning of the word. (*careless*)
- **Concept Vocabulary** Words that help develop understanding of a concept. (*space, sun, Earth, satellite, planet, asteroid*)
- **Classification and Categorization** Sorting words by related meanings. (*colors, shapes, animals, foods*)

**Contextual Word Lists** Teaching vocabulary in context is another way to secure understanding of unknown words. Grouping words by subject area such as science, social studies, math, descriptive words, new words, and so on enables students to connect word meanings and build vocabulary understanding.

- **Figurative Language** Idioms, metaphors, similes, personification, puns, and novel meanings need to be specifically taught, especially for English language learners.

- **Derivational Word Lists** Presenting groups of words derived from particular languages or with specific roots or affixes is an effective way to reinforce meanings and spellings of foreign words and word parts.

## Vocabulary Strategies for Unknown Words

Different strategies have been shown to be particularly effective for learning completely new words. These strategies are included in the *Spelling and Vocabulary Skills* activities.

**Key Word** This strategy involves providing or having students create a mnemonic clue for unknown vocabulary. For example, the word *mole* is defined in chemistry as a "gram molecule." By relating *mole* to *molecule*, students have a key to the meaning of the word.

**Definitions** Copying a definition from a dictionary is somewhat effective in learning new vocabulary. Combining this with using the word in writing and speaking adds to the effectiveness of this strategy. Requiring students to explain a word or use it in a novel sentence helps to ensure that the meaning is understood.

**Context Clues** Many words are learned from context, particularly with repeated exposure to words in reading and listening. Without specific instruction in consciously using context clues, however, unknown words are often ignored.

- **Syntax** How a word is used in a sentence provides some clue to its meaning.
- **External Context Clues** Hints about a word's meaning may appear in the setting, words, phrases, or sentences surrounding a word in text. Other known words in the text may be descriptive, may provide a definition (apposition), may be compared or contrasted, or may be used synonymously in context. Modeling and teaching students to use context to infer a word's meaning can help in learning unknown words.

**Word Structure** Examining the affixes and roots of a word may provide some clue to its meaning. Knowing the meaning of at least part of the word can provide a clue to its meaning. (For example, *unenforceable* can be broken down into meaningful word parts.)

**Semantic Mapping** Having students create a semantic map of an unknown word after learning its definition helps them to learn it. Have students write the new word and then list in a map or web all words they can think of that are related to it.

**Semantic Feature Analysis** A semantic feature analysis helps students compare and contrast similar types of words within a category to help secure unknown words. Have students chart, for example, the similarities and differences between different types of sports, including new vocabulary such as *lacrosse* and *cricket*.

# Developing Vocabulary

## Purpose

Vocabulary is closely connected to comprehension. Considerable vocabulary growth occurs incidentally during reading. A clear connection exists between vocabulary development and the amount of reading a person does, and there are strong indications that vocabulary instruction is important and that understanding the meaning of key words helps with comprehension.

In *Open Court Reading,* vocabulary is addressed before, during, and after reading. Before reading, the teacher presents vocabulary words from the selection. Students use skills such as context clues, apposition, and structural analysis to figure out the meaning of the words. These selection vocabulary words are not only important to understanding the text but are also high-utility words that can be used in discussing and writing about the unit theme.

During reading, students monitor their understanding of words and text. When they do not understand something, they stop and clarify what they have read. Students will use these same skills—context clues, apposition, structural elements, and the like—to clarify the meanings of additional words encountered while reading. Figuring out the meanings of words while reading prepares students for the demands of independent reading both in and out of school.

After reading, students review the vocabulary words that they learned before reading the selection. They also review any interesting words that they identified and discussed during reading. Students record in their Writer's Notebook both the selection vocabulary words and the interesting words they identified during their reading and are encouraged to use both sets of words in discussion and in writing.

## Procedure

Before students read a selection, the teacher uses an overhead transparency to introduce the selection vocabulary to the class. The transparency contains two sentences for each selection vocabulary word. Students must use context clues, apposition, or word structure in the sentences to figure out the meaning of the underlined vocabulary words. If students cannot figure out the meaning of the word using one of these skills, they can consult the glossary or dictionary.

Below are suggestions for modeling the use of context clues, apposition, or word structure to figure out the meaning of a word.

## Modeling Using Context Clues

Have students read the sentences on the transparency. Explain to students that they will use *context clues,* or other words in the sentence, to figure out the meaning of the underlined word. For example, if the word is "treacherous," the sentences might include:

1. Mrs. Frisby must undertake a <u>treacherous</u> journey to bring her son some medicine.

2. We took a <u>treacherous</u> walk near a swamp filled with crocodiles.

Have students look for clues in the sentences that might help them understand the meaning of the underlined word. Point out that a good clue in the second sentence is "near a swamp filled with crocodiles." This clue should help them understand that *treacherous* probably has something to do with danger. Guide students until they can give a reasonable definition of *treacherous.* To consolidate understanding of the word, ask another student to use the definition in a sentence.

## Modeling Using Apposition

Have students read the sentences on the transparency. Explain to students that they will use *apposition* to figure out the meaning of the word. In apposition, the word is followed by the definition, which is set off by commas. For example, if the word is "abolitionist," the sentences might include the following:

1. The conductor thought he was an <u>abolitionist</u>, a person who wanted to end slavery.

2. John Brown was a famous <u>abolitionist</u>, a person who wanted to end slavery.

It should be pretty clear to students using apposition that the definition of the word *abolitionist* is "a person who wanted to end slavery."

## Modeling Using Word Structure

Have students read the sentences on the transparency. Explain to students that they will use *word structure,* or parts of the selection vocabulary word, to figure out the meaning. For example, if the word is "uncharted," the sentences might include:

1. The strong wind blew Ivan's ship away into <u>uncharted</u> seas.

2. The explorers Lewis and Clark went into <u>uncharted</u> territory.

Have students look at the word *uncharted* and break it into parts: the prefix *un-*, *chart*, and the suffix *–ed.* Students should know that the suffix *un-* means "not," and that the suffix *–ed* usually indicates the past tense of a verb. However, you may need to remind students about the meanings of these affixes. Ask students for the meaning of the word *chart.*

Students should know that a chart could be a "map" or a "table." Guide them as they put together the definitions of the word parts, *un-* (not), *charted* (mapped or tabled). They should be able to come up with the definition "not mapped" or "unmapped" or even "unknown." Have them substitute their definition in the sentences to see if the definition makes sense. So, for instance, the first sentence would read "The strong wind blew Ivan's ship away into unmapped (or unknown) seas." Confirm with students that the new sentence makes sense, and then repeat the same process for the second sentence.

# Reading Comprehension

Everything the students learn about phonemic awareness, phonics, and decoding has one primary goal—to help them understand what they are reading. Without comprehension, there is no reading.

## Reading Comprehension Strategies

### Purpose

The primary aim of reading is comprehension. Without comprehension, neither intellectual nor emotional responses to reading are possible— other than the response of frustration. Good readers are problem solvers. They bring their critical faculties to bear on everything they read. Experienced readers generally understand most of what they read, but just as importantly, they recognize when they do not understand, and they have at their command an assortment of strategies for monitoring and furthering their understanding.

The goal of comprehension strategy instruction is to turn responsibility for using strategies over to the students as soon as possible. Research has shown that students' comprehension and learning problems are not a matter of mental capacity but rather their inability to use strategies to help them learn. Good readers use a variety of strategies to help them make sense of the text and get the most out of what they read. Trained to use a variety of comprehension strategies, students dramatically improve their learning performance. In order to do this, the teacher models strategy use and gradually incorporates different kinds of prompts and possible student think-alouds as examples of the types of thinking students might do as they read to comprehend what they are reading.

### Setting Reading Goals

Even before they begin reading and using comprehension strategies, good readers set reading goals and expectations. Readers who have set their own goals and have definite expectations about the text they are about to read are more engaged in their reading and notice more in what they read. Having determined a purpose for reading, they are better able to evaluate a text and determine whether it meets their needs. Even when the reading is assigned, the reader's engagement is enhanced when he or she has determined ahead of time what information might be gathered from the selection or how the selection might interest him or her.

### Comprehension Strategies

Descriptions of strategies good readers use to comprehend the text follow.

### Summarizing

Good readers sum up to check their understanding as they read. Sometimes they reread to fill in gaps in their understanding. Good readers use the strategy of summarizing to keep track of what they are reading and to focus their minds on important information. The process of putting the information in one's own words not only helps good readers remember what they have read, but also prompts them to evaluate how well they understand the information. Sometimes the summary reveals that one's understanding is incomplete, in which case it might be appropriate to reread the previous section to fill in the gaps. Good readers usually find that the strategy of summarizing is particularly helpful when they are reading long or complicated text.

### Monitoring and Clarifying

Good readers constantly monitor themselves as they read in order to make sure they understand what they are reading. They note the characteristics of the text, such as whether it is difficult to read or whether some sections are more challenging or more important than others are. In addition, when good readers become aware that they do not understand, they take appropriate action, such as rereading, in order to understand the text better. As they read, good readers stay alert for problem signs such as loss of concentration, unfamiliar vocabulary, or lack of sufficient background knowledge to comprehend the text. This ability to self-monitor and identify aspects of the text that hinder comprehension is crucial to becoming a proficient reader.

### Asking Questions

Good readers ask questions that may prepare them for what they will learn. If their questions are not answered in the text, they may try to find answers elsewhere and thus add even more to their store of knowledge. Certain kinds of questions occur naturally to a reader, such as clearing up confusion or wondering why something in the text is as it is. Intentional readers take this somewhat informal questioning one step further by formulating questions with the specific intent of checking their understanding. They literally test themselves by thinking of questions a teacher might ask and then by determining answers to those questions.

### Predicting

Good readers predict what will happen next. When reading fiction, they make predictions about what they are reading and then confirm or revise those predictions as they go.

### Making Connections

Good readers make connections between what they are reading and what they already know from past experience or previous reading.

### Visualizing

Good readers visualize what is happening in the text. They form mental images as they read. They picture the setting, the characters, and the action in a story. Visualizing can also be helpful when reading expository text. Visualizing helps readers understand descriptions of complex activities or processes. When a complex process or an event is being described, the reader can follow the process or the event better by visualizing each step or episode. Sometimes an author or an editor helps the reader by providing illustrations, diagrams, or maps. If no visual aids have been provided, it may help the reader to create one.

### Monitoring and Adjusting Reading Speed

Good readers understand that not all text is equal. Because of this, good readers continuously monitor what they are reading and adjust their reading speed accordingly. They skim parts of the text that are not important or relevant to their reading goals and they purposely slow down when they encounter difficulty in understanding the text.

## Procedures

### Modeling and Thinking Aloud

One of the most effective ways to help students use and understand the strategies good readers use is to make strategic thinking public. Modeling these behaviors and encouraging students to think aloud as they attempt to understand text can demonstrate for everyone in a class how these behaviors are put into practice. Suggestions for think-alouds are provided throughout the **Teacher's Edition.**

The most effective models you can offer will be those that come from your own reading experiences. What kinds of questions did you ask yourself? What kinds of things surprised you the first time you read a story? What kinds of new information did you learn? What kinds of things were confusing until you reread or read further? Drawing on these questions and on your students' questions and comments as they read will make the strategic reading process more meaningful to the students. Below are suggestions for modeling each of the comprehension strategies.

■ **Modeling Setting Reading Goals.** To model setting reading goals, engage students in the following:

■ **Activate prior knowledge.** As you approach a new text, consider aloud what you already know about the subject or what your experiences have been in reading similar material.

■ **Browse the text.** To get an idea of what to expect from a text, look at the title and the illustrations. Look for potential problems, such as difficult words. Have students glance quickly at the selection, looking briefly at the illustrations and the print. Have them tell what they think they might be learning about as they read the selection.

■ **Decide what to expect from the text.** Anticipate enjoying the story, the language of the text, or the new information you expect to gain from the selection.

■ **Modeling Summarizing.** Just as the strategy of summarizing the plot and then predicting what will happen next can enhance a student's reading of fiction, so too can the same procedure be used to the student's advantage in reading nonfiction. In expository text, it is particularly logical to stop and summarize at the end of a chapter or section before going on to the next. One way to model the valuable exercise of making predictions and at the same time expand knowledge is to summarize information learned from a piece of expository writing and then predict what the next step or category will be. Appropriate times to stop and summarize include the following:

■ when a narrative text has covered a long period of time or a number of events

■ when many facts have been presented

■ when an especially critical scene has occurred

■ when a complex process has been described

■ any time there is the potential for confusion about what has happened or what has been presented in the text

■ when returning to a selection

■ **Modeling Monitoring and Clarifying.** A reader may need clarification at any point in the reading. Model this strategy by stopping at points that confuse you or that may confuse your students. Indicate that you are experiencing some confusion and need to stop and make sure you understand what is being read. Difficulty may arise from a challenging or unknown word or phrase. It may also stem from the manner in which the information is presented. Perhaps the author did not supply needed information. As you model this strategy, vary the reasons for stopping to clarify so that the students understand that good readers do not simply skip over difficult or confusing material—they stop and figure out what they don't understand.

■ **Modeling Asking Questions.** Learning to ask productive questions is not an easy task. Students' earliest experiences with this strategy take the form of answering teacher-generated questions. However, students should be able to move fairly quickly to asking questions like those a teacher might ask. Questions that can be answered with a simple yes or no are not typically very useful for helping them remember and understand what they have read. Many students find it helpful to ask questions beginning with *Who? What? When? Where? How?* or *Why?* As students become more accustomed to asking and answering questions, they will naturally become more adept at phrasing their questions. As their question-asking becomes more sophisticated, they progress from simple questions that can be answered with explicit information in the text to questions that require making inferences based on the text.

> *Good readers use a variety of strategies to help them make sense of the text and get the most out of what they read.*

■ **Modeling Predicting.** Predicting can be appropriate at the beginning of a selection— on the basis of the titles and the illustrations—or at any point while reading a selection. At first, your modeling will take the form of speculation about what might happen next, but tell students from the start what clues in the text or illustrations helped you predict, in order to make it clear that predicting is not just guessing. When a student makes a prediction—especially a far-fetched one—ask what in the selection or in his or her own experience the prediction is based on. If the student can back up the prediction, let the prediction stand; otherwise, suggest that the student make another prediction on the basis of what he or she already knows. Often it is appropriate to sum up before making a prediction. This will help students consider what has come before as they make their predictions about what will happen next. When reading aloud, stop whenever a student's prediction has been confirmed or contradicted. Have students tell whether the prediction was correct. If students seem comfortable with the idea of making predictions but rarely do so on their own, encourage them to discuss how to find clues in the text that will help them.

■ **Modeling Making Connections.** To model making connections, share with students any thoughts or memories that come to mind as you read the selection. Perhaps a character in a story reminds you of a childhood friend, allowing you to better identify with interactions between characters. Perhaps information in an article on Native-American life in the Old West reminds you of an article that you have read on the importance of the bison to Native Americans. Sharing your connections will help students become aware of the dynamic nature of reading and show them another way of being intentional, active learners.

■ **Modeling Visualizing.** Model visualizing by describing the mental images that occur to you as you read. A well-described scene is relatively easy to visualize, and if no one does so voluntarily, you may want to prompt students to express their own visualizations. If the author has not provided a description of a scene, but a picture of the scene would make the story more interesting or comprehensible, you might want to model visualizing as follows: "Let's see. The author says that the street was busy, and we know that this story is set during the colonial period. From what I already know about those times, there were no cars, and the roads were different from the roads of today. The street may have been paved with cobblestones. Horses would have been pulling carriages or wagons. I can almost hear the horses' hoofs going clip-clop over the stones." Remind students that different readers may picture the same scene quite differently, which is fine. Every reader responds to a story in her or his own way.

■ **Modeling Monitoring and Adjusting Reading Speed.** Just as readers need to monitor for problems, they need to be aware that different texts can be approached in different ways. For example, if reading a story or novel for enjoyment, the reader will typically read at a relaxed speed that is neither so fast as to be missing information nor as slow as they might read a textbook. If on the other hand, the reader is reading a textbook, he or she will probably decrease speed to assure understanding and make sure that all important information is read and understood. When modeling this strategy, be sure you indicate why you, as the reader, have chosen to slow down or speed up. Good readers continually monitor their speed and ability to understand throughout reading.

## Reading Comprehension (continued)

### Reading Aloud

At the beginning of the year, students should be encouraged to read selections aloud. This practice will help you and them understand some of the challenges posed by the text and how different students approach these challenges.

Reading aloud helps students build fluency, which in turn will aid their comprehension. Students in grades K–3 can use **Decodable Books** to build fluency, while students in grades 4–6 can use the literature from the **Student Anthologies.** Fluent second graders read between 82 and 124 words per minute with accuracy and understanding, depending on the time of the year (fall/spring). Fluent third graders can be expected to read between 107 and 142 words per minute; fourth (125/143); fifth (126/151); sixth (127/153).

Make sure that you set aside time to hear each student read during the first few days of class—the days devoted to Getting Started are perfect for this—so that you can determine students' abilities and needs. **Workshop** is also a good time to listen to any students who do not get to read aloud while the class is reading the selection together.

If your students have not previously engaged in the sort of strategic thinking aloud that is promoted throughout the *SRA/Open Court Reading* program, you will have to do all or most of the modeling at first, but encourage the students to participate as soon as possible.

As the year progresses, students should continue reading aloud often, especially with particularly challenging text. Model your own use of strategies, not only to help students better understand how to use strategies, but also to help them understand that actively using strategies is something that good, mature readers do constantly.

Most students are unaccustomed to thinking out loud. They will typically stand mute as they try to figure out an unfamiliar word or deal with a confusing passage. When this happens, students should be encouraged to identify specifically what they are having difficulty with. A student might identify a particular word, or he or she may note that the individual words are familiar but the meaning of the passage is unclear.

### Active Response

Not only are good readers active in their reading when they encounter problems, but they respond constantly to whatever they read. In this way they make the text their own. As students read they should be encouraged to:

- Make as many connections as they can between what they are reading and what they already know.

- Visualize passages to help clarify their meanings or simply to picture appealing descriptions.

- Ask questions about what they are reading. The questions that go through their minds during reading will help them to examine, and thus better understand, the text. Doing so may also interest them in pursuing their own investigations. The questions may also provide a direction for students' research or exploration.

- Summarize and make predictions as a check on how well they understand what they are reading.

## Tips

- Remember that the goal of all reading strategies is comprehension. If a story or article does not make sense, the reader needs to choose whatever strategies will help make sense of it. If one strategy does not work, the reader should try another.

- Always treat problems encountered in text as interesting learning opportunities rather than something to be avoided or dreaded.

- Encourage students to think out loud about text challenges.

- Encourage students to help each other build meaning from text. Rather than telling each other what a word is or what a passage means, students should tell each other how they figured out the meanings of challenging words and passages.

- Assure students that these are not the only strategies that can be used while reading. Any strategy that they find helpful in understanding text is a good useful strategy.

- Encourage students to freely share strategies they have devised on their own. You might want to write these on a large sheet of paper and tape them to the board.

- An absence of questions does not necessarily indicate that students understand what they are reading. Be especially alert to students who never seem to ask questions. Be sure to spend tutorial time with these students occasionally, and encourage them to discuss specific selections in the context of difficulties they might have encountered and how they solved them as well as their thoughts about unit concepts.

- Observing students' responses to text will enable you to ascertain not only how well they understand a particular selection but also their facility in choosing and applying appropriate strategies. Take note of the following:

- ✓ Whether the strategies a student uses are effective in the particular situation.

- ✓ Whether the student chooses from a variety of appropriate strategies or uses the same few over and over.

- ✓ Whether the student can explain to classmates which strategies to use in a particular situation and why.

- ✓ Whether the student can identify alternative resources to pursue when the strategies she or he has tried are not effective.

- ✓ Whether students' application of a given strategy is becoming more effective over a period of time.

Becoming familiar and comfortable with these self-monitoring techniques gives readers the confidence to tackle material that is progressively more difficult. A good, mature reader knows that he or she will know when understanding what he or she is reading is becoming a problem and can take steps to correct the situation.

# Reading Comprehension Skills

## Purpose

An important purpose of writing is to communicate thoughts from one person to another. The goal of instruction in reading comprehension skills is to make students aware of the logic behind the structure of a written piece. If the reader can discern the logic of the structure, he or she will be more able to understand the author's logic and gain knowledge both of the facts and the intent of the selection. By keeping the organization of a piece in mind and considering the author's purpose for writing, the reader can go beyond the actual words on the page and make inferences or draw conclusions based on what was read. Strong, mature readers utilize these "between the lines" skills to get a complete picture of not only what the writer is saying, but what the writer is trying to say.

Effective comprehension skills include:

### Author's Point of View

Point of view involves identifying who is telling the story. If a character in the story is telling the story, that one character describes the action and tells what the other characters are like. This is first-person point of view. In such a story, one character will do the talking and use the pronouns *I*, *my*, *me*. All other characters' thoughts, feelings, and emotions will be reported through this one character.

If the story is told in third-person point of view, someone outside the story who is aware of all of the characters' thoughts and feelings and actions is relating them to the reader. All of the characters are referred to by their names or the pronouns *he/she*, *him/her*, *it*.

If students stay aware of who is telling a story, they will know whether they are getting the full picture or the picture of events as seen through the eyes of only one character.

### Sequence

The reader can't make any decisions about relationships or events if he or she has no idea in which order the events take place. The reader needs to pay attention to how the writer is conveying the sequence. Is it simply stated that first this happened and then that happened? Does the writer present the end of the story first and then go back and let the reader know the sequence of events? Knowing what the sequence is and how it is presented helps the reader follow the writer's line of thought.

### Fact and Opinion

Learning to distinguish fact from opinion is essential to critical reading and thinking. Students learn what factors need to be present in order for a statement to be provable. They also learn that an opinion, while not provable itself, should be based on fact. Readers use this knowledge to determine for themselves the validity of the ideas presented in their reading.

### Main Idea and Details

An author always has something specific to say to his or her reader. The author may state this main idea in different ways, but the reader should always be able to tell what the writing is about.

To strengthen the main point or main idea of a piece, the author provides details to help the reader understand. For example, the author may use comparison and contrast to make a point, provide examples, provide facts, give opinions, give descriptions, give reasons or causes, or give definitions. The reader needs to know what kinds of details he or she is dealing with before making a judgment about the main idea.

### Compare and Contrast

Using comparison and contrast is one of the most common and easiest ways a writer uses to get his or her reader to understand a subject. Comparing and contrasting unfamiliar thoughts, ideas, or things with familiar thoughts, ideas, and things gives the reader something within his or her own experience base to use in understanding.

### Cause and Effect

What made this happen? Why did this character act the way he or she did? Knowing the causes of events helps the reader to see the whole story. Using this information to identify the probable outcomes (effects) of events or actions will help the reader anticipate the story or article.

### Classify and Categorize

The relationships of actions, events, characters, outcomes, and such in a selection should be clear enough for the reader to see the relationships. Putting like things or ideas together can help the reader understand the relationships set up by the writer.

### Author's Purpose

Everything that is written is written for a purpose. That purpose may be to entertain, to persuade, or to inform. Knowing why a piece is written—what purpose the author had for writing the piece—gives the reader an idea of what to expect and perhaps some prior idea of what the author is going to say.

If a writer is writing to entertain, then the reader can generally just relax and let the writer carry him or her away. If, on the other hand, the purpose is to persuade, it will help the reader understand and keep perspective if he or she knows that the purpose is to persuade. The reader can be prepared for whatever argument the writer delivers.

### Drawing Conclusions

Often, writers do not directly state everything—they take for granted their audience's ability to "read between the lines." Readers draw conclusions when they take from the text small pieces of information about a character or event and use this information to make a statement about that character or event.

### Making Inferences

Readers make inferences about characters and events to understand the total picture in a story. When making inferences, readers use information from the text, along with personal experience or knowledge, to gain a deeper understanding of a story event and its implications.

## Procedure

### Read the Selection

First, have students read the selection using whatever strategies they need to help them make sense of the selection. Then discuss the selection to assure that students did, indeed, understand what they read. Talk about any confusion they may have, and make any necessary clarifications.

### Reread

Revisiting or rereading a selection allows the reader to note specific techniques that authors use to organize and present information in narratives and expository genres. Once students have a basic understanding of the piece, have them reread the selection in whole or in part, concentrating on selected skills. Choose examples of how the writer organized the piece to help the reader understand.

Limit this concentration on specific comprehension/writing skills to one or two that can be clearly identified in the piece. Trying to concentrate on too many things will just confuse students and make it harder for them to identify any of the organizational devices used by the writer. If a piece has many good examples of several different aspects, then go back to the piece several times over a span of days.

### Write

Solidify the connection between how an author writes and how readers make sense of a selection by encouraging students to incorporate these organizational devices into their own writing. As they attempt to use these devices, they will get a clearer understanding of how to identify them when they are reading.

Remind students often that the purpose of any skill exercise is to give them tools to use when they are reading and writing. Unless students learn to apply the skills to their own reading—in every area of reading and study—then they are not gaining a full understanding of the purpose of the exercise.

# Grammar, Usage, and Mechanics

*Writing is a complicated process. A writer uses handwriting, spelling, vocabulary, grammar, usage, genre structures, and mechanics skills with ideas to create readable text. In addition, a writer must know how to generate content, or ideas, and understand genre structures in order to effectively present ideas in writing. Many students never progress beyond producing a written text that duplicates their everyday speech patterns. Mature writers, however, take composition beyond conversation. They understand the importance of audience and purpose for writing. They organize their thoughts, eliminating those that do not advance their main ideas, and elaborating on those that do so that their readers can follow a logical progression of ideas in an essay or story. Mature writers also know and can use the conventions of grammar, usage, spelling, and mechanics. They proofread and edit for these conventions, so their readers are not distracted by errors.*

## Purpose

### The Study of English Conventions

Over the years the study of grammar, usage, and mechanics has gone in and out of favor. In the past century much research has been done to demonstrate the effectiveness of traditional types of instruction in the conventions of English. Experience and research have shown that learning grammatical terms and completing grammar exercises have little effect on the student's practical application of these skills in the context of speaking or writing. These skills, in and of themselves, do not play a significant role in the way students use language to generate and express their ideas—for example during the prewriting and drafting phases of the writing process. In fact, emphasis on correct conventions has been shown to have a damaging effect when it is the sole focus of writing instruction. If students are evaluated only on the proper use of spelling, grammar, and punctuation, they tend to write fewer and less complex sentences.

Knowledge of English conventions is, however, vitally important in the editing and proofreading phases of the writing process. A paper riddled with mistakes in grammar, usage, or mechanics is quickly discounted. Many immature writers never revise or edit. They finish the last sentence and turn their papers in to the teacher. Mature writers employ their knowledge of English language conventions in the editing phase to refine and polish their ideas.

The study of grammar, usage, and mechanics is important for two reasons.

1. Educated people need to know and understand the structure of their language, which in large part defines their culture.

2. Knowledge of grammar gives teachers and students a common vocabulary for talking about language and makes discussions of writing tasks more efficient and clearer.

## Procedure

The key issue in learning grammar, usage, and mechanics is *how* to do it. On the one hand, teaching these skills in isolation from writing has been shown to be ineffective and even detrimental if too much emphasis is placed on them. On the other hand, not teaching these skills and having students write without concern for conventions is equally ineffective. The answer is to teach the skills in a context that allows students to directly apply them to a reading or writing activity. Students should be taught proper use of punctuation or subject/verb agreement at the same time they are taught to proofread for those conventions. As they learn to apply their knowledge of conventions during the final stages of the writing process, they will begin to see that *correcting* errors is an editorial, rather than a composition skill.

## History of English

A basic understanding of the history and structure of the English language helps students understand the rich but complex resource they have for writing.

### Old English

The English language began about AD 450 when the Angles, Jutes, and Saxons—three tribes that lived in northern Europe—invaded the British Isles. Much of their language included words that had to do with farming (*sheep, dirt, tree, earth*). Many of their words are the most frequently used words in the English language today. Because of Latin influences, English became the first of the European languages to be written down.

### Middle English

In 1066 William the Conqueror invaded England and brought Norman French with him. Slowly Old English and Norman French came together, and Middle English began to appear. Today 40% of Modern English comes from French. With the introduction of the printing press English became more widespread.

### Modern English

With the Renaissance and its rediscovery of classical Greek and Latin, many new words were created from Greek and Latin word elements. This continued intensively during the Early Modern English period. This rich language was used in the writings of Shakespeare and his contemporaries and profoundly influenced the nature and vocabulary of English. With dictionaries and spelling books, the English language became more standardized, although it continues to be influenced by other languages and new words and trends. These influences continue to make English a living, dynamic language.

## Punctuation

Early writing had no punctuation or even spaces between words. English punctuation had its beginning in ancient Greece and Rome. Early punctuation reflected speaking, rather than reading. By the end of the eighteenth century, after the invention of printing, most of the rules for punctuation were established, although they were not the same in all languages.

## The Structure of English

**Grammar** is the sound, structure, and meaning system of language. People who speak the same language are able to communicate because they intuitively know the grammar system of that language, the rules of making meaning. All languages have grammar, and yet each language has its own grammar.

Traditional grammar study usually involves two areas:

- **Parts of speech** (nouns, verbs, adjectives, adverbs, pronouns, prepositions, conjunctions) are typically considered the content of grammar. The parts of speech involve the *form* of English words.

- **Sentence structure** (subjects, predicates, objects, clauses, phrases) is also included in grammar study. Sentence structure involves the *function* of English.

**Mechanics** involves the conventions of punctuation and capitalization. Punctuation helps readers understand writers' messages. Proper punctuation involves marking off sentences according to grammatical structure. In speech students can produce sentences as easily and unconsciously as they can walk, but in writing they must think about what is and what is not a sentence.

In English there are about 14 punctuation marks (period, comma, quotation marks, question mark, exclamation point, colon, semicolon, apostrophe, hyphen, ellipsis, parentheses, brackets, dash, and underscore). Most immature writers use only three: period, comma, and question mark. The experienced writer or poet with the command of punctuation adds both flexibility and meaning to his or her sentences through his or her use of punctuation.

**Usage** is the way in which we speak in a given community. Language varies over time, across national and geographical boundaries, by gender, across age groups, and by socioeconomic status. When the variation occurs within a given language, the different versions of the same language are called *dialects*. Every language has a *prestige dialect* associated with education and financial success. In the United States, this *dialect* is known as Standard English and is the language of school and business.

Usage involves the word choices people make when speaking certain dialects. Word choices that are perfectly acceptable in conversation among friends may be unacceptable in writing. Usage is often the most obvious indicator of the difference between conversation and composition. Errors in word usage can make a writer seem ignorant and thus jeopardize his or her credibility, no matter how valid or important his or her overall message might be. Usage depends on a student's cultural and linguistic heritage. If the dialect students have learned is not the formal language of school settings or if it is not English, students must master another dialect or language in order to write Standard English.

The English Language Conventions lessons in *Open Court Reading* are structured to focus on grammar and usage or mechanics skills presented in a logical sequence. A skill is introduced on the first day of the lesson with appropriate models and then practiced in reading and writing on subsequent days to ensure that skills are not taught in isolation. Encourage students to use the focused English language convention presented in each lesson as they complete each Writing Process Strategies activity. Also encourage them to reread their writing, checking for proper use of the conventions taught. With practice, students should be able to apply their knowledge of conventions to any writing they do.

## Tips

- Some of the errors students make in writing are the result simply of not carefully reading their final drafts. Many errors occur because the writer's train of thought was interrupted and a sentence is not complete or a word is skipped. These may look like huge errors that a simple rereading can remedy. Most often the writer can correct these types of errors on his or her own. A major emphasis of any English composition program should be to teach the editing and proofreading phases of the writing process so students can eliminate these types of errors themselves. This involves a shift in perception—from thinking of grammar as a set of discrete skills that involve mastery of individual rules, to understanding grammar as it applies to the act of communicating in writing.

- As students learn English language conventions, they should be expected to incorporate them into their written work. A cumulative student checklist of the grammar, usage, and mechanics skills covered in a grade level appears in the back of the ***Writer's Workbook.***

Sometimes, students write sentences that raise grammatically complex problems that require a deep understanding of English grammar. Use the Sentence Lifting strategies outlined in the **Proofreading** part of the Appendix to identify and discuss these more sophisticated types of errors that can include:

- **Faulty Parallelism.** Parts of a sentence parallel in meaning are not parallel in structure.
- **Nonsequitors.** A statement does not follow logically from something said previously.
- **Dangling Modifiers.** A phrase or clause does not logically modify the word next to it.
- **Awkwardness.** Sentences are not written simply.
- **Wordiness.** Thoughts are not written in as few words as possible.
- **Vocabulary.** Precise words are not used.

# Listening, Speaking, Viewing

*Some people are naturally good listeners, and others have no trouble speaking in front of groups. Many people, however, need explicit instruction on how to tune in for important details and how to organize and make an oral presentation. While some people naturally critique what they read, hear, and see, many others need specific guidance to develop skills for analyzing what they encounter in images and the media. The abilities to listen appropriately and to speak in conversations and in groups, as well as to critically evaluate the information with which they are presented, are fundamental skills that will serve students throughout their lives.*

## Purpose

In addition to reading and writing, listening, speaking, and viewing complete the language arts picture. Through the development of these language arts skills, students gain flexibility in communicating orally, visually, and in writing. When speaking and listening skills are neglected, many students have difficulty speaking in front of groups, organizing a speech, or distinguishing important information they hear. A top anxiety for many adults is speaking in front of groups. Much of this anxiety would not exist if listening, speaking, and viewing skills were taught from the early years.

The Listening, Speaking, and Viewing instruction focuses on the literature selection or the Writing Process Strategies to provide context, reinforce other elements of the lesson, and integrate the other language arts. Many of the Listening, Speaking, and Viewing skills are very similar to reading or writing skills. For

example, listening for details is the same type of skill as reading for details. Preparing an oral report employs many of the same skills as preparing a written report. Learning to use these skills effectively gives students flexibility in how they approach a task.

## Procedure

Listening, speaking, and viewing skills are presented with increasing sophistication throughout every grade level of *Open Court Reading* in the Language Arts part of each lesson. Every unit includes at least one lesson on each of the following skills so that students encounter the skills again and again throughout a grade level:

- **Listening.** Listening skills include comprehending what one hears and listening for different purposes, such as to identify sequence or details, to summarize or draw conclusions, or to follow directions.
- **Speaking.** Speaking skills include speaking formally and conversationally, using appropriate volume, giving oral presentations, and using effective grammar. Speaking skills also include using descriptive words, using figurative language, and using formal and informal language.
- **Viewing.** Viewing skills include comprehending main ideas and messages in images, mass media, and other multimedia.
- **Interaction.** Interaction instruction focuses on a combination of listening and speaking skills. These include asking and responding to questions, nonverbal cues such as eye contact, facial expression, and posture, and contributing to and interacting in group settings.
- **Presenting Information.** The last Listening, Speaking, and Viewing lesson in every unit usually focuses on presentation skills. These include sharing ideas, relating experiences or stories, organizing information, and preparing for speeches. These lessons often parallel the Writing Process Strategies instruction, so that students can prepare their information in written or oral form.

## Tips

- Point out the parallels among the language arts skills: providing written and oral directions, telling or writing a narrative, and so on. Encourage students to see that they have choices for communicating. Discuss the similarities and differences between different forms of communication, and determine whether one is preferable in a given situation.

- Ensure that all students have opportunities to speak in small groups and whole-class situations.

- Provide and teach students to allow appropriate wait time before someone answers a question.

# Writing

The ability to write with clarity and coherence is essential to students' success in school as well as in life. Communicating through writing is becoming more and more important in this age of computers. Yet, writing remains a major problem for students at all levels, as well as adults in the workplace.

## Purpose

Writing is a complex process. It requires the ability to use a variety of skills (penmanship, grammar, usage, mechanics, spelling, vocabulary) fluently and appropriately at the same time one's creative and critical thinking processes create and structure an idea. Familiarity with the structures of writing and different genres, audiences, and purposes is necessary to write appropriately as well. The art of writing well also involves writer's craft, the ability to manipulate words and sentences for effect.

As strange as it may seem, the better a writer is, the *harder* he or she works at writing. The best writers are not the best because they are naturally talented. They are the best usually because they work the hardest. Good writers really do take *more* time than others in the planning and revising stages of the writing process. Poorer writers make writing look easy by writing without planning and typically build a composition sentence by sentence. They turn in their papers with little or no correction.

The goals of writing instruction have many facets:

- To model and practice writing in a variety of writing genres so that students can choose and write in an appropriate form.
- To model and practice a writing process to help students develop routines for planning their work and then revising and editing it.
- To practice using spelling, vocabulary, and English language conventions skills in writing so that students can use them fluently.
- To develop writing traits: ideas, organization, voice, word choice, sentence fluency, and presentation so that students become effective writers.

Just as the goal of phonics instruction is to teach students to read, the Writing Process Strategies instruction in *Open Court Reading* focuses on skills, structures, and strategies for writing. The goal of this instruction is to learn how to write, rather than to develop a particular idea. From this instruction, students will have a comprehensive bank of tools for writing, which they can then employ in the development of their Research and Inquiry investigations in each unit or in any other writing application.

## Procedures

### Writing Genres

There are several different genres students are typically asked to write. These usually

> *The best writers are not the best because they are naturally talented. They are the best usually because they work the hardest. Good writers really do take more time than others in the planning and revising stages of the writing process.*

include many creative stories and a few reports. The only narrative writing most adults do, however, is summaries of meetings. The bulk of adult writing consists of writing reports, letters, analyses, memos, and proposals. College students, as well, typically write research reports or critiques. A literate student needs to be able to choose and write in an appropriate genre.

- Narrative writing is story writing, which has a beginning, middle, and end. It includes myth, realistic fiction, historical fiction, biography, science fiction, fantasy, folktale, and legend.
- Expository writing is informational writing. It includes research reports, scientific investigation, summaries, and explanations of a process.
- Descriptive writing is observational writing that includes details. It has descriptive paragraphs that may be part of narrative or expository writing.
- Poetry writing involves particular attention to word choice and rhythm. Poetry may be free form, ballad, rhyming, or a variety of other forms.
- Personal writing is functional writing to help record ideas, thoughts, or feelings or to communicate with others and may include E-mail, journals, lists, and messages.
- Persuasive writing involves the development of a persuasive argument. It includes posters, persuasive essays, and advertisements.

In *Open Court Reading* the first unit of every grade teaches the writing process and traits of writing. Each subsequent unit focuses on a particular genre appropriate for the unit content. Expository and persuasive writing are typically in the units with research themes such as medicine or business; personal, narrative, descriptive, and poetry writing are in units with universal themes, such as friendship and courage. Exemplary models of each form of writing are included either in the literature selection, on the *Language Arts*

*Transparencies,* or in the *Language Arts Handbook.*

Each genre has its own form and function. For example:

- A personal narrative is probably best ordered as a straightforward chronological retelling of events. Dialogue may help to tell the story.
- A process description should be told in a step-by-step order. The draft should include as much information as possible; each step must be clear. If the piece needs cutting, the student can always do it later.
- A persuasive piece appeals to feelings. It requires facts as well as expert opinions.
- An interview could be written as a series of questions and answers.
- The order of details in a descriptive piece must be easy to follow—from left to right, top to bottom, or whatever order makes sense.
- A fictional story must include details describing characters, setting, and the characters' actions. Dialogue also helps to tell the story.

The goal is not to develop full-blown novels and compositions, but to experience the structures of different forms of writing.

### Structures of Writing

Structures of writing involve the effective development of sentences, paragraphs, and compositions. In *Open Court Reading* structures of writing are taught within the context of the Writing Process Strategies activities rather than in isolation, so that students integrate their practice of writing structures as they develop different writing genres.

### Writer's Craft

Writer's Craft involves the elements and choices writers make to add drama, suspense, or lightheartedness to a written work. These elements may include foreshadowing, use of figurative language, dialogue, or enhancement of setting or use of description to affect the mood and tone. In *Open Court Reading,* along with structures of writing, the writer's craft is pointed out in the literature selection and then taught and practiced within the context of the Writing Process Strategies activities.

### Writing Traits

Writing traits are those elements and qualities in a composition that enhance the effectiveness of the writing. These include:

- Ideas/Content. Not only the quality of the idea, but the development, support, and focus of the idea makes a strong composition.

- Organization. In quality writing, the organization develops the central idea. The order and structure move the reader through the text easily. The beginning grabs the reader's attention and the conclusion adds impact.

- Voice. Voice is the overall tone of a piece of writing. Good writers choose a voice appropriate for the topic, purpose, and audience. As students develop writing skills, a unique style begins to emerge. The writing is expressive, engaging, or sincere, demonstrating a strong commitment to the topic.

- Word Choice. In quality writing words convey the intended message in an interesting, precise, and natural way appropriate to audience and purpose.

- Sentence Fluency. Sentence fluency enhances the flow and rhythm of a composition. In good writing sentence patterns are somewhat varied, contributing to ease in oral reading.

- Conventions. Good writers demonstrate consistent use and awareness of English language conventions.

- Presentation. A quality piece of writing includes an impressive presentation with attention to format, style, illustration, and clarity.

In *Open Court Reading,* the traits of writing are taught in the first unit and then practiced in every Writing Process Strategies activity as an integral part of the writing process.

### The Writing Process

Providing a routine or process for students to follow will help them to learn a systematic approach to writing. By following the steps of the writing process, students will learn to approach everything they write with purpose and thought. They learn that although writing takes time and thought, there are steps they can take to make their writing clear, coherent, and appealing to their audience.

In *Open Court Reading,* the first unit of every grade provides an overview and teaching of the writing process, including strategies and examples for getting ideas, determining audience and purpose for writing, organizing writing, drafting, revising, editing, and presenting. The vehicle used to apply this instruction is a student autobiography. The autobiographies can be collected in a school portfolio to assess writing development over the course of the elementary years.

# Prewriting

## Purpose

Prewriting is that phase of the writing process when students think through an idea they want to write about. To improve their writing, students should think about their ideas, discuss them, and plan how they want readers to respond. It is important for students to take time before writing to plan ahead so that they can proceed from one phase of the writing process to another without spending unnecessary time making decisions that should have been made earlier. Prewriting is the most time-consuming phase of the writing process, but it may be the most important.

> *The goal is not to develop full-blown novels and compositions, but to familiarize and practice the structures of different forms of writing.*

## Procedure

### Good student writers

- Listen to advice about time requirements and plan time accordingly.
- Spend time choosing, thinking about, and planning the topic.
- Spend time narrowing the topic.
- Determine the purpose for writing.
- Consider the audience and what readers already know about the topic.
- Conduct research, if necessary, before writing.
- Get information from a lot of different sources.
- Use models for different types of writing, but develop individual plans.
- Organize the resource information.
- Make a plan for writing that shows how the ideas will be organized.
- Elaborate on a plan and evaluate and alter ideas as writing proceeds.

### Noting Writing Ideas

Students can make notes of writing ideas at any time, with a special time being set aside following the discussion of each reading selection. The writing ideas students get from a discussion might be concerned with the topic of the selection they just read or with an aspect of the author's style. You should keep such a list of writing ideas also, and think aloud occasionally as you make writing idea notes.

Students must make many decisions during the prewriting phase of the writing process. Most students can benefit from talking with a partner or a small group of classmates about these decisions. They may want to discuss some of the following points.

- **Genre** or format of each writing piece. Having decided to use a writing idea such as "a misunderstanding on the first day of school," the student must decide how to use it—for example, as a personal narrative, a realistic fiction story, a poem, a fantasy story, a play, a letter, and so on.

- **Audience**. Although students' writing pieces will be shared with classmates and with you, some may ultimately be intended for other audiences.

- **Writing Purpose**. Each student should write a sentence that tells the purpose of the piece he or she plans to write. The purpose statement should name the intended audience and the effect the writer hopes to have on that audience. For example, a writer may want to describe her first day in school. The intended audience is kindergarten students, and she intends her story to be humorous. Her purpose statement would read, "I want to write a funny story for other students about my first day in kindergarten."

- **Planning**. Some writers may find it helpful to brainstorm with a partner or small group to list words and phrases they might use in a piece of writing. Sometimes this list can be organized into webs of related ideas or details. This kind of prewriting activity might be particularly useful for planning a descriptive piece. For planning a comparison/contrast piece, a writer might use another kind of visual organizer, such as a Venn diagram. Students planning fiction pieces might use a story frame or plot line.

## Tips

- Circulate as students make notes on writing ideas or work in small groups on prewriting activities.

- Notice which students are having difficulty coming up with writing ideas. It may help to pair these students with students who have many ideas.

- Do not worry if this phase of the process seems noisy and somewhat chaotic. Students must be allowed to let their imaginations roam in free association and to play around with words and ideas until they hit on something that seems right. They must be permitted to share ideas and help each other.

- Do not worry if, in the early sessions, the class as a whole seems to have few ideas. Through the reading and discussion of selections in the reading anthology, most students will soon have more writing ideas than they can use.

**PROGRAM APPENDIX**

## Writing (continued)

# Drafting

## Purpose

During the drafting phase of the writing process, students shape their planning notes into main ideas and details. They devote their time and effort to getting words down on paper. Whether students are drafting on scrap paper or on computer screens, your role is to encourage each writer to "get it all down." You must also provide a suitable writing environment with the expectation that there will be revision to the draft and to the original plan.

### Good Student Writers

- Express all their ideas in the first draft.
- Stop and think about what is being written while drafting.
- Evaluate and alter ideas while drafting.
- Change or elaborate on original plans while drafting.
- Discover that they need more information about certain parts of their writing.
- Learn a lot more about the topic while drafting.

## Procedure

Here are some points to share with students before they begin drafting:

- Drafting is putting your ideas down on paper for your own use. Writers do not need to worry about spelling or exact words. They just need to get their ideas down.
- Write on every other line so that you will have room to make revisions.
- Write on only one side of a page so that when you revise you can see all of your draft at once.
- As you draft, keep in mind your purpose for writing this piece and your intended audience.
- Use your plan and your notes from research to add details.

### Using Word Processors for Drafting

Many students enjoy drafting on the screen of a computer more than drafting on paper. Once they have mastered the keyboard, they may find it easier to think as they write. Their first attempts look less sloppy, and they are often more willing to make changes and experiment as they draft. They will certainly find it neater to use the delete key on the word processor than to correct their mistakes by crossing out. The Basic Computer Skills instruction in the Language Arts Overview of every lesson provides instruction on using the computer.

## Tips

Sometimes the hardest part of drafting is getting the first sentence down on paper. It may help a student even before she or he starts writing to begin a story in the middle or to write the word "Draft" in big letters at the top of the paper.

- If a student feels stuck during drafting, he or she may need to go back and try a different prewriting technique.
- After an initial fifteen or twenty minutes of imposed silence, some students may work better and come up with more ideas if they share as they write.
- You may find that it is difficult to get students to "loosen up" as they draft. Remember, most students have been encouraged to be neat and to erase mistakes when they write. It may help to share some of your own marked-up manuscripts with students.

# Revising

## Purpose

The purpose of revising is to make sure that a piece of writing expresses the writer's ideas clearly and completely. It has been said that there is no good writing, just good rewriting. A major distinction between good writers and poor writers is the amount of time and effort they put into revision. Poor writers look for spelling and grammatical errors if they do read their work.

### Good Student writers

- Evaluate what has been written.
- Read the draft as a reader, not the writer.
- Identify problems with focus, giving enough information, clarity, and order.
- Think of solutions to problems and understand when solutions will and won't work.
- Recognize when and how the text needs to be reorganized.
- Eliminate sentences or paragraphs that don't fit the main idea.
- Identify ideas that need elaboration.
- Do more research if needed to support or add ideas.
- Identify and eliminate unnecessary details.
- Ask for feedback from peer and teacher conferences.
- Take advantage of classroom and outside resources.
- Check the accuracy of facts and details.
- Give credit for any ideas from other people or sources.

## Procedure

Model asking questions like the following when revising various kinds of writing:

- About a narrative:
  - ✓ Does my first sentence get my readers' attention?
  - ✓ Are events in the story told in an order that makes sense?
  - ✓ Have I included dialogue to help move the story along?
  - ✓ Does the story have a clear focus?
- About a description:
  - ✓ Have I used details that appeal to the senses?
- About a comparison/contrast piece:
  - ✓ Have I made a separate paragraph for each subject discussed?
- About an explanation:
  - ✓ Will readers understand what I am saying?
  - ✓ Are the steps of the explanation in a clear order?
  - ✓ Have I made effective use of signal words?
  - ✓ Have I included enough information?
- About fiction:
  - ✓ Have I described my characters and setting?
  - ✓ Does the plot include a problem, build to a climax, and then describe the resolution of the problem?
- About persuasive writing:
  - ✓ Have I made my position clear?
  - ✓ Does my evidence support my position?
  - ✓ Have I used opinions as well as facts, and have I said whose opinions I used?
  - ✓ Have I directed my writing to my audience?

Help students understand the value of asking questions such as the following as they revise:

- About each paragraph:
  - ✓ Does each sentence belong in it?
  - ✓ Does each sentence connect smoothly with the next?
  - ✓ Does each sentence say something about the main idea?
- About each sentence:
  - ✓ Do the sentences read smoothly?
  - ✓ Have I combined sentences that were too short?
  - ✓ Have I broken sentences that were too long into two shorter sentences?
  - ✓ Have I varied the beginnings of the sentences?
- About the words:
  - ✓ Have I changed words that were repeated too often?
  - ✓ Do transition words connect ideas?

## Tips

■ Use the student Writing Folder to review student progress. Check first drafts against revised versions to see how each student is able to apply revision strategies.

■ You may find that some students are reluctant to revise. You might then try the following:

✓ If a student doesn't see anything that needs to be changed or doesn't want to change anything, get him or her to do something to the paper—number the details in a description or the steps in a process, circle exact words, underline the best parts of the paper. Once a paper is marked, the student may not be so reluctant to change it.

✓ One reason many students do not like to revise is that they think they must recopy everything. This is not always necessary. Sometimes writers can cut and paste sections that they want to move. Or they can use carets and deletion marks to show additions and subtractions from a piece.

✓ Give an especially reluctant student a deadline by which she or he must revise a piece or lose the chance to publish it.

✓ Students will hopefully be writing in other classes and on a variety of topics. Revision techniques can be used to improve writing in any curriculum area. Stress to students the importance of focusing on their intended audience as they revise.

# Proofreading

## Purpose

Writing that is free of grammatical, spelling, and technical mistakes is clearer and easier for readers to understand. By proofreading their pieces, students will also notice which errors they make repeatedly and will learn not to make them in the future.

After a piece of writing has been revised for content and style, students must read it carefully line by line to make sure that it contains no errors. This activity, the fourth phase of the writing process, is called proofreading and is a critical step that must occur before a piece of writing can be published. Students can begin proofreading a piece when they feel that it has been sufficiently revised.

### Good Student Writers

■ Edit the work to allow the reader to understand and enjoy the words.

■ Correct most errors in English language conventions.

■ Use resources or seek assistance to address any uncertainties in English language conventions.

## Procedure

### Using What They Have Learned

Students should be expected to proofread at a level appropriate to their grade. Young authors should not be held responsible for skills they have not yet learned. Older students will be able to check for a greater variety of errors than younger students and should be expected to take greater responsibility for their proofreading. For example, students in first grade can be expected to check for and correct omitted capital letters at the beginning of sentences, but they should not necessarily be expected to understand and correct capital letters in proper nouns or in names of organizations. Older students will have mastered many more grammatical, mechanical, usage, and spelling skills and can be expected to perform accordingly. When you spot an error related to a skill beyond a student's level, make clear to the student that you do not expect her or him to be responsible for the mistake, but do explain that the error still needs to be corrected. The following suggestions may be useful as you introduce proofreading to the students and help them develop their proofreading skills.

### Proofreading Checklist

Have students use a proofreading checklist similar to the one shown here to help them remember the steps for effective proofreading.

✓ Read each sentence.

✓ Does each sentence begin with a capital letter and end with correct punctuation?

✓ Do you notice any sentence fragments or run-on sentences?

✓ Are words missing from the sentence?

✓ Is any punctuation or capitalization missing from within the sentence?

✓ Do you notice any incorrect grammar or incorrect word usage in the sentence?

✓ Do you notice any misspelled words?

✓ Are the paragraphs indented?

✓ Can very long paragraphs be broken into two paragraphs?

✓ Can very short paragraphs be combined into one paragraph?

### Tips

■ **Proofreader's Marks** Students should use standard Proofreader's Marks to indicate the changes they wish to make. Explain to students that these marks are a kind of code used to show which alterations to make without a long explanation. Students may also be interested to know that professional writers, editors, and proofreaders use these same marks. You may want to review these marks one by one, illustrating on the board how to use them. For example, they may

insert a word or a phrase by using a caret (^). If students wish to insert more text than will fit above the line, they may write in the margin or attach another sheet of paper. It may be a good idea, when such extensive corrections are made, for students to proofread their final copy carefully to make sure they have included all their alterations.

■ **Sentence lifting** is a very effective method of showing students how to proofread their own work. Because students are working on their own sentences, they will be more inclined to both pay attention to what is going on and better understand the corrections that are made.

✓ Choose several pieces of student writing and look for common errors.

✓ On an overhead transparency, write several sentences. Include at least one sentence that has no errors.

✓ Tell students that you are going to concentrate on one type of error at a time. For example, first you will concentrate on spelling.

✓ Ask students to read the first sentence and point out any words they feel are spelled incorrectly. Do not erase errors. Cross them out and write the correctly spelled word above the crossed out word.

✓ Next move to a different type of error. Ask students to check for capitalization and punctuation.

✓ Continue in this way, correcting errors as you go through the sample sentences.

■ **Using a Word Processor.** If the students are using a word processor to write their pieces, they may wish to run a spell check on their document. Caution them, however, that even the most sophisticated computer cannot catch every spelling error. Misuse of homophones and typographical errors may not be caught by the computer if the misused words appear in the computer's dictionary. For example, if a student types *form* instead of *from*, the computer will not register a mistake because *form* is also a word.

Circulate as students are proofreading on their own or in pairs.

✓ Are students able to check references when they are unsure of a spelling or usage?

✓ Are students criticizing each other's work constructively?

✓ Does a student no longer omit end punctuation because he or she noticed this error repeatedly during proofreading?

✓ Note students who are having difficulty. You may wish to address these difficulties during individual conferences.

**Writing** (continued)

# Publishing

## Purpose

Publishing is the process of bringing private writing to the reading public. The purpose of writing is to communicate. Unless students are writing in a journal, they will want to present their writing to the public. Such sharing helps students to learn about themselves and others, provides an opportunity for them to take pride in their hard work, and thus motivates them to further writing.

Publishing their work helps motivate students to improve such skills as spelling, grammar, and handwriting. Publishing can be as simple as displaying papers on a bulletin board or as elaborate as creating a class newspaper. Publishing will not—indeed should not—always require large blocks of class time. Students will wish to spend more time elaborately presenting their favorite pieces and less time on other works. If students take an inordinate amount of time to publish their work, you may want to coach them on how to speed up the process.

### Good Student Writers

- Present the work in a way that makes it easy to read and understand.
- Consider format, style, illustration, and clarity in the presentation of the work.
- Show pride in the finished work.

## Procedure

### Preparing the Final Copy

When students feel that they have thoroughly proofread their pieces, they should copy the work onto another sheet of paper, using their best handwriting, or type the work on a computer or typewriter. They should then check this copy against the proofread copy to make sure that they made all the changes correctly and did not introduce any new errors. You may need to proofread and correct students' papers one final time before publishing to make sure that they have caught all errors.

### Publishing Choices

In publishing, students need to decide

✓ how to prepare the piece for publication.
✓ what form the published work should take.
✓ whether to illustrate their writing with photographs, drawings, or charts with captions, as necessary.
✓ where to place any art they are using.

### Publishing Checklist

The following checklist will help students when they are publishing their work. (Not every question applies to every form of publishing.)

✓ Have I revised my work to make it better?
✓ Have I proofread it carefully?
✓ Have I decided upon my illustrations?
✓ Have I recopied my piece carefully and illustrated it?
✓ Have I numbered the pages?
✓ Have I made a cover that tells the title and my name?

## Tips

- Read through the piece, and tell the student if any corrections still need to be made. Also make some suggestions about the best way to publish a piece if a student has trouble coming up with an idea.
- Make suggestions and give criticism as needed, but remember that students must retain ownership of their publishing. Leave final decisions about form and design of their work up to individual students.
- Remind students to think about their intended audience when they are deciding on the form for their published piece. Will the form they have selected present their ideas effectively to the people they want to reach?

# Writing Seminar

## Purpose

The purpose of Writing Seminar (Levels 1–6) is for students to discuss their work in progress and to share ideas for improving it.

Writing Seminar is one of the activities in which students may choose to participate during Workshop. Students will meet in small groups to read and discuss one another's writing. One student reads a piece in progress. Other students comment on the writing and ask questions about the ideas behind the writing. The student whose work is being critiqued writes down the comments made by his or her classmates and decides how to use these comments to make the writing better.

## Procedure

To begin the seminar, have one student writer read his or her revised draft as other students listen carefully. When the student has finished, invite other students to retell the story in their own words. If they have trouble retelling the story, the writer knows that he or she must make some ideas clearer.

Then have listeners who wish to comment raise their hands. The writer calls on each in turn. The listeners ask questions or make comments about the writing, telling, for example, what they like about it or what they might change to make it better. After several comments have been made, the writer notes any information that she or he might use. Another student then reads his or her piece.

## Guidelines for Peer Conferencing

In an early session, work with students to establish guidelines for peer conferencing. You might suggest rules such as the following:

✓ Listen quietly while someone else is speaking.
✓ Think carefully before you comment on another person's work.
✓ Make your comments specific.
✓ Comment on something that you like about the piece before you comment on something that needs to be improved.
✓ Discuss your work quietly so as not to disturb the rest of the class.

## Modeling Seminar Behavior

You may need to model meaningful comments and questions. For example:

✓ What was your favorite part?
✓ I like the part where (or when)
✓ I like the way you describe
✓ What happened after . . . ?
✓ I'd like to know more about
✓ Why did _____ happen?
✓ What do you think is the most important part?

## Teacher Conferencing

During Writing Seminar, you will want to schedule individual conferences with students to help them evaluate their writing so that they can recognize problems and find ways to solve them. Teacher conferences are useful during all phases of the writing process, but they are crucial during the revising phase. Conferences give you an opportunity to observe students as they evaluate their writing, solve problems, make decisions about their work, and take responsibility for the development and completion of their work. The basic procedure for conferences is:

- Have the student read his or her work aloud.
- Review any feedback the student has received so far.
- Identify positive elements of the work.
- Use one or more of these strategies to help the student improve his or her work.

✓ Have students explain how they got their ideas.

✓ Have students think aloud about how they will address the feedback they have received.

✓ Ask students to help you understand any confusion you may have about their writing.

✓ Have the student add, delete, or rearrange something in the work and ask how it affects the whole piece.

✓ Think aloud while you do a part of what the student was asked to do. Ask the student to compare what you did to what he or she did.

✓ Have the student prescribe as if to a younger student how to revise the work.

- Ask two or three questions to guide students through revising (see below).
- Conclude by having the student state a plan for continuing work on the piece.

## Writing Conference Questions

### Ideas
- Who is your audience?
- What is your purpose for writing?
- How does the reader know the purpose?
- Is there enough information about the topic?
- Do you like one part of your work more than the rest? Why?
- Is your main idea clear?
- Is there a better way to express this idea?
- Is this a good topic sentence?
- Is your introduction engaging?
- Are any important details left out?
- Are any not-so-important details left in?
- Do you use specific details and examples?
- Are your ideas accurate and, if necessary, supported by research?
- Does your conclusion sum up or restate your purpose for writing?
- What might be another way to end the work?

### Organization
- Is the writing organized in a way that makes the most sense based on the main idea?
- Is the structure clear for the reader? Is there a clear beginning, middle, and end?
- Are there smooth transitions from one part to the next?
- Are supporting details ordered in the most logical way?
- Can you combine any smaller paragraphs or separate larger ones?

### Voice
- Do you sound confident and knowledgeable?
- Does the voice you use reflect the purpose of your writing? Does your writing sound funny or serious when you want it to be?
- Is your voice appropriate for your audience?
- Do you sound interested in the subject?
- Have you confidently stated your opinion? Have you used the pronoun "I" if appropriate?
- Does your writing sound like you?
- Is your voice too formal or informal?
- Will this writing get a strong response from the reader?
- Does your writing make the reader care about your topic?

### Word Choice
- Do you use the same word/phrase repeatedly?
- Could you say the same thing with different words?

- Have you defined words your audience may not understand?
- Have you used precise words to describe or explain?
- Is there a better word to express this idea?
- Have you used your own words when summarizing information from another text?
- Do you use time and order words such as *first, next, then,* and *last* to help the reader understand when events take place?

### Sentence Fluency
- Are your sentences clear and to the point?
- Have you used different kinds and lengths of sentences to effectively present your ideas?
- Could any of your sentences be combined?
- Is there a rhythm to your sentences?
- Does each sentence introduce a new idea or a new piece of information?
- Do some sentences repeat what has already been stated? If so, cut or change them.
- Have you used transition words such as *in contrast, however,* and *on the other hand* to move smoothly from one subject to the other?
- Have you used transitional phrases, such as *according to, in addition to,* or *at the same time* to link sentences?
- Have you used conjunctions such as *and, but,* and *or* to combine short, choppy sentences?

## Tips
- Completed pieces as well as works in progress can be shared during Writing Seminar.
- Concentrate on one phase of the writing process at a time.
- Remember to keep conferences brief and to the point. If you are calling the conference, prepare your comments in advance. Be sure that you confer regularly with every student if only to check that each one is continuing to write, revise, and publish.
- During teacher conferences, you might use the following responses to student writing.
  - ✓ To open communication with the writer:
    - How is the writing going?
    - Tell me about your piece.
    - How did you get your ideas?
  - ✓ To give encouragement:
    - I like the part where . . . .
    - I like the way you open your piece by . . . .
    - I like your description of . . . .
  - ✓ To get the writer to clarify meaning:
    - I wonder about . . . .
    - What happened after . . . .
    - Why did . . . ?
  - ✓ To get the writer to think about direction and about writing strategies:

- What do you plan to do with your piece?
- How will you go about doing that?
- What could I do to help you?

- As you confer with students, also recognize growth—evidence in the text that a student has applied what he or she learned in earlier conferences to another piece of writing.
- Some cues to look for when evaluating a student's growth as a writer include:
  - ✓ The writer identifies problems.
  - ✓ The writer thinks of solutions to a problem.
  - ✓ The writer recognizes when and how the text needs to be reorganized.
  - ✓ The writer identifies ideas in the text that need elaboration.
  - ✓ The writer makes thoughtful changes and pays attention to detail.
  - ✓ The writer takes advantage of peer and teacher conferences, books, and other resources to improve his or her writing.

### Teaching Strategies for Writing

The teacher's role in writing instruction is critical. Certain strategies have been shown to be particularly effective in teaching writing.

**Teacher Modeling** Students learn best when they have good models. Models for the forms of writing appear in the literature selections, *Language Arts Transparencies,* and *Language Arts Handbook.* The Writing Process Strategies include instruction and models for all phases of the writing process. Teachers can also model the writing process for students every time they write.

**Feedback.** The most effective writing instruction is the feedback good teachers give to individual student work. Unfortunately many teachers simply mark errors in spelling, grammar, usage, and mechanics. The *Routine Card* and the *Writer's Workbook* provide questions that teachers can consider to offer constructive and meaningful feedback to students.

**Clear Assignments.** A well-written assignment makes clear to students what they are supposed to do, how they are supposed to do it, who the students are writing for, and what constitutes a successful response. When students have this information, they can plan, organize, and produce more effective work.

**Instruction.** Having students write a lot does not make them good writers. Few people become good writers, no matter how much they write. For many, the effect of years of practice is simply to produce increasingly fluent bad writing. Students need specific instruction and practice on different forms of writing and on different phases of the writing process, which they receive with instruction, modeling, practice, and feedback.

# Classroom Discussion

The more students are able to discuss what they are learning, voice their confusions, and compare perceptions of what they are learning, the deeper and more meaningful their learning becomes.

## Purpose

It is in discussions that students are exposed to points of view different from their own, and it is through discussion that they learn how to express their thoughts and opinions coherently. Through discussion, students add to their own knowledge that of their classmates and learn to explain themselves coherently. They also begin to ask insightful questions that help them better understand what they have read and all that they are learning through their inquiry/research and explorations. The purpose of classroom discussion is to provide a sequence through which discussion can proceed.

## Procedure

### Reflecting on the Selection

After students have finished reading a selection, provide an opportunity for them to engage in **whole-group** discussion about the selection. Students should:

- Check to see whether the questions they asked before reading have been answered. Encourage them to discuss whether any unanswered questions should still be answered and if so have them add those questions to the Concept/Question Board.

- Discuss any new questions that have arisen because of the reading. Encourage students to decide which of these questions should go on the Concept/Question Board.

- Share what they expected to learn from reading the selection and tell whether expectations were met.

- Talk about whatever has come to mind while reading the selection. This discussion should be an informal sharing of impressions of, or opinions about, the selection; it should never take on the aspects of a question-and-answer session about the selection.

- Give students ample opportunity to ask questions and share their thoughts about the selection. Participate as an active member of the group, making your own observations about information in a selection or modeling your own appreciation of a story. Be especially aware of unusual and interesting insights suggested by students so that these insights can be recognized and discussed. To help students learn to keep the discussion student-centered, have each student choose the next speaker instead of handing the discussion back to you.

### Recording Ideas

As students finish discussions about their reactions to a selection, they should be encouraged to record their thoughts, feelings, reactions, and ideas about the selection or the subject of the selection in their Writer's Notebooks. This will not only help keep the selections fresh in students' minds; it will strengthen their writing abilities and help them learn how to write about their thoughts and feelings.

Students may find that the selection gave them ideas for their own writing, or it could have reminded them of some person or incident in their own lives. Perhaps the selection answered a question that has been on their minds or raised a question they had never thought before. Good, mature writers—especially professional writers—learn the value of recording such thoughts and impressions quickly before they fade. Students should be encouraged to do this also.

### Handing Off

Handing off (Levels 1–6) is a method of turning over to students the primary responsibility for controlling discussion. Often, students who are taking responsibility for controlling a discussion tend to have all "turns" go through the teacher. The teacher is the one to whom attention is transferred when a speaker finishes, and the teacher is the one who is expected to call on the next speaker—the result being that the teacher remains the pivotal figure in the discussion.

Having the students "hand off" the discussion to other students instead of the teacher encourages them to retain complete control of the discussion and to become more actively involved in the learning process. When a student finishes his or her comments, that student should choose (hand the discussion off to) the next speaker. In this way, students maintain a discussion without relying on the teacher to decide who speaks.

When handing off is in place, the teacher's main roles are to occasionally remind students to hand off and to monitor the discussion to ensure that everyone gets a chance to contribute. The teacher may say, for example, "Remember, not just boys (or girls)," or "Try to choose someone who has not had a chance to talk yet."

In order for handing off to work effectively, a seating arrangement that allows students to see one another is essential. A circle or a semicircle is effective. In addition, all of the students need to have copies of the materials being discussed.

Actively encourage this handing-off process by letting students know that they, not you, are in control of the discussion.

If students want to remember thoughts about, or reactions to, a selection, suggest that they record these in the Writing Journal section of the Writer's Notebook. Encourage students to record the thoughts, feelings, or reactions that are elicited by any reading they do.

### Exploring Concepts Within the Selection

To provide an opportunity for collaborative learning and to focus on the concepts, have students form small groups and spend time discussing what they have learned about the concepts from this selection. Topics may include new information that they have acquired or new ideas that they have had.

Students should always base their discussions on postings from the Concept/Question Board as well as on previous discussions of the concept. The small-group discussions should be ongoing throughout the unit; during this time students should continue to compare and contrast any new information with their previous ideas, opinions, and impressions about the concepts. Does this selection help confirm their ideas? Does it contradict their thinking? Has it changed their outlook?

As students discuss the concepts in small groups, circulate around the room to make sure that each group stays focused upon the selection and the concepts. After students have had some time to discuss the information and the ideas in the selection, encourage each group to formulate some statements about the concept that apply to the selection.

### Sharing Ideas about Concepts

Have a representative from each group report and explain the group's ideas to the rest of the class. Then have the class formulate one or more general statements related to the unit concepts and write these statements on the Concept/Question Board. As students progress through the unit, they will gain more and more confidence in suggesting additions to the Concept/Question Board.

**Visual Aids** During this part of the discussion, you may find it helpful to use visual aids to help students as they build the connections to the unit concepts. Not all units or concepts will lend themselves to this type of treatment; however, aids such as time lines, charts, graphs, or pictographs may help students see how each new selection adds to their growing knowledge of the concepts.

Encourage students to ask questions about the concepts that the selection may have raised. Have students list on the Concept/Question Board those questions that cannot be answered immediately and that they want to explore further.

## Exploring Concepts Across Selections

As each new selection is read, encourage students to discuss its connection with the other selections and with the unit concepts. Also encourage students to think about selections that they have read from other units and how they relate to the concepts for this unit.

Ultimately, it is this ability to make connections between past knowledge and new knowledge that allows any learner to gain insights into what is being studied. The goal of the work with concepts and the discussions is to help students to start thinking in terms of connections—how is this like what I have learned before? Does this information confirm, contradict, or add a completely different layer to that which I already know about this concept? How can the others in the class have such different ideas than I do when we just read the same selection? Why is so much written about this subject?

Learning to make connections and to delve deeper through self-generated questions gives students the tools they need to become effective, efficient, lifelong learners.

## Tips

- Discussions offer a prime opportunity for you to introduce, or seed, new ideas about the concepts. New ideas can come from a variety of sources: students may draw on their own experiences or on the books or videos they are studying; you may introduce new ideas into the discussion; or you may, at times, invite experts to speak to the class.

- If students do not mention an important idea that is necessary to the understanding of some larger issue, you may "drop" that idea into the conversation and, indeed, repeat it several times to make sure that it does get picked up. This seeding may be subtle ("I think that might be important here.") or quite direct ("This is a big idea, one that we will definitely need to understand and one that we will return to regularly.").

> *Discussion is an integral part of learning.*

- In order to facilitate this process for each unit, you must be aware of the unit concepts and be able to recognize and reinforce them when they arise spontaneously in discussions. If central unit concepts do not arise naturally, then, and only then, will you seed these ideas by direct modeling. The more you turn

discussions over to students, the more involved they will become, and the more responsibility they will take for their own learning. Make it your goal to become a participant in, rather than the leader of, class discussions.

- Help students to see that they are responsible for carrying on the discussion. After a question is asked, always wait instead of jumping in with a comment or an explanation. Although this wait time may be uncomfortable at first, students will come to understand that the discussion is their responsibility and that you will not jump in every time there is a hesitation.

- As the year progresses, students will become more and more adept at conducting and participating in meaningful discussions about what they have read. These discussions will greatly enhance students' understanding of the concepts that they are exploring.

## Discussion Starters

- I didn't know that . . . .
- Does anyone know . . . .
- I figured out that . . . .
- I liked the part where . . . .
- I'm still confused about . . . .
- This made me think . . . .
- I agree with _____ because . . . .
- I disagree with _____ because . . . .
- The reason I think . . . .

# Inquiry and Investigation

Research and Investigation form the heart of the *SRA/Open Court Reading* program. In order to encourage students to understand how reading can enhance their lives and help them to become mature, educated adults, they are asked in each unit to use what they are learning in the unit as the basis for further exploration and research. The unit information is simply the base for their investigations.

There are two types of units in the *SRA/Open Court Reading* program—units based on universal topics of interest such as Friendship, Perseverance, and Courage and research units that provide students a very solid base of information upon which they can begin their own inquiry and research. Units delving into such areas as fossils, astronomy, and medicine invite students to become true researchers by choosing definite areas of interest—problems or questions to research in small cooperative groups and then to present to their classmates. In this way, students gain much more knowledge of the subject than they would have simply by reading the selections in the unit.

The selections in the units are organized so that each selection will add more information or a different perspective to students' growing bodies of knowledge.

## Investigating through Reflective Activities

### Purpose

The units in *SRA/Open Court Reading* that deal with universal topics will be explored through reflective activities. These units—such as Courage, Friendship, and Risks and Consequences—are organized to help students expand their perspectives in familiar areas. As they explore and discuss the unit concepts related to each topic, students are involved in activities that extend their experiences and offer opportunities for reflection. Such activities include writing, drama, art, interviews, debates, and panel discussions. Throughout each unit, students may be involved in a single ongoing investigative activity, or they may participate in a number of different activities. They may choose to produce a final written project or a visual aid. They will share with the rest of the class the new knowledge that they have gained from their reflective activities. During **Workshop** students will work individually or in collaborative groups on their investigation and/or projects.

The reflective activities will be activities of students' own choosing that allow them to explore the unit concepts more fully. They are free, of course, to make other choices or to devise activities of their own.

## Procedure

### Choosing an Area to Investigate

Students may work on activities alone, in pairs, or in small groups. They have the option of writing about or presenting their findings to the whole group upon completion. Before choosing a reflective activity, students should decide what concept-related question or problem they wish to explore. Generally, it is better for students to generate questions or problems after they have engaged in some discussion but before they have had a chance to consult source materials. This approach is more likely to bring forth ideas that students actually wonder about or wish to understand. Students may also look at the questions posted on the Concept/Question Board or introduce fresh ideas inspired by material they have just finished reading. Students who are working in pairs or in small groups should confer with one another before making a decision about what to explore. Some of the students may need your assistance in deciding upon, or narrowing down, a question or a problem so that it can be explored more easily. A good way to model this process for students is to make webs for a few of your own ideas on the board and to narrow these ideas down to a workable question or problem.

## Organizing the Group

After a question or a problem has been chosen, the students may choose an activity that will help them to investigate that problem or question. The students' next responsibility is to decide who is going to investigate which facet of the question or the problem (when they are conducting a literature search, for example) or who is going to perform which task related to the particular reflective activity (when they are writing and performing an original playlet or puppet show, for example). Lastly, students need to decide how, or if, they want to present their findings. For instance, after conducting a literature search, some students may want to read and discuss passages from a book with a plot or theme that relates to a unit concept. Other students may prefer acting out and discussing scenes from the book.

### Deciding How to Investigate

The following suggestions may help you and your students choose ways in which to pursue their investigations. You may want to post this list in the classroom so that groups have access to it as they decide what they want to investigate and how they want to proceed.

## Investigation Activities

- Conduct a literature search to pursue a question or a problem. Discussion or writing may follow.
- Write and produce an original playlet or puppet show based on situations related to the concepts.
- Play a role-playing game to work out a problem related to the concepts.
- Stage a panel discussion with audience participation on a question or problem.
- Hold a debate on an issue related to the concept.
- Write an advice column dealing with problems related to the concepts.
- Write a personal-experience story related to the concepts.
- Invite experts to class. Formulate questions to ask.
- Conduct an interview with someone on a subject related to the concepts.
- Produce and carry out a survey on an issue or question related to the concept.
- Produce a picture or photo essay about the concept.

**EXAMPLE:** In the Heritage unit in grade 5 of **SRA/Open Court Reading,** students read "In Two Worlds: A Yup'ik Eskimo Family." This selection is about how three generations of Eskimos living in Alaska near the Arctic strive to adopt the best of modern ways without abandoning their traditional values. During the class discussion, some students may note that Alice and Billy Rivers want their students to learn both the new and the old ways of living. As the discussion continues, many students may conclude from the story that the older generations hope that future generations will continue to value their roots and their cultural traditions. Students then relate this story to their own heritage. Some students may share information about their customs or traditions.

Students choose some reflective activities that will help them learn more about family heritage and that will answer some of their questions about the unit concepts. Some students may be interested in interviewing family members or close family friends about their cultural traditions and heritages. These students review what they know about interviewing. They proceed by:

- Contacting in advance the person(s) they want to interview.
- Preparing a list of questions to ask.
- Preparing a list of subjects to discuss, deciding how to record the interview (by audiotape, videotape, or taking notes).
- Deciding whether to photograph the person and, if so, getting permission to do so in advance—collecting the equipment necessary for conducting the interview.

After they conduct the interviews, students decide how they wish to present the information that they have collected.

> *Investigating through reflective activities allows students to gain a wider perspective on a concept by relating it to their own experiences. Students quickly become aware that it is their responsibility to learn and to help their peers learn more about the unit concepts.*

**EXAMPLE:** Another group of students in the same fifth-grade class may be more interested in planning a photo essay about one family or about a neighborhood with many families belonging to a particular culture. These students may decide to re-examine "In Two Worlds" to notice how the text and the photographs complement each other and what information is conveyed in each photograph. They may also decide to examine some photo essays listed in the unit bibliography. These students will need to make some advance preparations as well. They proceed by:

- Determining which neighborhood and which family or families to photograph.
- Contacting in advance the persons to be interviewed and photographed.
- Touring the neighborhood in advance of the photo shoot.
- Making a list of questions to ask the family or families about their heritage or about their neighborhood.

- Thinking about what information to include in their essay so that they can determine what photographs to take.
- Collecting the equipment necessary for conducting interviews and photographing subjects.

After students collect the information and take photographs, they may write and organize the photo essay and present it to the class. The teacher should remind students of the phases of the writing process, and encourage them to revise and proofread their work until they are completely pleased with it. Students can continue discussing family heritage and raising any new questions that they wish to investigate. The teacher should remind them that as they read further, they may think of a variety of ways to explore the unit concepts. The teacher should then ask students to post on the Concept/Question Board any new questions they have about family heritage. Students should sign or initial their questions so that they can identify classmates with similar interests and exchange ideas with them. The teacher should encourage students to feel free to write an answer or a note on someone else's question or to consult the board for ideas for their own explorations. From time to time, the teacher should post his or her own questions on the Concept/Question Board.

## Tips

- The *Leveled Classroom Library* contains books related to the unit concepts. Remind students that these are good sources of information and that they should consult them regularly— especially when they are investigating concept-related ideas and questions.
- Some students work better within a specified time frame. Whenever they are beginning a new activity, discuss with the students a reasonable period of time within which they will be expected to complete their investigations. Post the completion date somewhere in the classroom so that students can refer to it and pace themselves accordingly. At first, you may have to help them determine a suitable deadline, but eventually they should be able to make this judgment on their own.

# Investigating through Research

## Purpose

Students come to school with a wealth of fascinating questions. Educators need to capitalize on this excitement for learning and natural curiosity. A classroom in which only correct answers are accepted and students are not allowed to make errors and consider alternative possibilities to questions can quickly deaden this natural curiosity and enthusiasm. The purpose of the research aspect of this program is to capitalize on students' questions and natural curiosity by using a proven structure. This structure helps students to not get lost or bogged down but at the same time to preserve the open-ended character of real research, which can lead to unexpected findings and to questions that were not originally considered.

There is a conventional approach to school research papers that can be found, with minor variations, in countless textbooks. It consists of a series of steps such as the following: select a topic, narrow the topic, collect materials, take notes, outline, and write. By following these steps, a student may produce a presentable paper, but the procedure does not constitute research in a meaningful sense and indeed gives students a distorted notion of what research is about. We see students in universities and even in graduate schools still following this procedure when they do library research papers or literature reviews; we see their dismay when their professors regard such work as mere cutting and pasting and ask them where their original contribution is.

Even elementary school students can produce works of genuine research—research that seeks answers to real questions or solutions to real problems. This skill in collecting and analyzing information is a valuable tool in the adult world in which adults, as consumers, are constantly analyzing new information and making informed decisions on the basis of this information. Preparing students for the analytic demands of adult life and teaching them how to find answers to their questions are goals of education.

## Procedure

In order to make the research productive, the following important principles are embodied in this approach:

1. Research is focused on problems, not topics.
2. Conjectures—opinions based on less than complete evidence or proof—guide the research; the research does not simply produce conjectures.

3. New information is gathered to test and revise conjectures.
4. Discussion, ongoing feedback, and constructive criticism are important in all phases of the research but especially in the revising of problems and conjectures.
5. The cycle of true research is essentially endless, although presentations of findings are made from time to time; new findings give rise to new problems and conjectures and thus to new cycles of research.

## Following a Process

While working with the research units, students are encouraged to follow a set pattern or cycle in order to keep their research activities focused and on track. Students may go through these steps many times before they come to the end of their research. Certainly for adult researchers, this cycle of question, conjecture, research, and reevaluation can go on for years and in some cases lifetimes.

This cycle uses the following process:

1. **Decide on a problem or question to research.** Students should identify a question or problem that they truly wonder about or wish to understand and then form research groups with other students who have the same interests.
   - My problem or question is _____

2. **Formulate an idea or conjecture about the research problem.** Students should think about and discuss with classmates possible answers to their research problems or questions and meet with their research groups to discuss and record their ideas or conjectures.
   - My idea/conjecture/theory about this question or problem is _____

3. **Identify needs and make plans.** Students should identify knowledge needs related to their conjectures and meet with their research groups to determine which resources to consult and to make individual job assignments. Students should also meet periodically with the teacher, other classmates, and research groups to present preliminary findings and make revisions to their problems and conjectures on the basis of these findings.
   - I need to find out _____
   - To do this, I will need these resources _____
   - My role in the group is _____
   - This is what I have learned so far _____
   - This is what happened when we presented our findings _____

4. **Reevaluate the problem or question based on what we have learned so far and the feedback we have received.**
   - My revised problem or question is _____

5. **Revise the idea or conjecture.**
   - My new conjecture about this problem is _____

6. **Identify new needs and make new plans.**
   - Based on what I found out, I still need to know _____
   - To do this, I will need these resources _____
   - This is what I have learned _____
   - This is what happened when we presented our new findings _____

## Procedure for Choosing a Problem to Research

1. Discuss with students the nature of the unit. Explain to students that the unit they are reading is a research unit and that they will produce and publish in some way the results of their explorations. They are free to decide what problems or questions they wish to explore, with whom they want to work, and how they want to present their finished products. They may publish a piece of writing, produce a poster, write and perform a play, or use any other means to present the results of their investigations and research. They may work with partners or in small groups.

2. Discuss with students the schedule you have planned for their investigations: how long the project is expected to take, how much time will be available for research, when the first presentation will be due. This schedule will partly determine the nature of the problems that students should be encouraged to work on and the depth of the inquiry students will be encouraged to pursue.

3. Have students talk about things they wonder about that are related to the unit subject. For example, in the grade 3 unit, Money, students might wonder where money in the money machine comes from or how prices are determined. Conduct a free-floating discussion of questions about the unit subject.

4. Brainstorm possible questions for students to think about. It is essential that the students' own ideas and questions be the starting point of all inquiry. *Helpful hint:* For the first research unit, you might wish to generate a list of your own ideas, having students add to this list and having them choose from it.

5. Using their wonderings, model for students the difference between a research topic and a research problem or question by providing several examples. For example, have them consider the difference between the topic California and the problem, *Why do so many people move to California?* Explain to them that if they choose to research the topic California, everything they look up under the subject heading or index entry *California* will be related in some way to their topic. Therefore, it will be quite difficult to choose which information to record. This excess of information also creates problems in organizing their research. Clearly, then, this topic is too broad and general. Choosing a specific question or problem, one that particularly interests them, helps them narrow their exploration and advance their understanding. Some possible ideas for questions can be found in the unit introduction. Ideas can also be generated as you and your students create a web of their questions or problems related to the unit concept. For example, questions related to the subject California might include the following:

 ■ Why do so many people move to California?

 ■ How have the different groups of people living in California affected the state?

6. A good research problem or question not only requires students to consult a variety of sources but is engaging and adds to the groups' knowledge of the concepts. Furthermore, good problems generate more questions. Help students understand that the question, *Why do so many people move to California?* is an easy one to research. Many sources will contribute to an answer to the question, and all information located can be easily evaluated in terms of usefulness in answering the question. *Helpful hint:* Students' initial responses may indeed be topics instead of problems or questions. If so, the following questions might be helpful:

 ■ What aspect of the topic really interests you?

 ■ Can you turn that idea into a question?

7. Remember that this initial problem or question serves only as a guide for research. As students begin collecting information and collaborating with classmates, their ideas will change, and they can revise their research problem or question. Frequently, students do not sufficiently revise their problems until after they have had time to consider their conjectures and collect information.

8. As students begin formulating their research problems, have them elaborate on their reasons for wanting to research their stated problems. They should go beyond simple expressions of interest or liking and indicate what is puzzling, important, or potentially informative, and so forth, about the problems they have chosen.

9. At this stage, students' ideas will be of a very vague and limited sort. The important thing is to start them thinking about what really interests them and what value it has to them and the class.

10. Have students present their proposed problems or questions, along with reasons for their choices, and have an open discussion of how promising proposed problems are. As students present their proposed problems, ask them what new things they think they will be learning from their investigations and how that will add to the group's growing knowledge of the concepts. This constant emphasis on group knowledge building will help set a clear purpose for students' research.

> *Even elementary school students can produce works of genuine research— research that seeks answers to real questions or solutions to real problems.*

11. Form research groups. To make it easier for students to form groups, they may record their problems on the board or on self-sticking notes. Final groups should be constituted in the way you find best for your class—by self-selection, by assignment on the basis of common interests, or by some combination of methods. Students can then meet during **Workshop** to agree on a precise statement of their research problem, the nature of their expected research contributions, and lists of related questions that may help later in assigning individual roles. They should also record any scheduling information that can be added to the planning calendar.

### Using Technology

The **Research Assistant CD-ROM** (Levels 2–6), an interactive software program, supports student research by helping them plan, organize, present, and assess their research.

Students and teachers can access the Web site **www.sra4kids.com** to find information about the themes in their grade level.

### Tips

 ■ If students are careful about the problems or questions they choose to research, they should have few problems in following through with the research. If the problem is too broad or too narrow, they will have problems.

 ■ Have students take sufficient time in assessing their needs—both knowledge needs and physical needs in relation to their research. Careful preplanning can help the research progress smoothly with great results.

 ■ Encourage students to reevaluate their needs often so they are not wasting time finding things they already have or ignoring needs that they haven't noticed.

 ■ Interim presentations of material are every bit as important, if not more so, than final presentations. It is during interim presentations that students have the opportunity to rethink and reevaluate their work and change direction or decide to carry on with their planned research.

# Workshop

Every teacher and every student needs time during the day to organize, take stock of work that is done, make plans for work that needs doing, and finish up incomplete projects. In addition, time is needed for differentiating instruction and for peer conferencing.

## Purpose

**Workshop** is the period of time each day in which students work independently or collaboratively to practice and review material taught in the lessons.

A variety of activities may occur during this time. Students may work on a specific daily assignment, complete an ongoing project, work on unit exploration activities, focus on writing, or choose from among a wide range of possibilities. With lots of guidance and encouragement, students gradually learn to make decisions about their use of time and materials and to collaborate with their peers.

A goal of **Workshop** is to get students to work independently. This is essential since **Workshop** is also the time during which the teacher can work with individuals or groups of students to reinforce learning, to provide extra help for those having difficulties, to extend learning, or to assess the progress of the class or of individuals.

## Procedure

Initially, for many students, you will need to structure **Workshop** carefully. Eventually, students will automatically go to the appropriate areas, take up ongoing projects, and get the materials they will need. **Workshop** will evolve slowly from a very structured period to a time when students make choices and move freely from one activity to the next.

Adhere firmly to **Workshop** guidelines. By the time the students have completed the first few weeks of school, they should feel confident during **Workshop**. If not, continue to structure the time and limit options. For young students, early periods of **Workshop** may run no more than five to eight minutes. The time can gradually increase to fifteen minutes or longer as the students gain independence. Older students may be able to work longer and independently from the very beginning of the school year.

### Introducing Workshop

Introduce **Workshop** to students by telling them that every day there will be a time when they are expected to work on activities on their own or in small groups. For young students in the beginning, you will assign the **Workshop** activities to help them learn to work on their own. Point out the shelf or area of the classroom where **Workshop** materials are stored. Tell students that when they finish working with the materials for one activity, they will choose something else from the **Workshop** shelf. New activity materials will be added to the shelf from time to time. Make sure that the students know that they may always look at books during **Workshop**.

Tell older students that they will have an opportunity each day to work on their unit explorations, their writing, and other projects. Students will be working independently and collaboratively during this time.

### Guidelines

- Make sure each student knows what he or she needs to do during **Workshop**.
- Demonstrate for the whole group any activity assigned for **Workshop**; for example, teaching the students a new game, introducing new materials or projects, or explaining different areas.
- For young students, it is essential to introduce and demonstrate different activities and games before the students do them on their own. With games, you may want to have several students play while the others watch. Make sure that all the students know exactly what is expected of them.
- In the beginning, plan to circulate among the students providing encouragement and help as necessary.
- Once students are engaged in appropriate activities and can work independently, meet with those students who need your particular attention. This may include individual students or small groups.
- Let the students know that they need to ask questions and clarify assignments during **Workshop** introduction, so that you are free to work with small groups.
- Be sure that students know what they are to do when they have finished an activity and where to put their finished work.

Establish and discuss rules for **Workshop** with the students. Keep them simple and straightforward. You may want to write the finalized rules on the board or on a poster. You may want to review these rules each day at the beginning of **Workshop** for the first few lessons or so. You may also wish to revisit and revise the rules from time to time. Suggested rules include:

✓ Be polite.
✓ Share.
✓ Whisper.
✓ Take only the materials you need.
✓ Return materials.

### Setting Up Your Classroom for Workshop

Carefully setting up your classroom to accommodate different **Workshop** activities will help assure that the **Workshop** period progresses smoothly and effectively. While setting up your classroom, keep the primary **Workshop** activities in mind. During **Workshop** the students will be doing independent and collaborative activities. In kindergarten and first grade, these activities may include letter recognition and phonemic awareness activities and writing or illustrating stories or projects. In addition, they will be working on individual or small group projects.

Many classrooms have centers that the students visit on a regular or rotating basis. Center time can be easily and efficiently incorporated into the **Workshop** concept. For example, the activities suggested during **Workshop** can be incorporated into reading and writing areas. Other typical classroom areas include an art center, math center, science table, play area, etc.

The following are suggestions for space and materials for use during **Workshop**:

1. **Reading Area** supplied with books and magazines. The materials in the Reading Area should be dynamic—changing with students' abilities and reflecting unit themes they are reading. You may wish to add books suggested in the *Leveled Classroom Libraries* and unit bibliographies available with each unit.

2. **Writing Area** stocked with various types and sizes of lined and unlined paper, pencils, erasers, markers, crayons, small slates, and chalk. The area should also have various **Letter Cards**, other handwriting models, and worksheets for those students who want to practice letter formation or handwriting. Students should know that this is where they come for writing supplies. In addition to the supplies described above, the Writing Area can also have supplies to encourage the students to create and write on their own:

✓ magazines and catalogs to cut up for pictures; stickers, paint, glue, glitter, etc. to decorate books and book covers; precut and stapled blank books for the students to write in. (Some can be plain and some cut in special shapes.)

✓ cardboard, tag board, construction paper, etc., for making book covers. (Provide some samples.)

✓ tape, scissors, yarn, hole punches for binding books.

✓ picture dictionaries, dictionaries, thesaurus, word lists, and other materials that may encourage independence.

3. **Listening Area** supplied with tape recorder, CD player, optional headphones, and tapes of stories, poems, and songs for the students to listen to and react to. You might also want to provide blank tapes and encourage the students to retell and record their favorite stories or make up and tell stories for their classmates to listen to on tape. You may also want to make available the ***Listening Library Audiocassettes/CDs*** that are available with the program.

4. **Workshop Activity Center** supplied with **Alphabet Flash Cards,** individual **Alphabet Sound Card** sets (Kindergarten), **Individual Sound/Spelling Cards** and **High-Frequency Word Flash Cards** (Grades 1-3), and other materials that enhance what the students are learning. Other commonly used classroom materials that enhance reading can be included (for example, plastic letters, puzzles, workbooks).

Since students will be working on their inquiry/investigations during **Workshop**, make sure there are adequate supplies to help them with their research. These might include dictionaries, encyclopedias, magazines, newspapers, and computers—preferably with Internet capability.

> *Workshop is the period of time each day in which students work independently or collaboratively to practice and review material taught in the lessons.*

Students thrive in an environment that provides structure, repetition, and routine. Within a sound structure, the students will gain confidence and independence. This setting allows you to differentiate instruction in order to provide opportunities for flexibility and individual choice. This will allow students to develop their strengths, abilities, and talents to the fullest.

## Suggestions for English Language Learners

**Workshop** affords students who are English Language Learners a wealth of opportunities for gaining proficiency in English. It also encourages them to share their backgrounds with peers. Since you will be working with all students individually and in small groups regardless of their reading ability, students who need special help with language will not feel self-conscious about working with you. In addition, working in small groups made up of students with the same interests rather than the same abilities will provide them with the opportunity to learn about language from their peers during the regular course of **Workshop** activities.

Some suggestions for meeting the special needs of students with diverse backgrounds follow:

■ Preread a selection with English Language Learners to help them identify words and ideas they wish to talk about. This will prepare them for discussions with the whole group.

■ Preteach vocabulary and develop selection concepts that may be a challenge for students.

■ Negotiate the meaning of selections by asking questions, checking for comprehension, and speaking with English Language Learners as much as possible.

■ Draw English Language Learners into small group discussions to give them a sense that their ideas are valid and worth attention.

■ Pair English Language Learners with native English speakers to share their experiences and provide new knowledge to other students.

■ Have English Language Learners draw or dictate to you or another student a description of a new idea they may have during **Workshop** activities.

## Workshop Management Tips

Use the following **Workshop** management tips to ensure that **Workshop** runs smoothly. Note that these suggestions for a weekly unit/lesson may not exactly correspond to a particular unit/lesson in a given grade level, but will give you a sense of how **Workshop** should progress.

**Unit 1, Lesson 1** Introduce **Workshop** to students. Make sure they know where materials are located. Post the rules on the board or other prominent place in the classroom. Keep **Workshop** time short (less than thirty minutes) and very directed during the first few weeks until students can work independently.

**Unit 1, Lesson 2** Discuss using small groups for pre/reteaching purposes and how you will indicate who will be in the groups. Start by forming one small group randomly and having other students do something specific such as a writing assignment. When you have finished with the small group, send them to do independent work. Call another small group of students to work with you. Continue this each day until students are accustomed to forming groups and working independently.

**Unit 1, Lesson 3 Reading Roundtable** is a student-formed and student-run book discussion. Encourage students participating in Reading Roundtable to choose a book that they all will read and discuss. Several different Reading Roundtable groups may form on the basis of the books students choose.

**Unit 1, Lesson 4** For the first few weeks of the school year, make sure each student has a plan for using **Workshop** time.

**Unit 1, Lesson 5** Allot time for presentation and discussion of research activities. Use a whole **Workshop** day and have all groups present their findings, or split the presentations over several days, depending on the small-group needs of your class.

**Unit 1, Lesson 6** Review how students have used **Workshop** during this unit. Have they used their time well? Do they have the materials they need? Discuss suggestions for improving their use of this time. Take a few minutes at the beginning of each **Workshop** to make sure students know what they will be doing.

**Unit 2, Lesson 1** Form small extra-practice groups with the more advanced students from time to time, as they also need special attention.

**Unit 2, Lesson 2** To keep the whole class informed about the independent research being done, every other day or so invite a research group to explain what it is doing, how the research is going, and any problems they are encountering.

## Workshop (continued)

**Unit 2, Lesson 3** Discuss the use of **Workshop** time for doing inquiry and research projects. Introduce students to the activities provided for use with this unit at **www.sra4kids.com.**

**Unit 2, Lesson 4** Make sure small extra-practice groups are formed based on your observations of students' work on the different daily lessons. Small groups should be fluid and based on demonstrated need rather than becoming static and unchanging.

**Unit 2, Lesson 5** One purpose of **Workshop** is to help students learn independence and responsibility. Assign students to monitor **Workshop** materials. They should alert you whenever materials are running low or missing, and they can be responsible for checking on return dates of library books and making sure the books are either returned or renewed.

**Unit 2, Lesson 6** Students sometimes have difficulty starting discussions in Reading Roundtable. Try some of these discussion starters with students, and print them on a poster paper for student use.

I didn't know that . . .    I liked the part where . . .
Does anyone know . . .    I'm still confused by . . .
I figured out that . . .    This made me think . . .
I agree/disagree with _____ because . . .

**Unit 3, Lesson 1** By this time students should be accustomed to the routines, rules, expectations, and usage of **Workshop** time and be moving smoothly from small teacher-led groups to independent work. Monitor small groups occasionally to see that they are on task and making progress on their activities.

**Unit 3, Lesson 2** Make a practice of reading aloud to students. All students enjoy being read to, no matter their age or grade. Encourage them to discuss the shared reading in Reading Roundtable groups and to bring books and read them aloud to their classmates.

**Unit 3, Lesson 3** Encourage cooperation and collaboration by providing students with opportunities to engage in small groups.

**Unit 3, Lesson 4** Spend a few minutes each day circulating around the room and monitoring what students are doing independently or in small groups. Students can then share any questions or problems they are having with you on a timely basis.

**Unit 3, Lesson 5** Take note of different small groups. Make sure that quieter students are able to participate in the discussions. Often the stronger, more confident students dominate such discussions. Encourage them to give all participants a chance to share their ideas.

**Unit 3, Lesson 6** If students are not productive during **Workshop**, keep them in the small group you are working with until they can successfully benefit from independent work.

Discuss strategies they could use to become more independent.

**Unit 4, Lesson 1** Different students can monitor **Workshop** materials and alert you when materials or supplies are running low or missing and can check that library books are either returned or renewed.

**Unit 4, Lesson 2** From time to time, join a Reading Roundtable group, and take part in their discussion. Make sure students lead the discussion.

**Unit 4, Lesson 3** Encourage responsibility and independence by reminding students to show respect for each other and the materials provided.

**Unit 4, Lesson 4** Be sure students discuss during Reading Roundtable what they like or dislike about a book, why they wanted to read it, and how the book either lived up to their expectations or disappointed them. Discussions should not be about basic comprehension but should help students think more deeply about the ideas presented in the book.

**Unit 4, Lesson 5** Make sure students continue to use the activities provided for use with this unit at **www.sra4kids.com.**

**Unit 4, Lesson 6** If students are not productive in **Workshop**, keep them in the small group you are working with until they can successfully benefit from independent work. Discuss strategies they could use to become more independent.

**Unit 5, Lesson 1** Students often make great tutors for other students. They are uniquely qualified to understand problems that others might be having. Encourage students to pair up during **Workshop** to help each other with their daily lessons.

**Unit 5, Lesson 2** Form small extra-practice groups with the more advanced students from time to time, as they also need special attention.

**Unit 5, Lesson 3** In order to keep the whole class informed about the independent research being done, every other day or so, invite a research/investigation group to explain what it is doing, how the research is going, and any problems they are encountering.

**Unit 5, Lesson 4** Most of the authors of the student anthology selections are well known and have written many, many pieces of fine literature. Encourage students who enjoy the anthology selections to find other books by the same author. Encourage them to think about and discuss what about that particular author's work attracts them.

**Unit 5, Lesson 5** Share your impressions of books from the *Leveled Classroom Library* or other reading during Reading Roundtable. Note which students initiate sharing and which are reluctant to share.

**Unit 5, Lesson 6** Review with students the time they have used in **Workshop**. Have they used their time well? Do they have the materials they need? Discuss suggestions for improving the use of this time.

**Unit 6, Lesson 1** Spend a few minutes each day circulating around the room and monitoring what students are doing independently or in small groups. Students can share any questions or problems they are having with you on a timely basis.

**Unit 6, Lesson 2** Students should be accustomed to the routines, rules, expectations, and usage of **Workshop** time and be moving smoothly from small teacher-led groups to independent work. Make sure to monitor small groups occasionally to see that they are on task and making progress with their activities.

**Unit 6, Lesson 3** Make sure students continue to use the activities provided for use with this unit at **www.sra4kids.com.**

**Unit 6, Lesson 4** Allot time for presentation and discussion of research activities. You may want to use a whole **Workshop** day and have all groups present their findings or split the presentations over several days, depending on the urgency of the small-group instruction your class needs.

**Unit 6, Lesson 5** Students often make great tutors for other students. The fact that they too are just learning the materials makes them uniquely qualified to understand problems that others might be having. Encourage students to pair up during **Workshop** to help each other on their daily lessons.

**Unit 6, Lesson 6** If the reading selection is an excerpt from a longer piece, encourage students to read the book from which the excerpt is taken and discuss how the excerpt fits into the larger work.

Assessment can be one of your most effective teaching tools if it is used with the purpose of informing instruction and highlighting areas that need special attention.

## Purpose

Assessment is a tool the teacher uses to monitor students' progress and to detect students' strengths and weaknesses. Evaluation of student learning is addressed in two ways: Informal Assessment and Formal Assessment. Informal, observational assessment, or a quick check of students' written work, is presented in the *Teacher's Edition* in the form of assessment suggestions. Formal Assessment consists of performance assessment (both reading and writing) and objective tests (multiple choice and essay).

## Procedure

### Informal Assessment
#### *Observation*

Observing students as they go about their regular classwork is probably the single most effective way to learn in depth your students' strengths and areas of need. The more students become accustomed to you jotting down informal notes about their work, the more it will become just another part of classroom life that they accept and take little note of. This gives you the opportunity to assess their progress constantly without the interference and possible drawback of formal testing situations.

In order to make informal assessment of student progress a part of your everyday classroom routine, you might want to start by preparing the materials you will need on hand.

- Enter students' names in the Teacher's Observation Log, found in *Program Assessment.*

- Before each day's lesson begins, decide which students you will observe.

- Keep the Teacher's Observation Log available so that you can easily record your observations.

- Decide what aspect of the students' learning you wish to monitor.

- During each lesson, observe this aspect in the performances of several students.

- Record your observations.

- It may take four to five days to make sure you have observed and recorded the performance of each student. If you need more information about performance in a particular area for some of your students, you may want to observe them more than once.

### Progress Assessment
#### *Written Work*

Students are writing one thing or another all day long. Each of these pieces of writing can provide you with valuable information about your students' progress. Two very helpful resources that students will work in daily are the *Comprehension and Language Arts Skills* (Levels 1–6) and the *Inquiry Journal* (Levels 2–6).

- The *Comprehension and Language Arts Skills* include skills practice lessons that act as practice and reinforcement for the skills lessons taught during the reading of the lesson or in conjunction with the Language Arts lesson. These skill pages give you a clear picture of students' understanding of the skills taught. Use them as a daily assessment of student progress in the particular skills taught through the program. In *Phonemic Awareness and Phonics Skills* (K), and *Phonics Skills* (1), students practice each of the skills taught in Part 1 of the program.

- The *Inquiry Journal* can give you invaluable information on how students are progressing in many different areas. In the *Inquiry Journal,* students

  ✓ Record what they know about the concepts and what they learn. You will be able to monitor their growing ability to make connections and use their prior knowledge to help them understand new concepts.

  ✓ Keep a record of their research: what resources they need, what they have used, where they have looked, and what they have found. You can keep track of students' growing ability to find the resources and knowledge base they need to answer the questions they pose.

  ✓ Keep track of their work with their collaborative groups. This will give you a good idea of students' growing ability to work with peers for a common goal—the acquisition of new knowledge.

  ✓ Practice study and research skills that will help them in all of their schooling. You can easily keep track of how well they are learning to use such things as library resources, reference books, visual organizers, and much, much more.

#### *Dictation*

In grades 1–3, students use dictation to practice the sound/spelling associations they are learning and/or reviewing. Collect the dictation papers and look through them to see how the students are doing with writing and with proofreading their words. Record notes on the papers and keep them in the student portfolios.

#### *Portfolios*

Portfolios are more than just a collection bin or gathering place for student projects and records. They add balance to an assessment program by providing unique benefits to teachers, students, and families.

- Portfolios help build self-confidence and increase self-esteem as students come to appreciate the value of their work. More importantly, portfolios allow students to reflect on what they know and what they need to learn. At the end of the school year, each student will be able to go through their portfolios and write about their progress.

- Portfolios provide the teacher with an authentic record of what students can do. Just as important, portfolios give students a concrete example of their own progress and development. Thus, portfolios become a valuable source of information for making instructional decisions.

- Portfolios allow families to judge student performance directly. Portfolios are an ideal starting point for discussions about a student's achievements and future goals during teacher/family conferences.

You will find that there are many opportunities to add to students' portfolios.

## Assessment (continued)

### Reading

- During partner reading, during **Workshop**, or at other times of the day, invite students, one at a time, to sit with you and read a story from an appropriate *Decodable Book* (grades 1–3) or from the *Student Anthology.*

- As each student reads to you, follow along and make note of any recurring problems the student has while reading. Note students' ability to decode unknown words as well as any attempt—successful or not—to use strategies to clarify or otherwise make sense of what they are reading. From time to time, check students' fluency by timing their reading and noting how well they are able to sustain the oral reading without faltering.

- If the student has trouble reading a particular **Decodable Book**, encourage the student to read the story a few times on her or his own before reading it aloud to you. If the **Decodable Book** has two stories, use the alternate story to reassess the student a day or two later.

- If after practicing with a particular **Decodable Book** and reading it on his or her own a few times, a student is still experiencing difficulty, try the following:
  - Drop back two **Decodable Books.** (Continue to drop back until the student is able to read a story with no trouble.) If the student can read that book without problems, move up one book.
  - Continue the process until the student is able to read the current Decodable Book.

### Preparing for Formal Assessment
#### Written Tests

- Have the students clear their desks.
- Make sure the students can hear and see clearly.
- Explain the instructions and complete one or two examples with students before each test to make sure they understand what to do.
- Give students ample time to finish each test.

> *Observing students as they go about their regular classwork is probably the single most effective way to learn in depth your students' strengths and areas of need.*

The assessment components of *Open Court Reading* are designed to help teachers make appropriate instructional decisions. The variety of assessments is intended to be used continuously and formatively. That is, students should be assessed regularly as a follow-up to instructional activities, and the results of the assessment should be used to inform subsequent instruction.

### Program Assessment

The Program Assessment is a series of three broad measures that are meant to be administered at the beginning of the school year, at midyear, and at the end of the year.

- The Pretest gives teachers a snapshot of students' entry-level skills. This information allows the teacher to provide supplemental instruction to students who have not mastered critical skills and to offer more challenging material to students who demonstrate advanced abilities. In addition, this Pretest can serve as a baseline against which to measure students' progress throughout the year.

- The Midyear Test reviews skills that were taught in the first half of the school year, allowing teachers to determine how well students are retaining what they have learned. In addition, the Midyear Test contains "anchor items" similar to those that appeared on the pretest. These items will allow teachers to measure student progress from the beginning of the year to the middle of the year.

- The Posttest is a review of the content that was taught throughout the year and is a summative measure that reflects exit-level skills. The Posttest also contains anchor items, so it is possible to compare students' performance on specific skills at three points in the school year.

In addition to the Pretest, Midyear Test, and Posttest, the Program Assessment also contains a Teacher's Observation Log. Informal assessment is a part of the everyday classroom routine. Teachers can record information quickly on this observation sheet, and they may extend their observations over several days, until they have had a chance to observe each student's performance in a particular area.

### Unit Assessments

Unit Assessments, as the name implies, reflect the instructional content and reading selections in each unit. The various measures within a unit assessment allow the teacher to see how well students have learned the skills that have recently been taught and to provide any additional instruction that is necessary.

Unit Assessments include a variety of measures that vary in form and difficulty so they are both motivating and challenging. Some of the questions are relatively easy, and most students should answer them correctly. Others are more difficult, but none are beyond the abilities of the majority of the students in a class. The skills featured on unit assessments are tied to reading success and reflect both state and national standards.

### Unit Assessments include:

- Individual lesson assessments that assess the skills taught in each lesson immediately after

instruction is delivered. These assessments will help you determine how well students are grasping the skills and concepts as they are taught.

- End-of-unit assessments that assess all of the skills taught throughout the unit. These assessments will help determine the students' ability and growing bank of knowledge as well as their ability to retain concepts over a limited period of time—generally six to eight weeks per unit.

### Diagnostic Assessments

For the majority of the students in a class, the Program Assessment component of *Open Court Reading* will provide the teacher with all the information needed to make appropriate instructional decisions. In certain circumstances, however, it may be necessary to gather additional information in order to provide students with appropriate instruction. Some students, for example, may have specific skill deficits that prevent them from making adequate progress. Other students may enter the class after the beginning of the school year. A third situation is when the teacher might want to group students who have the same skill deficit. For these circumstances, we provide Diagnostic Assessments.

The Diagnostic Assessments offer a variety of measures that allow the teacher to identify students' strengths and weaknesses. The results of the assessment can help the teacher develop intervention strategies and choose the right supplemental instruction that will meet each student's needs. General and specific instructions are provided so that the teacher can use the Diagnostic Assessments efficiently without disrupting the instructional routine.

## Tips

- When observing students, do not pull them aside; rather, observe students as part of the regular lesson, either with the whole class or in small groups.

- Encourage students to express any confusion they may be experiencing. The questions students ask can give you valuable insight into their progress and development.

- The more comfortable students become with standardized-test formats—usually multiple choice—the more confident you and they will be in the fact that the test is testing their knowledge of a subject rather than their test-taking skills.

- Make sure students know that the ultimate purpose of assessment is to keep track of their progress and to help them continue to do better.

# Assessment

## Rubrics

A rubric is an established rule or criterion. Rubrics provide criteria for different levels of performance. Rubrics established before an assignment is given are extremely helpful in evaluating the assignment. When students know what the rubrics for a particular assignment are, they can focus their energies on the key issues.

### Using Comprehension Strategies Rubrics

The following rubrics can be used to gauge the students' growing knowledge of the comprehension strategies and how adept they are becoming in their use. The rubrics are simply a guide. Students may and probably will develop strategies of their own. The important thing to consider is whether or not students are becoming strategic, active readers—do they employ these and other strategies, or do they continue to simply plough through text unaware of any problems they might be having? The rubrics indicate the types of behaviors strategic readers use and will help you identify the growing facility your students can gain in dealing with text of all sorts.

### Grade 1: Comprehension Strategies Rubrics

#### Predicting

- The student makes predictions about what the text is about.
- The student updates predictions during reading, based on information in the text.

#### Visualizing

- The student visualizes ideas or scenes described in the text.

### Grades 2-6: Comprehension Strategies Rubrics

#### Summarizing

- The student paraphrases text, reporting main ideas and a summary of what is in the text.
- The student decides which parts of the text are important in his/her summary.
- The student draws conclusions from the text.
- The student makes global interpretations of the text, such as recognizing the genre.

#### Asking Questions

- The student asks questions about ideas or facts presented in the text and attempts to answer these questions by reading the text.

#### Predicting

- The student makes predictions about what the text is about.
- The student updates predictions during reading, based on information in the text.

#### Making Connections

- The student activates prior knowledge and related knowledge.
- The student uses prior knowledge to explain something encountered in text.
- The student connects ideas presented later in the text to ideas presented earlier in the text.
- The student notes ideas in the text that are new to him/her or conflict with what he/she thought previously.

#### Visualizing

- The student visualizes ideas or scenes described in the text.

#### Monitoring and Clarifying

- The student notes characteristics of the text, such as whether it is difficult to read or whether some sections are more challenging or more important than others are.
- The student shows awareness of whether he/she understands the text and takes appropriate action, such as rereading, in order to understand the text better.
- The student rereads to reconsider something presented earlier in the text.
- The student recognizes problems during reading, such as a loss of concentration, unfamiliar vocabulary, or a lack of sufficient background knowledge to comprehend the text.

#### Monitoring and Adjusting Reading Speed

The student changes reading speed in reaction to text, exhibiting such behavior as

- Skimming parts of the text that are not important or relevant.
- Purposely reading more slowly because of difficulty in comprehending the text.

### Research Rubrics

Throughout each unit, students engage in research and inquiry activities based on the unit concepts. They will present the findings of their research to the class. In this way they exhibit the wealth of knowledge and understanding they have gained about that particular concept. In addition to gaining knowledge about the concepts, students will be honing their research skills. With each unit, they will progress with their research in the same manner in which professional researchers do.

With each new unit of study, students should also become more and more sophisticated in their ability to formulate questions, make conjectures about those questions, recognize their own information needs, conduct research to find that information, reevaluate their questions and conjectures as new information is added to their knowledge base, and communicate their findings effectively. In addition, they will become more and more adept at working as a team and being aware of the progress being made as individuals and as a group. The Research Rubrics will help you to assess the students' progress as researchers and as members of collaborative teams.

#### Formulating Research Questions and Problems

1. With help, identifies things she/he wonders about in relation to a topic.
2. Expresses curiosity about topics; with help, translates this into specific questions.
3. Poses an interesting problem or question for research; with help, refines it into a researchable question.
4. Identifies something she/he genuinely wonders about and translates it into a researchable question.

#### Making Conjectures

1. Offers conjectures that are mainly expressions of fact or opinion. ("I think the Anasazi lived a long time ago." "I think tigers should be protected.")
2. Offers conjectures that partially address the research question. ("I think germs make you sick because they get your body upset." "I think germs make you sick because they multiply really fast.")
3. Offers conjectures that address the research question with guesses. ("I think the Anasazi were wiped out by a meteor.")
4. Offers reasonable conjectures that address the question and that can be improved through further research.

#### Recognizing Information Needs

1. Identifies topics about which more needs to be learned. ("I need to learn more about the brain.")
2. Identifies information needs that are relevant though not essential to the research question. ("To understand how Leeuwenhoek invented the microscope, I need to know what size germs are.")
3. Identifies questions that are deeper than the one originally asked. (Original question: "How does the heart work?" Deeper question: "Why does blood need to circulate?")

#### Finding Needed Information

1. Collects information loosely related to topic.
2. Collects information clearly related to topic.
3. Collects information helpful in advancing on a research problem.
4. Collects problem-relevant information from varied sources and notices inconsistencies and missing pieces.

## Assessment (continued)

5. Collects useful information, paying attention to the reliability of sources and reviewing information critically.

### Revising Problems and Conjectures

1. No revision.
2. Produces new problems or conjectures with little relation to earlier ones.
3. Tends to lift problems and conjectures directly from reference material.
4. Progresses to deeper, more refined problems and conjectures.

### Communicating Research Progress and Results

1. Reporting is sparse and fragmentary.
2. Report is factual; communicates findings but not the thinking behind them.
3. Report provides a good picture of the research problem, of how original conjectures were modified in light of new information, and of difficulties and unresolved issues.
4. A report that not only interests and informs the audience but also draws helpful commentary from them.

### Overall Assessment of Research

1. A collection of facts related in miscellaneous ways to a topic.
2. An organized collection of facts relevant to the research problem.
3. A thoughtful effort to tackle a research problem, with some indication of progress toward solving it.
4. Significant progress on a challenging problem of understanding.

### Collaborative Group Work

1. Group members work on separate tasks with little interaction.
2. Work-related decisions are made by the group, but there is little interaction related to ideas.
3. Information and ideas are shared, but there is little discussion concerned with advancing understanding.
4. The group clearly progresses in its thinking beyond where individual students could have gone.

### Participation in Collaborative Inquiry

1. Does not contribute ideas or information to team or class.
2. Makes contributions to Concept/Question Board or class discussions when specifically called upon to do so.
3. Occasionally contributes ideas or information to other students' inquiries.
4. Takes an active interest in the success of the whole class's knowledge-building efforts.

## Writing Rubrics

Rubrics are particularly effective for writing assignments, which do not have simple right or wrong answers. The rubrics included in the *Unit Assessments* for writing cover different elements of the writing. They are intended to help teachers provide criteria and feedback to students.

*Open Court Reading* provides four-point rubrics for writing in each of four areas. This enables teachers to clearly distinguish among different levels of performance.

1. Point score indicates that a student is performing below basic level.
2. Point score indicates that a student's abilities are emerging.
3. Point score indicates that a student's work is adequate and achieving expectations.
4. Point score indicates that a student is exceeding expectations.

### Conventions

The conventions rubrics provide criteria for evaluating a student's understanding and ability to use English language conventions, which include:

- Grammar and Usage
- Mechanics: Punctuation
- Mechanics: Capitalization
- Sentence Structure
- Spelling
- Overall grammar, usage, mechanics, and spelling

### Genre

Genre rubrics, found in the *Unit Assessment,* enable evaluation of students' grasp of the different structures and elements of each of these different forms of writing:

- Descriptive Writing
- Expository Structure
- Genre
- Narrative
- Narrative Character
- Narrative Plot
- Narrative Setting
- Persuasive
- Personal
- Poetry

### Writing Process

Writing process rubrics allow teachers to evaluate students' abilities in these areas:

- Getting Ideas
- Prewriting—Organizing Writing
- Drafting
- Revising
- Editing
- Presentation/Publishing

- Self-Management
- Language Resources

### Writing Traits

Writing traits rubrics, found in the *Unit Assessment,* provide criteria for different elements of written composition to identify a student's strengths and weaknesses.

- Audience
- Citing Sources
- Elaboration (supporting details and examples that develop the main idea)
- Focus
- Ideas/Content
- Organization
- Sentence Fluency
- Voice
- Word Choice

# Audiovisual and Technology Resource Directory

This directory is provided for the convenience of ordering the Technology Resources listed on the Technology pages in each Unit Overview.

## BFA Educational Media Coronet/MTI

Phoenix Learning Group
2349 Chaffee Drive
St. Louis, MO 63146
800-221-1274

## Dorling Kindersley

95 Madison Avenue
New York, NY 10016
212-213-4800
FAX: 212-213-5240
www.dk.com

## Great Plains National Instructional Television Library

GPN Educational Media
University of Nebraska-Lincoln
1800 North 33rd Street
Lincoln, NE 68583
402-472-4076
http://gpn.unl.edu

## Grolier Incorporated

90 Sherman Turnpike
Danbury, CT 06816
800-353-3140
www.grolier.com

## Innovative Educators

P.O. Box 520
Montezuma, GA 31063
1-888-252-KIDS
FAX: 888-536-8553
http://www.innovative-educators.com

## Library Video Company

P.O. Box 580
Wynnewood, PA 19096
800-843-3620
FAX: 610-645-4040
http://www.libraryvideo.com

## Live Oak Media

P.O. Box 652
Pine Plains, NY 12567
800-788-1121
FAX: 866-398-1070
http://www.liveoakmedia.com

## Macmillan/McGraw-Hill

220 East Danieldale Road
DeSoto, TX 75115-9960
800-442-9685
FAX: 972-228-1982
www.mhschool.com

## MCA Video MCA Records/Universal Studios

100 Universal City Plaza
Universal City, CA 91608
818-777-1000

## Mindscape, Inc.

The Learning Company
88 Rowland Way
Novato, California 94945
415-895-2000
Fax: 415-895-2102
www.mindscape.com

## Multicom Publishing

Multimedia 2000
2017 Eighth Avenue, 3rd Floor
Seattle, WA 98101
800-850-7272
Fax: 206-622-4380
www.m-2K.com

## Orange Cherry Software

P.O. Box 390
69 Westchester Ave.
Pound Ridge, NY 10576
914-764-4104
Fax: 914-764-0104
www.orangecherry.com

## Paramount

780 N. Gower
Hollywood, CA 90038
800-699-1085
www.paramount.com

## Queue, Inc.

338 Commerce Drive
Fairfield, CT 06432
800-232-2224
Fax: 203-336-2481
www.queueinc.com

## Scholastic

555 Broadway
New York, NY 10012-3999
800-SCHOLASTIC
http://www.scholastic.com

## Sony Wonder

Sony Corporation of America
550 Madison Avenue
Floor 19
New York, NY 10022
212-833-6800
http://www.sonywonder.com

## SRA/McGraw-Hill

220 East Danieldale Road
DeSoto, TX 75115-9960
888-SRA-4543
Fax: 972-228-1982
www.sra4kids.com

## Tom Snyder Productions

80 Coolidge Hill Road
Watertown, MA 02472
800-342-0236
Fax: 800-304-1254
www.tomsnyder.com

# Scope and Sequence

## Reading

| | K | 1 | 2 | 3 | 4 | 5 | 6 |
|---|---|---|---|---|---|---|---|
| **Print/Book Awareness (Recognize and understand the conventions of print and books)** | | | | | | | |
| Capitalization | ✔ | ✔ | ✔ | | | ✔ | ✔ |
| Constancy of Words | | | | | | ✔ | |
| End Punctuation | ✔ | ✔ | | | | ✔ | ✔ |
| Follow Left-to-right, Top-to-bottom | ✔ | ✔ | | | | | |
| Letter Recognition and Formation | ✔ | ✔ | | | | | |
| Page Numbering | | ✔ | | | | | |
| Picture/Text Relationship | ✔ | | | | ✔ | | |
| Quotation Marks | ✔ | ✔ | ✔ | | | ✔ | ✔ |
| Relationship Between Spoken and Printed Language | | ✔ | | | | | |
| Sentence Recognition | | | | | | | |
| Table of Contents | ✔ | ✔ | | | | | |
| Word Length | ✔ | | | | | | |
| Word Boundaries | | ✔ | | | | | |
| **Phonemic Awareness (Recognize discrete sounds in words)** | | | | | | | |
| Oral Blending: Words/Word Parts | ✔ | ✔ | ✔ | | | | |
| Oral Blending: Initial Consonants/Blends | ✔ | ✔ | ✔ | ✔ | | | |
| Oral Blending: Final Consonants | ✔ | ✔ | ✔ | ✔ | | | |
| Oral Blending: Initial Vowels | | ✔ | | | | | |
| Oral Blending: Syllables | | ✔ | | | ✔ | | |
| Oral Blending: Vowel Replacement | | | | | ✔ | | |
| Segmentation: Initial Consonants/Blends | ✔ | ✔ | ✔ | ✔ | | ✔ | |
| Segmentation: Final Consonants | ✔ | ✔ | ✔ | ✔ | | | |
| Segmentation: Words/Word Parts | ✔ | ✔ | ✔ | ✔ | ✔ | ✔ | |
| Rhyming | ✔ | ✔ | | | ✔ | ✔ | |
| **How the Alphabet Works** | | | | | | | |
| Letter Knowledge | ✔ | ✔ | ✔ | ✔ | | | |
| Letter Order (Alphabetic Order) | ✔ | ✔ | | | | | |
| Letter Sounds | ✔ | ✔ | ✔ | ✔ | ✔ | | |
| Sounds in Words | ✔ | ✔ | ✔ | ✔ | ✔ | | |
| **Phonics (Associate sounds and spellings to read words)** | | | | | | | |
| Blending Sounds into Words | ✔ | ✔ | | | | | |
| Consonant Clusters | | ✔ | | ✔ | | | |
| Consonant Digraphs | | ✔ | | ✔ | ✔ | | |
| Consonant Sounds and Spellings | ✔ | ✔ | ✔ | ✔ | | | |
| Phonograms | ✔ | ✔ | | ✔ | | | ✔ |
| Syllables | ✔ | ✔ | | | ✔ | | |
| Vowel Diphthongs | | ✔ | | ✔ | | | ✔ |
| Vowels: Long Sounds and Spellings | ✔ | ✔ | ✔ | ✔ | ✔ | ✔ | ✔ |
| Vowels: r-controlled | | ✔ | ✔ | ✔ | ✔ | ✔ | ✔ |
| Vowels: Short Sounds and Spellings | ✔ | ✔ | ✔ | ✔ | ✔ | ✔ | ✔ |

☐ Skills, strategies, and other teaching opportunities    ✔ Formal, progress, or informal testing opportunities

# Reading (continued)

| | Level | | | | | | |
|---|:-:|:-:|:-:|:-:|:-:|:-:|:-:|
| | K | 1 | 2 | 3 | 4 | 5 | 6 |
| **Comprehension Strategies** | | | | | | | |
| Asking Questions/Answering Questions | | ✔ | ✔ | ✔ | ✔ | ✔ | ✔ |
| Making Connections | | ✔ | ✔ | ✔ | ✔ | ✔ | ✔ |
| Monitoring and Clarifying | | ✔ | ✔ | ✔ | ✔ | ✔ | ✔ |
| Monitoring and Adjusting Reading Speed | | ✔ | ✔ | ✔ | ✔ | ✔ | ✔ |
| Predicting/Confirming Predictions | ✔ | ✔ | ✔ | ✔ | ✔ | ✔ | ✔ |
| Summarizing | | ✔ | ✔ | ✔ | ✔ | ✔ | ✔ |
| Visualizing | | ✔ | ✔ | ✔ | ✔ | ✔ | ✔ |
| **Comprehension Skills** | | | | | | | |
| Author's Point of View | | | ✔ | ✔ | ✔ | ✔ | ✔ |
| Author's Purpose | | | ✔ | ✔ | ✔ | ✔ | ✔ |
| Cause and Effect | ✔ | ✔ | ✔ | ✔ | ✔ | ✔ | ✔ |
| Classify and Categorize | ✔ | ✔ | ✔ | ✔ | ✔ | ✔ | ✔ |
| Compare and Contrast | ✔ | ✔ | ✔ | ✔ | ✔ | ✔ | ✔ |
| Drawing Conclusions | ✔ | ✔ | ✔ | ✔ | ✔ | ✔ | ✔ |
| Fact and Opinion | | | ✔ | ✔ | ✔ | ✔ | ✔ |
| Main Idea and Details | ✔ | ✔ | ✔ | ✔ | ✔ | ✔ | ✔ |
| Making Inferences | | ✔ | ✔ | ✔ | ✔ | ✔ | ✔ |
| Reality/Fantasy | ✔ | ✔ | | ✔ | | | |
| Sequence | | ✔ | ✔ | ✔ | ✔ | ✔ | ✔ |
| **Vocabulary** | | | | | | | |
| Antonyms | ✔ | ✔ | ✔ | ✔ | ✔ | ✔ | ✔ |
| Comparatives/Superlatives | | ✔ | ✔ | ✔ | ✔ | ✔ | ✔ |
| Compound Words | ✔ | ✔ | ✔ | ✔ | ✔ | ✔ | ✔ |
| Connecting Words (Transition Words) | | | | | | ✔ | ✔ |
| Context Clues | | ✔ | ✔ | ✔ | ✔ | ✔ | ✔ |
| Contractions | | | ✔ | ✔ | ✔ | ✔ | |
| Figurative Language | | | | ✔ | | ✔ | |
| Greek and Latin Roots | | | | ✔ | ✔ | | |
| High-Frequency Words | ✔ | ✔ | ✔ | ✔ | ✔ | ✔ | ✔ |
| Homographs | | | ✔ | ✔ | ✔ | ✔ | |
| Homophones/Homonyms | | ✔ | ✔ | ✔ | ✔ | ✔ | ✔ |
| Idioms | | | | | ✔ | ✔ | ✔ |
| Inflectional Endings | | ✔ | ✔ | ✔ | ✔ | ✔ | ✔ |
| Irregular Plurals | | | | ✔ | | ✔ | ✔ |
| Multiple Meaning Words | | | ✔ | ✔ | ✔ | ✔ | ✔ |
| Multisyllabic Words | | | ✔ | ✔ | | ✔ | |
| Position Words | ✔ | ✔ | | | | ✔ | |
| Prefixes | | | ✔ | ✔ | ✔ | ✔ | ✔ |
| Question Words | | ✔ | | | | | |
| Base or Root Words | | ✔ | ✔ | ✔ | ✔ | ✔ | ✔ |
| Selection Vocabulary | ✔ | ✔ | ✔ | ✔ | ✔ | ✔ | ✔ |
| Suffixes | | ✔ | ✔ | ✔ | ✔ | ✔ | ✔ |
| Synonyms | | ✔ | ✔ | ✔ | ✔ | ✔ | ✔ |
| Time and Order Words (Creating Sequence) | | | | | ✔ | ✔ | ✔ |
| Utility Words (Colors, Classroom Objects, etc.) | ✔ | ✔ | | | | | |
| Word Families | | | ✔ | ✔ | ✔ | ✔ | ✔ |

## Scope and Sequence (continued)

# Inquiry and Research

| Study Skills | K | 1 | 2 | 3 | 4 | 5 | 6 |
|---|---|---|---|---|---|---|---|
| | | | | | | Level | |
| Charts, Graphs, and Diagrams/Visual Aids | | | ✔ | | ✔ | ✔ | ✔ |
| Collaborative Inquiry | | | ✔ | ✔ | ✔ | ✔ | ✔ |
| Communicating Research Progress Results | | | ✔ | ✔ | ✔ | ✔ | ✔ |
| Compile Notes | | | | | | ✔ | ✔ |
| Conducting an Interview | | | | | | | ✔ |
| Finding Needed Information | | | ✔ | ✔ | ✔ | ✔ | ✔ |
| Follow Directions | ✔ | | | ✔ | | | |
| Formulate Questions for Inquiry and Research | | | ✔ | | | ✔ | ✔ |
| Give Reports | | | | | ✔ | ✔ | ✔ |
| Make Outlines | | | | ✔ | | ✔ | ✔ |
| Making Conjectures | | | ✔ | ✔ | ✔ | ✔ | ✔ |
| Maps and Globes | | | | | ✔ | | ✔ |
| Note Taking | | | ✔ | ✔ | ✔ | ✔ | ✔ |
| Parts of a Book | | | ✔ | ✔ | ✔ | | |
| Planning Investigation | | | ✔ | ✔ | ✔ | ✔ | ✔ |
| Recognizing Information Needs | | | ✔ | ✔ | ✔ | ✔ | ✔ |
| Revising Questions and Conjectures | | | ✔ | ✔ | ✔ | ✔ | ✔ |
| Summarize and Organize Information | | | | | ✔ | ✔ | ✔ |
| Time Lines | | | | | ✔ | ✔ | ✔ |
| Use Appropriate Resources (Media Source, Reference Books, Experts, Internet) | | | | | ✔ | ✔ | ✔ |
| Using a Dictionary/Glossary | | ✔ | ✔ | ✔ | ✔ | ✔ | ✔ |
| Using a Media Center/Library | | | | | ✔ | | ✔ |
| Using a Thesaurus | | | ✔ | ✔ | ✔ | ✔ | ✔ |
| Using an Encyclopedia | | | | | ✔ | | ✔ |
| Using Newspapers and Magazines | | | | | ✔ | | ✔ |
| Using Technology | | | | | | | |

Skills, strategies, and other teaching opportunities   ✔ Formal, progress, or informal testing opportunities

# Language Arts
## Writing/Composition

**PROGRAM APPENDIX**

| | Level | K | 1 | 2 | 3 | 4 | 5 | 6 |
|---|---|---|---|---|---|---|---|---|
| **Approaches** | | | | | | | | |
| Collaborative Writing | | | ✔ | | | | | |
| Group Writing | | | | | | | | |
| **Process** | | | | | | | | |
| Brainstorming/Prewriting | | ✔ | ✔ | | ✔ | ✔ | ✔ | |
| Drafting | | ✔ | ✔ | | ✔ | ✔ | ✔ | |
| Revising | | ✔ | ✔ | | ✔ | ✔ | ✔ | |
| Proofreading | | ✔ | ✔ | | ✔ | ✔ | ✔ | |
| Publishing | | ✔ | ✔ | | ✔ | ✔ | ✔ | |
| **Forms** | | | | | | | | |
| Biography/Autobiography | | ✔ | ✔ | ✔ | ✔ | ✔ | ✔ | ✔ |
| Business Letter | | | | | ✔ | ✔ | ✔ | ✔ |
| Describe a Process | | | ✔ | ✔ | ✔ | ✔ | | ✔ |
| Descriptive Writing | | ✔ | ✔ | ✔ | ✔ | ✔ | ✔ | ✔ |
| Expository/Informational Text | | ✔ | ✔ | ✔ | ✔ | ✔ | ✔ | ✔ |
| Folklore (Folktales, Fairy Tales, Tall Tales, Legends, Myths) | | | | ✔ | ✔ | ✔ | | |
| Friendly Letter | | | ✔ | ✔ | ✔ | ✔ | ✔ | ✔ |
| Historical Fiction | | | | | | | ✔ | ✔ |
| Journal Writing | | | ✔ | ✔ | ✔ | ✔ | ✔ | ✔ |
| Narrative | | | ✔ | ✔ | ✔ | ✔ | ✔ | ✔ |
| Personal Writing | | | ✔ | ✔ | ✔ | ✔ | ✔ | ✔ |
| Persuasive Writing | | ✔ | ✔ | ✔ | ✔ | ✔ | ✔ | ✔ |
| Play/Dramatization | | | | | ✔ | ✔ | ✔ | ✔ |
| Poetry | | | ✔ | ✔ | ✔ | ✔ | ✔ | ✔ |
| Realistic Story | | | | | ✔ | | | |
| **Writer's Craft** | | | | | | | | |
| Characterization | | | | ✔ | ✔ | ✔ | ✔ | ✔ |
| Descriptive Writing | | ✔ | ✔ | ✔ | ✔ | ✔ | ✔ | ✔ |
| Dialogue | | | ✔ | ✔ | ✔ | ✔ | ✔ | ✔ |
| Effective Beginnings | | | | ✔ | ✔ | ✔ | ✔ | ✔ |
| Effective Endings | | | | ✔ | ✔ | ✔ | ✔ | ✔ |
| Event Sequence | | | ✔ | ✔ | ✔ | ✔ | ✔ | ✔ |
| Figurative Language | | ✔ | | ✔ | ✔ | ✔ | ✔ | ✔ |
| Identifying Thoughts and Feelings | | ✔ | | ✔ | ✔ | ✔ | ✔ | ✔ |
| Mood and Tone | | | | | ✔ | ✔ | ✔ | ✔ |
| Plot (Problem/Solutions) | | ✔ | ✔ | ✔ | ✔ | ✔ | ✔ | ✔ |
| Point of View | | | | | ✔ | ✔ | ✔ | |
| Rhyme | | ✔ | ✔ | ✔ | ✔ | ✔ | ✔ | |
| Sensory Details | | | | | ✔ | | ✔ | ✔ |
| Sentence Variety | | | | | ✔ | | ✔ | ✔ |
| Sentence Elaboration | | | | | ✔ | | ✔ | ✔ |
| Setting | | ✔ | | ✔ | ✔ | | ✔ | ✔ |
| Suspense and Surprise | | | | ✔ | ✔ | ✔ | ✔ | |
| Topic Sentences | | | | ✔ | ✔ | ✔ | ✔ | ✔ |
| Using Comparisons | | | | | | | ✔ | |
| **Purposes** | | | | | | | | |
| Determining Purposes for Writing | | ✔ | ✔ | | | | ✔ | |

### Scope and Sequence (continued)

## Language Arts

**Grammar**

| | Level K | 1 | 2 | 3 | 4 | 5 | 6 |
|---|---|---|---|---|---|---|---|
| **Parts of Speech** | | | | | | | |
| Adjectives | ✔ | ✔ | ✔ | ✔ | ✔ | ✔ | ✔ |
| Adverbs | | | ✔ | ✔ | ✔ | ✔ | ✔ |
| Conjunctions | | | ✔ | ✔ | ✔ | ✔ | ✔ |
| Nouns | ✔ | ✔ | ✔ | ✔ | ✔ | ✔ | ✔ |
| Prepositions | ✔ | | | ✔ | ✔ | ✔ | ✔ |
| Pronouns | ✔ | ✔ | ✔ | ✔ | ✔ | ✔ | ✔ |
| Verbs | ✔ | ✔ | ✔ | ✔ | ✔ | ✔ | ✔ |
| **Sentences** | | | | | | | |
| Fragments | | | | | ✔ | ✔ | ✔ |
| Parts (Subjects/Predicates) | | ✔ | ✔ | ✔ | ✔ | ✔ | ✔ |
| Subject/Verb Agreement | ✔ | ✔ | ✔ | ✔ | ✔ | ✔ | ✔ |
| Structure (Simple, Compound, Complex) | | | | ✔ | ✔ | ✔ | ✔ |
| Types (Declarative, Interrogative, Exclamatory, Imperatives) | ✔ | ✔ | ✔ | ✔ | ✔ | ✔ | ✔ |
| Verb Tenses | ✔ | ✔ | ✔ | ✔ | ✔ | ✔ | ✔ |
| Verbs (Action, Helping, Linking, Regular/Irregular) | ✔ | ✔ | ✔ | ✔ | ✔ | ✔ | ✔ |
| **Usage** | | | | | | | |
| Adjectives | ✔ | ✔ | | ✔ | ✔ | ✔ | ✔ |
| Adverbs | | | ✔ | ✔ | ✔ | ✔ | ✔ |
| Articles | ✔ | ✔ | ✔ | ✔ | ✔ | ✔ | ✔ |
| Nouns | ✔ | ✔ | ✔ | ✔ | ✔ | ✔ | ✔ |
| Pronouns | ✔ | ✔ | ✔ | ✔ | ✔ | ✔ | ✔ |
| Verbs | ✔ | ✔ | ✔ | ✔ | ✔ | ✔ | ✔ |
| **Mechanics** | | | | | | | |
| Capitalization (Sentence, Proper Nouns, Titles, Direct Address, Pronoun "I") | ✔ | ✔ | ✔ | ✔ | ✔ | ✔ | ✔ |
| Punctuation (End Punctuation, Comma Use, Quotation Marks, Apostrophe, Colon, Semicolon, Hyphen, Parentheses) | ✔ | ✔ | ✔ | ✔ | ✔ | ✔ | ✔ |
| **Spelling** | | | | | | | |
| Contractions | | ✔ | ✔ | ✔ | | ✔ | |
| Inflectional Endings | | | ✔ | ✔ | ✔ | ✔ | |
| Irregular Plurals | | | ✔ | ✔ | ✔ | ✔ | ✔ |
| Long Vowel Patterns | | ✔ | ✔ | ✔ | ✔ | ✔ | ✔ |
| Multisyllabic Words | | | ✔ | ✔ | | ✔ | |
| Phonograms | | ✔ | ✔ | ✔ | | | ✔ |
| r-controlled Vowel Spellings | | ✔ | ✔ | ✔ | ✔ | ✔ | ✔ |
| Short Vowel Spellings | | ✔ | ✔ | ✔ | ✔ | ✔ | ✔ |
| Silent Letters | | | | ✔ | | | |
| Sound/Letter Relationships | | ✔ | ✔ | ✔ | | | |
| Special Spelling Patterns (-ough, -augh, -all, -al, -alk, -ion,-sion, -tion) | | ✔ | ✔ | ✔ | ✔ | ✔ | ✔ |

▢ Skills, strategies, and other teaching opportunities    ✔ Formal, progress, or informal testing opportunities

# Language Arts (continued)

### Listening/Speaking/Viewing

| | Level | | | | | | |
|---|:--:|:--:|:--:|:--:|:--:|:--:|:--:|
| | K | 1 | 2 | 3 | 4 | 5 | 6 |
| **Listening/Speaking** | | | | | | | |
| Analyze/Evaluate Intent and Content of Speaker's Message | | ✔ | ✔ | ✔ | ✔ | ✔ | ✔ |
| Ask and Answer Questions | ✔ | ✔ | ✔ | ✔ | ✔ | ✔ | ✔ |
| Determine Purposes for Listening | | | ✔ | ✔ | ✔ | | |
| Follow Directions | ✔ | ✔ | ✔ | ✔ | ✔ | ✔ | ✔ |
| Learn about Different Cultures through Discussion | | | | | ✔ | ✔ | ✔ |
| Listen for Poetic Language (Rhythm/Rhyme) | ✔ | ✔ | ✔ | ✔ | | | |
| Participate in Group Discussions | | ✔ | ✔ | ✔ | ✔ | ✔ | ✔ |
| Respond to Speaker | ✔ | ✔ | ✔ | ✔ | ✔ | ✔ | ✔ |
| Use Nonverbal Communication Techniques | ✔ | ✔ | ✔ | ✔ | ✔ | ✔ | ✔ |
| **Speaking** | | | | | | | |
| Describe Ideas and Feelings | ✔ | ✔ | ✔ | ✔ | ✔ | ✔ | ✔ |
| Give Directions | | | | | ✔ | ✔ | ✔ |
| Learn about Different Cultures through Discussion | | | | ✔ | ✔ | ✔ | ✔ |
| Participate in Group Discussions | ✔ | ✔ | ✔ | ✔ | ✔ | ✔ | ✔ |
| Present Oral Reports | | | ✔ | ✔ | ✔ | ✔ | ✔ |
| Read Fluently with Expression, Phrasing, and Intonation | | | ✔ | ✔ | ✔ | ✔ | ✔ |
| Read Orally | | ✔ | ✔ | ✔ | ✔ | ✔ | ✔ |
| Share Information | ✔ | ✔ | ✔ | ✔ | ✔ | ✔ | ✔ |
| Speak Clearly at Appropriate Volume | ✔ | ✔ | ✔ | ✔ | ✔ | ✔ | ✔ |
| Summarize/Retell Stories | ✔ | ✔ | ✔ | ✔ | ✔ | ✔ | ✔ |
| Understand Formal and Informal Language | ✔ | ✔ | ✔ | ✔ | ✔ | ✔ | ✔ |
| Use Appropriate Vocabulary for Audience | | ✔ | ✔ | ✔ | ✔ | ✔ | ✔ |
| Use Elements of Grammar in Speech | | | | ✔ | ✔ | ✔ | ✔ |
| **Viewing** | | | | | | | |
| Analyze Purposes and Techniques of the Media | | | | | ✔ | ✔ | ✔ | ✔ |
| Appreciate/Interpret Artist's Techniques | | | | | | | |
| Compare Visual and Written Material on the Same Subject | ✔ | | | | ✔ | | |
| Gather Information from Visual Images | ✔ | ✔ | ✔ | ✔ | ✔ | ✔ | ✔ |
| View Critically | | ✔ | ✔ | ✔ | ✔ | ✔ | ✔ |
| View Culturally Rich Materials | ✔ | ✔ | ✔ | | ✔ | ✔ | ✔ |
| **Penmanship** | | | | | | | |
| Cursive Letters | | | ✔ | ✔ | ✔ | ✔ | ✔ |
| Manuscript Letters | ✔ | ✔ | ✔ | | | | |
| Numbers | ✔ | ✔ | ✔ | ✔ | | | |

**PROGRAM APPENDIX**

# Unit Themes

| | LEVEL K | LEVEL 1 | LEVEL 2 |
|---|---|---|---|
| Unit 1 | School | Let's Read! | Sharing Stories |
| Unit 2 | Shadows | Animals | Kindness |
| Unit 3 | Finding Friends | Things That Go | Look Again |
| Unit 4 | The Wind | Our Neighborhood at Work | Fossils |
| Unit 5 | Stick to It | Weather | Courage |
| Unit 6 | Red, White, and Blue | Journeys | Our Country and Its People |
| Unit 7 | Teamwork | Keep Trying | |
| Unit 8 | By the Sea | Games | |
| Unit 9 | | Being Afraid | |
| Unit 10 | | Homes | |

| LEVEL 3 | LEVEL 4 | LEVEL 5 | LEVEL 6 |
|---|---|---|---|
| Friendship | Risks and Consequences | Cooperation and Competition | Perseverance |
| City Wildlife | Dollars and Sense | Astronomy | Ancient Civilizations |
| Imagination | From Mystery to Medicine | Heritage | Taking a Stand |
| Money | Survival | Making a New Nation | Beyond the Notes |
| Storytelling | Communication | Going West | Ecology |
| Country Life | A Changing America | Journeys and Quests | A Question of Value |

# Leveled Classroom Library Books

## LEVEL K

**Unit 1 School:** *Mouse Views: What the Class Pet Saw; The 100th Day of School; Billy and the Big New School; Vera's First Day of School; Bea and Mr. Jones; The Kissing Hand*

**Unit 2 Shadows:** *Footprints and Shadows; Shadows Are About; I Have a Friend; My Shadow; What Makes Day and Night?; Sun Up, Sun Down*

**Unit 3 Finding Friends:** *My Friends; Yo! Yes?; Will You Be My Friend?; George and Martha One Fine Day; Friends; May I Bring a Friend?*

**Unit 4 The Wind:** *The Wind Blew; One Windy Wednesday; The Sun, the Wind, and the Rain; What Makes the Wind?; Millicent and the Wind; Feel the Wind*

**Unit 5 Stick to It:** *The Carrot Seed; Leo the Late Bloomer; You'll Soon Grow into Them, Titch; JoJo's Flying Side Kick; Paul Bunyan: A Tall Tale; Liang and the Magic Paintbrush*

**Unit 6 Red, White, and Blue:** *The Pledge of Allegiance; 'Night, America; This Land Is Your Land; Happy Birthday, America; The Flag We Love; Mr. Lincoln's Whiskers*

**Unit 7 Teamwork:** *Can I Help?; Animal Orchestra; Tippy Bear Hunts for Honey; Helping Out; Stone Soup; The Great Trash Bash*

**Unit 8 By the Sea:** *Oceans; In the Ocean; Tacky the Penguin; Fish Faces; The Seashore Book; Commotion in the Ocean*

## LEVEL 1

**Unit 1 Let's Read!:** *America: My Land Your Land Our Land; I Read Signs; Miss Malarkey Doesn't Live in Room 10; The Old Woman Who Loved to Read; A Cake for Herbie; More Than Anything Else*

**Unit 2 Animals:** *Sweet Dreams: How Animals Sleep; Moo Moo, Brown Cow; Here Is the African Savanna; Is Your Mama a Llama?; A Pinky Is a Baby Mouse; Wolf Watch*

**Unit 3 Things That Go:** *I Spy a Freight Train; Wheels Around; This Plane; This Is the Way We Go to School; The Listening Walk; Firehorse Max*

**Unit 4 Our Neighborhood at Work:** *Communities; Night Shift Daddy; My Town; One Afternoon; Career Day; Mommy Works, Daddy Works*

**Unit 5 Weather:** *Snow; Snowballs; Rain; Red Rubber Boot Day; Twister; Snow Is Falling*

**Unit 6 Journeys:** *Rosie's Walk; The Train Ride; Amelia's Fantastic Flight; I'm Not Moving, Mama!; Ferryboat Ride!; The Josefina Story Quilt*

**Unit 7 Keep Trying:** *Flap Your Wings and Try; The Chick and the Duckling; One Duck Stuck; One Fine Day; The Purple Coat; The Story of a Blue Bird*

**Unit 8 Games:** *This Is Baseball; Take Me Out to the Ballgame; What's What? A Guessing Game; Leon and Bob; Moongame; James and the Rain*

**Unit 9 Being Afraid:** *Sheila Rae, the Brave; Henry and Mudge and the Bedtime Thumps; First Day Jitters; Let's Go Home Little Bear; Can't You Sleep, Little Bear?; Feelings*

**Unit 10 Homes:** *My House Mi Casa: A Book in Two Languages; To Market, To Market; The Someday House; Homeplace; The Little House; Livingstone Mouse*

## LEVEL 2

**Unit 1 Sharing Stories:** *Just Like Me; Mouse Tales; The Wednesday Surprise; Dear Annie; Jeremiah Learns to Read; Painted Words*

**Unit 2 Kindness:** *Abe Lincoln's Hat; Jamaica's Find; The Bat in the Boot; The Giving Tree; Uncle Willie and the Soup Kitchen; A Chair for My Mother*

**Unit 3 Look Again:** *The Trek; Who's Hiding Here?; The Mixed-Up Chameleon; A Color of His Own; What Do You Do When Something Wants to Eat You?; Hiding Out*

**Unit 4 Fossils:** *Dinosaur Babies; The Day of the Dinosaur; A Boy Wants a Dinosaur; If the Dinosaurs Came Back; Archaeologists Dig for Clues; How Big Were the Dinosaurs?*

**Unit 5 Courage:** *White Dynamite and Curly Kidd; What's Under My Bed?; Ruth Law Thrills a Nation; Jamaica and the Substitute Teacher; Birdie's Lighthouse; The Buffalo Jump*

**Unit 6 Our Country and Its People:** *Dancing with the Indians; A Picnic in October; Amelia's Road; Dragon Parade; The Lotus Seed; Dumpling Soup*

## LEVEL 3

**Unit 1 Friendship:** *Charlotte's Web; And To Think That We Thought That We'd Never Be Friends; Best Friends; Amigo; The Mountain that Loved a Bird; Alex Is My Friend*

**Unit 2 City Wildlife:** *Wild in the City; Come Back, Salmon: How a Group of Dedicated Kids Adopted Pigeon Creek and Brought It Back to Life; Farewell to Shady Glade; Coyotes in the Crosswalk: True Tales of Animal Life in the Wilds of the City!; City Park; Birds, Nests and Eggs*

**Unit 3 Imagination:** *Behind the Couch; My Life with the Wave; Maria's Comet; Frederick; How I Spent My Summer Vacation; Crocodile's Masterpiece*

**Unit 4 Money:** *Lemonade for Sale; Round and Round the Money Goes; Saturday Sancocho; The Treasure; Our Money; Screen of Frogs*

**Unit 5 Storytelling:** *Tell Me a Story, Mama; The Worry Stone; May'naise Sandwiches & Sunshine Tea; One Grain of Rice; A Storyteller's Story; Firetalking*

**Unit 6 Country Life:** *The Raft; Night in the Country; Mowing; Winter Wheat; A River Ran Wild; Unseen Rainbows, Silent Songs: The World Beyond Human Senses*

| LEVEL 4 | LEVEL 5 | LEVEL 6 |
|---|---|---|

**Unit 1 Risks and Consequences:** *The Big Balloon Race; A Day's Work; Poppy; Sarah, Plain and Tall; The Landry News; From the Mixed-Up Files of Mrs. Basil E. Frankweiler*

**Unit 2 Dollars and Sense:** *Max Malone Makes a Million; What's Cooking, Jenny Archer?; The Toothpaste Millionaire; Brainstorm! The Stories of Twenty American Kid Inventors; Odd Jobs; Better Than a Lemonade Stand!*

**Unit 3 From Mystery to Medicine:** *Germs Make Me Sick!; Pasteur's Fight Against Microbes; Marie Curie and the Discovery of Radium; Kids to the Rescue! First Aid Techniques for Kids; The First Woman Doctor; Fever: 1793*

**Unit 4 Survival:** *Harry the Poisonous Centipede; My Grandmother's Journey; Whichaway; Frozen Fire; Island of the Blue Dolphins; The Voyage of the Frog*

**Unit 5 Communication:** *Prairie Dogs Kiss and Lobsters Wave: How Animals Say Hello; Burton and Stanley; Dear Mr. Henshaw; The Chimpanzee Family Book; The Cat's Elbow and Other Secret Languages; Julie's Wolf Pack*

**Unit 6 A Changing America:** *Sleds on Boston Common: A Story from the American Revolution; The Discovery of the Americas; Stranded at Plimoth Plantation, 1626; . . . If You Traveled West in a Covered Wagon; The Louisiana Purchase; Gold Rush! The Young Prospector's Guide to Striking It Rich*

**Unit 1 Cooperation and Competition:** *The Big Bike Race; The Kid Who Ran For President; The Wheel on the School; Iditarod Dream: Dusty and His Sled Dogs Compete in Alaska's Jr. Iditarod; The View From Saturday; A World in Our Hands: In Honor of the 50th Anniversary of the United Nations*

**Unit 2 Astronomy:** *The Planets; Comets, Meteors, and Asteroids; Adventure in Space: The Flight to Fix the Hubble; The Young Astronomer; Edwin Hubble: American Astronomer; Tales of the Shimmering Sky: Ten Global Folktales with Activities*

**Unit 3 Heritage:** *Appalachia: The Voices of Sleeping Birds; This Land Is My Land; Going Back Home: An Artist Returns to the South; In the Year of the Boar and Jackie Robinson; The Great Ancestor Hunt: The Fun of Finding Out Who You Are; Do People Grow on Family Trees?*

**Unit 4 Making a New Nation:** *Samuel's Choice; Toliver's Secret; Johnny Tremain; A Young Patriot: The American Revolution as Experienced by One Boy; Mr. Revere and I; Come All You Brave Soldiers: Blacks in the Revolutionary War*

**Unit 5 Going West:** *Boom Town; Striking It Rich: The Story of the California Gold Rush; Black-Eyed Susan; By the Great Horn Spoon!; Children of the Wild West; Caddie Woodlawn*

**Unit 6 Journeys and Quests:** *Alicia's Treasure; Grass Sandals: The Travels of Basho; El Güero; Coast to Coast; Orphan Train Rider: One Boy's True Story; Call It Courage*

**Unit 1 Perseverance:** *The Most Beautiful Place in the World; Wilma Unlimited: How Wilma Rudolph Became the World's Fastest Woman; Littlejim's Dreams; The Circuit: Stories from the Life of a Migrant Child; Where the Lilies Bloom; The Wright Brothers: How They Invented the Airplane*

**Unit 2 Ancient Civilizations:** *Androcles and the Lion; Ancient Romans at a Glance; Painters of the Caves; Pyramids!; Dig This! How Archaeologists Uncover Our Past; Religions of the World*

**Unit 3 Taking a Stand:** *Aunt Harriet's Underground Railroad in the Sky; Jane Addams: Pioneer Social Worker; Number the Stars; Run Away Home; Kids at Work: Lewis Hine and the Crusade Against Child Labor; Red Scarf Girl: A Memoir of the Cultural Revolution*

**Unit 4 Beyond the Notes:** *The Jazz Man; A Mouse Called Wolf; Play Me a Story: Nine Tales about Musical Instruments; The Sea King's Daughter: A Russian Legend; Dragonsong; Music*

**Unit 5 Ecology:** *The Great Kapok Tree; Lifetimes; Elephant Woman: Cynthia Moss Explores the World of Elephants; The Missing 'Gator of Gumbo Limbo; Ecology for Every Kid: Easy Activities that Make Learning Science Fun; The Most Beautiful Roof in the World*

**Unit 6 A Question of Value:** *Abuelita's Heart; The Golden Bracelet; Lily's Crossing; The Black Pearl; The Monkey Thief; Wringer*

# Glossary of Reading Terms

This glossary includes linguistic, grammatical, comprehension, and literary terms that may be helpful in understanding reading instruction.

**acronym** a word formed from the initial letter of words in a phrase, **scuba (self-contained underwater breathing apparatus).**

**acrostic** a kind of puzzle in which lines of a poem are arranged so that words or phrases are formed when certain letters from each line are used in a sequence.

**adjective** a word or group of words that modifies a noun.

**adventure story** a narrative that features the unknown or unexpected with elements of excitement, danger, and risk.

**adverb** a word or group of words that modifies a verb, adjective, or other adverb.

**affective domain** the psychological field of emotional activity.

**affix** a word part, either a prefix or a suffix, that changes the meaning or function of a word root or stem.

**affricate** a speech sound that starts as a stop but ends as a fricative, the /ch/ in **catch.**

**agreement** the correspondence of syntactically related words; subjects and predicates are in agreement when both are singular or plural.

**alliteration** the repetition of the initial sounds in neighboring words or stressed syllables.

**alphabet** the complete set of letters representing speech sounds used in writing a language.

**alphabet book** a book for helping young children learn the alphabet by pairing letters with pictures whose sounds they represent.

**alphabetic principle** the principle that there is an association between sounds and the letters that represent them in alphabetic writing systems.

**alveolar** a consonant speech sound made when the tongue and the ridge of the upper and lower jaw stop to constrict the air flow, as /t/.

**anagram** a word or phrase whose letters form other words or phrases when rearranged, for example, **add** and **dad.**

**analogy** a likeness or similarity.

**analytic phonics** also deductive phonics, a whole-to-part approach to phonics in which a student is taught a number of sight words and then phonetic generalizations that can be applied to other words.

**antonym** a word that is opposite in meaning to another word.

**appositive** a word that restates or modifies a preceding noun. For example, **my daughter, Charlotte.**

**aspirate** an unvoiced speech sound produced by a puff of air, as /h/ in **heart.**

**aspirated stop** a stop consonant sound released with a puff of air, as /k/, /p/, and /t/.

**auditory discrimination** the ability to hear phonetic likenesses and differences in phonemes and words.

**author's purpose** the motive or reason for which an author writes, includes to entertain, inform, persuade, and explain how.

**automaticity** fluent processing of information, requiring little effort or attention.

**auxiliary verb** a verb that precedes another verb to express time, mood, or voice, includes verbs such as **has, is, will.**

**ballad** a narrative poem, composed of short verses to be sung or recited, usually containing elements of drama and often tragic in tone.

**base word** a word to which affixes may be added to create related words.

**blank verse** unrhymed verse, especially unrhymed iambic pentameter.

**blend** the joining of the sounds of two or more letters with little change in those sounds, for example /spr/ in **spring,** also **consonant blend** or **consonant cluster.**

**blending** to combine the sounds represented by letters to sound out or pronounce a word, contrast with **oral blending.**

**breve** the symbol placed above a vowel to indicate that it is a short vowel.

**browse** to skim through or look over in search of something of interest.

**canon** in literature, the body of major works that a culture considers important at a given time.

**case** a grammatical category that indicates the syntactic/semantic role of a noun phrase in a sentence.

**cause-effect relationship** a stated or implied association between an outcome and the conditions that brought it about, also the comprehension skill associated with recognizing this type of relationship as an organizing principle in text.

**chapter book** a book long enough to be divided into chapters, but not long or complex enough to be considered a novel.

**characterization** the way in which an author presents a character in a story, including describing words, actions, thoughts, and impressions of that character.

**choral reading** oral group reading to develop oral fluency by modeling.

**cinquain** a stanza of five lines, specifically one that has successive lines of two, four, six, eight, and two syllables.

**cipher** a system for writing in code.

**clarifying** a comprehension strategy in which the reader rereads text, uses a dictionary, uses decoding skills, or uses context clues to comprehend something that is unclear.

**clause** a group of words with a subject and a predicate used to form a part of or a whole sentence, a dependent clause modifies an independent clause, which can stand alone as a complete sentence.

**collaborative learning** learning by working together in small groups.

**command** a sentence that asks for action and usually ends with a period.

**common noun** in contrast to **proper noun**, a noun that denotes a class rather than a unique or specific thing.

**comprehension** the understanding of what is written or said.

**comprehension skill** a skill that aids in understanding text, including identifying **author's purpose, comprehending cause and effect relationships, comparing and contrasting** items and events, **drawing conclusions,** distinguishing **fact from opinion,** identifying **main ideas,** making **inferences,** distinguishing **reality from fantasy,** and understanding **sequence.**

**comprehension strategy** a sequence of steps for understanding text, includes asking questions, clarifying, making connections, predicting, summarizing, and visualizing.

**conjugation** the complete set of all possible inflected forms of a verb.

**conjunction** a part of speech used to connect words, phrases, clauses, or sentences, including the words **and, but, or.**

**consonant** a speech sound, and the alphabet letter that represents that sound, made by partial or complete closure of part of the vocal tract, which obstructs air flow and causes audible friction.

**context clue** information from the immediate text that helps identify a word.

**contraction** a short version of a written or spoken expression in which letters are omitted, for example, **can't.**

**convention** an accepted practice in spoken or written language, usually referring to spelling, mechanics, or grammar rules.

**cooperative learning** a classroom organization that allows students to work together to achieve their individual goals.

**creative writing** prose and poetic forms of writing that express the writer's thoughts and feelings imaginatively.

**cuing system** any of the various sources of information that help to identify an unrecognizable word in reading, including phonetic, semantic, and syntactical information.

**cumulative tale** a story, such as The Gingerbread Man, in which details are repeated until the climax.

**dangling modifier** usually a participle that because of its placement in a sentence modifies the wrong object.

**decodable text** text materials controlled to include a majority of words whose sound/spelling relationships are known by the reader.

**decode** to analyze spoken or graphic symbols for meaning.

**diacritical mark** a mark, such as a breve or macron, added to a letter or graphic character, to indicate a specific pronunciation.

**dialect**  a regional variety of a particular language with phonological, grammatical, and lexical patterns that distinguish it from other varieties.

**dialogue**  a piece of writing written as conversation, usually punctuated by quotation marks.

**digraph**  two letters that represent one speech sound, for example /sh/ or /ch/.

**diphthong**  a vowel sound produced when the tongue glides from one vowel sound toward another in the same syllable, for example /oi/ or /ou/.

**direct object**  the person or thing that receives the action of a verb in a sentence, for example, the word **cake** in this sentence: **Madeline baked a cake**.

**drafting**  the process of writing ideas in rough form to record them.

**drama**  a story in the form of a play, written to be performed.

**edit**  in the writing process, to revise or correct a manuscript.

**emergent literacy**  the development of the association of meaning and print that continues until a child reaches the stage of conventional reading and writing.

**emergent reading**  a child's early interaction with books and print before the ability to decode text.

**encode**  to change a message into symbols, for example, to change speech into writing.

**epic**  a long narrative poem, usually about a hero.

**exclamatory sentence**  a sentence that shows strong emotion and ends with an exclamation mark.

**expository writing** or **exposition**  a composition in writing that explains an event or process.

**fable**  a short tale that teaches a moral.

**fantasy**  a highly imaginative story about characters, places, and events that do not exist.

**fiction**  imaginative narrative designed to entertain rather than to explain, persuade, or describe.

**figure of speech**  the expressive, nonliteral use of language usually through metaphor, simile, or personification.

**fluency**  freedom from word-identification problems that hinder comprehension in reading.

**folktale**  a narrative form of genre such as an epic, myth, or fable that is well-known through repeated storytellings.

**foreshadowing**  giving clues to upcoming events in a story.

**free verse**  verse with irregular metrical pattern.

**freewriting**  writing that is not limited in form, style, content, or purpose, designed to encourage students to write.

**genre**  a classification of literary works, including tragedy, comedy, novel, essay, short story, mystery, realistic fiction, poetry.

**grammar**  the study of the classes of words, their inflections, and their functions and relations in sentences; includes phonological, morphological, syntactic, and semantic descriptions of a language.

**grapheme**  a written or printed representation of a phoneme, such as **c** for /k/.

**guided reading**  reading instruction in which the teacher provides the structure and purpose for reading and responding to the material read.

**handing off**  a method of turning over to the students the primary responsibility for controlling discussion.

**indirect object**  in a sentence, the person or thing to or for whom an action is done, for example, the word **dog** in this sentence: **Madeline gave the dog a treat**.

**inference**  a conclusion based on facts, data, or evidence.

**infinitive**  the base form of a verb, usually with the infinitive marker, for example, **to go**.

**inflectional ending**  an ending that expresses a plural or possessive form of a noun, the tense of a verb, or the comparative or superlative form of an adjective or adverb.

**interrogative word**  a word that marks a clause or sentence as a question, including **interrogative pronouns who**, **what**, **which**, **where**.

**intervention**  a strategy or program designed to supplement or substitute instruction, especially for those students who fall behind.

**invented spelling**  the result of an attempt to spell a word based on the writer's knowledge of the spelling system and how it works, often with overemphasis on sound/symbol relationships.

**irony**  a figure of speech in which the literal meaning of the words is the opposite of their intended meaning.

**journal**  a written record of daily events or responses.

**juvenile book**  a book written for children or adolescents.

**legend**  a traditional tale handed down from generation to generation.

**leitmotif**  a repeated expression, event, or idea used to unify a work of art such as writing.

**letter**  one of a set of graphic symbols that forms an alphabet and is used alone or in combination to represent a phoneme, also **grapheme**.

**linguistics**  the study of the nature and structure of language and communication.

**literary elements**  the elements of a story such as **setting**, **plot**, and **characterization** that create the structure of a narrative.

**macron**  a diacritical mark placed above a vowel to indicate a long vowel sound.

**main idea**  the central thought or chief topic of a passage.

**mechanics**  the conventions of capitalization and punctuation.

**metacognition**  awareness and knowledge of one's mental processes or thinking about what one is thinking about.

**metaphor**  a figure of speech in which a comparison is implied but not stated, for example, **She is a jewel**.

**miscue**  a deviation from text during oral reading in an attempt to make sense of the text.

**modeling**  an instructional technique in which the teacher serves as an example of behavior.

**mood**  the literary element that conveys the emotional atmosphere of a story.

**morpheme**  a meaningful linguistic unit that cannot be divided into smaller units, for example, **word**; **a bound morpheme** is a morpheme that cannot stand alone as an independent word, for example, the prefix **re-**; **a free morpheme** can stand alone, for example, **dog**.

**myth**  a story designed to explain the mysteries of life.

**narrative writing** or **narration**  a composition in writing that tells a story or gives an account of an event.

**nonfiction**  prose designed to explain, argue, or describe rather than to entertain with a factual emphasis, includes biography and autobiography.

**noun**  a part of speech that denotes persons, places, things, qualities, or acts.

**novel**  an extended fictional prose narration.

**onomatopoeia**  the use of a word whose sound suggests its meaning, for example, **purr**.

**oral blending**  the ability to fuse discrete phonemes into recognizable words; oral blending puts sounds together to make a word, **see also segmentation**.

**orthography**  correct or standardized spelling according to established usage in a language.

**oxymoron**  a figure of speech in which contrasting or contradictory words are brought together for emphasis.

**paragraph**  a subdivision of a written composition that consists of one or more sentences, deals with one point, or gives the words of one speaker, usually beginning with an indented line.

**participle**  a verb form used as an adjective, for example, **the skating party**.

**personification**  a figure of speech in which animals, ideas, or things take on human characteristics.

**persuasive writing**  a composition intended to persuade the reader to adopt the writer's point of view.

**phoneme**  the smallest sound unit of speech, for example, the /k/ in **book**.

**phonemic awareness**  the ability to recognize that spoken words are made up of discrete sounds and that those sounds can be manipulated.

## Glossary of Reading Terms (continued)

**phonetic spelling** the respelling of entry words in a dictionary according to a pronunciation key.

**phonetics** the study of speech sounds.

**phonics** a way of teaching reading that addresses sound/symbol relationships, especially in beginning instruction.

**phonogram** a letter or symbol that represents a phonetic sound.

**plot** the literary element that provides the structure of the action of a story, which may include rising action, climax, and falling action leading to a resolution or denouement.

**plural** a grammatical form of a word that refers to more than one in number; an **irregular plural** is one that does not follow normal patterns for inflectional endings.

**poetic license** the liberty taken by writers to ignore conventions.

**poetry** a metrical form of composition in which language is chosen and arranged to create a powerful response through meaning, sound, or rhythm.

**possessive** showing ownership either through the use of an adjective, an adjectival pronoun, or the possessive form of a noun.

**predicate** the part of the sentence that expresses something about the subject and includes the verb phrase; a **complete predicate** includes the principal verb in a sentence and all its modifiers or subordinate parts.

**predicting** a comprehension strategy in which the reader attempts to figure out what will happen and then confirms predictions as the text is read.

**prefix** an affix attached before a base word that changes the meaning of the word.

**preposition** a part of speech in the class of function words, such as **of**, **on**, **at**, that precede noun phrases to create prepositional phrases.

**prewriting** the planning stage of the writing process in which the writer formulates ideas, gathers information, and considers ways to organize them.

**print awareness** in emergent literacy, a child's growing recognition of conventions and characteristics of written language, including reading from left to right and top to bottom in English, and that words are separated by spaces.

**pronoun** a part of speech used as a substitute for a noun or noun phrase.

**proofreading** the act of reading with the intent to correct, clarify, or improve text.

**pseudonym** an assumed name used by an author, a pen name or nom de plume.

**publishing** the process of preparing written material for presentation.

**punctuation** graphic marks such as comma, period, quotation marks, and brackets used to clarify meaning and give speech characteristics to written language.

**question** an interrogative sentence that asks a question and ends with a question mark.

**realistic fiction** a story that attempts to portray characters and events as they actually are.

**rebus** the use of a picture or symbol to suggest a word or syllable.

**revise** in the writing process, to change or correct a manuscript to make its message more clear.

**rhyme** identical or very similar recurring final sounds in words, often at the ends of lines of poetry.

**rime** a vowel and any following consonants of a syllable.

**segmentation** the ability to break words into individual sounds; **see also oral blending**.

**semantic mapping** a graphic display of a group of words that are meaningfully related to support vocabulary instruction.

**semantics** the study of meaning in language, including the meanings of words, phrases, sentences, and texts.

**sentence** a grammatical unit that expresses a statement, question, or command; a **simple sentence** is a sentence with one subject and one predicate; a **compound sentence** is a sentence with two or more independent clauses usually separated by a comma and conjunction, but no dependent clause; a **complex sentence** is a sentence with one independent and one or more dependent clauses.

**sentence combining** a teaching technique in which complex sentence chunks and paragraphs are built from basic sentences.

**sentence lifting** the process of using sentences from children's writing to illustrate what is wrong or right to develop children's editing and proofreading skills.

**sequence** the order of elements or events.

**setting** the literary element that includes the time, place, and physical and psychological background in which a story takes place.

**sight word** a word that is taught to be read as a whole word, usually words that are phonetically irregular.

**simile** a figure of speech in which a comparison of two things that are unlike is directly stated usually with the words **like** or **as**, for example, **She is like a jewel**.

**spelling** the process of representing language by means of a writing system.

**statement** a sentence that tells something and ends with a period.

**study skills** a general term for the techniques and strategies that help readers comprehend text with the intent to remember, includes following directions, organizing, locating, and using graphic aids.

**style** the characteristics of a work that reflect the author's particular way of writing.

**subject** the main topic of a sentence to which a predicate refers, including the principal noun; a **complete subject** includes the principal noun in a sentence and all its modifiers.

**suffix** an affix attached at the end of a base word that changes the meaning of the word.

**summarizing** a comprehension strategy in which the reader constructs a brief statement that contains the essential ideas of a passage.

**syllable** a minimal unit of sequential speech sounds comprised of a vowel sound or a vowel-sound combination.

**symbolism** the use of one thing to represent something else in order to represent an idea in a concrete way.

**synonym** a word that means the same as another word.

**syntax** the grammatical pattern or structure of word order in sentences, clauses, and phrases.

**tense** the way in which verbs indicate past, present, and future time of action.

**text structure** the various patterns of ideas that are built into the organization of a written work.

**theme** a major idea or proposition that provides an organizing concept through which by study, students gain depth of understanding.

**topic sentence** a sentence intended to express the main idea of a paragraph or passage.

**tragedy** a literary work, often a play, in which the main character suffers conflicts and which presents a serious theme and has an unfortunate ending.

**usage** the way in which a native language or dialect is used by the members of the community.

**verb** a word that expresses an action or state that occurs in a predicate of a sentence; an **irregular verb** is a verb that does not follow normal patterns of inflectional endings that reflect past, present, or future verb tense.

**visualizing** a comprehension strategy in which the reader constructs a mental picture of a character, setting, or process.

**vowel** a voiced speech sound and the alphabet letter that represents that sound, made without stoppage or friction of the air flow as it passes through the vocal tract.

**vowel digraph** a spelling pattern in which two or more letters represent a single vowel sound.

**word calling** proficiency in decoding with little or no attention to word meaning.

**writing** also **composition** the process or result of organizing ideas in writing to form a clear message, includes persuasive, expository, narrative, and descriptive forms.

**writing process** the many aspects of the complex act of producing a piece of writing, including prewriting, drafting, revising, proofreading, and publishing.

*Open Court Reading* develops handwriting skills through weekly Penmanship lessons. The instruction for these lessons appears in the Language Arts part of the lesson in every grade level. The purpose of these lessons is to develop important handwriting skills necessary for producing legible, properly spaced documents. Penmanship practice reinforces the vocabulary in the lesson selection.

In addition to the board, the overhead projector can be a very effective device for teaching penmanship. Students can move their pencils at the same time the teacher forms letters on the transparency. It also helps to recite the descriptions or chants that go with each letter.

## Penmanship in Levels K to 2

Beginning in kindergarten, the Penmanship lessons expand on the sound/spelling instruction by introducing letters the students study in Sounds and Letters. Students learn that those letters are made of four basic lines: curved lines, horizontal lines, vertical lines, and slanted lines.

Next, students learn letter and number formation. The students practice letter formation by writing the letter being studied and then words from the literature selection that contain the particular letter. This instruction continues in Level 1 and is tied to the letter formation instruction in Phonics and Fluency.

## Cursive Handwriting Models

Penmanship is developed and practiced through Level 6, with cursive instruction beginning in the final unit of Level 2. Students are taught that most cursive letters are comprised of four strokes: undercurve, downcurve, overcurve, and slanted lines. These lessons teach students the essentials of cursive handwriting, such as proper slant; loops; joining; and spacing between letters, words, and sentences. As in the earlier levels, the students practice letter formation by writing the letters in the Writer's Notebook and then words from the literature selection that contain the particular letter.

The writing exercises progress with each level. Students begin writing words in kindergarten and graduate to writing sentences by the end of Level 1 and into Level 2. Level 3 eases students into cursive by having them practice words from the literature, with a transition to sentences in Level 4, and paragraphs in Levels 5 and 6.

## Hand and Paper Positioning

The **hand and paper positioning** models are for teachers' reference and enhance the written instruction of positioning lessons. The diagrams give teachers a visual aid so that they may better understand and demonstrate an effective technique of positioning.

A right-handed student should hold the pencil loosely about one inch above the point, between the thumb and middle finger. A left-handed student should hold the pencil the same way, but up to one half inch farther away from the point. The index fingers of both writers should rest lightly on the top of the pencil. The wrist should be level and just slightly raised from the desk.

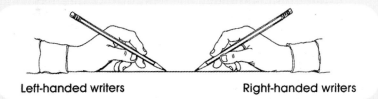

Left-handed writers        Right-handed writers

For both kinds of writers, the paper should lie straight in front of the student with the edges parallel to the edges of the desk. A left-handed writer may find it easier to slant the paper slightly to the right and parallel to the left forearm. A right-handed writer's writing hand should be kept well below the writing. The left hand should hold down the paper.

Left-handed writers        Right-handed writers

### Penmanship (continued)

## Cursive Handwriting Models

The models of cursive handwriting provide teachers with a systematic method for teaching students to form uppercase and lowercase letters of the alphabet. The dots on the letters indicate starting points for the students. The numbered arrows show the students in what order and what direction the line should go to form the particular letter. Teachers may use the chants to describe the letter step by step as he or she models the formation on the board. Students may also say the chants in unison as they practice the formation, whether they are writing the letter or tracing it on the board.

The four basic cursive strokes diagram aids teachers by giving examples of the strokes that recur frequently in cursive handwriting. Students can form most cursive letters by using one or more of these strokes. The letters in the Penmanship lessons are grouped according to the strokes particular to each letter.

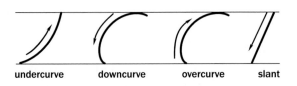

undercurve     downcurve     overcurve     slant

## Undercurve letters

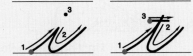  

**i**   Starting point, undercurve
Slant down, undercurve to endpoint, dot exactly above: small *i*

**t**   Starting point, undercurve
Slant down, undercurve to endpoint
Starting point, straight across: small *t*

**u**   Starting point, undercurve
Slant down, undercurve
Slant down, undercurve: small *u*

**w**   Starting point, undercurve
Slant down, undercurve, slant down, undercurve, small curve to right: small *w*

**r**   Starting point, undercurve
Slant right
Slant down, undercurve: small *r*

**s**   Starting point, undercurve
Curve down and back, undercurve: small *s*

## Downcurve letters

**p**   Starting point, undercurve
Slant, loop back
Overcurve
Curve back, undercurve: small *p*

**j**   Starting point, undercurve
Slant down
Loop back
Overcurve to endpoint
Dot exactly above: small *j*

**a**   Starting point, downcurve
Undercurve to starting point
Slant down, undercurve: small *a*

**c**   Starting point, downcurve
Undercurve: small *c*

**d**   Starting point, downcurve
Undercurve past starting point
Slant down, undercurve: small *d*

**q**   Starting point, downcurve
Undercurve to starting point
Slant down and loop forward, undercurve:
small *q*

**g**   Starting point, downcurve
Undercurve to starting point
Slant down and loop back, overcurve: small *g*

**o**   Starting point, downcurve
Undercurve
Small curve to right: small *o*

## Cursive Handwriting Models

### Overcurve letters

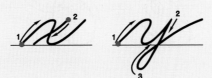

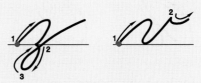

**n** Starting point, overcurve
Slant down, overcurve
Slant down, undercurve: small *n*

**m** Starting point, overcurve
Slant down, overcurve
Slant down, overcurve
Slant down, undercurve: small *m*

**x** Starting point, overcurve
Slant down, undercurve to endpoint
Starting point slant down: small *x*

**y** Starting point, overcurve
Slant down
Undercurve, slant down
Loop back into overcurve: small *y*

**z** Starting point, overcurve
Slant down, overcurve, down
Loop into overcurve: small *z*

**v** Starting point, overcurve
Slant down
Undercurve
Small curve to right: small *v*

### Letters with loops

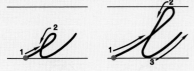

**e** Starting point, undercurve
Loop back, slant down
Undercurve: small *e*

**l** Starting point, undercurve
Loop back, slant down
Undercurve: small *l*

**h** Starting point, undercurve
Loop back, slant down
Overcurve, slant down
Undercurve: small *h*

**k** Starting point, undercurve
Loop back, slant down
Overcurve, curve forward and under
Slant down, undercurve: small *k*

**f** Starting point, undercurve
Loop back, slant down
Loop forward into undercurve: small *f*

**b** Starting point, undercurve
Loop back, slant down
Undercurve, small curve to right:
small *b*

## Penmanship (continued)

## Cursive Handwriting Models

### Downcurve letters

**A** Starting point, downcurve
Undercurve to starting point
Slant down, undercurve: capital *A*

**C** Starting point, loop
Downcurve, undercurve: capital *C*

**E** Starting point, loop
Downcurve
Loop back, downcurve
Undercurve: capital *E*

**O** Starting point, downcurve
left into undercurve
Loop and curve right: capital *O*

### Curve forward letters

**N** Starting point, loop
Curve forward
Slant down
Retrace up slant
Overcurve down into undercurve:
capital *N*

**M** Starting point, loop
Curve forward, slant down
Retrace up slant, overcurve
Slant down, retrace up slant
Overcurve down into undercurve:
capital *M*

### Curve forward letters

**K** Starting point, loop
Curve forward, slant down to end point
Starting point
Doublecurve back to slant
Curve forward
Undercurve up: capital *K*

**H** Starting point, loop
Curve forward, slant down to end point
Starting point
Curve back and slant down
Retrace up slant, loop left and
curve right: capital *H*

**U** Starting point, loop
Curve forward, slant down into
undercurve
Slant down, undercurve: capital *U*

**Y** Starting point, loop
Curve forward, slant down
Undercurve up, slant down
Loop back, overcurve: capital *Y*

**Z** Starting point, loop
Curve forward, slant down
Overcurve, curve down
Loop into overcurve: capital *Z*

**V** Starting point, loop
Curve forward and slant down,
undercurve up and overcurve:
capital *V*

## Cursive Handwriting Models

### Doublecurve letters

### Overcurve letters

   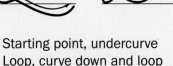

**X** Starting point, loop
Curve forward, slant down
Undercurve to end point
Starting point, slant down: capital X

**W** Starting point, loop
Curve forward, slant down into undercurve
Slant down into undercurve
Overcurve: capital W

**F** Starting point, loop
Curve forward and right to endpoint
Starting point
Doublecurve, curve up
Curve right, slant down: capital F

**T** Starting point, loop
Curve forward to endpoint
Starting point
Doublecurve, curve up
Curve right: capital T

**I** Starting point, overcurve
Curve down and up
Curve right: capital I

**J** Starting point, overcurve
Slant down and loop back
Overcurve: capital J

### Letters with loops

**Q** Starting point, loop
Curve forward, slant down
Loop back, curve under: capital Q

**G** Starting point, undercurve
Loop, curve up
Double curve, curve up
Curve right: capital G

**S** Starting point, undercurve
Loop, curve down and up
Curve right: capital S

**L** Starting point, undercurve
Loop, curve down and loop
Curve under: capital L

**D** Starting point, slant down
Loop, curve down and up
Loop and curve right: capital D

### Undercurve-slant letters

**P** Starting point, undercurve
Slant down, retrace up
Curve forward and back: capital P

**R** Starting point, undercurve
Slant down, retrace up
Curve forward to slant
Curve forward
Undercurve: capital R

**B** Starting point, undercurve
Slant down, retrace up
Curve forward, loop
Curve forward and back
Curve right: capital B

## Penmanship (continued)

### Numbers

**1** Starting point, straight down: *1*

**2** Starting point, around right, slanting left and straight across right: *2*

**3** Starting point, around right, in at the middle, around right: *3*

**4** Starting point, straight down
Straight across right
Starting point, straight down, crossing line: *4*

**5** Starting point, curving around right and up
Starting point, straight across right: *5*

**6** Starting point, slanting left, around the bottom curving up around right and into the curve: *6*

**7** Starting point, straight across right, slanting down left: *7*

**8** Starting point, curving left, curving down and around right, slanting up right to starting point: *8*

**9** Starting point, curving around left all the way, straight down: *9*

**10** Starting point, straight down
Starting point, curving left all the way around to starting point: *10*

**!** Starting point, straight down
Dot exactly below: exclamation point

**?** Starting point, curving around right, straight down
Dot exactly below: question mark

# Introduction to Sounds

| LESSON | PHONICS SKILLS | DECODABLE BOOKS |
|---|---|---|
| **Getting Started** | | |
| **DAY 1** | review /ā/ spellings; review /ē/ spellings | 1 Dave the Brave<br>2 Sleepy Steve |
| **DAY 2** | review /ī/ spellings; review /ō/ spellings | 3 The Shy Bird's Trick<br>4 Chinlow of Singboat |
| **DAY 3** | review /ū/ spellings; review /aw/ spelled *au_, aw* | 5 Mrs. Music<br>6 Paul, Aunt Maud,<br>and Claude |
| **DAY 4** | review /ow/ spelled *ou_, ow;* review /oi/ spelled *oi, _oy* | 7 Flower the Cow<br>8 Toy Store Explorer |
| **DAY 5** | review /o͞o/ spelled *oo;* review /o͞o/ spelled *u, u_e, _ew, _ue, oo* | 9 A Book for Mr. Hook<br>10 Root Stew |
| **Unit 1** | | |
| **LESSON 1** | /ī/ spelled *i_e, _y, igh;* endings *-ed, -ing, -s, -ful, -er;* review /ā/;<br>review short vowels | 11 The Frog Who<br>Wanted to Fly |
| **LESSON 2** | plural *–s;* inflectional endings; homographs; comparative and superlative<br>adjectives; /e/ spelled *e;* special spelling pattern /m/ spelled *mb;* /e/ spelled *ea;*<br>review short vowel;cvc – closed syllables | 12 Up to Bat |
| **LESSON 3** | antonyms; homophones; prefix *re-;* related words; review /ī/;<br>/ā/ spelled *a, ai_, a_e, _ay* | 13 Baking Princess |
| **LESSON 4** | suffixes *-ly, -ed, -ing;* contractions; /ō/; /ē/ spelled *e, ea, e_e, _y, ee, _ie_* | 14 City Girl |
| **LESSON 5** | suffix *-tion;* prefixes and suffixes; frequently misspelled words;<br>plural forms of nouns that end in *y;* /ū/ spellings; /ī/ spelled *i, _y, i_e, _ie, igh* | 15 The Prince's Foolish Wish |
| **LESSON 6** | inflectional endings and suffixes added to base words; /k/ spelled *c;* nouns;<br>review short vowels; /ō/ spelled *o, _ow, o_e, oa_, _oe* | 16 Rose, the Brave |
| **Unit 2** | | |
| **LESSON 1** | antonyms; synonyms; compound words; suffix *-y;* prefix *un-;*<br>spelling patterns /ar/ and *air;* review /ū/ spelled *u, u_e, _ue, _ew* | 17 Hugo Bugle |
| **LESSON 2** | compound words; homophones; suffix *-tion;* suffix *-ly;* /er/ spelled *ur* and *ir;*<br>/or/ spelled *or* and *ore;* review long vowels with open syllables | 18 Queen Kit |
| **LESSON 3** | word families; synonyms; /əl/ spelled *-le;* open syllables with vowel digraphs | 19 Dead as a Dodo,<br>Bald as an Eagle |
| **LESSON 4** | compound words; related words; vivid verbs; /ow/ spelled *ou_* and *ow;*<br>open syllables - vcv; closed syllables; multisyllabic words with long vowels;<br>/s/ spelled *s, ce, ci_;* special spelling pattern: /s/ spelled *sc* | 20 The Lives of Sea Turtles |
| **LESSON 5** | contractions; suffixes *-ly, -ing;* prefix *un-;* /oi/ spelled *oi* and *_oy;*<br>multisyllabic words with long and short vowels ending *-le* | 21 Nesting and Burrowing<br>Birds |
| **LESSON 6** | compound words; suffix *-ed;* antonyms; vivid verbs; /əl/; /ow/; /oi/; /er/;<br>multisyllabic words with long and short vowels | 22 Loop and Hook a Dream |

## Introduction to Sounds (continued)

**LEVEL APPENDIX**

| LESSON | PHONICS SKILLS | DECODABLE BOOKS |
|--------|----------------|-----------------|
| **Unit 3** | | |
| LESSON 1 | compound words; homophones; related words; /c/ spelled *s, ce, ci_;* /ā/ spelled *a, a_e, ai_, ay_;* review multisyllabic words with long and short vowels; special spelling patterns /n/ spelled *n, kn_,* and *gn_;* /m/ spelled *mb;* /g/ spelled *gh;* /l/ spelled *sl;* word families with spelling changes | 23 Sweet and Sour Soup |
| LESSON 2 | suffixes *-ful, -ly, -ing;* contractions; irregular past tense verbs; /ē/ spelled *ea, ee;* review diphthongs; /r/ spelled *er, ir, ur, ar;* /ə/ spelled *o* | 24 No Noise! |
| LESSON 3 | base words with suffixes; compound words; comparatives and superlatives (-er/-est); related words; /ī/ spelled *i_e, igh;* review diphthongs; suffixes *-ing, -ly, -er, -est* | 25 Summer Pen Pals |
| LESSON 4 | cardinal and ordinal numbers; suffixes; comparative and superlative endings *-er, -est;* /ō/ spelled *o* and *o_e;* diphthongs; prefixes *un-, re-, pre-, bi-, mis-, dis-* | 26 Joyce Writes a Good Story |
| LESSON 5 | prefixes and suffixes; /o͞o/ spelled *u_e, _ew;* diphthongs | 27 Little Hare |
| LESSON 6 | suffix *-ed;* comparatives; plural forms of words that end in *f;* homographs; related words; review long vowels; affixes as syllables | 28 Ralph, a Bug |
| **Unit 4** | | |
| LESSON 1 | homophones; base words and suffixes *-ed, -ment, -tion, -sion;* word families; double consonants | 29 Kitty and the Nothing Day |
| LESSON 2 | synonyms; base words with suffixes *-ly, -able;* final double consonants | 30 Traveling Star |
| LESSON 3 | compound words; /ā/ spelled *a_e, ai_, _ay;* contractions; base words with affixes; base words with suffixes: *-ful, -er, -tation* | 31 Whales |
| LESSON 4 | base words with suffixes *-ful, -ly, -ed, -ing;* /ē/ spelled *_ie_, ei* | 32 The Stone Wall |
| LESSON 5 | compound words; suffixes *-ed, -ing, -ial;* plural endings *-s* and *-es* | 33 Say It in Code |
| LESSON 6 | suffix *-ment;* antonyms; related words; special spelling patterns: *nk,* /t/ spelled *bt,* /n/ spelled *gn;* compound words | 34 Peace and Quiet |
| LESSON 7 | compound words; suffixes *-ment, -tion, -sion* | 35 School Days Long Ago |

## Introduction to Sounds (continued)

| LESSON | PHONICS SKILLS | DECODABLE BOOKS |
|---|---|---|
| **Unit 5** | | |
| **LESSON 1** | synonyms; hard *g*; /ā/ spelled *eigh*, consonant blends | |
| **LESSON 2** | antonyms; base words with suffixes -*ed*, -*able*, -*ation*, -*ative*; prefix *re*-; spellings *wr_*, *kn_*, *wh* | |
| **LESSON 3** | compound words; /wh/ spelled *wh*-; base words and suffix -*ness*; silent *l* in *lf*; /ch/ spelled ■*tch*; silent *g* in *gn* | |
| **LESSON 4** | homographs; /k/ spelled *c*, *k*, ■*ck*; base words with suffixes -*tion*, -*sion*; /ə/ | |
| **LESSON 5** | base words with prefixes and suffixes; /ā/ and /ī/; suffix -*ed*; /ē/ spelled _*ie*; /kw/ spelled *qu* | |
| **LESSON 6** | base words with prefix *be*-, *re*-; compound words; /s/ spelled *s* and *ce* and *ci_*; /j/ spelled *ge* | |
| **LESSON 7** | base words with suffixes -*ed*, -*ing*, -*y*, -*es*; review spelling patterns | |
| **Unit 6** | | |
| **LESSON 1** | vivid verbs; base words with suffixes -*ible* and -*ness*; irregular plurals | |
| **LESSON 2** | short vowel base words ending in -*tch* and the suffix -*ed*; long vowel base words ending in silent *e* with the suffix -*ing*; compound words; double consonants ending with -*y* | |
| **LESSON 3** | comparatives and superlatives; vivid verbs and adjectives; homophones; /f/ spelled *lf*; /m/ spelled *lm*; words ending in suffixes -*er*, -*est* | |
| **LESSON 4** | compound words; base words with the prefix *auto*-; plural words; Latin roots | |
| **LESSON 5** | compound words; prefix *un*-; suffix -*less*; Greek roots | |
| **LESSON 6** | compound words; suffix -*est*; prefix *re*-; French, Spanish, and German roots | |
| **LESSON 7** | contractions; vivid adjectives; irregular plurals | |

**L E V E L   A P P E N D I X**

# High-Frequency Word List

| | | | | | |
|---|---|---|---|---|---|
| a | cold | grow | may | said | too |
| about | come | had | me | saw | try |
| after | could | has | much | say | two |
| again | cut | have | must | see | under |
| all | did | he | my | seven | up |
| always | do | help | myself | shall | upon |
| am | does | her | never | she | us |
| an | done | here | new | show | use |
| and | don't | him | no | sing | very |
| any | down | his | not | sit | walk |
| are | draw | hold | now | six | want |
| around | drink | hot | of | sleep | warm |
| as | eat | how | off | small | was |
| ask | eight | hurt | old | so | wash |
| at | every | I | on | some | we |
| ate | fall | if | once | soon | well |
| away | far | in | one | start | went |
| be | fast | into | only | stop | were |
| because | find | is | open | take | what |
| been | first | it | or | tell | when |
| before | five | its | our | ten | where |
| best | fly | jump | out | thank | which |
| better | for | just | over | that | white |
| big | found | keep | own | the | who |
| black | four | kind | pick | their | why |
| blue | from | know | play | them | will |
| both | full | laugh | please | then | wish |
| bring | funny | let | pretty | there | with |
| brown | gave | light | pull | these | work |
| but | get | like | put | they | would |
| buy | give | little | ran | think | write |
| by | go | live | read | this | yellow |
| call | goes | long | red | those | yes |
| came | going | look | ride | three | you |
| can | good | made | right | to | your |
| carry | got | make | round | today | |
| clean | green | many | run | together | |

# Sound/Spelling Card Stories

## Card 1: /a/ Lamb

I'm Pam the Lamb, I am.
This is how I tell my Mommy where
    I am: /a/ /a/ /a/ /a/ /a/.

I'm Pam the Lamb, I am.
This is how I tell my Daddy where I
    am: /a/ /a/ /a/ /a/ /a/.

I'm Pam the Lamb, I am.
That young ram is my brother Sam.
This is how I tell my brother where
    I am: /a/ /a/ /a/ /a/ /a/.

I'm Pam the Lamb; I'm happy where
    I am.
Can you help me tell my family where
    I am? *(Have the children respond.)* /a/ /a/ /a/ /a/ /a/

## Card 2: /b/ Ball

Bobby loved to bounce his basketball.
He bounced it all day long.
This is the sound the ball made:
    /b/ /b/ /b/ /b/ /b/.

One day, while Bobby was bouncing
    his basketball,
Bonnie came by on her bike.

Bonnie said, "Hi, Bobby. I have a little
    bitty ball.
May I bounce my ball with you?"

Bobby said, "Sure!" and Bonnie
    bounced her little bitty ball.
What sound do you think Bonnie's ball
    made?
*(Encourage a very soft reply.)* /b/ /b/ /b/ /b/ /b/

Soon Betsy came by. "Hi, Bobby. Hi, Bonnie," she said.
"I have a great big beach ball. May I bounce my ball with you?"

Bobby and Bonnie said, "Sure!" and Betsy bounced her
    big beach ball.
What sound do you think the beach ball made?
*(Encourage a louder, slower reply.)* /b/ /b/ /b/ /b/ /b/

*(Designate three groups, one for each ball sound.)*
Now when Bobby, Bonnie, and Betsy bounce their balls
    together, this is the sound you hear:
*(Have all three groups make their sounds in a chorus.)*
    /b/ /b/ /b/ /b/ /b/

## Card 3: /k/ Camera

Carlos has a new camera. When he
    takes pictures, his camera makes a
    clicking sound like this:
    /k/ /k/ /k/ /k/ /k/.

In the garden, Carlos takes pictures of
    caterpillars crawling on cabbage:
    /k/ /k/ /k/ /k/ /k/.
At the zoo, Carlos takes pictures of a
    camel, a duck, and a kangaroo:
    /k/ /k/ /k/.
In the park, Carlos takes pictures of his
    cousin flying a kite: /k/ /k/ /k/ /k/ /k/.
In his room, Carlos takes pictures of his
    cute kitten, Cozy: /k/ /k/ /k/ /k/ /k/.

Can you help Carlos take pictures with his camera?
*(Have the children join in.)* /k/ /k/ /k/ /k/ /k/ /k/ /k/

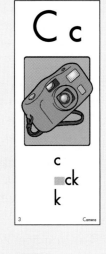

## Card 4: /d/ Dinosaur

Dinah the Dinosaur loves to dance.
She dances whenever she gets the chance.
Whenever that dinosaur dips and whirls,
This is the sound of her dancing twirls:
/d/ /d/ /d/ /d/ /d/ /d/!

Dinah the Dinosaur dances all day.
From dawn to dark, she dances away.
And when Dinah dances, her dinosaur feet
make a thundering, thudding, extremely
    loud beat:
*(loudly, with an exaggerated rhythm)*
/d/ /d/ /d/ /d/ /d/ /d/!

Now if you were a dinosaur just like Dinah,
you would certainly dance just as finely as she.
And if you were a Dino, and you had a chance,
what sound would your feet make when you did a dance?
*(Have the children join in.)* /d/ /d/ /d/ /d/ /d/ /d/

## Sound/Spelling Card Stories (continued)

### Card 5: /e/ Hen

Jem's pet hen likes to peck, peck, peck.
She pecks at a speck on the new red deck.
This is how her pecking sounds:
/e/ /e/ /e/ /e/ /e/.

Jem's pet hen pecks at corn in her pen.
She pecks ten kernels, then pecks again.
This is how her pecking sounds:
/e/ /e/ /e/ /e/ /e/.

Jem's hen pecks at a cracked egg shell.
She's helping a chick get out, alive and well.
This is how her pecking sounds:
/e/ /e/ /e/ /e/ /e/.

Can you help Jem's hen peck?
*(Have children say:)* /e/ /e/ /e/ /e/ /e/.

### Card 6: /f/ Fan

/f/ /f/ /f/ /f/ /f/—What's that funny sound?
It's Franny the Fan going round and round,
and this is the sound that old fan makes:
/f/ /f/ /f/ /f/ /f/.

When it gets too hot, you see,
Franny cools the family: /f/ /f/ /f/ /f/ /f/.
She fans Father's face
and Foxy's fur
and Felicity's feet.
Hear the Fan whir: /f/ /f/ /f/ /f/ /f/.

Can you make Franny the Fan go fast?
*(Have the children say quickly:)*
/f/ /f/ /f/ /f/ /f/.
Faster? /f/ /f/ /f/ /f/ /f/
Fastest? /f/ /f/ /f/ /f/ /f/

### Card 7: /g/ Gopher

Gary's a gopher.
He loves to gulp down food.
/g/ /g/ /g/ /g/ /g/, gulps the gopher.

Gary the Gopher gulps down grass
because it tastes so good.
/g/ /g/ /g/ /g/ /g/, gulps the gopher.

Gary the Gopher gulps down grapes—
gobs and gobs of grapes.
/g/ /g/ /g/ /g/ /g/, gulps the gopher.

Gary the Gopher gobbles green beans
and says once more,
/g/ /g/ /g/ /g/ /g/. He's such a hungry gopher!

Gary the Gopher gobbles in the garden
until everything is gone.

What sound does Gary the Gopher make?
*(Ask the children to join in.)* /g/ /g/ /g/ /g/ /g/

### Card 8: /h/ Hound

Harry the Hound dog hurries around.
Can you hear Harry's hurrying hound-
    dog sound?
This is the sound Harry's breathing
    makes when he hurries:
/h/ /h/ /h/ /h/ /h/ /h/!

When Harry the Hound dog sees a
    hare hop by,
he tears down the hill, and his four
    feet fly.
Hurry, Harry, hurry! /h/ /h/ /h/ /h/ /h/ /h/!

How Harry the Hound dog loves to hunt
    and chase!
He hurls himself from place to place.
Hurry, Harry, hurry! /h/ /h/ /h/ /h/ /h/ /h/!

When Harry the Hound dog sees a big skunk roam,
He howls for help and heads for home.

What sound does Harry make when he hurries?
*(Have the children answer.)* /h/ /h/ /h/ /h/ /h/ /h/

### Sound/Spelling Card Stories (continued)

## Card 9: /i/ Pig

This is Pickles the Pig.
If you tickle Pickles, she gets the giggles.
This is the sound of her giggling:
/i/ /i/ /i/ /i/ /i/.

Tickle Pickles the Pig under her chin.
Listen! She's giggling: /i/ /i/ /i/ /i/ /i/.
Wiggle a finger in Pickles' ribs.
Listen! She's giggling: /i/ /i/ /i/ /i/ /i/.

Give Pickles the Pig a wink,
and what do you think? First comes a grin.
    Then listen!
She's giggling again: /i/ /i/ /i/ /i/ /i/.

Quick! Tickle Pickles the Pig. What will
    she say? *(Have the children join in.)* /i/ /i/ /i/ /i/ /i/

## Card 10: /j/ Jump

When Jenny jumps her jump rope,
    it sounds like this: /j/ /j/ /j/ /j/ /j/.
When Jackson jumps his jump rope,
    it sounds like this: /j/ /j/ /j/ /j/ /j/.

The judges generally agree
that Jenny jumps most rapidly:
*(quickly)* /j/ /j/ /j/ /j/ /j/.

When Jenny jumps, she jumps to this jingle:
"Jump, jump, jump so quick.
Whenever I jump, I like to kick."
    /j/ /j/ /j/ /j/ /j/

The Judges generally agree
that Jackson jumps most quietly:
*(quietly)* /j/ /j/ /j/ /j/ /j/.

When Jackson jumps, he jumps to this jingle:
"Jump, jump, nice and quiet.
See what happens when you try it." /j/ /j/ /j/ /j/ /j/

*(to the children)* Jump rope like Jenny.
*(quickly)* /j/ /j/ /j/ /j/ /j/
*(to the children)* Jump rope like Jackson.
*(quietly)* /j/ /j/ /j/ /j/ /j/

## Card 11: /k/ Camera

Carlos has a new camera. When he
    takes pictures,
His camera makes a clicking sound like this:
/k/ /k/ /k/ /k/ /k/.

In the garden, Carlos takes pictures of
    caterpillars crawling on cabbage:
/k/ /k/ /k/ /k/ /k/.
At the zoo, Carlos takes pictures of a camel,
    a duck, and a kangaroo:
/k/ /k/ /k/.
In the park, Carlos takes pictures of his
    cousin flying a kite: /k/ /k/ /k/ /k/ /k/
In his room, Carlos takes pictures of his
    cute kitten, Cozy. /k/ /k/ /k/ /k/ /k/

Can you help Carlos take pictures with his camera?
*(Have the children join in.)* /k/ /k/ /k/ /k/ /k/ /k/ /k/

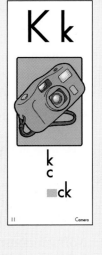

## Card 12: /l/ Lion

Look! It's Leon the Lion.
Leon loves to lap water from lakes,
and this is the sound the lapping lion
    makes: /l/ /l/ /l/ /l/ /l/.

Let's join Leon. Quick!
Take a little lick: /l/ /l/ /l/ /l/ /l/.

Are you a thirsty lass or lad?
Then lap until you don't feel bad:
    /l/ /l/ /l/ /l/ /l/.

What sound do you make when you lap
    like Leon the Lion?
*(Have the children say:)* /l/ /l/ /l/ /l/ /l/.

## Card 13: /m/ Monkey

For Muzzy the Monkey, bananas
    are yummy.
She munches so many, they fill up
    her tummy.
When she eats, she says:
    /m/ /m/ /m/ /m/ /m/!

Bananas for breakfast, bananas
    for lunch.
Mash them up, mush them up,
Munch, munch, munch, munch!
What does Muzzy the Monkey say?
*(Have the children say:)* /m/ /m/ /m/ /m/ /m/.

Bananas at bedtime? I have a hunch
Muzzy will mash them up, mush them up,
Munch, munch, munch, munch!
Then what will Muzzy the Monkey say?
*(Have the children say:)* /m/ /m/ /m/ /m/ /m/.

### Sound/Spelling Card Stories (continued)

## Card 14: /n/ Nose

When Norman Newsome has a cold,
    his nose just won't work right.
It makes a noisy, stuffy sound
    through morning, noon, and night.
When Norman has a cold, his nose goes:
    /n/ /n/ /n/ /n/ /n/!

When Norman Newsome has a cold,
    it's hard to just be quiet.
His nose just sniffs and snuffs
    and snarls.
Norman wishes he could hide it!
Instead, his poor, sick, noisy nose just goes:
    /n/ /n/ /n/ /n/ /n/!

Norman doesn't hate his nose;
It just does as it pleases!
Even when he sniffs a rose,
he nearly always sneezes.
Then Norman Newsome's nose
again goes *(Have the children say:)*
/n/ /n/ /n/ /n/ /n/.

## Card 15: /o/ Fox

Bob the Fox did not feel well at all.
He jogged to the doctor's office.
"Say /o/ Mr. Fox! /o/ /o/ /o/."

"My head is hot, and my throat hurts a lot,"
    said the fox.
"Say /o/ Mr. Fox! /o/ /o/ /o/ /o/."

"Yes, you've got a rotten cold," said
    the doctor.
"Say /o/ Mr. Fox! /o/ /o/ /o/."

"Find a spot to sit in the sun," said the doctor.
"Say /o/ Mr. Fox! /o/ /o/ /o/."

He sat on a rock in the sun.
Soon he felt much better.
*(with a satisfied sigh)* "/o/" said Mr. Fox.
/o/ /o/ /o/

## Card 16: /p/ Popcorn

Ping and Pong liked to pop corn. As
    it cooked, it made this sound:
    /p/ /p/ /p/ /p/ /p/ /p/ /p/.
One day Ping poured a whole package of
    popcorn into the pot. It made this sound:
    /p/ /p/ /p/ /p/ /p/ /p/ /p/.

The popcorn popped and popped. Ping filled
    two pots, and still the popcorn popped:
    /p/ /p/ /p/ /p/ /p/ /p/ /p/.
Pong filled three pails with popcorn, and still
    it kept popping: /p/ /p/ /p/ /p/ /p/ /p/ /p/.

"Call all your pals," said their pop. "We'll have a party."
    And the popcorn kept popping.
*(Have the children say the /p/ sound very fast.)*

## Card 17: /kw/ Quacking ducks

Quincy the Duck couldn't quite quack
    like all the other quacking ducks.
Oh, he could say /kw/ /kw/ /kw/ /kw/,
    but it never seemed just right.
When Quincy tried to quack quietly *(softly)*
    /kw/ /kw/ /kw/ /kw/
    his quack came out loudly *(loudly)*
    /kw/ /kw/ /kw/ /kw/!
When he tried to quack slowly *(slowly)*
    /kw/ . . . /kw/ . . . /kw/ . . . /kw/
    his quack came out quickly *(quickly)*
    /kw/ /kw/ /kw/ /kw/!
Quincy just couldn't quack right!

One day Quincy was practicing quacks.
    His friend Quip quacked along with him.
"Repeat after me," said Quip
    *(quietly)* /kw/ /kw/ /kw/ /kw/.
But Quincy quacked back,
    *(in normal voice)* /kw/ /kw/ /kw/ /kw/ /kw/!
Quincy still couldn't quack quite right.

But Quincy kept quacking. He said, "I won't quit until I quack
    like the best quackers around."
Can you show Quincy how quacking ducks quack?
*(Have the children join in.)*
/kw/ /kw/ /kw/ /kw/ /kw/ /kw/ /kw/ /kw/

## Card 18: /r/ Robot

Little Rosie Robot just runs and runs and runs.
She races round and round to get her chores
    all done.
Here's how Rosie sounds when she's working:
    /r/ /r/ /r/ /r/ /r/!

Rosie can rake around your roses.
Here comes that running robot!
    /r/ /r/ /r/ /r/ /r/!

Rosie can repair your wrecked radio.
Here comes that racing robot!
    *(softly)* /r/ /r/ /r/ /r/ /r/

Rosie can mend your round red rug.
Here comes that roaring robot!
    *(loudly)* /r/ /r/ /r/ /r/ /r/!

Rosie rarely does anything wrong.
But there are two things that Rosie can't
    do: rest and relax.
Here comes that roaring robot!
What does she say?
*(Have the children call out the answer:)*
    /r/ /r/ /r/ /r/ /r/.

L
E
V
E
L

A
P
P
E
N
D
I
X

## Card 19: /s/ Sausages

Sue and Sammy had a nice place in
the city.
On Saturday, Sue and Sammy decided
to have sausages for supper.
Sammy put seven sausages in
a skillet. /s/ /s/ /s/ /s/ /s/ /s/ /s/

Soon the smell of sausages filled
the air.
/s/ /s/ /s/ /s/ /s/, sizzled the sausages.

"Pull up a seat, Sue," said Sammy.
"The sausages are almost ready to serve."
/s/ /s/ /s/ /s/ /s/, sizzled the sausages.

Sue and Sammy ate the delicious sausages.
Soon they wanted more, so Sam put six more sausages in the
frying pan.
/s/ /s/ /s/ /s/ /s/, sizzled the sausages.

If you were cooking sausages with Sammy and Sue,
What sound would the sausages make as they sizzled?
*(Have the children join in:)* /s/ /s/ /s/ /s/ /s/ /s/.

## Card 20: /t/ Timer

When Tom Tuttle cooks, he uses
his timer.
Tom Tuttle's timer ticks like this:
/t/ /t/ /t/ /t/ /t/ /t/ /t/

Tonight Tom Tuttle wants tomatoes
on toast.
Tom turns on the oven.
Tom puts tomatoes on toast in the oven.
Tom sets the timer.
The timer will Ding! when Tom's toast
and tomatoes are done.
Until the timer dings, it ticks: /t/ /t/ /t/ /t/ /t/ /t/ /t/.

Tomatoes on toast take ten minutes.
/t/ /t/ /t/ /t/ /t/ /t/ /t/
Tom can hardly wait. /t/ /t/ /t/ /t/ /t/ /t/ /t/
He taps out the time: /t/ /t/ /t/ /t/ /t/ /t/ /t/.

What is the sound of Tom Tuttle's ticking timer?
*(Have the children join in.)* /t/ /t/ /t/ /t/ /t/ /t/ /t/
Ding! Time for dinner, Tom Tuttle!

## Card 21: /u/ Tug

Tubby the Tugboat can huff and puff
and push and pull to move big stuff.
/u/ /u/ /u/ /u/ /u/ /u/ /u/
That's the sound of Tubby the Tug.

If a boat is stuck and will not budge,
Tubby the Tugboat can give it a nudge. /u/ /u/ /u/ /u/ /u/ /u/ /u/
It's Tubby the Trusty Tug.

If a ship is caught in mud and muck,
Tubby the Tugboat can get it unstuck.
/u/ /u/ /u/ /u/ /u/ /u/ /u/
It's Tubby the Trusty Tug.

Can you help Tubby push and pull?
*(Have the children join in.)*
/u/ /u/ /u/ /u/ /u/ /u/ /u/

## Card 22: /v/ Vacuum

Vinny the Vacuum is cleaning again.
Before visitors visit, he always begins.
This is the sound of his very loud voice:
/v/ /v/ /v/ /v/ /v/!
If only that Vinny could clean without noise!

Vinny sucks up the crumbs baby Vicki dropped.
/v/ /v/ /v/ /v/ /v/!
He visits nearly everywhere except the tabletop.
/v/ /v/ /v/ /v/ /v/!
Three vine leaves, two vitamins, part of a vase—
all vanish when Vinny goes over the
place! /v/ /v/ /v/ /v/ /v/

As Vinny vacuums the velvety rug
a van full of visitors starts to drive up.
But Vinny's not done with the very last room!
Will you help Vinny the Vacuum vacuum?
*(Ask groups of children to say /v/ in a round to make
the continuous sound of a vacuum cleaner.)*

## Card 23: /w/ Washer

Willie the Washer washed white clothes all week.
When he washed, he went:
/w/ /w/ /w/ /w/ /w/ /w/ /w/.

All winter, Willie worked well.
/w/ /w/ /w/ /w/ /w/ /w/ /w/
But last Wednesday, Willie was weak. *(softly)*
/w/ /w/ /w/ /w/ /w/ /w/ /w/
This week, he got worse. *(slower and slower)*
/w/. . . /w/. . . /w/. . .
Poor Willie was worn out. *(slowly)* /w/

Then a worker came and fixed Willie's wires.
Willie felt wonderful. *(more loudly)*
/w/ /w/ /w/ /w/ /w/ /w/ /w/!
Now Willie can wash and wash wildly!
*(quickly)* /w/ /w/ /w/ /w/ /w/ /w/ /w/!

How does Willie the Washer sound now when he washes?
*(Have the children join in.)* /w/ /w/ /w/ /w/ /w/ /w/ /w/
Can you wash just like Willie?
*(Children together:)* /w/ /w/ /w/ /w/ /w/ /w/ /w/.

### Sound/Spelling Card Stories (continued)

## Card 24: /ks/ Exit

Rex is called the Exiting X;
he runs to guard the door.
To get past Rex, make the sound of X:
    /ks/ /ks/ /ks/ /ks/.
That is what Rex expects!

The ox knows the sound of X,
so she says /ks/ /ks/ /ks/ /ks/
    and gets past Rex.

The fox knows the sound of X,
so he says /ks/ /ks/ /ks/ /ks/
    and gets past Rex.

Can you say /ks/ /ks/ /ks/ /ks/
    and get past Rex the Exiting X?
*(Have the children respond:)* /ks/ /ks/ /ks/ /ks/!
Did we get past Rex?
*(Have the children say:)* Yes!

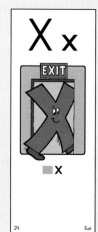

## Card 25: /y/ Yaks

Yolanda and Yoshiko are yaks.
They don't yell.
They don't yelp.
They don't yodel.
They don't yawn.
These young yaks just yak.
Yakety-yak, yakety-yak!
Can you hear the sound they make?
/y/ /y/ /y/ /y/ /y/ /y/ /y/.

Yolanda and Yoshiko yak in the yard.
/y/ /y/ /y/ /y/ /y/ /y/ /y/
They yak on their yellow yacht.
/y/ /y/ /y/ /y/ /y/ /y/ /y/
They yak in the yam patch.
/y/ /y/ /y/ /y/ /y/ /y/ /y/
These yaks yak all year!
/y/ /y/ /y/ /y/ /y/ /y/ /y/

Do you think these yaks like to yak?
*(Have the children answer:)* Yes!
*(Ask the children to yak like Yolanda and Yoshiko.)*

## Card 26: /z/ Zipper

Zack's jacket has a big long zipper.
The zipper zips like this: /z/ /z/ /z/ /z/.

When little Zack goes out to play,
he zips the zipper up this way:
    /z/ /z/ /z/ /z/.
Later, when he comes back in,
Zack zips the zipper down again:
    /z/ /z/ /z/ /z/.

Can you help Zack zip his jacket zipper?
*(Have the children join in.)* /z/ /z/ /z/ /z/

## Card 27: /ar/ Armadillo

Arthur Armadillo likes to whistle,
    hum, and sing.
But when he gets a head cold,
    his voice won't do a thing.

To sing and still sound charming—
and not sound so alarming—
Arthur has thought up the thing
of very often gargling.

Then Arthur Armadillo sounds like this:
    /ar/ /ar/ /ar/ /ar/ /ar/.

Arthur gargles in the park. /ar/ /ar/ /ar/
    /ar/ /ar/
He gargles in the dark. /ar/ /ar/ /ar/ /ar/ /ar/
He gargles on the farm. /ar/ /ar/ /ar/ /ar/ /ar/
He gargles in the barn. /ar/ /ar/ /ar/ /ar/ /ar/
Arthur is great at gargling! /ar/ /ar/ /ar/ /ar/ /ar/

What does Arthur Armadillo's gargling sound like?
*(Have the children respond.)* /ar/ /ar/ /ar/ /ar/ /ar/

## Card 28: /hw/ Whales

Look! It's Whitney the Whispering Whale!
Listen to her whisper: /hw/ /hw/ /hw/ /hw/ /hw/.

When Whitney meets with other whales,
she entertains them, telling tales.
She whispers: /hw/ /hw/ /hw/ /hw/ /hw/.
She's Whitney the Whispering Whale.

What ocean wonders does Whitney relate?
Does she whisper of whirlpools or whales
    that are great?
We're only people, so we'll never guess.
She's Whitney the Whispering Whale!
    /hw/ /hw/ /hw/.

Whatever Whitney whispers must be fun.
The other whales whistle when she's done.
They whoop and whack the white-capped waves.
They love Whitney the Whispering Whale! /hw/ /hw/ /hw/.

If you were Whitney, what sounds would you whisper
to your whale friends as they gathered to listen?
*(Have the children whisper:)* /hw/ /hw/ /hw/ /hw/ /hw/.

## Card 29: /er/ Bird

Bertie the Bird is the oddest bird
    that anyone has ever heard.
He doesn't caw like a crow or a gull,
    or tweet like a robin or a wren.
Instead, he makes a chirping sound—
    over and over again!
/er/ /er/ /er/ /er/ /er/ /er/!

Bert can't fly, since his wings are too short.
He arranges his feathers in curls.
He admits, "I've short wings and I don't really sing,
But I still am an interesting bird!"
/er/ /er/ /er/ /er/ /er/ /er/

Can you chirp like Bertie the Bird?
*(Have children say:)* /er/ /er/ /er/, /er/ /er/ /er/!

## Card 30: /sh/ Shell

Sheila and Sharon went to the seashore.
They saw lots of shells.
Sheila rushed from shell to shell.
Sharon held a shell to Sheila's ear.

"Do you hear anything?" asked Sharon.
"Yes, it sounds like the ocean crashing on
    the shore," shouted Sheila,
"/sh/ /sh/ /sh/ /sh/ /sh/."

"Let's try different shaped shells," said Sharon.
She found a big shell. It made a loud /sh/
    /sh/ /sh/ /sh/.
Sheila found a small shell. It made a soft /sh/ /sh/ /sh/ /sh/.
They found a thin shell. It made a high /sh/ /sh/ /sh/ /sh/.
They found a fat shell. It made a deep /sh/ /sh/ /sh/ /sh/.

Sheila and Sharon listened to lots of shells. But no matter
What the size and shape, what do you think Sheila and Sharon
Heard in every shell?
*(Have the children join in.)* /sh/ /sh/ /sh/ /sh/

## Card 31: /th/ Thimble

Theodore Thimble is a thinker.
Theodore thinks and thinks and thinks.
And when he thinks, he rubs his head.
/th/ /th/ /th/ /th/ /th/ /th/ /th/ /th/ /th/

Theodore thinks of thumbs—
Thin thumbs
Thick thumbs
All different kinds of thumbs.
/th/ /th/ /th/ /th/ /th/ /th/ /th/ /th/ /th/

Theodore thinks of thread—
Red thread
Blue thread
All different color thread.
/th/ /th/ /th/ /th/ /th/ /th/ /th/ /th/ /th/

Thread and thumb
Thumb and thread
These are the thoughts
In Theodore's head.
/th/ /th/ /th/ /th/ /th/ /th/ /th/ /th/ /th/

## Card 32: /ch/ Chipmunk

Chipper the chipmunk is cheerful and chubby.
He chats and he chatters all day.
/ch/ /ch/ /ch/ /ch/ /ch/ /ch/
He sits on a chimney.
Can you hear him chat?
He chats and he chatters this way:
/ch/ /ch/ /ch/ /ch/ /ch/ /ch/.

Chipper stuffs cherries into his cheek.
Then he chatters /ch/ /ch/ /ch/ /ch/ /ch/ /ch/.
Chipper likes chestnuts and acorns to eat.
Then he chatters /ch/ /ch/ /ch/ /ch/ /ch/ /ch/.

Can you children chatter like Chipper?
*(Have the children answer.)*
/ch/ /ch/ /ch/ /ch/ /ch/ /ch/

Now chat with the chipmunk child beside you.
*(Ask partners to have chipmunk conversations.)*
/ch/ /ch/ /ch/ /ch/ /ch/ /ch/

## Card 38: /ng/ Gong

The young king has slept much
    too long.
Let's go and awaken the king with
    a gong.

A pinging gong? It makes a quiet song:
*(softly)* /ng/ /ng/ /ng/ /ng/ /ng/.

That gong is wrong.
*(softly)* /ng/ /ng/ /ng/ /ng/
We need a louder gong!

A dinging gong? It makes this song:
*(a bit louder)* /ng/ /ng/ /ng/ /ng/ /ng/ /ng/.

That, too, is wrong.
*(as before)* /ng/ /ng/ /ng/ /ng/
We need an even louder gong!

A clanging gong?
It makes this song: *(loudly)* /ng/ /ng/ /ng/ /ng/ /ng/!

That's just the thing! /ng/ /ng/ /ng/ /ng/ /ng/!
That's the gong we needed all along!

Now, which gong should we bring to awaken the King?
*(Have children make the /ng/ sound loud enough to wake
    the king.)* /ng/ /ng/ /ng/ /ng/ /ng/

**Note:** Cards 33 through 37 are long vowel cards and do not have
corresponding stories.

## Sound/Spelling Card Stories (continued)

### Card 39: /ow/ Cow

Wow! Can you see poor Brownie
   the Cow?
She got stung by a bee and look at
   her now!
She jumps up and down with an
   /ow/ /ow/ /ow/ /ow/.

Poor Brownie found that a big buzzing sound
meant bees all around—in the air, on the ground.
Just one little bee gave Brownie a sting.
Now you can hear poor Brownie sing:
/ow/ /ow/ /ow/ /ow/.

Now if you were a cow and a bee found you
You'd probably jump and shout out too!
*(Have the children join in.)* /ow/ /ow/ /ow/ /ow/

ow
ou__

39     Cow

### Card 40: /aw/ Hawk

Hazel the Hawk never cooks her food;
Instead, she eats it raw.
And when she thinks of dinnertime
She caws: /aw/ /aw/ /aw/ /aw/.

Hazel the Hawk likes rabbits and mice
and catches them with her claws.
In August, she flies high above the fields
and spies them below, in the straw.
Sometimes she even snatches a snake!
And when she's caught one, she caws:
/aw/ /aw/ /aw/ /aw/.

If you were a hawk thinking of dinnertime,
   what do you think you'd say?
*(Have the children answer.)* /aw/ /aw/ /aw/ /aw/

aw
au__

40     Hawk

### Card 41: /o͞o/ Goo

/o͞o/ /o͞o/ /o͞o/ /o͞o/
What can be making that sound?
Could it be a new flute playing a tune?
No. It's goo!
/o͞o/ /o͞o/ /o͞o/ /o͞o/
The goo is oozing all over my hand.
/o͞o/ /o͞o/ /o͞o/ /o͞o/
The goo is oozing on my boots.
/o͞o/ /o͞o/ /o͞o/ /o͞o/
The goo is oozing off the roof.
The goo is oozing everywhere!
/o͞o/ /o͞o/ /o͞o/ /o͞o/
The goo is as sticky as glue.
It is as thick as stew.
/o͞o/ /o͞o/ /o͞o/ /o͞o/
Soon the goo will fill the school!
/o͞o/ /o͞o/ /o͞o/ /o͞o/

oo    _ew
u_e    _ue
u

41     Goo

Soon the goo will reach the moon!
/o͞o/ /o͞o/ /o͞o/ /o͞o/
What sound does the oozing goo make?
*(Have the children join in.)* /o͞o/ /o͞o/ /o͞o/ /o͞o/

### Card 42: /o͝o/ Foot

Mr. Hood took off his shoes and socks
   And went out walking in the wood.
He kicked a rock and hurt his foot.
   /o͝o/ /o͝o/ /o͝o/ /o͝o/
"Look, look!" said Mr. Hood. "There's a
   babbling, bubbling brook. I'll walk
   in the brook, so I won't hurt my foot."
So he stepped in the water, and guess what?
   /o͝o/ /o͝o/ /o͝o/ /o͝o/
Mr. Hood stepped on a hook!
   /o͝o/ /o͝o/ /o͝o/ /o͝o/
Mr. Hood stood. He shook his foot.
   /o͝o/ /o͝o/ /o͝o/ /o͝o/
"This isn't good," said Mr. Hood.
"I think I'll go home and read a book.
At least that won't hurt my foot."
*(Have the children join in.)* /o͝o/ /o͝o/ /o͝o/ /o͝o/

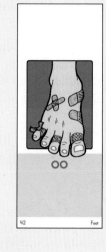

oo

42     Foot

### Card 43: /oi/ Coil

Boing! Boing! Boing! Boing!
Roy the Coil is a bouncing toy,
and this is the sound of his bounce:
/oi/ /oi/ /oi/ /oi/ /oi/.

Doing! Doing! Doing! Doing!
Roy the Coil just dances for joy.
This is the sound of his dance:
/oi/ /oi/ /oi/ /oi/ /oi/.

Ke-boing! Ke-boing!
Roy the Coil springs over a boy.
What springing sound does he make?
*(Have the children join in.)*
/oi/ /oi/ /oi/ /oi/ /oi/

oi
_oy

43     Coil

# Index (continued)

**INDEX**

# Index (continued)

**INDEX**

# Index (continued)

# Z

# Notes

Use this page to record lessons or elements that work well
or need to be adjusted for future reference.

## Lessons that work well.

_____
_____
_____
_____
_____
_____
_____
_____
_____
_____
_____
_____
_____

## Lessons that need adjustments.

_____
_____
_____
_____
_____
_____
_____
_____
_____
_____
_____
_____
_____

# Notes

Use this page to record lessons or elements that work well
or need to be adjusted for future reference.

## Lessons that work well.

_____

_____

_____

_____

_____

_____

_____

_____

_____

_____

_____

_____

_____

_____

## Lessons that need adjustments.

_____

_____

_____

_____

_____

_____

_____

_____

_____

_____

_____

_____

_____

_____

# Notes

Use this page to record lessons or elements that work well
or need to be adjusted for future reference.

## Lessons that work well.

_____
_____
_____
_____
_____
_____
_____
_____
_____
_____
_____
_____
_____

## Lessons that need adjustments.

_____
_____
_____
_____
_____
_____
_____
_____
_____
_____
_____
_____
_____
_____
_____
_____

# Notes

Use this page to record lessons or elements that work well
or need to be adjusted for future reference.

## Lessons that work well.

_____
_____
_____
_____
_____
_____
_____
_____
_____
_____
_____
_____
_____
_____

## Lessons that need adjustments.

_____
_____
_____
_____
_____
_____
_____
_____
_____
_____
_____
_____
_____
_____

# Notes

Use this page to record lessons or elements that work well
or need to be adjusted for future reference.

## Lessons that work well.

_____
_____
_____
_____
_____
_____
_____
_____
_____
_____
_____
_____
_____

## Lessons that need adjustments.

_____
_____
_____
_____
_____
_____
_____
_____
_____
_____
_____
_____
_____
_____

# Notes

Use this page to record lessons or elements that work well
or need to be adjusted for future reference.

## Lessons that work well.

_____

_____

_____

_____

_____

_____

_____

_____

_____

_____

_____

_____

_____

_____

## Lessons that need adjustments.

_____

_____

_____

_____

_____

_____

_____

_____

_____

_____

_____

_____

_____

_____

_____

# Notes

Use this page to record lessons or elements that work well
or need to be adjusted for future reference.

## Lessons that work well.

_____
_____
_____
_____
_____
_____
_____
_____
_____
_____
_____
_____
_____
_____

## Lessons that need adjustments.

_____
_____
_____
_____
_____
_____
_____
_____
_____
_____
_____
_____
_____
_____
_____

# Notes

Use this page to record lessons or elements that work well
or need to be adjusted for future reference.

## Lessons that work well.

## Lessons that need adjustments.

# Notes

Use this page to record lessons or elements that work well
or need to be adjusted for future reference.

## Lessons that work well.

_____
_____
_____
_____
_____
_____
_____
_____
_____
_____
_____
_____
_____

## Lessons that need adjustments.

_____
_____
_____
_____
_____
_____
_____
_____
_____
_____
_____
_____
_____
_____
_____

# Florida Resources

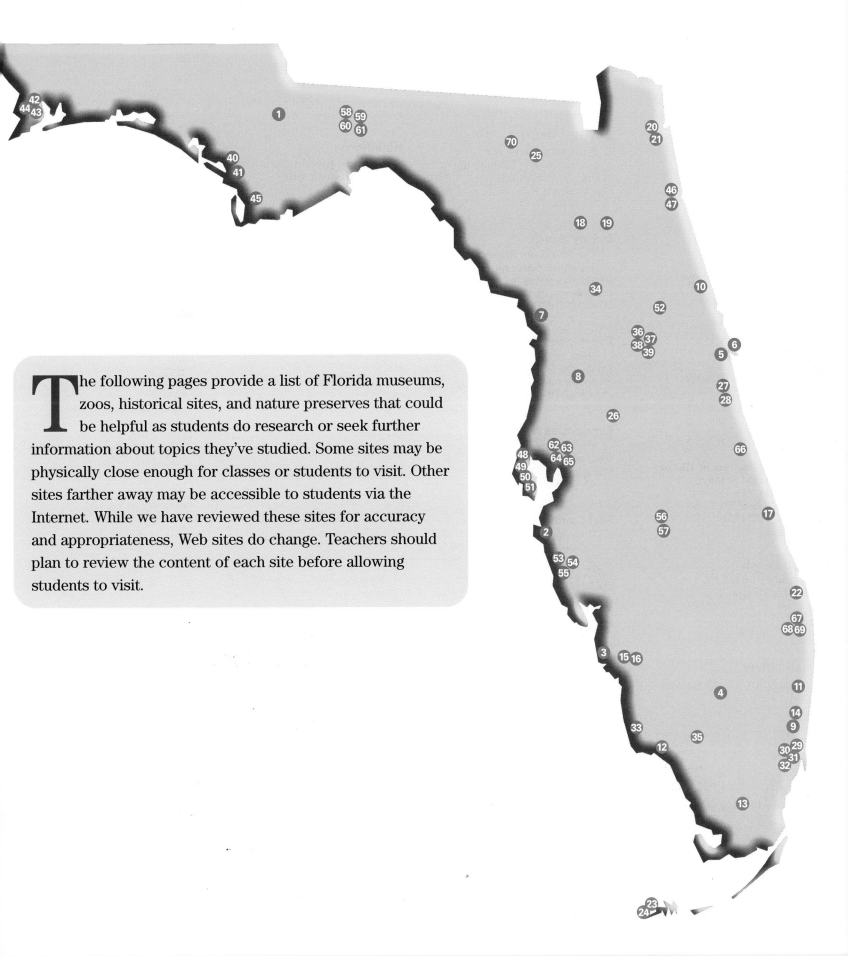

The following pages provide a list of Florida museums, zoos, historical sites, and nature preserves that could be helpful as students do research or seek further information about topics they've studied. Some sites may be physically close enough for classes or students to visit. Other sites farther away may be accessible to students via the Internet. While we have reviewed these sites for accuracy and appropriateness, Web sites do change. Teachers should plan to review the content of each site before allowing students to visit.

# Florida Resources

### Blountstown
**1 Panhandle Pioneer Settlement**
17879 N.W. Pioneer Settlement Road
Blountstown, FL 32424
Phone: (850) 674-3050
http://www.panhandlepioneersettlement.org

### Bradenton
**2 South Florida Museum, Bishop Planetarium, and Parker Manatee Aquarium**
201 10th Street West
Bradenton, FL 34205
Phone: (941) 746-4131
http://www.sfmbp.org/Museum/museum2.htm

### Cape Coral
**3 The Children's Science Center**
2915 NE Pine Island Road
Cape Coral, FL 33909
Phone: (941) 997-0012
http://www.cyberstreet.com/csc/

### Clewiston
**4 Ah-Tah-Thi-Ki Museum**
HC 61 Box 21A
Clewiston, FL 33440
Phone: (954) 792-0745
http://www.seminoletribe.com/museum

### Cocoa
**5 Brevard Museum of History and Natural Science**
2201 Michigan Avenue
Cocoa, FL 32926-5618
Phone: (321) 632-1830
http://www5.palmnet.net/~brevardmuseum

### Cocoa Beach
**6 Kennedy Space Center Visitor Complex**
Box 21066
Cocoa Beach, FL 32815
Phone: (321) 452-2121
http://www.kennedyspacecenter.com

### Crystal River
**7 Crystal River Archaeological State Park**
3400 N. Museum Point
Crystal River, FL 34428
Phone: (352) 795-3817
http://www8.myflorida.com/communities/learn/stateparks/district2/crystalriver/index.html

### Dade City
**8 Pioneer Florida Museum**
P.O. Box 335
Dade City, FL 33526-0335
Phone: (352) 567-0262
http://www.dadecity.com/museum

### Dania Beach
**9 Graves Museum of Archaeology & Natural History**
481 South Federal Highway
Dania Beach, FL 33004
Phone: (954) 925-7770
http://www.gravesmuseum.org

### Daytona Beach
**10 Museum of Arts and Sciences and Planetarium**
1040 Museum Boulevard
Daytona Beach, FL
Phone: (904) 255-0285
http://www.moas.org

### Delray Beach
**11 The Morikami Museum and Japanese Gardens**
4000 Morikami Park Road
Delray Beach, FL 33446
Phone: (561) 495-0233
http://www.morikami.org

### Everglades City
**12 Museum of the Everglades**
105 West Broadway
Everglades City, FL 34139
Phone: (941) 695-0008
http://www.colliermuseum.com

### Everglades National Park
**13 Everglades National Park**
40001 State Road 9336
Homestead, FL 33034-6733
Phone: (305) 242-7700
http://www.nps.gov/ever/

### Fort Lauderdale
**14 Museum of Discovery and Science**
401 SW Second Street
Fort Lauderdale, FL 33312
Phone: (954) 467-6637
http://www.MODS.org

### Fort Myers
**15 Calusa Nature Center and Planetarium**
3450 Ortiz Avenue
Fort Myers, FL 33905
Phone: (941) 275-3435
http://www.calusanature.com

**16 Imaginarium Hands-On Museum and Aquarium**
2000 Cranford Avenue
Fort Myers, FL 33916
Phone: (941) 337-3332
http://www.cityftmyers.com/Attractions/Imagin.htm

### Fort Pierce
**17 Harbor Branch Oceanographic Institution**
5600 US 1 North
Fort Pierce, Florida 34946
Phone: (561) 465-2400 ext. 517
http://www.hboi.edu

### Gainesville
**18 Florida Museum of Natural History**
University of Florida - Powell Hall
SW 34th Street and Hull Road
PO Box 112710
Gainesville FL 32611-2710
Phone: (352) 846-2000
http://www.flmnh.ufl.edu

### Hawthorne
**19 Marjorie Kinnan Rawlings State Historic Site**
Rte. 3, Box 92
Hawthorne, FL 32640
Phone: (352) 466-3672
http://www8.myflorida.com/communities/learn/stateparks/district2/marjoriekinnanrawlings/index.html

### Jacksonville
**20 Jacksonville Zoological Gardens**
8605 Zoo Parkway
Jacksonville, FL 32218
Phone: (904) 757-4463
http://www.jaxzoo.org

**21 Timucuan Ecological and Historic Preserve**
12713 Fort Caroline Road
Jacksonville, FL 32225
Phone: (904) 641-7155
http://www.nps.gov/timu

### Juno Beach
**22 Marinelife Center of Juno Beach**
14200 US 1, Loggerhead Park
Juno Beach, FL 33408
Phone: (561) 627-8280
http://www.marinelife.org

### Key West
**23 Audubon House & Tropical Gardens**
205 Whitehead Street
Key West, FL 33040
Phone: (305) 294-4513
http://www.audubonhouse.com

**24 Ernest Hemingway Home and Museum**
907 Whitehead Street
Key West, FL 33040
Phone: (305) 294-1136
http://www.hemingwayhome.com

### Lake City
**25 Florida Sports Hall of Fame**
601 Hall of Fame Dr.
Lake City, FL 32055
Phone: (904) 758-1310
http://www.floridasports.org

### Lakeland
**26 Polk Museum of Art**
800 East Palmetto Street
Lakeland, FL 33801
Phone: (863) 688-7743
http://www.polkmuseumofart.org

### Melbourne
**27 Brevard Museum of Art and Science**
1463 Highland Avenue
Melbourne, FL 32936
Phone: (321) 242-0737
http://www.artandscience.org

**28 Brevard Zoo**
8225 N. Wickham Road
Melbourne, FL 32940
Phone: (321) 254-9453
http://www.brevardzoo.org

### Miami
**29 Historical Museum of South Florida**
101 West Flagler Street
Miami, FL 33130
Phone: (305) 375-1492
http://www.historical-museum.org

**30 Miami Art Museum**
101 West Flagler Street
Miami, FL 33130
Phone: (305) 375-3000
http://www.miamiartmuseum.org

**31 Miami Metrozoo**
12400 S.W. 152nd Street
Miami, FL 33177
Phone: (305) 251-0400
http://www.metro-dade.com/parks/metrozoo.htm

**32 Miami Museum of Science & Space Transit Planetarium**
3280 South Miami Avenue
Miami, FL 33129-2899
Phone: (305) 854-4247
http://www.miamisci.org

### Naples
**33 Collier County Museum**
3301 Tamiami Trail East
Naples, FL 34112
Phone: (941) 774-8476
http://www.colliermuseum.com

### Ocala
**34 The Appleton Museum of Art**
4333 NE Silver Springs Blvd.
Ocala, FL 34470-7100
Phone: (352) 236-7100
http://www.fsu.edu/~appleton/

### Ochopee
**35 Big Cypress National Preserve**
HCR 61, Box 110
Ochopee, FL 33141
Phone: (941) 695-2000
http://www.nps.gov/bicy/

### Orlando
**36 Mennello Museum of American Folk Art**
900 East Princeton Street
Orlando, FL 32803
Phone: (407) 246-4278
http://www.mennellomuseum.com

**㊲ Orange County Regional History Center**
65 East Central Boulevard
Orlando, FL 32801
Phone: (407) 836-8500
http://www.thehistorycenter.org

**㊳ Orlando Museum of Art**
2416 N. Mills Avenue
Orlando, FL 32803
Phone: (407) 896-4231
http://www.omart.org

**㊴ Orlando Science Center**
777 East Princeton Street
Orlando, FL 32803-1291
Phone: (407) 514-2000
http://www.osc.org

## Panama City
**㊵ Junior Museum of Bay County**
1731 Jenks Avenue
Panama City, FL 32405
Phone: (850) 769-6128
http://www.panamacity.com/recreation/
JrMuseum/scripts/index.asp

**㊶ Visual Arts Center of Northwest Florida**
19 East 4th Street
Panama City, FL 32401
Phone: (850) 769-4451
http://www.visualartscenter.org

## Pensacola
**㊷ Historic Pensacola Village**
205 East Zaragoza Street
Pensacola, FL 32501
Phone: (850) 595-5985 x100
http://www.historicpensacola.org

**㊸ National Museum of Naval Aviation**
1750 Radford Boulevard
Pensacola Naval Air Station
Pensacola, FL 32508
Phone: (850) 452-3604
http://www.naval-air.org

**㊹ Pensacola Museum of Art**
407 South Jefferson Street
Pensacola, FL 32501
Phone: (850) 432-6247
http://www.artsnwfl.org/pma

## Port St. Joe
**㊺ Constitution Convention State Museum**
200 Allen Memorial Way
Port St. Joe, FL 32456
Phone: (850) 229-8029
http://www8.myflorida.com/communities/
learn/stateparks/district1/constitution/
index.html

## St. Augustine
**㊻ Castillo de San Marcos National Monument**
One South Castillo Drive
St. Augustine, FL 32084
Phone: (904) 829-6506
http://www.nps.gov/casa/

**㊼ Spanish Quarter Village**
29 St. George Street
St. Augustine, FL 32085
Phone: (904) 825-6830
http://www.oldcity.com/spanishquarter/

## St. Petersburg
**㊽ Great Explorations – The Hands-On Museum**
3rd Floor, The Pier
800 Second Ave. N.E.
St. Petersburg, FL 33701
Phone: (727) 821-8992
http://www.greatexplorations.org

**㊾ Museum of Fine Arts, St. Petersburg**
255 Beach Drive N.E.
St. Petersburg, FL 33701
Phone: (727) 896-2667
http://www.fine-arts.org

**㊿ Pier Aquarium**
2nd Floor, The Pier
800 Second Avenue N.E.
St. Petersburg, FL 33701
Phone: (727) 822-9520
http://www.stpete-
pier.com/attrax/aquarium.htm

**51 St. Petersburg Museum of History**
335 Second Avenue N.E.
St. Petersburg, FL 33701
Phone: (727) 894-1052
http://www.museumofhistoryonline.org

## Sanford
**52 Central Florida Zoological Park**
3755 NW Highway 17-92
Sanford, FL
Phone: (407) 323-4450
http://www.centralfloridazoo.org

## Sarasota
**53 Gulf Coast Wonder and Imagination Zone**
1001 Boulevard of the Arts
Sarasota, FL 34236
Phone: (941) 906-1851
http://www.gwiz.org

**54 Mote Marine Aquarium**
1600 Ken Thompson Parkway
Sarasota, FL 34236
Phone: (941) 388.4441
http://www.mote.org

**55 Ringling Museum of Art**
5401 Bay Shore Road
Sarasota, FL 34243
Phone: (941) 359-5700
http://www.ringling.org

## Sebring
**56 Children's Museum of the Highlands**
219 N. Ridgewood Drive
Sebring, FL 33870
Phone: (863) 385-5437
http://www.highlandsonline.net/children

**57 Museum of Florida's Art and Culture**
13238 US Highway 98
Sebring, FL 33876
Phone: (941) 382-6900
http://www.mofac.org

## Tallahassee
**58 Lake Jackson Mounds Archaeological State Park**
1022 DeSoto Park Drive
Tallahassee, FL 32301
Phone: (850) 922-6007
http://www8.myflorida.com/communities/
learn/stateparks/district1/lakejackson/
index.html

**59 Mary Brogan Museum of Art and Science**
350 South Duval Street
Tallahassee, FL 32301
Phone: (850) 513-0700
http://www.thebrogan.org

**60 Museum of Florida History**
500 South Bronough Street
Tallahassee, FL 32399-0250
Phone: (850) 488-1484
http://www.dos.state.fl.us/dhr/museum/

**61 Tallahassee Museum of History and Natural Science**
3945 Museum Drive
Tallahassee, FL 32310-6325
Phone: (850) 576-1636
http://www.tallahasseemuseum.org

## Tampa
**62 The Florida Aquarium**
701 Channelside Drive
Tampa, FL 33602
Phone: (813) 273-4000
http://www.flaquarium.net

**63 Lowry Park Zoo**
1101 West Sligh Avenue
Tampa, FL 33604-4756
Phone: (813) 935-8552
http://www.lowryparkzoo.com

**64 MOSI (Museum of Science and Industry)**
4801 E. Fowler Avenue
Tampa, FL 33617-2017
Phone: (813) 987-6100
http://www.mosi.org

**65 Tampa Museum of Art**
600 North Ashley Drive
Tampa, FL 33602
Phone: (813) 274-8130
http://www.tampamuseum.com/
visitor_info.htm

## Vero Beach
**66 Center for the Arts**
3001 Riverside Park Drive
Vero Beach, FL 32963
Phone: (561) 231-0707
http://www.vero-beach.fl.us/cfta

## West Palm Beach
**67 Norton Museum of Art**
1451 S. Olive Avenue
West Palm Beach, FL 33401
Phone: (561) 832-5196
http://www.norton.org

**68 Palm Beach Zoo at Dreher Park**
1301 Summit Street
West Palm Beach, FL 33405-3098
Phone: (561) 533-0887
http://www.palmbeachzoo.org

**69 South Florida Science Museum**
4801 Dreher Trail North
West Palm Beach, FL 33405
Phone: (561) 832-1988
http://www.sfsm.org/mainpage.htm

## White Springs
**70 Stephen Foster State Folk Culture Center**
Post Office Drawer G
White Springs, FL 32096
Phone: (386) 397-2733
http://www8.myflorida.com/communities/
learn/stateparks/district2/stephenfoster/
index.html

# Florida Resources

## Phonetic Problems Linked to Students' First Language

The following table focuses on some of the main pronunciation problems English Language Learners from eight language groups may encounter while learning English. The purpose of this table is to help teachers decide which steps to take in order to address chronic pronunciation problems. The table is by no means exhaustive and is meant to serve only as a guide. It shows pronunciation variances that students may make while learning English. For example, a student whose first language is Spanish may say something like cot when trying to pronounce the word cat. An empty cell indicates that the English sound listed poses no particular problem for students from the given language group.

| English Element | Spanish | Vietnamese |
|---|---|---|
| /a/ cat | /o/ cot | /o/ cot |
| /ē/ tea | | |
| /e/ bet | /ā/ bait | /a/ bat |
| /i/ ship | /ē/ sheep | /ē/ sheep |
| /ō/ cloak | | |
| /o/ clock | /ô/ clawk | |
| /u/ cup | /o/ cop, /ōō/ coop | |
| /ōō/ pull | /ōō/ pool | /ōō/ pool |
| /ə/ | Nonexistent. Replaced by another vowel sound. | |
| /b/ bad | | |
| /f/ fan | | |
| /j/ jar | /h/ har, /y/ yar | /z/ zar |
| /n/ need | | |
| /r/ rock, terrible | Rolled or trilled. | |
| /v/ vet | /b/ bet, /f/ fet | |
| /w/ week | /v/ veek, /ōō/ ooeek | |
| /z/ zoo | /s/ soo | |
| /zh/ measure | /z/ meazure | |
| /th/ think | /s/ sink, /t/ tink | /s/ sink, /t/ tink |
| /th/ though | /d/ doe | /d/ doe, /z/ zoh |
| /sh/ shoe | /ch/ chew | /s/ sue, /ch/ chew |
| Initial /s/ stop | Adds /e/ estop | |
| Final consonants /f/, /th/, etc. life, path... | | Final consonants unpronounced. lie, pa... |
| Final /p/, /t/, /k/ tip, sit, sick | | |
| Final /s/ after consonants. cats, rocks | | None. cat, rock |
| Final /v/ love | | /b/ lub, /p/ lup |
| Final consonant blends | Rare. One or more sounds dropped | None. One or more sounds dropped. |
| Polysyllabic words | | None. All words monosyllabic. |
| Intonation of sentences | | None. Tone of individual words changes meaning. |

**1** The sound contrasts for Hmong are based on information about Thai-Lao/English contrasts.

**2** The sound contrasts for Haitian Creole are based on information about French/English contrasts.

| Hmong[1] | Cantonese | Tagalog | Haitian Creole[2] (French) | Portuguese | Khmer |
|---|---|---|---|---|---|
| /o/ *cot* | | /o/ *cot* | /o/ *cot* | /o/ *cot* | /u/ *cut*, /e/ *yet* |
| /ü/ like French *tu* | | | /i/ *ti* | | |
| | All vowel sounds will vary, depending on the consonant sounds combined with them. | /ā/ *bait* | | /ā/ *bait* | |
| | | /ē/ *sheep* | /ē/ *sheep* | /ē/ *sheep* | /ē/ *sheep* |
| /o/ *clock* | | | | | /o/ *clock* |
| | | /ô/ *clawk* | | /ō/ *cloak* | |
| | | /o/ *cop* | /ä/ (father) *cap* | /a/ *cap*, /ä/ (father)*cäp* | |
| | | /o͞o/ *pool* | /o͞o/ *pool* | /o͞o/ *pool* | |
| Nonexistent. Replaced by another vowel sound. | | Nonexistent. Replaced by another vowel sound. | | Sound difficult, especially at the beginning of the word. | Nonexistent. Replaced by another vowel sound. |
| /p/ *pad* | | | | May sound close to /y/. | |
| | | /p/ *pan* | | | Sound difficult. May be dropped. |
| | | /y/ *yar* | /zh/ *zher* (as in *measure*) *zher* | /y/ *yar* | /ch/ *char* |
| | /l/ *leed* | | | | |
| | /l/ *lock, tellable* | | Pronounced as uvular r. | Pronounced too far back, close to /h/. | |
| | /f/ *fet* | /b/ *bet*, /f/ *fet* | | /w/ *wet*, /b/ *bet* | /w/ *wet*, /b/ *bet* |
| /h/ *heek* | | /v/ *veek*, /o͞o/ *ooeek* | | | |
| /s/ *soo* | /s/ *soo* | /s/ *soo* | | /s/ *soo* | /s/ *soo* |
| | /z/ *meazure*, /sh/ *meashur* | /z/ *meazure* | | /z/ *meazure*, /s/ *meassure* | /j/ *meajure* |
| /t/ *tink* | /t/ *tink* | /t/ *tink* | /s/ *sink* | /s/ *sink*, /t/ *tink* | /t/ *tink* |
| /d/ *doe* | /d/ *doe* | /d/ *doe* | /z/ *zoe* | /d/ *doe* | /d/ *doe* |
| | /s/ *sue* | | | /ch/ *chew* | /ch/ *chew* |
| | | | | Adds /e/ *estop* | May sound close to /h/. |
| Many final consonants dropped. *lifuh, pathuh* | Many final consonants dropped or vocalized. | | | | Difficult. Often dropped |
| /b/ *tib*, /d/ *sid*, /g/ *sig* | Often dropped or vocalized. *situh* | | Not aspirated. Confusion with *b, d,* and *g.* | | Often dropped. |
| None. *cat, rock* | None. *cat, rock* | None. *cat, rock* | | | |
| Often dropped. | Often dropped. | | | | Often dropped. |
| None. One or more sounds dropped. | None. One or more sounds dropped. | | | Rare. One or more sounds dropped. | None. One or more sounds dropped |
| Rare. Most words monosyllabic. | Rare. Most words monosyllabic | | | | |
| None. Tone of individual words changes meaning. | None. Tone of individual words changes meaning. | | | | |

# Florida Resources

## Florida Writes!

**What Florida Writes! Is.** Beginning in 2000, the Florida Writing Assessment Program, also known as Florida Writes!, was called FCAT (Florida's Comprehensive Assessment Test) Writing. Florida Writes! is a performance test given in January to all public school students in grades 4, 8, and 10 throughout the state of Florida.

The test measures expository and narrative writing for 4th graders, persuasive and expository writing for 8th and 10th graders. The test is used to evaluate student progress, monitor writing trends, and to compare school systems across the state.

**How the Test Is Administered.** Every year one expository and one narrative prompt are developed. In each 4th grade class, both expository and narrative writing prompts are assigned randomly. Along with a prompt, students are given a folder with two lined sheets of paper for writing and a blank sheet for planning. Students have 45 minutes to plan, write, and edit a draft paper that incorporates the various elements of good writing—organization, focus, and support. All work is done individually.

**How the Test Is Scored.** All papers are scored holistically on a six point (0–6)rubric, which sets standards for focus, organization, support, and conventions. Judges are trained to evaluate the entire paper and do not focus exclusively on any one element. Each paper is read by at least two people and the scores are averaged. A copy of the Scoring Method, a sample rubric from 1998, and the Description of Writing Scores are included for convenience. These may also be found on the Florida Department of Education Florida Writes! home page. **www.firn.edu/doe/sas/fwaphome.htm.**

**Florida Writes! Resources in _Open Court Reading_.** Within its Language Arts strand, **_Open Court Reading_** gives students thorough development of the writing skills and strategies they need to do well on Florida Writes!

- The first unit of every grade level provides explicit instruction in writing process strategies of prewriting, drafting, revising, editing/proofreading, and publishing.

- Throughout each grade level, students have weekly practice in writing process strategies.

- Every weekly writing activity provides instruction for writing traits in revision and editing (ideas, organization, word choice, sentence fluency, voice, conventions).These are the same elements of the Florida Writes! scoring method: focus, organization, support, and conventions.

- Each grade level includes a complete scope and sequence of explicit instruction in English language conventions of grammar, usage, mechanics, and penmanship. Spelling and vocabulary skills and strategies are taught and practiced throughout each grade level as well.

- Unit assessments include on-demand writing prompt performance assessment that parallels the Florida Writes! assessment.

### Florida Writing Assessment Program (FLORIDA WRITES!)

#### Holistic Scoring Method

**Definition of Holistic Scoring** Holistic scoring is a method by which trained readers evaluate a piece of writing for its overall quality. The holistic scoring used in Florida requires readers to evaluate the work as a whole, while considering four elements: focus, organization, support, and conventions. This method is sometimes called focused holistic scoring. In this type of scoring, readers are trained not to become overly concerned with any one aspect of writing but to look at a response as a whole.

**Focus** Focus refers to how clearly the paper presents and maintains a main idea, theme, or unifying point. Papers representing the higher end of the point scale demonstrate a consistent awareness of the topic and do not contain extraneous information.

**Organization** Organization refers to the structure or plan of development (beginning, middle, and end) and whether the points logically relate to one another. Organization refers to (1) the use of transitional devices to signal the relationship of the supporting ideas to the main idea, theme, or unifying point and (2) the evidence of a connection between sentences. Papers representing the higher end of the point scale use transitions to signal the plan or text structure and end with summary or concluding statements.

**Support** Support refers to the quality of the details used to explain, clarify, or define. The quality of support depends on word choice, specificity, depth, credibility, and thoroughness. Papers representing the higher end of the point scale provide fully developed examples and illustrations in which the relationship between the supporting ideas and the topic is clear.

**Conventions** Conventions refer to punctuation, capitalization, spelling, and variation in sentence used in the paper. These conventions are basic writing skills included in Florida's Minimum Student Performance Standards and the Uniform Student Performance Standards for Language Arts. Papers representing the higher end of the scale follow, with few exceptions, the conventions of punctuation, capitalization, and spelling and use a variety of sentence structures to present ideas.

## Florida Writing Assessment Program (FLORIDA WRITES!)

### Fourth Grade Rubric for 1998

The rubric further interprets the four major areas of consideration into levels of achievement. The rubric used to score papers in spring 1998 is shown below.

**6 points** The writing is focused on the topic, has a logical organizational pattern (including a beginning, middle, conclusion and transitional devices), and has ample development of the supporting ideas. The paper demonstrates a sense of completeness or wholeness. The writing demonstrates a mature command of language including precision of word choice. Subject/verb agreement and verb and noun forms are generally correct. With few exceptions, the sentences are complete, except when fragments are used purposefully. Various sentence structures are used.

**5 points** The writing focuses on the topic with adequate development of the supporting ideas. There is an organizational pattern, although a few lapses may occur. The paper demonstrates a sense of completeness or wholeness. Word choice is adequate but may lack precision. Most sentences complete, although a few fragments may occur. There may be occasional errors in subject/verb agreement and in standard forms of verbs and nouns, but not enough to impede communication. The conventions of punctuation, capitalization, and spelling are generally followed. Various sentence structures are used.

**4 points** The writing is generally focused on the topic but may include extraneous or loosely related material. An organizational pattern is evident, although lapses may occur. The paper exhibits some sense of completeness or wholeness. In some areas of the response, the supporting ideas may contain specifics and details, while in other areas, the supporting ideas may not be developed. Word choice is generally adequate. Knowledge of the conventions of punctuation and capitalization is demonstrated, and commonly used words are usually spelled correctly. There has been an attempt to use a variety of sentence structures, although most are simple constructions.

**3 points** The writing is generally focused on the topic but may include some extraneous or loosely related material. Although an organizational pattern has been attempted and some transitional devices have been used, lapses may occur. The paper may lack a sense of completeness or wholeness. Some of the supporting ideas may not be developed with specifics and details. Word choice is adequate but limited, predictable, and occasionally vague. Knowledge of the conventions of punctuation and capitalization is demonstrated, and commonly used words are usually spelled correctly. There has been an attempt to use a variety of sentence structures, although most are simple constructions.

**2 points** The writing may be slightly related to the topic or may offer little relevant information and few supporting ideas or examples. The writing that is relevant to the topic exhibits little evidence of an organizational pattern or use of transitional devices. Development of the supporting ideas may be inadequate or illogical. Word choice may be limited or immature. Frequent errors may occur in basic punctuation and capitalization, and commonly used words may frequently be misspelled. The sentence structure may be limited to simple constructions.

**1 point** The writing may only minimally address the topic because there is little, if any, development of supporting ideas, and unrelated information may be included. The writing that is relevant tot the topic does not exhibit an organizational pattern; few, if any, transitional devices are used to signal movement in the text. Supporting ideas may be sparse, and they are usually provided through lists, cliches, and limited or immature word choice. Frequent errors in spelling, capitalization, punctuation, and sentence structure may impede communication. The sentence structure may be limited to simple constructions.

**Unscorable**
The paper is unscorable because:
6. the response is not related to what the prompt requested the student to do.
7. the response is simply a rewording of the prompt.
8. the response is a copy of a published work.
9. the student refused to write.
10. the response is written in a foreign language.
11. the response is illegible.
12. the response is incomprehensible (words are arranged in such a way that no meaning is conveyed.
13. the response contains an insufficient amount of writing to determine if the student was attempting to address the prompt.
14. the writing folder is blank.

# Florida Resources

## Correlation to Florida Sunshine State Standards  Grade K

| Strand A: Reading | Unit 1 | Unit 2 | Unit 3 |
|---|---|---|---|
| **STANDARD 1: The student uses the reading process effectively.** | | | |
| **BENCHMARK LA.A.1.1.1 The student predicts what a passage is about based on its title and illustrations. The student:** | | | |
| 1. uses titles and illustrations to make oral predictions. | T46, T81, T236, T328 | T98 | T31, T38, T98, T226 |
| **BENCHMARK LA.A.1.1.2 The student identifies words and constructs meaning from text, illustrations, graphics, and charts using the strategies of phonics, word structure, and context clues. The student:** | | | |
| 1. understands how print is organized and read (for example, locates print on a page, matches print to speech, knows parts of a book, reads top-to-bottom and left-to-right, sweeps back to left for the next line). | T28, T49, T71, T81, T85, T93, T110, T111, T117, T132, T133, T137, T153, T162, T173, T241, T261, T265, T269, T287 | T37, T43, T52, T92, T101, T162, T220, T229, T233 | T33, T45, T51, T105, T147, T231 |
| 2. knows the names of the letters of the alphabet (both upper and lower case). | T55, T62, T108, T130, T170, T234, T235, T263, T265, T298, T316, T323 | T24, T37, T66, T78, T103, T107, T112, T114, T116, T125, T126, T128, T138, T146, T148, T164, T176, T186, T198 | T25, T35, T41, T47, T52, T78, T101, T109, T120, T158, T208, T233, T282, T284 |
| 3. knows the sounds of the letters of the alphabet. | | | T174 |
| 4. understands the concept of words and constructs meaning from shared text, illustrations, graphics, and charts. | T127, T143, T145, T157, T159, T167, T168, T169, T177, T199, T313 | T33-T35, T51, T52, T63-T65, T101, T103, T112-T113, T125-T127, T139, T147, T162, T173 | T22, T33, T51, T79, T93, T94, T117, T119, T120, T135, T183, T222, T223, T245, T246, T259, T273, T274 |
| 5. understands basic phonetic principles (for example, knows rhyming words; knows words that have the same initial and final sounds; knows which sound is in the beginning, middle, end of a word; blends individual sounds into words). | T65, T91, T107, T111, T129, T133, T145, T149, T159, T163, T169, T187, T191, T201, T213, T223, T227, T233, T251, T279 | T34, T64, T76, T92, T112, T126, T138, T146, T184, T204, T220, T262, T278, T286 | T22, T23, T35, T52, T53, T68, T69, T76, T77, T148, T149, T172, T173, T184, T185, T192, T193, T198, T200, T206, T247, T260 |
| 6. understands that print conveys meaning. | T39, T61, T81, T97, T277, T323, T333 | T33, T45, T51, T61, T63, T125, T245, T261, T289 | T33, T155, T183, T191, T197, T206, T233, T237, T239, T259, T282 |
| **BENCHMARK LA.A.1.1.3 The student uses knowledge of appropriate grade-, age-, and developmental-level vocabulary in reading. The student:** | | | |
| 1. identifies frequently used words. | T173, T236, T237, T328 | T130, T149, T180, T181, T207, T289 | T43, T78, T79, T109, T158, T159, T208, T233, T284 |
| 2. identifies words that name persons, places, or things and words that name actions. | T39, T61, T81, T89, T97, T127, T143, T157, T199, T211, T277, T295, T313 | T93, T111, T125, T137, T145, T153, T203, T211, T245, T261, T277, T285 | T117, T133, T147, T155, T163, T183, T191, T259, T281, T289 |
| 3. identifies and sorts common words from within basic categories (such as colors, shapes, foods). | T39, T61, T81, T89, T97, T106, T111, T128, T144, T211, T212, T222, T239, T277, T278, T295, T313 | T93, T111, T125, T137, T145, T153, T245, T261, T277, T285, T293 | T33, T51, T67, T75, T83, T117, T133, T147, T155, T163, T183, T191, T197, T245, T259, T273, T281, T289 |
| 4. uses a variety of sources to build vocabulary (for example, word walls, other people, life experiences). | T39, T46, T61, T66, T81, T89, T97, T114, T134, T150, T194, T199, T206, T211, T231, T241, T258, T284, T302 | T40, T56, T68, T98, T111, T116, T125, T130, T137, T145, T153, T168, T178, T190, T203, T211, T226, T245, T261 | T33, T38, T51, T54, T67, T75, T83, T98, T117, T122, T133, T136, T147, T155, T163, T178, T183, T197, T205, T213, T225 |
| 5. develops vocabulary by discussing characters and events from a story. | T36, T59, T61, T73, T119, T121, T125, T141, T143, T150, T153, T155, T164, T197, T261, T267 | T59, T61, T105, T107, T109, T116, T119, T121, T123, T130, T133, T142, T171, T181, T241 | T29, T49, T54, T57, T59, T61, T63, T65, T72, T73, T107, T115, T191, T229, T235, T237, T239 |
| **BENCHMARK LA.A.1.1.4 The student increases comprehension by rereading, retelling, and discussion. The student:** | | | |
| 1. uses strategies to comprehend text (for example, retelling, discussing, asking questions). | T36, T59, T71, T73, T79, T87, T119, T121, T125, T127, T137, T139, T141, T143, T150, T153, T155, T157, T164, T167 | T29, T33, T47, T49, T51, T59, T61, T63, T68, T71, T73, T75, T83, T105, T107, T109, T116, T119, T121, T123, T130 | T29, T41, T49, T54, T57, T59, T61, T63, T65, T67, T72, T73, T79, T83, T107, T111, T115, T125, T127, T129, T131, T136 |
| **STANDARD 2: The student constructs meaning from a wide range of texts.** | | | |
| **BENCHMARK LA.A.2.1.1: The student determines the main idea or essential message from text and identifies supporting information. The student:** | | | |
| 1. knows the main idea or essential message from a read-aloud story or informational piece. | T295 | T49, T259 | T115, T243 |
| **BENCHMARK LA.A.2.1.2: The student selects material to read for pleasure. The student:** | | | |
| 1. selects materials to read for pleasure. | T174 | | T160 |
| **BENCHMARK LA.A.2.1.3: The student reads for information to use in performing a task and learning a new task. The student:** | | | |
| 1. supports oral and written responses with details from the informative text. | | T73, T257, T259, T269, T271 | T129, T139 |

| Unit 4 | Unit 5 | Unit 6 | Unit 7 | Unit 8 |
|---|---|---|---|---|
| T42, T190, T246 | T40, T224 | T26, T40, T104, T184, T240 | T26, T40, T108, T194, T250 | T26, T42, T112, T192, T242 |
| T42, T45, T114, T200, T222 | T47, T56 | T31, T43, T47, T58, T70, T107, T124, T138, T148, T184, T194, T255 | T31, T43, T47, T49, T60, T70, T119, T194, T204, T253, T259, T261 | T33, T53, T115, T119, T121, T123, T245, T247, T249, T255, T257 |
| T35, T49, T57, T77, T87, T92, T97, T129, T141, T153, T165, T170, T175, T199, T206, T226, T282, T310 | T24, T52, T54, T114, T126, T178, T186, T231 | T22, T33, T36, T51, T56, T65, T100, T113, T115, T148, T150, T178, T187, T202, T210-T211, T216, T234, T257, T273 | T24, T45, T47, T74, T104, T111, T113, T117, T126, T146, T160, T197, T212, T220, T228, T246, T253, T269, T312 | T39, T53, T60, T108, T123, T127, T132, T245, T281 |
| T24-T27, T37-T39, T47, T60, T61, T145, T154-T157, T167-T169 | T22-T25, T34-T37, T54, T55, T69-T71, T77-T79, T93-T95, T107, T113-T115, T124-T127, T138-T140, T147, T148, T165-T167 | T22-T25, T34-T37, T54-T57, T66-T70, T82-T85, T100-T101, T120-T123, T134-T137, T148-T151, T158-T162, T177-T180 | T23-T25, T34-T37, T56-T59, T71-T74, T87-T89, T103-T105, T127-T129, T144-T147, T158-T161, T169-T172, T186-T190 | T22-T25, T37-T39, T59-T61, T78-T81, T89-T92, T107-T109, T131-T133, T147-T149, T160-T163, T238-T239, T263-T264 |
| T58, T88, T114, T129, T158, T166, T246 | T33, T40, T67, T76, T98, T124, T175, T201, T202, T224, T241, T246, T273 | T33, T53, T104, T147, T199, T264 | T33, T83, T157, T194, T204 | T42, T45, T47, T62, T77, T197 |
| T22, T23, T37-T39, T58-T61, T78, T80, T81, T89-T91, T93, T106, T107, T109-T111, T119, T121, T283, T286, T299, T300, T301 | T22, T23, T25, T34-37, T52-T55, T68-T71, T76-T79, T92-T95, T107, T218-T221, T229, T242-T245, T258-T262, T274-T276, T282 | T22-T25, T34-T37, T54-T57, T66-T70, T82-T85, T98-T99, T107, T109, T113, T121-T123, T135-T137, T148-T150, T158-T162 | T22-T25, T33-T37, T56-T59, T71-T74, T87-T88, T93, T102-T105, T127-T129, T143-T145, T157-T161, T168-T172, T187-T190 | T22-T25, T37-T39, T59-T61, T78-T79, T81, T88-T89, T91-T92, T107-T109, T130-T133, T146-T149, T161-T163, T170-T173 |
| T35, T47, T57, T77, T87, T97, T123, T125, T141, T165, T213, T221, T231 | T43, T51, T75, T105, T107, T155, T193, T227, T233 | T45, T109, T147, T291 | T123, T125, T235 | T145, T159, T197, T229, T261 |
| T49, T92, T93, T121, T170, T226, T249, T298, T310, T311 | T103, T128, T151, T196, T197, T263, T285 | T70, T162, T180, T220, T234, T296, T306 | T24, T55, T70, T86, T161, T172 | T22, T35, T57, T77-78, T81, T91-92, T109, T130, T149, T163 |
| T35, T57, T77, T87, T97, T129, T141, T153, T165, T175, T195, T205, T213, T265, T281, T297, T305, T315 | T33, T51, T67, T75, T83, T111, T123, T137, T145, T155, T175, T185, T193, T241, T257, T273, T281, T289 | T33, T53, T65, T81, T89, T119, T147, T157, T167, T259, T273, T291, T301, T311 | T167, T273 | T35, T57, T77, T88, T145, T159, T275, T291 |
| T35, T57, T77, T87, T97, T129, T141, T153, T165, T175, T265, T281, T297, T305, T315 | T33, T51, T67, T75, T83, T111, T123, T137, T145, T155, T191, T241, T257, T273, T281 | T33, T65, T119, T133, T147, T157, T167, T215, T259, T273, T291, T311 | T125, T157, T167, T177, T273, T291, T309, T321, T331 | T35, T57, T77, T87, T97, T160 |
| T35, T57, T62, T77, T87, T97, T114, T129, T134, T141, T146, T153, T158, T165, T175, T190, T195, T200, T205, T213, T221 | T33, T51, T67, T75, T83, T111, T123, T137, T145, T241 | T33, T53, T65, T81, T89, T119, T133, T147, T157, T167, T215, T259 | T55, T69, T85, T93, T125, T157, T167, T177, T273 | T35, T57, T77, T87, T97, T129, T145, T159, T169, T197, T207, T266, T275 |
| T31, T55, T57, T65, T67, T69, T71, T73, T75, T77, T82, T83, T93, T117, T123, T141, T193, T261 | T29, T49, T51, T59, T61, T65, T72, T109, T121, T123, T131, T133, T135, T142, T235, T239, T249 | T30, T75, T77, T79, T117, T127, T129, T131, T141, T145, T257, T267, T269, T271, T281, T283 | T39, T79, T123, T143, T271, T281, T283, T285, T287, T289, T291, T299 | T57, T82, T137, T139, T141, T143, T145, T153, T155, T157, T195, T205, T207, T269, T271 |
| T31, T35, T51, T55, T65, T67, T69, T71, T73, T75, T82, T83, T85, T93, T117, T123, T125, T127, T137, T139, T149, T151 | T29, T49, T59, T61, T63, T65, T72, T73, T103, T109, T119, T121, T131, T133, T135, T142, T151, T155, T173, T180, T183, T197 | T30, T51, T61, T63, T70, T75, T77, T79, T117, T127, T129, T131, T141, T143, T145, T162, T180, T194, T257, T267, T269, T271 | T30, T39, T53, T63, T65, T67, T74, T79, T81, T83, T123, T133, T135, T137, T139, T141, T151, T153, T155, T162, T190 | T31, T41, T55, T65, T67, T69, T71, T73, T75, T127, T137, T139, T141, T143, T153, T155, T157, T165, T179, T195, T205, T269 |
| T193, T263 | T49, T65, T239, T271 | T51, T63, T79, T81, T311 | T53, T123, T271, T307, T321 | T31 |
|  | T80 |  |  | T83, T300 |
| T31, T263 |  |  | T314 |  |

# Florida Resources

## Correlation to Florida Sunshine State Standards — Grade K

### Strand A: Reading

| | Unit 1 | Unit 2 | Unit 3 |
|---|---|---|---|
| **BENCHMARK LA.A.2.1.4:** The student knows strategies to use to discover whether information presented in a text is true, including asking others and checking another source. The student: | | | |
| **1.** understands that illustrations reinforce the information in a text. | T71, T119, T121, T153, T211, T273, T289, T293, T305 | T29, T73, T107, T184, T241 | T67, T107, T125, T155, T239, T281 |
| **BENCHMARK LA.A.2.1.5:** The student uses simple materials of the reference system to obtain information. The student: | | | |
| **1.** knows alphabetical order of letters. | T26, T42, T64, T84, T92, T130, T160, T170, T188, T202, T214 | T36, T78, T128, T148, T222, T248, T249, T264, T280, T281 | T134, T148 |
| **2.** uses pictures, environmental print and people to obtain information. | T28, T39, T97, T174, T231, T261, T277, T295, T313, T323, T333 | T29, T47, T55, T61, T71 | |
| **3.** asks "how" and "why" questions about a topic. | | T26, T29 | |

### Strand B: Writing

| | Unit 1 | Unit 2 | Unit 3 |
|---|---|---|---|
| **STANDARD 1:** The student uses writing processes effectively. | | | |
| **BENCHMARK LA.B.1.1.1:** The student makes a plan for writing that includes a central idea and related ideas. The student: | | | |
| **1.** uses prewriting strategies (such as drawing pictures, recording or dictating questions for investigation). | T36, T95, T125, T175, T177, T199, T211, T219, T221, T231, T241, T315, T329, T331 | T26, T30, T49, T80, T150, T208, T226, T261, T283 | T26, T80, T81, T133, T153, T161, T191, T210, T259, T278, T287 |
| **2.** generates ideas through brainstorming, listening to text read by teacher, discussion. | T127, T143, T157, T167, T177, T277, T313 | T80, T245 | T117, T183, T245 |
| **BENCHMARK LA.B.1.1.2:** The student drafts and revises simple sentences and passages, stories, letters, and simple explanations that: <br>• express ideas clearly; <br>• show an awareness of topic and audience; <br>• have a beginning, middle, and ending; <br>• effectively use common words; <br>• have supporting detail; and <br>• are in legible printing. <br>The student: | | | |
| **1.** dictates messages (such as news and stories). | | | |
| **2.** uses basic writing formats (for example, labels, lists, notes, captions, stories, messages). | T39, T175, T331 | | T33, T51, T67, T75, T83, T117, T133, T147, T155, T163, T197, T205, T210, T213, T273, T281 |
| **3.** demonstrates ability to sequence events during shared writing exercises. | T221, T277 | T203 | |
| **4.** revises by adding details to pictures, dictation, or letters. | T315 | | T155, T205, T281 |
| **BENCHMARK LA.B.1.1.3:** The student produces final simple documents that have been edited for: <br>• correct spelling; <br>• appropriate end punctuation; <br>• correct capitalization of initial words, "I," and names of people; <br>• correct sentence structure; and <br>• correct usage of age-appropriate verb/subject and noun/pronoun agreement. <br>The student: | | | |
| **1.** uses spelling approximations in written work. | | | |
| **2.** uses directionality of print in writing (including but not limited to left-to-right, top-to-bottom, spacing between words). | T238, T278, T331 | T150, T291 | T163, T213, T289 |
| **3.** identifies and attempts to use end punctuation (such as the period, question mark, exclamation point). | T329 | T137, T153, T173, T183, T195, T231, T241, T245, T250, T261, T277, T293 | T103, T113, T159, T163, T206, T213, T233, T237, T239, T289 |
| **STANDARD 2:** The student writes to communicate ideas and information effectively. | | | |
| **BENCHMARK LA.B.2.1.1:** The student writes questions and observations about familiar topics, stories, or new experiences. The student: | | | |
| **1.** dictates or writes with pictures or words a narrative about a familiar experience. | T241, T313, T333 | | T80, T160 |
| **2.** contributes ideas during a shared writing activity. | T61, T89, T143, T157, T211, T313 | | T117, T183, T210, T245 |

| Unit 4 | Unit 5 | Unit 6 | Unit 7 | Unit 8 |
|---|---|---|---|---|
| T123, T165, T257 | T51, T103, T137, T235, T289 | | T314 | T224 |
| | T36, T70, T78, T94, T166, T186, T260, T276 | T36, T68, T120, T136, T150, T160, T192, T218, T262, T276 | T58, T72, T88, T126, T170, T200, T228, T276, T294 | T83 |
| T31, T257, T261 | | T109, T117 | | T65, T67, T69, T71, T73 |
| T31, T94 | | | | |
| T32, T94, T95, T113, T190, T211, T227, T228, T246 | T49, T51, T72, T81, T97, T123, T142, T143, T169, T183, T185, T206, T223, T239, T257 | T53, T86, T133, T164, T199, T222, T273, T299 | T55, T143, T162, T174, T209, T291, T319 | T57, T85, T94, T145, T167, T207, T226, T227, T275, T296 |
| T32 | T30, T33, T111, T143, T152, T175, T183, T239, T241 | T33, T259 | T33, T125, T190, T199, T273 | T35, T129, T197 |
| | T206, T233 | | T164, T174, T317-T318 | T164, T166, T294 |
| T211 | T67, T137, T143, T155, T206, T273 | T86, T164, T222 | | T77, T85, T94, T159, T213, T226, T291 |
| | T111, T123, T145 | | | |
| | T75, T145, T201, T281 | T81, T153, T157, T215, T299, T301 | T85, T165, T167, T225 | T87, T169, T221 |
| T94 | | | T309 | T94 |
| T94, T209, T228, T285, T313 | T142, T143, T193, T206, T289 | T86, T164, T225, T263, T299, T311 | T217, T232 | T94, T167, T224, T305 |
| T47, T53, T117, T123, T125, T227, T251, T255, T311 | T83, T101, T105, T229 | T89, T167, T189, T199, T207, T259, T291, T311 | T190, T267 | T117, T223-T224 |
| | T137, T143, T206 | T154 | | T84-T85 |
| T129 | T206 | T119 | | |

# Florida Resources

## Correlation to Florida Sunshine State Standards  Grade K

| Strand B: Writing | Unit 1 | Unit 2 | Unit 3 |
|---|---|---|---|
| **BENCHMARK L.A.B.2.1.2:** The student uses knowledge and experience to tell about experiences or to write for familiar occasions, audiences, and purposes. The student: | | | |
| **1.** dictates and writes with pictures or words to record ideas and reflections. | T97, T143, T211, T221, T231, T295 | T130, T150, T275 | T33, T67, T83, T133, T147, T191, T197, T213 |
| **BENCHMARK LA.B.2.1.3:** The student uses basic computer skills for writing, such as basic word-processing techniques such as keying words, copying, cutting, and pasting; using e-mail; and accessing and using basic educational software for writing. The student: | | | |
| **1.** uses basic computer skills for writing (including but not limited to using a mouse, locating numbers/letters on keyboard, turning computer on/off, and locating and opening application icon). | | | |
| **BENCHMARK LA.B.2.1.4:** The student composes simple sets of instructions for simple tasks using logical sequencing of steps. The student: | | | |
| **1.** dictates or writes simple informational texts (such as descriptions, labels, lists). | T39, T61, T174, T221, T238, T295 | T253, T257, T259, T269, T271 | T51, T75 |

## Strand C: Listening, Viewing, and Speaking

| | Unit 1 | Unit 2 | Unit 3 |
|---|---|---|---|
| **STANDARD 1:** The student uses listening strategies effectively. | | | |
| **BENCHMARK LA.C.1.1.1:** The student listens for a variety of informational purposes, including curiosity, pleasure, getting directions, performing tasks, solving problems, and following rules. The student: | | | |
| **1.** follows two-step oral directions. | T24, T25, T27, T40, T41, T43, T46, T49, T51, T53, T55, T57, T59, T62-T66, T69, T71, T75, T77, T82-T85, T87, T90-T94 | T22-T25, T34-T37, T43, T45, T52, T54-T56, T64-T67, T76-T78, T92-T95, T98, T101, T103, T107, T112-T115, T126-T129 | T22, T23, T25, T34, T35, T41, T43, T45, T47, T52, T53, T68-T73, T76, T77, T80, T92-T94, T101, T105, T109, T113, T118-T120 |
| **2.** listens to oral language in different forms (such as stories read aloud, audio tapes, nursery rhymes, songs). | T24-T26, T28, T30, T40-T43, T48-T59, T64, T65, T68-T79, T82, T83-T85, T87, T90, T92, T93, T108, T110, T111, T116-T125, T130 | T22, T25, T26, T37, T42-T49, T52-T55, T58-T61, T64-T67, T70-T73, T76, T78, T92, T94, T95, T100-T109, T112, T114, T115 | T26, T33, T34, T40-T49, T52, T56-T65, T92, T100-T115, T118, T124-T131, T138-T145, T148, T152, T156, T158, T172 |
| **3.** listens for pleasure. | T196, T197 | | |
| **BENCHMARK LA.C.1.1.2:** The student recognizes personal preferences in listening to literature and other material. The student: | | | |
| **1.** knows personal preferences for listening to literature and other material (such as nursery rhymes, songs, stories). | T79, T311, T330 | T290 | T287 |
| **BENCHMARK LA.C.1.1.3:** The student carries on a conversation with another person, seeking answers and further explanations of the other's ideas through questioning and answering. The student: | | | |
| **1.** follows rules of conversation (such as taking turns speaking and listening). | T231 | | T203, T271 |
| **BENCHMARK LA.C.1.1.4:** The student retells specific details of information heard, including sequence of events. The student: | | | |
| **1.** listens for specific information, including sequence of events. | T41, T63, T83, T91, T129, T213, T223, T233, T251, T279, T313 | T163, T174, T175 | T23, T34, T69, T75, T118, T152, T222, T247, T261, T275, T283 |
| **STANDARD 2:** The student uses viewing strategies effectively. | | | |
| **BENCHMARK LA.C.2.1.1:** The student determines the main idea in a nonprint communication. The student: | | | |
| **1.** understands the main idea in a nonprint communication. | T167, T219, T229, T231 | T201 | T195, T203 |
| **BENCHMARK LA.C.2.1.2:** The student recognizes simple nonverbal cues, such as use of eye contact, smiles, simple hand gestures. The student: | | | |
| **1.** understands simple nonverbal cues (such as smiling, gesturing). | | | T205, T211 |
| **STANDARD 3:** The student uses speaking strategies effectively. | | | |
| **BENCHMARK LA.C.3.1.1:** The student speaks clearly and at a volume audible in large- or small-group settings. The student: | | | |
| **1.** speaks clearly and uses appropriate volume in different settings (such as choral speaking, informal conversations, shared readings). | T107, T129, T202, T213, T231, T252 | T22 | T163, T174, T195, T203 |

| Unit 4 | Unit 5 | Unit 6 | Unit 7 | Unit 8 |
|---|---|---|---|---|
| T35, T57, T77, T94, T97, T129, T141, T153, T165, T175, T195, T205, T213, T221, T228 | T152, T239 | | T163 | T35, T129 |
| T34, T128, T172, T194 | | | | |
| T25, T114, T149, T151, T161, T172, T173 | T30, T61, T119, T199, T239 | T65, T147, T207, T222, T291, T299 | T63 | |

| Unit 4 | Unit 5 | Unit 6 | Unit 7 | Unit 8 |
|---|---|---|---|---|
| T22, T24, T26, T27, T37-T39, T42, T45, T47, T49, T53, T58-T62, T78-T81, T88-91, T93-T95, T106, T107, T109-T111, T114, T117 | T22-T25, T31, T34-T37, T43, T47, T52-T56, T67-T73, T76-T81, T92-T95, T98, T101, T105, T107, T112-T116, T124-T127 | T22-T25, T34-T37, T43, T47, T49, T51, T54-T58, T66-T70, T72, T82-T86, T98-T101, T104, T107, T109, T111, T113, T115, T120-T124 | T22-T25, T34-T37, T40, T43, T47, T49, T51, T53, T56-T60, T71-T74, T76, T86-T90, T102-T105, T111, T113, T115, T117, T119, T121 | T22-T25, T36-T39, T49, T53, T55, T58-T62, T78-T81, T83-T84, T88-T92, T94, T106-T109, T115, T117, T119, T121, T123, T125, T127 |
| T22, T25, T28, T36, T44-T55, T58, T64-T75, T80, T83, T88, T90, T92, T106, T108, T109, T116-T127, T130, T132 | T26, T36, T42-49, T52, T54, T55, T58-65, T68, T70, T76, T78, T100-109, T112, T114, T115, T118-121, T124, T130-135 | T24, T26, T36, T42-51, T54, T56, T57, T60-63, T68, T70, T74-79, T84, T85, T98, T100, T106-117, T122, T126-131, T136 | T22, T24, T26, T36, T42-53, T56, T58, T59, T62-67, T70, T72, T74, T78-83, T88-89, T104, T110-123, T126, T128, T132-T141 | T26, T36, T38, T44-55, T58, T64-75, T78, T84, T92, T114-127, T136-143, T146, T152-157, T174, T188, T194-195, T198 |
| | | T309 | | |
| T303, T312 | T286 | T308-T309 | T249, T328 | T289, T304 |
| T203 | T145, T199 | T81, T155 | T85 | T87 |
| T23, T24, T37-T38, T60, T79, T80, T88-T90, T106, T109, T110, T132, T143, T144, T155, T156, T167, T168, T184-T186, T198 | T25, T36, T53, T54, T58-T65, T70, T77, T78, T92, T94, T113, T114, T125, T126, T166, T188, T204, T244, T260, T275 | T81, T100 | T24, T58, T72, T88, T104, T128, T160-T161, T170, T202, T212, T220, T228, T246, T276, T294, T312 | T58, T148-T149, T238, T294 |
| T211, T219 | T145, T191, T199 | T205, T213, T301 | T167, T215, T223 | T211, T219 |
| | T281 | | | T87, T221 |
| T203, T302, T303 | T199, T201, T209 | T81, T152, T155 | T215, T223, T232, T319 | T297, T299 |

# Florida Resources

## Correlation to Florida Sunshine State Standards
### Grade K

| Strand C: Listening, Viewing, and Speaking | Unit 1 | Unit 2 | Unit 3 |
|---|---|---|---|
| **BENCHMARK LA.C.3.1.2: The student asks questions to seek answers and further explanation of other people's ideas. The student:** | | | |
| **1.** asks and responds to questions. | T36, T45, T59, T71, T79, T119, T128, T132, T137, T139, T141, T148, T153, T155, T190, T197, T204, T219, T229, T250, T255 | T29, T39, T49, T52, T59, T61, T68, T71, T73, T97, T105, T107, T109, T112, T121, T123, T133, T142, T146, T181, T189 | T29, T37, T49, T57, T59, T61, T63, T65, T107, T111, T125, T127, T129, T131, T136, T139, T141, T143, T145, T186, T189 |
| **BENCHMARK LA.C.3.1.3: The student speaks effectively in conversations with others. The student:** | | | |
| **1.** uses basic speaking vocabulary to convey a message in conversation (such as numbers, adjectives, action words, shapes, colors, categories). | T30, T36, T37, T45, T46, T53, T71, T73, T79, T89, T94, T106, T113, T114, T119, T121, T137, T139, T141, T153, T155, T174 | T25, T39, T40, T47, T55, T56, T61, T68, T80, T81, T98, T105, T107, T109, T116, T119, T121, T123, T130, T133, T142 | T29, T31, T37, T49, T54, T57, T59, T61, T63, T65, T72, T73, T98, T107, T111, T115, T122, T125, T127, T129, T131, T136 |
| **BENCHMARK LA.C.3.1.4: The student uses eye contact and simple gestures when speaking. The student:** | | | |
| **1.** uses eye contact and appropriate gestures to enhance oral delivery. | | | |

## Strand D: Language

| | Unit 1 | Unit 2 | Unit 3 |
|---|---|---|---|
| **STANDARD 1: The student understands the nature of language.** | | | |
| **BENCHMARK LA.D.1.1.1: The student recognizes basic patterns in and functions of language (patterns such as characteristic sounds and rhythms and those found in written forms; functions such as asking questions, expressing oneself, describing objects or experience, and explaining). The student:** | | | |
| **1.** knows patterns of sound in oral language (such as rhyming, choral poetry, chants). | T65, T91, T107, T129, T145, T149, T159, T163, T169, T191, T201, T213, T223, T227, T233, T251, T277, T279, T295, T297 | T34, T76, T92, T112, T126, T128, T138, T146, T184, T196, T203, T204, T220, T262, T278, T286 | T22, T52, T68, T76, T148, T172, T184, T192, T198, T206, T260, T274, T282 |
| **BENCHMARK LA.D.1.1.2: The student recognizes the differences between language that is used at home and language that is used at school. The student:** | | | |
| **1.** recognizes the differences between less formal language that is used at home and more formal language that is used at school and other public settings. | | | T262 |
| **STANDARD 2: The student understands the power of language.** | | | |
| **BENCHMARK LA.D.2.1.1: The student understands that word choice can shape ideas, feelings, and actions. The student:** | | | |
| **1.** word choice can shape feelings, actions. | T199, T211, T221, T231, T241 | T75, T173, T183, T203 | T33, T51, T67, T75, T83, T183, T191, T197, T205, T213 |
| **BENCHMARK LA.D.2.1.2: The student identifies and uses repetition, rhyme, and rhythm in oral and written text. The student:** | | | |
| **1.** uses repetition, rhyme, and rhythm in oral and written texts (such as recites songs, poems, and stories with repeating patterns; substitutes words in a rhyming pattern). | T42, T63, T82, T83, T129, T201, T213, T251, T255, T277, T295, T297, T313, T323, T333 | T22, T76, T126, T146, T196, T204, T285 | T172, T184, T206 |
| **2.** understands the use of alliteration. | T255 | T285 | |
| **BENCHMARK LA.D.2.1.3: The student recognizes that use of more than one medium increases the power to influence how one thinks and feels. The student:** | | | |
| **1.** understands that the use of more than one medium can influence how one thinks and feels (for example, music, illustrations). | T219, T221, T229, T231, T241, T323 | T201 | T195, T197, T203, T205, T213 |
| **BENCHMARK LA.D.2.1.4: The student knows various types of mass media. The student:** | | | |
| **1.** knows various types of mass media (such as film, video, television). | | | T37, T225 |

## Strand E: Literature

| | Unit 1 | Unit 2 | Unit 3 |
|---|---|---|---|
| **STANDARD 1: The student understands the common features of a variety of literary forms.** | | | |
| **BENCHMARK LA.E.1.1.1: The student knows the basic characteristics of fables, stories, and legends. The student:** | | | |
| **1.** knows a variety of familiar literary genres (such as fiction, nonfiction, picture books, fairy tales, legends). | | T109, T116, T130, T273 | |
| **BENCHMARK LA.E.1.1.2: The student identifies the story elements of setting, plot, character, problem, and solution/resolution. The student:** | | | |
| **1.** knows the sequence of events, characters, and setting of stories (such as read-aloud stories). | T125, T164, T165, T261, T320 | T142, T282 | T49, T54, T65, T136, T152, T160, T210, T229, T243, T253, T255, T257, T265, T267, T269 |

| Unit 4 | Unit 5 | Unit 6 | Unit 7 | Unit 8 |
|---|---|---|---|---|
| T22, T28, T31, T41 T51, T55, T65, T67, T69, T73, T75, T123, T137, T149, T172, T193, T203, T211, T219, T245, T246, T263 | T26, T29, T39, T40, T45, T49, T97, T103, T121, T131, T133, T135, T191, T223, T237, T239, T249, T251, T253 | T30, T39, T51, T61, T63, T75, T77, T79, T103, T117, T127, T129, T131, T141, T143, T145, T154, T183, T205, T213, T257, T267 | T26, T30, T53, T65, T67, T79, T81, T83, T123, T133, T135, T137, T139, T141, T151, T153, T155, T197, T215, T223 | T31, T45, T47, T51, T55, T65, T67, T69, T71, T73, T75, T127, T137, T139, T141, T143, T153, T155, T241, T259, T269, T271, T289 |
| T28, T31, T33, T41, T51, T55, T62, T71, T75, T83, T123, T127, T134, T137, T139, T146, T149, T151, T158, T161 | T26, T29, T31, T39, T40, T49, T56, T59, T65, T73, T80, T97, T103, T109, T115, T116, T119, T121, T131, T133, T135 | T30-T31, T39-T40, T63, T75, T77, T79, T103-T104, T117, T138, T154, T183, T197, T205, T213, T239-T240, T301, T308 | T26, T30-T31, T40, T67, T76, T81, T83, T107-T108, T133, T137, T139, T141, T193, T215, T223, T250, T271, T321 | T26, T31, T33, T41-42, T45, T47, T51, T55, T65, T67, T69, T71, T73, T75, T111-T112, T169, T191, T211, T219, T242, T273, T289 |
| T85, T302, T303, T305 | T281 | T152, T155 | T225, T232, T319 | T87, T221, T297 |
| T22, T58, T78, T106, T130, T142, T154, T166, T184, T196, T214, T222, T266, T306 | T22, T52, T68, T76, T92, T112, T146, T164, T201, T242, T282 | T34, T54, T66, T82, T98, T107, T109, T113, T176, T190, T260, T274 | T85 | T146 |
| | T98, T281 | | | T299 |
| T35, T57, T77, T87, T97, T195, T205, T213, T221, T231 | T111, T123, T137, T145, T155, T175, T185, T271 | T187, T189 | | T45, T47, T49, T51 |
| T25, T58, T88, T130, T154, T184, T196, T214, T222, T266 | T52, T68, T76, T112, T146, T186, T201, T282 | T34, T54, T66, T109, T148, T176, T200 | T85, T86, T210, T221, T310 | T24, T80, T106, T146, T300 |
| T184, T214, T222, T266 | T186, T282 | T66, T148, T200 | T86, T210, T221, T310 | T24, T80, T281, T300 |
| T195, T205, T211, T213, T219, T221, T231 | T175, T185, T191, T193, T199, T201, T209 | T157, T187, T189, T205 | T209, T215, T223, T235, T309 | T211, T219, T221 |
| | | | | |
| T35, T77, T195, T231, T265, T273 | T33, T39, T75, T83, T137, T175, T183, T185, T209, T241, T257, T281, T289 | | T33, T193, T249 | T35 |
| T51, T82, T83, T263, T279, T295 | T45, T59, T61, T63, T65, T72, T73, T135, T237, T255, T263, T278 | T298 | T30, T164, T174, T281, T285, T289, T316-T318 | T85, T157, T167 |

# Florida Resources

## Correlation to Florida Sunshine State Standards — Grade K

### Strand A: Reading

| | Unit 1 | Unit 2 | Unit 3 |
|---|---|---|---|
| **STANDARD 2: The student responds critically to fiction, nonfiction, poetry, and drama.** | | | |
| **BENCHMARK LA.E.2.1.1:** The student uses personal perspective in responding to a work of literature, such as relating characters and simple events in a story or biography to people or events in his or her own life. The student: | | | |
| 1. relates characters and simple events in a read-aloud to own life. | T36, T141, T173, T209 | T97, T149 | T153, T181, T186, T189 |
| 2. uses a variety of personal interpretations to respond to stories and poems (such as talk, movement, music, art, drama, writing). | T87, T221, T231, T241, T301, T305 | T115, T195, T203, T211, T265, T275, T281, T288 | T52, T197, T205, T211, T213 |
| **BENCHMARK LA.E.2.1.2:** The student recognizes rhymes, rhythm, and patterned structures in children's texts. The student: | | | |
| 1. knows rhymes, rhythms, and patterned in children's text (such as repetitive text, pattern books, nursery rhymes). | | T281, T288 | |

## Grade 1

### Strand A: Reading

| | Unit 1 | Unit 2 | Unit 3 | Unit 4 |
|---|---|---|---|---|
| **STANDARD 1: The student uses the reading process effectively.** | | | | |
| **BENCHMARK LA.A.1.1.1 The student predicts what a passage is about based on its title and illustrations. The student:** | | | | |
| 1. uses prior knowledge, illustrations, and text to make predictions. | T92, T148, T234, T238, T239, T273, T293, T315, T318 | T52, T74, T76, T166, T184, T202, T224, T228, T256, T278, T298 | T48, T66, T68, T71, T82, T100, T162, T182, T198, T254, T281 | T35, T49, T67, T68, T85, T86, T101, T102, T126, T146, T164, T226 |
| **BENCHMARK LA.A.1.1.2 The student identifies words and constructs meaning from text, illustrations, graphics, and charts using the strategies of phonics, word structure, and context clues. The student:** | | | | |
| 1. uses basic elements of phonetic analysis (for example, hears, segments, substitutes, and blends sounds in words). | T25, T26, T32, T33, T42, T43, T44, T60, T61, T62, T64, T80, T81, T82, T84, T98, T99, T101, T108, T124, T125, T128, T134 | T23-T26, T29, T30, T40-T48, T54, T62-T66, T68-T70, T84-T93, T104-T112, T116, T135, T138-T141 | T22-T25, T27, T28, T40, T43, T58–T60, T62, T64, T76, T77, T79, T80, T84, T94-T97, T120-T122, T140, T141 | T22, T23, T25, T38–T42, T45, T58–T60, T62, T64, T67, T78–T81, T94–T97, T118, T119, T121, T122, T138-T141 |
| 2. uses sound/symbol relationships as visual cues for decoding. | T46, T47, T64, T65, T100, T101, T128, T135 | T25, T26, T29, T30, T43, T47, T48, T65, T66, T68, T69, T70, T87-T93, T107-T112, T137, T141, T159-T164, T176, T179 | T39, T58, T59, T95, T121, T141, T154, T175, T193, T216, T217, T233, T246, T281 | T22, T39, T94, T95, T119, T158, T159, T193, T195, T196, T217, T239, T256, T257, T271, T285 |
| 3. uses beginning letters (onsets) and patterns (rhymes) as visual cues for decoding. | T46, T64, T83, T100, T128, T141, T146, T161, T166, T172, T179, T244, T321 | T29, T41, T47, T69, T91, T111, T141, T163, T183, T201, T223, T253, T273, T295 | T24, T36, T39, T58, T59, T76, T94, T120, T121, T174, T192, T217, T232 | T40 |
| 4. uses structural cues (for example, word order, sentence boundaries) to decode words. | T137, T286 | T67, T271, T292 | T61, T77, T96, T155, T180, T192, T217, T218 | T24, T40, T60, T85, T138, T143, T177, T195, T218, T239, T240, T251, T259 |
| 5. uses context clues (for example, illustrations, knowledge of the story and topic) to construct meaning (meaning cues). | T102, T190, T191, T195, T207, T233, T243, T261, T272, T276, T281, T303, T323 | T94, T114, T118, T146, T147, T151, T281, T301 | T49, T50, T83, T135, T254 | T49, T67, T70, T85, T228, T229, T247, T248, T262, T263, T299 |
| 6. cross checks visual, structural, and meaning cues to figure out unknown words. | | | | |
| **BENCHMARK LA.A.1.1.3 The student uses knowledge of appropriate grade-, age-, and developmental-level vocabulary in reading. The student:** | | | | |
| 1. identifies and classifies common words from within basic categories. | T41, T51, T59, T79, T97, T115, T159, T237 | T39, T61, T83, T103, T125, T155, T175, T193, T215, T263, T265, T287 | T37, T57, T69, T75, T85, T87, T93, T103, T105, T111, T139, T153, T173, T191 | T37, T53, T57, T69, T71, T73, T77, T87, T93, T103, T109, T237, T255, T269, T297 |
| 2. uses knowledge of individual words in unknown compound words to predict their meaning. | T323 | | T77 | T137, T157, T175, T177, T191, T194, T207 |
| 3. uses resources and references such as beginning dictionaries and available technology to build upon word meanings. | T105, T151, T271, T310, T313, T315 | T261, T341 | T90, T187, T198, T238, T242, T260, T273, T276 | T84, T100, T181, T255, T260, T269, T283, T292, T297 |
| 4. uses knowledge of suffixes (including –er, -est, -ful) to determine meanings of words. | | | | |
| 5. develops vocabulary by listening to and discussing both familiar and conceptually challenging selections read aloud. | T41, T66, T102, T107, T148, T186, T315 | T53, T147, T152, T164, T207, T211, T215, T228, T229, T265, T317, T335 | T28, T44, T49, T64, T67, T80, T83, T88, T98, T101, T106, T124-T126, T131, T134, T144, T149, T153, T163, T183 | T26, T44, T45, T49, T64, T98, T101, T127, T132, T145, T147, T152, T162, T165, T170, T198, T199, T223 |
| **BENCHMARK LA.A.1.1.4 The student increases comprehension by rereading, retelling, and discussion. The student:** | | | | |
| 1. uses a variety of strategies to comprehend text (for example, retelling stories in correct sequence, recalling details, rereading). | T133, T234, T252, T257, T273, T277, T293 | T54, T117, T147, T151, T167, T171, T257, T259, T299, T303, T334 | T45, T49, T66, T100, T146, T165, T169, T182, T187, T198, T200, T224, T238, T257, T270, T272, T286 | T127, T130, T145, T147, T148, T150, T153, T165, T166, T168, T171, T181, T184, T199, T201, T278, T292 |

| Unit 4 | Unit 5 | Unit 6 | Unit 7 | Unit 8 |
|---|---|---|---|---|
| T41, T75, T171, T245 | | T63, T70, T145, T197 | T39, T67, T83, T141 | T47, T195, T259, T295 |
| T75, T95, T213, T221, T231 | T142, T193, T201, T209, T239, T278 | T207, T215, T225, T299 | T162, T174, T217, T225, T235, T316 | T213, T221, T229 |
| T58 | T49, T112 | T109 | T174, T259 | T300 |

| Unit 5 | Unit 6 | Unit 7 | Unit 8 | Unit 9 | Unit 10 |
|---|---|---|---|---|---|
| T48, T128, T194, T230 | T34, T50, T66, T102, T132, T148, T150, T164, T180, T182, T196 | 11FF, 12C, 12, 16, 18, 23C, 26M, 260, 30, 32, 34, 38, 40, 98C | 102C, 112C, 124M, 132C, 154M, 154, 162, 164, 166, 168, 170, 172, 174, 180M, 182, 188, 190 | 12C, 16, 22, 24, 26, 36M, 38E, 54, 56, 58, 59, 62, 64, 70C, 84N | 158M |
| T22, T23, T25, T26, T27, T38, T39, T40, T43, T60, T61, T62, T63, T64, T79, T81, T94, T95, T98, T99 | T23, T26, T42, T43, T45, T54, T62, T63, T65, T68, T78, T79, T81, T82, T86, T96-T100, T104 | 11HH, 11Y, 11Z, 12A, 12B, 12, 14, 16, 18, 20, 25E, 25F, 25H, 28, 30, 32, 34, 36, 38, 40, 45F, 45G, 45H, 45I, 45J | 101W, 101FF, 102A, 102B, 102, 104, 106, 108, 109, 111E, 111F, 112A, 116, 120, 123E, 123F, 124K, 126, 129F | 11W, 11X, 11FF, 12A, 12B, 12, 35E, 35F, 35G, 35H, 36K, 36L, 36, 38A-38D, 38, 54K, 54L, 54 | 137W, 137X, 137FF, 138A, 138B, 149E, 149F, 150A, 150B, 157E, 157F, 158K, 179F, 179G, 179H, 179I |
| T23, T27, T39, T43, T61, T63, T81, T94, T95, T99, T122, T123, T124, T127, T145, T158, T161, T175 | T22, T24, T25, T27, T42, T43, T45, T52, T54, T62, T63, T65, T68, T79, T81, T86, T97, T99, T104, T122, T123 | 11Y, 11Z, 11HH, 12A, 12B, 14, 16, 18, 20, 22, 25E, 25F, 25G, 25H, 26K, 26L, 26, 28, 30, 34, 36, 38, 40, 45F, 45G | 101W, 101X, 101FF, 102A, 102B, 102E, 104, 106, 108, 111E, 111F, 112A, 112B, 112E, 116, 120, 123E, 123F, 124K, 124L, 1240, 126, 129F, 132A | 11W, 11FF, 12B, 12E, 12, 35E, 35F, 35G, 35H, 36K, 36, 37D, 37E, 38A, 38, 53E, 53F, 53G, 54K, 54, 67F | 137X, 137FF, 138A, 149E, 149F, 150A, 150B, 157E, 157F, 179F, 179G, 179H, 179I, 179J, 180K, 197F, 197G, 200A, 205E, 205F, 206K, 220A |
| T22, T38, T60, T64, T81, T165, T193 | T42, T122, T143, T190 | 18, 36, 48, 66, 76, 86 | 104, 109, 143, 154, 160 | 12A, 70A, 84K | 137X, 180L |
| T78, T159 | T161, T216, T217 | 18, 36, 48, 66, 86 | 107, 134, 143, 154, 160 | 135G | 137X, 138B, 150B, 158L, 200B, 206L, 220B, 236L, 261J |
| T37, T52, T59, T68, T70, T77, T84, T86, T93, T104, T113, T141, T157 | | 14, 25E, 25F, 25G, 50, 66, 68, 69, 70, 72, 76, 92 | 114, 116, 121F, 125, 136, 144, 148, 151C, 156, 172, 182, 189 | 12D, 25, 36N, 37E, 38F, 40, 53E, 53F, 54N, 70D, 70, 72, 74, 78 | 138F, 149, 150E, 157, 1580, 179, 1800, 191, 192, 197, 200E, 205 |
| T150 | T81, T99, T106 | | 102E, 112E, 1240, 132E, 1540, 1800 | 19, 37E, 38H | 146, 157F, 179J |
| T201, T239, T254, T261, T283, T303, T315 | T56, T72, T108, T136, T168, T184, T202, T227 | 23B, 43B, 45H, 45I, 65G, 65H, 65I, 81B | 109B, 111E, 111F, 121B, 123E, 127B, 151B, 177B, 193B, 195G | 33B, 35E, 35F, 35G, 37B, 39, 41, 43, 45 | 139, 145, 149E, 149F, 157E, 158N |
| T51, T152, T279 | | 11Z | 112A, 134, 135, 169 | 13, 90A, 105, 119E, 119F, 119G | 193, 197G, 205E, 261G |
| T34 | T49, T54, T70, T85, T102, T132 | 12F, 46N, 65C, 65D | 132D | 11CC, 17, 53D, 67C, 67D, 83D | 197C, 197D, 205D |
| | T217, T218 | 12A, 12D, 25F | 101W, 132B, 170 | 67G, 67H | |
| T37, T59, T77, T113, T247, T268, T288, T296 | T7, T41, T51, T56, T67, T71, T72, T85, T90, T100, T103, T105, T108, T126, T131 | 23B, 25E-25G, 26N, 43B, 63B, 81B, 89B, 92N, 95B | 102D, 109B, 112D, 113, 117, 121B, 124N, 127B, 132D, 135, 136, 138, 151B, 154N, 172, 177B, 179G | 11Y, 12D, 33B, 36N, 37B, 38F, 51B, 65B, 70D, 81B, 120N, 121B, 122F, 133B | 137Y, 138E, 142, 147B, 150D, 155B, 158N, 177B, 181, 191, 195B |
| T50, T52, T70, T178, T179, T194, T224, T225, T232, T246, T268, T277, T288 | T39, T51-T57, T67-T73, T82, T84-T89, T100, T101, T103, T104-T106, T109, T127 | 12F, 12-23, 23C, 24, 26-43, 43C, 44, 460, 46Q, 46-62, 64, 66P, 66, 68-82, 86-89, 260 | 102-120, 121C, 122, 124, 126, 128, 132E, 132-152, 1540, 154-177, 177C, 178, 1800, 180-192, 193C, 194 | 12E, 12F, 12-33, 33C, 38G, 38H, 38-48, 51C, 51E, 540, 54P, 54-64, 65C, 70E, 70F | 138F, 150E, 1580, 158, 160, 162, 164, 166, 168, 170, 172, 174, 176, 180D |

# Florida Resources

## Correlation to Florida Sunshine State Standards  Grade 1

### Strand A: Reading

| | Unit 1 | Unit 2 | Unit 3 | Unit 4 |
|---|---|---|---|---|
| **STANDARD 2: The student constructs meaning from a wide range of texts.** | | | | |
| **BENCHMARK LA.A.2.1.1 The student determines the main idea or essential message from text and identifies supporting information. The stude** | | | | |
| 1. knows the main idea or theme and supporting details of a story or informational piece. | | T147, T167, T171, T189, T231, T259, T261 | | T127, T129, T132, T147, T149, T152, T165, T167, T170, T181, T183, T185-T189 |
| 2. uses specific details and information from a text to answer literal questions. | T243, T261, T281, T303 | T35, T71, T75, T76, T92, T93, T95, T97, T99, T113, T117, T120, T143, T185, T203 | T28, T33, T44, T51, T64, T99, T124-T126, T143, T270, T286, T287, T289 | T45, T65, T83, T99, T122, T129, T132, T145, T149, T152, T167, T170, T183 |
| 3. makes inferences based on text and prior knowledge such as regarding traits, characters, and problems | T210, T257, T272, T276, T298, T314, T318 | T74, T171, T281 | T72, T106, T134, T202 | T49, T66, T67, T71, T85, T87, T101, T132, T152, T170, T86, T202, 263, T277, T279 |
| 4. identifies similarities and differences between two texts such as in topics, characters, and problems). | T110, T170 | T52 | | |
| **BENCHMARK LA.A.2.1.2 The student selects material to read for pleasure. The student:** | | | | |
| 1. selects material to read for pleasure such as favorite books and stories. | | | | |
| 2. reads aloud familiar stories, poems, or passages. | T103 | T71, T92, T93, T113, T143, T165, T185, T203, T225, T275 | T45, T64, T99, T124, T125, T126, T144, T158, T178, T237, T251, T289 | T27, T45, T65, T83, T99, T199, T275, T291 |
| **BENCHMARK LA.A.2.1.3 The student reads for information to use in performing a task and learning a new task. The student:** | | | | |
| 1. reads for information used in performing tasks such as graphs, charts, signs, captions. | T77 | T152, T231, T262, T279 | | T253 |
| **BENCHMARK LA.A.2.1.4 The student knows strategies to use to discover whether information presented in a text is true, including asking others and checking another source. The student:** | | | | |
| 1. uses background knowledge, teacher opinion, and supporting reasons from the text to determine whether a story/text is fact or fiction. | T57, T233, T235, T237, T239, T253, T315, T317 | T278, T318, T336 | | T30, T126, T226 |
| **BENCHMARK LA.A.2.1.5 The student uses simple materials of the reference system to obtain information. The student:** | | | | |
| 1. uses simple reference material to obtain information (such as table of contents, fiction and nonfiction books, picture dictionaries, audio visual software). | T50, T55, T88, T106, T132, T152, T170, T175, T176, T190, T232, T272 | T37, T283 | T7, T35, T108, T137, T146, T150, T169, T242, T276 | T35, T48, T66, T84, T100, T126, T146, T164, T180, T200, T226, T244 |
| 2. alphabetizes words according to the initial letter. | | | T242 | T58, T78, T158 |
| 3. uses alphabetical order to locate information. | | T101 | T108, T150, T230, T242 | |

### Strand B: Writing

| | Unit 1 | Unit 2 | Unit 3 | Unit 4 |
|---|---|---|---|---|
| **STANDARD 1: The student uses writing processes effectively.** | | | | |
| **BENCHMARK LA.B.1.1.1 The student makes a plan for writing that includes a central idea and related ideas. The student:** | | | | |
| 1. generates ideas before writing on self-selected topics and assigned tasks (such as brainstorming). | T41, T59, T79, T97, T115, T179, T215 | 58, T100, T172, T234, T284 | T228 | T37, T74, T137, T237 |
| 2. makes a plan before writing the first draft. | T141, T161, T179, T199, T215 | T58, T122, T262 | | T37, T57, T137, T157, T237, T255 |
| 3. focuses on a central idea (for example, familiar person, place, object, experience). | T179, T199, T215 | | T37, T54, T57, T75, T93, T111, T139, T148, T207, T231 | T37, T57, T77, T137, T157, T237, T255 |
| **BENCHMARK LA.B.1.1.2 The student drafts and revises simple sentences and passages, stories, letters, and simple explanations that**<br>• *express ideas clearly;*<br>• *show an awareness of topic and audience;*<br>• *have a beginning, middle, and ending;*<br>• *effectively use common words;*<br>• *have supporting detail; and*<br>• *are in legible printing.*<br>**The student:** | | | | |
| 1. writes legibly using manuscript form (for example, prints numbers and upper- and lowercase letters; uses left to right sequencing; spaces between words and sentences). | T28, T29, T30, T31, T33, T45, T63, T75, T83, T100, T101, T111, T115, T126, T127, T129, T145-T147, T165, T184 | T125, T237, T341 | T111, T171, T179, T207, T260, T268, T284, T295 | T61, T109, T160, T207, T241, T273, T297 |

| Unit 5 | Unit 6 | Unit 7 | Unit 8 | Unit 9 | Unit 10 |
|---|---|---|---|---|---|
| T51, T69, T85, T105, T107, T179, T253, T255 | T55, T69, T71, T87, T89, T133 | 67, 69, 71, 73, 75, 77, 79 | 135, 139, 143, 145, 147, 149, 151, 177 | 107, 109, 111, 113, 115 | 177A, 201, 203C |
| T65, T86, T108, T128, T202, T209, T224, T225, T247, T253, T268, T288 | T37, T47, T56, T71, T72, T89, T90, T101, T146, T147, T154, T168, T179 | 11DD, 13, 23, 24, 25, 28, 43, 44, 45, 64, 65, 81, 82, 83, 89, 90, 91, 95-97 | 101BB, 109, 110, 111, 117, 121-123, 127, 128, 129, 133, 151, 152, 153, 177 | 11CC, 33, 33A, 35, 37A, 37E, 37, 51A, 51, 53, 65A, 65, 67, 81A | 137BB, 138D, 141, 147, 147A, 149, 155A, 157, 177A, 179, 195A, 197 |
| T230 | T56, T72, T90, T108, T136, T154, T168, T184, T202, T228, T248 | 11DD, 18, 23E, 25C, 43, 63C, 81, 89, 95 | 109, 137, 145, 151, 193 | 33A, 35, 37A, 51A, 53, 65A, 67, 77, 79, 81A, 83, 87A, 89, 101, 103 | 147, 147A, 149, 155A, 157, 177A, 179, 180M, 195, 195A, 197, 200C, 203 |
| | | 45, 63E, 65, 71, 83, 91, 97 | 123, 129, 150, 153, 179, 195 | 37, 53, 67, 75, 81E, 83, 86, 103 | |
| T271 | T45, T153, T167, T196, T201, T227, T289 | 26M, 43 | | 22, 70C, 84D, 84M, 120D | |
| T65, T179, T195, T225, T247 | | 17, 23A, 460, 660 | 195D | | |
| T231 | T84, T85, T103, T109 | 34 | | 30, 79, 81C | 147E, 147F, 195E, 235D |
| T66, T197 | T84 | 12C, 26M, 46M, 66M | 102C, 109A, 112C, 124M, 132C, 154M, 180M | | 215 |
| T35, T48, T85, T198 | T50, T66, T84, T91, T102, T109, T130, T137, T164, T171, T196, T222, T230, T242 | 12C, 26M, 46M, 460, 65C | 101DD, 112C, 129D, 153A, 153C | 11CC, 12C, 33A, 36M, 37A, 38E, 51A, 53D, 54M, 67C, 67D, 81A, 83C, 83D, 84M, 87A, 90C | 138D, 149D, 150C, 158N, 179D, 180M, 197C, 197D, 200C, 205D, 2060 |
| | | 65C, 65D | 129C | 35D | 149D |
| | | 65C, 65D | 129C, 129D | 35D, 53D | 149D |
| T37, T141, T189, T239, T276 | T41, T141, T233 | 11HH, 43C, 45F, 65F, 83F, 97F | 101FF, 109F, 111E, 129F, 179F, 195F | 11FF, 20, 37D, 50, 67F, 85, 89F, 117E, 121D | 137FF, 179F, 197F, 219F, 261F |
| T59, T141, T261 | T61, T159, T253 | 25E, 45G, 65G, 83G, 97G | 111E, 153E, 179G, 195G | 35E, 37E, 67G, 119E, 135E | 149E, 179G, 197G, 219G, 261G |
| T59, T141, T189, T261 | T61, T110, T159, T186, T253 | 25E, 45G, 65G, 83G, 97G | 111E, 153E, 179G, 195G | 35E, 37E, 67G, 119E, 135E | 149E, 179G, 197G, 219G, 261G |
| T97, T113, T173, T209, T243, T265, T283, T286, T306, T315 | T113, T207, T307 | 12B, 25G, 25H, 45J, 65J, 91F, 99L | 123F, 153H, 179J, 195R | 35H, 53G, 83F, 119H, 135N | 157F, 179J, 205F, 235F, 235G, 261P |

# Florida Resources

## Correlation to Florida Sunshine State Standards     Grade 1

| Strand B: Writing | Unit 1 | Unit 2 | Unit 3 | Unit 4 |
|---|---|---|---|---|
| **2.** knows the differences among individual letters, words, sentences, and paragraphs. | T28, T29, T30, T31, T42, T45, T59, T60, T63, T73, T80, T82, T85, T91, T98, T100 | T150, T207, T229, T230, T232, T257, T260, T266, T279, T282, T296, T299 | T26, T37, T38, T39, T49, T53, T57, T60, T71, T75, T80, T96, T120, T122, T139, T140 | T23, T38, T67, T77, T79, T118, T158, T159, T192, T217, T218, T245, T255 |
| **3.** maintains a single idea/topic in writing. | T243, T303, T318, T323 | T304, T323, T341 | T70 | T72, T175, T281 |
| **4.** uses descriptive words to convey ideas in writing. | | T39, T61, T83, T287, T341 | T149, T187, T277 | |
| **5.** uses an organizational structure in writing (including beginning, middle, and ending; using supporting details). | T281 | | T188 | T175, T269 |
| **6.** uses strategies for narrative writing (for example, including story elements, using some dialogue). | | | | |
| **7.** evaluates own and other's writing (for example, rereads own writing to check for meaning; responds constructively to other's writing). | | T83, T103, T125, T212, T341 | | T93, T283 |
| **8.** revises by adding or substituting text and using a caret. | | T39, T61, T83, T125 | T143, T179 | T191 |

### BENCHMARK LA.B.1.1.3 The student produces final simple documents that have been edited for
- **correct spelling;**
- **appropriate end punctuation;**
- **correct capitalization of initial words, "I," and names of people;**
- **correct sentence structure; and**
- **correct usage of age-appropriate verb/subject and noun/pronoun agreement.**
**The student:**

| | Unit 1 | Unit 2 | Unit 3 | Unit 4 |
|---|---|---|---|---|
| **1.** uses spelling approximations in written work. | T179 | T212, T262 | T27 | |
| **2.** uses directionality of print in writing (including but not limited to left-to-right, top-to-bottom, spacing between words). | T75, T111 | T307, T308 | T79, T97, T123, T157, T179, T195, T221, T249, T269, T285 | T24, T42, T62, T63, T109, T143, T161, T176 |
| **3.** identifies and attempts to use end punctuation (such as the period, question mark, and exclamation point). | T243, T261, T281, T307 | T155, T160, T175, T180, T193, T237, T265, T287, T307 | | T137, T157, T175, T207, T237, T255, T269, T297 |
| **4.** uses spelling approximations and some conventional spelling. | T185, T203 | | | |
| **5.** spells commonly used, phonetically regular words at first grade or higher level. | T309 | T28, T47, T68, T90, T104, T110, T134, T162, T176, T194, T200, T215, T272 | | |
| **6.** uses end punctuation and capitalizes initial words of sentences, names of people, the pronoun "I", days of the week, and months of the year. | T59, T79, T141, T161, T179, T243, T261, T281 | T57, T155, T175, T265, T287, T294, T307 | | T37, T53, T57, T77, T109, T207, T237, T255, T269, T297 |
| **7.** uses complete sentences in writing. | | | | T207 |

### STANDARD 2: The student writes to communicate ideas and information effectively.

### BENCHMARK LA.B.2.1.1 The student writes questions and observations about familiar topics, stories, or new experiences. The student:

| | Unit 1 | Unit 2 | Unit 3 | Unit 4 |
|---|---|---|---|---|
| **1.** writes stories about experiences, people, objects, or events. | | T287 | | |
| **2.** contributes ideas during a group writing activity. | | T58, T100, T172, T262, T284, T304 | T57, T58, T93, T103, T139, T162, T188, T198, T263, T295 | T54, T74, T75, T107, T281 |

### BENCHMARK LA.B.2.1.2 The student uses knowledge and experience to tell about experiences or to write for familiar occasions, audiences, and purposes. The student:

| | Unit 1 | Unit 2 | Unit 3 | Unit 4 |
|---|---|---|---|---|
| **1.** writes informal texts (for example, journal entries, reading response). | T175, T196, T277, T318 | T56, T58, T262 | T70, T134, T148, T153, T171, T173, T191, T207, T245 | T55, T72 |
| **2.** writes for familiar occasions, audiences, and purposes (including but not limited to explaining a process or telling a story). | | T152, T307 | T91, T171, T189 | T269 |

### BENCHMARK LA.B.2.1.3 The student uses basic computer skills for writing, such as basic word processing techniques such as keying words, copying, cutting, and pasting; using e-mail; and accessing and using basic educational software for writing. The student:

| | Unit 1 | Unit 2 | Unit 3 | Unit 4 |
|---|---|---|---|---|
| **1.** uses basic word processing skills and basic educational software for writing (including but not limited to typing words/sentences, using software to draw and label, printing pictures/stories, locating and opening a file, and saving and naming a file). | T140, T242 | T38, T154, T264 | T36, T138 | T36, T136, T236 |

| Unit 5 | Unit 6 | Unit 7 | Unit 8 | Unit 9 | Unit 10 |
|---|---|---|---|---|---|
| T77, T94, T142, T174, T176, T192, T218, T240, T262, T263, T284 | T51, T77, T160, T173, T275 | 25G, 99C | 101FF, 111F, 153F, 179H, 195H | 12B, 35F, 53E, 67H, 84L, 90B, 122C, 135H | 149F, 179H, 206L, 235E |
| T77, T157, T283 | T77, T173, T275 | 45H, 65H, 83H | 109F, 111F, 121F, 153F, 179H | 35F, 67H, 119F, 135F | 144, 149F, 179H, 197H |
| T57, T59, T77, T239, T261, T276, T283 | | 25G, 83F, 83G, 83H, 91E, 99C | 111F, 123E, 153F, 179H, 195H | 51E, 67H, 89F, 119E, 119F, 121B, 135F | 179I, 197H, 205E |
| T283 | T77 | 25F, 43F, 45H, 65H, 83H, 99C | 123E, 195H | 119D | 235E, 235F, 259F, 261H, 2610 |
| | | 25F, 45H, 65H, 83H, 99C, 99K | | | 219F, 219G, 235E, 259E |
| T93, T157, T303 | T95, T189, T295 | 12B, 45I, 65I, 99K | 153G, 179I, 195Q | 35G, 53F, 83E, 119G, 135M | 157E, 179I, 205E, 235F, 2610 |
| T303 | T295 | 25G | 179I | | 179I |
| | T77, T207 | 43F, 153F | 153F | | |
| T173, T244, T266, T287, T315 | T78, T96, T98 | 11Z, 12B, 26L, 46L, 98B, 99L | 123F | 35H, 53G, 65F, 83F, 119H | 137X, 138B, 150B, 158L, 200B, 205F, 206L, 220B, 236L, 261J |
| T113, T307, T315 | T26, T65, T98, T113, T145, T177, T185, T203, T219, T257, T298 | 11Z, 25H, 26L, 45J, 65J, 66L, 92L, 98B, 99L | 101X, 111E, 111F, 112B, 123F, 132B, 153H, 154L, 180L, 195F, 195H, 195J, 195R | 36K, 36L, 38B, 53G, 67F, 67G, 67H, 70B, 84L, 90B, 115 | 157F, 235G, 261P |
| | T45, T65, T81, T99, T113, T125, T145, T163, T177, T193, T207, T219 | 11HH, 25G, 25H, 45F, 45G, 45H, 45I, 45J, 65F, 65G, 65H, 65I, 65J | 101FF, 111E, 111F, 123E, 123F, 129F, 153E, 153F, 153G, 153H, 179F, 179G | 51C, 67H | 137FF, 149E, 149F, 157E, 157F, 179F, 179G, 179H, 179I, 179J, 197F, 197G |
| T113 | T45, T207 | 11Z, 12B, 25H, 26L, 45J, 46L, 65J, 66L, 86B, 91F, 92L, 98B, 99L | 101X, 102B, 112B, 123F, 124L, 132B, 153H, 154L, 179J, 180L, 195J, 195R | 11X, 12B, 35H, 36L, 38B, 38C, 53G, 54L, 70B, 83F, 84L, 90B, 120L, 135N | 179J, 205F, 235G, 261P |
| T113, T315 | T26, T65, T98, T113, T145, T177, T207, T219, T257, T258, T279 | 11Z, 25H, 26L, 45J, 65J, 66L, 92L, 98B | 101X, 112B, 123F, 132B, 153H, 154L, 179J, 180L, 195J, 195R | 36L, 38B, 54L, 70B, 84L, 90B, 120L, 122C, 135H | 157F, 235G, 261F, 261G, 261H, 261P |
| T315 | T113 | 23B, 45J, 63B, 65J, 81B, 89B, 93F, 99L | 109B, 121F, 129F, 127B, 151B, 153E, 153F, 177B, 179J, 193B | 67H | 157F, 200A, 261P |
| | T186 | 25F, 45H, 65H, 83H | | | 259F |
| T57, T276 | T41, T58, T105 | | 151E, 195P | 20, 26, 47, 50, 62, 117E, 119H | 143, 157F, 179J, 185, 205F, 224, 233F, 235G |
| T167 | T56, T72, T110 | 23A, 25A, 25H, 43A, 63A, 65A, 81A, 83A, 89A, 95A | 109A, 121A, 127A, 139, 151A, 177A, 193A | 33A, 37A, 51A, 59, 81A, 87A, 117A, 121A, 133A | 184, 230 |
| | T159, T173, T189 | 25F, 65H, 83H | 107, 195G, 195H, 195Q | 19, 50 | 144, 239 |
| T283, T303, T315 | T275 | 45E, 83H, 99K | 111F, 153F, 195H | | |

# Florida Resources

## Correlation to Florida Sunshine State Standards                 Grade 1

| Strand B: Writing | Unit 1 | Unit 2 | Unit 3 | Unit 4 |
|---|---|---|---|---|
| **BENCHMARK LA.B.2.1.4 The student composes simple sets of instructions for simple tasks using logical sequencing of steps. The student:** | | | | |
| **1.** writes simple informational texts (such as two-step instructions in sequence, directions, reports). | | | T279, T295 | |

### Strand C: Listening, Viewing, Speaking

| | Unit 1 | Unit 2 | Unit 3 | Unit 4 |
|---|---|---|---|---|
| **STANDARD 1: The student uses listening strategies effectively.** | | | | |
| **BENCHMARK LA.C.1.1.1 The student listens for a variety of informational purposes, including curiosity, pleasure, getting directions, performing tasks, solving problems, and following rules. The student:** | | | | |
| **1.** follows three-step oral directions. | T97 | T211 | T198 | |
| **2.** listens and responds to a variety of media (such as stories, books, audiotapes, videotapes). | T27, T60, T62, T144, T145, T176, T200, T226, T246, T264, T284, T306, T321 | T32, T44, T62, T104, T107, T119, T122, T137, T190, T197, T248, T285 | T23, T30, T59, T77, T95, T120, T128, T141, T155, T193, T265, T266, T281 | T22, T26, T33, T39, T45, T65, T79, T95, T119, T139, T147, T271, T285 |
| **BENCHMARK LA.C.1.1.2 The student recognizes personal preferences in listening to literature and other material. The student:** | | | | |
| **1.** knows personal preferences for listening to literature and other material (such as nursery rhymes, songs, stories, informational books). | | T337 | T7 | |
| **BENCHMARK LA.C.1.1.3 The student carries on a conversation with another person, seeking answers and further explanations of the other's ideas through questioning and answering. The student:** | | | | |
| **1.** uses basic conversation strategies (including but not limited to asking questions to clarify or get information, taking turns, raising hand to speak, staying on topic and conveying a message, facing the speaker). | T54, T71, T74, T75, T92, T136, T149, T156, T175, T194, T210, T257, T315, T319 | T52, T53, T54, T56, T57, T75, T78, T95, T98, T99, T114, T120, T122, T147, T150, T151, T166, T169, T170, T178 | T52, T70, T88, T106, T129, T130, T134, T148, T168, T182, T185, T186, T202, T226, T240, T258, T274, T275 | T22, T33, T65, T99, T103, T191, T232, T247, T250, T283 |
| **BENCHMARK LA.C.1.1.4 The student retells specific details of information heard, including sequence of events. The student:** | | | | |
| **1.** listens for specific information in stories (including but not limited to sequence, story details). | | T147, T167, T298, T337 | T30, T35, T49, T93 | |
| **STANDARD 2: The student uses viewing strategies effectively.** | | | | |
| **BENCHMARK LA.C.2.1.1 The student determines the main idea in a nonprint communication. The student:** | | | | |
| **1.** understands the main idea or common theme in pictures and symbols. | T318 | T52, T103, T115, T147, T149, T167, T169, T187, T209, T229, T231, T251 | T82, T107, T130, T135, T149, T162, T182, T198, T240, T254 | T226, T247, T263 |
| **BENCHMARK LA.C.2.1.2 The student recognizes simple nonverbal cues, such as use of eye contact, smiles, simple hand gestures. The student:** | | | | |
| **1.** understands simple nonverbal cues (such as eye contact, facial expressions, gesturing). | T52, T156, T247, T301, T306 | T87, T188, T210, T211, T260, T263, T270, T305, T310, T337 | T59, T95, T106, T121, T148, T168, T186, T189, T202, T226, T258 | T23, T79, T95, T107, T140, T271 |
| **STANDARD 3: The student uses speaking strategies effectively.** | | | | |
| **BENCHMARK LA.C.3.1.1 The student speaks clearly and at a volume audible in large- or small group settings. The student:** | | | | |
| **1.** speaks clearly and uses appropriate volume in a variety of settings (such as large or small groups, learning centers). | T108, T156, T199, T301 | T212, T234, T247, T263, T284, T285, T297, T304, T337 | T91, T150, T185, T189, T191, T243, T273, T275 | T75, T107, T176, T216, T235, T283, T284 |
| **BENCHMARK LA.C.3.1.2 The student asks questions to seek answers and further explanation of other people's ideas. The student:** | | | | |
| **1.** asks questions to seek answers and further explanation of other people's ideas. | T67, T71, T75, T103, T107, T111, T171, T210, T298, T315, T318, T319 | T53, T54, T57, T95, T99, T122, T215, T232, T233, T260, T282, T302, T304, T320 | | T67, T227, T228, T245, T261, T262 |
| **BENCHMARK LA.C.3.1.3 The student speaks effectively in conversations with others. The student:** | | | | |
| **1.** uses speaking vocabulary to convey a message in conversation (such as descriptive words, singular and plural nouns, compound words). | T110, T154, T210, T298 | | T173 | T137, T157, T175, T191, T207 |
| **BENCHMARK LA.C.3.1.4 The student uses eye contact and simple gestures when speaking. The student:** | | | | |
| **1.** uses eye contact and appropriate gestures to enhance oral delivery. | T156, T195 | T211, T263, T305, T337, T339 | T189, T242, T275 | T107, T235 |

| Unit 5 | Unit 6 | Unit 7 | Unit 8 | Unit 9 | Unit 10 |
|---|---|---|---|---|---|
| T59, T77, T93, T231 | T173, T275 | | | | |
| T122, T218 | | 95F | 127B | 135D | 157E, 203E, 219D |
| | T43, T51, T79, T97, T105, T107, T123, T131, T161, T175 | 11A, 12F, 25G, 260, 26P, 46P, 66P, 81F, 86F, 92P, 98D, 99F, 99G | 101Y, 102E, 109E, 112F, 1240, 124, 132E, 132F, 1540, 154P, 177E, 1800 | 11CC, 33A, 37A, 38G, 51A, 540, 70E, 840, 90E, 135M | 137BB, 259E |
| T271 | | 46P, 66M, 66P, 99G | 109E, 151E, 195M | 70C, 84M, 90C | 251 |
| T70, T108, T169, T198 | T56, T69, T72, T79, T82, T90, T93, T102, T108, T109, T127, T136, T142, T154, T168, T184, T190 | 19, 23, 23A, 43A, 43F, 63A, 99A, 99K | 105, 109A, 109D, 111, 121A, 127A, 151A, 153D, 177A, 193A, 195P | 33A, 35G, 37A, 51A, 65A, 81A, 83E, 94, 117A, 121A, 133A, 135D | 147A, 155A, 157A, 177A, 195A, 195E, 203A, 217A, 217F, 219D, 223, 233F, 259A, 261D, 2610 |
| T48, T69, T85, T105, T171, T247, T255, T275, T277 | T50, T66, T84, T102, T130, T180, T196, T222, T242, T264 | 12D, 12E, 12F, 26N, 260, 26P, 46M, 460, 46P, 66M, 660, 66P, 86C, 86E | 112D, 112F, 124M, 132C, 132F, 154N, 180M, 180P | 12D, 12F, 36M, 36N, 54N, 54P, 70C, 70F, 84N, 90D, 95, 122F, 122H | 138F, 150E, 1580, 1800, 200E, 206Q, 220G, 2360 |
| T51, T72, T88, T168 | T87, T95 | 13, 65I, 84 | 101DD, 113, 130, 133, 137, 145, 147, 149, 153G, 187, 190 | 13, 17, 29, 40, 55, 56, 57, 68, 115, 117, 119G | 214 |
| T36, T122, T142, T238, T240, T304 | T78, T79, T91, T93, T174 | 63F, 91E | | 23 | 217F, 219D, 235F, 261D, 261E |
| T169, T189, T276 | T58, T91, T93, T96, T107, T276 | 12E, 25, 260, 43A, 45I, 45, 65, 83, 91, 97 | 111, 123, 123E, 129, 153, 179, 195, 195D, 195Q | 37, 37B, 38G, 51C, 53F, 81C, 89D, 120N, 122G, 135D | 150E, 1580, 179I, 1800, 195E, 200E, 206Q, 219D, 220G, 233F, 2360, 259F |
| T57, T67, T72, T75, T84, T88, T103, T149, T152, T165, T168, T181 | T52, T56, T58, T72, T74, T88, T90, T91, T102, T108, T136, T138, T154, T168 | 11EE, 25B, 25C, 45B, 45C, 63A, 83B, 88, 91B | 114, 120, 123C, 123E, 129D, 146, 158, 187, 188 | 12, 18, 20, 28, 30, 32, 33A, 37A, 38, 51A, 540, 65A | 137BB, 147A, 155A, 177A, 195A, 195E, 203A, 217A, 233A, 259A |
| T77 | | 65I | 119, 179I | 35F, 119E, 119F, 119G | 197G, 205E, 261G |
| T169, T276 | T91 | 12, 91E | 195D | 37B, 81C, 92, 107, 117E, 135D | 195E, 217F, 219D, 235F, 261D |

# Florida Resources

## Correlation to Florida Sunshine State Standards — Grade 1

### Strand D: Language

| | Unit 1 | Unit 2 | Unit 3 | Unit 4 |
|---|---|---|---|---|
| **STANDARD 1: The student understands the nature of language.** | | | | |
| **BENCHMARK LA.D.1.1.1 The student recognizes basic patterns in and functions of language (patterns such as characteristic sounds and rhythms and those found in written forms; functions such as asking questions, expressing oneself, describing objects or experience, and explaining). The student:** | | | | |
| 1. uses repetition, rhyme, and rhythm in a variety of activities (such as chants, songs, or story innovations). | T24, T27, T42, T45, T60, T62, T80, T89, T98, T106, T108, T113, T124 | T22, T44, T62, T65, T83, T87, T179, T216, T218, T246, T248, T269, T308, T310 | T23, T39, T59, T95, T120, T121, T140, T174, T216, T233, T265, T266 | T22, T23, T39, T59, T79, T95, T139, T192, T217, T271, T285 |
| **BENCHMARK LA.D.1.1.2 The student recognizes the differences between language that is used at home and language that is used at school. The student:** | | | | |
| 1. recognizes the differences between less formal language that is used at home and more formal language that is used at school and other public settings. | T303 | T199 | | |
| **STANDARD 2: The student understands the power of language.** | | | | |
| **BENCHMARK LA.D.2.1.1 The student understands that word choice can shape ideas, feelings, and actions. The student:** | | | | |
| 1. understands that word choice can shape ideas, feelings, and actions (such as multiple meaning words, figurative language). | T88 | T53, T181, T229, T279 | T37, T82, T131, T149, T187, T199, T279 | |
| **BENCHMARK LA.D.2.1.2 The student identifies and uses repetition, rhyme, and rhythm in oral and written text. The student** | | | | |
| 1. uses repetition, rhyme, and rhythm in oral and written texts (such as uses rhyming words orally; distinguishes between rhyming and non-rhyming words). | T24, T42, T90, T107, T110, T141, T142, T153, T161, T171, T173, T179, T199, T213, T215, T224, T282, T304, T314, T321 | T22, T23, T27, T139, T207 | T23, T58 | T237, T255, T269, T283, T297 |
| **BENCHMARK LA.D.2.1.3 The student recognizes that use of more than one medium increases the power to influence how one thinks and feels. The student:** | | | | |
| 1. understands that the use of more than one medium increases the power to influence how one thinks and feels. | | T265 | T137 | T91, T93 |
| **BENCHMARK LA.D.2.1.4 The student knows various types of mass media. The student:** | | | | |
| 1. knows various types of mass media (such as radio, television, billboards, newspapers). | | T99, T171, T189 | T107, T187 | T91 |

### Strand E: Literature

| | Unit 1 | Unit 2 | Unit 3 | Unit 4 |
|---|---|---|---|---|
| **STANDARD 1: The student understands the common features of a variety of literary forms.** | | | | |
| **BENCHMARK LA.E.1.1.1 The student knows the basic characteristics of fables, stories, and legends. The student:** | | | | |
| 1. knows various broad literary genres (such as nonfiction, fiction, poetry). | T49, T69, T87, T105, T131, T151, T169, T189, T205, T231, T235, T255, T271, T313 | T50, T72, T114, T122, T144, T204, T206, T226, T228, T276 | T47, T128, T150, T188, T252 | T46, T124, T224 |
| **BENCHMARK LA.E.1.1.2 The student identifies the story elements of setting, plot, character, problem, and solution/resolution. The student:** | | | | |
| 1. knows beginning, middle, and ending. | | | | |
| 2. knows main characters, setting, and simple plot in a story. | T234, T235, T237, T238, T256 | T49, T165 | | |
| **STANDARD 2: The student responds critically to fiction, nonfiction, poetry, and drama.** | | | | |
| **BENCHMARK LA.E.2.1.1 The student uses personal perspective in responding to a work of literature, such as relating characters and simple events in a story or biography to people or events in his or her own life. The student:** | | | | |
| 1. relates characters and simple events in a story to own life. | T256 | T228 | T50, T66, T86, T89, T106, T130, T224, T226, T238, T240, T272 | T265 |
| **BENCHMARK LA.E.2.1.2 The student recognizes rhymes, rhythm, and patterned structures in children's texts. The student:** | | | | |
| 1. knows rhymes, rhythm, and patterned structures in a variety of children's texts (such as poetry). | T175, T177, T179, T319 | T207 | T135, T137, T252, T257 | T260 |

| Unit 5 | Unit 6 | Unit 7 | Unit 8 | Unit 9 | Unit 10 |
|---|---|---|---|---|---|
| | T42, T79, T91, T142, T191 | 12 | 125, 127, 127B | 36N, 36, 83E | |
| T303 | | | 121F, 181 | 36 | |
| T37 | | 23E, 99 | 111E, 111F, 121E, 123E, 172, 195G | 33E, 121B | 205E |
| T142, T240, T276 | T42 | 12C, 20 | 123E, 127, 127B, 179H, 179J | 35G, 36, 83E, 120M, 135F | |
| T36, T140, T238 | | 65I | 177D | | 137EE, 179E, 197E, 205E, 219E, 261E |
| T69 | T230 | | 177D | | |
| T226, T228, T248, T270, T290, T292 | T128, T194, T220, T240, T262, T282 | 11E, 23A, 26A, 26M, 43E, 46A, 66M, 86C, 86, 99A | 101M, 112C, 124A, 124M, 132C, 154A, 154M, 177E, 180A, 180M | 11DD, 36A, 36M, 51E, 54A, 54M, 84A, 90C, 120A, 122E, 122H, 131 | 137M, 158A, 158M, 180A, 206A, 215, 236A, 237, 239, 241, 245, 247, 249 |
| | T269 | 20, 36, 95C | 109C, 151E, 193F | 51E, 65E, 87E | |
| | | 20, 23E, 31, 63E, 93, 95 | 109E, 195M | 31, 33E, 51C, 51E, 55, 65E, 71, 77, 81E, 87, 87E, 129 | |
| T50, T68, T70, T84, T104, T105, T109, T166, T169, T182, T200, T232, T274 | T134, T150, T152, T166, T169 | 19, 23, 45, 46, 50, 54, 65, 68, 74, 78, 80, 83, 91, 94, 97 | 101BB, 109D, 111, 115, 121C, 122, 123, 123A, 129, 140, 142, 146, 150 | 14, 26, 33E, 56, 60, 65C, 72, 73, 74, 76, 79, 85, 90, 94 | |
| | T97 | | 124M, 125, 127, 127B | 121 | 177E |

# Florida Resources

## Correlation to Florida Sunshine State Standards     Grade 2

| Strand A: Reading | Unit 1 | Unit 2 |
|---|---|---|
| **STANDARD 1: The student uses the reading process effectively.** | | |
| **BENCHMARK LA.A.1.1.1: The student predicts what a passage is about based on its title and illustrations. The student:** | | |
| 1. uses prior knowledge, illustrations, and text to make and confirm predictions. | 14O, 21A, 26O, 41A, 46O, 59A, 62O, 79A, 84O, 103A | 108O, 117A, 135A, 138O, 153A, 156O, 180O, 195A, 198, 200O, 220O |
| **BENCHMARK LA.A.1.1.2: The student identifies words and constructs meaning from text, illustrations, graphics, and charts using the strategies of phonics, word structure, and context clues. The student:** | | |
| 1. blends sound components into words. | 14, 23F-23J, 43F-43J, 81F-81J, 105F-105J, 14K-14N, 14P, 26K, 26L, 26N, 26P, 26, 46K-46N, 46P, 47 | 108K-N, 108P, 108-115, 119F, 119H, 120K-120N, 120P, 120-124, 126-130, 132, 137G, 137J, 155F, 177G, 197F |
| 2. applies knowledge of beginning letters (onsets) and spelling patterns (rhymes) in single and multi-syllable words as visual clues for decoding. | 14K-14N, 14P, 14, 26K-26N, 26P, 26, 43F-43I, 46P, 46K-46N, 47, 62L-62N, 62P, 62 | 108K-108N, 108P, 120K-120N, 120P, 120, 132, 138K-138N, 138P, 138, 142, 145, 147, 156K-156N, 156P, 156, 157, 159 |
| 3. applies knowledge of a variety of developmentally appropriate structural cues (for example, word order, prefixes, suffixes, verb endings) to decode unfamiliar words. | 14N, 14P, 23G, 26L, 26N, 26P, 26, 46L, 46P, 47, 61G, 61H, 62L, 62N, 62P, 62 | 108P, 108-116, 120P, 120, 121, 123, 124, 126-130, 135, 138P, 138, 140, 143, 144, 146, 148-150, 152, 156P |
| 4. applies knowledge of a variety of context cues (for example, illustrations, diagrams, information in the story, titles and headings, sequence) to construct meaning (meaning cues). | 14P, 17, 28, 29P, 43G-43I, 46P, 59C, 62P, 67, 84P, 86, 88, 100 | 108P, 120P, 138P, 156P, 180P, 194, 200P, 202, 222P |
| 5. cross-checks visual, structural, and meaning cues to figure out unknown words. | 14P, 26P, 46P, 62P, 84P | 108P, 120P, 138P, 156P, 180P, 200P, 222P |
| 6. uses context cues to define multiple meaning words. | | |
| **BENCHMARK LA.A.1.1.3: The student uses knowledge of appropriate grade-, age-, and developmental-level vocabulary in reading. The student:** | | |
| 1. identifies simple, multiple-meaning words. | | 177G-177I, 197G-197I, 235G |
| 2. uses knowledge of contractions, base words, and compound words to determine meaning of words. | 14M, 14P, 26K, 26, 46K, 47 | 108P, 119G-119I, 120P, 138P, 156P, 180K, 180, 188, 200K, 200, 201, 205 |
| 3. uses knowledge of prefixes (including –un-, re-, pre-, mis-) and suffixes (including –er, -est, -ful) to determine meaning of words. | 46K, 47, 62K, 62 | 108P, 108-116, 120P, 120, 121, 127, 135, 138P, 138, 140, 143, 144, 146, 148-150, 152, 156P, 156, 160, 164 |
| 4. knows homophones, synonyms, and antonyms for a variety of words. | 21B, 41B, 59B, 62N, 79B, 103B | 137G-137I, 221G-221I, 235H-235I |
| 5. develops vocabulary by reading independently and listening to and discussing both familiar and conceptually challenging selections. | 21A, 21D, 41B, 59A, 60, 67, 79A, 80, 103A | 117A, 118, 135A, 136, 153A, 154, 175A, 176, 196, 220, 234 |
| 6. uses resources and references to build upon word meanings (such as dictionaries, glossaries). | 14P, 17, 28, 81G-81I, 86, 105G, 105H | 108P, 120P, 138P, 156P, 180P, 200P, 222P |
| **BENCHMARK LA.A.1.1.4: The student increases comprehension by rereading, retelling, and discussion. The student:** | | |
| 1. uses a variety of strategies to comprehend text (for example, self-monitoring, predicting, retelling, discussing, restating ideas). | 20, 21C, 40, 51, 54, 58, 59C, 67, 69, 72, 78, 92, 95, 96 | 110, 114, 116, 117A, 120, 122, 124, 130, 132, 134, 142, 146, 148, 150, 152, 153C, 160, 162, 164, 168, 170, 172 |
| **STANDARD 2: The student constructs meaning from a wide range of texts.** | | |
| **BENCHMARK LA.A.2.1.1: The student determines the main idea or essential message from text and identifies supporting information. The stude** | | |
| 1. summarizes information in texts (including but not limited to central idea, supporting details, connections between texts). | 14R, 27, 29, 31, 33, 35, 37, 41C | 201, 203, 205, 207, 209, 211, 213, 215, 217, 219, 219C |
| 2. uses specific ideas, details, and information from text to answer literal questions. | 21, 23, 25, 41, 43, 45, 59, 61, 79, 81, 103, 105 | 117, 119, 135, 137, 153, 155, 175, 177, 195, 197, 219, 221, 233, 235 |
| 3. makes connection and inferences based on text and prior knowledge (such as order of events, possible outcomes). | 47, 49, 51, 53, 55, 57, 59, 63, 65, 67, 69, 71, 73, 75, 77, 79, 79C, 85, 87, 89, 91, 93, 95, 97, 99, 101, 103, 103C | 109, 111, 113-116, 117C, 121, 123, 125, 127, 129, 131, 133, 135, 135C-D, 139, 141, 143, 145, 147, 149, 151 |
| 4. understands similarities and differences across texts (such as topics, characters, problems). | 21C, 43A, 61, 81, 92, 103E, 105 | 119, 137, 150, 155, 177, 197, 221, 233F, 235 |
| **BENCHMARK LA.A.2.1.2: The student selects material to read for pleasure. The student:** | | |
| 1. selects materials to read for pleasure, as a group or independently. | 14D, 23A, 26D, 46D, 62D, 81A, 84D | 120D, 138D, 156D, 180D, 200D |
| 2. reads aloud with fluency and expression (including but not limited to reads phrases rather than word-by-word; attends to punctuation; interjects a sense of feeling, anticipation, characterization) from developmentally appropriate material. | 14N, 14Q, 26L, 26N, 26Q, 44, 46L, 46N, 46Q, 62L, 62N, 62Q, 81A, 84L, 84N, 84Q | 108L, 108N, 108Q, 120L, 120N, 120Q, 138L, 138N, 138Q, 156L, 156N, 156Q, 180L, 180N, 180Q, 200L, 200N, 200Q |

| Unit 3 | Unit 4 | Unit 5 | Unit 6 |
|---|---|---|---|
| 2380, 249A, 2520, 263A, 2680, 291A, 2960, 311A, 3140, 331A, 3340, 357A | 14M, 27A, 30M, 37A, 40, 42M, 62, 64M, 82M, 92M | 122M, 143A, 146, 148M, 155A, 160M, 173A, 178M, 193A, 196M, 209A | 248M, 265A, 268M, 281A, 284M, 295A, 298M, 311A, 316M, 331A, 336M, 359A |
| 238K-238N, 238P, 238-248, 251G, 252K-252N, 252P, 252-263, 265G, 268K-268N, 268P, 268-272, 274, 275, 277 | 14K, 14L, 14N, 14-18, 20-27, 30K, 30L, 30N, 30-37, 42K, 42L, 42N, 42-50, 52-59, 82K, 82L, 82N, 82-89, 92K, 92L | 122K, 122N, 148K, 148N, 160K, 160N, 178K, 178N, 196K, 196N, 212K, 212N | 248K, 248L, 248N, 2480, 248, 251-256, 258-263, 267F, 268K, 268L, 268N, 268, 270-272, 274-280, 284K |
| 238K-238N, 238P, 238-240, 242, 243, 245, 247, 248, 252K-252N, 252P, 268K-268N, 268P, 268-271, 274 | 14K, 14L, 14N, 14, 16, 18, 20, 22, 25, 30K, 30L, 30N, 30-34, 42K, 42L, 42N, 420, 42, 64K, 64L, 64N, 64, 65 | 122L, 122N, 122, 148L, 148N, 160L, 160N, 178L, 178N, 178, 196L, 196N, 196, 212L, 212N, 212 | 248L, 248N, 2480, 248, 251, 253-263, 268L, 268N, 268, 272, 275-277, 279, 280, 284L, 284N, 284-293 |
| 238L, 238P, 238-241, 244, 246, 252N, 252P, 268N, 268P, 268, 272, 275, 277-279, 284-286, 289, 296N | 14N, 14, 15, 17, 19, 21, 23-27, 30, 31, 33, 35-37, 42N, 420, 42-46, 49-51, 53, 54, 56-59, 64N, 64-68, 71-75 | 122L, 122N, 122, 148L, 148N, 148, 160L, 160N, 160, 178L, 178N, 196L, 196N, 196, 212L, 212N, 212 | 248L, 248N, 248, 252, 254, 256, 259, 260, 263, 267F-267I, 268L, 268N, 268, 270-273, 275, 284L, 284N, 2840 |
| 238P, 252P, 268P, 296P, 311C, 314P, 334P | 14M, 140, 30N, 300, 42N, 50, 64N, 82N, 92N | 122N, 138, 148N, 160N, 162, 178N, 196N, 212N, 224 | 248N, 268N, 284N, 298N, 311C, 316N, 336N, 362N |
| 238P, 252P, 268P, 296P, 311C | 140, 20, 300, 42N, 64N, 82N, 92N | 122N, 148N, 160N, 178N, 196N, 212N | 248N, 268N, 284N, 298N, 316N |
|  |  | 188 | 311C |
| 242, 244 | 82K | 160K | 333G-333I |
| 238P, 251G-251I, 252P, 268K, 268L, 268P, 268, 272, 275, 277, 285, 286, 293G-293I | 14K, 14, 18, 19, 27, 30K, 30, 31, 33, 35-37, 42N, 64N, 82K, 82N, 82, 83, 92N | 160K, 175G-175I, 196K, 204, 205, 212K | 248N, 268N, 284K, 297G-297I, 298N, 316K, 316N, 336N, 362K, 362N, 362 |
| 238K, 238P, 238, 241, 244, 246, 252P, 265G, 265I, 268M, 268P, 296P, 311C, 313H-313I, 334M, 334P, 359G, 359I | 14K, 14, 15, 17, 21, 23, 26, 42K, 42N, 42, 46, 48, 54, 64K, 64N, 64, 66, 68, 73, 77, 82K, 82N, 82, 84-89, 92N | 122K, 148K, 160K, 178K, 195G, 195H, 196K | 248K, 248N, 248, 252, 268K, 268N, 270-273, 283G-283I, 284N, 298N, 316K, 316N, 316, 319, 320, 326, 336N |
|  | 39G-39I, 41A, 79G-79I, 82L, 119H-119I | 145G-145H, 157G-157I, 160K, 178L, 212K, 245H, 245I | 268K, 281B, 295B, 298K, 311B, 313G-313I, 316K, 331B, 336K, 362K, 373B |
| 249A, 249B, 250, 263A, 263B, 264, 291A, 292, 296R, 311A, 311B, 312, 331A, 331B, 332 | 27B, 29G, 37B, 59B, 77B, 89B, 117B | 143A, 155A, 173A, 174, 193A, 194, 210, 243A, 244 | 265A, 265B, 266, 267G-267I, 281A, 281B, 282, 295A, 295B, 296, 311A, 311B, 312, 331A |
| 238P, 251H, 252P, 268P, 296P, 311C, 314P, 334P, 321 | 20, 30N, 300, 42N, 64N, 82N, 92N | 122N, 148N, 160N, 178N, 196N, 212N | 248N, 268N, 284N, 297H, 298N, 316N, 336N, 362N |
| 240, 244, 246, 248, 249A, 249C, 252, 254, 256, 258, 262, 263A, 268, 272, 274, 276, 278, 280 | 16, 18, 20, 22, 24, 27C, 32, 36, 44, 46, 50, 52, 54, 58, 61G-61I, 64, 66, 68, 74, 76, 84, 86, 88, 94, 96, 98, 100 | 122, 124, 128, 130, 132, 134, 136, 138, 140, 142, 143A, 148, 152, 154, 155A, 155C, 162, 164, 166, 168, 170, 173A | 248, 250, 252, 254, 256, 258, 260, 262, 264, 265A, 268, 270, 272, 274, 278, 280, 281A, 284, 286, 288, 290, 294 |
| 240, 244, 249C, 272, 276, 282, 286, 300, 304, 306, 310, 330, 335, 337 | 22, 37A, 43, 45, 46, 47, 49, 51, 58, 59D, 61, 86, 93, 95, 97, 99, 101-105, 107, 109, 111, 113, 115, 117 | 150, 152, 155C, 166, 182, 186, 187, 189, 191, 193, 195, 196, 200, 204, 222, 228, 238, 242, 245 | 254, 256, 262, 274, 278, 304, 310, 322, 328, 338, 346, 350, 354, 358, 359C |
| 249, 251, 263, 265, 291, 293, 311, 313, 331, 333, 357, 359 | 29, 37, 39, 59, 61, 77, 79, 89, 91, 117, 119 | 143, 145, 155, 157, 173, 175, 193, 195, 209, 211, 243, 245 | 265, 267, 281, 283, 295, 297, 311, 313, 331, 333, 359, 361, 373, 375 |
| 239, 241, 243, 245, 247, 249, 253-259, 261, 263, 263C, 268, 269, 271, 273-280, 281, 283-285, 287 | 15, 17, 19, 21, 23, 25, 27, 32, 53, 55, 57, 59, 65, 67, 69, 71, 73, 75, 77, 83-85, 87, 89, 89C, 106, 110 | 123, 125, 127, 129, 131, 133, 135, 137, 139, 141, 143, 143C, 149, 151, 153, 155, 161, 163, 165, 167, 169, 171, 173 | 249, 251, 253, 255, 257, 259, 261, 263, 265, 265C, 265D, 269, 270, 271, 273, 275, 277, 279, 281, 281C |
| 263E, 265, 293, 296R, 313, 333, 359 | 39, 61, 79, 91, 119 | 145, 157, 175, 178P, 195, 211, 245 | 283, 295B, 295C, 295D, 297, 297A, 313, 331E, 333, 359C, 359D, 361, 361A, 375 |
| 238D, 252D, 268D, 296D, 314D, 334D | 14D, 30D, 42D, 64D, 82D, 92D | 122D, 148D, 160D, 178D, 196D, 212D | 248D, 268D, 284D, 298D, 316D |
| 238L, 238N, 238Q, 252L, 252N, 252Q, 262, 268L, 268N, 268Q, 290, 296L, 296N, 296Q, 314L, 314N, 314Q | 14L, 140, 30L, 300, 42L, 420, 64L, 640, 82L, 820, 92L, 920 | 122L, 1220, 148L, 1480, 160L, 1600, 178L, 1780, 196L, 1960, 212L, 2120 | 248L, 2480, 2680, 284L, 2840, 298L, 2980, 336L, 3360, 3620 |

## Correlation to Florida Sunshine State Standards                    Grade 2

### Strand A: Reading

| | Unit 1 | Unit 2 |
|---|---|---|
| **BENCHMARK LA.A.2.1.3: The student reads for information to use in performing a task and learning a new task. The student:** | | |
| 1. reads informational texts for specific purposes (including to perform a task, to learn a new task, to sequentially carry out the steps of a procedure, to locate information to answer a question). | | 117F, 153F, 155C, 175E, 219E |
| **BENCHMARK LA.A.2.1.4: The student knows strategies to use to discover whether information presented in a text is true, including asking others and checking another source. The student:** | | |
| 1. uses strategies to clarify the accuracy of a text (such as discussion, checking other sources). | | 175F |
| **BENCHMARK LA.A.2.1.5: The student uses simple materials of the reference system to obtain information. The student:** | | |
| 1. uses simple reference material (such as table of contents, dictionary, index, glossary). | 14P, 26P, 46P, 62P, 84P | 108P, 117F, 120P, 138P, 156P, 180P, 200P, 222P, 235D |
| 2. alphabetizes words according to initial and second letter. | 23D | 235D |
| 3. uses parts of a book to locate information, including chapter titles, guide words, and indices. | 43D | 117F, 219E, 235D |
| 4. generates questions about topics of personal interest. | 13R, 14B, 23B, 23C, 26B, 43B, 43C, 46B, 61B, 62B, 84B | 108B, 119B, 120B, 137B, 138B, 156B, 180B, 200B, 222B |

### Strand B: Writing

| | Unit 1 | Unit 2 |
|---|---|---|
| **STANDARD 1: The student uses writing processes effectively.** | | |
| **BENCHMARK LA.B.1.1.1: The student makes a plan for writing that includes a central idea and related ideas. The student:** | | |
| 1. generates ideas before writing on self-selected topics and assigned tasks. | 14B, 23B, 23C, 23F-23J, 25A, 26B, 43B, 43C, 45A, 61B, 62B, 84B | 108B, 119B, 119C, 119F, 120B, 137F, 138B, 155F, 156B, 180B |
| 2. makes a plan before writing the first draft (such as drawing pictures, using graphic organizers). | 43F-J | 137G, 155G |
| 3. focuses on a central idea and groups related ideas. | 61F | 119D, 119I |
| **BENCHMARK LA.B.1.1.2: The student drafts and revises simple sentences and passages, stories, letters, and simple explanations that**<br>• *express ideas clearly;*<br>• *show an awareness of topic and audience;*<br>• *have a beginning, middle, and ending;*<br>• *effectively use common words;*<br>• *have supporting detail; and*<br>• *are in legible printing.*<br>**The student:** | | |
| 1. writes and revises a variety of simple texts (for example, sentences, paragraphs, stories, letters, explanations telling why or how, picture books, poems). | 25A, 105C | 119F-119J, 137F-137J, 155F-155J, 221F-221J, 235F-235J |
| 2. writes legibly. | 23J, 43J, 61J, 81J, 105J | 119J, 137J, 155J, 177J, 197J, 221J, 235J |
| 3. uses one or more paragraphs to focus on separate ideas in writing and uses transition words where appropriate. | | 177G |
| 4. writes for a specific audience. | | 119G |
| 5. writes a story that includes most story elements (character, setting, problem, sequence of events, resolution). | | |
| 6. uses strategies to support ideas in writing (including but not limited to using several sentences to elaborate upon an idea; using specific word choice and relevant details such as reasons or examples). | | 137G |
| 7. evaluates own and other's writing (for example, determining how own writing achieves its purposes, asking questions, making comments, responding constructively to other's comments, helping classmates apply conventions). | 81G | |
| 8. revises writing to improve supporting details and word choice by adding or substituting text. | 81F-81J | |
| **BENCHMARK LA.B.1.1.3: The student produces final simple documents that have been edited for**<br>• *correct spelling;*<br>• *appropriate end punctuation;*<br>• *correct capitalization of initial words, "I," and names of people;*<br>• *correct sentence structure; and*<br>• *correct usage of age-appropriate verb/subject and noun/pronoun agreement.*<br>**The student:** | | |
| 1. spells frequently used words correctly. | 105F | |

| Unit 3 | Unit 4 | Unit 5 | Unit 6 |
|---|---|---|---|
| 263F | 29A, 82P | 145A, 155E | 248P, 265E, 283D, 295F, 298P, 305, 311D-311F |
| | | | |
| 263F, 357F | 31 | 155E | |
| 238P, 252P, 263F, 268P, 296P, 314P, 333D, 334P, 357E, 359D | 29D | 160, 175A, 195D | 248N, 267D, 268N, 283D, 284N, 298N, 316N, 336N, 362N |
| 357F | | | |
| 263F, 333D, 357E, 357F | 61D | 195D | 283D, 295F |
| 238B, 251A-251C, 252B, 265B, 268B, 293B, 296B, 313B, 314B, 333B, 334B | 14B, 29A, 29C, 30B, 39B, 42B, 61B, 64B, 79B, 82B, 91B, 92B, 119B | 122B, 145C, 148B, 157C, 160B, 178B, 195A, 195B, 196B, 211B, 212B | 248B, 267B, 267C, 268B, 283B, 284B, 297B, 298B, 313B, 316B, 333B, 336B |
| | | | |
| 238B, 251B, 251C, 252B, 265B, 268B, 293B, 296B, 313B, 314B, 333B, 334B | 29A, 29B, 39B, 39C, 42B, 61B, 64B, 79B, 79F, 82B, 91B, 92B, 119B | 122B, 145B, 145C, 147A, 148B, 157B, 157C, 160B, 178B, 195B, 196B, 211B, 212B | 248B, 267B, 267C, 268B, 283B, 284B, 297B, 298B, 313B, 315A, 316B, 333B |
| | | 145G, 175G, 195G, 211G | 283G, 297G, 313G |
| 238B, 251A, 251H, 252B, 268B, 296B, 314B, 334B | 29C | | |
| | | | |
| 251H-251J, 263D, 291C, 331C, 357C | 29H-29J, 39H-39J, 61H-61J, 79H-79J, 91H-91J | 145H-145J, 157H-157J, 173D, 175H-175J, 193D, 195H-195J, 211H-211J, 245H-245J | 265C, 265E, 281F, 283A, 283H-283J, 295C, 297D, 311C, 313H-313J |
| 251J, 265J, 293J, 313J, 333J, 359J | 29J, 39J, 61J, 79J, 91J, 119J | 145J, 157J, 175J, 195J, 211J, 245J | 267J, 283J, 297J, 313J, 333J, 361J, 375J |
| 313H-313I | | | |
| | 39G, 61G, 91G | | 267G, 297G, 375G |
| | | 175F-175J, 211H-211I | |
| 357C | 29H-29I | 195H | 297H |
| | | | |
| | 29J, 39I | | |
| | | | |
| | | | 298L, 316L |

## Correlation to Florida Sunshine State Standards
### Grade 2

### Strand B: Writing

| | Unit 1 | Unit 2 | |
|---|---|---|---|
| **2.** uses references to edit writing (for example, word lists, dictionaries, charts). | | | |
| **3.** uses conventions of punctuation (including but not limited to periods, question marks, exclamation points; commas in dates, series of words, and in greetings and closures in letters). | 105H | 137F-137H, 177F-177H, 221F-221H | |
| **4.** capitalizes initial words of sentences, the pronoun "I," and proper nouns. | 105G | 119F-119H | |
| **5.** revises and edits for sentence structure and age-appropriate usage (including nouns, action verbs, adjectives, adverbs). | 61H, 105H | | |
| **6.** uses strategies to "finish" a piece of writing (such as incorporates illustrations, photos, charts, and graphs; prepares a final copy). | 105J | 119J, 137J, 221J | |

**STANDARD 2: The student writes to communicate ideas and information effectively.**

**BENCHMARK LA.B.2.1.1: The student writes questions and observations about familiar topics, stories, or new experiences. The student:**

| | | | |
|---|---|---|---|
| **1.** write questions or makes notes about familiar topics, stories, or new experiences. | 23, 43, 61, 81, 105 | 119, 137, 155, 177, 177F-177J, 197, 221, 235 | |

**BENCHMARK L.A.B.2.1.2: The student uses knowledge and experience to tell about experiences or to write for familiar occasions, audiences, and purposes. The student:**

| | | | |
|---|---|---|---|
| **1.** writes informally (such as journal entries, reading response, and poetry). | 13S, 21B, 23, 41B, 43, 45A, 59B, 79B, 81, 105 | 117B, 119, 135B, 137, 153B, 155, 175B, 177, 177F-177J, 195B, 197, 199A, 219B | |
| **2.** uses effective word choice in written work to tell about experiences (including but not limited to anecdotal detail and figurative language such as similes). | | 199A | |
| **3.** writes for familiar occasions, audiences and purposes (including but not limited to entertaining, informing, responding to literature). | | 119G, 175B, 199A | |

**BENCHMARK LA.B.2.1.3: The student uses basic computer skills for writing, such as basic word-processing techniques such as keying words, copying, cutting, and pasting; using e-mail; and accessing and using basic educational software for writing. The student:**

| | | | |
|---|---|---|---|
| **1.** uses basic word processing skills and basic educational software for writing (including proofreading, using appropriate fonts and graphics, using technology to 'publish' writing). | 13F, 14D, 23E, 26D, 46D, 61E, 105E-105J | 119B, 119J | |

**BENCHMARK LA.B.2.1.4: The student composes simple sets of instructions for simple tasks using logical sequencing of steps. The student:**

| | | | |
|---|---|---|---|
| **1.** writes simple informational texts (such as three-step instructions in sequence, expository pieces). | | 177F-177J | |

### Strand C: Listening, Viewing, and Speaking

**STANDARD 1: The student uses listening strategies effectively.**

**BENCHMARK LA.C.1.1.1: The student listens for a variety of informational purposes, including curiosity, pleasure, getting directions, performing tasks, solving problems, and following rules. The student:**

| | | | |
|---|---|---|---|
| **1.** listens for information and pleasure. | 13M, 22, 23I, 24, 42, 44, 59E, 60, 79F, 80, 81A, 104 | 119I, 198, 235C | |

**BENCHMARK LA.C.1.1.2: The student recognizes personal preferences in listening to literature and other material. The student:**

| | | | |
|---|---|---|---|
| **1.** knows personal preferences for listening to literature and other material (such as poetry, songs, stories, informational books). | 22, 23I, 42, 60, 80, 104 | 118, 136, 154, 176, 196, 220 | |

**BENCHMARK LA.C.1.1.3: The student carries on a conversation with another person, seeking answers and further explanations of the other's ideas through questioning and answering. The student:**

| | | | |
|---|---|---|---|
| **1.** uses strategies to contribute to group conversations (including but not limited to recounting personal experiences, initiating conversation, asking questions, reporting on personal knowledge of a topic). | 23A, 59E, 79, 81A, 103C, 105I | 221A | |

**BENCHMARK LA.C.1.1.4: The student retells specific details of information heard, including sequence of events. The student:**

| | | | |
|---|---|---|---|
| **1.** listens for specific details and information (including but not limited to logical sequence and flow of events, story elements, concluding events). | 23A | 137A, 155C, 197D, 198, 221C, 235C | |

**STANDARD 2: The student uses viewing strategies effectively.**

**BENCHMARK LA.C.2.1.1: The student determines the main idea in a nonprint communication. The student:**

| | | | |
|---|---|---|---|
| **1.** understands the main idea or common theme in pictures, symbols, film, and works of art. | 21B, 21E, 81I, 82, 103B | 117B, 177I, 178-179, 199B, 219B, 233D | |

**BENCHMARK LA.C.2.1.2: The student recognizes simple nonverbal cues, such as use of eye contact, smiles, simple hand gestures. The student:**

| | | | |
|---|---|---|---|
| **1.** understands and uses simple nonverbal cues (such as eye contact, facial expressions, gesturing). | 25B | 197I, 221C, 233A | |

| Unit 3 | Unit 4 | Unit 5 | Unit 6 |
|---|---|---|---|
| | 29H, 61I, 79H | | |
| 251F-H | | | |
| | | 145F-145H | |
| 313H | 29H, 79H, 91H | 157H | |
| | | 145E, 157E, 175E, 195E, 195J, 211E, 245E | 375J |
| 251, 251B, 265, 265B, 293, 293B, 293J, 313, 313B | 39B, 61, 79, 91, 91B, 119B, 119 | 1220, 145, 145B, 145C, 157, 157B, 175, 195, 195B | 267, 267B, 267C, 283, 297, 313, 333, 361, 375 |
| 249B, 251, 263B, 265, 291B, 293, 311B, 313, 331B | 27B, 37B, 59B, 117B | 1220, 145, 147A, 157, 159, 173B, 175, 193B | 265B, 281B, 283, 295B, 297, 311B, 313, 315, 331B, 333, 359B, 361, 373B, 375 |
| | 39I, 61J | | |
| 249B, 291B, 293G, 311B, 357B | 61G | 175G, 211G | 265B, 311B, 359B, 373B |
| 251B, 265B, 265E, 293B, 293E, 313B, 313E, 333B, 333E, 359B, 359E | 39B, 61B, 79B, 91B, 119B | 145B, 157B, 175B, 195B, 211B, 245B | 267B, 283B, 297B, 313B, 333B, 361B, 375B |
| 251G, 333G-333J | | | |
| 251I, 265H, 267B, 333A, 359C | 59F, 62, 63B, 91A, 119C | 143A, 144, 145A, 155A, 156, 158, 159B, 173A, 174, 193A | 266, 282, 296, 312, 332, 359E, 361D |
| 250, 264, 292, 312, 332, 358 | 28, 38, 78, 90 | 144, 156, 174, 194, 210, 244 | 266, 282, 296, 312, 332, 360, 374 |
| 249A, 263A, 291A, 293A, 311A, 313A, 331A, 333I, 357A | 27A, 29I, 37A | 143A, 175I | 298M, 311E, 311F, 313A, 333A, 353, 359E, 361I, 362M, 364, 373F, 375C |
| 251I, 265J, 291D, 293D, 333A | 27A, 37A, 59F, 91A, 119C | 145A, 145I, 159B, 211J, 245J | 259, 267I, 359E, 361D, 375C |
| 294, 357B, 359I | 63B, 89B | 173B, 176, 177, 195I, 209B, 245A | 257, 281B, 311, 311A, 311F, 313A, 313I, 331B, 334, 335, 359E |
| 359C | 41B | 211I | |

# Florida Resources

## Correlation to Florida Sunshine State Standards — Grade 2

### Strand C: Listening, Viewing, and Speaking

| | Unit 1 | Unit 2 |
|---|---|---|
| **STANDARD 3: The student uses speaking strategies effectively.** | | |
| **BENCHMARK LA.C.3.1.1: The student speaks clearly and at a volume audible in large- or small-group settings. The student:** | | |
| 1. uses volume, phrasing, and intonation appropriate for different situations (such as large or small group settings, sharing oral stories, dramatic activities). | 21A, 41A, 43I, 59A, 79A, 81A, 103A, 105M | 135A, 137I, 235C |
| 2. speaks for different purposes (such as to inform, to entertain, to express ideas). | 21A, 23A, 26O, 41A, 41F, 59A, 59E, 79A, 79F, 81A, 103A, 103C, 105M | 117A, 119A, 135A, 153A, 175A, 195A, 219A, 233A, 235C, 235I |
| **BENCHMARK LA.C.3.1.2: The student asks questions to seek answers and further explanation of other people's ideas. The student:** | | |
| 1. uses oral communication to clarify understanding of a topic or ideas (such as making comments, asking questions to gain information, asking for clarification of unfamiliar words and ideas). | 21A, 41A, 59A, 61D, 79A, 103A, 105I | 117A, 135A, 153A, 175A, 195A, 219A, 233A, 221C, 235A, 235C |
| **BENCHMARK LA.C.3.1.3: The student speaks effectively in conversations with others. The student:** | | |
| 1. uses speaking to convey a message in conversation vocabulary (such as synonyms, antonyms, complex sentence structures). | | 175A, 221C, 235C |
| **BENCHMARK LA.C.3.1.4: The student uses eye contact and simple gestures when speaking. The student:** | | |
| 1. uses eye contact and appropriate gestures to enhance oral presentations. | | 197I, 235C |

### Strand D: Language

| | Unit 1 | Unit 2 |
|---|---|---|
| **STANDARD 1: The student understands the nature of language.** | | |
| **BENCHMARK LA.D.1.1.1: The student recognizes basic patterns in and functions of language (patterns such as characteristic sounds and rhythms and those found in written forms; functions such as asking questions, expressing oneself, describing objects or experience, and explaining). The student:** | | |
| 1. knows patterns used in standard English. | 61F-61J | 119F, 119G, 119J, 137F-137I, 155F-155J, 177F, 177I, 197F-197J, 221F |
| 2. knows different functions of language (such as asking questions, describing, explaining). | 45B, 61D, 81A, 81I, 105I | 155I, 177I, 221A |
| **BENCHMARK LA.D.1.1.2: The student recognizes the differences between language that is used at home and language that is used at school. The student:** | | |
| 1. understands the differences between less formal language that is used at home and more formal language that is used at school and other public settings. | 61I | 221C |
| **STANDARD 2: The student understands the power of language.** | | |
| **BENCHMARK LA.D.2.1.1: The student understands that word choice can shape ideas, feelings, and actions. The student:** | | |
| 1. understands that word choice can shape ideas, feelings, and actions (such as language appropriate to the subject, synonyms, antonyms). | 41E, 45B, 96, 103E | 111, 117A, 125, 141, 175D, 186, 199A, 219D, 221C |
| **BENCHMARK LA.D.2.1.2: The student identifies and uses repetition, rhyme, and rhythm in oral and written text. The student:** | | |
| 1. uses repetition, rhyme, and rhythm in oral and written text (such as choral reading of poems, songs, rhymes, and stories; identifying rhymes, repeated sounds, onomatopoeia). | 25A, 45A, 59D | 119I, 128, 155H, 155I, 177H, 184 |
| **BENCHMARK LA.D.2.1.3: The student recognizes that use of more than one medium increases the power to influence how one thinks and feels. The student:** | | |
| 1. understands that the use of multimedia forms (for example, illustrations, music) can influence how one thinks and feels. | | 166, 174, 199B, 233D |
| **BENCHMARK LA.D.2.1.4: The student recognizes various types of mass media. The student:** | | |
| 1. knows various types of mass media (such as magazines, newspapers, radio, television, billboards). | 23H | 221D |

### Strand E: Literature

| | Unit 1 | Unit 2 |
|---|---|---|
| **STANDARD 1: The student understands the common features of a variety of literary forms.** | | |
| **BENCHMARK LA.E.1.1.1: The student knows the basic characteristics of fables, stories, and legends. The student:** | | |
| 1. knows basic characteristics of a variety of genres (such as fables, stories, fiction, nonfiction, poetry, fairy tales, folktales, legends, myths, pictures and predictable books). | 21A, 26O, 41A, 59A, 79A, 84O, 103A | 117A, 120O, 135A, 153A, 175A, 200O, 219A, 222O, 233A |

| Unit 3 | Unit 4 | Unit 5 | Unit 6 |
|---|---|---|---|
| 249A, 263A, 267B, 291A, 311A, 331A, 357A, 359C | 27A, 37A, 39I, 41B, 59A, 59F, 77A, 89A, 117A, 119C | | 265A, 281A, 295A, 297J, 311A, 315B, 331A, 359A, 373A, 375C |
| 249A, 263A, 265I, 267B, 291A, 311A, 313I, 331A, 333A, 357A, 359C | 41B, 59A, 59F, 63B, 77A, 89A, 91I, 117A, 119C | 143A, 145A, 155A, 155E, 157A, 157I, 173A, 193A, 209A, 243A | 265A, 281A, 295A, 311A, 331A, 333A, 359A, 361I, 373A, 375C, 375I |
| 249A, 263A, 291A, 311A, 331A, 357A, 359C | 27A, 37A, 59A, 77A, 89A, 91I, 117A | 143A, 155A, 173A, 193A, 209A, 243A | 265A, 281A, 295A, 311A, 331A, 359A, 361I, 373A, 375C |
| 249B, 263B, 291A, 311B, 331A | 39I, 63B | 143A, 245I | 265A, 281A, 295A, 311A, 331A, 359A, 373A |
| 359C | 59F | 211I | 375C |
| | | | |
| 251F, 251G, 251J, 265F-265J, 293F-293J, 313F-313J, 333F-333J, 359F-359J | 29F-29J, 39F-39J, 61F-61J, 79F-79J, 91F-91J, 119F-119J | 145F-145J, 157F-157J, 175F-175J, 195F-195J, 245F-245J | 333J, 361F, 361H, 361J |
| 265I, 293I, 333I | 91I | 175I | 283I |
| | | | 361C |
| 267A, 293I, 331E, 350 | 37E, 39H, 61I, 79H | 138, 145G, 157I, 159A | 265C, 283H, 297I, 315A, 315B, 373E |
| 274, 291D, 311D | 39J, 41B, 119I | 159A | 315A |
| 268, 296, 359I | 27D, 41A, 79I | | 361D |
| | 27D, 59E, 63B, 79I | | 313D, 361D, 375D |
| | | | |
| 249A, 263A, 291A, 291D, 311A, 331A, 333A, 357A | 27A, 30M, 37A | 122M, 143A, 155A, 160M, 173A, 173E, 178M, 193A, 196M, 209A, 243A | 265A, 281A, 281E, 295A, 311A, 331A, 359A, 373A |

# Florida Resources

## Correlation to Florida Sunshine State Standards

### Grade 2

| Strand E: Literature | Unit 1 | Unit 2 |
|---|---|---|
| **BENCHMARK LA.E.1.1.2: The student identifies the story elements of setting, plot, character, problem, and solution/resolution. The student:** | | |
| **1.** understands problem(s) and solution(s) in a story. | 21C | 117E, 207, 216, 233D |
| **STANDARD 2: The student responds critically to fiction, nonfiction, poetry, and drama.** | | |
| **BENCHMARK LA.E.2.1.1: The student uses personal perspective in responding to a work of literature, such as relating characters and simple events in a story or biography to people or events in his or her own life. The student:** | | |
| **1.** understands connections between characters and events in literature and people, events, and experiences in own life. | 21C, 54, 65, 79, 79C | 153B, 155A, 175B, 195B, 208, 219B, 233B, 235A |
| **BENCHMARK LA.E.2.1.2: The student recognizes rhymes, rhythm, and patterned structures in children's texts. The student:** | | |
| **1.** knows rhymes, rhythms, and patterned structures in a variety of children's texts (such as prose, poetry). | 25A, 45A, 48, 59D | 128 |

### Grade 3

| Strand A: Reading | Unit 1 | Unit 2 |
|---|---|---|
| **STANDARD 1: The student uses the reading process effectively.** | | |
| **BENCHMARK LA.A.1.2.1 The student use a table of contents, index, headings, captions, illustrations, and major words to anticipate or predict content and purpose of a reading selection. The student:** | | |
| **1.** uses text features to predict content and monitor comprehension (for example, uses table of contents, indexes, captions, illustrations, key words, preview text). | 14O, 28P, 45G-45J, 48O, 64O, 79C, 82O, 93D, 94O | 114O, 126O, 136O, 148O, 160O, 163D, 182O |
| **2.** uses knowledge of formats, ideas, plots, and elements from previous reading to generate questions and make predictions about content of text. | 43E | 120, 126, 138, 140, 142, 148O, 166O, 170, 179E |
| **BENCHMARK LA.A.1.2.2 The student selects from a variety of simple strategies, including the use of phonics, word structures, context clues, self-questioning, confirming simple predictions, retelling, and using visual cues to identify words and construct meaning from various texts, illustrations, graphics, and charts. The student:** | | |
| **1.** uses decoding strategies to clarify pronunciation (for example, less common vowel patterns, homophones). | 14L, 27F-27J, 28M, 45F-45J, 48K, 48M, 61F-61J, 81F-81J, 93F-93J, 94K, 111F-111J | 125F-125J, 126K, 126M, 133F-133J, 136M, 145F-145J, 163F-163J, 181F-181J, 195F-195J |
| **2.** uses context clues (for example, known words, phrases, structures) to infer the meaning of new and unfamiliar words, including synonyms, antonyms, and homophones. | 14P, 25B, 27I, 28P, 43B, 48K, 48P, 59B, 64P, 91B | 114K, 114P, 123B, 125G, 126K, 126P, 131B, 136P, 143B, 145H, 148P, 163G-163J, 166P, 181G-181I, 195G-195I |
| **3.** makes, confirms, and revises predictions. | | 120, 140, 142 |
| **4.** uses a variety of word structures and forms to construct meaning (for example, affixes, roots, homonyms, antonyms, synonyms, word analogies). | 48K, 61G-61J | 114K, 126K, 136K, 148K |
| **5.** establishes a purpose for reading (for example, for entertainment; to skim for facts; to answer a specific question). | 14P, 28P, 48O, 64P, 82P, 93P | 114P, 126P, 136P, 145H, 148P, 166P, 182P |
| **BENCHMARK LA.A.1.2.3 The student uses simple strategies to determine meaning and increase vocabulary for reading, including the use of prefixes, suffixes, root words, multiple meanings, antonyms, synonyms, and word relationships. The student:** | | |
| **1.** uses a variety of strategies to determine meaning and increase vocabulary (for example, prefixes, suffixes, root words, less common vowel patterns, homophones, compound words, contractions). | 28K, 82P, 94K, 94P | 114K, 125G-125J, 126K, 145G-145J, 166P, 182P |
| **2.** discusses meanings of words and develops vocabulary through meaningful real-world experiences. | 27G | 123B, 131B, 143B, 161B, 179B, 193B |
| **BENCHMARK LA.A.1.2.4 The student clarifies understanding by rereading, self-correction, summarizing, checking other sources, and class or group discussion. The student:** | | |
| **1.** uses a variety of strategies to monitor reading in third-grade or higher texts (for example, rereading, self-correcting, summarizing, checking other sources, class and group discussions, reading on, trying alternative pronunciations, asking questions). | 24, 42, 58, 78, 81G-81J, 90, 93G-93J, 108 | 118, 120, 122, 130, 133H, 133I, 145I, 142, 148, 150, 160, 178, 184, 186, 190, 192, 195I |
| **STANDARD 2: The student constructs meaning from a wide variety of texts.** | | |
| **BENCHMARK LA.A.2.2.1 The student reads text and determines the main idea or essential message, identifies relevant supporting details and facts, and arranges events in chronological order. The student:** | | |
| **1.** understands explicit and implicit ideas and information in third-grade or higher texts (for example, main idea, implied message, relevant supporting details and facts, chronological order of events). | 83, 85, 89, 91C, 95, 97, 99, 101, 103, 105, 107, 109 | 133G-133J, 161, 163A, 163G-163J, 195G |

| Unit 3 | Unit 4 | Unit 5 | Unit 6 |
|---|---|---|---|
| | | 209E | 331E, 373A |
| | | | |
| | | 124, 128, 134, 140, 148, 168, 172, 206, 211A, 214, 216, 218 | 298P, 311E, 331B, 333A, 333B, 344, 350, 353, 356, 359C, 361A |
| 25RR, 291D, 311D | | 159A | |

| Unit 3 | Unit 4 | Unit 5 | Unit 6 |
|---|---|---|---|
| 1980, 2160, 2240, 2400, 243, 2500, 2600 | 14M, 23C, 26M, 38M, 47H, 48M, 58M, 72M, 94M | 108M, 120M, 128M, 146M, 158M, 168M, 170, 180M | 198M, 204M, 216M, 236M, 247G, 247I, 250M, 262M, 284M |
| 216, 218, 230, 2500, 254, 256 | 23C. 58M, 64, 74, 82, 86, 102 | 110, 112, 138, 140, 146M, 170, 174 | 222, 226, 228, 236M, 250M, 252, 254, 256, 262M, 270, 272, 284M, 286 |
| 198K, 198M, 213F-213J, 216M, 223F-223J, 237F-237J, 240M, 249F-249J, 250K, 259F-259J, 260K, 269F-269J | 25F-24J, 35F-35J, 48K, 58K, 94K, 105F-105J | 108K, 117F-117J, 127F-127J, 143F-143J, 146K, 155F-155J, 158K, 165F-165J, 168K, 179F-179J, 180K, 193F-193J | 213F-213J, 236K, 250K, 261G, 262K, 283F-283J, 284K, 295F |
| 198P, 216P, 240P, 249G-249I, 259H | 14K, 14N, 26K, 26N, 38N, 47G-47J, 72K, 93G-93J | 108N, 120K, 120N, 127G, 128N, 146N, 158N | 198N, 203G, 204K, 204N, 213H, 213I, 233G-233J, 239B, 250N, 259B, 283G-283I, 295G |
| 216, 218, 230, 256 | 23C, 64, 102 | 110, 112, 138, 140, 162, 174, 190 | 222, 224, 226, 228, 252, 254, 268, 270 |
| 223G-223J, 237G-237J, 240M | 14K, 25G-25J, 26K, 38K, 48K, 55G-55J, 58K, 72K, 105H | 108K, 120K, 128K, 146K, 158K | 203G-203J, 213G, 213H, 216K, 236K, 247F-247J, 261G-261J, 262K, 283G-283J, 295G-295J |
| 198M, 198P, 216P, 224P, 240P, 250P, 260P, 269J | 14N, 14P, 26N, 38N, 48N, 58N, 58N, 72M, 94N | 108N, 120N, 128N, 146M, 158N, 168N, 180N | 198N, 203M, 216N, 236N, 284N |
| 198K, 198M, 213G-213J, 216K, 224K, 224M, 240P, 250P, 260P, 269J | 14K, 26K, 26N, 35G-35J, 38K, 47G-47J, 48N, 58K, 58N, 71G-71J, 72K, 72N, 93F-93J, 94K, 94N, 105F-105J | 108K, 120K, 128K, 143G-143J, 146K, 146N, 158K, 158N, 165G-165J, 168K, 168N, 179G-179J, 180N, 193G, 193H | 198K, 204K, 236K, 236N, 250K, 250N, 261G, 261I, 262K, 262N, 284N, 295G |
| 211B, 221B, 224B, 224P, 235B, 247B, 257B, 267B | 23B, 33B, 45B, 53B, 69B, 69C, 91B, 103B | 115B, 125B, 141B, 153B, 163B, 165G-165J, 168N, 177B, 191B, 193D | 201B, 211B, 231B, 245B, 259B, 261G, 281B |
| 200, 204, 206, 208, 210, 216, 218, 220, 234, 235A, 244, 246, 256, 266, 269H | 16, 20, 22, 26, 30, 32, 42, 44, 47G, 50, 52, 60, 64, 68, 69C, 71, 71G, 71I, 90, 96, 102, 103C, 105I | 108, 110, 112, 113, 117I, 120, 122, 123, 127G-125J, 140, 143H, 146, 147, 148, 149, 151-153, 153C, 155I, 158, 160, 162, 165G, 170, 176, 180, 186, 190, 193G | 198, 200, 203G, 210, 213H, 230, 238, 240, 242, 244, 245A, 245C, 252, 254, 256, 258, 262, 270, 272, 276, 280, 281A, 290, 292 |
| 225, 227, 229, 231, 233, 235, 235C, 235D | 17, 19, 21, 23, 25, 39, 41, 43, 45, 53, 53A, 55, 69, 73, 77, 79, 81, 85, 87, 89, 91, 91C, 93, 105, 115C | 109, 111, 113, 115, 117G-117J, 153, 153A, 155, 155G-155J, 159, 163, 163A, 165, 169, 171, 173, 175, 177, 177A | 207, 209, 211, 211C, 211D, 259, 259A, 263, 265, 267, 276, 281, 281A, 281C, 283G-283J, 285, 287, 289, 291, 293 |

# Florida Resources

## Correlation to Florida Sunshine State Standards
### Grade 3

### Strand A: Reading

| | Unit 1 | Unit 2 |
|---|---|---|
| **BENCHMARK LA.A.2.2.2 The student identifies the author's purpose in a simple text. The student:** | | |
| 1. identifies author's purpose in a simple text. | | 183, 185, 187, 189, 191, 193, 193C |
| **BENCHMARK LA.A.2.2.3 The student recognizes when a text is primarily intended to persuade. The student:** | | |
| 1. begins to recognize when a text is intended primarily to persuade. | | |
| **BENCHMARK LA.A.2.2.4 The student identifies specific personal preferences relative to fiction and nonfiction reading. The student:** | | |
| 1. knows personal preferences for literary texts (for example, fiction, stories, poems). | | 143C |
| 2. knows personal preference for nonfiction (for example, biographies, journals, magazines, interviews). | | |
| **BENCHMARK LA.A.2.2.5 The student reads and organizes information for a variety of purposes, including making a report, conducting an interview, taking a test, and performing an authentic task. The student:** | | |
| 1. reads and organizes information (for example, in story maps, graphs, charts) for different purposes (for example, to be informed, to follow directions, to make a report, to conduct interviews, to take a test, to perform a task). | 111G, 111H, 111J | 123F, 125I, 145J, 163I-163J, 195D 195F, 195J |
| **BENCHMARK LA.A.2.2.6 The student recognizes the difference between fact and opinion presented in a text. The student:** | | |
| 1. knows the difference between a fact and an opinion. | | |
| **BENCHMARK LA.A.2.2.7 The student recognizes the use of comparison and contrast in a text. The student:** | | |
| 1. understands the use of comparison and contrast within a selection. | 49, 51, 53, 55, 57, 59, 59C, 59D, 111I | 181I |
| **BENCHMARK LA.A.2.2.8 The student selects and uses a variety of appropriate reference materials, including multiple representations of information, such as maps, charts, and photos, to gather information for research project. The student:** | | |
| 1. uses a variety of representations to gather information (such as maps, charts, photos). | 25E | 133D, 133G, 145D, 195A, 195G |

### Strand B: Writing

| | Unit 1 | Unit 2 |
|---|---|---|
| **STANDARD 1: The student uses writing processes effectively.** | | |
| **BENCHMARK LA.B.1.2.1 The student prepares for writing by recording thoughts, focusing on a central idea, grouping related ideas, and identifying the purpose of writing. The student:** | | |
| 1. uses a variety of strategies to prepare for writing (such as lists, mapping ideas, rehearsing ideas, grouping related ideas, story webs). | 27F-27J | 125A, 125F-125G, 133F-133G, 145F, 163F-163G, 181F-181G, 195F-195G |
| 2. establishes a purpose for writing (including but not limited to informing, entertaining, explaining). | 45F-45J, 81D | 125F-125G, 133F-133G, 145F, 163F, 181F-181G, 195G |
| **BENCHMARK LA.B.1.2.2 The student drafts and revises writing in cursive that** • *focuses on the topic;* • *has a logical organizational pattern, including a beginning, middle, conclusion, and transitional devices;* • *has ample development of supporting ideas;* • *demonstrates a sense of completeness or wholeness;* • *generally has correct subject/verb agreement;* • *generally has correct verb and noun forms;* • *with few [exceptions], has sentences that are complete, except when fragments are use purposefully;* • *uses a variety of sentence structures; and* • *generally follows the convections of punctuation, capitalization, and spelling.* **The student:** | | |
| 1. focuses on a central idea or topic (excludes irrelevant or repetitious information). | | 125G-125I, 133G, 145G, 163F, 163H, 195H |
| 2. uses an organizational pattern (including but not limited to having a beginning, middle, and end; organizing ideas sequentially or around major points of information). | | 125G, 145G-145H, 163G, 195H |
| 3. uses supporting ideas, descriptive details, and specific information that clearly relate to the focus. | | 145G |
| 4. uses strategies to achieve a sense of completeness or wholeness in writing (including but not limited to using clear and specific vocabulary, using complete information). | 81F-81J | 125I, 163I, 181I, 195I |
| 5. understands the purpose of a first draft (for example, to get ideas on paper). | 61F-61J | 181H |
| 6. uses effective sentence variety. | 81F-81J | 163I, 181I, 195I |
| 7. generally follows the conventions of punctuation, capitalization, and spelling appropriate at third-grade or higher level [see benchmark LA.B.1.2.3 for specifics]. | 93F-93J, 111F | 125J, 133J, 145J, 163J, 181J, 195F, 195J |

| Unit 3 | Unit 4 | Unit 5 | Unit 6 |
|---|---|---|---|
| 199, 201, 203, 205, 207, 209, 211 | 49, 51, 53, 53C | 121, 123, 125, 127, 129, 131, 135, 137, 141, 141C, 141D | 237, 239, 241, 243, 245 |
|  |  | 141C, 141D |  |
| 257A | 105B | 155A, 165A |  |
| 257A | 105B | 155A, 165A | 245D |
| 211E | 33F, 45E, 55D, 93D, 105D | 115F, 117H, 155A | 203E, 203I, 213E, 233E, 283I |
|  | 25H | 141C, 141D, 159, 161, 163, 163C, 163D | 207, 209, 211, 211C, 211D |
| 241, 243, 245, 247, 247C, 247D | 105H | 199, 201 |  |
| 249D | 23F, 25D, 33F, 45E, 71D, 93D, 105D | 115F, 125D, 141F, 143D, 165F | 233A, 247A, 247D, 261D, 283D |
| 213F-213G, 223G, 237G, 249A, 249G, 259G, 269G | 25C, 25G, 35C, 35G, 47G, 55G, 71G, 93A, 93G, 105G | 117G, 127G, 143G, 155G, 165G, 179G, 193G | 203A, 203D, 203G, 213G, 233G, 247G, 261G, 283G, 295G |
| 223F, 237F, 249F, 259F, 269F | 25C, 25F, 35F, 47F, 55F, 71F, 910, 93F, 103C, 105F | 117F, 127F, 127G, 143F, 155F, 165F, 179F, 193F | 203F, 213F, 233F, 247F, 261F, 283F, 295F |
| 213H, 237H | 25I, 55H |  | 283G |
| 213H, 223I, 237G-237H, 269H | 35G, 91C, 105I |  |  |
| 213H, 237H, 269H | 93H | 145B | 247I |
| 213I, 269I, 237I | 25I, 35I, 47I, 55I, 71I |  | 203I, 261F, 261I |
| 223H, 237H, 249H, 259H | 35H, 47H, 55H, 71H, 105H |  | 203H, 213H, 247H, 283H |
| 213I, 269H-269I | 25I, 55I, 71G, 93I | 155H | 203J, 283I |
| 213J, 223J, 237J, 249J, 259J, 269F, 269J | 25J, 35J, 47J, 55J, 71J, 93J, 105J | 117J, 127J, 143J, 155J, 165J, 179J, 193F, 193J | 203J, 213J, 233H, 233J, 247J, 261J, 283J, 295F, 295J |

# Florida Resources

## Correlation to Florida Sunshine State Standards  Grade 3

| Strand B: Writing | Unit 1 | Unit 2 |
|---|---|---|
| **BENCHMARK LA.B.1.2.3 The student produces final documents that have been edited for**<br>• *correct spelling;*<br>• *appropriate use of punctuation, including commas in a series, dates, and addresses, and beginning and ending quotation marks;*<br>• *correct capitalization of proper nouns;*<br>• *correct paragraph indentation;*<br>• *correct usage of subject/verb agreement, verb and noun forms, and sentence structure; and*<br>• *correct formatting according to instructions.*<br>**The student:** | | |
| **1.** uses a variety of spelling strategies (such as knowing root words, prefixes, and suffixes; using word families, syllabication). | | |
| **2.** uses conventions of punctuation (including but not limited to, commas in a series, dates, and addresses; quotation marks to indicate dialogue; apostrophes to indicate singular possession; periods in abbreviations). | 93F-93H, 111F-111H | 125F-125H, 133F-133H, 145F-145H, 181F-181H, 195F-195H |
| **3.** uses principles of agreement in written work (including but not limited to, subject/verb and noun/pronoun). | 45F-45H, 61F-61H, 93H, 111F-111H | |
| **4.** uses parts of speech in written work (including but not limited to, verb tenses, plurals of common irregular nouns, comparative and superlative adjectives and adverbs). | 27F-27H, 81F-81H, 111F-111H | 145H, 145J |
| **5.** uses basic features of page format (for example, paragraph indentations, margins). | 111F-111J | 145H, 145J |
| **STANDARD 2: The student writes to communicate ideas and information effectively.** | | |
| **BENCHMARK LA.B.2.2.1: The student writes notes, comments, and observations that reflect comprehension of content and experiences from a variety of media. The student:** | | |
| **1.** writes notes, comments, and observations that generally reflect comprehension of content and experiences from a variety of media. | 27J | 125J, 195F |
| **BENCHMARK L.A.B.2.2.2: The student organizes information using alphabetical and numerical systems. The student:** | | |
| **1.** attempts to use simple alphabetical and numerical systems to organize information. | 61H | |
| **BENCHMARK LA.B.2.2.3: The student writes for a variety of occasions, audiences, and purposes. The student:** | | |
| **1.** writes for a variety of occasions, audiences, and purposes (such as letters to invite or thank, stories or poems to entertain, information to record). | 81D | 133G, 145F, 145G, 195F |
| **BENCHMARK LA.B.2.2.4: The student uses electronic technology, including word-processing software and electronic encyclopedias, to create, revise, and verify information. The student:** | | |
| **1.** uses electronic technology (including word-processing software and electronic encyclopedias) to create, revise, retrieve, and verify information. | | 145I, 181H |
| **BENCHMARK LA.B.2.2.5 The student creates narratives in which ideas, details, and events are in logical order and are relevant to the story line. The student:** | | |
| **1.** attempts to establish a single story focus on a topic through the use of suspense, humor, creativity or fantasy. | | |
| **2.** exhibits an awareness of topic with little irrelevant information. | | |
| **3.** attempts to develop a story line that is easy to follow and paraphrase. | | 181G |
| **4.** generally chooses specific detail and adequate word choice to support the story line. | | 161D |
| **5.** attempts to create logical organizational pattern appropriate to narrative writing (beginning, middle, end). | | |
| **6.** attempts to use transitions to move the narrative forward in time. | | 125H |
| **7.** generally creates a sense of story completeness. | | |
| **8.** attempts to use varied sentences within the story. | | |
| **BENCHMARK LA.B.2.2.6 The student creates expository responses in which ideas and details follow an organizational pattern and are relevant to the purpose. The student:** | | |
| **1.** attempts to focus on an expository topic with no irrelevant or repetitious information. | | 133F, 133H, 145I, 163I |
| **2.** develops supporting ideas with information that relates to the focus. | | 133H-133I, 145I, 163I |
| **3.** develops anecdotes or examples to support reasons. | | 145H |
| **4.** begins to present facts and examples objectively. | | 133H-133I |
| **5.** creates a logical organizational pattern (including an effective beginning, middle, and end) appropriate to expository writing. | | 125H, 133H-133I, 163H, 181H |

| Unit 3 | Unit 4 | Unit 5 | Unit 6 |
|---|---|---|---|
| | 14K, 38K, 58K | 120K, 128K | 198K, 204K, 233F-233J, 247F-247J, 261F-261J, 283F-283J, 295H |
| 223F-223H, 269F-269H | 47F-47H, 105F-105H | 127F-127H, 143F-143H, 193F-193H | 203F-203H, 213F-213H, 233F-233H, 247F-247H, 283F-283H, 295F-295H |
| | 55F-55H, 71F-71H, 105F-105H | | 233F-233H, 283F-283H |
| 213F-213H, 237F-237H, 249F-249H, 259F-259H, 269F-269H | 55F-55J, 71F-71J, 93F-93H, 105F-105J | 165J | 203F-203J, 233F-233J, 233F-233H, 261F-261H, 283F-283H, 295F, 295G, 295J |
| 213J, 237J, 269J | 25H, 55J, 105J | 165J | 233J |
| 269D | 71H, 93J | 155H | 203J, 245C, 261G, 261J, 295D, 295J |
| 213D, 249H, 269D | | | 213G, 203E, 213E, 233E |
| 223H, 249H, 259H, 269H | 47G | 117H, 119B | 211E, 213G, 213I, 215A, 215B, 233G, 247G, 283H |
| 213E, 213I, 223E, 223H-223I, 237E, 249E, 249H-249J, 259E, 259H-259J, 269E, 269J | | | 247E, 261E, 283E, 295E, 295H-295I |
| | | 117H, 165G, 179G, 193H | |
| | | 117I, 127H, 179I | |
| | | 127H, 143H, 165H | |
| | | 117G, 143G, 195A | |
| 213D | | 117H, 143H | |
| | | 127G, 179H | |
| | 105H | 117H, 155I | 203H |
| | | 117I, 127I, 143I, 155H, 165I, 193I | |
| | | | |
| | 93H | 145B | |
| | 93H | | |
| | | | |
| | | | |

# Florida Resources

## Correlation to Florida Sunshine State Standards      Grade 3

### Strand B: Writing

| | Unit I | Unit 2 |
|---|---|---|
| **6.** attempts to use appropriate expository transitions to relate ideas. | | 125H |
| **7.** attempts to use a variety of sentence structures to present ideas. | 61I, 81G, 81I | |

### Strand C: Listening, Viewing, and Speaking

**STANDARD 1: The student uses listening strategies effectively.**

**BENCHMARK LA.C.1.2.1: The student listens and responds to a variety of oral presentations, such as stories, poems, skits, songs, personal accounts, informational speeches. The student:**

| | Unit I | Unit 2 |
|---|---|---|
| **1.** listens and responds to a variety of oral presentations such as stories, poems, skits, songs, personal accounts, or informational speeches. | 27I, 46, 79E, 109E | |
| **2.** follows multiple-step oral directions. | 14M, 14N, 28L, 28N, 48L, 48N, 64L, 64N, 82L, 82N, 94L, 94N | 114L, 114N, 126L, 126N, 136L, 136N, 148L, 148N, 166L, 166N, 182L |

**BENCHMARK LA.C.1.2.2: The student identifies specific personal listening preferences regarding fiction, drama, literary nonfiction, and informational presentations. The student:**

| | | |
|---|---|---|
| **1.** knows personal listening preferences (for example, poetry, songs, stories, fiction, nonfiction, drama, informational speeches). | 27I | 114Q, 123B, 126Q, 128R, 136Q, 148R, 166R, 182R |

**BENCHMARK LA.C.1.2.3: The student carries on an extended conversation with a group of friends. The student:**

| | | |
|---|---|---|
| **1.** interacts with peers in a variety of situations to develop and present familiar ideas (such as group activities, peer conferences, literature groups). | 25A, 27H, 43A, 59A, 79A, 81A, 91A, 93A | 109A, 123A, 123, 126Q, 131A, 143A, 161A |

**BENCHMARK LA.C.1.2.4: The student listens attentively to the speaker, including making eye contact and facing the speaker. The student:**

| | | |
|---|---|---|
| **1.** listens attentively to the speaker, including making eye contact and facing the speaker. | 27I, 93I | 163G |

**BENCHMARK LA.C.1.2.5: The student responds to speakers by asking questions, making contributions, and paraphrasing what is said. The stud[ent:]**

| | | |
|---|---|---|
| **1.** uses strategies to respond to speakers (such as asking questions, making contributions, paraphrasing). | 43F, 111I | 125I, 181H, 181I |

**STANDARD 2: The student uses viewing strategies effectively.**

**BENCHMARK LA.C.2.2.1: The student determines the main concept and supporting details in nonprint media messages. The student:**

| | | |
|---|---|---|
| **1.** understands the main concept and supporting details in nonprint media messages. | 81I | 163I |

**BENCHMARK LA.C.2.2.2: The student recognizes and responds to nonverbal cues used in a variety of nonprint media, such as motion pictures, television advertisements, and works of art. The student:**

| | | |
|---|---|---|
| **1.** understands nonverbal cues (such as music, color, motion) used in a variety of media. | 43B, 59B, 91B | 131B, 143B, 146 |

**STANDARD 3: The student uses speaking strategies effectively.**

**BENCHMARK LA.C.3.2.1: The student speaks clearly at an understandable rate and uses appropriate volume. The student:**

| | | |
|---|---|---|
| **1.** uses strategies to speak clearly (such as appropriate rate, volume, pitch). | 45I | 133I, 148Q, 165B |

**BENCHMARK LA.C.3.2.2: The student asks questions and makes comments and observations to clarify understanding of content, processes, and experiences. The student:**

| | | |
|---|---|---|
| **1.** asks and responds to questions and makes comments and observations (for example, clarifies ideas, paraphrases information shared by others). | 27H, 45A, 45I, 61A, 61C, 81A, 93A, 109A, 109C, 111A, 111I | 118, 125A, 125I, 126, 128, 130, 133A, 138, 145A, 145H, 148, 150, 160, 161A, 161C, 170, 179A, 181I, 192, 195A, 195H |

**BENCHMARK LA.C.3.2.3: The student speaks for specific occasions, audiences, and purposes, including conversations, discussions, projects, and informational or imaginative presentations. The student:**

| | | |
|---|---|---|
| **1.** gives oral presentations for different purposes (including but not limited to reporting, explaining, persuading). | 47B | 123F, 131F, 181J, 195A |

**BENCHMARK LA.C.3.2.4: The student uses eye contact and gestures that engage the audience. The student:**

| | | |
|---|---|---|
| **1.** uses eye contact and gestures that engage the audience. | 93I | 123F |

**BENCHMARK LA.C.3.2.5: The student participates as a contributor and occasionally acts as a leader in a group discussion. The student:**

| | | |
|---|---|---|
| **1.** actively participates in class discussions (for example, asks and responds to questions, explains information, listens to discussion members). | 45A, 81A, 93A, 111A | 133A, 145A, 179A, 181I, 195A |

| Unit 3 | Unit 4 | Unit 5 | Unit 6 |
|---|---|---|---|
| 237G | | | |
| | | 117F, 117G | |

| Unit 3 | Unit 4 | Unit 5 | Unit 6 |
|---|---|---|---|
| 211E, 215B, 221F | 23E, 91A, 103A | 115F, 117I, 119B, 125F, 141D, 145B, 153A, 163A, 177A, 193J | 201F, 211F, 215B, 231F, 249B |
| 198L, 198N, 216L, 216N, 224L, 224N, 240L, 240N, 250L, 250N, 260L, 260N | 14L, 26K, 38L, 48L, 58L, 72L, 93L | 108L, 120L, 128L, 146L, 158L, 168L, 180L | 204L, 216L, 236L, 250L, 262L, 284L, 295I |
| 198Q, 211B, 215B, 216Q, 221B, 223A, 224Q, 235B, 240Q, 250Q, 260Q | 14O, 47O, 72O, 94O, 103A | 108O, 115D, 120O, 128O, 146O, 158O, 168O, 180O | 198O, 201B, 204O, 213B, 216O, 236O, 250O, 262O, 284O |
| 211A, 213I, 215B, 221A, 235A, 247A, 249A, 257A, 267A | 23A, 33A, 45A, 53A, 58O, 69A, 71, 71I, 91A, 103A | 115A, 125A, 141A, 145B, 153A, 163A, 165C, 177A, 179A, 179J, 191A, 193A | 198L, 201A, 211A, 215B, 231A, 233I, 259A, 261I, 281A, 293A |
| 215B | 105I | 141F, 143G, 145B, 155G, 165G, 193A | 215B, 283C, 295I |
| 221F, 259I, 269I | 23E, 45F, 71I | 145B, 165I | 203I, 211F, 231F, 233H |
| 215B, 243 | 55I | 155I | |
| 221B, 243, 249I | 23B | 156 | 211B, 231B, 234, 281B |
| 215B, 223I, 240Q, 250, 271B | 37B, 48O, 72O, 94O | 119B, 145B, 146O, 158O, 166, 168O, 180O, 193I, 194 | 211E, 213I, 231B, 236O, 249B, 250O, 262O, 283I, 284O |
| 200, 204, 206, 208, 211C, 211E, 213A, 223A, 226, 232, 234, 237A, 254, 259I, 264, 269I | 16, 22, 23E, 25C, 25I, 30, 42, 44, 47A, 74, 80, 91A, 93A, 103A, 105G | 108, 115F, 117A, 120, 125C, 125F, 141D, 143A, 145B, 148, 153A, 165I, 179I | 198, 201F, 210, 211EE, 211F, 215B, 218, 224, 230, 261I |
| 213I, 235F | 23E, 33F, 45E, 45F | 115E, 115F, 125F, 145B, 179I, 193I | 201F, 211E, 211F, 215B, 231F, 249B, 283I |
| 215B, 235F | 105I | 145B, 177E | 215B |
| 211E, 213A, 223A, 237A, 259I | 23E, 25C, 25I, 49A, 55A, 71A, 71I, 91A, 103A, 105A | 115E, 115F, 117A, 125F, 127C, 143A, 153A, 163A, 165B, 165I, 177A, 179A, 191A | 201F, 203A, 211F, 231F, 249B, 259A, 261I, 293A |

# Florida Resources

## Correlation to Florida Sunshine State Standards — Grade 3

| Strand C: Listening, Viewing, and Speaking | Unit 1 | Unit 2 |
|---|---|---|
| **BENCHMARK LA.C.3.2.6: The student organizes a speech using a basic beginning, middle, and ending. The student:** | | |
| **1.** expresses thoughts in an organized manner. | | 195I |

### Strand D: Language

| | Unit 1 | Unit 2 |
|---|---|---|
| **STANDARD 1: The student understands the nature of language.** | | |
| **BENCHMARK LA.D.1.2.1: The student understands that there are patterns and rules in the syntactic structure, symbols, sounds, and meanings conveyed through the English language. The student:** | | |
| **1.** uses elements of grammar in speech (including but not limited to subject-verb agreement, singular and plural nouns, comparatives, superlatives, verb tenses). | | |
| **BENCHMARK LA.D.1.2.2: The student understands that language formality varies according to situations and audiences. The student:** | | |
| **1.** uses language appropriate to situation and audience (including, but not limited to appropriate vocabulary and examples appropriate to topic and audience). | 61I | |
| **STANDARD 2: The student understands the power of language.** | | |
| **BENCHMARK LA.D.2.2.1: The student understands that word choices can shape reactions, perceptions, and beliefs. The student:** | | |
| **1.** understands that word choices can shape reactions, perceptions, and beliefs. | 47B | 145I |
| **BENCHMARK LA.D.2.2.2: The student identifies and refers to symbol, theme, simile, alliteration, and assonance in oral and written texts. The student:** | | |
| **1.** understands similes, symbols, and idiomatic language. | | |
| **BENCHMARK LA.D.2.2.3: The student recognizes different techniques used in media messages and their purposes. The student:** | | |
| **1.** understands different techniques used in media messages and their purposes. | | |
| **BENCHMARK LA.D.2.2.4: The student selects and uses appropriate technologies to enhance efficiency and effectiveness of communication. The student:** | | |
| **1.** understands the usefulness of various technologies for different tasks. | 27E, 45D, 61E, 81E, 93E, 111E | 125E, 133D, 133E, 145E, 163E, 181E, 195E |
| **BENCHMARK LA.D.2.2.5: The student understands that a variety of messages can be conveyed through mass media. The student:** | | |
| **1.** distinguishes fact from opinions in newspapers, magazines, and other media. | | |

### Strand E: Literature

| | Unit 1 | Unit 2 |
|---|---|---|
| **STANDARD 1: The student understands the common features of a variety of literary forms.** | | |
| **BENCHMARK LA.E.1.2.1: The student identifies the distinguishing features among fiction, drama, and poetry and identifies the major characteristics of nonfiction. The student:** | | |
| **1.** understands the distinguishing features of literary texts (such as fiction, drama, poetry, fairy tales, fables, fantasy, biography). | 25A, 43A, 59A, 109A, 109D | 123A, 137, 139, 141, 143, 143A, 143C, 143E |
| **2.** understands the distinguishing features of nonfiction texts (such as directions, biographies, journals, interviews, magazines, textbooks). | 91A, 91E | 131A, 131E, 161A |
| **3.** reads a variety of self-selected and assigned literary and informational texts (such as fiction, drama, poetry, realistic fiction, fables, fantasy, biography, autobiography). | 14, 28, 48 | 114, 123B, 126, 136 |
| **BENCHMARK LA.E.1.2.2: The student understands the development of the plot and how conflicts are resolved in a story. The student:** | | |
| **1.** understands the development of plot in a story. | 43E | |
| **2.** understands how conflicts are resolved in a story, including problem solution or resolution. | 43, 43E | |
| **3.** makes inferences and draws conclusions regarding story elements (such as the traits, actions, and motives of characters; textual events, setting). | 59E, 79D, 109 | 125, 127, 129, 131C, 131 |
| **BENCHMARK LA.E.1.2.3: The student knows the similarities and differences among the characters, settings, and events presented in various texts. The student:** | | |
| **1.** knows the similarities and differences of characters presented within third grade or higher level selections. | 55, 59, 79D | 123D |
| **2.** knows the similarities and differences of settings presented within third grade or higher level selections. | 49, 53, 59C, 59D | 123C, 179E |
| **3.** knows the similarities and differences of events presented within third grade or higher level selections. | 57, 59C, 59D | |

| Unit 3 | Unit 4 | Unit 5 | Unit 6 |
|---|---|---|---|
| | 93I | 179I | |
| | 35I | 117G | 295G, 295H |
| 223I | | 127D | 215B |
| 213F-213H, 215A, 215B, 247B, 249G-249J, 259G-259J, 269H | 47I, 93H | 119A, 143I, 195A | 215B, 249A |
| 223G, 237I | 71H | 117H, 145A | 211E, 233I |
| 211E, 233I | | 115F | |
| 213E, 223E, 237E, 249E, 259E, 269E | 25D, 25E, 33F, 35E, 45E, 47E, 55E, 71E, 93E, 105E | 117E, 127E, 143E, 155C, 155D, 155E, 165E, 179E, 193E | 203E, 213E, 233E, 247E, 247I, 261E, 283E, 295E |
| | 25H, 55I | 158P, 163C | 211C |
| 211A, 221A, 235A, 257A | 23A, 33A, 53A, 53E, 69A, 91A, 103A | 115A, 115E, 117A, 141A, 163A, 177A, 177D, 191A | 201A, 211A, 231A, 231E, 259A, 281A, 293A, 293E |
| 247A, 247E | 45A, 45D, 91A | 125D, 146M, 153A, 153D | 245A, 245D |
| 198, 211B, 216, 221B, 223A, 240 | 140, 14, 26, 33C, 470, 580, 72, 940, 103C | 108, 115D, 120, 1460, 155A, 1580, 165A, 1680, 179A, 1800, 193A | 198, 201B, 204, 213B, 216, 2360, 2500, 2620, 2840 |
| | 23D, 91A | 181, 183, 185 | 259E |
| | 23D | | 259E |
| 225, 227, 229, 231, 233, 235, 235C, 235D | 15, 17, 19, 21, 23, 53, 59, 61, 63, 91A, 95, 97, 99, 101, 103 | 153, 177 | 217, 219, 221, 223, 225, 227, 229, 231, 231C, 231D, 259, 285, 289, 291, 293, 293C, 293D |
| 2500 | 33E, 55, 91A, 93, 103D, 105 | 163, 179, 180M, 193 | 261, 262M, 283 |
| 2500, 257E | | 180M, 193 | 201D, 236M, 247, 261, 262M, 265, 283, 285 |
| | 55, 71, 93, 105 | 155, 158M, 165, 179, 180M, 193 | 236M, 283 |

# Florida Resources

## Correlation to Florida Sunshine State Standards

Grade 3

**Strand E: Literature**

| | Unit 1 | Unit 2 |
|---|---|---|
| **BENCHMARK LA.E.1.2.4: The student knows that the attitudes and values that exist in a time period affect the works that were written during that time period. The student:** | | |
| **1.** makes connections between information in texts and stories and historical events. | 280, 820, 91, 940 | |
| **BENCHMARK LA.E.1.2.5: The student identifies and uses literary terminology appropriate to the grade level, including symbol, theme, simile, alliteration, and assonance. The student:** | | |
| **1.** identifies and uses literary terminology appropriate to third grade or higher level (including theme, simile, alliteration, metaphor). | 46 | 165A, 193E |
| **STANDARD 2: The student responds critically to fiction, nonfiction, poetry, and drama.** | | |
| **BENCHMARK LA.E.2.2.1: The student recognizes cause-and-effect relationships in literary texts. The student:** | | |
| **1.** recognizes cause-and-effect relationships in literary texts. | 29, 31, 33, 35, 37, 39, 41, 43, 43C, 65, 67, 69, 71, 73, 75, 77, 79 | 149, 151, 153, 155, 157, 159, 161, 167, 169, 171, 173, 175, 177, 179, 179C |
| **BENCHMARK LA.E.2.2.2: The student recognizes and explains the effects of language, such as sensory words, rhymes, and choice of vocabulary and story structure, such as patterns, used in children's texts. The student:** | | |
| **1.** recognizes the techniques of language used in children's literature (such as sensory words, rhymes, and choice of vocabulary). | 47A | 135A, 165A, 193E |
| **2.** recognizes the use of story structure used in children's literature (such as patterns). | | |
| **BENCHMARK LA.E.2.2.3: The student responds to a work of literature by explaining how the motives of the characters or the causes of events compare with those in his or her own life. The student:** | | |
| **1.** responds to literature by explaining how the motives of the characters compare with those of own life. | 25C | |
| **2.** responds to literature by explaining how the causes of events compare with those of own life. | 25C | 174 |
| **BENCHMARK LA.E.2.2.4: The student identifies the major theme in a story or nonfiction text. The student:** | | |
| **1.** recognizes the major theme in a story. | 27, 45, 61, 109 | 125, 145, 178, 192, 195 |
| **2.** recognizes the major information in a nonfiction text. | 93 | 133, 160, 161C |
| **BENCHMARK LA.E.2.2.5: The student forms his or her own ideas about what has been read in a literary text and uses specific information from the text to support these ideas. The student:** | | |
| **1.** uses specific information from the text to defend interpretations. | 91 | 123A, 127, 129, 131A, 131C, 143A, 161A, 179A, 193C |

Grade 4

**Strand A: Reading**

| | Unit 1 | Unit 2 |
|---|---|---|
| **STANDARD 1: The student uses the reading process effectively.** | | |
| **BENCHMARK LA.A.1.2.1: The student uses a table of contents, index, headings, captions, illustrations, and major words to anticipate or predict content and purpose of a reading selection. The student:** | | |
| **1.** uses text features to make predictions and monitor comprehension (for example, glossary, headings, side-headings, sub-headings; paragraphs; organization by main ideas, details, cause-and-effect, comparison and contrast, sequence of events). | 20M, 20P, 32M, 32P, 48M, 66M, 66P, 82M, 82P, 100M, 116M, 116P | 126P, 132M, 132P, 146M, 146P, 156M, 156P, 172P, 188M, 188O, 202M, 202P |
| **2.** uses prior knowledge integrated with text features to generate questions and make predictions about content of text. | 20M, 32M, 48M, 66M, 82M, 100M, 116M | 126M, 132M, 146M, 156M, 188M, 199C, 202M |
| **BENCHMARK LA.A.1.2.2: The student selects from a variety of simple strategies, including the use of phonics, word structure, context clues, self-questioning, confirming simple predictions, retelling, and using visual cues to identify words and construct meaning from various texts, illustrations, graphics, and charts. The student:** | | |
| **1.** extends the expectations of the third grade with increasingly complex reading selections and assignments and tasks. | 20, 20K, 20N, 32K, 32N, 36, 48K, 48N, 49, 53, 66, 66K, 66N, 82K, 82N, 84, 86, 88, 90, 92, 95, 100, 100K, 100N, 103 | 126, 126K, 126N, 132, 132K, 132N, 146, 146K, 146N, 156, 156K, 156N, 172K, 172N, 188K, 188N, 196, 199C, 202K |

| Unit 3 | Unit 4 | Unit 5 | Unit 6 |
|---|---|---|---|
|  | 94M, 103F | 122, 127, 177 |  |
| 215A, 257E, 261, 263, 271A | 65, 67, 69, 69D, 91A | 145A, 163E, 187, 189, 191, 191E | 211E, 213, 281E |
|  | 27, 29, 31, 33, 33C, 95, 97, 99, 101, 103 | 195A | 261C, 269, 271, 273, 275, 277, 279, 281, 281A |
| 215A, 221E, 259G-259J, 269I | 37A, 69D | 119A, 141E, 167A, 167B, 195A, 195B | 211E, 215A |
| 2500 | 91 | 167A |  |
| 210, 2600, 262, 266 | 20, 26, 60, 78, 84, 88 | 122, 130, 136, 158M, 166, 182 | 288 |
| 266 | 20, 26, 45C, 58M, 60, 78, 84, 88 | 182 | 266, 288 |
| 213, 223, 237, 257, 259, 269 | 25, 35, 53, 69, 80, 91, 102, 105 | 117, 143, 165, 176, 177C | 203, 213, 224, 230, 233, 259, 259A, 259E, 261, 281, 283, 293, 295A |
| 247, 249 | 47, 91 | 120, 125C, 127, 153 | 245, 247 |
| 211A, 221A, 235A, 247A, 247B, 267A | 23A, 33A, 45A, 69A | 115A, 125A, 141A, 153, 153A, 163A, 177A, 191A | 201A, 211A, 217, 219, 221, 223, 225, 227, 229, 231, 231C, 231D, 245A, 259A, 293A |

| Unit 3 | Unit 4 | Unit 5 | Unit 6 |
|---|---|---|---|
| 208M, 208P, 209, 211, 213, 215, 217, 219, 221, 226M, 242M, 242P, 243, 245, 247, 248, 258M, 264M, 288M, 289 | 322M, 322P, 323, 324, 325, 326, 327, 328, 331C, 334M, 334P, 335, 337, 339, 341, 351, 353, 355, 357, 360M, 360P | 416M, 416P, 417, 419, 421, 421C, 426M, 434M, 446M, 4460, 446, 448, 452, 461, 463, 465, 476M | 484M, 484P, 485, 487, 489, 492M, 502M, 508M, 508P, 509, 511, 513, 515, 517, 517C, 522M, 522P, 523, 527, 529, 529C |
| 208M, 226M, 242M, 258M, 264M, 288M, 308M | 322M, 324, 326, 328, 334M, 360M, 362, 378, 378M, 392M, 406M | 416M, 426M, 434M, 446M, 460M, 476M | 484M, 492M, 502M, 508M, 522M, 532M, 542M |
| 208K, 208N, 212, 226N, 242K, 242N, 244, 248, 249, 250, 258, 258K, 258N, 264K, 264N, 270, 272, 274, 288K | 322K, 322N, 324, 326, 328, 331C, 334K, 334N, 335, 338, 342, 360, 360K, 360N, 378K, 378N, 380, 381, 382, 383, 384 | 416, 416K, 416M, 416N, 426K, 426M, 428, 434K, 434M, 443E, 446M, 446N, 4460, 448, 452, 460K, 460M, 460N, 460 | 484, 484K, 484M, 484N, 486, 487, 488, 492, 492K, 492N, 494, 495, 502, 502K, 502N, 508K, 508N, 522K, 522N, 529 |

# Florida Resources

## Correlation to Florida Sunshine State Standards

Grade 4

### Strand A: Reading

| | Unit 1 | Unit 2 |
|---|---|---|
| **BENCHMARK LA.A.1.2.3:** The student uses simple strategies to determine meaning and increase vocabulary for reading, including the use of prefixes, suffixes, root words, multiple meanings, antonyms, synonyms, and word relationships. The student: | | |
| **1.** uses a variety of strategies to determine meaning and increase vocabulary (for example, multiple meaning words, antonyms, synonyms, word relationships, root words, homonyms). | 20K, 48K, 65G, 65H, 66K, 70, 73, 77B, 82K, 95B, 100K, 116K, 117, 121B | 126K, 131G, 131H, 132K, 133, 137, 138, 140, 146K, 156K, 172K |
| **2.** develops vocabulary by reading independently. | 20D, 32D, 48D, 66D, 82D, 100D, 116D | 126D, 132D, 146D, 156D, 172D, 188D |
| **3.** develops vocabulary by listening to and discussing both familiar and conceptually challenging selections read aloud. | 29B, 45B, 47A, 63B, 77B, 95B, 111B | 129B, 141B, 151B, 169B, 185B, 199B, 203B |
| **4.** uses resources and references such as dictionary, thesaurus, and context to build word meanings. | 20N, 48N, 66N, 79D, 97D, 116N | 126N, 132N, 156N, 172N, 188N |
| **BENCHMARK LA.A.1.2.4:** The student clarifies understanding by rereading, self-correction, summarizing, checking other sources, and class or group discussion. The student: | | |
| **1.** uses a variety of strategies to monitor reading in fourth-grade or higher texts (for example, rereading, self-correcting, summarizing, checking other sources, class and group discussions, questioning whether text makes sense, searching for cues, identifying miscues). | 28, 29A, 44, 45A, 63A, 76, 77A, 94, 95A, 110, 111A, 120, 121A, 123D | 129A, 132O, 134, 136, 138, 141A, 141C, 146O, 148, 150, 151A, 151C, 156O, 158, 162, 164, 169A, 172O, 176, 178 |
| **STANDARD 2:** The student constructs meaning from a wide range of texts. | | |
| **BENCHMARK LA.A.2.2.1:** The student reads text and determines the main idea or essential message, identifies relevant supporting details and facts, and arranges events in chronological order. The student: | | |
| **1.** understands ideas and information in fourth-grade or higher texts (for example, knows main idea or essential message, connects important ideas with corresponding details, makes inferences about information, distinguishes between significant and minor details, knows chronological order of events). | 29A, 45A, 63A, 77A, 83, 85, 87, 89, 91, 93, 95, 95A, 101, 103, 105, 107, 109, 111, 111A, 111C, 117, 119, 121, 121A | 126P, 127, 129, 129A, 129C, 132P, 133, 135, 137, 139, 141, 141A, 147, 149, 151, 151A, 157, 159, 161, 163, 165, 167 |
| **BENCHMARK LA.A.2.2.2:** The student identifies the author's purpose in a simple text. The student: | | |
| **1.** identifies and discusses the author's purpose in text. | | |
| **BENCHMARK LA.A.2.2.3:** The student recognizes when a text is primarily intended to persuade. The student: | | |
| **1.** recognizes text that is written primarily to persuade. | | |
| **BENCHMARK LA.A.2.2.4:** The student identifies specific personal preferences relative to fiction and nonfiction reading. The student: | | |
| **1.** uses knowledge of author's styles, themes, and genres to choose own reading. | | |
| **BENCHMARK LA.A.2.2.5:** The student reads and organizes information for a variety of purposes, including making a report, conducting interviews, taking a test, and performing an authentic task. The student: | | |
| **1.** reads and organizes information (for example, in outlines, timelines, graphic organizers) throughout a single source for a variety of purpose (for example, to discover models for own writing, to make a report, to conduct interviews, to take tests, to perform a task). | 47D, 65C | 187D, 205D |
| **BENCHMARK LA.A.2.2.6:** The student recognizes the difference between fact and opinion presented in a text. The student: | | |
| **1.** knows if specific information from text is fact, fiction, or opinion. | | |
| **BENCHMARK LA.A.2.2.7:** The student recognizes the use of comparison and contrast in a text. The student: | | |
| **1.** understands a variety of textual organizations (for example, comparison and contrast, cause-and-effect, sequence of events). | 21, 23, 25, 27, 29, 29C, 33, 35, 37, 41, 45, 45C, 67, 69, 71, 73, 75, 77, 77C | 133, 135, 137, 139, 141, 157, 159, 161, 163, 179, 181, 183, 185, 202P, 203 |
| **2.** understands how comparison or contrast impacts the meaning of a text. | 35, 45 | 179, 181, 183, 185 |
| **BENCHMARK LA.A.2.2.8:** The student selects and uses a variety of appropriate reference materials, including multiple representations of information, such as maps, charts, and photos, to gather information for research projects. The student: | | |
| **1.** uses appropriate reference materials from multiple sources to gather information for a research project (such as maps, charts, photos). | 31D | 131D, 143C |
| **2.** uses a systematic research process (including but not limited to selects a topic, formulates questions, narrows the focus of a topic, develops a plan for gathering information). | 47C, 65C | 131C, 143C, 153C, 171C, 187C |

### Strand B: Writing

| | Unit 1 | Unit 2 |
|---|---|---|
| **STANDARD 1:** The student uses writing processes effectively. | | |
| **BENCHMARK LA.B.1.2.1:** The student prepares for writing by recording thoughts, focusing on a central idea, grouping related ideas, and identifying the purpose of writing. The student: | | |
| **1.** uses a variety of strategies to prepare for writing (such as brainstorming, making lists, mapping ideas, grouping related ideas, keeping a notebook of ideas, observing surroundings, answering questions posed by others). | 20N, 31B, 31C, 31F, 31G, 31H, 31I , 31J, 32M, 47B, 47F, 47G, 47H, 47I, 47J, 63E, 65B, 79B, 97B, 113B, 123B | 131B, 131C, 131F, 131G, 143B, 143F, 143G, 153B, 153F, 153G, 171B, 171F, 171G, 187B, 187F, 187G, 201B, 201F, 201G, 205B, 205F, 205G |

| Unit 3 | Unit 4 | Unit 5 | Unit 6 |
|---|---|---|---|
| 208K, 208N, 212-219, 226N, 258K, 264K, 288K, 296, 308K | 322K, 334K, 378K, 389G, 389H, 389I, 395, 397, 398, 401B, 403G-403I, 406K, 413G, 413I | 416K, 423H, 426K, 433G, 433H, 434K, 443H, 446K, 459H, 460K, 473H, 476K, 481H | 484K, 486-488, 492K, 508K, 508N, 519G-519I, 522K, 522N, 531G-531I, 532K, 532N, 542K, 542N, 547G-547I |
| 208D, 226D, 242D, 258D, 264D, 288D | 322D, 334D, 360D, 378D, 392D, 406D | 416D, 426D, 434D, 446D, 460D, 476D | 484D, 492D, 502D, 508D, 522D, 532D |
| 221B, 237B, 253B, 261B, 285B, 305B, 317B | 331B, 357B, 373B, 387B, 401B, 411B | 421B, 431B, 441B, 457B, 471B, 479B | 489B, 497B, 505B, 517B, 529B, 539B, 545B |
| 208N, 226K, 226N, 242N, 264N, 288N, 308N | 322N, 334L, 334N, 360N, 361, 375D, 378N, 392N, 406N | 416N, 426N, 434N, 446N, 476N | 484N, 492N, 502N, 508N, 522N, 532N, 542N |
| | | | |
| 2080, 210, 212, 216, 218, 220, 221A, 2260, 228, 221C, 232, 236, 237A, 2420, 252, 253A | 330, 331A, 334, 3340, 336,342, 344, 350, 352, 354, 356, 357A, 357C, 3600, 372, 373A, 3780, 380, 384, 386 | 4160, 416, 418, 420, 421A, 426, 428, 430, 431A, 4340, 434, 436, 438, 440, 441A, 441C, 4460, 456, 457A, 4600, 460 | 4840, 486, 488, 489A, 4920, 494, 496, 497A, 502, 5020, 504, 505A, 505C, 508, 5080, 510, 512, 514, 516, 517A |
| | | | |
| 209, 211, 213, 215, 217, 219, 221, 221A, 227, 229, 231, 237A, 237C, 253A, 261A, 265, 267, 269, 271, 273, 275, 277 | 323, 325, 327, 329, 331, 331A, 335, 337, 339, 341, 343, 345, 347, 349, 351, 353, 355, 357, 357A, 373A, 379, 381 | 416P, 417, 419, 421, 421C, 439, 441 | 485, 487, 489, 489A, 489C, 493, 495, 497, 497A, 497C, 503, 505, 505A, 517A, 523, 527, 529, 529A, 529C, 529E, 533 |
| | | | |
| 233, 235, 315, 317 | 361, 363, 365, 373C | 431E, 434P, 435, 437, 446P | 503, 505, 529E |
| | | 423F, 431E | |
| | 333B, 373E, 389B | | |
| | | | |
| 208, 223A, 223D | 359C | | 497F, 499D, 505E, 537 |
| | | | |
| 259, 261, 261C | 366, 371, 393 | 426P, 427, 429, 431, 431C, 441D, 477 | |
| | | | |
| 215, 217, 219, 221, 242P, 243, 245, 247, 288P, 289, 293, 295, 297, 299, 301, 303 | 322P, 323, 325, 327, 360P, 367, 369, 371, 373 | 460P, 461, 463, 465 | 508P, 511, 513, 515, 517, 517C, 523, 525, 527, 529, 529C, 532P, 533, 535, 537, 539 |
| 243, 245, 247, 273, 275, 277, 279, | | | 511, 513, 515, 517, 517C |
| | | | |
| 239D, 287D | 333C, 333D, 375D, 389D | 423C, 473D | 491C, 531C |
| 223A, 223C, 239C, 255C, 263C, 287C | 333C, 359C, 389C | 423D, 433C, 443D | 491C, 499C, 507C, 519C |
| | | | |
| | | | |
| 223B, 223C, 223F, 239B, 255B, 263B, 263F, 287B, 307B, 319B | 331A, 333B, 333F, 333G, 359B, 359F, 359G, 375B, 375F, 375G, 377B, 389B, 389F, 389G, 391A, 403F, 403G, 413B, 413F, 413G | 423F, 423G, 433F, 433G, 443F, 443G, 459F, 459G, 473G, 481F, 481G | 491B, 491F, 491G, 499B, 499F, 499G, 507B, 507F, 507G, 519B, 519F, 519G, 531B, 531F, 531G, 541B, 541F, 541G, 547B, 547F, 547G |

# Florida Resources

## Correlation to Florida Sunshine State Standards

**Grade 4**

| Strand B: Writing | Unit 1 | Unit 2 |
|---|---|---|
| **2.** establishes a purpose for writing (including but not limited to, to explain, to inform, to tell a story, to make a request). | 47F, 47J | 131G, 143C, 143G, 153G, 171G, 187G, 201G, 205G |

**BENCHMARK LA.B.1.2.2: The student drafts and revises writing in cursive that**
- *focuses on the topic;*
- *has a logical organizational pattern, including a beginning, middle, conclusion, and transitional devices;*
- *has ample development of supporting ideas;*
- *demonstrates a sense of completeness or wholeness;*
- *generally has correct subject/verb agreement;*
- *generally has correct verb and noun forms;*
- *with few [exceptions], has sentences that are complete, except when fragments are used purposefully;*
- *uses a variety of sentence structures; and*
- *generally follows the conventions of punctuation, capitalization, and spelling.*
**The student:**

| | Unit 1 | Unit 2 |
|---|---|---|
| **1.** focuses on one aspect of a topic (including but not limited to using organization that conveys central idea, including a beginning that sets a context for the topic, excluding irrelevant or repetitious information). | 65G-65J | 131I, 143I, 153H, 187I, 205H, 205I |
| **2.** uses an organizational pattern appropriate to purpose and audience. | 65G-65J, 79I | 131H, 131I, 143H, 153I |
| **3.** uses devices to develop relationships among ideas (such as transitions; paragraphs that show a change in time, idea, or place; cause-and-effect relationships). | 65H, 65J | 131H, 171H, 187H |
| **4.** uses supporting ideas, details, and facts from a variety of sources (including personal anecdotes) to develop and elaborate the topic. | 65H, 65J | 171I, 201H, 201I |
| **5.** uses strategies to achieve a sense of completeness or wholeness in writing (such as using appropriate voice in writing; using descriptive language to clarify ideas and create vivid images; using accurate representation of events and sequence; using elements of style, such as appropriate tone and sentence variation). | 65I, 65J, 79F-79J, 97F-97J | |
| **6.** uses varied sentence structures (such as simple, compound; short and long fragments, where appropriate). | 79J, 97H | |
| **7.** generally follows the conventions of punctuation, capitalization, and spelling [see benchmarks, LA.B.1.2.3, for specifics]. | 113I, 113J | |

**BENCHMARK LA.B.1.2.3: The student produces final documents that have been edited for:**
- *correct spelling;*
- *correct use of punctuation, including commas in series, dates, and addresses, and beginning and ending quotation marks;*
- *correct capitalization of proper nouns;*
- *correct paragraph indentation;*
- *correct usage of subject/verb agreement, verb and noun forms, and sentence structure; and*
- *correct formatting according to instructions.*
**The student:**

| | Unit 1 | Unit 2 |
|---|---|---|
| **1.** uses a variety of strategies (such as base words and common spelling patterns) and resources (such as dictionaries and thesauruses) to spell words. | 31F, 31G, 31H, 47F, 47H, 65H, 79G, 97F-97I, 113F-113J, 123F-123I | 131F, 131H-131J |
| **2.** uses conventions of punctuation (including but not limited to commas in a series, dates, and addresses; beginning and ending quotation marks). | 77E, 113G, 113H, 113J, 123H, 123J | 153J, 171J, 185D, 187J, 201J |
| **3.** uses conventions of capitalization (including but not limited to proper nouns, titles, first word of a direct quotation). | 113H, 113J, 123H | 143J, 185D, 205J |
| **4.** uses various parts of speech in writing (such as subject/verb agreement, nouns and verb forms, demonstrative pronouns, coordinating conjunctions). | 113I, 113J, 123H | 143J |
| **5.** uses correct paragraph indentation. | 123F, 123J | 185D |
| **6.** uses appropriate page format for different genre. | 123F-123J | |

**STANDARD 2: The student writes to communicate ideas and information effectively.**

**BENCHMARK LA.B.2.2.1: The student writes notes, comments, and observations that reflect comprehension of content and experiences from a variety of media. The student:**

| | Unit 1 | Unit 2 |
|---|---|---|
| **1.** writes notes, comments, and observations that reflect comprehension of content and experiences from a variety of media. | 31B, 47B, 47D, 65B, 79B, 97B, 123B | 131B, 143B, 153B, 171B, 187B, 201B, 205B |

**BENCHMARK LA.B.2.2.2: The student organizes information using alphabetical and numerical systems. The student:**

| | Unit 1 | Unit 2 |
|---|---|---|
| **1.** uses alphabetical and numerical systems such as outlining to organize information. | | |

| Unit 3 | Unit 4 | Unit 5 | Unit 6 |
|---|---|---|---|
| 263G | 333G, 359G, 375G, 389G, 403G, 413G | 423G, 433G, 443G, 459G, 473G, 481G | 491G, 499G, 507G, 519G, 531G, 547G |
| | | | |
| 223H, 223I | 333H, 389I | 433H, 443I, 459H, 473H | 491H-491I, 499H-499I, 507H-507I, 519H-519I, 531H-531I, 541G, 547H |
| 263I | 389H, 413H | 423I, 433I, 443H, 481I | 491H, 491I, 499H, 499I, 507H, 507I, 519H, 519I, 531H, 531I, 541G |
| | 403H, 403I | 481H | 541H, 541I |
| | 333I | 423H, 473I | |
| | 375H, 375I | 459I | 491H, 491I, 499H, 499I, 507H, 507I, 519H, 519I, 531H, 531I |
| | | | 491H, 491I, 499H, 499I, 507H, 507I, 519H, 519I, 531H, 531I |
| | 413I | | 491H, 491I, 499H, 499I, 507H, 507I, 519H, 519I, 531H, 531I |
| | | | |
| 223F, 223H, 239F, 239H, 255F, 255H, 263F, 263H, 287F, 287H, 307H, 319H | 333F, 333H, 359F-359H, 375F, 375H, 389H, 403H, 403J, 413H, 413J | 423J | 491H, 499H, 507H, 541H |
| 223J | | | 499J, 507J |
| 223J | | | 547J |
| | 333J, 359J, 403J | 459J | 491J, 499J, 507J, 519J, 531J, 541J |
| | | | 541J |
| | 389J, 413J | 433J, 443J, 473J | 491J, 499J, 507J, 519J, 531J, 541J |
| | | | |
| 223B, 239B, 255B, 263B, 287B, 307B, 319B | 333B, 359B, 375B, 389B, 403B, 413B | | 491B, 499B, 507B, 519B, 531B, 541B, 547B |
| | | 459H | |

# Florida Resources

## Correlation to Florida Sunshine State Standards — Grade 4

### Strand B: Writing

| | Unit 1 | Unit 2 |
|---|---|---|
| **BENCHMARK LA.B.2.2.3: The student writes for a variety of occasions, audiences, and purpose. The student:** | | |
| 1. writes for a variety of occasions, audiences, and purposes (such as journals to reflect upon, ideas, a report to describe a scientific observation). | 20N, 32M, 63E, 95A, 111A, 121A, 121E | 131G, 143G, 171G, 187G, 201G, 205G |
| **BENCHMARK LA.B.2.2.4: The student uses electronic technology, including word-processing software and electronic encyclopedias, to create, revise, retrieve, and verify information. The student:** | | |
| 1. uses electronic technology (including word-processing software and electronic encyclopedias) to create, revise, retrieve, and verify information. | | 131E, 131I, 143E, 143I, 153D, 153E, 153I, 171D, 171E |
| **BENCHMARK LA.B.2.2.5: The student creates narratives in which ideas, details, and events are in logical order and are relevant to the story line. The student:** | | |
| 1. creates a central focus through the use of suspense, humor, creativity, or fantasy. | 121E | |
| 2. exhibits a consistent awareness of topic with little or no irrelevant information. | | |
| 3. develops a story line that is easily followed. | 77C | |
| 4. chooses specific detail and precise word choice to support the story line. | | |
| 5. creates a logical organizational pattern (including a beginning, middle, and end) appropriate to narrative writing. | | |
| 6. uses transitions to move the narrative story forward in time. | 77C | |
| 7. creates a sense of story completeness. | | |
| 8. attempts to use a variety of sentence structures to support the story. | | |
| **BENCHMARK LA.B.2.2.6: The student creates expository responses in which ideas and details follow an organizational pattern and are relevant to the purpose. The student:** | | |
| 1. attempts to establish a clear focus with little or no irrelevant or repetitious information. | | 131G, 143G-143I, 153G-153I, 171G, 171H, 187G, 201G, 201I |
| 2. develops supporting ideas by presenting facts and information that relate to the focus. | | 187H, 201H |
| 3. develops anecdotes or examples to support and elaborate upon reasons. | | 171I, 201J |
| 4. generally presents facts, examples, and definitions objectively. | | 131I |
| 5. creates a logical organizational pattern (including a beginning, middle, and end) appropriate to expository writing. | | 131H, 153J, 171J, 187J |
| 6. uses appropriate expository transitions to relate ideas within and between paragraphs. | | |
| 7. uses a variety of sentence structures to present ideas. | | 143J |

### Strand C: Listening, Viewing, and Speaking

| | Unit 1 | Unit 2 |
|---|---|---|
| **STANDARD 1: The student uses listening strategies effectively.** | | |
| **BENCHMARK LA.C.1.2.1: The student listens and responds to a variety of oral presentations, such as stories, poems, skits, songs, personal accounts, informational speeches. The student:** | | |
| 1. understands information presented orally (for example, key points, details, different interpretations). | 19M, 31I, 123C | 125N, 131I, 205C |
| **BENCHMARK LA.C.1.2.2: The student identifies specific personal listening preferences regarding fiction, drama, literary nonfiction, and informational presentations. The student:** | | |
| 1. knows personal listening preferences (for example, chapter books, poetry, stories about diverse groups and cultures, nonfiction, drama, informational speeches). | 20O, 29C, 32O, 45C, 48O, 63C, 66O, 77C, 82O, 95C, 100O, 111C, 116P, 121C | 126O, 129C, 132O, 141C, 146O, 151C, 156O, 169C, 172O, 185C, 188O, 199C |

| Unit 3 | Unit 4 | Unit 5 | Unit 6 |
|---|---|---|---|
| 221C, 223F-223J, 237C, 239F-239J, 255F-255J, 263F-263J, 287F-287J, 305C, 307F-307J, 319F-319J | 333G, 359G, 375G, 389G, 403G, 413G | 423G, 433G, 443G, 459G, 473G, 481G | 489A, 491G, 497A, 499G, 505A, 507G, 517A, 519G, 529A, 531G, 539A, 541G |
| 223E, 239E, 255E, 263E, 287E, 307E, 319E | 331E, 333B, 333D | 423J, 443I, 459I, 473H, 481H, 481I | 491H-491J, 499H-499I, 505F, 507B, 507H-507I, 519H-519I, 531H-531I, 539E, 541G |
| | 375H, 413H | | |
| | 333J, 389H, 413I | | |
| | 359I | | |
| | 333I, 359J, 403I | | |
| | 333H, 359I, 375I | | |
| | 403H, 403J | | |
| | 389I-389J, 413J | | |
| | 375J | | |
| | | | |
| | | | |
| | | | |
| | | | |
| | | | |
| | | | |
| | | | |
| 223I, 255I, 307C, 319C | 321P, 401F | 423I, 424, 474 | 483N, 520 |
| 2080, 221C, 2260, 237C, 2420, 253C, 261C, 285C, 305C | 3220, 331C, 3340, 357C, 3600, 373C, 3780, 387C, 3920, 401C, 4060, 411C | 4160, 421C, 4260, 431C, 4340, 441C, 4460, 457C, 4600, 471C, 4760, 479C | 4840, 489C, 4920, 497C, 5020, 505C, 5080, 517C, 5220, 529C, 5320, 539C |

# Florida Resources

## Correlation to Florida Sunshine State Standards · Grade 4

| Strand C: Listening, Viewing, and Speaking | Unit 1 | Unit 2 |
|---|---|---|
| **BENCHMARK LA.C.1.2.3: The student carries on an extended conversation with a group of friends. The student:** | | |
| **1.** interacts with peers in a variety of situations to develop and present familiar ideas (such as conversations, whole group interactions, discussions). | 29A, 31A, 45A, 63A, 65A, 77A, 79A, 95A, 97A, 111A, 113A, 113B, 121A, 123A | 128, 129A, 131A, 141A, 143A, 131A, 151A, 169A, 185A, 199A, 201A, 203A |
| **BENCHMARK LA.C.1.2.4: The student listens attentively to the speaker, including making eye contact and facing the speaker. The student:** | | |
| **1.** listens attentively to the speaker, including making eye contact and facing the speaker. | 31I | 205C |
| **BENCHMARK LA.C.1.2.5: The student responds to speakers by asking questions, making contributions, and paraphrasing what is said. The student:** | | |
| **1.** uses strategies to respond to speakers (such as asking questions, making contributions, summarizing, reflecting on ideas). | 123C | 131I, 187I, 205C |
| **STANDARD 2: The student uses viewing strategies effectively.** | | |
| **BENCHMARK LA.C.2.2.1: The student determines main concept and supporting details in nonprint media messages. The student:** | | |
| **1.** understands the main concept and supporting details in nonprint media messages. | | 171I |
| **BENCHMARK LA.C.2.2.2: The student recognizes and responds to nonverbal cues used in a variety of nonprint media, such as motion pictures, television advertisements, and works of art. The student:** | | |
| **1.** discusses and reacts to nonverbal cues used in a variety of media (such as motion pictures, television, advertisements, works of art). | 98, 123I | 129B, 151B, 154, 169B, 199B |
| **STANDARD 3: The student uses speaking strategies effectively.** | | |
| **BENCHMARK LA.C.3.2.1: The student speaks clearly at an understandable rate and uses appropriate volume. The student:** | | |
| **1.** uses strategies to speak clearly (such as rate, volume, tone, projection). | 47I, 115B | |
| **BENCHMARK LA.C.3.2.2: The student asks questions and makes comments and observations to clarify understanding of content, processes, and experiences. The student:** | | |
| **1.** asks questions and makes comments and observations (for example, clarifies understanding of content, processes, and experiences; seeks the ideas and opinions of others; supports own opinions). | 29A, 45A, 63A, 65, 77A, 95A, 111A, 113B, 121A | 129A, 141A, 151A, 169A, 185A, 187I, 199A, 203A |
| **BENCHMARK LA.C.3.2.3: The student speaks for specific occasions, audiences and purposes, including conversations, discussions, projects, and informational or imaginative presentations. The student:** | | |
| **1.** prepares for and gives presentations for specific occasions, audiences, and purposes (including but not limited to group discussions, informational or dramatic presentations). | 79C, 113C, 123C | 141E, 141F, 143I, 145B |
| **BENCHMARK LA.C.3.2.4: The student uses eye contact and gestures that engage the audience. The student:** | | |
| **1.** uses eye contact and gestures that engage the audience. | 97I, 113C | 201C |
| **BENCHMARK LA.C.3.2.5: The student participates as a contributor and occasionally acts as a leader in a group discussion. The student:** | | |
| **1.** uses discussion strategies (for example, acts as participant and leader; volunteers relevant information; responds to opinions and ideas of others; summarizes information heard). | 29A, 45A, 63A, 77A, 95A, 111A, 121A | 129A, 141A, 151A, 169A, 185A, 199A, 203A |
| **BENCHMARK LA.C.3.2.6: The student organizes a speech using a basic beginning, middle, and ending. The student:** | | |
| **1.** presents a speech in an organized manner (including but not limited to organizing and sequencing details, information, and directions). | | 201C, 201I |

### Strand D: Language

| | Unit 1 | Unit 2 |
|---|---|---|
| **STANDARD 1: The student understands the nature of language.** | | |
| **BENCHMARK LA.D.1.2.1: The student understands that there are patterns and rules in the syntactic structure, symbols, sounds, and meanings conveyed through the English language. The student:** | | |
| **1.** uses elements of grammar in speech (including but not limited to present, past, and future verb tenses; subject-verb agreement; pronouns as subjects). | 31H, 47H, 65H, 79H, 97H, 123H | 131H, 201C |
| **2.** uses sentence variety in speech. | | 131H, 143I, 201C |
| **BENCHMARK LA.D.1.2.2: The student understands that language formality varies according to situations and audiences. The student:** | | |
| **1.** varies language according to situation, audience, and purpose (for example, appropriate tone, content, vocabulary). | 65I | |

| Unit 3 | Unit 4 | Unit 5 | Unit 6 |
|---|---|---|---|
| 221A, 232A, 239A, 253A, 255A, 261A, 263A, 285A, 287A, 287I, 305A, 307A | 331A, 333A, 357A, 373A, 375A, 387A, 389A, 401A, 403A, 411A | 421A, 431A, 441A, 457A, 459C, 471A, 479A, 481C | 489A, 489F, 497A, 499A, 505A, 517A, 529A, 531I, 539A, 541A, 545A |
| 319C | 413C | 481C | 547C |
| 223I, 307C | 401F, 403I, 413C | 423I, 481C | 531I, 541I, 547C |
|  |  | 433A, 443C, 473C |  |
| 221B, 256, 263I, 285B, 305B, 317B | 333E, 357B, 359E, 375E, 387B, 389E, 401B, 403E, 404, 411B, 413E | 433A, 443C, 473C | 489B, 497B, 500, 517B |
| 239I, 241B, 263D, 319C | 391B | 425B, 459C, 475B | 491I, 499I, 521B, 541C, 547D |
| 221A, 237A, 253A, 261A, 285A, 287C, 287I, 305A, 307C, 317A, 319C | 331A, 357A, 373A, 387A, 401A, 403I, 411A, 413C | 423C, 481C | 489A, 497A, 505A, 517A, 529A, 539A, 545A, 547C |
| 263D, 287C, 307C, 319C, 319I | 331E, 359A, 375C, 389C, 403C, 413C, 413J | 459C, 473C, 481C | 491I, 541C, 547C |
| 307I, 319C |  | 459C | 541C, 547D |
| 221A, 237A, 253A, 261A, 285A, 287I, 305A, 317A | 331A, 357A, 373A, 387A, 401A, 411A | 421A, 431A, 441A, 457A, 471A, 479A | 489A, 497A, 505A, 517A, 529A, 531I, 539A, 545A |
| 319D | 333I, 413I | 481C, 481I | 547C, 547I |
|  |  |  |  |
| 223H, 239H, 263H, 287H, 319H | 333H, 359H, 359I, 375H, 389H, 403H, 413H | 423H, 433H, 433I, 443H, 459C, 459H, 473H, 481H | 491H, 507H, 531H, 541C, 541H, 547H |
| 263D, 319C |  | 433I, 459C, 473H | 499H, 541C, 547D, 547H |
| 263G, 287F-287J | 333G, 359G, 375G, 389G, 403G, 413G | 423G, 459G, 473G, 475B | 491G, 499G, 507G, 531G, 541C, 547G |

# Florida Resources

## Correlation to Florida Sunshine State Standards                           Grade 4

| Strand D: Language | Unit 1 | Unit 2 |
|---|---|---|
| **STANDARD 2: The student understands the power of language.** | | |
| **BENCHMARK LA.D.2.2.1: The student understands that word choices can shape reactions, perceptions, and beliefs. The student:** | | |
| **1.** uses appropriate words to shape reactions, perceptions, and beliefs (for example, synonyms, antonyms, figurative language). | 115A | |
| **BENCHMARK LA.D.2.2.2: The student identifies and refers to symbol, theme, simile, alliteration, and assonance in oral and written texts. The student:** | | |
| **1.** understands similes, metaphors, analogies, and alliteration. | 114, 115A | |
| **BENCHMARK LA.D.2.2.3: The student recognizes different techniques used in media messages and their purposes. The student:** | | |
| **1.** uses a technique employed in media messages to achieve a specific purpose. | 113I | |
| **BENCHMARK LA.D.2.2.4: The student selects and uses appropriate technologies to enhance efficiency and effectiveness of communication. The student:** | | |
| **1.** uses appropriate available technologies to enhance communication. | 31E, 47E, 65E, 79E, 97E, 113E, 123C, 123E | 131E, 143E, 171E, 187E, 201E |
| **BENCHMARK LA.D.2.2.5: The student understands that a variety of messages can be conveyed through mass media. The student:** | | |
| **1.** interprets messages conveyed through mass media. | | 171I |

## Strand E: Literature

| | Unit 1 | Unit 2 |
|---|---|---|
| **STANDARD 1: The student understands the common features of a variety of literary forms.** | | |
| **BENCHMARK LA.E.1.2.1: The student identifies the distinguishing features among fiction, drama, and poetry and identifies the major characteristics of nonfiction. The student:** | | |
| **1.** understands the distinguishing features of literary texts (such as fiction, drama, poetry, biography, historical fiction, chapter books). | 29A, 32A, 45A, 48M, 63E, 77A, 81A, 95A, 95E, 115A, 116M, 121A, 121E | 132A, 141D, 145, 199A, 199D, 203A, 203D |
| **2.** understands the distinguishing features of nonfiction texts (such as biography, reference materials, magazines, newspapers). | 82M, 95A, 95E, 111A | 126M, 129A, 132A, 141A, 141D, 151A, 151D, 169A, 169E |
| **3.** reads a variety of literary and informational texts (such as fiction, drama, poetry, biography, historical fiction, reference materials, chapter books, magazines, newspapers). | 20, 20A, 32, 32A, 48, 48A, 66, 66A, 80, 82, 82A, 100, 100A, 114, 116, 116A | 126, 126A, 132, 144, 146, 146A, 156A, 172, 172A, 188, 188A, 202A |
| **BENCHMARK LA.E.1.2.2: The student understands the development of plot and how conflicts are resolved in a story. The student:** | | |
| **1.** understands relationships between the development of plot and changes in other story elements (such as character, setting, solution/resolution). | 29E, 45E, 111E | |
| **2.** understands how story events contribute to the plot and/or solution of the problem. | 29E | |
| **3.** understands how conflicts are resolved in a story. | 29E | |
| **BENCHMARK LA.E.1.2.3: The student knows the similarities and differences among the characters, settings, and events presented in various texts. The student:** | | |
| **1.** knows the similarities and differences of characters presented within and across fourth grade or higher level selections. | 33, 35, 39, 43, 45, 45C, 45D, 45E, 47, 65, 110, 111E, 123 | 131, 153A, 179, 185, 187, 205 |
| **2.** knows the similarities and differences of settings presented within and across fourth grade or higher level selections. | 29E | 183 |
| **3.** knows the similarities and differences of events presented within and across fourth grade or higher level selections. | 29E, 113 | 143, 143A, 153A, 171, 181, 187, 187A, 199D, 201, 205 |
| **BENCHMARK LA.E.1.2.4: The student knows that the attitudes and values that exist in a time period affect the works that are written during that time period. The student:** | | |
| **1.** knows that the attitudes and values that exist in a time period affect stories and informational articles written during that time period. | 121A | |
| **BENCHMARK LA.E.1.2.5: The student identifies and uses literary terminology appropriate to the grade level, including symbol, theme, simile, alliteration, and assonance. The student:** | | |
| **1.** identifies and uses literary terminology appropriate to fourth grade or higher level (including theme, simile, alliteration, metaphor). | 81A, 115A | |
| **STANDARD 2: The student responds critically to fiction, nonfiction, poetry, and drama.** | | |
| **BENCHMARK LA.E.2.2.1: The student recognizes cause-and-effect relationships in literary texts. The student:** | | |
| **1.** identifies cause-and-effect relationships in literary texts. | 21, 23, 25, 27, 29, 29C, 67, 69, 71, 123 | 203 |

| Unit 3 | Unit 4 | Unit 5 | Unit 6 |
|---|---|---|---|
|  | 375G, 375H, 375I | 433A, 443I | 491G, 499G, 507G, 519G-519H, 531H |
| 255G, 255I, 319G-319I | 337, 360K, 377A | 473G, 473H, 473I, 475A | 499G, 499H, 507H-507I |
|  |  | 433F-433J, 443C, 473C, 481C, 481F-481J |  |
| 223E, 239E, 255E, 263E, 287E, 307E, 319E | 333E, 359E, 375E, 389E, 403E, 413E | 423E, 433J, 443E, 459E, 473E, 481E | 491J, 499J, 519I, 541G |
| 263I | 389I | 433A, 443C, 459I |  |
| 225A, 237A, 237E, 253A, 285A, 305A, 305E, 317A | 331A, 357A, 373A, 373E, 375F, 387A, 389F, 403F, 413F, 413G | 475A, 476A | 491F, 499F, 505A, 507F, 517A, 517E, 519F, 521A, 531F |
| 208M, 221A, 221D, 237E, 258M, 261A, 261E, 305A, 305E | 357A, 375D, 401A, 403F, 411A | 416A, 421E, 426A, 434A, 446A, 457D, 460A | 489A, 489E, 497A, 505A, 529A, 539A, 545A |
| 208, 208A, 223B, 224, 226A, 239D, 240, 242, 242A, 258A, 264, 264A, 288A, 308, 308A | 322, 322A, 334, 334A, 360A, 376, 378, 378A, 390, 392, 392A, 406A | 416, 425B, 426, 434, 460, 475B | 484, 484A, 492, 492A, 502, 502A, 508, 508A, 521B, 522, 522A, 532, 532A, 542, 542A |
| 255I, 285E, 317D | 331D, 387D | 471E | 505D |
| 255I, 285E, 317D | 331D, 387D |  |  |
| 255I, 285E, 317D | 331D, 387D |  |  |
| 239, 253A, 253E, 255H, 285E, 287, 301, 307 | 331D, 389, 389A, 399, 403, 413 | 459, 473, 481 | 505D, 507, 515, 517 |
| 255G, 285E | 331D |  | 491, 507, 531, 541 |
| 239, 255, 285E, 297, 299, 303, 305, 319 | 331D, 333, 359, 375, 389A, 399, 403, 413, 413A | 443, 459, 473, 481 | 491, 499, 507, 513, 519, 531, 541 |
|  | 401E | 421A, 479A |  |
| 246 | 337, 377A, 360K | 475A | 491F, 497, 499F, 507F-507H, 519F |
| 289, 291, 293, 305C | 367, 369, 371, 373 |  | 539D, 543, 545, 545C |

# Florida Resources

## Correlation to Florida Sunshine State Standards

**Grade 4**

| Strand E: Literature | Unit 1 | Unit 2 |
|---|---|---|
| **BENCHMARK LA.E.2.2.2: The student recognizes and explains the effects of language, such as sensory words, rhymes, and choice of vocabulary and story structure, such as patterns, used in children's texts. The student:** | | |
| **1.** recognizes the uses of language found in children's literature (such as sensory words, rhymes, and choice of vocabulary). | | |
| **2.** understands the effects of text structure used in children's literature (such as rhyme schemes in poetry and story patterns). | | |
| **BENCHMARK LA.E.2.2.3: The student responds to a work of literature by explaining how the motives of the characters or the causes of events compare with those in his or her own life. The student:** | | |
| **1.** responds to literature by explaining how the motives of the characters compare with those of own life. | 31A, 65A, 70, 79A | 185C |
| **2.** responds to literature by explaining how the causes of events compare with those of own life. | 31A, 65A, 70, 79A | 185C |
| **BENCHMARK LA.E.2.2.4: The student identifies the major theme in a story or nonfiction text. The student:** | | |
| **1.** understands the major theme in a story. | 31, 47, 65, 79, 123 | 185, 185A, 199A, 201, 203A, 205, 205G |
| **2.** understands the major information in a nonfiction text. | 95A, 97, 111A, 113 | 129A, 129, 131, 141, 141A, 143, 151A, 153, 169 |
| **BENCHMARK LA.E.2.2.5: The student forms his or her own ideas about what has been read in a literary text and uses specific information from the text to support these ideas. The student:** | | |
| **1.** forms ideas about what has been read in a literary text and uses specific information from the text to support these ideas. | 29A, 45A, 63A, 65D, 77A, 111A, 121A | 185A, 199A, 203A, 205G-205J |

**Grade 5**

| Strand A: Reading | Unit 1 | Unit 2 |
|---|---|---|
| **STANDARD 1: The student uses the reading process effectively.** | | |
| **BENCHMARK LA.A.1.2.1: The student uses a table of contents, index, headings, captions, illustrations, and major words to anticipate or predict content and purpose of a reading selection. The student:** | | |
| **1.** uses text features to make predictions and monitor comprehension (for example, print variations, such as italics, bold face, underlines, appendices). | | 114M, 128M, 140M, 146, 149D |
| **BENCHMARK LA.A.1.2.2: The student selects from a variety of simple strategies, including the use of phonics, word structure, context clues, self-questioning, confirming simple predictions, retelling, and using visual cues to identify words and construct meaning from various texts, illustrations, graphics, and charts. The student:** | | |
| **1.** refines previously learned knowledge and skills of the fifth grade with increasingly complex reading texts and assignments and tasks. | 30, 33B, 35G-35J, 36K, 36L, 45G-45J, 48K, 55G-55J, 58K, 58N, 66K, 66N, 86K, 86L, 86N, 99I, 91J | 102K, 102N, 111B, 113H-113J, 114K, 114L, 114N, 120N, 125C, 128K, 128N, 137G, 140K, 140N, 152K, 152L |
| **BENCHMARK LA.A.1.2.3: The student uses simple strategies to determine meaning and increase vocabulary for reading, including the use of prefixes, suffixes, root words, multiple meanings, antonyms, synonyms, and word relationships. The student:** | | |
| **1.** uses a variety of strategies to determine meaning and increase vocabulary (for example, homonyms, homophones, homographs, prefixes, suffixes, word-origins, multiple meanings, antonyms, synonyms, word relationships). | 20K, 33B, 43B, 53B, 55G-55J, 58K, 63B, 65H-65J, 83B, 85G-85J, 86K, 97B, 99G-99J | 102K, 111B, 113G, 113J, 117B, 119G-119J, 120N, 125B, 127G-127J, 128K, 128N, 137G-137J, 140K, 151G-151J, 152K, 161G-161J, 166K, 177G |
| **2.** identifies, classifies, and demonstrates knowledge of levels of specificity among fifth-grade or higher level words from a variety of categories. | | 133, 157, 159C, 159D |
| **BENCHMARK LA.A.1.2.4: The student clarifies understanding by rereading, self-correction, summarizing, checking other sources, and class or group discussion. The student:** | | |
| **1.** uses a variety of strategies to monitor reading in fifth-grade or higher texts (for example, adjusting reading rate according to purpose and text difficulty, rereading, self-correcting, summarizing, checking other sources, class and group discussions, trying an alternate word). | 33A, 43A, 53A, 63A, 65G-65J, 83A, 85G, 85I, 85J, 97A | 108, 111A, 111C, 114M, 117A, 117C, 122, 124, 125A, 125C, 128D, 130, 135A, 144, 149A, 149C, 154, 159A, 166, 175A |

| Unit 3 | Unit 4 | Unit 5 | Unit 6 |
|---|---|---|---|
| | | | |
| 225B | 359D, 391A | | |
| 225B | 391A, 411E | | |
| | | | |
| 255B, 255H, 255I, 255J, 317C | 359A, 375B, 394, 403B | | |
| 255B, 255H, 317C | 324, 359A, 375B, 394, 403A, 403B | | |
| | | | |
| 253A, 285A, 317A | 331A, 372, 373A, 387A | 479A | 517A |
| 221A, 223, 237A, 239, 261A, 263, 305A | 357A, 401A, 411A | 421A, 431A, 441A, 457A, 471A | 489A, 497A, 505A, 529A, 539A, 545A |
| | | | |
| 237A, 253A, 255J, 285A, 305A, 317A | 331A, 373A, 387A, 401A, 411A | 479A | 517A |

| Unit 3 | Unit 4 | Unit 5 | Unit 6 |
|---|---|---|---|
| | | | |
| 192M, 248M | 313C | 459C | 522 |
| | | | |
| 180L, 180N, 191G-191J, 192K, 192L, 192N, 212K, 212L, 223B, 225I, 228K, 228N, 243B, 248K, 248L, 248N, 252, 275C, 278K, 278N, 285G, 285I, 285J | 288N, 307G, 307H, 307J, 310K, 310N, 316L, 316N, 332K, 332N, 350K, 350N, 350, 354, 356, 366K, 366N, 380K, 380N, 387G, 387J | 390K, 390L, 390N, 406K, 406L, 406N, 430, 430K, 430L, 430N, 432, 436, 440, 446K, 446L, 446N, 446, 450, 452, 456, 458 | 510K, 510N, 512, 514, 516, 518, 522K, 522N, 524, 528, 530, 532, 537B, 537C, 542K, 542N, 566K, 566N, 574, 576, 580 |
| | | | |
| 180L, 192K, 192L, 209G-209J, 212K, 212L, 223B, 225G, 225J, 228K, 228L, 248K, 238L, 277G-277J, 278K, 285G, 285H, 285J | 288K, 305B, 307I, 310K, 331L, 313B, 315G-315J, 316K, 316L, 332K, 347G-347J, 350K, 350L, 365G-365J, 366K, 366L, 379G, 379J, 380K, 380L, 387H-387J | 390K, 390L, 405G-405J, 406K, 406L, 427H-427J, 430K, 430L, 443G-443J, 446K, 446L, 461G-461J, 462K, 474K, 493B, 495G-495J, 507G, 507I, 507J | 510K, 521F-521J, 522K, 537B, 539F-539J, 542K, 565G-565J, 566K, 583H-583J, 586K, 602K, 625G-625J |
| 245G-245J | 337, 339, 341, 343, 345, 345C, 345D | 446K, 446L | |
| | | | |
| 182, 188, 189A, 194, 198, 200, 206, 207A, 214, 218, 220, 223A, 225H, 230, 232, 234, 236, 238, 243A, 250, 252, 256 | 288, 290, 292, 296, 300, 304, 305A, 310, 312, 313A, 316, 318, 320, 322, 324, 326, 328, 329A, 332, 334, 336, 338, 340, 342 | 390, 392, 394, 398, 400, 402, 403A, 405H, 408, 410, 414, 416, 418, 420, 422, 424, 425A, 427G, 430, 432, 434, 436 | 512, 514, 516, 518, 519A, 522, 524, 526, 528, 530, 532, 534, 536, 537A, C, 542, 544, 546, 548, 550, 552, 554, 556, 558 |

# Florida Resources

## Correlation to Florida Sunshine State Standards

Grade 5

### Strand A: Reading

| | Unit 1 | Unit 2 |
|---|---|---|
| **STANDARD 2: The student constructs meaning from a wide range of texts.** | | |
| **BENCHMARK LA.A.2.2.1: The student reads text and determines the main idea or essential message, identifies relevant supporting details and facts, and arranges events in chronological order. The student:** | | |
| 1. summarizes and paraphrases information in fifth-grade or higher texts (for example, main idea, implied message, supporting ideas and facts, chronological order of events). | 37, 39, 41, 43, 43C, 43D, 63, 63C, 63D, 83, 97 | 108, 115, 117, 125, 125A, 129, 135, 135C, 144, 149C, 167, 169, 171, 173, 175 |
| **BENCHMARK LA.A.2.2.2: The student identifies the author's purpose in a simple text. The student:** | | |
| 1. describes author's purpose and describes how an author's perspective influences the text. | 87, 89, 91, 93, 97C-97E | 177 |
| **BENCHMARK LA.A.2.2.3: The student recognizes when a text is primarily intended to persuade. The student:** | | |
| 1. knows characteristics of persuasive text. | 97E | 137I |
| **BENCHMARK LA.A.2.2.4: The student identifies specific personal preferences relative to fiction and nonfiction reading. The student:** | | |
| 1. uses a variety of criteria to choose own reading (for example, author's style, themes, knowledge of genres, text difficulty, recommendations of others). | | 119A, 127A |
| **BENCHMARK LA.A.2.2.5: The student reads and organizes information for a variety of purposes, including making a report, conducting interviews, taking a test, and performing an authentic task. The student:** | | |
| 1. [reads and organizes information] to support opinions, predictions, and conclusions, to write a research report, to conduct interviews, to take a test, to perform tasks. | 45D, 55A, 65A, 85D | 111, 111B, 125, 125B, 127A, 127C, 135B, 135F, 137C, 137D, 149, 149B, 159, 159B, 175, 175B |
| **BENCHMARK LA.A.2.2.6: The student recognizes the difference between fact and opinion presented in a text. The student:** | | |
| 1. extends the expectations of the fourth grade with increasingly complex reading selections, assignments, and tasks. | | 153 |
| **BENCHMARK LA.A. 2.2.7: The student recognizes the use of comparison and contrast in a text. The student:** | | |
| 1. extends the expectations of the fourth grade with increasingly complex reading selections, assignments, and tasks. | 67, 69, 71, 79, 81, 83, 83C, 83D | 141, 145, 147, 149, 153, 155, 159C |
| **BENCHMARK LA.A.2.2.8: The student selects and uses a variety of appropriate reference materials, including multiple representations of information, such as maps, charts, and photos, to gather information for research projects. The student:** | | |
| 1. uses appropriate reference materials from multiple sources to gather information for a research project (such as reference books, photos, timelines). | 55A, 85D | 113A |
| 2. uses strategies to identify a research topic (such as brainstorming, listing questions, using idea webs). | 45C | 113C |
| 3. uses key words, indexes, cross-references, and letters on volumes to locate information for research topics. | 35D | 127D, 151D |
| 4. compiles information into written reports or oral presentations. | 99C | 161C |

### Strand B: Writing

| | | |
|---|---|---|
| **STANDARD 1: The student uses writing processes effectively.** | | |
| **BENCHMARK LA.B.1.2.1: The student prepares for writing by recording thoughts, focusing on a central idea, grouping related ideas, and identifying the purpose of writing. The student:** | | |
| 1. uses a variety of strategies to prepare for writing (such as brainstorming, making lists, mapping, outlining, grouping related ideas, using graphic organizers, taking notes). | 35F, 35G, 45F-45J, 55D, 55F, 83D | 111C, 119F |
| 2. establishes a purpose for writing (including but not limited to informing, entertaining, explaining). | 35G-35I | 137G, 151H |
| **BENCHMARK LA.B.1.2.2: The student drafts and revises writing in cursive that** | | |
| • *focuses on the topic,* | | |
| • *has a logical organizational pattern, including a beginning, middle, conclusion, and transitional devices,* | | |
| • *has ample development of supporting ideas,* | | |
| • *demonstrates a sense of completeness or wholeness,* | | |
| • *generally has correct subject/verb agreement,* | | |
| • *generally has correct verb and noun forms,* | | |
| • *with few [exceptions], has sentences that are complete, except when fragments are used purposefully,* | | |
| • *uses a variety of sentence structures, and* | | |
| • *generally follows the conventions of punctuation, capitalization, and spelling* | | |
| **The student:** | | |

| Unit 3 | Unit 4 | Unit 5 | Unit 6 |
|---|---|---|---|
| 182, 188, 193, 195, 198, 206, 207, 231, 235, 237, 239, 241, 243C, 243D, 247B, 279, 281, 283 | 292, 300, 304, 305, 311, 312, 313, 318, 324, 326, 328, 329, 336, 342, 344, 345, 360, 363, 363E, 365D, 368, 372, 377 | 394, 400, 405, 407, 408, 409, 411, 415, 416, 417, 419, 420, 421, 422, 423, 424, 425, 425C, 425D, 427, 437, 439, 441 | 511, 515, 519, 519C, 521, 537, 539, 543, 544, 547, 548, 549, 551, 552, 557, 561, 563, 565, 568, 570 |
| | 377E | 403E | 567, 569, 571, 573, 575, 577, 579, 581, 581C |
| | 385E, 387D | | |
| 191A | | 443A | 583D |
| 189, 189B, 191A, 207B, 225A, 243, 243B, 245D, 275, 275B, 283, 283B | 305F, 313, 313B, 313E, 315D, 329, 329B, 331C, 345, 345B, 347A, 354, 363, 363B, 363C, 377, 377B, 385, 385B | 403, 403B, 425, 425B, 432, 440, 441, 441B, 443A, 443C, 450, 452, 458, 459, 459B, 459C, 466, 470, 471, 471B, 473D | 512, 521A, 537C, 565A, 565C, 583C |
| | 367, 369, 371, 373, 375, 377, 377C, 377D | 403E, 475, 477, 479, 481, 483, 485, 487, 489, 491, 493C, 493D | 545, 553, 555 |
| 199, 201, 203, 205, 207, 207C | 327, 329 | 455, 457, 459 | |
| 191A, 277D | 307A | 443A, 507D | |
| 191C, 191D, 209C | 307C, 315C | 405C, 427C | 521C |
| | 379A | 443A, 443D | |
| 285C | 379C | 495C | 625C |
| 191D, 191F, 209F, 225F, 245F, 277F, 285F | 331G, 347F, 365F, 379F | 405J, 443F, 443G, 461F, 461G, 473F, 473G, 495F, 495G, 507F, 507G | 521F, 521G, 539F, 539G, 565F, 565G, 583F, 583G, 601F, 601G, 625F, 625G |
| 189D, 191G, 207F, 209G, 225F, 225G, 245G, 277G, 285G | 315G, 347F, 347G, 365F, 365G | 405F, 443F, 443G, 461F, 461G, 473F, 473G, 495F, 495G, 507F, 507G | 521G, 539G, 565G, 583G, 601G, 625G |

# Florida Resources

## FLORIDA RESOURCES

## Correlation to Florida Sunshine State Standards    Grade 5

| Strand B: Writing | Unit 1 | Unit 2 |
|---|---|---|
| **1.** focuses on a central idea or topic (including but not limited to using facts and details from several sources, excluding irrelevant or repetitious information). | 35H, 45G, 55I, 85F, 99J | 113F, 119G, 127G, 137H, 151G-151I, 177F |
| **2.** uses an appropriate organizational pattern (including but not limited to, topic sentences, supporting sentences, and sequence, develops new ideas in separate paragraphs, concludes with effectiveness). | 55G, 85G | 113G, 113H, 119G, 135D, 151J, 161G, 177G |
| **3.** uses strategies to achieve a sense of completeness or wholeness in writing (such as considers voice, audience, word choice, tone, and imagery, revises for clarity and interest to reader). | 65F-65J, 85F, 85H, 85J | 161F, 161H |
| **4.** uses varied sentence structures (simple, compound, complex). | 85I | 119J |
| **5.** generally follows the conventions of punctuation, capitalization, and spelling [see benchmark, LA.B.1.2.3, for specifics]. | 35F, 99J | 113E-113H, 119E, 119F, 119G, 119H, 119J, 127E-127H, 137E-137H, 151E-151H |

**BENCHMARK LA.B.1.2.3: The student produces final documents that have been edited for:**
- *correct spelling,*
- *correct use of punctuation, including commas in series, dates, and addresses, and beginning and ending quotation marks,*
- *correct capitalization of proper nouns,*
- *correct paragraph indentation,*
- *correct usage of subject/verb agreement, verb and noun forms, and sentence structure, and*
- *correct formatting according to instructions.*

**The student:**

| | | |
|---|---|---|
| **1.** uses strategies to spell words (for example, using resources such as dictionary or thesaurus to confirm spelling). | 35G, 66L, 99F, 99G | |
| **2.** uses conventions of punctuation (including but not limited to commas in a series, dates, and addresses, beginning and ending quotation marks, hyphens in compound words). | 65F-65H, 99F, 99G, 99H, 99J | 113J, 127F-127H, 137F, 137G, 137H, 137J, 151F-151H, 161F-161I, 177F, 177G, 177H, 177J |
| **3.** uses conventions of capitalization (including but not limited to the names of organizations, nationalities, races, languages, and religions, the heading, salutation, and closing of a letter). | 35F-35H, 65F-65H, 99F, 99J | 113F, 113G, 113H, 113J, 119F-119H |
| **4.** uses various parts of speech in written work (including but not limited to substituting pronouns for nouns, using singular and plural possessive forms of nouns, using common and proper nouns, using correct forms of adjectives, verbs, and adverbs). | 35H, 45F, 45H, 55F-55H | |
| **5.** uses a variety of strategies to format written work (such as chapter book, reference source, electronic formatting). | | 117C |
| **6.** evaluates own and other's writing (for example, identifies the best features of a piece of writing, determines how own writing achieves its purpose, asks for feedback, responds to classmate's writing). | 53E, 85I, 99I | 117C, 128G, 161J, 177I |

**STANDARD 2: The student writes to communicate ideas and information effectively.**

**BENCHMARK LA.B.2.2.1: The student writes notes, comments, and observations that reflect comprehension of content and experiences from a variety of media. The student:**

| | | |
|---|---|---|
| **1.** writes notes, comments, and observations that reflect comprehension of content and experiences from a variety of media. | 33A, 43A, 45D, 47, 53A, 55D, 63A, 83A, 97A, 99A | 111A, 117A, 120P, 127, 128P, 135A, 149A, 151G, 151H, 159A, 161D, 163, 165, 175A |

**BENCHMARK LA.B.2.2.2: The student organizes information using alphabetical and numerical systems. The student:**

| | | |
|---|---|---|
| **1.** uses alphabetical and numerical systems such as outlining to organize information. | | 137D |

**BENCHMARK LA.B.2.2.3: The student writes for a variety of occasions, audiences, and purpose. The student:**

| | | |
|---|---|---|
| **1.** writes for a variety of occasions, audiences, and purposes (such as letters to persuade or request, humorous or suspenseful stories to entertain, instructions to inform). | 47A, 47B, 53D, 63D, 97D | 111C, 117D, 163A, 165A, 175C |

**BENCHMARK LA.B.2.2.4: The student uses electronic technology, including word-processing software and electronic encyclopedias, to create, revise, retrieve, and verify information. The student:**

| | | |
|---|---|---|
| **1.** uses electronic technology (including word-processing software and electronic encyclopedias) to create, revise, retrieve, and verify information. | 99G | |

**BENCHMARK LA.B.2.2.5: The student creates narratives in which ideas, details, and events are in logical order and are relevant to the story line. The student:**

| | | |
|---|---|---|
| **1.** uses strategies to create an effective central theme or focus (suspense, humor, creativity, or fantasy). | 35I | |
| **2.** exhibits a consistent awareness of topic with no irrelevant information. | 65G | |
| **3.** develops a story line that is easy to follow and paraphrase. | 45J | 125C |
| **4.** chooses specific detail and precise word choice to support the story line. | 65F, 65J | |
| **5.** creates a logical organizational pattern (including an effective beginning, middle, end, and transitions) appropriate to narrative writing. | 35J | |

| Unit 3 | Unit 4 | Unit 5 | Unit 6 |
|---|---|---|---|
| 191G, 209I, 245J, 277J, 285J | 345D | 461H, 461I, 495I, 507H | |
| 191H, 191J, 209H, 209J, 245J, 277I, 285I, 285J | 315H, 365G, 379I, 387G | 443H, 443I, 461H, 461I, 507H | 539H |
| 225G, 225I, 245H, 277H, 277I, 285H, 285I | 347I, 365G, 387G-387H | 461H, 461I, 473H, 473J, 495I, 507I | 521I, 565I, 583I, 601I, 625I |
| | 331H, 347I | | 521H |
| | | | |
| | 387I | | 539J, 625J |
| | 347J, 363E, 387I | 427F-427H, 443F, 443G, 443H, 443J, 461F, 461G, 461H, 461J, 473F-473H, 495F-495H, 507F-507H | 539J, 625J |
| | 331LJ, 347J, 387I | 443F, 443G, 443H, 443J, 461F, 461G, 461H, 461J, 507F-507H | 625J |
| 191F-191H, 209F-209H | 347H | | |
| 225J | 347J, 365J | | 565J |
| | 305D | 425D, 459C, 505D | 521I, 539I, 565I, 581C, 583I, 601I, 625I |
| 180P, 189A, 189B, 191D, 192P, 207A, 207B, 209D, 211, 212P, 223A, 243A, 247 | 288P, 305A, 313A, 329A, 345A, 350P, 363A, 363B, 366P, 377A, 379A, 385A | 403A, 425A, 427D, 441A, 459A, 471A, 493A, 505A | 510P, 519A, 522P, 537A, 542P, 563A, 566P, 581A, 599A, 602P, 623A |
| | 347D, 379H | | 615, 617, 623C |
| 207D | 315F, 345D, 377D, 385D | 403D, 405G-405J, 427F, 427H, 427I, 427J, 461G, 473H | 521G, 539G, 565G, 583G, 601G, 625G |
| 277D | 315D | 427I, 427J, 495D | 539D |
| | 379F | 441D | 565H, 583H, 601H |
| | | | 565H |
| | | | 565H, 583H |
| | | | 565H, 601H, 625I, 625J |
| | | | 519D, 583H |

# Florida Resources

## Correlation to Florida Sunshine State Standards
Grade 5

| **Strand B: Writing** | **Unit 1** | **Unit 2** |
|---|---|---|
| **6.** uses transitions effectively to move the narrative story forward in time. | 55H, 85J | |
| **7.** creates a clear sense of story completeness. | | |
| **8.** uses a variety of sentence structures to reinforce the story. | | |
| **BENCHMARK LA.B.2.2.6: The student creates expository responses in which ideas and details follow an organizational pattern and are relevant to the purpose. The student:** | | |
| **1.** establishes a clear, central focus with little or no irrelevant or repetitious material. | | 119H, 119J, 127F, 127H |
| **2.** creates ample development of supporting ideas by presenting facts and information that clearly relates to the focus. | 35H | 127H, 137G, 177G, 177H |
| **3.** develops extended anecdotes or examples to support reasons. | | 127H, 151A |
| **4.** presents facts, examples, and definitions objectively. | | 161H |
| **5.** creates a logical organizational pattern (including an effective beginning, middle, end, and transitions) appropriate to expository writing. | | 113H, 137G, 151G, 161G, 177I |
| **6.** uses a variety of effective expository transitions to relate ideas within and between paragraphs. | | 113I, 113J, 161G, 177I |
| **7.** uses a variety of sentence structures to reinforce ideas. | 85I | 119I, 119J, 177I, 177J |

## Strand C: Listening, Viewing, and Speaking

| **STANDARD 1: The student uses listening strategies effectively.** | | |
|---|---|---|
| **BENCHMARK LA.C.1.2.1: The student listens and responds to a variety of oral presentations, such as stories, poems, skits, songs, personal accounts, informational speeches. The student:** | | |
| **1.** understands information presented in a variety of forms (for example, informational speeches, humor, persuasive messages, and directions). | 35I, 46, 47B, 99A | |
| **2.** uses listening strategies in non-interactive settings (for example, assemblies, visual media, formal presentations). | 46, 99A | 162, 164, 177C |
| **BENCHMARK LA.C.1.2.2: The student identifies specific personal listening preferences regarding fiction, drama, literary nonfiction, and informational presentations. The student:** | | |
| **1.** knows personal listening preferences (for example, audio tapes, editorials, nonfiction, drama, informational speeches). | 36O, 48P, 58P, 66P, 86P | 102P, 114P, 140P, 152P, 166P |
| **BENCHMARK LA.C.1.2.3: The student carries on an extended conversation with a group of friends. The student:** | | |
| **1.** interacts with peers in a variety of situations to develop and present familiar ideas (such as summarizes information from group activities, recognizes different perspectives). | 33A, 35, 43A, 45, 45C, 53A, 55, 55C, 63A, 65, 83A, 85, 85A, 85C, 97A, 99 | 111A, 113, 119, 119C, 119D, 119I, 125A, 127, 127C, 135A, 137, 137I, 149A, 151, 151C, 161, 175A, 177 |
| **BENCHMARK LA.C.1.2.4: The student listens attentively to the speaker, including making eye contact and facing the speaker. The student:** | | |
| **1.** listens attentively to the speaker, including making eye contact and facing the speaker. | 35I, 85A, 99A, 99C | 163B, 177C |
| **BENCHMARK LA.C.1.2.5: The student responds to speakers by asking questions, making contributions, and paraphrasing what is said. The student:** | | |
| **1.** uses strategies to respond to speakers (such as asking questions, paraphrasing to confirm understanding, summarizing, making contributions, offering feedback). | 85I, 99C | 113I, 151I, 161C, 177C |
| **STANDARD 2: The student uses viewing strategies effectively.** | | |
| **BENCHMARK LA.C.2.2.1: The student determines main concept and supporting details in nonprint media messages. The student:** | | |
| **1.** identifies and explains the main concept and supporting details in a nonprint media message. | 65I | |
| **BENCHMARK LA.C.2.2.2: The student recognizes and responds to nonverbal cues used in a variety of nonprint media, such as motion pictures, television advertisements, and works of art. The student:** | | |
| **1.** understands persuasive messages used in nonprint media (such as television commercials, advertisements, commands, requests). | | |
| **STANDARD 3: The student uses speaking strategies effectively.** | | |
| **BENCHMARK LA.C.3.2.1: The student speaks clearly at an understandable rate and uses appropriate volume. The student:** | | |
| **1.** uses strategies to speak clearly (such as rate, volume, phrasing, enunciation). | 36O, 45D, 48O, 58O, 66O, 85A, 86O, 99C | 102O, 140O, 152O, 163B, 165B, 166O, 177C |

| Unit 3 | Unit 4 | Unit 5 | Unit 6 |
|---|---|---|---|
| | 305D | 441D | 519D |
| | | | 583H, 625C |
| | | | 521H |
| | | | |
| 207D | 307H-307J, 331I, 365I | | |
| | 387J | | |
| | 331I, 365I, 387J | | |
| | 365I | | |
| | | | |
| | | | |
| | | | |
| 191I, 210, 285C | 307D, 385E, 387A | 427D | 625C |
| 210, 246 | 387A | 507C | 625C |
| 1800, 192P, 228P, 2480, 2780 | 2880, 3100, 3160, 3320, 3660, 3800 | 427D, 4620, 4740, 4960 | |
| 189A, 191, 207A, 209, 209C, 223A, 225C, 243A, 247B, 275A, 277, 277C, 283A, 285 | 305A, 307, 313A, 315, 315C, 315H, 329A, 331, 331C, 345A, 347, 363A, 365, 365C, 365I, 377A, 379, 385A, 387 | 403A, 405I, 425A, 427C, 441A, 443C, 459A, 471A, 473C, 473I, 493A, 505A | 519A, 521I, 537A, 539C, 563A, 565C, 581A, 599A, 623A |
| 285C | 387C | 507C | 625C |
| 285C | 379C, 385E, 387C | 405I, 495C, 507C | 625C |
| 245I | 307D, 387A | | |
| 245I | 307I, 387A, 387D | | |
| 209I, 211B, 2280, 2480, 2780, 285C | 309, 309B, 315I, 3160, 3320, 3660, 3800, 385E, 387C | 3900, 4060, 4460, 4620, 4960, 507C | 5100, 539I, 540, 541B, 5420, 5660, 625C, 626, 627B |

# Florida Resources

## Correlation to Florida Sunshine State Standards · Grade 5

### Strand C: Listening, Viewing, and Speaking

| | Unit 1 | Unit 2 | |
|---|---|---|---|
| **BENCHMARK LA.C.3.2.2: The student asks questions and makes comments and observations to clarify understanding of content, processes, and experiences. The student:** | | | |
| 1. asks relevant questions and makes comments and observations (for example, gives feedback, draws conclusions, reflects on information, clarifies understanding of content, processes, and experiences). | 85I, 99C | 101O, 137I, 151I, 177C | |
| **BENCHMARK LA.C.3.2.3: The student speaks for specific occasions, audiences, and purposes, including conversations, discussions, projects, and informational or imaginative presentations. The student:** | | | |
| 1. prepares for and gives presentations for specific occasions, audiences, and purposes (including but not limited to informational or imaginative presentations, research reports, extemporaneous talks). | 47B, 55I, 58G, 85A, 99C | 119D, 161C, 161I, 177C, 177I | |
| 2. uses visual aids, technology, or demonstrations to support a presentation. | 65I, 99D | 119D, 161C, 161I, 177C | |
| **BENCHMARK LA.C.3.2.4: The student uses eye contact and gestures that engage the audience. The student:** | | | |
| 1. uses nonverbal strategies (such as eye contact, gestures, posture, facial expressions) to engage the audience. | 99C | 177C | |
| **BENCHMARK LA.C.3.2.5: The student participates as a contributor and occasionally acts as a leader in a group discussion. The student:** | | | |
| 1. uses discussion strategies (for example, acts as a participant and leader, organizes information for a group, uses evidence to support ideas). | 33A, 43A, 53A, 63A, 83A, 97A | 111A, 117A, 125A, 135A, 137C, 149A, 159A, 175A | |
| **BENCHMARK LA.C.3.2.6: The student organizes a speech using a basic beginning, middle, and ending. The student:** | | | |
| 1. presents a speech in an organized manner (including but not limited to including content appropriate to the audience, using notes or other memory aids, summarizing main points). | 99I | 161D, 177I | |

### Strand D: Language

| | Unit 1 | Unit 2 | |
|---|---|---|---|
| **STANDARD 1: The student understands the nature of language.** | | | |
| **BENCHMARK LA.D.1.2.1: The student understands that there are patterns and rules in the syntactic structure, symbols, sounds, and meanings conveyed through the English language. The student:** | | | |
| 1. uses elements of grammar in speech (including but not limited to present, past, future, and progressive verb tenses, subject-verb agreement, pronoun references, word order). | | 119I | |
| 2. uses sentence variety in speech. | | 119I | |
| **BENCHMARK LA.D.1.2.2: The student understands that language formality varies according to situations and audiences. The student:** | | | |
| 1. varies language according to situation, audience, and purpose (for example, uses appropriate content, examples, vocabulary). | 55I | | |
| **STANDARD 2: The student understands the power of language.** | | | |
| **BENCHMARK LA.D.2.2.1: The student understands that word choices can shape reactions, perceptions, and beliefs. The student:** | | | |
| 1. uses appropriate words to shape reactions, perceptions, and beliefs (for example, connotative and idiomatic meaning, synonyms, antonyms, sensory words). | | 127I, 161F | |
| **BENCHMARK LA.D.2.2.2: The student identifies and refers to symbol, theme, simile, alliteration, and assonance in oral and written texts. The student:** | | | |
| 1. extends awareness of similes, metaphors, symbols, analogies, alliteration, and idiomatic language learned in Third and Fourth Grades. | 55J | 159E, 165A | |
| **BENCHMARK LA.D.2.2.3: The student recognizes different techniques used in media messages and their purposes. The student:** | | | |
| 1. uses a technique employed in media messages to achieve a specific purpose. | | 127I | |
| **BENCHMARK LA.D.2.2.4: The student selects and uses appropriate technologies to enhance efficiency and effectiveness of communication. The student:** | | | |
| 1. uses appropriate available technologies to enhance communication. | | 127B, 137B | |
| **BENCHMARK LA.D.2.2.5: The student understands that a variety of messages can be conveyed through mass media. The student:** | | | |
| 1. understands techniques used to convey messages conveyed in mass media (for example, fact and opinion, persuasive devices). | | 127I, 137I | |

| Unit 3 | Unit 4 | Unit 5 | Unit 6 |
|---|---|---|---|
| 285C | 385E, 387C | 507C | 521I, 565I, 625C |
| | | | |
| 211B, 247B, 285C, 285D, 285I | 309B, 313F, 345F, 363F, 379C, 385E, 387A, 387C | 495C, 507C, 507I | 521C, 625C, 625I |
| 285D | 379C, 379D | 495C, 507C | 625I |
| 277I, 285C | 385E, 387C | 507C | 601I, 625C |
| 189A, 207A, 223A, 243A, 245C, 275A, 283A | 305A, 307I, 313A, 329A, 345A, 347C, 363A, 365I, 377A, 385A | 403A, 425A, 441A, 443I, 459A, 461C, 471A, 473I, 493A, 505A | 519A, 537A, 563A, 581A, 583C, 599A, 623A |
| 285I | 379I, 385E, 387I | 495I | 625I |
| | | | |
| | | | |
| | 307H, 315F-315H, 387H | 427I | |
| | | | |
| | | | |
| 209I, 245G | 307H, 331I | | 583I |
| | | | |
| 225I, 243E, 247A, 277J | 329D, 331G-331J | 427I, 443I, 457, 473G, 473I, 473J, 507H | 521G-521J, 581E, 583A, 601G, 601I, 601J, 625G, 625J |
| | 307G, 307H, 387D | 461I | |
| 285D | 315B, 331B, 347B, 379D, 387B | | 583I |
| | 307D, 307H, 347I, 387A, 387D | | |

# Florida Resources

## Correlation to Florida Sunshine State Standards    Grade 5

| Strand E: Literature | Unit 1 | Unit 2 |
|---|---|---|
| **STANDARD 1: The student understands the common features of a variety of literary forms.** | | |
| **BENCHMARK LA.E.1.2.1: The student identifies the distinguishing features among fiction, drama, and poetry and identifies the major characteristics of nonfiction. The student:** | | |
| 1. understands the distinguishing features of literary texts (such as fiction, drama, poetry, folktales, myths, poems, historical fiction, autobiographies). | 47A | 111D, 125D, 163A, 175D |
| 2. understands the distinguishing features of nonfiction texts (such as textbooks, letters, scientific procedures, magazines). | | 111D, 111F, 135E |
| 3. reads a variety of literary and informational texts (such as fiction, drama, poetry, biography, myths, fantasies, historical fiction, biographies, autobiographies, textbooks, manuals, magazines). | | 120-125, 128-135 |
| **BENCHMARK LA.E.1.2.2: The student understands the development of plot and how conflicts are resolved in a story. The student:** | | |
| 1. understands relationships between the development of plot and changes in other story elements (such as character, setting, solution/resolution). | 43E, 83E | |
| 2. understands how story events contribute to the plot and/or solution of the problem. | 63E, 83E | |
| **BENCHMARK LA.E.1.2.3: The student knows the similarities and differences among the characters, settings, and events presented in various texts. The student:** | | |
| 1. knows the similarities and differences of characters presented within and across fifth grade or higher level selections. | 45, 53E, 55, 63, 65, 65D, 85, 99 | |
| 2. knows the similarities and differences of settings presented within and across fifth grade or higher level selections. | 43E, 53E | |
| 3. knows the similarities and differences of events presented within and across fifth grade or higher level selections. | 45, 53E, 63E | |
| **BENCHMARK LA.E.1.2.4: The student knows that the attitudes and values that exist in a time period affect the works that are written during that time period. The student:** | | |
| 1. knows that the attitudes and values that exist in a time period affect stories and informational articles written during that time period. | | |
| **BENCHMARK LA.E.1.2.5: The student identifies and uses literary terminology appropriate to the grade level, including symbol, theme, simile, alliteration, and assonance. The student:** | | |
| 1. identifies and uses literary terminology appropriate to fifth grade or higher level (including theme, simile, alliteration, metaphor). | | 159E, 165A |
| **STANDARD 2: The student responds critically to fiction, nonfiction, poetry, and drama.** | | |
| **BENCHMARK LA.E.2.2.1: The student recognizes cause-and-effect relationships in literary texts. The student:** | | |
| 1. understands cause-and-effect relationships in literary texts. | | |
| **BENCHMARK LA.E.2.2.2: The student recognizes and explains the effects of language, such as sensory words, rhymes, and choice of vocabulary and story structure, such as patterns, used in children's texts. The student:** | | |
| 1. understands how the author's choices of language (such as sensory words and vocabulary choice) and story structure (such as rhymes and story patterns) contribute to the overall quality of a literary work. | 47A, 53C, 53D | |
| **BENCHMARK LA.E.2.2.3: The student responds to a work of literature by explaining how the motives of the characters or the causes of events compare with those in his or her own life. The student:** | | |
| 1. responds to literature by explaining how the motives of the characters compare with those of own life. | 33E, 35, 99 | 121, 123, 151, 161 |
| 2. responds to literature by explaining how the causes of events compare with those of own life. | 65 | |
| **BENCHMARK LA.E.2.2.4: The student identifies the major theme in a story or nonfiction text. The student:** | | |
| 1. knows themes that recur across literary works. | | |
| 2. identifies the major information in a nonfiction text. | | 135, 135C |
| **BENCHMARK LA.E.2.2.5: The student forms his or her own ideas about what has been read in a literary text and uses specific information from the text to support these ideas. The student:** | | |
| 1. uses specific information from text to support ideas about content in literary texts (such as advances judgments, refers to text, other works, other authors, nonprint media, and personal knowledge to support ideas). | 21, 23, 25, 27, 29, 31, 33A, 33E, 35, 39, 41, 43, 43A, 43C, 43D, 45, 53, 53A, 55, 63, 63A, 65, 83A, 85, 97A, 99 | 103, 105, 107, 109, 111, 111A, 113, 117, 117A, 119, 125, 125A, 127, 135A, 137, 149, 149A, 151, 159, 159A, 161, 175A |

| Unit 3 | Unit 4 | Unit 5 | Unit 6 |
|---|---|---|---|
| 189E, 211A, 247A | | 459D, 505E | 519E, 541A, 627A |
| | 313D, 345E, 385E | 425E, 493E | 537D |
| 180-189, 192-207, 210-211, 214-223 | 288-305, 308-309, 350-363, 366-377 | | 510-519, 521D, 586-599 |
| 275D | | 471E | 599D |
| 275D | | 471E, 473A | |
| 191, 209, 225, 277, 285 | 377A | 441E, 453, 459, 473, 495 | 512, 521, 521D, 539, 539A, 599D, 601, 625, 625D |
| 283D | | 453, 507 | 539A, 625D |
| 225 | | 405, 427, 453, 459, 461, 507 | 539A, 565, 625D |
| | 308, 315A, 331A | 461D | |
| 207E, 247A | 329D, 331G, 331H, 331J | 429A, 457, 473G, 473I, 473J, 507H | 541A, 601G, 601I, 601J, 623D, 625D, 627A |
| | 289, 291, 293, 295, 297, 299, 301, 303 | 497, 499, 501, 503, 505, 505C, 505D | 523, 525, 527, 529, 531, 533, 535, 537 |
| 183, 185, 187, 223D, 259 | 309A | 469 | 541A, 563D, 583 |
| 189B, 218, 222, 223C, 282 | | 443 | 583, 601 |
| 223C | | | 590, 599C |
| 207E, 245 | | 425C, 427, 443, 461, 473, 495, 507 | 537, 541, 563, 623A, 623D, 625D |
| 193, 195, 207A | | | |
| 189, 189A, 191, 207, 207A, 209, 213, 215, 217, 219, 221, 223, 223A, 225, 231, 235, 237, 239, 241, 243, 243A, 243C, 243D, 245, 247B, 249, 251, 253, 255, 275, 275A, 283, 283A, 285 | 305A, 307, 313A, 315, 329A, 331, 345A, 347, 351, 353, 355, 357, 359, 363A, 363C, 363D, 365, 377A, 379, 387, 387A | 391, 393, 395, 397, 399, 401, 403, 403A, 403C, 403D, 405, 425A, 427, 441A, 441E, 447, 449, 451, 459, 459A, 461, 463, 465, 467, 471, 471A, 471C, 471D, 473, 493, 493A, 495, 505, 505A, 507 | 519A, 537A, 539, 563A, 565, 581, 581A, 599A, 601, 623, 625 |

# Florida Resources

## Notes

Use this page to record lessons or elements that work well
or need to be adjusted for future reference.

### Lessons that work well.

_____
_____
_____
_____
_____
_____
_____
_____
_____
_____
_____
_____
_____

### Lessons that need adjustments.

_____
_____
_____
_____
_____
_____
_____
_____
_____
_____
_____
_____
_____

# Notes

Use this page to record lessons or elements that work well
or need to be adjusted for future reference.

## Lessons that work well.

_____
_____
_____
_____
_____
_____
_____
_____
_____
_____
_____
_____
_____
_____

## Lessons that need adjustments.

_____
_____
_____
_____
_____
_____
_____
_____
_____
_____
_____
_____
_____
_____

# Florida Resources

Use this page to record lessons or elements that work well
or need to be adjusted for future reference.

## Lessons that work well.

_____
_____
_____
_____
_____
_____
_____
_____
_____
_____
_____
_____
_____

## Lessons that need adjustments.

_____
_____
_____
_____
_____
_____
_____
_____
_____
_____
_____
_____
_____
_____

# Notes

Use this page to record lessons or elements that work well
or need to be adjusted for future reference.

## Lessons that work well.

_____
_____
_____
_____
_____
_____
_____
_____
_____
_____
_____
_____
_____
_____

## Lessons that need adjustments.

_____
_____
_____
_____
_____
_____
_____
_____
_____
_____
_____
_____
_____
_____

# Florida Resources

Use this page to record lessons or elements that work well
or need to be adjusted for future reference.

## Lessons that work well.

_____
_____
_____
_____
_____
_____
_____
_____
_____
_____
_____
_____
_____

## Lessons that need adjustments.

_____
_____
_____
_____
_____
_____
_____
_____
_____
_____
_____
_____
_____